Regulating Wall Street

Founded in 1807, John Wiley & Sons is the oldest independent publishing company in the United States. With offices in North America, Europe, Australia, and Asia, Wiley is globally committed to developing and marketing print and electronic products and services for our customers' professional and personal knowledge and understanding.

The Wiley Finance series contains books written specifically for finance and investment professionals as well as sophisticated individual investors and their financial advisors. Book topics range from portfolio management to e-commerce, risk management, financial engineering, valuation, and financial instrument analysis, as well as much more.

For a list of available titles, visit our Web site at www.WileyFinance.com.

Regulating Wall Street

The Dodd-Frank Act and the New Architecture of Global Finance

VIRAL V. ACHARYA
THOMAS F. COOLEY
MATTHEW RICHARDSON
INGO WALTER

WILEY

John Wiley & Sons, Inc.

Published by John Wiley & Sons, Inc., Hoboken, New Jersey.
Published simultaneously in Canada.

ISDA® is a registered trade mark of the International Swaps and Derivatives Association, Inc.

For general information on our other products and services or for technical support, please contact our Customer Care Department within the United States at (800) 762-2974, outside the United States at (317) 572-3993 or fax (317) 572-4002.

Wiley also publishes its books in a variety of electronic formats. Some content that appears in print may not be available in electronic books. For more information about Wiley products, visit our web site at www.wiley.com.

Library of Congress Cataloging-in-Publication Data:

Regulating Wall Street : the Dodd-Frank Act and the new architecture of global finance /
   Viral V. Acharya ... [et al.].
      p.   cm. — (Wiley finance series)
   Includes index.
   ISBN 978-0-470-76877-8 (cloth); ISBN 978-0-470-94984-9 (ebk);
   ISBN 978-0-470-94985-6 (ebk); ISBN 978-0-470-94986-3 (ebk)
   1. Financial institutions—Government policy—United States.   2. Banks and
banking—State supervision—United States.   3. Financial crises—United States.
4. International finance—Law and legislation.   5. United States—Economic
policy—2009– I. Acharya, Viral V.
   HG181.R357 2010
   332'.042—dc22   2010034668

Printed in the United States of America

10 9 8 7 6 5 4 3 2 1

To our outstanding colleagues and contributors,
who embraced this project
with relentless energy and enthusiasm

Contents

Foreword

This book continues the collaborative effort and scholarship of the New York University Stern School of Business faculty. I was amazed that part of the group that published the series of white papers that became the book *Restoring Financial Stability: How to Repair a Failed System*, published by John Wiley & Sons in March 2009, would have the energy and dedication to undertake this economic analysis of the complete Dodd-Frank Wall Street Reform and Consumer Protection Act of 2010. And I was amazed that they would do so in such a short period of time and with such a level of comprehension and clarity as to the issues to consider and evaluate, and also be able to provide new insights into methods that would lead to economically sound financial market reform. In the various sections, Acharya, Cooley, Richardson, Walter, and their colleagues at the Stern School not only consider the benefits and costs of the various sections of the Dodd-Frank Act, but also articulate clearly the Act's possible success in meeting the objectives, the likely consequences and unintended consequences, and the costs of the reforms in each of its sections. They should be commended for this effort.[*]

I was also amazed that this volume is not just an amplification of the original book but pushes academic and applied research to a new level. New work on measurement of systemic risk probabilities and costs, a new proposal for taxing banks differentially for systemic risk contributions, analysis of new forms of contingent capital, a clear discussion of the Volcker Rule and its consequences, and exploration of the likely effects of taking over entities to resolve failures—all these are thought-provoking. In the words of a scientist, "Why didn't I think of many of the issues raised in the book?" For example, when the government takes over a bank, the bank must pay employees to stay to unwind it—they won't stay on government salaries. Does the new financial protection agency help or hurt consumers—and does it mitigate systemic risk?

---

[*]I will refer to the "book" in my comments because it is a collaborative effort by so many on the Stern School faculty. I would worry that I was not giving proper credit or was incorrectly identifying the sources of the arguments and analysis.

Although others perhaps won't give the authors proper attribution (for all good ideas are copied freely), the arguments and analysis in this book will be used by bankers and other market constituents to make the case for forms of regulation that they deem appropriate and to point out to the regulatory bodies the unintended consequences of other regulations. Regulators, in turn, will use the book's structure and economic arguments to counter and to develop more appropriate regulations. With inputs and analyses from this book, along with the work of others, my hope is that a sensible balance will arise that will neither cripple the financial system nor create a false sense that the new financial regulatory architecture will prevent failures in the future.

In the summer and fall of 2008 the global financial system was in chaos. Since then, there have been myriad discussions, conferences, television shows, Internet discourses, books, and articles about the crisis, its causes, who was to blame, and the failures. There have been congressional hearings, commissions, G-20 meetings, government and central-bank proposals, et cetera. There was, and is still, anger directed at Wall Street, the bailouts, and the bonus awards, and against central bankers and legislative bodies for not acting sooner to constrain the excesses of the financial system or for promoting them. As the book discusses, although the independence of the Federal Reserve is intact, its wings have been clipped as a lender of last resort. Moreover, we might have lost the opportunity to examine whether an active monetary policy should target only inflation and not changes in asset prices and risk, or whether inflation-targeting policies exacerbated the crisis (as some suggest). And this crisis has had a direct effect on jobs and on those who have owned homes and had leveraged balance sheets. As the book suggests, although government support of housing, mortgage finance, the government-sponsored enterprises (GSEs), and the rating agencies should have been the core of the Dodd-Frank Act, 25 percent of this legislation is devoted to moving liquid over-the-counter interest rate swaps to clearing corporations, where, paradoxically, more than 50 percent of swaps among dealers are already cleared, a large increase occurring subsequent to the crisis. The book clearly addresses these issues of housing finance as well as what is left out of the Act.

The Dodd-Frank Act arose from anger and cries for retribution against Wall Street. I had hoped that the chaos would provide the opportunity to reflect, to understand, and to learn from the crisis, and that from that learning financial entities would change practices (such as in clearing swaps) on their own and that gaps in regulatory rules would be corrected or old rules would be adjusted to reflect modern realities. Understanding takes discussion, argument, effort, and, most important, time to gather data and to conduct analyses of that data. At 2,319 pages, the Act requires that 243 new formal rules be adopted by 11 different regulatory agencies, all within a year and a half of its passage. This is a massive undertaking. It is shocking that so many failures in the system have now come to light. Or is it the case that Congress really could not pinpoint the causes of the crisis or know how to prevent future crises? Why did Congress fail to define the new rules precisely? Why did it pass on the actual rule-making responsibility to the agencies that will make new rules either to punish or to garner new jobs from Wall Street? And why, if these failures are now so important and devastating, do new requirements need to be phased in over such long time frames? Why are the rules so vague (such as transactions that include "a material conflict of interest" between the bank and its clients are prohibited)? And why might the Volcker Rule, which limits proprietary trading and constrains hedge fund and private equity investments to some extent, not actually be implemented, in part, for up to four years and perhaps as long as seven years? The book provides excellent discussions of these difficulties.

I am not sure that market failures and externalities (that were mispriced) were the only causes of the crisis. An important cause was also the poor infrastructure to manage financial innovations. If rules were insufficient for the Treasury or the Federal Reserve Bank to unwind failing institutions or too many agencies without expertise were watching over various financial entities, then the makeup and constitution of regulatory bodies should be changed. I am suspicious that this became important only after Lehman Brothers' default caused a much larger mess than regulators expected. And I think that the Dodd-Frank Act buried only one agency.

Since successful innovations are hard to predict, economic theory suggests that infrastructure to support financial innovations will, by and large, follow them, which increases the probability that controls will be insufficient at times to prevent breakdowns in governance mechanisms. It would be too expensive to build all of the information links, legal rules, risk management controls, and so forth in advance of new product introductions. Too many don't succeed in incurring large support costs in advance of market acceptance. For this reason, those financial innovations that grow rapidly are more likely to fail and to create crises—such as failures in mortgage finance, failures in subprime mortgage product innovations, failures to monitor mortgage originators, failures to provide mortgage bankers with the correct incentive systems, failures in adjustable-rate mortgages, failures in rating agency modeling of mortgage products and their synthetics, failures of investment banks in monitoring the growth of their mortgage products, and failures by those entities insuring mortgage products. There was a lack of infrastructure in place at large banks such as Citibank and with regard to credit default swaps at American International Group (AIG). Unfortunately, failures in mortgage finance tend to have vast consequences for homeowners as well as for the industries that service them.

Failures are expected. Some will be low-cost, whereas others will exact a large cost. And not all fast growing innovations fail. Before the fact, failures are hard to identify. Failures, however, do not lead to the conclusion that reregulation will succeed in stemming future failures. As this book clearly argues, while governments are able to regulate organization forms such as banks or insurance companies, they are unable to regulate the services provided by competing entities, many as yet unborn in the global community. Innovation benefits society, and innovation has costs. This crisis has caused many to conclude that the Dodd-Frank Act should have slowed down innovation to prevent too rapid growth, but it is hard to justify this conclusion, as the book's discussion of the role of government oversight and guaranteeing of systemic entities suggests.

The response to this dilemma is difficult. Infrastructure to support innovation is a business decision. The senior management of financial entities must decide when more resources are necessary to monitor and to understand innovation. They must decide whether the returns to innovation are worth the risks, including the risks of having incomplete information systems and controls; and they must decide whether the returns are measured correctly and whether the capital supporting innovation is sufficient. Financial entities are building entirely new risk systems in response to the crisis. Innovation risks are being incorporated into decision making from the outset. Measurement technologies are being built to provide senior management with the information they need to make informed decisions about product lines and their controls. In the past, risk management had been a reporting and a regulatory requirement within a bank. That is changing as risks and returns are being evaluated as part of the optimization process. That banks relied on the Bank for International Settlements to set risk rules is inappropriate. For example, their value at risk metrics, which rely on portfolio theory, did not allow for the possibility that liquidity shocks could result in asset prices around the world becoming highly correlated. The book goes to great length to model and discuss appropriate regulatory capital rules and their consequences that address some of these pitfalls of current rules.

We don't yet have a deep understanding of the intermediation process. Markets work because intermediaries are willing to step in and buy when sellers want to sell before buyers want to buy, and vice versa. Financial intermediaries provide liquidity or risk transfer services in mostly nontraded markets, and service the idiosyncratic needs of consumers, students, commercial or residential mortgage holders, corporations, pension funds, insurance companies, and others. The demand for intermediation services is not constant. The price of liquidity changes—increasing with lack of synchronicity in demand and supply, and becoming extreme at times of shock when intermediaries no longer have confidence in the value of the underlying assets and rationally withdraw from the provision of intermediation services as a result of an inability to determine new valuations quickly. With a shock, liquidity prices and valuations change simultaneously; sometimes liquidity prices change much more than valuation changes or vice versa.

Central bankers have always operated under the assumption that they provide collateral for good value to smooth out liquidity crises until markets work again. But, if this were true, no liquidity crisis would occur. Every intermediary would know of valuations, and as prices deviated from equilibrium values they would step in to reduce spreads and make large returns on capital. The uncertainty about what proportion of the price decline or increase was caused by changes in liquidity or fundamental value is extremely difficult to parse out quickly. Sometimes it takes a short time; sometimes it takes much longer. If it takes a long time, however, markets are chaotic; and as time expands, fundamental values continue to change.

I believe the economics of innovation and intermediation are key reasons why financial crises have such broad effects. Shocks affect intermediation across unrelated segments of the financial markets as shocks in one market are transmitted by intermediaries that reduce risk in one market in light of losses to other intermediaries, who in turn reduce risk in other markets.

The book discusses the consequences of rapid innovation and breakdowns in the intermediation process. Innovation affects compensation, for without measurement or adequate risk controls, senior management has difficulty discerning skill from risk taking. Innovation leads to seeming moral hazard issues. Lenders often don't spend resources in the short run to monitor instances in which others will step in to protect them. (For example, since AIG posted collateral to each of its counterparties and bankruptcy laws allowed them to seize the collateral in the event of AIG's default, the counterparties did not have to monitor the credit or the size of AIG's business. This was obviously true of government foreign debt holders, for example.) The true moral hazard in the system is that debt holders suffer little loss during a financial crisis. If they did, they would monitor or force management to monitor innovations.

The intermediation process must break down from time to time. This is the nature of markets. Markets work. In a sense the market breakdown can be considered a failure, but it is a failure only in that markets don't operate in times of crisis as they do when times are calm. The fact that markets work this way does not mean that regulators can do a better job of controlling markets. They watch the water from afar. The picture is far different up close.

As I read through the book's excellent discussion of the Dodd-Frank Act and its likely good or bad consequences, I was unable to discern whether regulators had addressed the innovation questions and whether they understood the nature of the intermediation business. The book, however, does discuss moral hazard issues, compensation programs, and accounting issues—mark-to-market and information systems within the firm and how they affect other firms. It tackles the role of government and how the government leads to bad innovations such as the GSEs or the monopoly of the rating agencies. In this vein, the book also covers the new role of central clearing agencies for the over-the-counter derivatives markets.

The 2008 financial crisis and its aftermath will cause financial entities to learn on their own. And this learning will mitigate the consequences of future shocks.

The Dodd-Frank Wall Street Reform and Consumer Protection Act of 2010 will take years to implement. The uncertainty about the form of these new rules will impede growth in our society. I am sure that I will return to this book regularly for its analysis as events unfold over the next number of years. Congratulations to the team for such a commendable accomplishment.

MYRON S. SCHOLES
Frank E. Buck Professor of Finance, Emeritus
Graduate School of Business
Stanford University

Preface

In the fall of 2008, at the peak of the crisis, we launched a project among the New York University Stern School of Business faculty to understand what had gone wrong, what the policy options were, and what seemed to be the best course of action at the time. This resulted in a series of white papers authored by 33 members of the faculty. These were widely circulated among politicians and their staff members, as well as practitioners and academics worldwide. Taken together, the white papers were guided by a public interest perspective and intended as an independent and defensible assessment of the key issues by people who understand the theoretical concepts and institutional practice of modern finance and economics. The result was a book, *Restoring Financial Stability: How to Repair a Failed System*, published by John Wiley & Sons in March 2009.

Drawing on the insights gathered in that effort, it seemed logical to think about a second project that would focus specifically on the myriad reform proposals under discussion, provide an objective evaluation of their merits, add some new ideas to fill in the gaps or improve outcomes, and suggest their likely impact on the global financial system and economy as a whole. A total of 40 members of the Stern School faculty and doctoral students—virtually all participants in the first project and several new members as well—stepped up to contribute to this effort. First, we produced an e-book in December 2009 that addressed the U.S. House of Representatives financial reform bill. This was followed by the Senate bill in April 2010, requiring important modifications in our analysis. This had to be repeated when the two bills were reconciled in conference and finally signed by President Obama on July 21, 2010—all the while keeping a weather eye on developments in Basel, London, Brussels, and other centers of global financial regulation.

Along the way, we have read the entire Act and its predecessors in detail, debated it among ourselves and professional colleagues, and identified strengths and weaknesses through the lens of modern financial economics. We like to think our first project helped to shape some of the debate leading up to the Dodd-Frank legislation as we commented on various versions of the proposed reforms in congressional testimony, speeches, workshops, and other forums around the world.

At the end of the day, the Dodd-Frank Wall Street Reform and Consumer Protection Act of 2010 is the keystone of the financial reform structure in the United States and will be influential worldwide. It is more or less aligned to some basic principles agreed on in G-20 meetings of heads of state during and after the crisis, as well as to parallel developments in the Basel Committee on Banking Supervision, the European Union, and at the national levels in the United Kingdom, continental Europe, and elsewhere. This book presents a comprehensive and objective analysis of the various initiatives legislated or proposed by the Act, along with their implications for financial firms, markets, and end users going forward. There will undoubtedly be a number of further surprises, as well as unintended consequences of what has now been legislated. We have tried to anticipate and face up to as many of them as possible. We feel confident that we have provided readers with a coherent and rigorous framework for thinking about whatever may lie ahead for global finance.

We are grateful for the many comments we received from readers of our first book. They did much to sharpen our thinking and inform our effort in this volume to look ahead. Special thanks are due to Joanne Hvala, Jessica Neville, and the rest of the staff at the Stern School, who supported our efforts, to Sanjay Agrawal and Anjolein Schmeits for their diligent reading and copyediting of the manuscript, and to Philipp Schnabl and Kermit (Kim) Schoenholtz, who provided invaluable editorial inputs in addition to contributing to book chapters. And certainly not least, we confess admiration of the entire team at John Wiley & Sons, with a special nod to Pamela van Giessen, for their incredible professionalism and some amazing turnaround times to get our thoughts into print.

New York   VIRAL V. ACHARYA
September 2010   THOMAS COOLEY
                                                                 MATTHEW RICHARDSON
                                                                 INGO WALTER

A Bird's-Eye View

The Dodd-Frank Wall Street Reform and Consumer Protection Act

Viral V. Acharya, Thomas Cooley, Matthew Richardson, Richard Sylla, and Ingo Walter

Recently, Friedrich Hayek's classic *The Road to Serfdom*, a warning against the dangers of excessive state control, was the number one best seller on Amazon. At the same time, the foundation of much modern economics and capitalism—Adam Smith's *The Wealth of Nations*—languished around a rank of 10,000. It is a telling reflection of the uncertain times we are in that precisely when confidence in free markets is at its all-time low, skepticism about the ability of governments and regulation to do any better is at its peak. So it is no trivial task for the United States Congress and the Obama administration to enact the Dodd-Frank Wall Street Reform and Consumer Protection Act of 2010 and convince a skeptical public that financial stability will be restored in the near future.

The Act is widely described as the most ambitious and far-reaching overhaul of financial regulation since the 1930s. Together with other regulatory reforms introduced by the Securities and Exchange Commission (SEC), the Federal Reserve (the Fed), and other regulators in the United States and Europe, it is going to alter the structure of financial markets in profound ways. In this Prologue, we provide our overall assessment of the Act in three different ways: from first principles in terms of how economic theory suggests we should regulate the financial sector; in a comparative manner, relating the proposed reforms to those that were undertaken in the 1930s following the Great Depression; and, finally, how the proposed reforms would have fared in preventing and dealing with the crisis of 2007 to 2009 had they been in place at the time.

THE BACKDROP FOR THE DODD-FRANK ACT OF 2010

The backdrop for the Act is now well understood but worth an encore.

When a large part of the financial sector is funded with fragile, short-term debt and is hit by a common shock to its long-term assets, there can be en masse failures of financial firms and disruption of intermediation to households and corporations. Having witnessed such financial panics from the 1850s until the Great Depression, Senator Carter Glass and Congressman Henry Steagall pushed through the so-called Glass-Steagall provisions of the Banking Act of 1933. They put in place the Federal Deposit Insurance Corporation (FDIC) to prevent retail bank runs and to provide an orderly resolution of troubled depository institutions—banks—before they failed. To guard against the risk that banks might speculate at the expense of the FDIC, they ring-fenced depositary banks' permissible activities to commercial lending and trading in government bonds and general-obligation municipals, requiring the riskier capital markets activity to be spun off into investment banks.

At the time it was legislated, and for several decades thereafter, the Banking Act of 1933 reflected in some measure a sound economic approach to regulation in case of market failure:

- *Identify the market failure*, or in other words, why the collective outcome of individual economic agents and institutions does not lead to socially efficient outcomes, which in this case reflected the financial fragility induced by depositor runs.
- *Address the market failure through a government intervention*, in this case by insuring retail depositors against losses.
- *Recognize and contain the direct costs of intervention, as well as the indirect costs due to moral hazard arising from the intervention*, by charging banks up-front premiums for deposit insurance, restricting them from riskier and more cyclical investment banking activities, and, through subsequent enhancements, requiring that troubled banks face a "prompt corrective action" that would bring about their orderly resolution at an early stage of their distress.

Over time, however, the banking industry nibbled at the perimeter of this regulatory design, the net effect of which (as we explain in some detail later) was to keep the government guarantees in place but largely do away with any defense the system had against banks' exploiting the guarantees to undertake excessive risks. What was perhaps an even more ominous development was that the light-touch era of regulation of the financial sector starting in the 1970s allowed a parallel (shadow) banking system to evolve. In hindsight, while at least some of this could be judged as inevitable innovation in financial technology, it is hard to dispute the claim—made, for instance, by Paul Volcker, the former chairman of the Federal Reserve—that much evolution of the parallel banking system was designed precisely to circumvent existing regulations.

The parallel banking system consisted of the following: money market funds collecting uninsured short-term deposits and funding financial firms, effectively reintroducing the fragile maturity mismatch of traditional banking that the Banking Act had attempted to fix; investment banks performing many functions of commercial banks and vice versa; and a range of derivatives and securitization markets providing tremendous liquidity for hitherto illiquid loans but operating unregulated (or at least weakly regulated) in the shadow of regulated banks. The result was a parallel banking sector that was both opaque and highly leveraged. The fact that much of this innovation took place outside of the banking system rendered ineffective other regulatory institutions, like the SEC, that had been introduced in 1930s to address information asymmetries in intermediation.

In many ways, the parallel banking system reflected *regulatory arbitrage*, the opportunity and the propensity of the financial sector to adopt organizational forms and financial innovations that would circumvent the regulatory apparatus designed to contain bank risk taking. Ignoring this regulatory arbitrage—or at least leaving it unchecked—was possible, in part, for several reasons: regulatory naiveté in the face of the ingenuity of the financial sector, the ideology of the times, and a cognitive failure by everyone to appreciate fully the unintended consequences of existing regulation and to develop the tools to deal with them.

As a result, the Banking Act began to be largely compromised. In four decades since its birth, the parallel banking system grew to over $10 trillion of intermediation in the U.S. economy and reached a scale similar to the deposit-based commercial banking system. Traditional banks gradually morphed into large, complex financial institutions (LCFIs). The increasing size and connectedness of traditional and shadow banks rendered many of them too big to fail or too systemic or interconnected to fail—or rather, to be *allowed* to fail. Deposit insurance, which was explicit, rule-based, and bundled with mechanisms to contain risk taking, was replaced by the effective insurance of the uninsured wholesale deposits of LCFIs—in other words, by anticipation of government intervention that was implicit, discretionary, and divorced from moral hazard concerns.

For sure, there were efforts to contain these financial behemoths. The increasingly global nature of the LCFIs and the threat that competition among countries to attract banking flows might produce a regulatory race to the bottom led, in late 1980s, to the setting of prudential capital standards. These were the Basel I requirements that provided a framework to assess the risk of banking assets and ensure they were not funded with too much leverage. But shadow banking allowed the behemoths easily to bypass these attempts at global containment, which suffered the same fate as their predecessor, the Banking Act, in much shorter time. The coarse buckets of Basel I risk categories were easily gamed at the edges. The requirements were found to be, at best, catching up with the fast-paced evolution of banking activities, rather than being ahead of the game; in the end, they turned out to be woefully inadequate. Perhaps their greatest folly was—and is—that, unlike the Banking Act that had identified a clear market failure and addressed it, the Basel I regulations were narrowly focused at the individual risk of institutions rather than their collective risk, a focus that would ensure financial stability of the system only if the institutions were, somewhat miraculously, all identical.

Fast-forward to 2004, which many argue was the year when a perfect storm began to develop that would eventually snare the global economy. Global banks were seeking out massive capital flows into the United States and the United Kingdom by engaging in short-term borrowing, increasingly through uninsured deposits and interbank liabilities, financed at historically low interest rates. They began to manufacture huge quantities of *tail risk*—that is, events of small likelihood but with catastrophic outcomes. A leading example was the so-called safe assets (such as the relatively senior—AAA-rated—tranches of subprime-backed mortgages) that would fail only if there was a secular collapse in the housing markets. As LCFIs were willing to pick up loans from originating mortgage lenders and pass them around or hold them on their own books after repackaging them, a credit boom was fueled in these economies. The government push for universal home ownership in the United States made subprime mortgages a particularly attractive asset class for manufacturing such tail risk. Given their focus on the individual institution's risk, prudential standards ignored the risk of an entire financial system manufacturing such tail risk, and they even encouraged—through lower-risk weights—the manufacturing of AAA-rated mortgage-backed tranches.

The net result of all this was that the global banking balance sheet grew twofold from 2004 to 2007, but its risk appeared small, as documented in the Global Financial Stability Report of the International Monetary Fund (IMF) in April 2008. The LCFIs had, in effect, taken a highly undercapitalized one-way bet on the housing market, joined in equal measure by the U.S. government's own shadow banks—Fannie Mae and Freddie Mac—and American International Group (AIG), the world's largest insurer. While these institutions seemed individually safe, collectively they were vulnerable. And as the housing market crashed in 2007, the tail risk materialized, and the LCFIs crashed, too, like a house of cards. The first big banks to fail were in the shadow banking world. They were put on oxygen in the form of Federal Reserve assistance, but the strains in the interbank markets and the inherently poor quality of the underlying housing bets even in commercial bank portfolios meant that when the oxygen ran out in the fall of 2008 some banks had to fail. A panic ensued internationally, making it clear that the entire global banking system was imperiled and needed—and markets expected it to be given—a taxpayer-funded lifeline.

In the aftermath of this disaster, governments and regulators began to cast about for ways to prevent—or render less likely—its recurrence. It was no surprise to discover that the regulatory framework needed rethinking; that had begun before the full onset of the crisis at the behest of United States Treasury Secretary Henry Paulson. The crisis created focus and led first to a bill from the House of Representatives, then one from the Senate, which were combined and distilled into the Dodd-Frank Wall Street Reform and Consumer Protection Act of 2010. The critical task for the Dodd-Frank Act is to address this increasing propensity of the financial sector to put the entire system at risk and eventually to be bailed out at taxpayer expense.

Does the Dodd-Frank Act do the job?

Before answering that, here are the Act's highlights:

- *Identifying and regulating systemic risk.* Sets up a Systemic Risk Council that can deem nonbank financial firms as systemically important, regulate them, and, as a last resort, break them up; also establishes an office under the U.S. Treasury to collect, analyze, and disseminate relevant information for anticipating future crises.
- *Proposing an end to too-big-to-fail.* Requires funeral plans and orderly liquidation procedures for unwinding of systemically important institutions, ruling out taxpayer funding of wind-downs and instead requiring that management of failing institutions be dismissed, wind-down costs be borne by shareholders and creditors, and if required, ex post levies be imposed on other (surviving) large financial firms.
- *Expanding the responsibility and authority of the Federal Reserve.* Grants the Fed authority over all systemic institutions and responsibility for preserving financial stability.
- *Restricting discretionary regulatory interventions.* Prevents or limits emergency federal assistance to individual institutions.
- *Reinstating a limited form of Glass-Steagall (the Volcker Rule).* Limits bank holding companies to de minimis investments in proprietary trading activities, such as hedge funds and private equity, and prohibits them from bailing out these investments.

- *Regulation and transparency of derivatives.* Provides for central clearing of standardized derivatives, regulation of complex ones that can remain traded over the counter (that is, outside of central clearing platforms), transparency of all derivatives, and separation of nonvanilla positions into well-capitalized subsidiaries, all with exceptions for derivatives used for commercial hedging.

In addition, the Act introduces a range of reforms for mortgage lending practices, hedge fund disclosure, conflict resolution at rating agencies, requirement for securitizing institutions to retain sufficient interest in underlying assets, risk controls for money market funds, and shareholder say on pay and governance. And perhaps its most popular reform, albeit secondary to the financial crisis, is the creation of a Bureau of Consumer Financial Protection (BCFP) that will write rules governing consumer financial services and products offered by banks and nonbanks.

ASSESSING THE DODD-FRANK ACT USING THE ECONOMIC THEORY OF REGULATION

Evaluating the Act in terms of the economic theory of regulation requires that we assess how well it addresses the market failures that led to the financial collapse of 2007 to 2009. First, does it address the relevant externalities? When an economic transaction imposes costs (or benefits) on individuals who are not party to the transaction, we call this an externality (also referred to as spillovers or neighborhood effects). In the instance of the financial crisis, the externality was the enormous buildup of systemic risk in the financial system, specifically the risk that a large number of financial firms funded with short-term debt would fail all at once if there was a correction in the housing market.

The full costs of an externality are not borne by parties in the transaction unless there are markets to appropriately price the externality. Typically, the markets for externalities are missing (think of carbon emissions, for example) and so, too, is the invisible hand operating through prices to produce externalities at the efficient level. Economists' preferred solution to this kind of market failure is generally to employ what are called Pigouvian taxes, named after Arthur Cecil Pigou, a British economist who was a contemporary of John Maynard Keynes. Such taxes are usually the least invasive way to remedy a market failure, because they do not require heavy-handed government intervention into the specific decisions made by households and firms. In the context of the financial crisis, these would take the form of taxes on financial firms that rise with their systemic risk contributions. They would also raise revenue that the government can use to reduce other taxes or employ to improve the infrastructure of financial markets or cover the costs of sorting out systemic failures. Unfortunately, these taxes are often not politically palatable, as the debate over the Dodd-Frank Act has made clear. Nevertheless, we argue throughout this book that such solutions are preferred, and we describe in detail how systemic risk could be measured and taxed.

Economic theory also explains why there are missing markets due to asymmetric information between parties to transactions and the limited ability to make binding commitments, which have been analyzed in great detail in the context of insurance markets. These market failures do not always have clean solutions, and much of modern regulation involves designing contractual or other arrangements to overcome them with minimal cost to economic efficiency. However, transaction costs preclude overcoming these failures completely, and we are always living in the world of second-best. As a result, the design of government intervention—say through a Pigouvian tax on systemic risk contributions of firms—must be robust to its unintended consequences.

Viewed using this lens of economic theory of regulation, does the Dodd-Frank Act address the relevant market failures while guarding well against the Act's unintended consequences?

The first reaction to the Act—which evolved from the House bill in late 2009, then the Senate bill, and then their "conference"—is that it certainly has its heart in the right place. It is highly encouraging that the purpose of the new financial sector regulation is explicitly aimed at developing tools to deal with systemically important institutions. And it strives to give prudential regulators the authority and the tools to deal with this risk. Requirement of funeral plans to unwind large, complex financial institutions should help demystify their organizational structure—and the attendant resolution challenges when they experience distress or fail. If the requirement is enforced well, it could serve as a tax on complexity, which seems to be another market failure in that private gains from it far exceed the social ones.

In the same vein, even though the final language in the Act is a highly diluted version of the original proposal, the Volcker Rule limiting proprietary trading investments of LCFIs provides a more direct restriction on complexity and should help simplify their resolution. The Volcker Rule also addresses the moral hazard arising from direct guarantees to commercial banks that are largely designed to safeguard payment and settlement systems and to ensure robust lending to households and corporations. Through the bank holding company structure, these guarantees effectively lower the costs for more cyclical and riskier functions such as making proprietary investments and running hedge funds or private equity funds. However, there are thriving markets for performing these functions, and commercial banking presence is not critical.

Equally welcome is the highly comprehensive overhaul of derivatives markets aimed at removing the veil of opacity that has led markets to seize up when a large derivatives dealer experiences problems (Bear Stearns, for example). Centralized clearing of derivatives and the push for greater transparency of prices, volumes, and exposures—to regulators and in aggregated form to the public—should enable markets to deal better with counterparty risk, in terms of pricing it into bilateral contracts, as well as understanding its likely impact. The Act also pushes for greater transparency by making systemic nonbank firms subject to tighter scrutiny by the Fed and the SEC.

However, when read in its full glory, some experts have dismissed the 2,300+-page script of the Dodd-Frank Act out of hand. The Act requires over 225 new financial rules across 11 federal agencies. The attempt at regulatory consolidation has been minimal and the very regulators who dropped the ball in the current crisis have garnered more, not less, authority. But, given that the massive regulatory failure of the financial crisis needs to be fixed, what options do we have? Given a choice between Congress and the admittedly imperfect regulatory bodies designing the procedures for implementing financial reform, it would not seem to be a difficult decision. The financial sector will have to live with the great deal of uncertainty that is left unresolved until the various regulators—the Fed, the SEC, and the Commodity Futures Trading Commission (CFTC)—spell out the details of implementation.

That said, from the standpoint of providing a sound and robust regulatory structure, the Act falls flat on at least four important counts:

1. The Act does not deal with the mispricing of pervasive government guarantees throughout the financial sector. This will allow many financial firms to finance their activities at below-market rates and take on excessive risk.
2. Systemically important firms will be made to bear their own losses but not the costs they impose on others in the system. To this extent, the Act falters in addressing directly the primary source of market failure in the financial sector, which is systemic risk.
3. In several parts, the Act regulates a financial firm by its form (bank) rather than function (banking). This feature will prevent the Act from dealing well with the new organizational forms likely to emerge in the financial sector—to meet the changing needs of global capital markets, as well as to respond to the Act's provisions.
4. The Act makes important omissions in reforming and regulating parts of the shadow banking system that are systemically important. It also fails to recognize that there are systemically important markets—collections of individual contracts and institutions—that also need orderly resolution when they experience freezes.

The net effect of these four basic faults is that implicit government guarantees to the financial sector will persist in some pockets and escalate in some others; capital allocation may migrate in time to these pockets and newer ones that will develop in the future in the shadow banking world and, potentially, sow seeds of the next significant crisis. Implementation of the Act and future regulation should guard against this danger.

Government Guarantees Remain Mispriced in the Financial System, Leading to Moral Hazard

In 1999, economists John Walter and John Weinberg, of the Federal Reserve Bank of Richmond, performed a study of how large the financial safety net was for U.S. financial institutions. Using fairly conservative criteria, they reported 45 percent of all liabilities ($8.4 trillion) received some form of guarantee. A decade later, the study was updated by Nadezhda Malysheva and John Walter with staggering results—now, 58 percent of all liabilities ($25 trillion) are under a safety net. Without appropriate pricing, government guarantees are highly distortionary: They lead to subsidized financing of financial firms, moral hazard, and the loss of market discipline, which, in turn, generate excessive risk taking. Examples include FDIC insurance provided for depository institutions, implicit backing of the government-sponsored enterprises (GSEs)—Fannie Mae and Freddie Mac—and the much discussed too-big-to-fail mantra of LCFIs. The financial crisis of 2007 to 2009 exposed the depth of the problem with the failure of numerous banks and the need to replenish FDIC funds, the now virtually explicit guarantee of GSE debt, and the extensive bailouts of LCFIs.

The Dodd-Frank Act makes little headway on the issue of government guarantees. While admittedly such guarantees have been a problem for many years, the Act nonetheless makes little attempt to readdress the pricing of deposit insurance, which until now has effectively returned insurance premiums to banks in good times. And while the GSEs are the most glaring examples of systemically important financial firms whose risk choices went awry given their access to guaranteed debt, the Act makes no attempt to reform them. The distortion here is especially perverse, given the convenience of having the GSEs around to pursue political objectives of boosting subprime home ownership and using them as so-called bad banks to avoid another titanic collapse of housing markets. Finally, there are several large insurance firms in the United States that can—and did in the past—build leverage through minimum guarantees in standard insurance contracts. Were these to fail, there is little provision in the Act to deal adequately with their policyholders: There are currently only the tiny state guarantee funds, which would never suffice for resolving the obligations of the large insurance firms. Under the Act, there would be no ex ante systemic risk charges on these firms, but it is highly unlikely that their policyholders will be allowed to be wiped out or that the large banks will be made to pay for these policies (as the Act proposes)! Taxpayer bailout of these policies is the more likely outcome. These institutions remain too big to fail and could be the centers of the next excess and crisis.

Of course, proponents of the Act would argue that at least the issue of being too big to fail has been dealt with once and for all through the creation of an orderly liquidation authority (OLA). But when one peels back the onion of the OLA, it is much less clear. Choosing an FDIC-based receivership model to unwind such large and complex firms creates much greater uncertainty than would a restructured bankruptcy code for LCFIs or the forced debt-to-equity conversions inherent in so-called living wills. Time will tell whether the OLA is considered credible enough to impose losses on creditors of too-big-to-fail firms (FDIC-insured depositors aside), but market prices of LCFI debt will be able to provide an immediate answer through a comparison of yield spreads with not-too-big-to-fail firms.

The Act Does Not Sufficiently Discourage Individual Firms from Putting the System at Risk

Since the failure of systemically important firms imposes costs beyond their own losses—to other financial firms, households, the real sector, and potentially, other countries—it is not sufficient to simply wipe out their stakeholders: management, shareholders, and creditors. These firms must pay in advance for contributing to the risk of the system. Not only does the Act rule this out, it makes the problem worse by requiring that other large financial firms pay for the costs, precisely at a time when they are likely to be facing the risk of contagion from failing firms. This is simply poor economic design for addressing the problem of externalities.

It is somewhat surprising that the Act has shied away from adopting an ex ante charge for systemic risk contributions of LCFIs. And, in fact, it has most likely compromised its ability to deal with their failures. It is highly incredible that in the midst of a significant crisis, there will be the political will to levy a discretionary charge on the surviving financial firms to recoup losses inflicted by failed firms: It would in fact be better to reward the surviving firms from the standpoint of ex ante incentives and relax their financing constraints ex post to boost the flagging economic output in that scenario. Under the proposed scheme, therefore, the likely outcomes are that the financial sector will most likely not pay for its systemic risk contributions—as happened in the aftermath of this crisis—and that to avoid any likelihood that they have to pay for others' mistakes and excesses, financial firms will herd by correlating their lending and investment choices. Both of these would increase, not decrease, systemic risk and financial fragility.

Equally problematic, the argument can be made that the Act has actually increased systemic risk in a financial crisis. While it is certainly true that the Financial Stability Oversight Council of regulators has more authority to address a systemic crisis as it emerges, there is the implicit assumption that the Council will have the wherewithal to proceed. Given the historical experience of regulatory failures, however, this seems like a tall order. In contrast, the Act reduces the ability of the Federal Reserve to provide liquidity to nondepository institutions, and, as just mentioned, does not prearrange funding for solvent financial institutions hit by a significant event. The Council will be so restricted that its only choice in a liquidity crisis may be to put the systemically important firm through the OLA process, which, given the uncertainty about this process, could initiate a full-blown systemic crisis. Much greater clarity on exact procedures underlying the OLA would be necessary to avoid such an outcome.

The Act Falls into the Familiar Trap of Regulating by Form Rather Than Function

The most salient example of this trap is the Act's overall focus on bank holding companies, after clarifying that nonbanks may get classified as systemically important institutions, too, and be regulated accordingly. As we just explained, the Act allows for provision of federal assistance to bank holding companies under certain conditions, but restricts such assistance to other systemically important firms, in particular, large swap dealers. This will create a push for the acquisition of small depositories just as nonbanks anticipate trouble, undermining the intent of restriction. There are also important concentrations of systemic risk that will develop, for instance, as centralized clearing of derivatives starts being implemented. And when their systemic risk materializes, employing the Fed's lender-of-last-resort function may be necessary, even if temporarily so, to ensure orderly resolution.

Consider a central clearinghouse of swaps (likely credit default swaps to start with, but eventually several other swaps, including interest rate swaps). As Mark Twain would put it, it makes sense to "put all one's eggs in a basket" and then "watch that basket." The Act allows for prudential standards to watch such a basket. But if the basket were on the verge of a precipitous fall, an emergency reaction would be needed to save the eggs—in this case, the counterparties of the clearinghouse. The restriction on emergency liquidity assistance from the Fed when a clearinghouse is in trouble will prove disastrous, as an orderly liquidation may take several weeks, if not months. The most natural response in such cases is to provide temporary federal assistance, eventual pass-through of the realized liquidation losses to participants in the clearinghouse, and its private recapitalization through capital contributions from participants. Why force intermediate liquidity assistance to go through a vote of the Council (and perhaps the Congress) to make an exception to the Act and have the markets deal with uncertainty around such regulatory discretion?

Regulatory Arbitrage Is Not Adequately Addressed, So Large Parts of the Shadow Banking Sector Remain in Their Current Form

The story of the financial crisis of 2007 to 2009 was that financial institutions exploited loopholes in capital requirements and regulatory oversight to perform risky activities that were otherwise meant to be well capitalized and closely monitored. Examples are numerous: (1) financial firms' choosing unqualified regulatory agencies to oversee them (e.g., AIG's choice of the Office of Thrift Supervision [OTS] for its financial products group); (2) the loading up of so-called AAA-rated securities in a regulatory setting ripe for conflict of interests between rating agencies, security issuers, and investors; and (3) the development of a parallel banking sector that used wholesale funding and over-the-counter (OTC) derivatives to conduct activities identical to those of commercial banks without being subject to bank rules and regulations.

To be fair, the Dodd-Frank Act does not ignore all of this in its financial reform. For example, it makes major steps forward to deal with the regulatory reliance and conflict of interest problem with rating agencies, OTC derivatives are brought back into the fold, and leverage-enhancing tricks like off-balance-sheet financing are recognized as a major issue. But the basic principle that similar financial activities, or, for that matter, economically equivalent securities should be subject to the same regulatory rules is not core to the Act.

For example, several markets—such as the sale and repurchase agreements (repos)—that now constitute several trillion dollars of intermediation flows have been shown to be systemically important. In what sense do these markets perform different functions than demand deposits, and why aren't they regulated as such? Moreover, these markets can experience a freeze if a few financial firms are perceived to be risky but their exact identity is unknown. Orderly resolution of a freeze and prevention of fire-sale asset liquidations in these markets remain unplanned. And ditto for dealing with runs on money market funds whose redemption risk following the collapse of Lehman brought finance to a standstill.

LEARNING FROM THE LESSONS OF THE 1930s

Next, we assess the Dodd-Frank Wall Street Reform and Consumer Protection Act of 2010 in a comparative sense, using the lessons we can learn from the history. Like the regulatory reforms of the 1930s, the Dodd-Frank Act was born of a severe financial crisis that immediately preceded it in 2007 to 2009 and the Great Recession that overlapped with it. The issues the Act covers were informed by many of the perceived failures of our financial architecture in the crisis. The Act is already being denounced by some for not going far enough to curb the risky behavior of financial institutions, and denounced by others for going too far and hampering innovation and efficiency in financial markets. We provide a somewhat more balanced and sober assessment of the likely success of the new regulatory architecture proposed by the Act, using history as benchmark.

Financial crises are recurring phenomena, just like the business cycle. The U.S. economic history of the pre-1934 era was one of repeated crises that brought the financial system to a halt and often led to sharp economic contractions. The most dramatic, of course, was the banking crisis that began in the 1920s and 1930s that led to the sharp and prolonged contraction of the Great Depression. And it was that crisis that inspired the great expansion of financial regulation and the creation of many of the central regulatory institutions—the FDIC and the SEC—that we rely on to this day.

Prior to the 1930s, there was relatively light regulation of the financial system and of securities markets in general. But the 1920s were a remarkable decade, driven by enormous technological change, large increases in wealth and inequality, and a rapid expansion of finance and of debt. The decade ended with a banking crisis that saw the failure of more than 4,000 banks between 1929 and 1932. It was clear that the institutions put in place in 1914 with the creation of the Federal Reserve System were not sufficient to forestall panic and halt bank runs. More intervention that dealt directly with bank failures and risk taking was needed.

What ensued was a series of bold moves to address the financial crisis. There were two goals. First and foremost was to create mechanisms to stop the panic that was unfolding. As we describe in the following paragraphs and in subsequent chapters, the result was a set of institutions that we relied on heavily in the financial crisis of 2007 to 2009 with mixed success. The second goal was to create institutions to address the market failures that led to the financial crisis, with the objective of making the system more stable for the future.

The actions taken in the 1930s were truly dramatic. Federal agencies were created to borrow on public credit and use the proceeds to make loans to, and investments in, private financial and nonfinancial firms. The monetary system changed from one based on the gold standard to one of fiat money domestically and a gold exchange standard internationally. In central banking, the powers of the Federal Reserve System were both increased and centralized. The banking system was restructured in important ways and made safer by the introduction of deposit insurance for retail deposits. Federal regulation of the securities industry came with the creation of the SEC and related measures.

Addressing the Panic

Providing Liquidity to Markets   In the early days of the banking crisis of the 1930s, it became clear that there was a huge shortage of liquidity in the economy. Congress created the Reconstruction Finance Corporation (RFC) in January 1932, on President Herbert Hoover's recommendation, to aid a variety of enterprises that had exhausted their ability to garner private credit in the depths of the Great Depression. The RFC's capitalization came from the federal government, and it was authorized to borrow several times that amount to make secured loans to banks, insurance companies, and railroad corporations. Subsequent amendments in 1932 extended RFC lending powers to states, farmers, and banks. Thousands of banks took advantage of these federal capital injections. But the RFC was eventually abolished.

The more important and lasting innovation was the Emergency Relief and Construction Act of 1932 that added paragraph 3 to Section 13 of the Federal Reserve Act. It said: "In unusual and exigent circumstances, the Board of Governors of the Federal Reserve System, by the affirmative vote of not less than five members, may" allow the Federal Reserve to lend money to "any individual, partnership, or corporation," as long as certain requirements are met. Provisions in the 1933 Emergency Banking Act further extended these powers.

Taken together, these represented an enormous expansion of the power of the Fed to intervene in the economy in a crisis in order to provide liquidity where it was needed. It was exactly this power that the Fed relied on in the financial crisis of 2007 to 2009 when it came to the aid of Bear Stearns, AIG, and others. The Fed's actions invoking Section 13(3) are given much credit for ameliorating the crisis, just as the 1930s reformers envisioned. But it is also true that the way it used that power, forcing arranged marriages of large institutions and rescuing some nonbanks and not others, drew enormous criticism. The Fed arguably exacerbated the problem of having institutions that are too big to (be allowed to) fail, and it engaged in what is essentially fiscal policy, the provenance of the Treasury.

In reaction to perceived mistakes that the Fed made, the Dodd-Frank Act poses some new limits on the Fed's Section 13(3) authority, curbs that could limit its effectiveness in a future crisis. This is an example of the trap of regulating by form rather than function. We argue in Chapter 2 that the provisions constraining the ability of the Fed to extend liquidity to specific nonbank firms may limit its flexibility in a crisis. We propose better ways to reduce the risks from temporary, quasi-fiscal actions by the Fed during a crisis.

Stopping Bank Runs   As Franklin D. Roosevelt took office in 1933, there was a full-fledged banking panic going on and cries for reform of the banking system. The response to those pressures could have been many—for example, nationalizing the banks, or a relaxation of restrictions on bank mergers or interstate banking, leading to a highly concentrated banking system—all solutions that had been adopted elsewhere and all actively debated at the time.

The immediate response to the panic was to declare a bank holiday in order to determine, as had been the case in 1907, whether individual banks were solvent, illiquid, or liquid enough to reopen. This helped to calm the system but only restored the status quo of the post-1907 world. The fundamental fragility of the fractional reserve banking system still existed. Banks borrowed deposits and made money by engaging in risky intermediation, holding only a fraction of reserves needed at any point of time to repay depositors; depositors had no easy way of assessing the risk of banks' failure to repay, leaving intact the possibility of panics and bank runs.

The Banking Act of June 1933, the so-called Glass-Steagall Act, contained several of the most important and long-lasting reforms to deal with panics and bank runs. It introduced deposit insurance by creating the FDIC, capitalized by a Treasury subscription and some of the surplus of the Federal Reserve banks. The Banking Act required all banks that were members of the Federal Reserve System to have their deposits insured, up to a limit, by the FDIC. Other banks could also be covered, subject to approval by the FDIC. Insured banks were required to pay premiums for their insurance based on their deposits. Within six months of the creation of the FDIC, 97 percent of all commercial bank deposits were covered by insurance.

The creation of the FDIC was arguably the most successful policy response to the banking crisis of the 1930s. The FDIC was economically successful because it solved a well-defined problem: uncertainty about the solvency of the banks among retail depositors. More importantly, it did so in a way that acknowledged the contradictions and risks inherent in fractional reserve banking, by making those responsible for managing the risks—the banks themselves—pay for insuring against them. These costs were passed through to bank borrowers, time depositors, and investors. Bank runs disappeared, and the number of bank failures dropped to an extremely low level compared with prior decades. Over time, the FDIC developed a highly effective mechanism for allowing insolvent banks to fail without disrupting markets.

The FDIC has evolved, becoming more effective in some ways and less effective in others. The glaring weaknesses that became apparent in the financial crisis of 2007 to 2009, however, were twofold. Much of financial intermediation had moved to the shadow banking system, which was immune to the solutions that worked for deposit-based commercial banking. Thus, we were again vulnerable to banks runs and panics in the shadow banking sector. Further, it became clear that the resolution mechanisms that worked so successfully for insolvent commercial banks were not workable for LCFIs.

The Dodd-Frank Act makes some progress in addressing the latter issue by expanding the role of the FDIC in dealing with large systemic institutions, but it does precious little to address the former issue of the shadow banking system. In particular, the likelihood of runs on money markets and repo markets remains a real threat in future financial crises. The Act is relatively impotent on this front, since it refuses to recognize that a large part of the deposits of the financial sector are no longer in the traditional form of insured FDIC deposits, but rather in the form of money market deposits and interbank repos. And, as noted earlier, it is completely silent on the problem of how the FDIC is to be funded and what the role of systemic risk assessments would be in that funding. This is something that the reformers of the 1930s viewed as crucial but that was eroded by regulatory capture over the decades.

Making the Financial System Safer

Constraining Risky Behavior   The Banking Act of 1933 not only created the FDIC to address bank panics, but it also required the separation of securities affiliates from commercial banks, and restricted the latter from granting credit for speculative purposes. It prohibited payment of interest on demand deposits. And it permitted national banks to branch within a state to the same extent that state banks were allowed to branch. In 1932, President Hoover and Senator Glass had tried, and failed, to pass a law separating commercial and investment banking, and also allowing national banks to branch statewide.

The 1933 Act became politically feasible in a time of great turmoil, because all of the politicians and private interests involved got something that they each wanted. Glass got the separation of commercial and investment banking and the restrictions on loans for speculative purposes. He thought these provisions made banking safer by eliminating conflicts of interest and risky lending practices that, in his view, had caused the stock market to crash and banks to fail. Steagall got deposit insurance to make banks safer in the eyes of depositors, and he staved off some of the more liberal branching provisions that might have accomplished the same end but only by posing a competitive threat to his small unit-bank constituents. Investment banks benefited because they would no longer have the investment banking affiliates of commercial banks as competitors. And commercial banks benefited by the ban on demand deposit interest because it reduced their costs, enhanced their charter values, and diffused incentives to take excessive risks. Many politicians liked the measure because they believed that payment of interest on demand deposits had contributed to the Depression's bank failures by encouraging banks to take more risks to pay those interest costs.

The 1930s banking reforms also made banks and savings institutions safer by protecting them from competition through a host of regulations and entry controls; in effect, they created a cartel in the U.S. commercial banking and thrift industry. This cartelization, which was also a hallmark of Roosevelt's approach to other industries, helps to explain why the banking reforms eventually stopped working. The commercial banking and thrift sector lost ground within the financial system, when depositors discovered in the 1970s that they could earn a higher return on their money and still use it for transactions by placing it in new financial market innovations—the money market funds and cash-management accounts offered by brokerage firms. These instruments faced no restrictions on the interest rates that could be paid on their deposits, and hence, they were able to invest in short-term commercial paper issued by highly rated financial firms and corporations, and partly pass through the greater, but riskier, return earned on this paper.

In the 1980s, Congress responded by increasing deposit insurance limits and removing some restrictions on deposit interest rates and permissible types of bank lending. However, this had the unintended consequence of encouraging riskier loan-making by banks, leading to more bank failures and a thrift institution crisis a decade later. In the 1990s, a major consolidation movement swept through the U.S. banking sector, aided by Congress's enactment of nationwide branch banking privileges in 1994, which followed a series of similar bilateral branching deregulations between states. A relatively small number of very large banks soon came to hold the lion's share of U.S. bank deposits.

The Glass-Steagall separation of commercial and investment banking of 1933 lasted for more than six decades before it was formally repealed in 1999. The move for its repeal had proceeded steadily since the 1970s on several fronts. Academic studies argued that before Glass-Steagall, commercial banks with investment banking affiliates were less, not more, risky than independent investment banks. Within the banking sector, large U.S.

commercial banks contended that they were at a competitive disadvantage relative to the universal banks allowed by other nations, banks that combined commercial with investment banking and other financial services. But nothing was put in place of Glass-Steagall to limit the risks in the system as banks became more complicated.

The only exception to this was the widespread enthusiasm for internationally agreed-upon capital standards, the Basel Accords, to provide a common risk-based assessment of bank assets and the required capital levels. The basic idea underlying the requirements was to bring the solvency risk of an individual bank to a desired level. The Accords dealt with the lending books of banks to start with, but soon incorporated value-at-risk-based capital charges for trading books. Eventually, they added further gradation of risk categories to refine the required capital calculations. Although the process of achieving international consensus might have had some merits, the end result has been a disaster. The standards have been both easy to game—they measured the risk of assets from the standpoint of individual banks' risk but ignored systemic risk, the primary rationale for bank regulation—and they ignored the new fragility that was developing on banks' liability side in the form of uninsured wholesale deposit funding.

Addressing Informational Asymmetries   Three weeks before it enacted the 1933 Glass-Steagall separation of investment and commercial banking, Congress began its reform of Wall Street with the Securities Act of May 1933. There were two major provisions: a requirement that *new* offerings of securities had to be registered with a government agency, the Federal Trade Commission (soon replaced by the yet-to-be-created SEC), and a requirement that potential investors in the new offering had to be furnished a prospectus containing sufficient information from the registration statement to allow them to judge the value of the offering.

Before 1933, there had been no federal regulation of the securities industry, although a couple of decades earlier, states had enacted the so-called blue-sky laws, requiring sellers of securities to provide information about them to buyers. Information is what the reforms were about—before the 1930s, information about most publicly traded companies was pretty much the province of insiders, corporate managers and directors, and investment bankers, who supplied capital and advice to the firms and managed their offerings of securities. To some extent, organized securities exchanges mitigated the asymmetry of information between investors and insiders by requiring companies whose securities were listed on the exchanges to provide some information to the exchanges and investors. But these listing requirements were not uniform and were subject to changes according to the exchanges' own interests. Losses suffered by many investors in the Crash of

1929 and the Great Depression posed a political challenge to the control of corporate information by insiders, particularly when congressional investigations uncovered evidence of market rigging and manipulation.

The Securities Exchange Act of June 1934 extended the registration and disclosure requirements of the 1933 act to *all* listed securities. It established the SEC and required corporations with listed securities to file annual financial reports (balance sheets and income statements) and quarterly earnings statements to the new agency. These were to be public information, and they were to be verified by independent auditors employing standardized accounting procedures. This was a boost to the accounting profession, and it would shortly lead to the emergence of a new profession, securities analysis.

Many later acts of Congress added to the new regulatory regime for the securities industry. It is not an exaggeration to say that many players on Wall Street and in corporate America in the 1930s hated the new regulatory regime imposed on them by these reforms. It reduced their power relative to that of investors and the government, and it raised their costs of doing business. But in the long run, as many of them would recognize, the new regulatory regime was one of the best things that ever happened for Wall Street and corporate America. Why? Because it created confidence among investors—then and in the decades to follow—that Wall Street finally had become a level playing field and that the informational asymmetries that had formerly plagued the game of investment had been greatly reduced, if not eliminated. Without the 1930s reforms, it is difficult to envision that the securities investing classes of the United States would have grown to the extent they did by the end of the century, or that institutional investors, such as mutual funds and pension funds, would have thrived to the extent they did.

The financial crisis of 2007 to 2009, however, revealed some glaring weaknesses of the institutional legacy of the 1930s. First, financial markets and financial firms have become ever more complex and difficult for the SEC and investors to understand. Over time, the SEC and other regulators grew to rely on external sources of information: the rating agencies, whose information was contaminated by a market failure. Further, many new products and firms have fallen outside the purview of the traditional regulatory institutions. Hedge funds, derivatives trading, and complex products are examples of innovations that have all increased the informational asymmetries in the world of finance.

The Dodd-Frank Act tries to address many of these increasing complexities. In particular, as we explain in the book, its attempt to unveil the opaque over-the-counter market for derivatives is to be lauded and can in fact be expanded to reveal to regulators—and, in some aggregated forms, even to market participants—information on counterparty exposures that would

be most relevant for assessing systemic risk. Similarly, the Act requires the
Office of Financial Research to be set up to collect and analyze data and
to provide timely reports on building concentrations of systemic risk in the
economy. This type of macro-prudential focus has been missing so far in the
existing supervision of banks and the financial sector, as the emphasis has
tended to be at the micro level of individual institutions. And, once again,
the Act greatly expands the responsibility and reach of the regulators in
ensuring these objectives can be met.

Turn Back the Clock?

Were the 1930s financial reforms responsible for the several decades of
financial stability that followed? Is the seemingly increased financial instability of the past two or three decades a result of dismantling parts of the
1930s regulatory structures? Today, some observers are tempted to answer
both questions in the affirmative. But the nostalgia for this earlier system is
probably misplaced.

Any evaluation of the success of the 1930s reforms in promoting a long
period of financial stability needs to take into account the larger context of
the United States in the world economy. In that light, it becomes apparent
that a good bit of the seeming success of the 1930s reforms was less inherent
in the reform legislation than a result of the unique position of economic
strength that the United States enjoyed in the world of the 1940s through the
1960s. World War II damaged the economies of every other large nation,
while it strengthened that of the United States.

As other nations recovered from the war and returned to more normal economic relationships with the United States, and the United States
embarked on an ill-conceived inflationary binge, the flaws in the 1930s financial regulatory structure became increasingly apparent. There were, for
instance, credit crunches and disintermediations in the late 1960s and 1970s
caused by regulated ceilings on deposit interest rates.

There have been too many changes in the world economy and national
and world financial systems in recent decades to support an argument that
an increased proneness to financial crises resulted from dismantling some of
the 1930s financial reforms. Parts of those reforms did contribute to some
of the financial instabilities of the 1970s and 1980s. However, Americans,
including bankers and bank investors, probably gained from the elimination
of regulated deposit interest rates and the liberalization of restrictions on
branch banking in the 1980s and 1990s.

There were early warning signs that the evolution of the financial system
was creating new risks that the old Glass-Steagall rubric could not deal with.
Glass-Steagall restrictions encouraged the rise of fragile shadow banks. To
restore stability, shadow banks needed to be treated more like banks, but this

did not happen. The collapse of Continental Illinois Bank in 1984 pointed to the dangers of wholesale funding of banks and was the first bank deemed too big to fail. The collapse of Long-Term Capital Management in 1998 highlighted the growth of systemic risk and the need for better bankruptcy mechanisms for financial firms. These warnings were ignored, despite reports immediately following these events pointing to new forms of systemic risk that were emerging and the need to nip them in the bud. By at least recognizing the problem of resolving and containing risks of large, complex financial institutions that are systemically important, the Dodd-Frank Act does take a giant step forward, even though critical implementation details remain to be fleshed out.

PREVENTING THE LAST CRISIS—HOW WOULD THE DODD-FRANK ACT HAVE PERFORMED?

It should be clear from the discussion thus far that designing effective regulatory policy is not easy. Unlike laboratory science that relies on a controlled environment, economic systems are inherently more dynamic, constantly evolving as changes in the nature of markets and institutions drive them in one direction or another. This evolution makes it difficult for policymakers to fully anticipate the direction or magnitude of change. But this does not mean that policymakers should not be thinking about the future. Ideally, what we want are policies that will stand up to changes in the environment and remain effective, without leaving a large footprint of unintended consequences. At a minimum, though, they must address current issues that are unlikely to go away.

Does the Dodd-Frank Act meet this minimum standard? Starting in 2003 and 2004 (years during which the credit boom took hold), until the fall of 2008 (when the financial system had to be rescued), how effective would the Act's provisions have been? Would the Act have prevented the enormous buildup of leverage on financial balance sheets, all betting against a material correction in the U.S. housing market? And would the Act have dealt adequately with the failures of Bear Stearns, Lehman Brothers, and AIG, along with the attendant stress in money markets?

This "back to the future" exercise has its limitations, to be sure. We do not want legislation that will help us to win the last war, or only the next one, but it is equally dangerous to think the next one will be different altogether. The exercise does point out some serious limitations of the protective umbrella that the Dodd-Frank Act is supposed to represent, and since much is still to be determined in the implementation of the Act, there is value in knowing those limitations. We have already mentioned as serious limitations the lack of a direct tax on systemically important institutions commensurate with their systemic risk contributions, and the failure to provide adequate resolution mechanisms for shadow banking institutions as serious limitations. But the question is: Would the Dodd-Frank Act have sufficed in other ways? We remain skeptical.

Let's go back to 2003. Recall the most staggering statistic of the credit boom of 2003 to the second quarter of 2007: The balance sheet size of the 10 largest global banks more than doubled, from about €7 trillion to €15 trillion during this period. And, during the same period, the regulatory assessment of the risk on their balance sheets (assessed for computing the banks' Tier 1 capital) moved far more gradually from €3.5 trillion to under €5 trillion. The system was deemed to be very well capitalized in the second quarter of 2007—indeed, better capitalized by this standard than in 2003. Something was clearly amiss.

The apparent safety of the financial sector's collective balance sheet was attributable to the fact that the top 10 global banks had amassed vast quantities of AAA-rated tranches backed by residential mortgages. These assets had historically been safer than similarly rated corporate loans. This was the principal reason behind their lower risk charge (by a factor of five) under the Basel capital requirement.[1] Even accepting that the AAA-rated mortgage-backed securities were indeed safer than corporate loans at the time—in itself a strong assumption for the period ahead—capital requirements ignored the fact that the entire system was at risk should mortgage defaults reach levels at which AAA-rated tranches could take some losses. Next, we explain that such financial fragility—the extraordinarily high level of exposure of the system to a common asset shock—would not have been discouraged by the Dodd-Frank Act.

The Dodd-Frank Act will require systemically important institutions to be identified and to be subjected to higher capital and liquidity requirements. These requirements are unlikely to be raised in the near future, given the weak state of global economic recovery. But assume a new 8 percent Tier 1 capital requirement had existed in place of the actual 4 percent in 2003. Would such a higher capital requirement have done the job? The problem in the buildup to the credit crisis was not the *level* of the capital requirement but its *form*. Suppose the level of the capital requirement is raised but there is no change in the Basel risk weights. The AAA-rated mortgage-backed securities would continue to enjoy a one-fifth risk-weight charge, compared with AAA-rated corporate loans. Consequently, the basic distortion favoring mortgage finance in the economy would remain. Worse, by raising the capital requirement, bankers face a lower return on equity (ROE). So to restore their ROE, bankers would tilt their portfolios even *more* toward mortgage-backed securities, in essence levering up more in an economic sense, yet remaining safer in a Basel risk-weighted sense.[2]

There are several things that could be done differently in the Dodd-Frank Act to avoid such a correlated buildup of mortgage exposures starting in 2003. First, rather than taking an a priori stance that one asset will remain safer than some other asset, the regulators could assess this by applying an annual stress test of the financial sector based on the composition of assets in different banks' portfolios. If all of them were concentrated in mortgages, they would hardly represent a safer asset class from a systemic risk standpoint. Or the systemic risk itself could be assessed in a reduced-form measure that investigates whether banks' equity returns imply greater systemic risk—for example, if they are more correlated with the overall market or the financial sector as a whole. If applied during the pre-2007 period, our research shows that such measures would have (1) noted that the most systemically risky institutions were the investment banks (which were also most highly leveraged), followed by Fannie Mae and Freddie Mac, and (2) suggested charging them with a higher capital requirement or a systemic risk tax instead of simply raising the level of capital requirement uniformly for all players.

Second, the regulators should have recognized that, if a particular asset were given capital relief relative to some other asset based on past performance, there would—in response to the capital relief—be greater allocation to that asset by the banks in question. This allocation would lead to lower-quality loans over time, and the two assets would converge in their risk qualities and possibly even swap risk rankings. Ignoring the response of asset allocators to policymaking and treating the design of capital requirements as a purely statistical exercise focused on estimating and buffering against past losses on assets are fatal flaws in the Basel tool kit that the Dodd-Frank Act has failed to correct.

Of course, the Dodd-Frank Act is not just focused on capital requirements. It proposes liquidity requirements, as well. But putting aside more liquidity would not have been difficult in 2003 because of the huge capital inflows from current-account-surplus countries, such as China, into current-account-deficit countries, such as the United States, the United Kingdom, and Spain. It is worth noting that the Dodd-Frank Act—notwithstanding the Bureau of Consumer Finance Protection it plans to set up—would have done little to prevent the enormous lending bubble specific to subprime mortgages in the United States. In large part, that bubble was the result of the intentional politically driven expansion of owner-occupied housing. The Act does nothing to address the worst-performing shadow banks—Fannie Mae and Freddie Mac—which were at the center of the housing expansion, had to be taken into government conservatorship in the early fall of 2008, and have cost U.S. taxpayers more than the total of all Wall Street institutions, with no end in sight. Although we are assured that this is the next policy priority, separating Fannie and Freddie from the financial reforms of the Dodd-Frank Act only highlights their intensely political role in mortgage finance, a role that is unfortunately highly distortionary from the standpoint of financial stability of the system.

It is also worth asking if the Volcker Rule provisions of the Dodd-Frank Act would have helped to stem the crisis by limiting the trading activities of banks like Citigroup. The way the Volcker rules are written, they would not have constrained the risk-taking activities of banks for a very long time (even now, they are likely to bind only for a few large players such as Goldman Sachs). But, assuming they were binding, would they have prevented the buildup of systemic risk? The answer is less than crystal clear. Proprietary trading is defined as short-term trading on your own accounts. Much risk was undertaken by commercial banks by simply borrowing short, lending long, and not holding adequate capital for the maturity mismatch. This form of risk taking is not technically called proprietary trading, but without adequate capital, maturity mismatch is just another form of a carry trade, which generates a small return most of the time, but can eventually blow up in a big way. A part of this maturity mismatch was possible as banks exploited weak capital requirements. A lot would thus depend on how the Volcker rules are interpreted for the process of moving assets into structured investment vehicles (SIVs) and conduits. It is not hard to imagine interpretations of the Volcker Rule that would make such activities more attractive (in a relative sense compared to short-term proprietary trading) and potentially create even more tail risk.

Finally, the Act also gives rights to prudential regulators to break up the systemically important institutions when they get into trouble and requires wind-down plans of these institutions in advance for resolving them in an orderly manner. We argue, however, that there remains substantial uncertainty that this is going to work well, if at all.

To illustrate this, assume a credit boom took hold in the financial sector from 2003 to the second quarter of 2007, followed by a housing price collapse across the board in the United States. In March 2008, Bear Stearns was beginning to experience trouble as a result of its poor equity base relative to its leverage (of course, it remained well capitalized from the Basel capital standpoint!). Bear's balance sheet had an asset side exposed to the housing market and a liability side that was extremely fragile and exposed to runs. In particular, Bear Stearns was rolling over each night in excess of $75 billion of repo contracts on mortgage-backed securities. These were AAA-rated for the most part but were anticipated to have losses in the future and rightly feared to be illiquid by the repo financiers, mainly money market mutual funds. Bear's primary money market financiers—Fidelity and Federated—feared having to liquidate the underlying collateral in an illiquid market at substantial fire-sale discounts (since they would not be able to hold long-term assets without violating their maturity restrictions). They refused to roll over the repos. Bear Stearns had to draw down on its $20 billion pool of liquidity, and within a week was brought to its knees with no assets on its balance sheet that could be pledged in markets without investors fearing the risk of rollover and thus charging substantial haircuts. Bear Stearns faced bankruptcy by the middle of March.

The first two weeks of March 2008 can be considered the run phase of the Bear Stearns collapse. As Bear faced bankruptcy, authorities had to decide whether to let it fail. Bankruptcy would lead to substantial liquidations of its assets backing the repos that were still outstanding, which would translate to losses to Bear's commercial paper providers—again, mainly money market mutual funds. In short, the failure of Bear Stearns could have led some money market funds to "break the buck" (net asset value falls below $1 per share), as the Reserve Primary Fund eventually did when Lehman Brothers was allowed to fail in mid-September of 2008. This would have precipitated redemptions from money market funds, in general, because many of them were exposed to investment banks with portfolios similar to Bear's. Also complicating the scenario was the fact that Bear Stearns was a primary clearer of a large number of credit default swaps, effectively performing the role of a clearing bank (if not exactly a clearinghouse) as a private entity side by side with its other investment banking activities. The failure of Bear would have thus created severe uncertainty about possible contagion spreading through the network of counterparty exposures—as the failure of AIG in mid-September 2008 would have had it not been backstopped by the government.

Now, suppose the Dodd-Frank Act had been in place at the time of Bear's collapse. The first thing to note is that the Federal Reserve would not have been able to act as swiftly to provide direct aid to Bear in the form of the guarantees that were required to facilitate its sale to JPMorgan Chase. The Dodd-Frank Act limits the Section 13(3) lending authority of the Fed. The Fed would have had to appeal to the Systemic Risk Council to begin the reorganization process. It is hard to know if the Council would have responded with sufficient speed and cohesion to meet the needs of the situation, but the constraints on the Fed could have arguably made the panic worse. Note also that even a forceful version of the Volcker Rule would have made no difference for the structure or risks on Bear's balance sheet because it does not restrict the proprietary trading activities of nonbanks.

One thing the Dodd-Frank Act does is increase transparency in markets in a number of ways, and that would have helped in the Bear Stearns case. One of the biggest problems confronting regulators at the time was uncertainty about counterparty exposures and their likely consequences. With the Dodd-Frank provisions in place, the credit default swaps that Bear was clearing would most likely have been cleared instead through a central clearinghouse. For their part, the clearinghouse and the regulators would have had access to full information on various counterparties, and therefore would have been able to assess whether there was, in fact, substantial settlement risk arising from reintermediation of swaps cleared by Bear Stearns. And, even if some of the swaps were not centrally cleared, the transparency requirements of the Dodd-Frank Act would have meant that information about counterparties to these swaps would have been in a centralized data repository such as the Depository Trust & Clearing Corporation (DTCC). Armed with this knowledge, regulators could have dealt with containing the damage and pacifying markets if there were no significant exposures, after taking account of the (greater) collateral or margin that would have been required under the Dodd-Frank Act.

The only uncertainty would arise if there were substantial uncollateralized exposures to another counterparty, say Goldman Sachs, that would now face a significant write-down. Without a clear plan to deal with this exposure, the regulators would struggle to release information to the market that Goldman Sachs was in trouble as a result of Bear's failure. But a lack of revelation of such information by regulators would itself be adverse information to markets! What would be required under such circumstances is a temporary mechanism to deal with the uncollateralized exposure—for example, making Goldman Sachs a conservative payment against its exposure through the Fed's emergency lending Section 13(3) assistance—but with a claw-back based on eventual reintermediation or liquidation costs incurred on these exposures.

The resolution process would have been triggered by Bear's difficulty, and the orderly liquidation of positions could take place in principle. But the important question remains: Would the regulators implementing the Act—the Treasury, the Fed, the FDIC—have been able to stick to its premise of passing along all losses on its counterparty exposures at a time when the whole system was subject to similar exposures? As we have said before, while the Act has its heart in the right place in wanting to eliminate the too-big-to-fail problem, there is a fair bit of uncertainty left in terms of exact resolution and wind-down procedures. While markets would certainly not digest such uncertainty well, history has shown over and again that regulators do not, either, and there would have been a call for emergency powers overriding the provisions of the Dodd-Frank Act.

The Bear Stearns example also highlights another generic problem with the Dodd-Frank Act: that it does not come to grips with the question of what is a bank and what is banking, and therefore it does not address many of the issues of the shadow banking system. It contains nothing that would deal with the commercial paper and repo market runs that triggered Bear's collapse. In cases when the liquidated values on repo contracts and anticipated recoveries on commercial paper holdings turn out to be substantially discounted, some of the money market funds providing the financing might get pushed to breaking the buck. Without a clear plan to resolve money market fund failures, the depositors of money market funds would now rush in to claim their deposits before others could, imposing further redemption issues for these funds. Some of the depositors might have deposits in other funds, too, and realizing losses on one set of savings, they might need to liquidate some others, inducing a contagious run on these other funds.

Once again, one would need the Fed to step in to temporarily provide liquidity to stop the redemptions—provisions that could be at conservative valuations of money market fund assets. And the unwinding of insolvent funds would have to be orderly in due course with additional losses clawed back from investors redeemed by the Fed. The same questions arise, however. Given that this is the Fed's Section 13(3) emergency lending to a nonbank holding company, would the Financial Stability Oversight Council approve it quickly enough, or would uncertainty about the outcome of the process lead investors to rush even faster to pull out their deposits, thus exacerbating the run?

Hence, in all likelihood, even with the Dodd-Frank Act in place, we would have seen something like what happened in the demise of Lehman Brothers if Bear had been allowed to collapse. While some may argue this may have been a good thing—letting Bear fail in March 2008 rather than Lehman in September 2008—the bigger point is that failures of both required orderly resolution. This, in turn, required temporary liquidity assistance to stem the run or the authority to suspend redemptions for a period, by which orderly unwinding of assets of failed institutions could be planned.

At the heart of the problem is the bankruptcy exemption given to repo and derivatives contracts, and the Dodd-Frank Act explicitly keeps that in place. It is clear that this exemption is needed, because without it, a large number of contracts could get stuck in the bankruptcy of a failing firm. The exemption, however, requires a systemic exception. When there were bank runs in the pre-FDIC era, commercial bank clearinghouses in New York would suspend redemption of individual bank deposits and convert those into joint liability certificates of the clearinghouse. Then, we put deposit insurance in place to deal with depositor runs more directly. In the crisis of 2007 to 2009, when we faced wholesale depositor runs, the Federal Reserve had to pull out all the stops—given the lack of FDIC coverage of such deposits—to effectively suspend the runs. And, in between these episodes, almost all massive bank failures have required such suspension. The systemic bankruptcy exception—that all claims immediately payable be stayed for a day or a few days—could work in the context of the Dodd-Frank Act, if the orderly resolution process acts swiftly enough. For instance, if the regulator has 24 hours to transfer the derivatives of a counterparty to a third party, and at that point the counterparty does not get to (or need to) terminate the contracts, then the liquidity problems would be much more muted. But this may require the Fed to employ its emergency lending facility, which the Dodd-Frank Act explicitly restricts in the context of individual nonbanks.

The good news is that the Dodd-Frank Act does leave substantial latitude to the prudential regulators—the FDIC and the Federal Reserve System—to design orderly resolution procedures. Our back-to-the-future tests make it clear that for the Act to succeed in putting an end to taxpayer-funded bailouts, prudential regulators need to design (1) resolution and wind-down plans not just for systemically important institutions, but also for system-ically important markets and collections of small institutions, and (2) ro-bust mechanisms to deal with runs on the system at large from short-term creditors—runs that can arise not just in retail deposits (which have been addressed since 1934), but also with wholesale finance (such as repos, com-mercial paper, and derivatives) that were at the heart of the recent financial crisis. What is clear is that we have not yet made plans to address this aspect of the issue.

CONCLUSION

As we prepare for the implementation of the new reforms to our financial regulatory system, it is useful to remember that the major round of reforms in the 1930s was appropriate based on the problems faced by policymakers and legislators in the wake of the Great Depression. Many of the reforms put in place had long-lasting benefits and are still with us. But the problems exposed by the current financial crisis are not the same as those of the 1930s, so it would be a mistake to think we can fix them simply by going back to the 1930s solutions. That is why we have to focus on their success at addressing the critical flaws that led to the financial crisis: our failure to make financial firms pay for government guarantees, our failure to control systemic risk, our failure to implement orderly resolution mechanisms for large systemic institutions, and our failure to bring the shadow banking system into the regulatory orbit.

In a somewhat less well-known passage from *The Wealth of Nations*, Adam Smith explains beautifully that:

> *To restrain private people, it may be said, from receiving in pay-ment the promissory notes of a banker for any sum, whether great or small, when they themselves are willing to receive them; or, to restrain a banker from issuing such notes, when all his neighbors are willing to accept of them, is a manifest violation of that natu-ral liberty, which it is the proper business of law not to infringe, but to support. Such regulations may, no doubt, be considered as*

in some respects a violation of natural liberty. But those exertions of the natural liberty of a few individuals, which might endanger the security of the whole society, are, and ought to be, restrained by the laws of all governments; of the most free, as well as of the most despotical. The obligation of building party walls, in order to prevent the communication of fire, is a violation of natural liberty, exactly of the same kind with the regulations of the banking trade which are here proposed.

The Dodd-Frank Act is right in charging depository banks—and their prudential regulators—to build party walls. But the fire can (and did) happen elsewhere in the shadow banking system.

The Dodd-Frank Act is right in demanding an orderly resolution to fires when they break out, but by putting hard brakes on emergency services that can extinguish fires, it exposes the system to serious risk in case the fire alarms fail and the sprinklers do not start.

The Dodd-Frank Act is right in putting an end to taxpayers' footing the bill to put out fires. But it makes little economic sense to charge neighbors for that and, especially so, when their houses are in great danger of catching fire too.

And alas, much of what the Dodd-Frank Act attempts to do may be for naught if the government continues to fund future fires through Fannie Mae and Freddie Mac with no walls around whatsoever!

In the end, we applaud the Dodd-Frank Act's ambition and its copious attempt to rewrite financial sector regulation. The Act does represent the culmination of several months of sincere effort on the part of the legislators, their staffers, the prudential regulators, academics, policy think tanks, and, of course, the financial industry (and the lobbyists!). But it is equally important to recognize that the most ambitious overhaul of the financial sector regulation in our times does not fully address private incentives of individual institutions to put the system at risk, leaves a great deal of uncertainty as to how we will resolve future crises, and is likely to be anachronistic, in parts, right from the day of its legislation. Not all is lost, though, and these limitations can be fixed in due course. To understand how, read the rest of the book!

OUTLINE

The remainder of the book is organized into five sections: **Financial Architecture, Systemic Risk, Shadow Banking, Credit Markets,** and **Corporate Control.** Each section consists of several chapters focusing on specific aspects of the Dodd-Frank Act as they relate to an important set of institutions, markets, risks, and means to control these risks. In turn, each chapter lays out the overall issue, our summary and assessment of the Dodd-Frank Act's legislations relating to the issue, how the failures and weaknesses of the Act in addressing the issue could be corrected in the future, and finally, what the implications of the legislations for global finance are going forward. Throughout, we have attempted—as in this Prologue—to couch the analysis under the umbrella of sound economic theory for regulating externalities (in this case, systemic risk) and to always be looking out for unintended consequences of proposed regulation as well as opportunities for the financial sector to engage in regulatory arbitrage around it.

In **Financial Architecture**, we examine three issues: what will broadly be **The Architecture of Financial Regulation** following the Dodd-Frank Act in terms of which regulators will cover which sets of institutions and markets and what are the important gaps; whether the Act was in the end sufficiently wise in guarding **The Power of Central Banks and the Future of the Federal Reserve System**, but whether it has put excessive restrictions on the Fed's ability to perform the lender-of-last-resort function that might be necessary for orderly resolution of systemically important firms; and whether the newly proposed **Consumer Finance Protection** agency is likely to serve a useful purpose for the society even though it seems somewhat of an aberration in terms of what was required to address systemic risk of financial firms.

In **Systemic Risk**, which frames the most important part of our book, we study in turn the Act's proposals for **Measuring Systemic Risk**, recommending that in addition to descriptive criteria, market-based measures be employed with regulatory stress tests and gathering of information on interconnectedness of financial firms. In **Taxing Systemic Risk**, we take a rather critical stand on the Act and argue that its reluctance, and ultimately refusal, to charge systemically important institutions for the guarantees they enjoy and for externalities of their failures is a significant logical error. In fact, we explain why some of the Dodd-Frank Act's proposals worsen incentives of firms to build up systemic risk. The Act prefers instead to adopt **Capital, Contingent Capital, and Liquidity Requirements**, and we assess the likely efficacy of various proposals on the table, including Basel III and some new ones, clarifying when and why they may not be sufficient as substitutes for a more direct systemic risk charge.

The next two chapters in the **Systemic Risk** section deal with direct restrictions on risk taking (**Large Banks and the Volcker Rule**) to separate short-term proprietary trading, hedge funds, and private equity funds from bank holding companies, whether the rule goes sufficiently far to address the too-big-to-fail problem, and if the much needed **Resolution Authority** to handle failures of large, complex financial institutions will be sufficiently effective in achieving its end purpose. On both issues, we remain skeptical, but especially so on whether orderly resolution is well thought through in the Dodd-Frank Act. In fact, we are somewhat concerned that even more uncertainty has been added to the process than in the past. In the final chapter of this section, we provide a detailed discussion of **Systemic Risk and the Regulation of Insurance Companies,** an issue that was at the center of the crisis through AIG's risk taking and failure but which, somewhat surprisingly, has remained unaddressed for most part in the Act.

In **Shadow Banking,** we examine those markets and institutions that have hitherto been unregulated or at least weakly regulated compared to functionally similar banking institutions. In **Money Market Funds,** we explain why the Dodd-Frank Act does not fully resolve the issue of dealing with a full-scale run on money market funds, as witnessed following the collapse of Lehman Brothers, and we propose an orderly resolution mechanism for the same. **The Repurchase Agreement (Repo) Market** represents another glaring omission even though the repo run on Bear Stearns was among the most salient failure mechanisms of the crisis. Again, we propose a repo resolution authority that regulators may consider in future for addressing repo runs. We then discuss whether some of the transparency proposals concerning asset management funds, namely **Hedge Funds, Mutual Funds, and ETFs,** go a touch too far. And finally, we explain why one of the biggest successes of the Dodd-Frank Act may in the end lie in **Regulating OTC Derivatives,** over 450 pages of the Act that propose a comprehensive reform of over-the-counter (OTC) derivative markets. While there is much to admire here—in particular, the central clearing and transparency proposals—a lot has also been left to prudential regulators. There are a number of adjustments and modifications that could make the Act's implementation in the years to come even stronger from the standpoint of reducing systemic risk linked to leverage and opacity of OTC markets.

In **Credit Markets,** we highlight the biggest omission of the Act, namely that it ignores completely **The Government-Sponsored Enterprises** (especially Fannie Mae and Freddie Mac) as the most systemically important institutions of the financial sector. We propose mechanisms to unwind Fannie and Freddie, and to reorganize U.S. mortgage finance—in the short run and in the long run—to develop a more vibrant, more privatized mortgage securitization market. We then consider the **Regulation of Rating Agencies** and whether the Dodd-Frank Act addresses the conflicts of interest in the issuer-pay model of rating securitized products, and next whether the **Securitization Reform** deals adequately with the incentive problems in the originate-to-distribute model of lending and the regulatory arbitrage problems in laying risks off the balance sheet evinced by the crisis.

In the final section of the book on **Corporate Control,** we tackle **Reforming Compensation and Corporate Governance,** whether the reforms are necessary, and if they are likely to be effective absent full internalization of systemic risk costs by large financial firms. Last, we dscuss **Accounting and Financial Reform** relating to mark-to-market accounting (whether it gives early signals of stress or exacerbates it), and accounting treatment of risks versus their regulatory treatment for capital purposes.

NOTES

1. This was true under Basel II capital requirements that applied to European banks. While Basel I capital requirements applicable to the U.S. commercial banks did not give the privileged capital treatment to AAA-rated tranches, these banks could reduce their capital requirements by a factor of five to 10, by putting assets off the balance sheet into conduits and structured investment vehicles (SIVs). And the U.S. investment banks were allowed to use their internal models to calculate risks in 2004, which reduced capital requirements on AAA-rated tranches practically to zero. For the sake of argument, however, we will stick to the Basel II requirements in our exercise.
2. Similarly, any propensity of commercial banks to offload assets into conduits and SIVs, and thereby lower regulatory capital, would also become only stronger.

PART One

Financial Architecture

CHAPTER 1

The Architecture of Financial Regulation

Thomas Cooley and Ingo Walter*

There are four pillars of effective regulatory architecture that are common across all financial systems. Good architecture should (1) encourage innovation and efficiency, (2) provide transparency, (3) ensure safety and soundness, and (4) promote competitiveness in global markets. Efforts to pursue these objectives at the same time inevitably create difficult policy trade-offs. Measures that assure greater financial robustness may make financial intermediation less efficient or innovative, for example. Efforts to promote financial innovation may erode transparency, safety, and soundness. Competitive pressure among financial centers may trigger a race to the bottom in terms of systemic robustness to internal and external shocks.

Unfortunately, benchmarks underlying the financial architecture, on which it is easy to find agreement, are far more difficult to define in detail—and even more difficult to calibrate in practice. We know that excessive regulation involves costs, but what are they? We also know that underregulation can unleash disaster, which can be observed only after the fact. So optimum regulation is the art of balancing the immeasurable against the unknowable. It is not surprising that financial crises are a recurrent phenomenon.

In this chapter we spell out the practical alternatives for financial regulation and identify the nature of their impact on key attributes of financial products, markets, and firms. We then narrow the range of regulatory options to those contained in the Dodd-Frank Wall Street Reform and Consumer Protection Act of 2010 and comparable regulatory initiatives around

---

*The authors benefited from discussions in "The Architecture of Financial Regulation" Working Group for the NYU Stern e-book *Real Time Solutions for Financial Reform*, which also included Lawrence J. White.

the world, and assess them in light of the four pillars of regulatory architecture underlying a financial system that successfully serves the public interest.

1.1 WALKING THE REGULATORY TIGHTROPE

The Prologue to this volume makes clear that financial intermediation is an essential economic activity that is fraught with difficulties. There are frequent market failures involving asymmetric information, costly state verification, and missing markets. Even in the simpler world of the early twentieth century, such problems brought the financial system to its knees repeatedly until a more robust regulatory structure—one that somehow managed to work tolerably well for a long time—was designed in the 1930s. Over the ensuing decades that structure was altered to accommodate new institutions, new financial instruments, financial globalization, and periodic shocks and market failures. Over time it began to resemble a structure that had been modified too many times and in too many ways to efficiently accommodate the growing complexities of modern financial intermediation. Eventually it reached a tipping point and failed spectacularly, with huge costs to the global economy.

Although the worst of the financial crisis of 2007 to 2009 has passed, the defects of the dominant institutions remain. They continue to pose grave risks to future financial stability. So a new regulatory architecture has become inevitable, and it is important to consider how it will perform.

Regulatory architecture is critical to resource allocation and economic growth. Economies with inefficient financial systems demonstrably waste more economic resources and grow more slowly than otherwise comparable economies with efficient financial systems. Economies with weak financial systems continue to plug into global financial markets in search of low-cost capital, so they are no longer immune to global shocks and sometimes contaminate the system with shocks of their own. Good financial architecture has to be robust to shocks that emanate from the financial system and the real economy both domestically and internationally.

Adding yet another layer of complexity are the institutions charged with executing regulatory mandates affecting the financial architecture. Should regulators be organized by function—such as commercial banking, investment banking and financial markets, asset management, and insurance—allowing them to gain enough industry expertise to have a reasonable understanding of what it is they are regulating? Or should they be structured in line with the firms they are regulating, ranging from financial conglomerates to community banks, so they can better oversee the complexities and avoid overinvestment in regulatory infrastructure where it isn't needed?

And who should monitor the buildup of systemic risk in the financial structure as a whole (macro-prudential risk), which goes well beyond the remit of regulators covering individual firms (micro-prudential risk)? This in turn raises the question of who gets to determine when firms have failed, and how to resolve them if they are no longer viable? And should those doing the resolving be the same people who created the failure or stood by and watched it happen in the first place?

In great architecture, "form follows function." Financial architecture is really no different. The institutional structure that should be created to implement the regulatory changes that have now been passed into law in the United States depends critically on certain macro decisions about the goals of the regulation. If some activities are carved out of financial conglomerates into independent financial specialists, for example, a sensible regulatory architecture may be very different from what would be needed if financial conglomerates are left intact, with all of their internal complexity, conflicts of interest, and opaqueness.

Finally, there is the critical issue of regulatory execution, which is almost always done by high-minded and overworked civil servants standing against the best and the brightest on the payrolls of those they are supposed to be regulating. Plenty of examples attest to the inequality of this battle, with well-intentioned regulation undermined by regulatory arbitrage that distorts its purpose and implementation.

There are many regulatory issues at stake. How do we protect consumers? What should we do about corporate pay? What should we do about mortgages? How should we regulate derivatives? And so on. All are important to someone, but there is one issue that is important to all: How do we construct a system of regulation in which decisions made in one or a few financial institutions cannot bring the entire system to a halt and the world's economies to their knees? This is the problem of containing systemic risk. Without question it is the single most important issue.

The U.S. Dodd-Frank Wall Street Reform and Consumer Protection Act of 2010 and the discussions being held elsewhere in the G-20 countries are at least in part a reflection of popular sentiment—notably a powerful emotional antipathy toward bankers—lobbying by special interests, and substantial political trade-offs and maneuvering. But that is the history of both our financial system and financial regulation. Here our goal is to offer informed commentary on the new structures for financial regulation that are on the table, and an idea of what might be done better. Since regulation and government intervention are an explicit acknowledgment of market failure, there is an inherent acceptance of the cliché that we should not let the perfect be the enemy of the good.

The regulatory dialectic in the financial services sector is both sophisticated and complex, and it often confronts heavily entrenched and politically well-connected players—and runs up against the personal financial interests of some of the brightest minds and biggest egos in business. The more complex the industry, the greater the challenge to sensible regulation, probably nowhere as strikingly as in the case of massive, complex, global financial services conglomerates that may be too hard to manage, too hard to oversee and govern, and almost certainly too hard to monitor and regulate.

To preview our line of thinking, we believe that by far the best way to address the most important issue of all—systemic risk—is to make the firms that create it pay a fair price for having created it. This requires measuring, pricing, and taxing systemic risk, as discussed in detail in Chapters 4 and 5 of this book. The only alternative is to require institutions that manufacture systemic risk to become simpler by separating their excessively risky activities into independent firms, as discuss in Chapter 7.

Whether derisking the financial system by correctly pricing systemic risk or by segregating highly risky functions into nonsystemic firms, a powerful regulatory capability is essential. The financial crisis of 2007 to 2009 has highlighted the failure of other approaches—such as managerial self-regulation, proper corporate governance, industry self-regulation, and market discipline—to successfully contain systemic risk. It is far too late for the financial industry to argue that lessons have been learned that ensure that firm-level and system-level risk management will work better next time.

1.2 ALTERNATIVE APPROACHES TO FINANCIAL REGULATION

The new regulatory architecture embodied in the Dodd-Frank Wall Street Reform and Consumer Protection Act of 2010 is a complicated brew—one that changes much but does so without an overarching and coherent structural design. Indeed, it deals only partially with one of the most striking and dangerous aspects of international finance that has developed over the past decade or two, namely the growth of the shadow banking system. These are firms or business units of financial conglomerates that perform key functions of banks but to a significant degree fall outside the regulatory system. They include hedge funds, private equity funds, mutual funds, derivatives, and repo markets that incur market risk, credit risk, liquidity risk, and operational risk. Like water channeling its way to the sea, financial flows seek the least costly and least regulated bypasses, mostly through the shadow banking system. So unless the regulatory architecture encompasses these flows, it is doomed eventually to fail.

Starting with the end of the 2007 to 2009 global financial crisis and taking on board the valuable lessons learned, we can identify four alternative routes to improve the financial architecture in terms of satisfying the criteria we have in mind: encouraging innovation and efficiency, providing transparency, ensuring safety and soundness, and promoting competitiveness in global markets.

Modified Laissez-Faire

The first option essentially involves maintaining the institutional status quo—the Gramm-Leach-Bliley rules permitting financial conglomerates in the United States and universal banking rules in other countries—and allowing banks or bank holding companies to engage in all forms of financial intermediation and principal investing worldwide, subject to certain firewalls and other safeguards. These safeguards would be modified to deal with systemic risk and incorporate the lessons of the financial crisis of 2007 to 2009. This option is heavily favored by the major financial firms in the United States, and major regulators elsewhere have recommitted themselves to the universal banking or financial conglomerate model. Despite much evidence to the contrary, they believe that bigger and broader are better.

Laissez-faire was the initial approach of the Obama administration, which in March 2009 announced a package of proposed regulatory reforms and new measures to deal with systemic risk. These principles are to a large extent reflected in the Dodd-Frank Act. The success of this approach depends critically on the government's ability to install and enforce an effective set of rules through a constellation of new or reinvigorated regulatory agencies covering a wide variety of different types of financial institutions in both the banking and the shadow banking worlds. With much financial intermediation having moved to the shadow banking sector and falling outside of the purview of the existing regulatory agencies, the consequence is a loss of transparency and a huge increase in the informational asymmetries in markets. So getting the regulatory architecture right poses an enormous challenge, given that the regulators themselves have had a dismal record of preventing crises through the enforcement of rules in the existing regulatory structure.

The key elements of a modified laissez-faire approach—one that would improve the safety and soundness of all financial intermediaries—involves (1) creating an appropriate mandate and tools for a systemic risk regulator, (2) pricing implicit public subsidies to systemic financial firms using capital and liquidity requirements, (3) improving the transparency of the financial system, and (4) creating the bankruptcy tools the financial system needs.

The 1930s U.S. financial reforms were truly revolutionary in their time, and in many ways visionary. The modified laissez-faire approach of today is more incremental. It mainly patches holes in a failed system and establishes early warning and corrective action, which would hopefully catch the next big crisis in time to prevent systemwide damage.

Could this modified laissez-faire approach succeed? Much depends on how well the new systemic risk regulator—the Federal Reserve—is able to do its job. Is it really likely that systemic institutions that have shown themselves to be too big and complex to manage and too big, complex, and interconnected to regulate by the past regulatory structure will in the end be rendered fail-safe under the evolutionary new regime?

There is also the issue of regulatory capture. The ease with which the investment banking industry was able to convince the Securities and Exchange Commission (SEC) to allow an increase in its leverage ratios in 2004, or the banking industry was able to capture the Federal Deposit Insurance Corporation (FDIC) politically and get in place limits on FDIC insurance contributions, or the commercial banking industry was able to undermine hard-fought progress on fair value accounting and permit banks to manipulate earnings in 2009 does not augur well for future regulatory capture. Nor does the 2010 report of the Lehman Brothers bankruptcy examiner regarding the firm's ability to collectively bamboozle regulators, auditors, rating agencies, lawyers, and investors by slipping through the cracks in the system—for example, by creatively using repo transactions. It will not be the last time. Much talent in the years ahead will be devoted to avoidance, evasion, obfuscation, and financial innovation with little or no commercial or social purpose.

Critics of the Federal Reserve as the lead regulator of systemic financial firms have argued that its track record in the run-up to the most recent crisis proved to be very poor indeed. Together with the U.S. Treasury, its damage-control efforts in the crisis broke all precedents and increased the amount of moral hazard and competitive concentration in the financial system. It was not necessarily worse than the combined efforts of the Bank of England and the Financial Services Authority in the United Kingdom, or the European Central Bank (which does not have a direct regulatory mandate) and the gaggle of national regulators in continental Europe. Like the United States, it's back to the drawing board for the regulatory architecture in major financial systems around the world.

Excessive pessimism is certainly premature, but the Fed's increased politicization is a virtual certainty going forward, as its mandate extends further from monetary policy into politically sensitive macro-prudential and micro-prudential domains. So it is surely a design weakness of the laissez-faire approach if it permits monetary policy to be distorted by these new mandates.

However, successful pricing of systemic risk using a combination of capital and liquidity requirements, along with the cost of more intense supervision, holds considerable promise. These are aforementioned taxes that are intended to internalize the negative externalities created by firms that produce systemic risk. Ultimately, their success will depend on how effectively they reflect the systemic risk of the financial institutions subject to them, and how these requirements are extended into the shadow banking system. If boards and managements are doing their jobs, they will carefully reexamine the costs and benefits of remaining massive financial conglomerates, for example, and find ways of escaping into less heavily taxed nonsystemic organizational forms.

Glass-Steagall 2.0

The argument for reinstating Glass-Steagall-like bank activity restrictions is that certain profitable but volatile activities of investment banks and other parts of the shadow banking system are incompatible with the special character of commercial banking—namely, operating the payments system, taking deposits and making commercial loans, and serving as the transmission belt for monetary policy. These activities include underwriting and dealing in corporate debt and equities, asset-backed debt and certain other securities, derivatives of such securities as credit default swaps, principal investing, and managing in-house hedge funds. These activities are also deemed to be incompatible with access to Federal Reserve discount facilities, debt guarantees, and other types of government support intended to safeguard the public-utility attributes of commercial banking.

Under this regulatory option, the legacy investment banks that converted to bank holding companies during the crisis in order to gain full access to the government safety net (Goldman Sachs and Morgan Stanley) would revert to broker-dealer status and would be functionally regulated as such, with additional oversight by the systemic risk regulator. The investment banking divisions of commercial banks would be sold, floated, or spun off to shareholders and similarly regulated. U.S. investment banking divisions of foreign financial conglomerates would be divested as well, or operate as separately capitalized subsidiaries of their foreign-based financial conglomerate parents.

Some have suggested that the Glass-Steagall constraints of 1933 may in fact have performed relatively well for over half a century, when benchmarked against all four of the criteria noted earlier—efficiency, innovation, robustness, and competitiveness. The epic battle between bank-based and capital-market-based finance, domestically and internationally, created competitive pressure for all financial intermediaries. The U.S. financial system was stable and prosperous in spite of many shocks and changing monetary standards during the 66 years Glass-Steagall was in effect.

An alternative view is that the U.S. financial system prospered *in spite of* the restrictions imposed by Glass-Steagall because of the country's uniquely powerful economic position in the aftermath of World War II. During this period, New York became the leading global center of finance, with London as its only serious rival. All of the continental financial centers, dominated as they were by universal banks, dropped by the wayside as their own investment banking units joined their chief global wholesale rivals in London and New York. Many investment banks gravitated to an integrated full-service business model and thrived without access to central bank liquidity facilities or public bailouts in the case of failures like Barings in London or Peregrine Securities in Hong Kong. The same was true of buy-side specialists in the mutual fund business (e.g., Fidelity and Vanguard), pension funds (e.g., TIAA-CREF in the United States and Hermes in the United Kingdom), and hedge funds (e.g., Soros and Tiger).

The survival and even prosperity of financial specialists in the presence of government-supported and -subsidized bank holding companies suggests that a modern version of Glass-Steagall would not turn out to be ruinous. Mergers and acquisitions (M&A) boutiques ranging from Perella Weinberg to Lazard Frères seem to be thriving on the basis of dispassionate corporate advice, as are midsize investment banks like Jefferies & Company, which do a viable midmarket business and make a point forgoing government support, as opposed to their conglomerate rivals.

This is anecdotal evidence, of course, but it suggests that a powerful nonbank financial intermediation industry would quickly emerge following Glass-Steagall-type reregulation, one populated by more transparent firms that lend themselves to relatively straightforward oversight by functional regulators in tandem with a systemic risk regulator.

Functional Carve-Outs, Size Constraints, and the Volcker Rule

A less draconian approach to limiting the scope of banking activity, as Glass-Steagall did, is to recognize that some financial activities should not be allowed within systemic multifunctional firms. Among these activities are:

- Management of in-house hedge funds.
- Creating off-balance-sheet affiliates having no commercial purpose and dedicated to evading regulatory constraints.

- Running large proprietary trading positions in cash securities and derivatives that are not integral to the core process for financial intermediation.
- Acting as principal investors in nonfinancial activities such as real estate and private equity.

Financial conglomerates persistently argue that such carve-outs would limit synergies that are essential to their business models. But it is not clear that those synergies actually exist to the extent claimed, or if they do, whether they are in the public interest.

An alternative or complement to carve-outs is to limit the size of financial conglomerates that incorporate commercial banking units, so that they are forced to become nonsystemic. Metrics to achieve this could include market share caps or deposit ceilings or asset ceilings. This would not involve activity prohibitions, but size-constrained financial conglomerates would soon lose critical mass in specific areas of engagement, and presumably would try to focus on the most profitable ones and divest others. This could be a more market-aligned and elegant solution than specific activity carve-outs.

Given murky evidence so far on the relationships between firm size and efficiency, stability, and competitiveness, size constraints may have some merit. Paradoxically, the general response of policymakers to the crisis thus far (except for Lehman Brothers) is to make financial Goliaths even bigger and even more systemic.

Global Alignment

One of the continuing themes in the discussions of financial regulation is the problem of global alignment versus fragmentation. Even supporters of the modified laissez-faire approach, discussed earlier, are concerned with global coordination and in particular with avoiding competitive distortions that would impede the continued globalization of finance.[1] The premise is that global mobility of capital has contributed significantly to world economic growth.

Observers point to the fact that national governments such as the United Kingdom, Switzerland, Japan, France, and the United States ultimately support the safety net covering financial conglomerates and other systemic firms based in their jurisdictions. In the case of large international firms based in small countries, the spillover from the systemic risk of institutional failure to sovereign risk is obvious. Compared to the United States, such countries therefore have an even greater incentive to implement serious safety and soundness policies for their financial firms, and then let the firms decide whether they should change their business models to avoid the costs. This incentive also suggests that most of the world's home countries of systemic financial firms would have a great interest in harmonization and coordination to make it all work.

Skeptics argue that most countries are so wedded to the universal banking model that they are unlikely to go along with any tougher regulatory architecture that may result in structural changes in financial conglomerates. Moreover, the decades it took to achieve the Basel Accords on capital adequacy and the ease with which they were evaded does not augur well for effective globally coordinated regulatory reforms. Indeed, the Basel Accords are the poster child for the failures of regulatory coordination. Basel III Accords are now under discussion, but most sovereign regulatory bodies recognize what a disaster Basel II was. This means it will take a long time to agree on regulations, and countries like the United States are unlikely to be bound by them.

An alternative is to force global systemic institutions to run their non-domestic financial operations as separately incorporated subsidiaries of the parent firm and regulated principally by the host countries where they do business. Host regulators, it is argued, are closer to the action and ultimately would have to carry the safety net, in effect ring-fencing local operations from support obligations on the part of the taxpayers of the parent firms' home countries. Understandably, this argument has been received most enthusiastically in small countries like Switzerland that are home to big, global, and systemically significant financial firms.

Like protectionism in international trade, the costs of regulatory fragmentation could be enormous, although these costs are often broadly dispersed and hard to measure. In the past, banks in many countries were protected from competition by entry restrictions and direct controls, in return for which they accepted the domestic regulations that were imposed on them. In today's global economy that is no longer feasible, and banks' ability to operate across national jurisdictions helps them to avoid regulations.

But that hardly means that countries have a built-in incentive to create porous regulatory environments. The United States and the United Kingdom, for example, have no reason to participate in a regulatory race to the bottom even if they pursue different approaches to regulation. Despite their recent problems, New York and London remain the two major financial centers in the world. Why? The answer is simple: good institutions, good legal systems, and a commitment to good regulation. Both will continue to be places where those with weaker institutions will want to do business, if only because the cost of capital is lower.

■   ■   ■

We conclude that, all things considered, given the facts on the ground, the most defensible approach to the new regulatory architecture in finance—assuming it can be carried out in a disciplined, consistent, internationally coordinated, and sustained manner with a firm eye to the public interest—is the first of these alternatives: modified laissez-faire.

By creating and enforcing a shadow price for systemic risk, universal banks and financial conglomerates will draw their own strategic conclusions in the context of the microeconomics and industrial organization of global wholesale financial intermediation. The hope is they will split themselves up into smaller, less systemic, more specialized, easier-to-regulate firms. Shareholders themselves can then decide what kinds of financial firms they want to own based on risk and return criteria, rather than being forced to own a fixed portfolio of businesses in the form of shares in financial conglomerates. Financial theory and empirical evidence suggest they will be better off as a result.[2]

But those who have become incurably cynical about politics and regulatory capture might think about advocating specific activity carve-outs (Option 3) as a second-best alternative, specifically as proposed under the original Volcker Rule. Either option stands some chance of forestalling another financial crisis—at least in the short run. If Option 1 turns out to fail this time, then Option 2 will surely be considered seriously after the next big financial debacle.

1.3 THE LEGISLATION

Based on the criteria that we have suggested ought to set the basis for reform of the financial architecture and the options that exist to meet those criteria, how does the Dodd-Frank Wall Street Reform and Consumer Protection Act of 2010 measure up?

Taken as a whole, the legislation does not incorporate a clear or consistent approach to the problem of regulating the financial sector. It incorporates elements from all four of the foregoing approaches, but mainly a great deal of modified laissez-faire plus a few restrictions on banks' activities. Perhaps its greatest failure is that it is not anchored in a serious consideration of the question of what is banking and what is a bank. As a result, it has no clear and coherent set of policies for dealing with the shadow banking system and bringing it under the regulatory umbrella in a systematic way. Indeed, the architectural compromises incorporated into the Act have resulted in a rather unwieldy structure.

A committee of regulators, the Financial Stability Oversight Council, is made responsible for monitoring systemic risk and taking measures to address it. The Federal Reserve is given a greatly expanded role in the supervision and regulation of systemic firms, including nonbanks, but the Fed's own powers to intervene in a crisis and to come to aid of the shadow banking system are constrained—as we discuss in the next chapter. It is hard to imagine a more complex and politicized task.

The Act requires that all bank holding companies with total consolidated assets of at least $50 billion, along with nonbank financial companies designated by the Council as systemically significant, will potentially be subject to heightened prudential standards promulgated and administered by the Fed. While the $50 billion threshold for bank holding companies is significant, the Fed retains important flexibility to distinguish between bank holding companies on the basis of their perceived riskiness, complexity, activities, size, and other factors in terms of which financial firms will be subject to stiffer prudential standards.

The Act does not set specific prudential requirements, but it identifies areas where the Council can recommend higher prudential standards and where the Fed must impose them. These stiffer standards include heightened capital requirements, rigorous leverage and liquidity requirements, risk management requirements, concentration limits (25 percent of capital stock and surplus), resolution plans (so-called living wills), and stress tests. Certain publicly traded companies supervised by the Fed will be required to establish independent risk committees.

Another significant feature of the legislation is that the Fed will be required to impose a strict 15:1 debt-to-equity leverage ratio on any financial company that the Council determines poses a "grave threat" to financial stability. The Fed will also be required to create an early remediation regime—similar in concept to the prompt corrective action (PCA) regime of the FDIC—in consultation with the Council and the FDIC.

The Fed will also have discretion to impose other prudential standards, including contingent capital requirements, enhanced public disclosure, short-term debt limits, and other measures the regulators decide are necessary to mitigate risk. The Act leaves open the possibility that the Fed may decide to require nonbank financial companies to segregate their financial activities into separate entities.

With respect to capital standards, the Act does take pains to avoid the Basel II trap. The Collins Amendment requires that the risk-based and leverage capital standards currently applicable to U.S. insured depository institutions be imposed on U.S. bank holding companies, including U.S. intermediate holding companies of foreign banking organizations, thrift holding companies, and systemically important nonbank financial companies. It requires that whatever capital and leverage standards are arrived at eventually will constitute a floor with respect to any future Basel III Accords.

The legislation shied away from size and line-of-business restrictions or activity carve-outs. Instead it envisions that the aforementioned, enhanced risk limitations can be successfully imposed and enforced by the Fed and the Council. The Act does not prevent the largest financial companies from growth by acquisition, but no financial company will be permitted to merge with another financial company if the consolidated liabilities of the combined firm exceed 10 percent of the total consolidated liabilities of all U.S. financial companies.

Large banks and other systemically important financial firms are otherwise left to function as they did before, although they will be being monitored more intensely and be subject to a variety of new nonsystemic regulatory constraints (consumer protection, derivatives trading, executive compensation, etc.).

The Act gives the Federal Reserve the authority to intervene in any systemically important financial company for the purpose of affecting liquidation, subject to a two-thirds vote of the Council of Regulators, provided that no government funds are used for any sort of creditor bailout without prior congressional approval. The bill includes a new orderly liquidation authority (OLA) that will replace the bankruptcy code and other applicable insolvency laws for liquidating financial companies and certain of their subsidiaries under certain circumstances. Under the new liquidation authority, the Treasury secretary would have the authority to appoint the FDIC as receiver of any financial company if certain conditions are satisfied.

A requirement for a dissolution insurance fund to be financed by annual premiums paid by systemically important firms was the focus of intense Republican opposition, and was ultimately dropped from the legislation. This omission was contrary to the advice of many observers in academia. Such a fund would have reimbursed the government for the too-big-to-fail subsidy of their borrowing costs as a way to set aside funds necessary for any future bailouts. Instead, the costs of remediation are to be borne by surviving firms—firms that turned out to be better managed and less risky. We continue to believe that this makes no sense whatsoever.

The Dodd-Frank Act does implement a much weakened form of the Volcker Rule (subject to further study) by limiting the amount banks may invest in proprietary hedge funds and private equity funds to 3 percent of Tier 1 capital, and prohibits proprietary trading in all but obligations of the U.S. government or its agencies and municipal debt. It also requires systemically important nonbank financial companies to carry additional capital and observe some limits on proprietary trading activities, but it does not expressly prohibit them. The Volcker Rule even in its weakened form is not effective until two years after enactment, and then there will be a two-year transition period with the possibility of additional extensions. Given those conditions, the Volcker Rule seems unlikely to be binding on the behavior of banks or shadow banks anytime soon, if ever.

A positive note is that the Act does a fair amount to improve the transparency of the financial system. It departs from the anything-goes culture of the past decade. It requires mandatory clearing of derivatives through regulated clearing organizations and mandatory trading through either regulated exchanges or swap execution facilities. It mandates new oversight and monitoring activities in the Fed, the Treasury, and the SEC. It falls short in coming to grips with the informational role played by rating agencies and understanding the key market failure that compromised their role in the past.[3]

Finally, the Dodd-Frank Act pays little real attention to international regulatory efforts or coordination. Members of Congress and the Obama administration assumed that whatever reforms come about in the United States will be the first to appear, and therefore would inevitably become the template for the world. The main exception is a willingness to be part of the discussion of revised minimum bank capital adequacy standards in the form of Basel III that could be implemented after substantial negotiation over an indeterminate period of time.

The organizational structure of the new regulatory system is unwieldy for sure. The Federal Reserve is at the center of it with greatly expanded responsibilities and some new powers to go with them. Equally, the Treasury and the FDIC have newly articulated roles in preserving financial safety and soundness and ending the too-big-to-fail problem and the inherent moral hazard that goes with it. Finally, the SEC has a greatly expanded mandate for rule making, monitoring, and ensuring transparency.

One of the glaring oversights of this new architecture, however, is that it doesn't pay enough attention to the financial needs of the regulators and, as a result, it preserves a strong political role in the regulatory process. The Federal Reserve will maintain its independence and is self-funded. But it is subject to stronger oversight than ever and less independence of action. The new Bureau of Consumer Financial Protection is independently funded by the Fed. The FDIC's independence seems to be even more limited than in the past because it has greatly expanded authority for resolving insolvent bank and nonbank firms but no authority to charge insurance premiums ex ante. Its ability to assess fees based on the risks it insures has always been limited by Congress and will continue to be so. It must now borrow from the Treasury to cover the costs of resolving insolvent large, complex financial institutions (LCFIs). The SEC has greatly expanded responsibilities, but, as in the past, no ability to fund itself. It will remain subject to the whims of congressional appropriations and thus vulnerable to political capture.

1.4 SUMMARY

As a general proposition, financial intermediaries and the structure of the financial architecture cannot be allowed to impose politically unacceptable costs on society, either by failing individuals deemed worthy of protection in financial matters or by permitting firm-level failure to contaminate other financial institutions and, ultimately, the system as a whole.

Protecting the financial system from misconduct and instability is fundamentally in the public interest. It inevitably presents policymakers with difficult choices between financial efficiency and innovation on the one hand and institutional and systemic safety and stability on the other. And because the services provided by banks and other financial intermediaries as allocators of capital affect nearly everything else in the economy, regulatory failure quickly becomes a traumatic event with important consequences for the real sector of the economy.

There is much still to be determined about the new shape of financial regulation. A great deal depends on rules yet to be written and decisions yet to be made in the process of implementing the Dodd-Frank Wall Street Reform and Consumer Protection Act of 2010. We suggest that correct pricing of systemic risk and successfully forcing the costs inside financial intermediaries is the first and best option for performing well against the four key criteria for financial architecture we have proposed. Financial intermediaries can then select strategic options that reduce net regulatory burdens, in the process reducing society's exposure to systemic risk.

NOTES

1. See, for example, Committee on Capital Markets Regulation (2006) and McKinsey & Co. (2008).
2. See, for example, Schmid and Walter (2009).
3. See Chapter 15 of this book.

REFERENCES

Acharya, Viral, and Matthew Richardson, eds. 2009. *Restoring financial stability.* Hoboken, NJ: John Wiley & Sons.

Bodnar, Gordan M., Charles Tang, and Joseph Weintrop. 1999. Both sides of corporate diversification: The value impacts of geographic and industrial diversification. Working paper, Johns Hopkins University.

Campa, Jose M., and Simi Kedia. 2002. Explaining the diversification discount. *Journal of Finance* 57:1731–1762.

Committee on Capital Markets Regulation. 2006. Interim report of the Committee on Capital Markets Regulation (The Paulson Report). Washington, DC: U.S. Government Printing Office.

DeLong, Gayle. 2001a. Focusing versus diversifying bank mergers: Analysis of market reaction and long-term performance. Working paper, CUNY.

DeLong, Gayle. 2001b. Stockholder gains from focusing versus diversifying bank mergers. *Journal of Financial Economics* 59:221–252.

Denis, David J., Diane K. Denis, and Keven Yost. 2002. Global diversification, industrial diversification, and firm value. *Journal of Finance* 57:1951–1979.

Fauver, Larry, Joel F. Houston, and Andy Naranjo. 2004. Cross-country evidence on the value of corporate industrial and international diversification. *Journal of Corporate Finance* 10:729–752.

Gande, Amar, Manju Puri, Anthony Saunders, and Ingo Walter. 1997. Bank underwriting of debt securities: Modern evidence. *Review of Financial Studies* 10 (4): 1175–1202.

Houston, Joel, and Michael Ryngaert. 1994. The overall gains from large bank mergers. *Journal of Banking and Finance* 18:1155–1176.

Kane, Edward J. 1987. Competitive financial reregulation: An international perspective. In *Threats to international financial stability*, ed. R. Portes and A. Swoboda. Cambridge: Cambridge University Press.

Kane, Edward J. 2001. Relevance and need for international regulatory standards. Brookings-Wharton Papers on Financial Services: 87–115.

McKinsey & Co. 2008. Sustaining New York's and the US' global financial services leadership. Report commissioned by Mayor Michael Bloomberg and Senator Charles Schumer. Mayor's Office of the City of New York. Available at www.nyc.gov/html/om/pdf/ny_report_final.pdf.

Puri, Manju. 1996. Commercial banks in investment banking: Conflict of interest or certification role? *Journal of Financial Economics* 40 (3): 373–401.

Saunders, Anthony, and Ingo Walter, 1994. *Universal banking in the United States.* New York: Oxford University Press.

Schmid, Markus M., and Ingo Walter. 2009. Do financial conglomerates create or destroy economic value? *Journal of Financial Intermediation* (October).

U.S. Department of the Treasury. 2009. Bank regulatory reform: Rebuilding financial supervision and regulation. Washington, DC: U.S. Government Printing Office.

Walter, Ingo, ed. 1986. *Deregulating Wall Street.* New York: John Wiley & Sons.

Walter, Ingo. 2004. *Mergers and acquisitions in banking and finance.* New York: Oxford University Press.

CHAPTER 2

The Power of Central Banks and the Future of the Federal Reserve System

Thomas Cooley, Kermit Schoenholtz, George David Smith, Richard Sylla, and Paul Wachtel*

The Federal Reserve System was born of a financial crisis, the Panic of 1907. Major changes in the structure and powers of the Federal Reserve were the result of subsequent crises, most notably the Great Depression of the 1930s. It is not surprising then that the financial crisis of 2007 to 2009 should lead to further changes in the power and scope of the Fed. The Dodd-Frank Wall Street Reform and Consumer Protection Act of 2010 mandates major changes in the role and responsibilities of the Federal Reserve System. The Fed will have enhanced responsibility for systemic risk assessment and regulation, and it will house and fund a new Bureau of Consumer Financial Protection (BCFP). The policy mandate of the Fed is also expanded. In addition to price stability and full employment, the Fed must now make financial stability an explicit goal. In addition to expanding the powers of the Fed, the Dodd-Frank bill also sets some new limits. In particular, the Fed's ability to lend and provide liquidity in a crisis will be curtailed, and its operations and lending programs will be subjected to more scrutiny.

The recent financial crisis highlighted the extraordinary power of the Federal Reserve and other central banks to intervene in the economy in a

---

*The authors benefited from discussions in the "Central Bank Independence and the Role of the Fed" Working Group for the NYU Stern e-book *Real Time Solutions for Financial Reform*, which also included David Backus, Itamar Drechsler, and Thomas Mertens.

crisis. Not surprisingly, the interventions led to a vigorous public debate about the choices the Fed made, the proper role of the Fed in a crisis, and the transparency of its actions. Never has a central bank been so deeply involved in providing liquidity to a weakened financial system.

The role of a central bank in financial crises is a topic with a long history. With the help of Walter Bagehot, the Bank of England learned in the 1860s and 1870s that proper behavior on the part of a lender of last resort is to furnish liquidity *to the market* by discounting freely when presented with good collateral, at a penalty rate of interest to provide incentives for borrowers to repay as soon as they are able and for banks to maintain adequate liquidity. In the recent crisis, the Fed developed a range of Bagehot-like facilities to deliver liquidity when and where it was needed.

But the Fed and some other central banks also went well beyond what Bagehot taught a century and a half ago. In addition to lending to the market, they lent to particular institutions in trouble, sometimes on dodgy collateral. Whenever a central bank acts as a lender of last resort, the decision to do so on behalf of particular institutions—no matter how dispassionately and professionally arrived at—has political ramifications.

Even in lending to the market, the Fed intervened to an unprecedented degree, reacting quickly to create vast reserves and shoring up institutions in novel ways to prevent a wholesale collapse of the U.S. financial system. The Fed expanded its traditional role as lender of last resort to become *an investor of last resort* as well. One could argue that this was an appropriate means to prevent a widespread systemic collapse of the financial system. Yet it was bound to add to concerns about the range of Fed powers.

However else these decisions are judged, the political fallout from what were intended as prudent professional decisions cannot be denied. We should not be surprised that when unelected leaders of powerful, independent financial institutions make political decisions, they invite a popular backlash. In the United States, public suspicion of seemingly unchecked power of banking authorities dates back to the colonial period.

Not surprisingly, Congress has turned its attention to ways to improve financial sector regulation and avert future crises. The changes to the role of the Fed that are introduced by the Dodd-Frank Act arise mostly out of serious thought about the role of central banks and the appropriate scope of their activity. But there also are lingering reflections of the public anger triggered by the crisis and the Fed's role in it. We will try to distinguish between the two.

We start with some historical background that highlights the longstanding American tradition of opposition to central banks. We then turn to the Dodd-Frank Act and distinguish between the expressions of public anger and the substantive issues that are worthy of scrutiny. To foreshadow our conclusions, we argue that the most egregious populist elements of the prior House and Senate reform drafts have been eliminated from the Dodd-Frank bill. At the same time, the bill weakens or eliminates some Fed powers that played an important role in mitigating the recent crisis. Instead, it relies heavily on new, complex, and potentially unwieldy regulatory and resolution mechanisms to prevent and tame future crises. If these new structures prove ineffective, the absence of emergency authority for some forms of Fed lending could make future crises even more devastating than the recent one.

2.1 THE HISTORICAL BACKGROUND

Hamilton and the First Central Bank

Widespread resistance to a powerful central bank is at least as old as the United States. When Treasury Secretary Alexander Hamilton proposed in 1790 that Congress charter a Bank of the United States for 20 years, he set off a controversy that would echo throughout U.S. history. A strong, centralized state such as Britain had recently posed a grave threat to American liberties. So had the Bank of England, which aided Britain's war efforts and operated under the British government's auspices. To many Americans, Hamilton appeared to be trying to create similar threatening institutions in the United States. They thought it better to have a more limited and weaker federal government, and smaller local financial institutions created by the states.

Issues of political power—rather than competing theories of economics —framed the debates among the founders regarding the role and structure of the federal government. In the various state constitutions, the powers of the executive were severely curbed, and under the federal Constitution, the central government's executive authority was to be hedged by a legislature that represented states' rights and interests. That the executive branch should sponsor an institution that represented a large concentration of financial power would prove immediately controversial.

Hamilton, however, was both more an economist and more accepting of an "energetic" central government than his opponents. He envisioned that the Bank of the United States would serve as an important adjunct to federal public financing operations. In a country with only three small local banks at the time, it would also serve the private sector as a bank of discount, deposit, and note issue with a nationwide system of branches. The Bank was to be a large private corporation, a feature aimed at the modern goal of limiting short-run political influences on it, what today would be called central bank independence. At the same time, Hamilton proposed that the federal government take a 20 percent stake in the corporation to signal its public ties and responsibilities, and he imposed on it an obligation to report on its condition regularly to the Treasury secretary.

Congress debated Hamilton's proposal in early 1791 and quickly passed the bill embodying it. In the House debates, however, where members were more sensitive to their constituents, James Madison argued that the Constitution had not conferred on Congress an explicit power to establish any corporation, including a bank. Edmund Randolph, the attorney general, and Thomas Jefferson, the secretary of state, furnished President George Washington with opinions that the proposed Bank of the United States was unconstitutional.

Hamilton responded with a lengthy defense of the bank, relying upon the "necessary and proper" clause of the Constitution, exposing flaws in the reasoning of his fellow cabinet members, and setting down for the first time the doctrine of a constitution's "implied powers" that later became an important worldwide principle of constitutional law. Washington was persuaded and signed the Bank of the United States bill into law.

The Bank served the U.S. economy well. It was an efficient fiscal agent for the Treasury. And since it received the note and deposit liabilities of a rapidly expanding system of state-chartered banks in payment of federal taxes, it could effectively regulate the U.S. banking system and credit conditions. It also took on limited lender-of-last-resort functions by aiding a few banks with temporary reserve deficiencies.

Nevertheless, Congress failed to renew the Bank's charter when it came up for renewal in 1811. In addition to issues of constitutionality and concentration of power, interest group lobbying also played a role. State-chartered banks—which numbered more than 100 by 1811—had the opportunity to rid themselves of a regulator and a competitor. With no Bank of the United States, they stood to gain the federal government's banking business. The self-interest of state-chartered banks prevailed over the preferences of now President Madison and Treasury Secretary Albert Gallatin, both of whom supported renewal of the Bank's federal charter.

The Second Bank

Without a Bank of the United States, financing the War of 1812 grew complicated and embarrassing. Except in New England, state banks suspended convertibility of their liabilities to base money, and there was considerable inflation. Chastened by the experience, Congress moved quickly after the war ended in 1815 to charter a second Bank of the United States, again for 20 years, starting in 1816. The second Bank was an enlarged version of the first. The federal government again took a 20 percent stake, and now it also appointed a fifth of the Bank's directors.

The second Bank of the United States performed as well as the first. It aided the Treasury in restoring convertibility of the currency after the war, although it was blamed for the period of tight credit necessary to reach that goal, as well as for the panic of 1819 prompted by the credit contraction. In the 1820s and early 1830s, Nicholas Biddle, the talented but arrogant Bank president for much of this period, was a true central banker. Biddle became so personally identified with the Bank that its friends and enemies alike could focus on a personality, a mixed blessing for the institution. Under Biddle, the Bank managed domestic and international payments systems, helped the Treasury to manage its debt, prevented the major British financial crisis of 1825 from spilling over into the United States, and presided over a period of rapid, noninflationary economic growth.

Nonetheless, when Congress approved a renewal of its charter in 1832, President Jackson vetoed it. His veto message, a classic of populist rhetoric, raised all the old arguments about the Bank's constitutionality and the threats posed by a large and powerful financial institution with a monopoly charter, as well as some new ones that included the specter of foreign ownership of the Bank's capital stock. Jackson severed the government's relationships with the Bank of the United States. The country would not have a central bank again until 1914.

Making Do without a Central Bank

The United States developed various substitutes for a central bank, but these failed to promote financial stability as well as the two Banks of the United States had done.[1] After 1836, some central banking functions were performed by the Treasury, by clearinghouses for banks in major cities, and—after the 1863 advent of the National Banking System during the Civil War—by large national banks in leading cities, especially the central reserve city of New York. The Treasury held its own reserves of base money and could inject them into the banking system to prevent or alleviate liquidity crises. Clearinghouses could issue loan certificates among their members during crises to make more base money reserves available to meet demands of panicky depositors.

Under the Bank of the United States regime, the country experienced only two banking crises, in 1792 and 1819, or one every 20 years. Thereafter, banking crises occurred on average about every 10 years: in 1837, 1839–1842, 1857, 1873, 1884, 1893, and 1907. Until the twentieth century, none of these crises was sufficient to overcome political resistance to more centralized control of banking and monetary policy. U.S. society remained largely rural, and most people could fall back on local resources in times of crisis. Those circumstances would change with mass urbanization and more economic specialization and interdependence in the twentieth century.

Introduction of the Federal Reserve

By 1907, the U.S. economy was the largest in the world, and it was embarrassing that it had more frequent banking crises than did European countries with central banks. In the 1907 panic, J. Pierpont Morgan, a private banker acting as a quasi central banker, effectively coordinated the means to stem the panic. That kind of power in private hands was as disconcerting a prospect as lodging it in the public domain. In the wake of the panic, Congress therefore set in motion the machinery that would lead to passage of the Federal Reserve Act in 1913, and the opening of the Fed in 1914. After 1914, banking crises did not disappear, but they once again became less frequent. The Federal Reserve Act reflected the crosscurrents of American history: It created a decentralized central bank.

The decentralized Federal Reserve, however, failed to prevent or mitigate the greatest financial crisis that ever confronted the United States. To a considerable extent, the depth and duration of the Great Depression reflected a widespread collapse of the U.S. financial system. The Fed did little to ease credit as the money supply and the price level plummeted. If anything, its perverse actions under the gold standard probably helped transmit the crisis abroad. Much of the problem was institutional. When it had been set up in 1914, the Federal Reserve System was all too federal, reflecting states' rights sentiments in Congress; that is, it was a weakly governed collection of regional Reserve Banks with the New York Reserve Bank taking the de facto lead in matters of money-center and international finance.

The decentralized structure of the Federal Reserve System helps to explain the lack of concerted action to stave off the massive bank runs and failures that ballooned into the thousands from late 1930 to early 1933. Not until 1935 did Utah banker Marriner Eccles preside over a restructuring of a more centralized, systemwide Board of Governors, based on banking legislation that, among other regulatory features, established most of the centralized Fed's powers as we know them today. Eccles used the new structure and his personal authority to stake out more central bank independence from the Treasury. Yet, the new Fed extended the Depression by its premature actions in 1936 and 1937 to absorb excess reserves. As a result of that experience and the Fed's efforts to help the Treasury finance wartime expenditures at low interest rates, the central bank became, in effect, a vassal of the Treasury until the Treasury Accord of 1951 began to restore Fed independence.

As far as broader U.S. finance was concerned, states' rights claims and populism were by no means gone. Until late in the twentieth century, American banks could have branches in at most one state. Many were confined to one city or even one office (so-called unit banking). Congress and federal regulatory authorities continued to defer to state and local preferences in finance. Powerful members of Congress representing constituencies for whom easy credit was important could be relied on to praise the Fed whenever it lowered interest rates, and to condemn it whenever it raised them. Only after the Fed's easy money policies led to soaring inflation and unprecedentedly high nominal interest rates in the 1970s did American populism enter a temporary quiet period. The independence of the Fed and the primacy of its price stability objective earned virtually universal support.

2.2 THE FEDERAL RESERVE AND THE DODD-FRANK BILL

Lingering Populism

The financial crisis that began in 2007 triggered widespread criticisms of the dramatic Fed interventions aimed at mitigating the economic fallout from the financial collapse. While the Fed has much to account for, members of Congress also found it convenient to blame the Fed for lapses before and during the crisis. Some observers singled out former Fed chairman Alan Greenspan as the single most culpable villain because of the long period of low interest rates on his watch that they contend led to an unsustainable bubble in housing prices. While most of the legislative provisions reflect a serious effort to improve the effectiveness of financial regulation, some portion of the legislation reflects lingering congressional anger about the crisis.

It is not difficult to find examples of the reaction. Congressman Ron Paul, a modern Andrew Jackson, wants to "End the Fed," and has a best-selling book with that title. His arguments have appealed to a much wider audience than his libertarian populist base. The Grayson-Paul amendment introduced in 2009 would have subjected Fed decision making to audits and quick second-guessing by Congress. Although the Dodd-Frank bill mutes the Paul proposals, it still poses a risk to Fed independence. For example, the comptroller general is asked to provide Congress with a full audit report of Fed activities in the recent crisis, as well as an evaluation of Fed governance. In addition, the bill allows the Government Accountability Office to perform additional audits of all lending activities of the Fed without explicitly exempting monetary policy operations. Such audits may seem a coercive threat to Fed policymakers who anticipate congressional second-guessing of policy decisions. While public anger regarding the Fed's actions may be on the wane as the economy recovers, these provisions could bode a return of politically motivated pressures on monetary policies that were regular features in U.S. financial history.

New Constraints on the Lender of Last Resort

Congress has added an explicit mandate for financial stability to the list of Fed objectives. It also has strengthened the Fed's focus on supervision by establishing a new vice chairman for supervision at the Board of Governors. And it has—at least implicitly—ratified the Fed's aggressive creation of broad-based Bagehot-like programs to provide liquidity during the crisis. At the same time, it has significantly altered the tools available to secure financial stability, sharply curtailing here, and adding substantially there. It is impossible to assess the comprehensive impact of these changes, partly because many of the changes will have to be spelled out by a newly formed group of regulators responsible for systemic regulation, the Financial Stability Oversight Council (FSOC).

At least some of the legislative changes will make it more difficult for the Fed to intervene in crises in a timely way when they occur. Specifically, there are limits placed on the Fed's emergency lending powers to nonbank entities. Beginning in the spring of 2008, the Fed relied repeatedly on the emergency lending powers expressed in Section 13(3) of the Federal Reserve Act, which allowed the central bank to extend loans to nonbanks ("individuals, partnerships, and corporations") in a financial exigency. To opponents of the Fed, its emergency loans to specific institutions (such as Bear Stearns and AIG) epitomize the central bank's willingness to use public funds to bail out financial institutions, and to do so beyond the scrutiny of any elected officials. To defenders of the central bank, this authority enabled the Fed and the U.S. government to respond quickly when the financial system faced a wave of defaults. Applied carefully, it can be consistent with Bagehot's approach of lending to anyone offering good collateral at a penalty rate. In the financial crisis, lending under the Fed's 13(3) authority probably helped prevent the turmoil from spreading beyond Lehman Brothers and AIG to other large, connected, and vulnerable institutions.

The Dodd-Frank Act markedly narrows this authority. First, the bill prohibits lending to specific nonbanks. Emergency lending can no longer be provided to any "individual, partnership, or corporation" but only to "participant[s] in any program or facility with broad-based eligibility." Second, it states that "any emergency lending program or facility is for the purpose of providing liquidity to the financial system, and not to aid a failing financial company, and that the security for emergency loans is sufficient to protect taxpayers from losses and that any such program is terminated in a timely and orderly fashion." The goal of these restrictions is presumably to reduce the moral hazard of so-called too-big-to-fail shadow banks and to prevent taxpayer assistance for the restructuring or liquidation of shadow banks. Such restructuring of nonbanks will be driven through the new Federal Deposit Insurance Corporation (FDIC)-led resolution mechanism created by the legislation (see Chapter 7 for an analysis of this facility).

Third, under the new Dodd-Frank regime, Fed programs that allow for the efficient distribution of liquidity in a crisis (à la Bagehot) to solvent financial institutions with acceptable collateral, such as the extraordinary facilities developed in the crisis, would require the approval of the Treasury secretary. It is not clear why the Treasury secretary should be involved in programs that are designed to provide liquidity *without* cost to the taxpayer. This approach adds to concerns about Fed independence. It also creates a new distinction between banks, where the Fed can provide liquidity without Treasury approval and without utilizing its authority under Section 13(3), and shadow banks, where approval and emergency authority are required.[2]

It is doubtful that the optimal approach to Fed emergency workout-related lending is to forbid it outright. By doing so, the bill eliminates (rather than just raises the cost of using) a policy safety valve that has been available for more than 75 years in the event of unforeseen circumstances. In effect, Congress is counting on other regulatory reforms and the new resolution mechanism to prevent or tame financial crises. Alternative policy approaches to Fed emergency lending might have been to require prior presidential approval (along with notification to Congress) of workout-like loans, to limit the size of such Fed lending without prohibiting it, or to require the President to include in an emergency supplementary budget proposal an appropriation to acquire all the workout-related assets from the Fed.

Some combination of these alternatives would mitigate the inevitable conflict between requiring accountability for quasi-fiscal actions by the central bank and securing the independence of monetary policy, while allowing a timely crisis response. In our view, a better approach would be to require the Treasury to facilitate removing non-Treasury or nonagency debt from the Fed's balance sheet in a timely way following any crisis stabilization effort. This approach would make it clear that the Fed can act temporarily in extremis as the government's bank when it serves as investor of last resort but cannot hold these assets on its balance sheet for long. Nothing in the Dodd-Frank bill directly addresses this confounding of fiscal and monetary policy.

The focus on limiting emergency funding only for nonbanks also appears misplaced. The problem of too-big-to-fail creating a moral hazard originated with the Fed lending to a large *bank* in distress (Continental Illinois in 1984). Yet the legislation does not constrain Federal Reserve lending to individual *banks*. The reason may be that the most unpopular Fed actions in 2008 were its moves to bail out the creditors of nonbanks (particularly those of Bear Stearns and AIG). The legislation seems designed to prevent a recurrence of these extraordinarily unpopular emergency actions.

Yet, from either an analytic or a commonsense perspective, there is little reason why the lender of last resort should distinguish between a bank and a nonbank if both pose an identical systemic threat. Why should the lender of last resort fail to underpin the financial system because of the legal label borne by a financial institution, regardless of its function? Bagehot articulated this pragmatic functional view back in the nineteenth century: "The holders of the cash reserve ... must lend to merchants, to minor bankers, to 'this man and that man' whenever the security is good."[3] Conceivably, one effect of the new rules may be to prompt shadow banks on the verge of trouble to convert into banks to facilitate access to Fed lending facilities—just as Goldman Sachs and Morgan Stanley did in the wake of Lehman's 2008 failure. If so, the goal of mitigating the too-big-to-fail problem could remain elusive. There is a related question of whether the bill as structured creates a stronger presumption for pushing a challenged nonbank through the resolution process than it does for a similarly situated bank. Will there be greater (perceived) forbearance for banks?

To be sure, a central bank in a democratic society must be subject to review and held accountable by elected officials. Its potent tools need to be carefully monitored. Thus, we would prefer a procedure that achieves political accountability for the central bank while maintaining its ability to make timely interventions in the interest of financial and economic stability. This problem could have been addressed by having a preauthorized standby authority (possibly limited in scale) to be used when a need arises in a crisis, accompanied by monitoring procedures that would spring into action as the standby authority came to be employed.[4]

Emergency lending facilities enable the Fed (and the government) to respond rapidly to unexpected systemic shocks. The proposed structure could delay and politicize decision making, especially compared with a parliamentary system where the executive branch can implement fiscal changes virtually overnight. It is not difficult to imagine an instance where the inability to act in a timely way on the part of the lender of last resort would pose a risk to national security, as well as to the financial system and the economy. One need only look at the experience of the Great Depression of 1930 to 1933 to see the negative consequences of inaction and delayed action by the Fed.

New Fed Disclosure Requirements

The Dodd-Frank bill makes some dramatic changes in the conduct of central bank business by requiring full public disclosure of the details, terms, and counterparties involved for virtually all Fed transactions. Such disclosure pertains to emergency lending programs as well as traditional forms of discount lending and open market operations. In all cases, disclosure occurs after a significant delay, one year after the end of a special lending program and roughly two years after each regular discount window or open market transaction. These information releases will make a plethora of data available to the research community and will keep the public fully informed about central bank transactions. It is hard to take issue with provisions that make the actions of an independent government agency transparent with a reasonable lag. The bill's disclosure delays should avoid the kind of instability that premature disclosure requirements helped spark during the Great Depression.[5]

However, it is reasonable to ask how the bill's new disclosure requirements will affect the Fed's policy tools. In our view, the bill's new disclosure requirements will tend to weaken discount window lending as a crisis-management tool. Banks have always feared that disclosure of borrowing from the Fed's discount window would signal their fragility and trigger a run. Partly as a result, discount window lending has been negligible in recent decades, outside of crises. And, of course, fears of a run are much greater in a crisis. Notably, Fed efforts since the 1990s to encourage greater use of the discount window and to strengthen its value as a policy tool have had little effect. The new disclosure requirement may make it even more difficult than in the past for the Fed to persuade banks to use the discount window when the financial system is threatened by an extraordinary liquidity shortfall.

Expanding Other Fed Powers and Changing Governance

The other major feature of the Dodd-Frank Act that relates directly to the Federal Reserve is the introduction of a new mechanism for the regulation of systemically important financial institutions. The Financial Stability Oversight Council (FSOC)—consisting of the major regulatory authorities—will be advised by a new Office of Financial Research within the Treasury. The Office will have broad authority to collect and analyze information on systemic risks in the financial system. The Council will have the authority to instruct the Federal Reserve to impose regulations on nonbank financial companies that present systemic risks.

The Fed's new FSOC-determined authority, along with the Board of Governors' new vice chairman for supervision, institutionalizes a heightened emphasis on financial regulation and stability within the Fed. This shakeup of previous regulatory arrangements will help to avoid the benign neglect of systemic issues that prevailed before the crisis. Yet it remains to be seen how well the new, complex apparatus will respond dynamically to the evolution of the financial industry, which will continue to have powerful incentives to take on systemic risks.

Some observers argue that the Fed has always had the ability to extend supervision over shadow banks and that these new structures are superfluous. However, the recent crisis highlights the need for explicit recognition of systemic risks arising in the shadow banking system. The Council will have the authority to direct the Fed's attention to areas where risks warrant additional regulation and to instruct the Fed to act. A key uncertainty is how effectively the various regulators will coordinate their activities among an analytic group (the Treasury's Office of Financial Research), a deliberative body (the Council that votes to extend regulation and authorize Fed action), and the regulator (the Federal Reserve). It also is unclear how far regulators will go to empower market discipline—through transparency and through charges for implicit government subsidies—as a means of revealing and taming systemic risk.

The Fed also plays a secondary role in a newly developed mechanism led by the FDIC for the orderly liquidation of failing financial institutions. The goal of the process is to unwind systemically significant failing companies without invoking "too big to fail" or imposing any costs on the taxpayers. The decision to start the liquidation process requires that the Treasury, the FDIC, and the Fed all agree that the institution in question is of systemic importance. The FDIC can then provide guarantees of deposits and other liabilities to the extent to which it anticipates being repaid. Naturally, this process is both complex and untried. Once again, its effectiveness will have to be proven by experience.

Finally, in contrast to earlier draft legislation, the Dodd-Frank bill avoids governance changes that could have seriously politicized top appointments at the Federal Reserve district banks and threatened Fed independence. The limited changes in the bill may be viewed as a cautious reaction to what some perceive as a too-cozy relationship between the financial sector and the Federal Reserve System. For example, the Government Accountability Office will conduct a study of the current system for appointing Federal Reserve Bank directors, to examine conflicts of interest and the effectiveness of public representation. The bill also prohibits the Federal Reserve Bank directors appointed by member banks (Class A directors) from voting for the Bank president.[6] Earlier proposals for more draconian changes (including one to make the president of the Federal Reserve Bank of New York a presidential appointee subject to Senate confirmation) are not included in the final legislation.

Consumer Financial Protection

A major ingredient of the Dodd-Frank legislation is the creation of a Bureau of Consumer Financial Protection (BCFP), an independent consumer watch-dog housed at and funded by the Federal Reserve. It would have the mandate to ensure that American consumers get the clear, accurate information they need to shop for mortgages, credit cards, and other financial products, and protect them from hidden fees, abusive terms, and deceptive practices. We discuss consumer finance protection separately in the next chapter, but it is worth commenting briefly on the implications for the Fed that stem from having that bureau located there. On the surface there are no implications, since it is to be funded by the Fed but is to have an independent director, appointed by the President and confirmed by the Senate. Because it is de-signed to be independent, it should have few implications for the normal functioning of the Fed. At the same time, there is no logical reason to house it in the Fed. Clearly, this is the result of some political wrangling. It en-abled the framers of the legislation to essentially hide the costs and avoid having to seek appropriations to cover them. There is potential for conflict. Consumer protection is inherently highly politicized because there are so many constituents—both businesses and consumers. That is why it has such populist political appeal. The logrolling circus that led up to the passage of the Dodd-Frank bill should be evidence enough that politicians can put tremendous pressure on regulators to protect consumers and business inter-ests in particular ways without concern for the larger consequences. It is not difficult to imagine circumstances in which actions taken—or not taken—by the BCFP could engender further political intrusions on the Fed.

2.3 THE POSTCRISIS ROLE OF A CENTRAL BANK: A BENCHMARK FOR MEASURING DODD-FRANK

Since the late seventeenth century, the role of central banks has always been in flux. In their earliest years, the primary function of central banks was to act as fiscal agents for governments. Later, in the nineteenth century, Walter Bagehot articulated the importance of the lender-of-last-resort function. The central bank's policy role in economic stabilization—setting policy interest rates and managing money growth—did not emerge as a key function until the middle of the twentieth century. Around the same time, central banks in many countries took on much of the responsibility for the supervision and regulation of banks. Most central banks also assumed responsibility for the integrity, efficiency, and accessibility of the payments and settlement systems.

The Dodd-Frank bill reflects changing views of the role of a central bank in the postcrisis world by providing an explicit new goal for the Federal Reserve. In addition to its existing mandate to attain maximum employment and stable prices, the Dodd-Frank Act gives the Federal Reserve an explicit financial stability function; Section 1108b states that "The Board of Governors shall identify, measure, monitor, and mitigate risks to the financial stability of the United States."

What Is a Central Bank Function and What Is Not?

Modern central bank functions fall into three areas: monetary policy, the supervision and regulation of individual financial institutions, and systemic regulation of the financial sector as a whole. This latter function includes both the traditional concern for the functioning of the payments system and a new set of concerns about systemwide risk arising from the increased complexity and interconnectedness of financial institutions and markets.

With these roles in mind, there are important elements in the structure of the Federal Reserve that inevitably limit its independence. The Fed is answerable to Congress, which created it. Its top officials are nominated by the executive branch and confirmed by the Senate. Unlike the European Central Bank (ECB), the Fed's mandate can be altered by a simple congressional majority. At the same time, the 12 Federal Reserve district banks are governed by independent boards and are formally owned by the member banks, making the Federal Reserve System subject to regulatory capture by the banks that it is supposed to supervise. Add to that the need to work closely with the Treasury in times of crisis, and you have a system that must always be sensitive to the risks of political interference in the setting of monetary policy. Keeping inflation expectations low and stable in this setting requires sustained policy vigilance.

While it forbids some quasi-fiscal actions by the Fed and adds to the possible range of Fed supervisory authority, the Dodd-Frank bill does not materially alter this reality. The Federal Reserve System remains the pragmatic result of decades of evolution and haggling to balance the public's mistrust of bankers with its similar mistrust of politicians. However imperfect, the Fed is widely viewed as among the most independent of government agencies. The same can be said when comparing the Fed with many other central banks in the industrial world. Even its fiercest critics typically admire the integrity, devotion, and expertise of the Fed's personnel.

Monetary Policy

Very few argue with the idea that monetary policy aimed at economic stabilization should rest in the hands of an independent central bank. Although there are those (such as Ron Paul and other libertarians) who advocate the abolition of central banks, economists and historians have amply documented that independent central banks achieve lower and less volatile inflation rates than those that are beholden to governments in power, and that they do so at no long-run cost to economic output.

The central bank can use its tools to guide the economy toward goals set forth by the government. In the United States, the Fed has a dual mandate to maintain stable prices and full employment. Many other central banks—the ECB is a notable example—have a single mandate to maintain price stability. A central bank influences interest rates and the growth of money and credit in order to attain its specified goals. An independent central bank can pursue these goals without concern for an election cycle that might tempt elected policymakers to pursue short-term goals, such as unsustainably high employment and real growth with little concern for longer-run inflationary implications.

Some argue that the function of a central bank should begin and end with monetary policy, and that any other obligation would distract the central bank from achieving its primary goal of economic stabilization. Indeed, an early Senate draft suggested just that, removing all other functions except the formulation of monetary policy from the central bank. However, this approach ignores important links between monetary policymaking, financial regulation, and prudential supervision that favor a wider role for a modern central bank.

Supervision, Regulation, and the Lender of Last Resort

As noted earlier, in the nineteenth century Bagehot introduced the idea that the central bank should serve broadly as a lender of last resort to the financial system. In fact, the modern notion of monetary policymaking evolved out of the central bank's lending activities. Traditionally, the central bank provided liquidity to the financial system. Its lending to the banking system influenced the aggregate economy even before the macroeconomic role of the central bank was acknowledged. Indeed, one of the first and rather successful policy efforts of the new Federal Reserve System was the provision of funds to counter seasonal funding shortfalls associated with the agricultural cycle. When special liquidity problems threatened the operation of the banking system, the central bank also would act as the lender of last resort. It is only logical that such a lender should have sufficient information about borrowers to be able to make sound loans. Thus, it is no accident that bank regulatory and supervisory functions are often associated with the lender of last resort.

Even as it circumscribes the Fed's emergency lending powers, the Dodd-Frank bill in other ways strengthens the connection between the lender of last resort and regulatory and supervisory functions. It enables the Fed—subject to recommendation from the new FSOC—to supervise systemically important nonbanks. It also ratifies the Fed's ability to provide nonbanks with emergency liquidity through facilities with broad access (but not with lending to individual nonbanks).

Some economists have claimed that the lender-of-last-resort role for central banks is obsolete.[7] They argue that in the presence of modern, well-developed financial markets, there should be no such thing as an illiquid but solvent firm. Solvent firms should always be able to arrange financing in the interbank market, the repo market, or longer-term credit markets. In the aftermath of the 2007 to 2009 crisis, this view, which harks back to the arrangements in place prior to the panic of 1907, seems to reflect an overly optimistic faith in the ability of financial markets to avoid collapses.

Conceivably, the supervision and regulation of individual banking institutions need not be a central bank function. In some countries, it is housed in other government agencies. And in the United States, the Fed has always shared these functions with state and national agencies responsible for chartering banks, as well as with the deposit insurance agency.

However, as the U.S. lender of last resort, it is crucial that the Fed be able to obtain timely information about any potential borrower. This is a linchpin of the argument that the central bank should have a leading role in bank supervision and regulation. One might ask whether the real issue is effective communication between the Federal Reserve and any other agencies with supervisory authority. In practice, however, instances where the role of supervisor and lender of last resort have been separated—such as in the United Kingdom, where the Bank of England acts as lender of last resort and the Financial Services Authority oversees the potential borrowers—have highlighted how difficult it is to communicate effectively in a crisis. As a result, UK Chancellor George Osborne recently announced plans to eliminate the Financial Services Authority and return a leading role in bank supervision to the Bank of England.

More importantly, the benefits of linking the lender of last resort and the role of supervision go beyond the advantages of rapid communication. The skills and expertise developed in the course of regulation and supervision may help the lender of last resort to innovate when necessary in a liquidity crisis. For example, the rapid, emergency introduction of several new Fed lending facilities during the crisis of 2007 to 2009 (e.g., the Treasury Auction Facility and the Primary Dealer Credit Facility) would have been difficult in the absence of extensive hands-on experience in the financial system on the part of Fed supervisors. Similarly, experience in regulation and supervision may be critical for the development and informed use of so-called macro-prudential powers, which aim to curb systemic financial threats.

Against this background, it is important to distinguish among the types of organizations to be supervised. The lender-of-last-resort role probably is of greatest relevance in dealing with institutions whose instability would pose a direct threat to the financial system as a whole. It is possible for a wide array of small financial institutions to pose such a systemic threat if they face a common exposure that makes them collectively vulnerable. The experience of money market mutual funds (MMMFs) in the recent crisis provides a case in point. Yet, there are few such examples. Even the thrifts crisis of the early 1980s was not truly systemic. Moreover, the experience of the recent crisis suggests that large, complex financial institutions (LCFIs) are more likely to be sources of systemic disruption. For this reason, there would appear to be a stronger case for linking the lender of last resort to the supervision of LCFIs than to the supervision of other financial institutions.

The Dodd-Frank bill largely preserves the supervisory role of the Federal Reserve district banks even with regard to small banks. The district banks were naturally reluctant to give up their supervisory role, since it is one of their major activities. Ensuring the soundness of banks large and small is viewed as integral to economic health of the regions they serve. Confidential information obtained in the course of supervising banks can be of use in setting monetary policy, especially when it helps policymakers to anticipate demand for and supply of credit. Nevertheless, the case for Fed supervision of smaller banks remains far less compelling than the case for supervision of systemically important financial institutions (SIFIs), including nonbanks.[8]

Systemic Risk Regulator

Although systemic risk is not a new idea, the notion of an explicit systemic risk regulatory function is new. Addressing systemic threats was an implicit function of the Fed because its lender of last resort facility was the only tool available to respond to systemic risk problems. When clearing failures, Y2K concerns, or the terrorist attacks of 9/11 threatened the operation of the financial system, the Fed's discount window was the tool available to address the problems. Until the crisis of 2007 to 2009, the biggest use of the Fed's discount window occurred in the week after 9/11, when the

Fed successfully met heightened liquidity needs that otherwise could have threatened financial system stability.

The Federal Reserve also had the authority to lend widely (that is, to nonbanks) in times of widespread financial exigency in order to manage a systemic threat. Until March 2008, however, these powers were hardly known and little understood because they had not been used after the 1930s, when they were created and employed. With the benefit of hindsight, we see that the evolution of discount lending authority in the twentieth century gave the Fed a valuable tool for responding to systemic risks. However, it did not make the Fed the actual systemic regulator with an obligation to monitor and prevent the rise of systemic risk. In fact, the recent crisis highlights what can happen when there is no one authority unambiguously responsible for responding to systemic risks.

The establishment of a systemic risk regulator is an important component of the Dodd-Frank bill. To be effective, such a regulatory authority has to have influence that stretches out in multiple directions. First, the systemic regulator needs to augment the oversight and supervision of institutions that are so large and interconnected that any insolvency would create systemic problems.

Second, it must be able to address systemic problems that can arise from smaller institutions facing a common vulnerability. For example, the 2008 run on money market mutual funds (MMMFs) highlights the risk posed by so-called shadow banks—those that lack deposit insurance and a lender of last resort even though their funds can be withdrawn at face value with little or no notice. A similar funding vulnerability affects those institutions—such as broker-dealers—that are dependent on the collateralized repo market. The FSOC should grant to the Fed the authority to regulate such risk-laden market funding practices, in addition to the behavior of any institution that itself can generate systemic risks.

Third, economic conditions can give rise to systemically risky activity. The extended period of low interest rates in the early 2000s created an environment that promoted rapid credit expansion and some of the excesses, particularly in the mortgage markets, that generated the crisis. In addition, new elements of monetary policy—so-called macro-prudential powers—constitute an important potential element of systemic risk management.

It is uncertain whether the Dodd-Frank FSOC will become the powerful systemic regulator that is needed. Rather than exercising direct authority, the FSOC will be able to authorize explicit Fed supervision of SIFIs. Such authority makes it possible in theory to rein in the systemically risky activities of any financial institutions—shadow banks, hedge funds, and insurance companies, for example—including ones that are not otherwise subject to regulatory oversight. If the behavior of any financial institution creates systemic threats, the regulator has reason to be concerned.

However, the Council is only a loose umbrella organization with the mission, among other things, "to identify risks to the financial stability of the United States that could arise from the material financial distress or failure, or ongoing activities, of large, interconnected bank holding companies or nonbank financial companies, or that could arise outside the financial services marketplace" and "make recommendations to primary financial regulatory agencies to apply new or heightened standards and safeguards for financial activities or practices that could create or increase risks of significant liquidity, credit, or other problems spreading among bank holding companies, nonbank financial companies, and United States financial markets."

The Council will play a largely indirect role: instructing regulators to tighten oversight when it deems that systemic risks warrant action. Thus, the systemic regulator is removed from the direct issues of systemic concern—supervision of institutions that can create systemic risks and monetary policy. And the Federal Reserve will be only one participant among several in the FSOC, without a leading role. The argument for giving the Federal Reserve System a more central role in systemic regulation is that so many of the functions and concerns of a systemic regulator are closely related to essential Fed functions.[9] The Fed monitors markets constantly and has to ensure the integrity and viability of the payments system. Business and financial cycles are closely linked: It is impossible to secure economic stability without a modicum of financial stability. Given its expertise and its degree of independence from the government, the Fed is a natural location for assessing the possible trade-offs between these two policy goals. It already has key tools for managing systemic threats and is developing new ones.

The bill preserves the Fed's role as the principal regulator of the largest banks. And it permits the Council to grant the Fed supervisory authority over other SIFIs. If the Council acts effectively in this way, most key issues of systemic concern eventually will be brought under the wing of the central bank. Still, the Dodd-Frank bill significantly narrows the Fed's emergency lending authority. A key issue some time in the future will be whether the new restrictions on emergency lending to individual nonbanks will inhibit a prompt and timely response to a crisis with potentially systemic implications.

2.4 SUMMARY

To many observers, the financial crisis of 2007 to 2009 had its roots in mistakes made by the Federal Reserve under Alan Greenspan. When the Fed wielded its enormous power to try to stem the financial meltdown, it strayed far from the normal precincts of monetary policy. It is not surprising, then, that financial reform should include some serious rethinking of the role of the Fed. A strong and independent central bank is an anomalous entity in a constitutional democracy that emphasizes accountability and the responsibility of elected officials.

Nevertheless, the Dodd-Frank Act leaves the independence of the Federal Reserve reasonably intact. Some of the challenges to central bank independence that were introduced in earlier congressional discussions were misguided and potentially counterproductive expressions of public anger regarding the recent financial crisis. Anger is a poor basis on which to craft effective reforms. Fortunately, the Dodd-Frank bill dropped the most egregious attacks on the Fed. However, it introduces restrictions on emergency lending and new structures for responding to systemic risks that will have to be judged when tested by events. It is far from clear that these complex new structures will be able to mitigate crises when they occur.

Finally, there is no escaping the fact that there are competing goals that make the role of the central bank difficult to determine. Although everyone agrees that monetary policy is a central bank concern and the raison d'être for central bank independence, there are wide differences of opinion regarding the extent to which the Fed should also have responsibility for the supervision and regulation of individual financial institutions and for systemic regulation of the financial sector as a whole. While a modicum of financial stability is necessary for economic stability, there are potential conflicts among the mandates of the central bank. Even the European Central Bank, which has the sole mandate of price stability, has been drawn into an expanded role by its decision (in the face of some fierce opposition) to hold the sovereign debt of member states that faced serious funding challenges, such as Greece, Spain, and Portugal.

We contend that strong linkages among the three functions of a central bank are sufficiently compelling that, with proper oversight, the central bank should have broad authority in all three of them. The Dodd-Frank Act goes some way in this direction, but not as far as it could or should have. A key concern is the prohibition or weakening of some Fed crisis-management tools before it is clear whether the new and potentially unwieldy apparatus to prevent and mitigate financial crises will prove effective. The bill also prevents use of some of the crisis-management tools that the Fed employed to mitigate financial instability in the recent crisis, at least until they might be authorized via the FSOC. Delayed crisis interventions could well prove to be less effective than timely ones. The history of financial crises indicates that strong leadership and timely interventions separate well-managed from poorly-managed economies. It is far from clear that a new, and hence untested, oversight council can provide stronger leadership in a crisis situation than would an experienced central banker.

NOTES

1. Banks in the United States were numerous and small by world standards. Well into the twentieth century, despite their federal charters, even New York's money-center "national" banks were constrained to function with a state and local focus, highlighting the continued concerns about size and power in the financial system and the continued influence of local banking interests. See George David Smith and Richard Sylla, "Capital Markets," *Encyclopedia of the United States in the Twentieth Century*, vol. 3, edited by S. I. Cutler (New York: Scribner, 1996).

2. The prohibition on Fed lending to swaps entities other than those associated with depositories further distinguishes between banks and nonbanks. The rationale appears to be that regulators can more easily contain the risks taken by swap entities associated with banks, but that remains to be seen.

3. Walter Bagehot, *Lombard Street*, page 51, as cited in Brian Madigan, "Bagehot's Dictum in Practice: Formulating and Implementing Policies to Combat the Financial Crisis," speech to the Federal Reserve Bank of Kansas City's Annual Economic Symposium at Jackson Hole, Wyoming, August 21, 2009.

4. For example, to restrict Fed assumption of credit risks and make the central bank accountable, Martin Feldstein has proposed that Congress explicitly authorize Treasury funding of such longer-term private credit allocations by the Fed. See Feldstein, "What Powers for the Federal Reserve?" *Journal of Economic Literature* 48 (March 2010), 134–145, at 135–136.

5. In 1932, when Congress required the Reconstruction Finance Corporation to disclose details regarding its borrowers (mostly banks), a new wave of bank runs ensued.

6. These changes appear to reflect congressional dismay over the actions of the former chairman of the board of directors of the Federal Reserve Bank of New York, Stephen Friedman, who simultaneously served on the board of Goldman Sachs when it became a bank holding company. Friedman came under criticism for personal financial transactions (for which Fed approval had been granted), while serving in both of these roles and while leading the search for a new president of the Bank, who, as it happened, came from Goldman Sachs.

7. For example, Marvin Goodfriend and Robert G. King, "Financial Deregulation, Monetary Policy, and Central Banking," in *Restructuring Financial Services in America* (Lanham, MD: AEI Studies, 1988), 481.

8. Alan Blinder ("How Central Should the Central Bank Be?" *Journal of Economic Literature* 48 [March 2010], 123–133, at 132) agrees with us that the case for Fed supervision of small banks is less than compelling and "peripheral to its core mission."

9. It is notable that the ECB is expected to enjoy such a central role in the new European Systemic Risk Board.

CHAPTER 3

Consumer Finance Protection

Thomas Cooley, Xavier Gabaix, Samuel Lee, Thomas Mertens,
Vicki Morwitz, Shelle Santana, Anjolein Schmeits,
Stijn Van Nieuwerburgh, and Robert Whitelaw

3.1 OVERVIEW

There has been growing concern in recent years that many consumers lack the knowledge to evaluate and make decisions about financial products. Some of the most important decisions consumers make in their lifetimes involve financial products: a mortgage to purchase a home, a loan to purchase an automobile, credit to make a large durable purchase, investments for retirement, and insurance to keep one's family secure. In the past, the government and employers often made financial decisions for households, for example by providing defined benefit retirement plans or Social Security; now, however, households are more frequently on their own. Furthermore, financial products have become increasingly complex over time, and consumers face a wide range of product options offered by different service providers, causing decision making to be more complicated. Consumers therefore need to be financially literate in order to make well-informed choices for such complex decisions.

Unfortunately, studies show that many consumers lack the basic financial knowledge needed to make informed decisions about financial products (Braunstein and Welch 2002; Lusardi 2008; Lusardi, Mitchell, and Curto 2009). Many consumers do not understand fundamental financial concepts such as compound interest, risk diversification, real versus nominal values, and the difference between stocks and bonds (Lusardi 2008). This lack of financial literacy then leads to suboptimal decision making. Consumers with higher levels of financial literacy plan more for retirement, while those with lower levels of literacy borrow more, save less, and have more trouble repaying their debt (Lusardi 2008). Even the average consumer has difficulty making financial decisions, given the complexity of financial information (Perry and Morris 2005), and the overall lack of financial capability of American consumers, in terms of their ability to make ends meet, plan ahead, or choose and manage financial products, is troubling (Lusardi 2010). For example, many American consumers have made suboptimal decisions about loans for their homes. Given the available product offerings, many people did not obtain competitively priced loans but selected loans that were suboptimal in terms of their risks relative to their benefits (Willis 2006).

Notably, this problem persists despite the presence of federally mandated disclosures. Even with these disclosures, consumers remain uninformed about important aspects of financial products and do not always make rational decisions (Bar-Gill and Warren 2008). One reason disclosures seem to fail is that too much information is provided to consumers; consumers therefore experience information overload, which often leads them to focus on only a few pieces of easily understood information but not necessarily the most important ones for effective decision making (Simon 1978). This is even more likely to occur for complex decisions where, despite the importance of accuracy and care, consumers often rely on simplifying heuristics in their decision making (Kahn and Baron 1995). A second reason disclosures fail is that consumers are overly optimistic and may interpret information provided to them in a manner that helps them to come to a desired conclusion, even if that conclusion is not rational (Kunda 1990). For example, a consumer might select a credit card with high penalty fees and interest rates if he mistakenly believes he will never need to make a late payment (Bar-Gill and Warren 2008).

To make matters worse, there is growing concern that some financial firms purposely design and proactively advertise products to mislead consumers about the benefits versus the risks (Braunstein and Welch 2002; Henderson and Pearson 2008). It has been alleged that many home buyers who qualified for conventional loans based on their credit scores instead selected higher-rate subprime loans. Stories abound of consumers who did not notice details concerning the repayment terms of loans. Studies have shown that consumers often do not notice, or they underestimate, the magnitude of fees and charges that are added to other more salient product costs, particularly when those fees are not made salient (Campbell 2006; Morwitz, Greenleaf, and Johnson 1998; Willis 2006), and firms may take advantage of this in financial markets (Gabaix and Laibson 2006). Certain groups of consumers—such as older Americans (Agarwal, Driscoll, Gabaix, and Laibson 2009; Lusardi, Mitchell, and Curto 2009); people with low levels of education; minorities; and women (Lusardi 2008)—may have lower financial literacy and be particularly vulnerable to unethical marketing practices for financial products. These concerns are the basis for past and proposed government intervention involving consumer protection.

3.2 THE CRISIS AND THE DODD-FRANK ACT

As part of the response to the current financial crisis, the Dodd-Frank Wall Street Reform and Consumer Protection Act creates the Bureau of Consumer Financial Protection (BCFP) as an independent bureau within the Federal Reserve System. Under the Dodd-Frank bill, the Federal Reserve, Federal Deposit Insurance Corporation (FDIC), and Office of the Comptroller of the Currency (OCC) continue to regulate banks for safety and soundness, but their powers to regulate consumer products are transferred to a new, independent BCFP. The intent of the BCFP is to unify the supervision and enforcement of existing protection laws in consumer finance in an effort to ensure that consumers are provided with understandable information about financial products, to enhance their financial literacy, and to protect them from abusive practices.

While we argue in other chapters of this book that the primary cause of the crisis was the risk taking of banks, consumer protection was certainly lacking, and we therefore strongly support the creation of such a bureau. While consumer protection, or lack thereof, was something of a sideshow in the financial crisis, it may well have played a minor supporting role. The systemic risk to which the financial sector was exposed was initially housing market risk. In other words, it was the decline in house prices that triggered many of the subsequent events during the crisis. This decline was the result of the prior unsupportable run-up in prices, which was itself a function of the speculative frenzy in the housing market that was facilitated by the availability of credit in the mortgage market. Thus, to the extent that more vigilant consumer protection would have dampened demand for housing via its effect on the mortgage market, the run-up and subsequent decline in house prices might have been less dramatic and the crisis less severe.

Despite this, it is difficult to determine the degree to which better consumer protection would have helped. For example, for some consumers, it may have been perfectly rational to take out adjustable-rate mortgages or negative-amortization loans with low or no down payments. For example, some consumers may rationally expect their incomes to increase over time (e.g., medical students), and these types of loans could enable them to buy properties that they could not otherwise afford at the time. In these cases, the associated risk was borne primarily by the lender, or by those to whom the original lender passed on the loans. Effective consumer protection should not prevent such individuals from taking these rational gambles. At the same time, other consumers were clearly induced to take on more risk than was optimal, in part by misleading or deceptive marketing, and these individuals would have been protected under a better system, with the associated benefit of reducing the fragility of the financial system as a whole. Of course, the bursting of the housing bubble did not have to result in a financial crisis. As we saw during the deflation of the technology bubble starting in 2000, there can be dramatic declines in wealth without an associated financial crisis. The fundamental issue rests with the risk-taking behavior of financial institutions.

Although consumer protection laws were in place prior to the recent financial crisis, they were clearly ineffective. The authority for enforcement is currently in the hands of at least 11 different agencies. All of them have responsibility for only a subgroup of financial firms, and their mandates partly conflict. Among the agencies, the Federal Trade Commission (FTC) is unique in having consumer protection on the list of its primary mandates. We see several major shortcomings of the current regulatory framework. First, consumer protection has an orphan status, with no single agency being responsible for regulation and enforcement. Hence, consumer protection does not receive enough attention. Second, financial organizations could, by changing from one form of financial institution to another (e.g., from a bank charter to a thrift charter), pick the regulator and set of regulations they prefer to deal with. Third, most of these agencies do not have any litigation experience. The sole exception—the FTC—has only limited jurisdiction over financial institutions. Fourth, due to the distributed control, agencies have underinvested in the collection of information. Thus, we agree that a unified federal bureau of consumer protection is an improvement over the current system.

The BCFP is charged with monitoring firms that offer financial services in order to protect the interests of consumers when they shop for mortgages, credit cards, and other financial products. The Bureau would unify the current regulatory framework without expanding the current legal framework, and consumer protection in many branches of the financial services industry would be subordinate to this single agency. The specific goals of the BCFP include the following: to aid consumers in understanding and using relevant information; to protect them from abuse, deception, and fraud by ensuring that disclosures for financial products are easy to understand; to conduct research; and to provide financial literacy education.

The bill assigns a number of responsibilities to the BCFP. First, the Bureau has its own function of data collection and research that allows it to monitor markets for consumer financial products and services and to evaluate the appropriateness of these products and services. Second, it has the authority to set rules under current consumer financial law and take appropriate enforcement action to address violations. Third, it is responsible for conducting financial education programs. Fourth, the Bureau is charged with collecting, investigating, and responding to consumer complaints. Fifth, the Bureau has a mandate to ensure that suitable financial products and services are made available to consumer groups and communities that have traditionally been underserved in these markets. Sixth, the Bureau has a mandate to protect vulnerable consumers, including older Americans and service personnel and their families. To help achieve these goals, there will be the following offices within the Bureau: the Office of Fair Lending and Equal Opportunity, the Office of Financial Education, the Office of Service Member Affairs, and the Office of Financial Protection for Older Americans.

Ten specific aspects of the bill are worth noting:

1. Several financial products are specifically excluded from regulation under the BCFP, including financing provided by automobile dealers, retailers, and sellers of modular homes. Products and services provided by insurance companies, real estate brokers, accountants, tax preparers, and lawyers, among others, are also exempt from regulation under the Bureau, leaving them under the current system of regulation.

2. While the BCFP can write rules for all depository institutions, smaller banks and credit unions with assets under $10 billion will not be subject to the Bureau's enforcement authority. Instead, regulations will be enforced by their current regulator.

3. In general, the bill does not preempt or annul state law, except in the case of national banks when the state consumer financial law would have a discriminatory effect on national banks relative to state-chartered banks, as determined by the OCC in consultation with the BCFP.

4. The BCFP is to be run by a director who is appointed by the President with the advice and consent of the Senate. The director will serve a five-year term. The Bureau is funded directly by the Federal Reserve System.

5. The bill provides for additional regulation of the mortgage market under the Mortgage Reform and Anti-Predatory Lending Act. Major provisions include: (1) prohibitions on steering incentives for mortgage brokers (i.e., payments to brokers for selling specific types of loans), (2) restrictions on prepayment penalties, (3) restrictions on high-cost mortgages, and perhaps most important, (4) a requirement that lenders make a "reasonable and good faith determination" that borrowers have a "reasonable ability to repay" the loan that they are taking out.

6. The bill also provides additional regulation for debit and credit card companies with more than $10 billion in assets under the Durban amendment. In particular, the bill requires that interchange fees be reasonable and proportional to incurred costs, as defined by the Fed. The

bill also states that payment card issuers and networks cannot include in their contracts with vendors prohibitions on giving discounts for cash, check, or debit card payments. They also cannot prohibit the vendor's decision to refuse to allow credit card purchases for transactions that are below some threshold.

7. Regulations prescribed by the BCFP can be set aside only if they threaten the safety and soundness of the financial system as determined by a two-thirds vote of the Financial Stability Oversight Council.
8. The BCFP, when proposing new rules and regulations, is required to consider input from other regulators, but is not required to enact their recommendations.
9. The regulations allow industry participants to engage in trial programs and market tests to develop disclosures that might be more effective than those prescribed by the BCFP.
10. The BCFP has the authority to prohibit or limit mandatory predispute arbitration, if warranted based on a study.

3.3 EVALUATION OF THE BCFP

In evaluating the current legislation, two models are particularly helpful: the FTC's Bureau of Consumer Protection and the Financial Consumer Agency of Canada. The FTC's Division of Financial Practices under the Bureau of Consumer Protection has the mandate to protect "consumers from deceptive and unfair practices in the financial services industry, including protecting consumers from predatory or discriminatory lending practices, as well as deceptive or unfair loan servicing, debt collection, and credit counseling or other debt assistance practices" (FTC web site 2009). While the FTC's goals and methods are well suited for providing consumer protection and financial education, its authority is limited to credit market activities by nondepository institutions, and thus is inadequate for protecting consumers across the wide range of financial products they face. The BCFP would take over many of the FTC's consumer financial protection responsibilities.

The Financial Consumer Agency of Canada supervises a broad range of financial service providers, including all banks, federally incorporated and registered insurance, trust and loan companies, and retail associations. Its mandate consists of consumer protection and consumer education and thus puts more emphasis on informing the public, compared with its U.S. counterpart. To enforce consumer protection laws, Canada's Financial Consumer Agency can seek a commitment from financial institutions to remedy issues in due time, impose monetary penalties or criminal sanctions, and take further actions if deemed necessary. Canada provided the Financial Consumer

Agency with a research arm that also gathers data. This function makes information available to the public—for example, databases on the rates and features of credit cards. Furthermore, the agency offers online quizzes that allow consumers to test their knowledge of credit cards and mortgages.

We endorse the creation of an independent consumer protection bureau in the United States, and the BCFP, as embodied in the current legislation, is an important step in this direction. While we are concerned that if not done effectively there is risk of overregulation, we agree with the mission to unify enforcement for consumer protection. We also agree that the BCFP's mission should include aiding consumers in understanding and using relevant information; protecting them from abuse, deception, and fraud; conducting research; and providing financial literacy education.

The independence of the Bureau is important, and its structure as an independent agency within the Federal Reserve System seems to achieve this goal, especially since the associated funding avoids the annual congressional appropriations process that can serve as a mechanism for imposing undesirable political pressure. However, housing the Bureau within the Fed also sends a signal that bank solvency comes before consumer protection. This idea may seem reasonable, but it also implies that there is a conflict between these two goals—something that is far less obvious. Appropriate consumer protection should not adversely affect financial institutions, but perhaps housing the Bureau in the Fed is a warning as to how likely we are to see appropriate regulation.

Ideally, the Bureau would have full rule-making and enforcement authority over all financial firms and products. While the Dodd-Frank Act does unify much of this authority in the BCFP, there are some troubling exceptions. For example, auto loans and annuities are two extremely popular products where abuses have been alleged in the past; however, auto dealers and insurance companies have been specifically excluded from oversight by the Bureau. Although the Dodd-Frank Act also empowers the Federal Trade Commission, the current regulator for automobile dealers, to write rules related to auto financing more quickly and easily, we still feel these carve-outs leave a significant part of consumers' assets underregulated. We are also concerned that since the BCFP will not have the power to enforce regulation for smaller banks and financial institutions, if the existing regulators fail to do their job, consumer protection may be inadequate. Worse yet, financial firms may be able to exploit these exclusions by engaging in regulatory arbitrage. For instance, financial firms can redirect their credit supply to less regulated sectors.

It is also important that the BCFP sets the federal floor but not ceiling for consumer protection. State protection laws are often stricter than federal laws, and the Dodd-Frank Act does a creditable job in achieving this goal.

As we argued earlier, many consumers are not sufficiently financially literate to assess complex financial products and might make misguided decisions. We agree with the broad mandate given to the BCFP for financial consumer education and information provision. The Bureau could, for instance, publish consumer guidelines, compare standard rates or contracts, and offer financial literacy tests. However, as research demonstrates that financial education may not be enough to protect all consumers from poor choices (Braunstein and Welch 2002), we believe that more is needed.

To aid those consumers for whom financial education does not suffice, the BCFP should actively intervene to improve overall welfare. Although it is not explicit in the Dodd-Frank Act, we recommend that the BCFP should have the option of requiring financial service providers to include a plain-vanilla product in their menu. This offering should be easy to understand, even for the inexperienced customer. It would also serve the purpose of a point of reference in comparison with other products. The BCFP should also ensure that default options are prudently chosen, since consumers, especially those who are inexperienced, are likely to refrain from active choices. Such a default option has proven successful in increasing participation in 401(k) retirement plans. When the default is for employees to participate, and opting out requires an active choice, participation rates increase substantially. In addition, the agency could consider marking certain products with a seal of approval. Uninformed customers would thus be given the chance to fall back on financial products that have been scrutinized by the BCFP and about which they can get independent information. While the current bill does not endow the BCFP with the authority and the mandate to implement such actions, they could be viewed as falling under the general objective of ensuring that "markets for consumer products are fair, transparent, and competitive."

Potentially harmful products might require additional measures. The BCFP has the ability to engage in litigation in cases of abuse, deception, or fraud. We also endorse the BCFP's right to prohibit the sale of financial products or practices as a last resort, something that is not contained explicitly in the bill. However, no product should be banned before it has been tried by the market. Bans should be imposed only if consumer litigation and extensive market research have proven that the products or services are widely misunderstood, misused, and detrimental to consumers. This proviso aims at curbing the danger of overregulation, which might leave some market participants worse off and might stifle financial innovation.

Last, the BCFP should focus not only on protecting consumers from misguided decisions, but also on improving the incentives for their brokers. To ensure good financial advice, the BCFP should review the licensing practices for brokers and set minimum standards. Furthermore, the Bureau should be given the authority to review and regulate brokers' compensation. The prohibition on steering incentives for mortgage brokers in the Mortgage Reform and Anti-Predatory Lending Act, which falls under the purview of the BCFP, is a good example of this type of regulation. Such measures may help to ensure that consumers receive the sound advice they need to make prudent long-term financial decisions.

It is obviously difficult to envision exactly how education, regulation, and intervention should look, even in markets that we currently understand well. It is impossible to anticipate what regulations will be needed for innovative products that have not yet been invented. One key to the future success of the BCFP is for the agency to continuously reevaluate its programs in a rigorous and systematic fashion. In other words, the agency must collect data on the effects of its ongoing regulatory efforts, and conduct and evaluate pilot programs for new products and markets or new efforts in existing fields. An excellent example is the study of the legislative experiment in which the State of Illinois required high-risk mortgage applicants in some areas to submit loan offers for review by financial counselors (Agarwal, Amromin, Ben-David, Chomsisengphet, and Evanoff 2009). This type of ongoing experimentation and monitoring is critical for improving outcomes. We therefore support the bill's requirement that the Bureau conduct assessments, using available evidence and data, of any significant rule or order it adopts and urge it to do so on a continuous basis.

What implications does the creation of the BCFP have for the future of financial institutions and financial services? Up front, it is critical to note that there is absolutely no inherent conflict between appropriate consumer protection and the safety and soundness of banks and other financial institutions. While it may be the case that increasing financial literacy and protecting consumers from misleading or deceptive practices reduces profits for some companies in some segments of the market, from a social welfare standpoint, it is tough to argue that prohibiting these practices is harmful. On the contrary, a well-functioning BCFP should not only protect consumers, but also provide additional benefits such as increased competition and the efficiencies that this competition engenders. Moreover, firms would have the incentive to develop value-increasing innovations rather than innovations that increase profits only through exploitation of poor decision making.

Of course, given experiences with government intervention in other facets of the economy, skeptics might doubt that the creation of the BCFP will, in fact, lead to appropriate consumer protection. The dangers of over- or misregulation are substantial. First, arbitrary restrictions on the types of products or services that are offered might easily reduce social welfare. For example, payday lending has come under attack at various times, but there is evidence that access to high-interest loans can mitigate individual financial distress in the face of natural disasters (Morse 2009). A better way to avoid the costs associated with the misuse of these products might be to mandate information disclosure designed to improve decision making by overcoming cognitive biases (Bertrand and Morse 2009). In the case of the Dodd-Frank Act, the restrictions on mortgage lending would appear to be of most concern. Elimination of prepayment penalties and restrictions on high-cost mortgages, while certainly motivated by abuses that have occurred in the past, will also almost certainly reduce the availability of credit, as will the responsibility placed on lenders to ensure that borrowers have a documented ability to repay their loans.

Second, haphazard regulation (i.e., regulation of some corporate forms but not others or rules based on arbitrarily defined product categories) is almost certain to create investment in technologies to avoid this regulation. The tax code and the responses to it are a perfect example of this type of effect. Complexity and the existence of exceptions, loopholes, and other carve-outs have fostered a whole industry devoted to tax avoidance in one form or another. In the context of consumer protection, not only would the goal of protecting consumers be undermined, but substantial resources could potentially be diverted from more productive uses. The bill excludes numerous financial services providers from oversight by the BCFP, and it is uncertain how the industry will adapt, if at all, to exploit these exclusions.

Third, overburdensome regulation could increase costs for companies offering financial products, and price controls could decrease revenues. An example of the latter would be limits on interest rates charged by credit card companies. In the short run, these cost increases or revenue decreases could threaten the profitability and even the viability of some, particularly smaller, companies. In the longer run, this type of regulation will lead companies to exit the market, as we have seen with insurance companies in various states; this is a disservice to consumers who benefit from active markets with vibrant competition. An illustration of this type of issue is the specific language in the bill permitting the BCFP to restrict interchange (debit card) fees. While minor in itself, it does provide a warning that heavy-handed regulation of financial services could occur as the BCFP stretches its regulatory muscle. Regulation can also inadvertently hurt traditionally underserved consumers and communities by limiting their access to financial products and services. While the concerns of overregulation remain, we support the bill's focus on balancing consumer protection with the needs of underserved markets and the viability of firms that offer financial products or services.

In sum, while there is clearly hope that an independent, well-financed, and appropriately staffed BCFP will make significant strides in educating and protecting consumers and therefore improving their welfare, there is a well-justified fear that the creation of such a bureau and the external pressures that may come to bear once it is in existence can potentially subvert this potential and cause more harm than good.

REFERENCES

Agarwal, Sumit, Gene Amromin, Itzhak Ben-David, Souphala Chomsisengphet, and Douglas D. Evanoff. 2009. Do financial counseling mandates improve mortgage choice and performance? Evidence from a legislative experiment. Ohio State University, Fisher College of Business, Working Paper 2008-03-019.

Agarwal, Sumit, John Driscoll, Xavier Gabaix, and David Laibson. 2009. The age of reason: Financial decisions over the life-cycle and implications for regulation. *Brookings Papers on Economic Activity*, no. 2:51–117.

Bar-Gill, Oren, and Elizabeth Warren. 2008. Making credit safer. *University of Pennsylvania Law Review* 157 (1): 1–101.

Bertrand, Marianne, and Adair Morse. 2009. Information disclosure, cognitive biases and payday borrowing. Working paper, University of Chicago.

Braunstein, Sandra, and Carolyn Welch. 2002. Financial literacy: An overview of practice, research, and policy. *Federal Reserve Bulletin*, November 1, 445–457.

Campbell, John. 2006. Household finance. *Journal of Finance* 61 (4): 1553–1604.

FTC web site. 2009. December 3. www.ftc.gov/bcp/bcpfp.shtm.

Gabaix, Xavier, and David Laibson. 2006. Shrouded attributes, consumer myopia, and information suppression in competitive markets. *Quarterly Journal of Economics* 121 (2): 505–540.

Henderson, Brian J., and Neil Pearson. 2008. The dark side of financial innovation. Working paper, George Washington University.

Kahn, Barbara E., and Jonathon Baron. 1995. An exploratory study of choice rules favored for high-stakes decisions. *Journal of Consumer Psychology* 4 (4): 305, 325–326.

Kunda, Ziva. 1990. The case for motivated reasoning. *Psychological Bulletin* 108 (3): 480–498.

Lusardi, Annamaria. 2008. Financial literacy: An essential tool for informed consumer choice? SSRN Working Paper No. 1336389.

Lusardi, Annamaria. 2010. Americans' financial capability. Report prepared for the Financial Crisis Inquiry Commission.

Lusardi, Annamaria, Olivia S. Mitchell, and Vilsa Curto. 2009. Financial literacy and financial sophistication among older consumers. NBER Working Paper No. w15469.

Morse, Adair. 2009. Payday lenders: Heroes or villains? Working paper, University of Chicago.

Morwitz, Vicki G., Eric Greenleaf, and Eric Johnson. 1998. Divide and prosper: Consumers' reactions to partitioned prices. *Journal of Marketing Research* 25 (November): 453–463.

Perry, Vanessa G., and Marlene D. Morris. 2005. Who is in control? The role of self-perception, knowledge, and income in explaining consumer financial behavior. *Journal of Consumer Affairs* 39 (2): 299–313.

Simon, Herbert A. 1978. Rationality as process and as product of thought. *American Economic Review* 68 (2): 1–16.

Willis, Lauren E. 2006. Decisionmaking and the limits of disclosure: The problems of predatory lending: Price. *Maryland Law Review* 65 (3): 707–840.

Systemic Risk

CHAPTER 4

Measuring Systemic Risk

Viral V. Acharya, Christian Brownlees, Robert Engle,
Farhang Farazmand, and Matthew Richardson*

4.1 OVERVIEW

The most important lesson from the financial crisis of 2007 to 2009 has been that failures of some large financial institutions can impose costs on the entire system. We call these systemically important financial institutions (SIFIs). Their failures invariably put regulators in a compromised situation since, absent prearranged resolution plans, they are forced to rescue the failed institutions to preserve a functioning financial system. In the recent crisis, this has involved protecting not just insured creditors, but sometimes uninsured creditors and even shareholders. The anticipation that these bailouts will occur compromises market discipline in good times, encouraging excessive leverage and risk taking. This reinforces the systemic risk in the system. It is widely accepted that systemic risk needs to be contained by making it possible for these institutions to fail, thus restraining their incentives to take excessive risks in good times. First and foremost, however, regulators need to ascertain which institutions are, in fact, systemically important. Indeed, the systemic risk of an individual institution has not yet been measured or quantified by regulators in an organized manner, even though systemic risk has always been one of the justifications for our elaborate regulatory apparatus.

---

*The authors benefited from discussions in the "Measuring Systemic Risk" Working Group for the NYU Stern e-book *Real Time Solutions for Financial Reform*, which also included Nicholas Economides, Sabri Öncü, Michael Pinedo, and Kermit L. Schoenholtz.

There are some institutions that follow highly cyclical activities and are thus heavily correlated with aggregate economic conditions. If these institutions are also highly levered, especially with short-term debt, then they face runs in the event of sufficiently adverse news about their condition. This makes them more prone to failure and liquidation. If their failure were unrelated to aggregate conditions, their liquidation would be straightforward, as there would be healthy players in the financial sector to acquire them or their assets. However, when institutions' asset risk is correlated with that of the economy, they are likely to fail when the rest of the financial sector is under stress too, and their liquidations are difficult and potentially destabilizing for other players if fire-sale asset prices lead to externalities. In this case, systemic risk propagates through the effect of firm failures on asset prices. Many observers attribute the markdowns in prices of illiquid so-called toxic assets during the crisis of 2007 to 2009 (at least partly) to several highly levered financial firms having taken a one-way bet on housing prices in the economy—a bet that went bad and produced difficult funding conditions for much less levered financial institutions that were holding similar assets.

Interconnection among financial firms can also lead to systemic risk under crisis conditions. Financial institutions are interconnected in a variety of networks in bilateral and multilateral relationships and contracts, as well as through markets. Under normal conditions, these interconnections are highly beneficial to the financial system and its constituents. For example, they can be used by financial institutions to diversify risk as well as to accumulate capital for specific functions. Under crisis conditions, this is not the case: First, these interconnections (including markets) may fail to function in their normal way, resulting in particular institutions' facing excessive and unexpected risks. Second, many interconnections and commitments cannot be altered quickly and therefore, in a crisis, may transfer risk and losses across financial firms, resulting in cascading failures. Third, certain institutions are central to key financial networks, and their failures can result in widespread failures. These institutions may be too large (to fail) but others may be highly interconnected, although not particularly big.

The failures of Bear Stearns, Lehman Brothers, and American International Group (AIG) all contributed to systemic risk in the form of uncertainty about which interconnections would transmit default risk. In the case of Bear Stearns, the risk was stemmed through government support. In the case of Lehman Brothers, the risk spread as losses on Lehman bonds caused the Reserve Primary Fund, a money market fund, to "break the buck," causing a run on it and several other money market funds. And in the case of AIG, its counterparty position was so large in terms of exposures of other potentially systemic institutions and municipalities, in the United States as well as in Europe, that it could not be allowed to fail.

Finally, while size by itself need not lead to systemic effects of failures, it may do so if large-scale liquidations are feared and lead to disruption of markets, interconnections, and the loss of intermediation functions that they might take months, or years, to rebuild. Cases in point are the Continental Illinois Bank's failure in 1984, the near collapse of Long-Term Capital Management in 1998, and that of Citigroup in the autumn of 2008. Of course, this brings with it the curse of too-big-to-fail expectations and the attendant moral hazard problems.

4.2 THE DODD-FRANK WALL STREET REFORM AND CONSUMER PROTECTION ACT

In June 2010 Congress integrated the Frank bill passed by the House in the fall of 2009 with the Dodd bill passed by the Senate in 2010. The White House signed the bill into law and the regulators are faced with the task of implementation. Many features of the Dodd-Frank Act are sensible and conform to the recommendations of the NYU Stern Book, *Restoring Financial Stability*, edited by Acharya and Richardson (2009), including chapters by many of the same authors included in this volume. Other features of the Act, however, are problematic for the financial system, and many are left to the implementation of various regulatory bodies.

The Act focuses on systemic risk. It establishes a Financial Stability Oversight Council, which is chaired by the Secretary of the Treasury and consists of the top financial officers from various governmental and regulatory agencies—the Federal Reserve, the Office of the Comptroller of the Currency (OCC), the Bureau of Consumer Financial Protection, the Securities and Exchange Commission (SEC), the Federal Deposit Insurance Corporation (FDIC), the Commodity Futures Trading Commission (CFTC), the Federal Housing Finance Agency (FHFA), and the National Credit Union Administration (NCUA)—and an independent member with insurance expertise. The role of this council is to "identify risks to the financial stability of the United States that could arise from the material financial distress or failure, or ongoing activities, of large, interconnected bank holding companies or nonbank financial companies or that could arise outside the financial services marketplace."[1] In addition, the council is to affirm the commitment of the government not to shield investors or counterparties from failures of such companies and to respond to any future emerging threat to the stability of the U.S. financial system.

In addition to identifying systemically risky U.S. bank and nonbank financial institutions, the Council can insist that a foreign bank or nonbank financial institution be supervised by the Federal Reserve Board of Governors. In taking this step, the Council must "determine that material financial distress at the . . . financial company, or the nature, scope, size, scale, concentration, interconnectedness, or mix of the activities of the . . . financial company, could pose a threat to the financial stability of the United States."[2] If a company is avoiding regulation by its organization or operations but would otherwise be considered systemically risky, the Council has the authority to insist that it be regulated by the Board of Governors. The Council annually reviews the institutions it considers systemically risky and can terminate some oversight.

The chief role of the Council is to identify systemic risks wherever they arise and recommend policies to regulatory bodies. As a quick rule of thumb, financial institutions that have a huge concentration in volume of one or more product areas are likely candidates for systemically risky institutions. These entities are generally likely to be making markets in that product and are likely to be systemic in that their failures would impose significant counterparty risk and disruptions on other financial institutions. Hence, they should be deemed as systemic regardless of any other criteria.

The Council is explicitly charged to "identify systemically important financial market utilities and payment, clearing, and settlement activities." We particularly endorse the addition to the systemic risk criteria of firms operating or significantly owning public utility functions that participate in the payments system and move reserves around in the economy—such as clearing (for instance, Bear Stearns for credit derivatives until its failure in March 2008 and JPMorgan Chase and Bank of New York for repurchase agreements) and payment and settlement (several large commercial banks that provide banking services to households and corporations). The Dodd-Frank Act authorizes "enhancements to the regulation and supervision of systemically important financial market utilities and the conduct of systemically important payment, clearing, and settlement activities by financial institutions," including standards for risk and liquidity management.[3]

It is an open question how regulators will treat these systemically risky entities housed in otherwise safe firms. Indeed, our recommendation— discussed in Chapter 13, "Regulating OTC Derivatives"—is to move the public utility function out of private financial firms (for instance, as clearinghouses) wherever possible (for instance, for standardized products with sufficient daily volume of trading) and to subject the public utility to sufficiently high capital standards, so as to eliminate most of the systemic risk associated with performance of the function. Going forward, as many over-the-counter (OTC) derivatives start being centrally cleared, clearinghouses would be important utilities that should be considered in the set of systemically important institutions and be subject to prudential risk standards. However, several over-the-counter derivatives will likely remain uncleared and may collectively add up to a substantial part of derivatives markets. Regulators would have to be particularly watchful in ensuring that critical entities in the uncleared derivatives market are also brought within their radar.

To the best of our knowledge, no specific list of systemic firms has yet been determined. Internationally, the Financial Stability Board (FSB), an international body of regulators and central bankers, based out of the Bank for International Settlements, has compiled a list of 28 global financial institutions; these firms are considered as "systemic risk institutions" for cross-border supervision exercises, such as drawing up so-called living wills or recovery and resolution plans. This list (see Appendix A) includes six insurance companies and 22 banks from the United Kingdom, continental Europe, North America, and Japan, even though the exact criteria employed have not been revealed.

Most important for systemic risk, the Dodd-Frank Act calls for stricter prudential standards for systemically important institutions. In particular,

> *In order to prevent or mitigate risks to the financial stability of the United States that could arise from the material financial distress, failure, or ongoing activities of large, interconnected financial institutions, the Council may make recommendations to the Board of Governors concerning the establishment and refinement of prudential standards and reporting and disclosure requirements applicable to nonbank financial companies supervised by the Board of Governors and large, interconnected bank holding companies, that are more stringent than those applicable to other nonbank financial companies and bank holding companies that do not present similar risks to the financial stability of the United States.*[4]

Moreover, these additional standards should be increasing in stringency based on:

> *(A) the extent of the leverage of the company; (B) the extent and nature of the off-balance-sheet exposures of the company; (C) the extent and nature of the transactions and relationships of the company with other significant nonbank financial companies and significant bank holding companies; (D) the importance of the company*

as a source of credit for households, businesses, and State and local governments and as a source of liquidity for the United States financial system; (E) the importance of the company as a source of credit for low-income, minority, or underserved communities, and the impact that the failure of such company would have on the availability of credit in such communities; (F) the extent to which assets are managed rather than owned by the company, and the extent to which ownership of assets under management is diffuse; (G) the nature, scope, size, scale, concentration, interconnectedness, and mix of the activities of the company; (H) the degree to which the company is already regulated by 1 or more primary financial regulatory agencies; (I) the amount and nature of the financial assets of the company; (J) the amount and types of the liabilities of the company, including the degree of reliance on short-term funding; and (K) any other risk-related factors that the Council deems appropriate.[5]

While factors A to K capture many important characteristics of risk, there is an obvious factor missing. At the core of a firm's systemic risk is the comovement of that firm's assets with the aggregate financial sector in a crisis. Moreover, all but two factors—factor C and the mention of interconnectedness in factor G—are about dealing with the risk of banks from an individual bank-by-bank standpoint.

The policies to be followed in regulating financial companies that are deemed systemically risky are not specified in the bill. Instead a range of policies are laid out and will be proposed by the Council for implementation by the Board of Governors. These policies include:[6]

- Risk-based capital requirements.
- Leverage limits.
- Liquidity requirements.
- Resolution plan and credit exposure report requirements.
- Concentration limits.
- A contingent capital requirement.
- Enhanced public disclosures.
- Short-term debt limits.
- Overall risk management requirements.

Our interpretation of the Act is that its intention is to give the Board of Governors flexibility to reduce the risk of the systemically most important firms that are identified by the Council. One necessary feature is to provide the Council with the tools to be able make such identifications possible. Therefore, in order to support the Council with its task of generating and analyzing data and information relevant for systemic risk assessment, the Act establishes the Office of Financial Research (OFR).

The purpose of the OFR is to support the Council in fulfilling its purposes and duties by "(1) collecting data on behalf of the Council, and providing such data to the Council and member agencies; (2) standardizing the types and formats of data reported and collected; (3) performing applied research and essential long-term research; (4) developing tools for risk measurement and monitoring; (5) performing other related services; and (6) making the results of the activities of the Office available to financial regulatory agencies."[7]

The director of the Office will report on the assessment by the Office of significant financial market developments and potential emerging threats to the financial stability of the United States. As an organizational structure, there are two core parts:[8]

1. *The Data Center* prepares and publishes, in a manner that is easily accessible to the public (1) a financial company reference database; (2) a financial instrument reference database; and (3) formats and standards for Office data, including standards for reporting financial transaction and position data to the Office.
2. *The Research and Analysis Center*, on behalf of the Council, will develop and maintain independent analytical capabilities and computing resources "(i) to develop and maintain metrics and reporting systems for risks to the financial stability of the United States; (ii) to monitor, investigate, and report on changes in system-wide risk levels and patterns to the Council and Congress; (iii) to conduct, coordinate, and sponsor research to support and improve regulation of financial entities and markets; (iv) to evaluate and report on stress tests or other stability-related evaluations of financial entities overseen by the member agencies; (v) to maintain expertise in such areas as may be necessary to support specific requests for advice and assistance from financial regulators; (vi) to investigate disruptions and failures in the financial markets, report findings, and make recommendations to the Council based on those findings; (vii) to conduct studies and provide advice on the impact of policies related to systemic risk; and (viii) to promote best practices for financial risk management."[9]

Since the OFR is funded by an assessment on systemically important financial firms and it is organized as an independent think tank within

Treasury, we generally support the idea of its existence. The organizational structure and funding seem flexible enough to allow the OFR to collect data and produce research that other government agencies (e.g., the Federal Reserve) may not be able to produce.

4.3 EVALUATION OF THE DODD-FRANK ACT

Our evaluation of the Dodd-Frank Act is centered around several themes: that the criteria for determining systemic institutions can be supplemented with market-based continuous measures of systemic risk; the need to assess systemic risk linked to the interconnectedness of institutions and what role the Office of Financial Research could play in such assessment; employing stress tests and aggregated risk exposure reports to assess the risk of the system as a whole (not just during crises but on a regular basis); and whether the list of systemic institutions should be made public.

Market-Based Measures of Systemic Risk

While we do not disagree with the list of criteria suggested by the Act, we do not recommend a pure reliance on classification-based criteria with specific thresholds. Suppose, for example, that banks are divided into systemic risk categories by size and that resolution plans apply only to the top size category. Clearly, there would be tremendous advantage for banks that are near the lower threshold of the top size category to remain just below that size. Indeed, larger banks may simply break themselves up yet retain their exposures to some common aggregate risky asset, for example, the housing market. In this case, the true systemic risk may not be substantially reduced, as the comovement in different parts of the financial sector remains, even though it is now contained in many more, smaller institutions. The same regulatory arbitrage rule applies for coarse categorization based on leverage. A corollary of this argument is that a group of institutions that are individually small but collectively exposed to the same risk—for example, money market funds—could all experience runs when there is an aggregate crisis and high-quality issuers of commercial paper fall into distress. These should be considered as part of a potentially systemic risk pocket of the economy.

An alternative to coarse categorization of systemic risk is to employ market-based measures that are more continuously variable. One possibility is to use market data to estimate which firms are most exposed, and therefore contribute most to the losses incurred, during an economy-wide downturn such as the Great Depression or the Great Recession of 2007 to 2009. Such measures would be inexpensive and responsive to market conditions, and would be natural complements to the more detailed investigations envisioned in the Act. The use of market-based measures has recently been studied by Acharya, Pedersen, Philippon, and Richardson (2010a, 2010b); Adrian and Brunnermeier (2008); Brownlees and Engle (2010); De Jonghe (2009); Gray and Jobst (2009); Huang, Zhou, and Zhu (2009); and Lehar (2005), among others.

These measures are generally based on stock market data because it is most commonly available at daily frequency and least affected by bailout expectations. For instance, a simple measure called Marginal Expected Shortfall (MES) estimates the loss that the equity of a given firm can expect if the broad market experiences a large fall. A firm with a high MES and also high leverage will find its capital most depleted in a financial crisis relative to required minimum solvency standards and therefore faces high risk of bankruptcy or regulatory intervention. It is such undercapitalization of financial firms that leads to systemic risk. An implementation of this idea is now available at the New York University Stern School of Business volatility laboratory (Vlab). It is updated regularly and posted daily on Vlab. These systemic risk rankings can be accessed at www.systemicriskranking .stern.nyu.edu and are described briefly in Section 4.4.

Overall, we see the two approaches—relying on simple systemic risk criteria such as size, leverage, and interconnectedness and relying on market-based estimates of systemic risk—as complementary. The first is more transparent and likely to flag obvious candidates; the second is a reality check based on market perceptions as to whether some candidates have been missed altogether (or some obvious ones are less systemic than they seem at first blush). For instance, securities dealers and brokers show up as being most systemic in every single year since 1963, based on stock market data (MES), even though they have remained essentially unregulated. By contrast, AIG is a natural one-way insurance provider of large quantities that is not identified by stock market data as being significantly systemic until six months into the crisis. Also, while systemic risk categories can be arbitraged by market participants, market-based systemic risk measures are more difficult to evade until the firm's true systemic risk has diminished.

Interconnectedness

A key issue that arises in measuring systemic risk is that interconnections of financial institutions are somewhat opaque, and their precise nature may be entirely different in a stressed scenario than under normal conditions. For instance, counterparty exposures can reverse signs when conditions change. And deep out-of-the-money options, such as those sold by AIG to banks as synthetic insurance, can lead to defaults due to margin or collateral calls even before the events being insured against materialize. There is no simple answer to these questions, but important steps can be taken.

In order to have any hope of assessing interconnectedness of a financial institution and its pivotal role in a network, detailed exposures to other institutions through derivative contracts and interbank liabilities are a must. This requires legislation that compels reporting, such that all connections are registered in a repository immediately after they are formed or when they are extinguished, along with information on the extent and form of the collateralization and the risk of collateral calls when credit quality deteriorates. These reports could be aggregated by risk and maturity types to obtain an overall map of network connections. What is important from the standpoint of systemic risk assessment is that such reports, and the underlying data, be rich enough to help estimate *potential exposures* to counterparties under infrequent but socially costly market- or economy-wide stress scenarios. For instance, it seems relevant to know for each systemically important institution (1) what are the most dominant risk factors in terms of losses likely to be realized in stress scenarios, and (2) what are its most important counterparties in terms of potential exposures in stress scenarios. A transparency standard that encompasses such requirements is provided in Chapter 13, "Regulating OTC Derivatives."

The establishment of the OFR is an important step in obtaining and employing the necessary data. It provides a framework in which the data can be reported and analyzed and made available to regulatory bodies. The choice of data to be collected is not made explicit in the legislation but will be determined by the OFR staff. Thus we encourage the OFR to obtain both position data and collateral agreements so that contingent positions can be examined in stress scenarios. The analysis of network effects in a stress test is extremely complex even if all of the data on positions are available. The response by counterparties to a particular stress event may depend on liquidity considerations, their own capital distress, netting conditions in stable and bankruptcy outcomes, and many other factors. This calculation will be feasible only under simplifying assumptions that ongoing research must evaluate. Presumably much of this analysis will be carried out within the OFR and the academic community and is a high priority. For some recent research related to the financial crisis, see Chan-Lau, Espinosa, Giesecke, and Sole (2009); Nier, Yang, Yorulmazer, and Alentorn (2007); and Upper (2007).

A further complexity is the international nature of such networks. As many counterparties may be foreign entities, the data to follow the stress event may not be available. Further, as subsidiaries of the company under examination may be foreign registered institutions, the flow of funds may be exceedingly difficult to follow. The Lehman bankruptcy illustrates many of these issues. Many clearing and settlement businesses are already international. For example, the Depository Trust & Clearing Corporation (DTCC) clears and warehouses the vast majority of swaps contracts in many segments of the financial space. They analyze positions and prices and provide information to the public and confidential data to regulators on these products. Such global organizations will be natural components of the regulatory environment, and their contributions should be warmly welcomed.

A very important feature of the Dodd-Frank Act is the section on over-the-counter (OTC) derivatives. As discussed in Chapter 13, "Regulation of OTC Derivatives," the legislation moves a wide range of OTC derivatives to centralized clearing and/or exchange trading. As a consequence, the counterparty risk that is inherent in OTC derivatives simply becomes risk relative to the central counterparty. The central counterparty will automatically set margins so that risk positions will be nearly marked to market. This remaining central counterparty risk is potentially systemic and must be carefully monitored. However, it is a risk that can be easily regulated because clearinghouses are public utilities and are naturally supervised. Thus improving the functioning of the OTC derivatives market will substantially reduce the difficulty in measuring the network effects of systemic institutions.

Stress Tests

In order to be able to project into infrequent future scenarios, such scenarios need to be modeled and considered in the first place. An attractive way of dealing with such projection is to conduct so-called stress tests—along the lines of the Supervisory Capital Assessment Program (SCAP) exercise conducted by the Federal Reserve during February to May 2009. (See Appendix B for a description of the SCAP exercise and its impact on the markets.) To report its objectives and findings, we quote from the report:[10]

> From the macroprudential perspective, the SCAP was a top-down analysis of the largest bank holding companies (BHCs), representing a majority of the U.S. banking system, with an explicit goal to facilitate aggregate lending. The SCAP applied a common, probabilistic scenario analysis for all participating BHCs and looked beyond the traditional accounting-based measures to determine the needed capital buffer. The macroprudential goal was to credibly reduce the probability of the tail outcome, but the analysis began at the microprudential level with detailed and idiosyncratic data on the

*risks and exposures of each participating BHC. This firm-specific,
granular data allowed tailored analysis that led to differentiation
and BHC-specific policy actions, e.g., a positive identified SCAP
buffer for 10 BHCs and no need for a buffer for the remaining
nine.*[11]

We believe stress tests should be a regular part of the Federal Reserve
tool kit to determine the risk of institutions in stressed systemic scenarios,
as well as to assess the overall systemic risk of the financial sector in such
scenarios. There has been valuable knowledge and experience developed in
the exercise of SCAP 2009, and this could be built upon. Indeed, we find
it comforting that the Dodd-Frank Act calls for systemic institutions to be
subject to periodic stress tests:

> *The Board of Governors, in coordination with the appropriate pri-
> mary financial regulatory agencies and the Federal Insurance Office,
> shall conduct annual analyses in which nonbank financial com-
> panies supervised by the Board of Governors and bank holding
> companies described in subsection (a) are subject to evaluation of
> whether such companies have the capital, on a total consolidated
> basis, necessary to absorb losses as a result of adverse economic
> conditions.*[12]

Moreover, systemically important financial institutions are required to
perform semiannual tests. Such assessments should be done more frequently
in a crisis and may complement the firm's own test (as recommended by the
Securities and Exchange Commission in SEC.1114, Stress Tests).

Finally, we document in Appendix C that academic research (Acharya,
Pedersen, Philippon, and Richardson 2010a) has found that market-based
measures of systemic risk such as Marginal Expected Shortfall and leverage
help explain the outcomes of the SCAP exercise conducted in 2009. Hence,
we view the historical-based systemic risk measures and projected systemic
risk measures through stress tests as complementary. Regulators should
embrace both as useful cross-checks and independent pieces of valuable
intelligence for assessment of systemic risk of financial firms.

Transparency

In terms of both the activities of the OFR and the government-run stress
tests, we recommend a fully transparent approach to systemic risk measurement and categorization. A key benefit of transparency is that releasing
valuable capitalization and counterparty exposure information can allow
market participants to price more accurately risk in contracts with each

other and to employ suitable risk controls. The primary objection to the public disclosure of systemically important institutions is that it implicitly confers too-big-to-fail or too-interconnected-to-fail guarantees on such institutions. However, the problem of implicit guarantees is best resolved by the creation of a resolution authority and a process that limits the fallout from failure. Unfortunately, however, forces against transparency gather momentum when a credit resolution mechanism or recapitalization plan is not in place. To wit, absent the ability to deal with potentially insolvent firms once they have been detected to be so, regulators would shy away from releasing this information and instead let such institutions fester and potentially risk the rest of the financial system to their even greater problems down the road. However, all the evidence (see Appendix B) suggests that the information released by the SCAP exercise of 2009 on relative strengths and weaknesses of banks in the United States was perceived as welcome news in the marketplace, since it was followed by a credible plan to get them to recapitalize—privately or through government capital injection, dilution of existing shareholders, and firing of existing management. Furthermore, continuously varying market-based measures of systemic risk such as MES are easily computable by market participants, and they obviate opacity.

Another key benefit of a requirement that regulators produce systemic risk reports that are based on information aggregated across institutions and markets and make them transparent, is that they help address another risk *within* an institution—the so-called operational risk—which can also lead to systemic risk concerns if it brings down a sufficiently large and systemically important firm. Operational risk is typically attributed to deficiencies in corporate processes (a company's risk management systems); in its people (due to incompetence, fraud, or unauthorized behavior); and in its technology (its information systems, quality of its data, its mathematical modeling, etc.). Risk management systems benefit considerably from information transparency (intra- as well as intercompany), while satisfying all corporate, regulatory, and privacy constraints. Within a company, there have to be rules for daily aggregation of positions that are reported to the higher levels in the company—preferably in conjunction with matching aggregate information received from the more important counterparties in order to reduce probabilities of errors and fraud. At the corporate level, the net positions of the separate divisions of the company have to be compiled and analyzed (including dependencies and risk correlation analyses). It is thus beneficial if a top-down structure from risk reports required by the systemic risk regulator is in place, whereby minimum standards are imposed on individual firms to gather and aggregate such information on their own exposures. At regular time intervals, the aggregate information would be shared with the regulator and other counterparties.

4.4 NYU STERN SYSTEMIC RISK RANKINGS

A daily updated systemic risk ranking of U.S. financial institutions is provided at the New York University Stern School of Business Vlab at http://vlab .stern.nyu.edu/welcome/risk. More details about the economic and statistical methodology underlying these rankings are available in Acharya, Pedersen, Philippon, and Richardson (2010a) and Brownlees and Engle (2010), which are available as links on this site.

At the core of these rankings is the analysis of Marginal Expected Shortfall (MES). MES is a prediction of how much the stock of a particular financial company will decline in a day if the whole market declines by (say) at least 2 percent. The measure incorporates the volatility of the firm and its correlation with the market, as well as its performance in extremes. MES can used to determine the capital shortfall that a firm would face in a crisis.

When the capital of the aggregate financial sector falls below prudential levels, systemic risk emerges because the sector has too little capital to cover its liabilities. This leads to the widespread failure of financial institutions and/or the freezing of capital markets, which greatly impairs financial intermediation.

For each financial institution, NYU Stern's Vlab produces a Systemic Risk Contribution, SRISK%, which equals the percentage contribution of each firm to the aggregate capital shortfall in the event of a crisis. Firms with a high percentage of capital shortfall in a crisis not only are the biggest losers in a crisis, but also are the firms that create or extend the crisis. Hence, SRISK% is an economically appealing measure of systemic risk of a financial firm.

This section is broken down into two subsections. The first presents a brief summary of the underlying statistical methodology used to estimate the systemic risk rankings (using SRISK% and MES). The second applies this methodology (in real time) to four events of particular interest related to the financial crisis of 2007 to 2009: (1) just prior to the crisis starting in late July 2007, (2) just prior to Bear Stearns's effective failure on March 14, 2008, (3) just prior to Lehman Brothers' bankruptcy on September 15, 2008, and (4) around the government's SCAP stress tests of the financial system in the spring of 2009.

Systemic Risk Methodology

To understand better how this risk ranking works, it is helpful to present in more detail the analysis behind the rankings and then to look at how these rankings performed before and during the crisis. The first step is the calculation of MES, and the next step is the calculation of SRISK%.

The econometric techniques used to calculate Marginal Expected Shortfall (MES) are detailed in the paper by Brownlees and Engle (2010). The essential idea is that the dynamic bivariate relationship between the equity of an individual financial company and a broad index reflects the market view of the systemic risk in the financial company. The MES is defined as the expected loss by equity holders on a day when the broad market falls by at least 2 percent. This can be written in a formula for firm i on day t, as:

$$MES_{i,t} = E_{t-1}\left(-R_{i,t} \mid R_{m,t} < -.02\right) \qquad (4.1)$$

This will be a number that is generally somewhat bigger than 2 percent, particularly for firms that are very sensitive to the aggregate market. The value of MES is calculated using time-series methods. The volatilities are estimated with asymmetric GARCH (generalized autoregressive conditional heteroskedasticity) models and the correlations are estimated with asymmetric DCC (dynamic conditional correlation) models. The contribution from the tails is estimated with a kernel smoother of the empirical bivariate density function of the residuals. The MES is the product of the volatility of the firm times its correlation with the market times the expected shortfall (ES) of the market plus a second term that depends on the tails.

$$MES_{i,t} = \sigma_{i,t}\rho_{i,m,t} E_{t-1}\left(-R_{m,t} \mid R_{m,t} < -.02\right) + tail\ correction \qquad (4.2)$$

These methods are described in the Brownlees and Engle paper. This is the first step in estimating the expected loss to equity holders in a financial crisis.

On the Vlab web site, this number is calculated for the largest 100 financial firms every day in the sample starting in 1990 or whenever the equity started trading, and goes to the present. For each day of at least a 2 percent decline in market values, we can compare the actual losses of these firms with the predicted losses. We can rank the firms from the smallest predicted loss to the greatest. Do the actual losses of these firms have the same rank order as predicted?

By computing the rank correlations, we find that the average rank correlation over all of the 2 percent down days is 0.38. During the financial crisis it was 0.44. On only a few days are these correlations not significantly different from zero. The firms that are expected to lose the most in a market downturn generally do so, although the ranking is not exact.

Next we translate this daily loss in a crisis into the total loss of equity value of a firm in a longer-duration (for example, a half-year-long) crisis by multiplying by a constant. The use of a constant multiplier is only an approximate solution to the multistep forecasting problem, but it is reasonable and simple and has a minimal effect on cross-sectional ranking.

The objective is to estimate the equity loss over six months if the market's cumulative return is worse, for example, than a 40 percent decline. Since returns are measured as log returns, they should be exponentiated before taking expectations, at least for long-horizon returns. For one-day calculations, the differences are quite slight (to the third decimal).

$$E_{t-1}\left(-\sum_{j=1}^{126} \exp\left(R_{i,t+j} \right) - 1 \left| \sum_{j=1}^{126} R_{m,t+j} < -.4 \right. \right) \approx \theta MES_{i,t} \qquad (4.3)$$

This entity can be described as the CrisisMES, and similarly, if it is estimated for the market itself, it can be called the Marginal Expected Shortfall in a crisis, CrisisES. It can be estimated by simulating the bivariate stochastic process for six months many times. Some of these simulated outcomes correspond to market returns that are worse than 40 percent. These outcomes are naturally ones with high volatilities and correlations. The average returns in these outcomes define the CrisisMES and CrisisES.

Using a set of typical parameters, which are estimates for Citibank over the sample period 1977 to 2009, the daily ES was 2.4 percent and the daily MES was 3.7 percent. From 10,000 simulations, the CrisisES was 38 percent and the CrisisMES was 53 percent. The ratio of the CrisisMES to daily MES is 14.3, which we approximate as $\theta = 18$ for the calculations. The exact number would be different for different parameters and starting conditions. Future research will investigate this relationship fully.

Finally, the contribution to systemic risk is measured by the capital shortage the firm would experience in a crisis. As firm equity values fall, debt equity ratios skyrocket, pushing firms toward insolvency. When a firm has insufficient capital, it may default on its obligations or otherwise fail to honor obligations. The extent of the capital shortage is the extent of the contribution to systemic risk. In doing this calculation, we use current market capitalization and the most recent Compustat data on quasi-leverage, defined to be the ratio of book debt to market value of equity. If equity falls sufficiently so that it is less than 8 percent of the value of the firm, then it is considered capital-constrained, and the capital shortfall is computed.

Letting D be the total book value of debt and E be the current market value of equity, surplus capital is given by:

$$SurplusCapital = E - .08(D + E) \qquad (4.4)$$

From the earlier calculation in equation (4.3), we have the distribution of E in a crisis, and the expected quantity of surplus capital is simply the expectation of equation (4.4). Assuming that the debt is relatively constant in value, the main random variable is the value of equity. When this surplus is negative, the firm is in distress and the size of the distress is the capital shortfall expected in a crisis. Thus,

$$Distress_{i,t} = \min [0, .92(1 - CrisisMES) - .08D] \qquad (4.5)$$

The sum of the capital shortfall for the whole financial sector is the aggregate capital shortfall. Each deficient firm is given a systemic risk contribution, which is its percentage of the aggregate capital shortfall. We call this SRISK%. It is this number that reflects the systemic contribution of each firm, and this is the variable that is used to form the NYU Stern systemic risk rankings.

On an ongoing basis, NYU Stern's Vlab provides MES and SRISK% for the largest 100 financial institutions in the United States. These results are being extended to financial institutions worldwide. The eventual goal is to create systemic risk measures for financial institutions not just in terms of their domestic market, but also their effect on global markets.

Systemic Risk Analysis of the Financial Crisis of 2007 to 2009

Here, we report and analyze MES and SRISK% for dates representing four important periods during the financial crisis:

1. July 1, 2007: While there is no official date to the financial crisis, some analysts point to the collapse of two highly leveraged Bear Stearns hedge funds on June 22, 2007. But a more reasonable time frame is when the markets suffered their first systemwide shock. The first event occurred at the end of July 2007 when the market for asset-backed security issuance froze.
2. March 1, 2008: The collapse of Bear Stearns on March 14, 2008, and then subsequent sale to JPMorgan on March 17 (with the government

backing Bear Stearns's mortgage-related assets) is considered the first of many failures of large, complex financial institutions during the crisis.

3. September 12, 2008: While there were numerous failures both before (e.g., Bear Stearns, IndyMac, Fannie Mae, and Freddie Mac), concurrently (e.g., Merrill Lynch and AIG), and after (e.g., Wachovia, Washington Mutual, and, some would argue, Citigroup), the major event of the crisis was Lehman Brothers' filing for bankruptcy on September 15, 2008.

4. March 31, 2009: The SCAP (i.e., unified stress tests of the large banks in the United States) was initiated in February 2009 and concluded in May 2009. The results of the tests showed which banks would be expected to suffer a shortfall in a market stress scenario.

The results are summarized in Table 4.1. Specifically, the table provides the MES and SRISK% calculations for the 10 most systemic financial institutions (in terms of SRISK%) at each of the four dates. Because the list obviously changes through time, the systemic risk ranks are provided for the firms at every date as long as the firm made it in the top 10 in at least one of the four periods; hence, the list covers 17 firms though it should be noted that seven of the firms drop out as they *effectively* failed during the crisis.

We believe it is worth making several observations based on Table 4.1. The first, and most important, point is that the methodology picks out the firms that created most of the systemic risk in the financial system. The major firms that effectively failed during the crisis (i.e., either went bust, were forced into a merger, or were massively bailed out)—Bear Stearns, Fannie Mae, Freddie Mac, Lehman Brothers, AIG, Merrill Lynch, Wachovia, Bank of America Corporation (BAC), and Citigroup—all show up early as systemic during the period in question. For example, all but Bank of America, AIG, and Wachovia are in the top 10 on July 1, 2007. And by March 2008, both Bank of America and AIG have joined the top 10, with Wachovia 11th ranked.

Second, most of the systemic risk in the system is captured by just a few firms. For example, in July 2007, just five firms capture 58.2 percent of the systemic risk in the financial sector. By March 1, 2008, however, as the crisis was impacting many more firms, the systemic risk is more evenly spread, with 43 percent covered by five firms. As the crisis was just about to go pandemic with massive failures of a few institutions, the concentration creeps back up, reaching 51.1 percent in September 2008 (where we note that the SRISK% values have been scaled up to account for the capital shortfalls of failed institutions). And as bailed-out firms were merged with

TABLE 4.1 Systemic Risk Rankings during the Financial Crisis of 2007 to 2009

	July 1, 2007			March 1, 2008			September 12, 2008			March 31, 2009		
	SRISK%	Rank	MES	SRISK%	Rank	MES	SRISK%	Rank	MES	SRISK%	Rank	MES
Citigroup	14.3	#1	3.27	12.9	#1	4.00	11.6	#1	6.17	8.8	#4	12.55
Merrill Lynch	13.5	#2	4.28	7.8	#3	5.36	5.7	#5	6.86	—	—	—
Morgan Stanley	11.8	#3	3.25	6.7	#6	3.98	5.2	#7	4.87	2.8	#7	9.16
JPMorgan Chase	9.8	#4	3.44	8.5	#2	4.30	8.6	#4	5.2	12.1	#2	10.55
Goldman Sachs	8.8	#5	3.6	5.3	#9	3.14	4.2	#9	3.58	3.7	#5	6.61
Freddie Mac	8.6	#6	2.35	5.9	#7	4.60				—	—	—
Lehman Brothers	7.2	#7	3.91	5.0	#10	4.88	4.6	#8	15.07	—	—	—
Fannie Mae	6.7	#8	2.47	7.1	#4	5.88	—	—	—	—	—	—
Bear Stearns	5.9	#9	4.4	2.9	#12	4.16	—	—	—	—	—	—
MetLife	3.6	#10	2.57	2.2	#15	2.93	1.9	#12	3.20	3.2	#6	11.93
Bank of America	0	#44	2.06	6.7	#5	3.60	9.6	#2	6.33	12.7	#1	13.41
AIG	0	#45	1.51	5.5	#8	4.63	9.6	#3	10.86			
Wells Fargo	0	#48	2.38	1.9	#16	4.14	3.0	#10	5.40	10.4	#3	12.15
Wachovia	0	#51	2.2	4.6	#11	4.64	5.7	#6	9.61			
Prudential Fin.	3.3	#11	3.09	2.6	#13	3.94	2.1	#11	4.17	2.6	#8	15.89
U.S. Bancorp	0	#40	1.62	0	#54	2.41	1.1	#15	5.20	2.6	#9	10.4
PNC Financial	0	#49	2.46	0	#43	2.84	0.3	#32	3.78	1.6	#10	10.03

Table 4.1 ranks the 10 most systemically risky financial firms among the 100 largest financial institutions for four dates ranging from July 1, 2007, through March 31, 2009. The Marginal Expected Shortfall (MES) measures how much the stock of a particular financial company will decline in a day, if the whole market declines by at least 2 percent. When equity values fall below prudential levels of 8 percent of assets, the Systemic Risk Contribution, SRISK%, measures the percentage of all capital shortfall that would be experienced by this firm in the event of a crisis. Note that the SRISK% calculations here incorporate existing capital shortfalls from failed institutions.

Source: www.systemicriskranking.stern.nyu.edu.

other firms and the industry became more concentrated, by March 2009, the four largest commercial banks—Bank of America, JPMorgan Chase, Wells Fargo, and Citigroup—covered 51.8 percent of the total systemic risk.

Third, and relatedly, consider the evolution of one of the largest commercial banks, namely Bank of America, as the crisis unfolded. In July 2007, compared to JPMorgan Chase and Citigroup, which were both heavily involved in capital market activities, Bank of America was considered a more conservative institution. Our systemic risk measures confirm this, as its rank is 44th with a very small expected contribution to aggregate capital shortfall in a crisis. By March 2008, Bank of America had already announced it would purchase Countrywide Financial, the largest nonprime mortgage lender. Equity markets incorporated such news, and its systemic risk rank skyrocketed to fifth with 6.7 percent of the financial sector's systemic risk. Just before the Lehman collapse, Bank of America was now ranked second with an adjusted SRISK% of 10.9 percent. Finally, by the time of March 2009, Bank of America had also merged with Merrill Lynch, one of the more systemic investment banks. Not surprisingly, Bank of America was now ranked as the most systemic institution with an SRISK% of 14.9 percent.

As a final comment, just prior to the crisis going pandemic with Lehman Brothers filing for bankruptcy on September 15, 2008, consider our estimates of MES (i.e., expected percent equity losses) of firms in the financial sector. From Table 4.1, three firms in particular stand out, namely Lehman Brothers, AIG, and Wachovia, which all have MES values (15.07 percent, 10.86 percent, and 9.61 percent, respectively) that are much larger than those of other firms. Not shown in the table is the only other firm with an MES at that level (albeit not in the top 10 SRISK% rank), namely Washington Mutual at 11.40 percent. Of course, all four of these firms failed in a spectacular manner either the week of September 15 or shortly thereafter.

The rankings of MES and SRISK% in Table 4.1 do indeed coincide with the narrative descriptions of which firms were systemic during the financial crisis. The ability of these rankings to identify systemically risky firms in advance of their actual default is a goal of this research that appears to have been successful. The demonstration that this approach to measuring systemic risk can successfully identify firms that posed systemic risks in the past suggests the promise of this methodology to identify firms to be more carefully scrutinized by the new systemic risk regulator and potentially subjected to systemic taxes or capital charges. (See Chapter 5, "Taxing Systemic Risk," and Chapter 6, "Capital, Contingent Capital, and Liquidity Requirements.")

APPENDIX A: SYSTEMIC RISK INSTITUTIONS

The following is a list of 28 international systemically risky institutions published by the Financial Stability Board (FSB):

North American Banks
Goldman Sachs (GS.N)
JPMorgan Chase (JPM.N)
Morgan Stanley (MS.N)
Bank of America—Merrill Lynch (BAC.N)
Royal Bank of Canada (RY.TO)

UK Banks
HSBC (HSBA.L)
Barclays (BARC.L)
Royal Bank of Scotland (RBS.L)
Standard Chartered (STAN.L)

European Banks
UBS (UBSN.VX)
Credit Suisse (CSGN.VX)
Société Général (SOGN.PA)
BNP Paribas (BNPP.PA)
Santander (SAN.MC)
BBVA (BBVA.MC)
Unicredit (CRDI.MI)
Banca Intesa, Deutsche Bank (DBKGn.DE)
ING (ING.AS)

Japanese Banks
Mizuho (8411.T)
Sumitomo Mitsui (8316.T)
Nomura (8604.T)
Mitsubishi UFJ (8306.T)

Insurers

AXA (AXA.PA)

Aegon (AEGN.AS)

Allianz (ALVG.DE)

Aviva (AV.l)

Zurich (ZURN.VX)

Swiss Re (RUKN.VX)

APPENDIX B: SUPERVISORY CAPITAL ASSESSMENT PROGRAM (SCAP)

From a macroeconomic perspective, the financial sector acts as the oil in the engine that drives the economy. It does so by serving as an intermediary between investors, helping with the transfer of capital from investors to the production side of an economy. An adverse shock as witnessed during the credit crisis can easily disrupt the transfer of capital and render an economy vulnerable to recession.

The Supervisory Capital Assessment Program (SCAP) initiated in the United States in February 2009 and concluded in May 2009 was originated amidst the credit crisis, which had cast into doubt the future solvency of many large and complex financial firms. A number of firms had already received financial aid through the Troubled Asset Relief Program (TARP), but with the credit crisis deepening, a pressing issue that arose was whether the financial sector would be able to withstand a potential worsening of the crisis.

During such a severe time of distress and huge uncertainty about the future solvency of financial firms, the Federal Reserve found it necessary to conduct a stress test in order to assess the financial ability of the largest U.S. bank holding companies (BHCs) to withstand losses in an even more adverse economic environment. Such an exercise was intended to provide policymakers with information on the financial stability of the system and on the potential need for limiting a large-scale financial meltdown with adverse effects on production and employment in the overall economy.

In the following paragraphs, the companies that were the focus of the test, the stress tests, and the main variable(s) used for measuring capital reserves are briefly introduced.

The SCAP focused on the 19 largest financial companies, which combined held two-thirds of assets and more than half of loans in the U.S. banking system, and whose failures were deemed to pose a systemic risk.

The technical goal of the exercise was by means of stress tests to assess the ability of the firms to maintain ongoing businesses in the case of a more severe negative shock.

Two scenarios were to be assessed. In the first *base* scenario the economy was assumed to follow the then-current consensus path with still negative expected outcomes. The second scenario was a more *adverse* path where a deeper downturn was assumed. Both scenarios were two-year-ahead what-if exercises and considered losses across a range of products and activities (such as loans, investments, mortgages, and credit card balances). Firms with trading assets in excess of $100 billion were asked to estimate potential trading losses and counterparty credit losses.

For both the base case and the adverse case, the Federal Reserve provided the companies with a common set of loss-rate ranges across specific loan categories as guidelines for estimation purposes. For example, under the base scenario an indicative two-year cumulative loss-rate range of 1.5 percent to 2.5 percent was provided for first-lien mortgages in the prime category. The corresponding indicative loss-rate range in the adverse scenario was set to 3 percent to 4 percent. As described in the May 7, 2009, report of the Federal Reserve containing the results of the SCAP stress tests, the indicative loss rates were derived from methods of predicting losses, including historical loss experiences and quantitative models relating loan performances to macroeconomic variables.

However, firms were allowed to diverge from the indicative loss rates where they could provide evidence of the appropriateness of their estimates. More importantly, the supervisors, recognizing the differences across firms, asked the firms to provide data about particular characteristics of their portfolios in order to make more tailored quantitative assessments of losses.

The goal of the test was to measure the ability of a firm to absorb losses in terms of its Tier 1 capital, with more emphasis on Tier 1 common capital, "reflecting the fact that common equity is the first element of the capital structure to absorb losses." Firms whose capital buffers were estimated to be small relative to estimated losses under the adverse scenario would be required to increase their capital ratios. The size of the SCAP buffer was determined in accordance with the estimated losses under the worst-case scenario and the ability of a firm to have a Tier 1 risk-based ratio in excess of 6 percent at year-end 2010 and its ability to have a Tier 1 common capital risk-based ratio in excess of 4 percent at year-end 2010.

The main finding was that 10 of the 19 original banks needed to raise additional capital in order to comply with the capital requirements set forth in the SCAP. In all cases, the additional buffer that had to be raised was due to inadequate Tier 1 common capital. In total, around $75 billion had to be raised, though there were significant variations across the firms, ranging from $0.6 billion to $33.9 billion. The number is much smaller than the estimated two-year losses, which were at $600 billion or 9.1 percent on total loans. The total amount of reserves already in place was estimated to be able to absorb much of the estimated losses. Using only data up to end of 2008, the required additional buffer that had to be raised was estimated at $185 billion. However, together with the adjustments after the first quarter of 2009, the amount was reduced to $75 billion. Tables 4.2 and 4.3 are both from the report on the SCAP results. They contain the results of the SCAP stress test on aggregate and firm level, respectively.

The stress test sought to determine the ability of a firm to withstand a large negative shock. To the extent that negative shocks increase the riskiness of a firm and their default risks, spreads on credit default swaps (CDSs) would be indicative of the market's reaction to SCAP and its findings. Figures 4.1 and 4.2 depict the time-series plots of CDS spreads for a subset of the firms in the SCAP study. All data are from Datastream.

Figure 4.1 depicts the subset of firms that were later on required to raise their capital buffers. These are in the G1 group. Note that to accommodate the spreads for GMAC in the G1 group we have posted the spreads for GMAC in the right-hand side scale. Figure 4.2 plots this for G2, the subset of firms that did not need additional buffers. These plots of CDS spreads show that subsequent to the collapse of Lehman Brothers all spreads increased substantially; this is the large group of spikes early in the sample. Interestingly, there is also an increase in CDS spreads around the announcement of the stress test. There is, though, a difference between the two groups. With respect to the G1 group, the spreads continue to linger around a higher level after the initiation of the test, whereas we observe a declining pattern for the G2 group subsequent to the announcement.

The pattern in the CDS spreads is suggestive of the fact that the transparency of the program may have aided the market participants to distinguish between the different groups. Market participants using the provided information may have been able to deduce the relative systemic riskiness of the firms well in advance of the Fed's announcement of the results. The drop in spreads for the firms in the G1 group subsequent to the announcement of the results could be indicative of better-than-anticipated results of the SCAP.

Another approach, illustrated in Figure 4.3, to observing the market's reaction to the SCAP is to consider option implied volatilities. The implied volatilities are those of the one-year at-the-money (ATM) forward call and put options obtained from Option Metrics standardized files. The presented volatilities are cross-sectional averages with each group (G1 and G2)

TABLE 4.2 Supervisory Capital Assessment Program, Aggregate Results for 19 Participating Bank Holding Companies for the More Adverse Scenario

Estimated for 2009 and 2010 for the More Adverse Scenario	More Adverse Scenario	
	$ Billions	As % of Loans
Total Estimated Losses (Before purchase accounting adjustments)	599.2	
First Lien Mortgages	102.3	8.8%
Second/Junior Lien Mortgages	83.2	13.8%
Commercial and Industrial Loans	60.1	6.1%
Commercial Real Estate Loans	53.0	8.5%
Credit Card Loans	82.4	22.5%
Securities (AFS and HTM)	35.2	NA
Trading & Counterparty	99.3	NA
Other (1)	83.7	NA
Memo: Purchase Accounting Adjustments	64.3	
Resources Other Than Capital to Absorb Losses in the More Adverse Scenario (2)	362.9	
SCAP Buffer Added for More Adverse Scenario		
(SCAP buffer is defined as additional Tier 1 common/contingent common)		
Indicated SCAP Buffer as of December 31, 2008	185.0	
Less: Capital Actions and Effects of Q1 2009 Results (3) (4)	110.4	
SCAP Buffer (5)	74.6	

Note: The estimates in this table represent a hypothetical "what-if" scenario that involves an economic outcome that is more adverse than expected. These estimates are not forecasts of expected losses or revenues.

(1) Includes other consumer and non-consumer loans and miscellaneous commitments and obligations.
(2) Resources to absorb losses include pre-provision net revenue less the change in the allowance for loan and lease losses.
(3) Capital actions include completed or contracted transactions since Q4 2008.
(4) Total includes only capital actions and effects of Q1 2009 results for firms that need to establish a SCAP buffer.
(5) There may be a need to establish an additional Tier 1 capital buffer, but this would be satisfied by the additional Tier 1 common capital buffer unless otherwise specified for a particular BHC.

Note: Numbers may not sum due to rounding.
Source: "The Supervisory Capital Assessment Program" (Hirtle, Schuermann, and Stiroh 2009).

TABLE 4.3 Supervisory Capital Assessment Program, Estimates for 19 Participating Bank Holding Companies ($ Billions)

	AmEx	BofA	BB&T	BNYM	CapOne	Citi	FifthThird	GMAC
Tier 1 Capital	10.1	173.2	13.4	15.4	16.8	118.8	11.9	17.4
Tier 1 Common Capital	10.1	74.5	7.8	11.0	12.0	22.9	4.9	11.1
Risk-Weighted Assets	104.4	1,633.8	109.8	115.8	131.8	996.2	112.6	172.7
Estimated for 2009 and 2010 for the More Adverse Scenario								
Total Loss estimates (Before purchase accounting adjustments)	11.2	136.6	8.7	5.4	13.4	104.7	9.1	9.2
First Lien Mortgages	NA	22.1	1.1	0.2	1.8	15.3	1.1	2.0
Second/Junior Lien Mortgages	NA	21.4	0.7	NA	0.7	12.2	1.1	1.1
Commercial & Industrial Loans	NA	15.7	0.7	0.4	1.5	8.9	2.8	1.0
Commercial Real Estate Loans	NA	9.4	4.5	0.2	1.1	2.7	2.9	0.6
Credit Card Loans	8.5	19.1	0.2	NA	3.6	19.9	0.4	NA
Securities (AFS and HTM)	NA	8.5	0.2	4.2	0.4	2.9	0.0	0.5
Trading & Counterparty	NA	24.1	NA	NA	NA	22.4	NA	NA
Other (1)	2.7	16.4	1.3	0.4	4.3	20.4	0.9	4.0
Total Loss Rate on Loans (2)	14.3%	10.0%	8.6%	2.6%	11.7%	10.9%	10.5%	6.6%
First Lien Morgages	NA	6.8%	4.5%	5.0%	10.7%	8.0%	10.3%	10.2%
Second/Junior Lien Mortgages	NA	13.5%	8.8%	NA	19.9%	19.5%	8.7%	21.2%
Commercial & Industrial Loans	NA	7.0%	4.5%	5.0%	9.7%	5.8%	11.0%	2.7%
Commercial Real Estate Loans	NA	9.1%	12.6%	9.9%	6.0%	7.4%	13.9%	33.3%
Credit Card Loans	20.2%	23.5%	18.2%	NA	18.2%	23.0%	22.3%	NA
Memo: Purchase Accounting Adjustments	0.0	13.3	0.0	0.0	1.5	0.0	0.0	0.0
Resources Other Than Capital to Absorb Losses in the More Adverse Scenario (3)	11.9	74.5	5.5	6.7	9.0	49.0	5.5	−0.5
SCAP Buffer Added for More Adverse Scenario								
(SCAP Buffer is defined as additional Tier 1 Common/contingent Common)								
Indicated SCAP buffer as of December 31, 2008	0.0	46.5	0.0	0.0	0.0	92.6	2.6	6.7
Less: Capital Actions and Effects of Q1 2009 Results (4) (5) (6) (7)	0.2	12.7	0.1	−0.2	−0.3	87.1	1.5	−4.8
SCAP Buffer (8) (9) (10)	0.0	33.9	0.0	0.0	0.0	5.5	1.1	11.5
MES at end of September 2008	6.6	7.6	5.0	7.0	6.9	6.9	8.3	NA

(1) Includes other consumer and non-consumer loans and miscellaneous commitments and obligations.

(2) Includes losses on other consumer and non-consumer loans.

(3) Resources to absorb losses include pre-provision net revenue less the change in the allowance for loan and lease losses.

(4) Capital actions include completed or contracted transactions since Q4 2008.

(5) For BofA, includes capital benefit from risk-weighted asset impact of eligible asset guarantee.

(6) For Citi, includes impact of preferred exchange offers announced on February 27, 2009.

(7) Total includes only capital actions and effects of Q1 2009 results for firms that need to establish a SCAP buffer.

(8) There may be a need to establish an additional Tier 1 capital buffer, but this would be satisfied by the additional Tier 1 Common capital buffer unless otherwise specified for a particular BHC.

(9) GMAC needs to augment the capital buffer with $11.5 billion of Tier 1 Common/contingent Common of which $9.1 billion must be new Tier 1 capital.

(10) Regions needs to augment the capital buffer with $2.5 billion of Tier 1 Common/contingent Common of which $400 million must be new Tier 1 capital.

Goldman	JPMC	KeyCorp	MetLife	Morgan Stanley	PNC	Regions	State St	SunTrust	USB	Wells	Total
55.9	136.2	11.6	30.1	47.2	24.1	12.1	14.1	17.6	24.4	86.4	836.7
34.4	87.0	6.0	27.8	17.8	11.7	7.6	10.8	9.4	11.8	33.9	412.5
444.8	1,337.5	106.7	326.4	310.6	250.9	116.3	69.6	162.0	230.6	1,082.3	7,814.8
17.8	97.4	6.7	9.6	19.7	18.8	9.2	8.2	11.8	15.7	86.1	599.2
NA	18.8	0.1	0.0	NA	2.4	1.0	NA	2.2	1.8	32.4	102.3
NA	20.1	0.6	0.0	NA	4.6	1.1	NA	3.1	1.7	14.7	83.2
0.0	10.3	1.7	0.0	0.1	3.2	1.2	0.0	1.5	2.3	9.0	60.1
NA	3.7	2.3	0.8	0.6	4.5	4.9	0.3	2.8	3.2	8.4	53.0
NA	21.2	0.0	NA	NA	0.4	NA	NA	0.1	2.8	6.1	82.4
0.1	1.2	0.1	8.3	NA	1.3	0.2	1.8	0.0	1.3	4.2	35.2
17.4	16.7	NA	NA	18.7	NA	NA	NA	NA	NA	NA	99.3
0.3	5.3	1.8	0.5	0.2	2.3	0.8	6.0	2.1	2.8	11.3	83.7
0.9%	10.0%	8.5%	2.1%	0.4%	9.0%	9.1%	4.4%	8.3%	7.8%	8.8%	9.1%
NA	10.2%	3.4%	5.0%	NA	8.1%	4.1%	NA	8.2%	5.7%	11.9%	8.8%
NA	13.9%	6.3%	14.1%	NA	12.7%	11.9%	NA	13.7%	8.8%	13.2%	13.8%
1.2%	6.8%	7.9%	0.0%	2.4%	6.0%	7.0%	22.8%	5.2%	5.4%	4.8%	6.1%
NA	5.5%	12.5%	2.1%	45.2%	11.2%	13.7%	35.5%	10.6%	10.2%	5.9%	8.5%
NA	22.4%	37.9%	NA	NA	22.3%	NA	NA	17.4%	20.3%	26.0%	22.5%
0.0	19.9	0.0	0.0	0.0	5.9	0.0	0.0	0.0	0.0	23.7	64.3
18.5	72.4	2.1	5.6	7.1	9.6	3.3	4.3	4.7	13.7	60.0	362.9
0.0	0.0	2.5	0.0	8.3	2.3	2.9	0.0	3.4	0.0	17.3	185.0
7.0	2.5	0.6	0.6	6.5	1.7	0.4	0.2	1.3	0.3	3.6	110.4
0.0	0.0	1.8	0.0	1.8	0.6	2.5	0.0	2.2	0.0	13.7	74.6
6.5	6.7	7.0	5.2	7.4	4.2	8.7	6.2	5.3	4.3	6.2	NA

Note: Numbers may not sum due to rounding.
Sources: The row containing information on MES is provided by the authors. All other information is obtained from "The Supervisory Capital Assessment Program" (Hirtle, Schuermann, and Stiroh 2009).

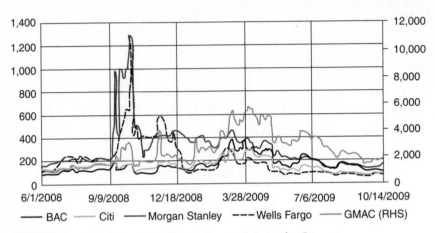

FIGURE 4.1   Five-Year Maturity Senior CDS Spreads, G1

for both calls and puts. Although the implied volatilities exhibit an increasing pattern well before the initiation of the SCAP, it is apparent that they peak around the time of the announcement and subsequently start on a declining pattern.

It is apparent that removing uncertainty about the near-future prospects of the firms was the main purpose of the SCAP exercise. The exercise estimated the potential additional buffer that needed to be raised to cover a

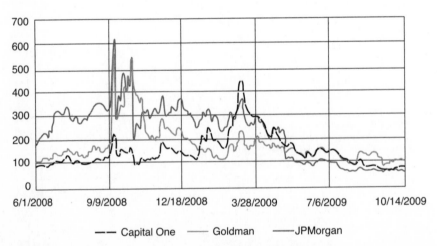

FIGURE 4.2   Five-Year Maturity Senior CDS Spreads, G2

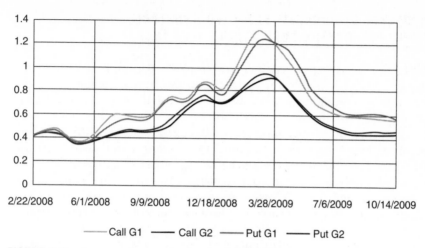

FIGURE 4.3   Average Groupwise Implied Volatilities

negative shock in the near future, and, by making the details and results of the test public, the Federal Reserve resolved or helped reduce, in a timely and quick fashion, a lot of uncertainty in an already volatile market. A great advantage of the stress test was its focus on scenario testing and the ability of firms to operate in an economy with a larger-than-expected downturn. Although issues can be raised about the underlying assumptions in the scenarios and the shortage of an adequate number of scenarios, the mere fact that large negative outcomes and the operational capabilities of firms were considered certainly seems to have provided much needed reassurance to the market participants.

Going forward, it is vital to learn from the lessons of the stress test and implement on an ongoing basis such scenario testing with the collaboration of firms and a supervisory entity. Discussing this in a speech on March 26, 2010, member of the Board of Governors Daniel K. Tarullo mentioned the Federal Reserve's plans to implement a supervisory system. The purpose of such a regular supervisory system is to monitor the health of firms and confirm the compliance of firms with the capital requirement regulations. It is the hope that such a system will gauge the riskiness of the firms' portfolios and provide the guidelines for adequate capital buffers that need to be in place in order to weather tough times. The proposed supervisory system will use both market and firm-specific data in making assessments. Once again, transparency can be an important side benefit by providing relevant information on systemic risk not just to the supervising institution but also to the market participants to impose timely market discipline.

APPENDIX C: MARGINAL EXPECTED SHORTFALL (MES) AND SUPERVISORY STRESS TEST (SCAP)

SCAP, the stress test exercise undertaken by the Federal Reserve System in spring 2009 and described in Appendix B, sought to determine the ability of a firm to withstand a large economy-wide negative shock. In order to do so it had to determine the loss to a firm in the event of such a shock.

Consider an estimate of Marginal Expected Shortfall (MES) of a firm, a market-based measure that, during a past period, on the worst days of the market, estimates the average percentage losses (negative stock return) of a firm. This is a simple nonparametric estimate of MES described in Sections 4.3 and 4.4. MES is an attempt to answer the question of how much systemic risk a firm has by asking what would happen to the firm in an environment of a large negative shock to the economy or the financial sector.

Thus, there is a distinct similarity between stress tests and MES, albeit with some differences also. The stress tests are forward-looking by nature. They test the what-if hypotheses of scenarios that may or may not unfold in the future. In contrast, by focusing on past stock market data, the MES estimate described earlier is constrained by projections based on history. If severely stressed outcomes are not present in the data, MES may paint an inaccurate picture of the firm's systemic risk compared to a stress test, which focuses on scenarios specified by the supervisors. On the flip side, MES can serve to keep the supervisory discretion in check and ensure oversight of the systemic risk of some firms as well as provide a benchmark for comparative purposes.

Hence, the results for the financial firms in the SCAP exercise of spring 2009 can in fact be used to measure the usefulness of MES.

Table 4.3 contains results of the 19 banks that were part of the SCAP stress test and their capital buffers and additional requirements. The last but one row (SCAP Buffer) refers to the capital shortfall or additional Tier 1 common capital that the banks needed to raise. The first two rows (Tier 1 Capital and Tier 1 Common Capital, respectively) refer to the Tier 1 and Tier 1 common capital that the banks already had in place. The last row of the table shows our calculation of MES for these firms computed during October 2007 to September 2008. Note that MES is not reported for GMAC, as it did not have publicly traded equity over this period.

Figure 4.4 shows the lineup of MES against the capital shortfall of the firms (SCAP Buffer) relative to their Tier 1 common capital. The presence of a strong positive relationship between MES and the findings of the SCAP stress tests emerges. In particular, there is a clear separation in level of MES between the firms that end up with a shortfall and those that do not.

This provides an important testimony to the information content of market-based systemic risk measures. In particular, in the cross-section of

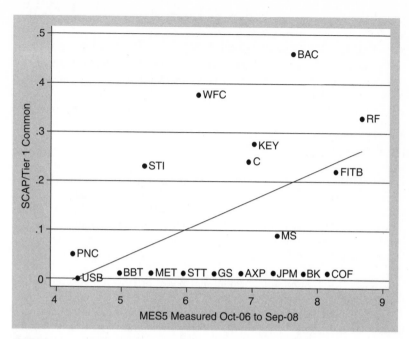

FIGURE 4.4   MES versus SCAP/Tier 1 Common Capital
Scatterplot of the marginal expected shortfall (MES) measure against
SCAP/Tier 1 Common. MES5 is the marginal expected shortfall of a stock given
that the *market return* is below its fifth percentile. The sample consists of 18 U.S.
financial firms included in the Federal Reserve's stress tests in the spring of 2009.
SCAP is the announced capital shortfall of each firm and Tier 1 Common is its
tangible common equity. MES5 was measured for each individual company
stock using the period October 2007 to September 2008.

financial firms, even the simplest nonparametric estimate of MES contained
the ability to explain their systemic risk using historical data, as was as-
certained through more exhaustive and laborious regulatory stress tests of
these firms.

NOTES

1. HR 4173, Title I, "Financial Stability," Subtitle A, "Financial Stability Oversight
   Council," Sec. 112, "Council Authority."
2. HR 4173, Title I, "Financial Stability," Subtitle A, "Financial Stability Oversight
   Council," Sec. 113, "Authority to require supervision and regulation of certain
   nonbank financial companies."

3. HR 4173, Title VIII, "Payment, Clearing, and Settlement Supervision," Sec. 802, "Findings and Purposes."
4. HR 4173, Title I, "Financial Stability," Subtitle A, "Financial Stability Oversight Council," Sec. 115, "Enhanced supervision and prudential standards for nonbank financial companies supervised by the Board of Governors and certain bank holding companies."
5. HR 4173, Title I, Subtitle A, Sec. 113, "Authority to require supervision and regulation of certain nonbank financial companies."
6. HR 4173, Title I, Subtitle A, Sec. 115.
7. HR 4173, Title I, Subtitle B, "Office of Financial Research," Sec. 153, "Purpose and Duties of the Office."
8. HR 4173, Title I, Subtitle B, "Office of Financial Research," Sec. 154, "Organizational structure; responsibilities of primary programmatic units."
9. HR 4173, Title I, Subtitle B, "Office of Financial Research," Sec. 154, " Organizational structure; responsibilities of primary programmatic units."
10. See the Federal Reserve Bank of New York report on the SCAP exercise (Hirtle, Schuermann, and Stiroh 2009).
11. Ibid.
12. HR 4173, Title I, Subtitle C, "Additional Board of Governors Authority for Certain Nonbank Financial Companies and Bank Holding Companies," Sec. 165, "Enhanced supervision and prudential standards for nonbank financial companies supervised by the Board of Governors and certain bank holding companies."

REFERENCES

Acharya, Viral V., Lasse H. Pedersen, Thomas Philippon, and Matthew Richardson. 2010a. Measuring systemic risk. Working paper, New York University Stern School of Business.

Acharya, Viral V., Lasse H. Pedersen, Thomas Philippon, and Matthew Richardson. 2010b. A tax on systemic risk. Forthcoming NBER publication on Quantifying Systemic Risk, ed. Joseph Haubrich and Andrew Lo.

Acharya, Viral V., and Matthew Richardson, eds. 2009. *Restoring financial stability: How to repair a failed system.* Hoboken, NJ: John Wiley & Sons.

Adrian, Tobias, and Markus Brunnermeier. 2008. CoVaR. Working paper, Federal Reserve Bank of New York.

Brownlees, Christian, and Robert Engle. 2010. Volatility, correlation and tails for systemic risk measurement. Working paper, New York University Stern School of Business.

Chan-Lau, Jorge, Marco Espinosa, Kay Giesecke, and Juan A. Sole. 2009. Assessing the systemic implications of financial linkages. *IMF Global Financial Stability Report* 2, April.

De Jonghe, Olivier. 2009. Back to the basics in banking? A micro-analysis of banking system stability. Forthcoming in the *Journal of Financial Intermediation.*

Gray, Dale, and Andreas A. Jobst. 2009. Tail dependence measures of systemic risk using equity options data implications for financial stability. Working paper, International Monetary Fund, Washington, D.C.

Hirtle, Beverly, Til Schuermann, and Kevin Stiroh. 2009. The Supervisory Capital Assessment Program. Federal Reserve Bank of New York. Available at http://newyorkfed.org/research/staff_reports/sr409.html.

Huang, Xin, Hao Zhou, and Haibin Zhu. 2009. A framework for assessing the systemic risk of major financial institution. *Journal of Banking and Finance* 33 (11): 2036–2049.

Lehar, A. 2005. Measuring systemic risk: A risk management approach. *Journal of Banking and Finance* 29:2577–2603.

Nier, Erland, Jing Yang, Tanju Yorulmazer, and Amadeo Alentorn. 2007. Network models and financial stability. *Journal of Economic Dynamics and Control* 31 (6): 2033–2060.

Upper, Christian. 2007. Using counterfactual simulations to assess the danger of contagion in interbank markets. Bank for International Settlements Working Paper No. 234.

CHAPTER 5

Taxing Systemic Risk

Viral V. Acharya, Lasse Pedersen, Thomas Philippon,
and Matthew Richardson*

5.1 SYSTEMIC RISK AND THE FINANCIAL CRISIS OF 2007 TO 2009

In the fall and winter of 2008 to 2009, the worldwide economy and financial markets fell off a cliff. The stock market fell 42 percent in the United States and, on a dollar-adjusted basis, the market dropped 46 percent in the United Kingdom, 49 percent in Europe at large, 35 percent in Japan, and around 50 percent in the larger Latin American countries. Likewise, global gross domestic product (GDP) fell by 0.8 percent (the first contraction in decades), with the decline in advanced economies a sharp 3.2 percent. Furthermore, international trade fell a whopping 12 percent.

When economists bandy about the term *systemic risk*, this is what they mean. Financial firms play a critical role in the economy, acting as intermediaries between parties that need to borrow and parties willing to lend or invest. Without such intermediation, it is difficult for companies to get credit and conduct business, and for people to get student loans and automobile loans, to save, and to perform a range of other financial transactions. Systemic risk emerges when the financial sector as a whole has too little capital to cover its liabilities. This leads to the widespread failure of financial institutions and/or the freezing of capital markets, which greatly impairs

*The authors are grateful to Anjolein Schmeits for helpful comments and suggestions. We benefited from discussions in the "Taxing Too-Big-to-Fail Institutions" Working Group for the NYU Stern e-book *Real Time Solutions for Financial Reform*, which also included Thomas Cooley and Ingo Walter.

financial intermediation, both in terms of the payments system and in terms of lending to corporations and households.

That some financial institutions contribute more than others to the overall capital shortfall in a crisis is a prototypical example of the negative externality of systemic risk in the financial sector. Markets do not price negative externalities, so if unchecked, they get produced in excess. As a remedy to this, economists prefer the solution of taxing the externality. Since the 1920s, this has been referred to as Pigouvian taxes, named after the British economist Arthur Cecil Pigou. Pigou argued that imposing these taxes was optimal because doing so didn't require heavy-handed government intervention into the decision making of market participants.

This chapter argues similarly for taxing the systemic risk of financial firms. The Dodd-Frank Wall Street Reform and Consumer Protection Act of 2010 unfortunately does not take this approach to financial reform, but instead prefers to focus on the ability of government to contain systemic risk through the design of capital adequacy requirements.

Some policymakers consider this to be a mistake. For example, Narayana Kocherlakota, the president of the Federal Reserve Bank of Minneapolis, in a July 2010 speech in Montreal, argued:

> *Knowing bailouts are inevitable, financial institutions fail to internalize all the risks that their investment decisions impose on society.... Taxes are a good response because they create incentives for firms to internalize the costs that would otherwise be external.... A financial firm should be taxed for the amount of risk it creates that is borne by taxpayers.... It seems to me that capital and liquidity requirements are intrinsically backwards-looking.... We need forward-looking instruments for what is intrinsically a forward-looking problem. And that's a key reason why taxes, based on market information, will work better.*

Like other regulation of financial firms, it is crucial that systemic risk taxation is not just directed at depository institutions, but is imposed equally across the financial sector. Specifically, given the interconnectedness of the modern financial sector and for the purposes of systemic regulation, one should think of "financial firms" as not just the commercial banks taking deposits and making loans, but also as investment banks, money market funds, insurance firms, and, potentially, even hedge funds and private equity funds. There are several types of systemic risk that can arise from the failure of a financial institution, and especially so during a financial crisis. These include counterparty risk, spillover risk due to forced asset sales, liquidity hoarding (inducing an interest rate contagion from weaker to safer firms), and the risk of contagious runs in the shadow banking system.

This is precisely what happened in September 2008. Some of our largest financial institutions—the government-sponsored enterprises (GSEs) (Fannie Mae and Freddie Mac), Lehman Brothers, American International Group (AIG), Merrill Lynch, Washington Mutual, Wachovia, and Citigroup—effectively failed. With the securitization market already frozen from the previous year, other key parts of the capital markets, such as short-term financing via money markets and commercial paper, also froze—with a dramatic widening of spreads in the loan and public debt markets as a result.

At the heart of the problem were the risk-taking incentives of the large, complex financial institutions (LCFIs) and the systemic risk they produce. The risk-taking activity of these institutions manifested itself in a specific way in this crisis. Firms exploited loopholes in regulatory capital requirements to take an undercapitalized $2 trillion to $3 trillion highly leveraged, one-way bet on credit portfolios, particularly tied to residential real estate but also to commercial real estate and other consumer credit. For the most part, this bet was safe, except in the case of a severe economic downturn. But market risk of this sort is the last thing these systemic institutions should be holding, because in a recession everything else held by these firms collapses, as well.

Why did these firms take those bets? They had access to cheap financing because of either implicit guarantees (e.g., too big to fail) or explicit guarantees (e.g., in case of the GSEs and deposit institutions) by the government. And because credit bets with market risk offer higher returns, these firms piled on market risk. All the benefits of the bets accrued to the shareholders of the firm, but the external cost of the firm's collapse—which led to failures of others and/or the freezing of capital markets—was ultimately borne by society.

We now know that guaranteeing the liabilities of major U.S. financial institutions seriously distorts the allocation of capital and the competition among financial intermediaries. The guarantee provides these firms with an unfair advantage, because they can raise capital at a lower cost. Because the guarantee is so valuable and pervasive, these giant intermediaries face little market discipline and have a perverse incentive to expand their scope, scale, risk exposure, leverage, and financial interconnectedness. The result is that the economy at large suffers a triple whammy: massive taxpayer-financed bailouts, a less competitive and less efficient financial system increasingly populated by firms that are deemed too big to fail, and a greater likelihood of future economic and financial crises.

The current problem with financial regulation is that the regulation seeks to limit each institution's risk in isolation. Unless the external costs of systemic risk are internalized by each financial institution, however, these institutions will have the incentive to take risks that are not borne just by the institution but instead by society as a whole. In other words, individually firms may take actions to prevent their own collapse, but not necessarily the collapse of the system. It is in this sense that the financial institution's risk is a negative externality on the system.[1]

This chapter assesses whether the Dodd-Frank Act suitably deals with this negative externality and is organized as follows. In Section 5.2, "Regulating Systemic Risk," we provide a first-best economic analysis of what the optimal policy should be in a perfect world. In Section 5.3, "The Dodd-Frank Wall Street Reform and Consumer Protection Act," we compare and contrast the Act's approach to the first-best analysis. Section 5.4, "A Tax on Systemic Risk," provides a proposal for how to implement the first-best policy. In Section 5.3, we also briefly relate our discussion of the Act to subsequent chapters on systemic risk: Chapter 6, "Capital, Contingent Capital, and Liquidity Requirements"; Chapter 7, "Large Banks and the Volcker Rule"; and Chapter 8, "Resolution Authority."

5.2 REGULATING SYSTEMIC RISK

There are three challenges to regulating systemic risk:

1. To identify and measure the systemic risk of financial firms.
2. To develop, based on systemic risk measures, an optimal policy whose main purpose is to have financial firms internalize the systemic risk costs imposed on the rest of the financial sector and external real economy.
3. To make sure that this policy is implementable, is not subject to future regulatory arbitrage, and mitigates the moral hazard problem inherent to government guarantees such as deposit insurance and being too big to fail.

To address these challenges, we first suggest an economic framework. Consider a model of a banking system in which each bank has limited liability and maximizes shareholder value. The regulator provides some form of a safety net (i.e., guarantees for some creditors such as deposit or too-big-to-fail insurance). The economy faces systemic risk (i.e., systemwide costs) in a financial crisis. We make the assumption that systemic risk emerges when the banking sector's equity capitalization falls below some fraction of its total assets, and that the costs of systemic risk are proportional to the magnitude of this shortfall.

Under these conditions, it is possible to show that the optimal policy would be for the regulator to tax (i.e., charge a premium to) each individual bank. This systemic risk tax would be an amount equal to the sum of two components:[2]

1. Expected losses of the firm upon default.
2. Expected systemic costs in a crisis × Contribution of the firm to these costs.

Let us consider these two components in turn.

1. *The firm's expected losses upon default:*
   That is, the **government guarantees in the system need to be priced,** or in other words, financial firms must pay for the guarantees they receive. Because the prices of these guarantees will vary across firms as a result of their specific risk characteristics, each firm will be induced to choose leverage and risk-taking activities more prudently. Currently, in the United States, the Federal Deposit Insurance Corporation (FDIC) chooses the level of FDIC premiums on a risk basis. However, in reality, premiums have been charged only when the fund was poorly capitalized, so the past FDIC scheme, in general, did not achieve this optimal policy (the FDIC scheme is revised under the Dodd-Frank Act, as described in Section 5.3).

2. *The firm's contribution to expected losses in the crisis (i.e., the contribution of each firm to aggregate losses above a certain threshold) multiplied by the expected systemic costs when the financial sector becomes undercapitalized:*
   Thus, the systemic risk also needs to be priced; that is, **financial institutions need to internalize the costs of the negative externality imposed on the system.** We explain later that the expected systemic costs in a crisis can be considered the *time-series* component of the tax (determining the overall level of the tax), and a firm's contribution to these systemic costs can be considered the *cross-sectional* component (determining which firms pay more of the tax). Furthermore, and consistent with economic intuition, the contribution of an individual institution to systemic costs will increase with lower initial capital, riskier asset holdings that contribute to the tail dependence between the institution and the system, institutional and aggregate volatility, and the severity of the externality.

In summary, from an economic point of view, therefore, the optimal policy to contain excessive systemic risk is to charge financial institutions for the implicit taxpayer guarantees they enjoy. They should pay what amounts to a tax, a bank levy, an insurance premium, or whatever the term, both for their expected losses in the event of failure (similar in theory, though not in practice, to the FDIC deposit insurance premium) and for expected losses when failure occurs in the context of a systemic crisis (broadly defined as the financial system as a whole becoming undercapitalized).

Charging the premium causes the financial institution on the margin to hold more initial capital up front (i.e., to be less levered) and to take less risky positions. That is, facing the tax, the financial institutions will organically choose to become less systemic. These firms will therefore be encouraged to rethink their business models. In particular, they will have to consider reducing their scope, scale, risk exposures, and interconnectedness, thus trading off the returns from such activities against the insurance premiums attached to them. Market discipline and managerial discretion would then work hand in hand with the correct pricing of systemic risk to create a more stable and efficient financial architecture. To the extent systemic risk still remains, it will be taxed and the costs borne by the shareholders of the financial institution, as opposed to taxpayers.

However, there are several difficulties with implementing this policy.

Obstacle 1: Measuring Systemic Risk

Can regulators ever perfectly measure bank risk, leverage, or interconnectedness, especially when the institutions under scrutiny are complex and perform almost all possible financial intermediation activities? Simply stated, if regulation is based on noisy observables, these institutions have an incentive to undertake "regulatory arbitrage" and load up risks on the dimension where regulation is most imprecise.

All is not lost, however. With respect to systemic risk, Chapter 4, "Measuring Systemic Risk," describes the various ways to identify and measure systemic risk. In that chapter, we provide a simple and intuitive way to measure the systemic risk contribution of each financial institution. Motivated by the economic theory just discussed, we argue that systemic risk costs can be measured as the *expected systemic costs* when the financial sector becomes undercapitalized (the time-series component) times *the financial institution's percentage contribution to the sector's undercapitalization* (the cross-sectional component). That is, on a relative basis, the systemic risk of a financial firm is the fraction of expected losses made by the financial firm in the systemic event that financial sector losses fall below a critical threshold.

The first term—*expected systemic costs*—measures the level of the systemic risk. There is empirical evidence on what leads to financial crises and the costs to economies of such crises beyond the impact of a normal economic downturn. In particular, there is growing evidence on what leads to financial crises and the large bailout costs and real economy welfare losses associated with banking crises (see, for example, Caprio and Klingebiel 1996; Honohan and Klingebiel 2000; Hoggarth, Reis, and Saporta 2002; Reinhart and Rogoff 2008; and Borio and Drehmann 2009). The bottom line from these studies is that there are leading indicators for banking crises, and these crises represent significant portions of GDP—in the order of 10 percent to 20 percent, on average, and much higher in the worst crises. The important conclusion is that, depending on the likelihood of a crisis, the systemic risk component of the tax may be quite important.

The second term—*percentage contribution of the institution to costs incurred in a financial sector collapse*—determines which institutions contribute to this risk. Empirical work suggests that this is related to the firm's contribution to sectorwide equity losses when the sector fails and to the firm's leverage. Acharya, Pedersen, Philippon, and Richardson (2010a) and Brownlees and Engle (2010) provide a methodology for estimating this contribution using publicly available equity (or, in principle, even bond market or credit default swap) data, information about leverage, and assumptions about what triggers a financial sector collapse.[3]

Using output from this methodology, Table 5.1 provides risk measures for the most systemic financial firms taken from the 100 largest financial firms in terms of equity market capitalization.

For illustrative purposes, we consider two dates—July 1, 2007, a month before the financial crisis started at the end of July 2007, and September 12, 2008, the weekend before the bankruptcy of Lehman Brothers (but after the collapse of Fannie Mae and Freddie Mac). We provide two measures, Marginal Expected Shortfall (MES), which represents the expected percentage daily loss of the firm's equity given at least a 2 percent fall in the aggregate market, and the Systemic Risk Contribution, SRISK%, which is the percentage contribution of the firm's losses to the aggregate capital shortfall in the event of a crisis. The rankings are based on SRISK%.

Several observations are in order:

- On both July 1, 2007, and September 12, 2008, the methodology picks out the firms that not only ended up failing but also that created much of the systemic risk in the financial system. For example, on July 1, 2007, Citigroup, Merrill Lynch, Freddie Mac, Lehman Brothers, Fannie Mae, and Bear Stearns all make the top 10. And by the weekend before Lehman's collapse, Bank of America, AIG, and Wachovia also join the top 10. This list covers all the major firms that either failed or received massive bailouts from the government.
- Most of the systemic risk in the system is captured by just a few firms. For example, in July 2007, 90.2 percent of the systemic risk (of publicly traded firms) is covered by just 10 firms, and 58.2 percent by just five

TABLE 5.1 Top 10 Systemically Risky Firms in July 2007 and September 2008

Firm (7/1/07)	SRISK%	MES	Firm (9/12/08)	SRISK%	MES
Citigroup	14.3	3.27	Citigroup	13.1	6.17
Merrill Lynch	13.5	4.28	Bank of America	10.9	6.33
Morgan Stanley	11.8	3.25	AIG	10.9	10.86
JPMorgan Chase	9.8	3.44	JPMorgan Chase	9.7	5.20
Goldman Sachs	8.8	3.60	Merrill Lynch	6.5	6.86
Freddie Mac	8.6	2.35	Wachovia	6.5	9.61
Lehman Brothers	7.2	3.91	Morgan Stanley	5.9	4.87
Fannie Mae	6.7	2.47	Lehman Brothers	5.2	15.07
Bear Stearns	5.9	4.40	Goldman Sachs	4.8	3.58
MetLife	3.6	2.57	Wells Fargo	3.4	5.40

Table 5.1 provides an overview of the 10 most systemically risky financial firms among the 100 largest financial institutions for July 1, 2007, and September 12, 2008. The Marginal Expected Shortfall (MES) measures how much the stock of a particular financial company will decline in a day, if the whole market declines by at least 2 percent. The measure incorporates the volatility of the firm and its correlation with the market, as well as its performance in extremes. The MES measure is used to determine the capital shortfall that a firm would face in a crisis. When equity values fall below prudential levels of 8 percent of assets, the Systemic Risk Contribution, SRISK%, measures the percentage of all capital shortfall that would be experienced by this firm in the event of a crisis. (See Chapter 4, "Measuring Systemic Risk.") *Source:* www.systemicriskranking.stern.nyu.edu.

firms. By September 12, 2008, as the crisis was in full swing and therefore affecting many firms, the risk is a little more evenly distributed, with 76.8 percent covered by 10 firms, and 51.1 percent by five firms.
- Of some note, the MES increased dramatically from the start of the crisis to September 2008, especially for Lehman Brothers, AIG, and Wachovia, which have MES values many times higher than other firms. Of course, all three firms failed spectacularly shortly thereafter in the fall of 2008.

Obstacle 2: Implementing the Tax on Systemic Risk

Given this measurement of systemic risk, what are the issues with implementation of a tax on financial institutions based on the extent to which they likely contribute to systemic risk?

In terms of charging for the expected loss of the financial firm's guaranteed liabilities (i.e., the *institution-risk* component), this is akin to the FDIC premium. But without a credible resolution authority for all other liabilities, it is not clear that the guarantees extend only to deposits. For example, other systemically risky short-term liabilities, such as uninsured deposits, foreign deposits, interbank loans, and repurchase agreements, may have implicit guarantees. If so, then these guarantees should also be priced to reduce moral hazard, or alternatively, a credible resolution authority must be set up to deal with these liabilities in default. Chapter 8 analyzes the issue of creating such a resolution authority.

In terms of charging for the *systemic risk* component (i.e., the expected systemic costs in a crisis times the financial institution's percentage contribution to the undercapitalization of the financial sector), we consider two implementable schemes to value this tax. The first, described shortly, is based on a direct regulatory tax for systemic risk, given our measure for each institution's contribution to systemic risk. The second approach, described in Section 5.4, is based on a market-based discovery of the price of systemic risk insurance that financial institutions must purchase jointly from the private sector and the government or the central bank.[4]

How would one estimate the expected systemic risk costs of a financial crisis? Empirically, this estimate should be based on the extensive time series of what causes crises; in other words, one would need to measure the probability of a crisis. Such signals might include systemwide leverage, asset bubbles, market volatility, and so forth (Reinhart and Rogoff 2009). By measuring the actual costs of past crises, along with the probability of a crisis, the regulator could then measure expected costs. A potentially nice feature of these calculations is that the regulator can adjust the expected costs to make them countercyclical—in other words, pushing them upward in good times and downward in bad times. The need for countercyclical measures is generally considered a key ingredient of financial reform, both by regulators abroad and among academics.[5]

Given these expected systemic costs, the regulator can then estimate the percentage contribution of each financial institution to the aggregate capital shortfall of the financial sector—our definition of a systemic trigger. Of course, the regulator might have a different definition, such as the degree of interconnectedness through all the firm's cross-exposures. The estimate of this relative contribution to systemic risk should be based on extensive cross-sectional analysis of how these firms might perform in crisis-type periods. Table 5.1 of this chapter provided an example of such a comparison. Multiplying this component by the one cited previously provides the level of necessary taxes.

If implemented perfectly, the financial firm would optimally choose to be less levered and to hold less systematically risky assets; in other words, it would be induced to impose its own capital requirement and Glass-Steagall-like restriction on risky activities. Since some systemic risk would remain, the financial firm would pay its contribution of the now-lower expected systemic costs, as all firms acting this way would reduce the probability of a systemic crisis.

As we see it, the primary difficulty lies with trying to estimate the overall expected systemic costs of a crisis. While there is considerable evidence that might help the regulator pin down the bailout and welfare costs of a crisis, estimating the likelihood of a crisis may prove evasive. This suggests that it might make sense for regulators to impose some constraints on leverage and asset risk—in other words, capital requirements and Glass-Steagall-like restrictions—in addition to the systemic risk tax. These constraints should be set so that they would most likely not bind if the tax level were estimated correctly. Chapters 6 and 7, respectively, examine the issue of capital requirements and Glass-Steagall restrictions on risk taking.

Obstacle 3: Is Moral Hazard Solved?

Because the government would now price and charge for both the *firm risk* and *systemic risk* components for each financial institution, less risk is produced and the moral hazard problem is mitigated. However, the actions of the financial firm are not fully observable, so once the premiums for the guarantees and systemic risk are set, and indeed capital requirements and Glass-Steagall restrictions imposed, the firm can in principle change its behavior. While a private market (like the one described in Section 5.4) may be better able to monitor the bank's actions than the regulator, the optimal contract usually calls for some type of state-contingent payoff to solve this problem.[6]

What would such a contract look like in this setting?

Theoretically, it would impose a severe penalty function in bad states to get the bank to avoid excessive risk-taking activities. The intuition here is similar to any standard insurance contract, which employs large deductibles in order to induce appropriate risk levels.

The problem with this contract is that, under a system of limited liability, the punishment is somewhat irrelevant, as shareholders are wiped out before it can be imposed. Nevertheless, Part Two on systemic risk (in particular, Chapters 6 and 8) discusses several ways to align incentives and thus bring back market discipline. These include: the creation of an insolvency regime for complex financial institutions that would allow the orderly failure or restructuring of insolvent firms (Chapter 8); a requirement that financial institutions employ in their capital structure a new kind of hybrid claim that has a *forced* debt-for-equity conversion whenever a prespecified threshold of distress (individual and systemic) is met (Chapter 6); punishing a firm's success, such as via a windfall profit tax, which would achieve the goal of systemic risk reduction, albeit at the cost of hurting legitimate profit-taking opportunities due to its taxation of ex post success; or even more extreme solutions, such as double liability for shareholders, a popular approach in the United States prior to the 1930s.[7]

5.3 THE DODD-FRANK WALL STREET REFORM AND CONSUMER PROTECTION ACT OF 2010

Given our own view of what the optimal policy should entail, how does the financial reform bill stack up in terms of addressing systemic risk?

Our preferred approach is to *disincentivize systemic risk* by having financial firms internalize the systemic risk costs imposed on the rest of the financial sector and the real economy. This way, the firms will organically dismantle themselves to become institutions with the appropriate size, leverage level, and risk profile. It is highly likely that this approach would greatly reduce the likelihood of a crisis and reduce the too-big-to-fail mantra.

The alternative approach taken in the Dodd-Frank Act is primarily to *manage systemic risk*, a method not dissimilar to the 1930s legislation described in the Prologue of the book. The risk of such an approach, however, is that it may not sufficiently reduce systemic risk, or worse, it may simply move it elsewhere in the system. That is, when the legislation does not adequately define systemic risk, and simply creates guidelines (albeit some sensible ones) to address a perceived problem, there is really no guarantee that it will be successfully implemented to tackle the issue at hand.

This point aside, one way to judge the Act's likelihood of success is to analyze how it addresses the three main challenges laid out at the beginning of Section 5.2 with respect to regulating systemic risk, namely: (1) identifying and measuring the systemic risk of financial firms, (2) using systemic risk measures to develop an optimal policy aimed at reducing the systemic risk in the financial sector and external real economy, and (3) making sure this policy is not subject to future regulatory arbitrage and that it mitigates the moral hazard problem inherent to government guarantees such as deposit insurance and too-big-to-fail guarantee.

Measuring Systemic Risk

With respect to the measurement issue, the Dodd-Frank Act considers a company as systemic if: (1) material financial distress at the company level could pose a threat to financial stability or the economy, or (2) the nature, scope, size, scale, concentration, interconnectedness, or mix of the company's activities could pose a threat to financial stability or the economy. In particular, the Act recommends that the systemic risk regulators consider the following criteria: (1) the amount and nature of the company's financial assets; (2) the amount and nature of the company's liabilities, including the degree of reliance on short-term funding; (3) the extent of the company's leverage; (4) the extent and nature of the company's off-balance-sheet exposures; (5) the extent and nature of the company's transactions and relationships with other financial companies; (6) the company's importance as a source of credit for households, businesses, and state and local governments and as a source of liquidity for the financial system; (7) the nature, scope, and mix of the company's activities; (8) the degree to which the company is already regulated by one or more federal financial regulatory agencies; and (9) the operation of, or ownership interest in, any clearing, settlement, or payment business of the company.

These criteria are all sensible. To the extent that the bill pushes the exact details onto the newly created Financial Stability Oversight Council, this too makes some sense. The Council will have 10 members, including the Treasury secretary (chair), an independent member, and heads of the Federal Reserve Board, FDIC, Securities and Exchange Commission (SEC), Commodity Futures Trading Commission (CFTC), Office of the Comptroller of the Currency (OCC), Federal Housing Finance Agency (FHFA), National Credit Union Administration (NCUA), and the new Bureau of Consumer Financial Protection (BCFP). It is hard to argue with this makeup, as most of the relevant regulators, who have access to the latest data, will be represented. Also, it is a good idea that the Act creates a new Office of Financial Research within Treasury that is staffed with economists, accountants, lawyers, former supervisors, and other specialists. This office will support the Council's work by collecting financial data and conducting economic analysis. Finally, the fact that the Act calls for the Federal Reserve, the most independent of the relevant agencies, to implement the Council's policies is reasonable, as the Fed is least likely to be captured by either financial institutions or politicians.

One glaring omission, however, is any recognition that along with leverage, the key characteristic of a systemically important institution is the *co-movement* of its asset returns with the aggregate financial sector during a crisis. While the measurement criteria described earlier are clearly related to this characteristic, the focus of the Act again is on individual institution risk. Given the theory outlined in Acharya, Pedersen, Philippon, and Richardson (2010a) and described in Section 5.2, there is a sense in which this comovement is *the key variable* we should care about with respect to systemic risk.

Reducing Systemic Risk

In terms of the broad issues relating to systemic risk, the Dodd-Frank Act has good intentions. It recognizes that systemic institutions must be subject to higher standards that should increase with the degree of systemic risk. Moreover, these prudential standards cover all the likely suspects. For example, the Act states:

> [I]*n order to prevent or mitigate risks to the financial stability of the United States that could arise from the material financial distress or failure of large, interconnected financial institutions, the Council may make recommendations to the Board of Governors concerning the establishment and refinement of prudential standards and reporting and disclosure requirements applicable to nonbank financial companies supervised by the Board of Governors and large, interconnected bank holding companies, that—(1) are more stringent than those applicable to other nonbank financial companies and bank holding companies that do not present similar risks to the financial stability of the United States; and (2) increase in stringency, based on the considerations identified in subsection (b)(3) [i.e., the systemic risk factors described earlier].*[8]

Moreover, these stricter standards should include "(1) risk-based capital requirements; (2) leverage limits; (3) liquidity requirements; (4) a contingent capital requirement; (5) resolution plan and credit exposure report requirements; (6) enhanced public disclosures; (7) concentration limits; (8) short-term debt limits; and (9) overall risk management requirements."[9]

In addition, the Act does impose some sensible Glass-Steagall-like restrictions on bank holding companies and nonbank financial companies that are deemed systemically risky. One is a limit on the ability of an institution to grow by merger if its liabilities exceed 10 percent of all liabilities of financial firms in the United States. The second is more binding, and prohibits bank holding companies (while placing curbs on systemically risky nonbank financial companies) from engaging in proprietary trading, defined as the trading of stocks, bonds, options, commodities, derivatives, or other financial instruments with the company's own money and for the company's own account. In the context of systemic risk, this issue is discussed in depth in Chapter 7.

Mitigating Moral Hazard

The Dodd-Frank Act falls short, however, with respect to our third and final criterion—namely, preventing regulatory arbitrage and mitigating moral hazard. In particular, the Act does not adequately address the too-big-to-fail problem in several important ways.

First, the Act's approach is soft on large financial institutions in that the stricter prudential standards involve capital, liquidity, and contingent capital requirements, which may not be costly to the institution. While these standards should reduce systemic risk, these financial institutions may remain large, have access to too-big-to-fail guarantees, and still take excessive risk.

Originally, the House bill, prior to its conference reconciliation with the Senate version, contained a $150 billion "systemic resolution fund." With respect to the pricing of the too-big-to-fail guarantee, the idea was to charge an assessment on all financial institutions that would go into a systemic fund to be used for future bailouts of the sector. This would have been similar to the FDIC premium but applied more broadly to systemic institutions, presumably to cover the bailout costs of systemic liabilities, such as uninsured household, business, and foreign deposits; interbank loans; repo transactions; and over-the-counter (OTC) derivatives, among others. Of course, the assessment would have been a disincentive to become a too-big-to-fail (and, more generally, a systemic) institution, which would have achieved its purpose.

Unfortunately, because the existence of a systemic resolution fund was unpalatable to many in Congress, the assessment on banks was dropped and replaced by a process that requires ex post funding by the financial sector for any costs not borne by shareholders and creditors of the failed institution. Since large amounts of systemic liabilities will most likely not be allowed to fail for fear of ensuing banklike runs, there exists a terrible free-rider problem. Banks that do not take excessive risks and instead act in a prudent fashion are made responsible for the failures of those that do take excessive risks. Thus, the moral hazard problem of the too-big-to-fail financial firm remains. The Act's solution is even more of a problem because it requires that, in a crisis, the solvent part of the financial sector should cover the losses of the failed part of the sector. This is the exact opposite inference one would draw from countercyclical capital requirements. In other words, when capital is most needed in the financial sector, it is being used to cover the mistakes of others.

Part of the problem is that the systemic resolution fund, as originally envisioned, was to help wind down failed institutions; instead, its purpose should have been to compensate those who suffer the collateral damage from systemic financial crises: the solvent financial institutions and businesses in the real economy that suffer when credit markets panic. The optimal policy laid out in Section 5.2 would solve this problem by bifurcating the fund into one piece that covers explicit and implicit government guarantees and another piece that is used to support solvent firms that are affected by the onslaught of systemic risk.

Consider Federal Reserve Chairman Ben Bernanke's oft-cited analogy for why bailouts, however distasteful, are sometimes necessary. Bernanke has described a hypothetical neighbor who smokes in bed and, through his carelessness, starts a fire that begins to burn down his house. You could teach him a lesson, Bernanke says, by refusing to call the fire department and letting the house burn to the ground. However, you would risk the fire spreading to other homes. So first you have to put out the fire. Only later should you deal with reform and retribution.

But let's change the story slightly. If the neighbor's house is burning, putting the fire out might risk the lives of the firefighters. You can still call the fire department, but instead of saving the neighbor's house, the firefighters stand in protection of your house and those of your other neighbors. If the fire spreads, they are ready to put it out. This approach could save lives, and it has the added benefit of chastening your guilty neighbor into refraining from smoking in bed, or perhaps into installing new fire alarms.

This is the purpose of a systemic risk fee on LCFIs.

Second, even if systemic risk were managed this way (which is not the case in the Dodd-Frank Act), the regulators would still need to price implicit guarantees (along with deposit insurance) and impose the costs on the financial institutions. But despite the number of pages in the Dodd-Frank Act, there is little or no attempt to address the question of whether systemically risky uninsured short-term liabilities are covered either through pricing of their implicit guarantee or via a credible mechanism within the resolution authority.[10] As discussed in Chapter 8, "Resolution Authority"; Chapter 10, "Money Market Funds"; and Chapter 11, "The Repurchase Agreement (Repo) Market," the Dodd-Frank Act provides little mention of this issue.

The Dodd-Frank Act does a much better job with respect to some of the issues related to FDIC insurance—the one guarantee that is explicitly recognized. Prior to the crisis, it was simply unacceptable that, when the FDIC's deposit insurance fund reserves exceeded a certain level, many banks were no longer required to pay fees into the fund. In fact, large banks did not pay any significant deposit insurance premiums for the decade leading up to the crisis, and the insurance funds are now depleted. By not charging for insurance during the run-up to the crisis, the government exacerbated the moral hazard problem.

The Dodd-Frank Act does correct this problem by getting rid of the upper limit for the reserve ratio (i.e., ratio of the FDIC-insured fund to total deposits). Moreover, the Act increases the minimum reserve ratio to 1.35 percent from 1.15 percent, with much of the increase eventually being paid by large banks (i.e., more than $10 billion in assets). Of course, given that the FDIC's fund is currently at −0.38 percent, with the possibility of falling further, these new rules are hardly restrictive. In fact, the Act gives the FDIC until 2020 to reach the 1.35 percent threshold. Thus, the issue of the upper limit will not come up for at least a decade.

In addition, the Dodd-Frank Act tilts the costs of the FDIC-insured fund toward large depository institutions. This will impose some additional costs on the firms that tend to be systemically more risky. On the margin, this should cause these firms to reduce their liabilities. Specifically, the Act calls for the FDIC to now base its assessment on the firm's total liabilities (its assets minus its tangible equity) as opposed to the prior rule that used just the firm's insured deposits.[11] Given that (1) the majority of the liabilities in the financial sector are held by just a few large firms, and (2) these firms use funding sources other than deposits, the effect of this clause will be to shift the costs much more toward these firms. In lieu of any meaningful reform to get these firms to internalize the costs they impose on the system, this part of the Dodd-Frank Act is a step in the right direction.

Third, the bill's preferred way to deal with the too-big-to-fail problem is through a resolution authority. But, as we argue later in this chapter and in greater detail in Chapter 8, this authority is inadequate for this purpose. If the Act's main defense against the too-big-to-fail problem is the resolution authority, then choosing a receivership model is not a particularly credible way to ensure that systemic liabilities will be left unprotected in a crisis. A more transparent and predictable design would be either a living will mechanism or one based on the bankruptcy code, possibly restructured to deal with LCFIs. As written, the resolution authority in the Act is a very risky way of managing systemic risk when a crisis emerges. It reads like a mismatch of the bankruptcy code and a receivership model, and may actually increase uncertainty about who is entitled to assets when the firm fails. As is well known, uncertainty is the bogeyman of a financial crisis. Thus, while the Act does provide the resolution authority with flexibility during the crisis, the Act may not be realistic for how it deals with failing firms. It would be much better to define rules up front.

For all nonguaranteed liabilities, we prefer a living will. The idea is to take these liabilities and separate them into classes of debt with different priorities. If the firm defaults on its debt, the equity of the firm is eliminated and the lowest-priority debt converts to new equity. If the removal of the low-priority debt is sufficient to afford the firm to cover its remaining debt obligations, then the firm would continue as is. If some of these debt obligations are still in default, however, then the process would continue until the debts are no longer in default or the highest-priority debt gets converted to equity. The living will is just one approach the regulator can take to create a credible plan that both avoids the costs of liquidation in bankruptcy and allows for creditors to pay for the risks they incur. This is important as it will bring back market discipline to the financial sector and remove some of the implicit government guarantees for the too-big-to-fail firms.

5.4 A TAX ON SYSTEMIC RISK

In this chapter, we have strongly argued that systemically important financial institutions need to internalize the systemic risk costs they impose on the financial system. Without a mechanism that leads to this outcome, financial firms will continue individually to maximize the value of their enterprises. These actions, in aggregate, result in too much systemic risk being produced and a more fragile financial system than is otherwise optimal.

Consider by way of analogy the congestion tax being charged in the city of London. Its purpose is not to charge each driver his or her share of the usage of London roads (though that might also make economic sense), but to get each driver to internalize his or her contribution to congestion; thus, those whose economic returns against incurring the charge are not too high would adopt other means of transportation. The charge is imposed during times and in areas where congestion is indeed costly for the city. And, most importantly, the charge is paid by each driver contributing to the congestion rather than by those who use the central London roads at night, after the congestion period has expired. As we emphasized in the Prologue of this book, regulation of pollution—one of the most classic problems of externalities in economics—deals with it much the same way: The polluter pays for its contributions.

Internationally, there seemed to be general support for such an approach to managing systemic risk. But as the Dodd-Frank Act was being revised to drop a tax on banks, so too did many of the G-20 countries. Australia, Canada, and India, which weathered the financial crisis relatively well, were among the primary opponents of the tax. The notable exceptions were the three largest economies in Europe—the United Kingdom, France, and Germany, some emerging market countries like Hungary, and international organizations like the International Monetary Fund (IMF).[12] Most of the proposed taxes are not particularly sophisticated and tend to be charged on either the firms' total assets or their risky liabilities (i.e., all their debts except insured deposits). For example, the United Kingdom has put forth a tax of 0.07 percent on risky liabilities. In July 2010, Hungary caused a bit of an uproar by pushing through a tax of 0.45 percent on assets. Many of the countries, like the United Kingdom, Hungary, and France, do not consider the tax as a way to fund bailouts per se, but more as incentive for firms to reduce risk and as a revenue source for government. This is consistent with the congestion tax argument.

Given the international interest in a systemic risk tax, it seems worthwhile to provide a more detailed discussion of how to implement the optimal tax (i.e., to offer a more sophisticated approach than just taxing the amount of liabilities). While much of this presentation is based on Acharya, Pedersen, Philippon, and Richardson (2010b), there are a number of other papers that also call for Pigouvian-type taxes (e.g., Perotti and Suarez 2009; Jeanne and Korinek 2010).

Section 5.2 described one way for the regulator to implement the systemic risk tax. One of the issues with using that methodology is that it involves using data (which may differ across types of financial firms), statistical estimates of tail events that are subject to error, and regulators who may not have the appropriate background. Therefore, a better approach may be to employ a market-based solution to estimating the systemic tax of each financial firm.

At the core of a market-oriented solution is the role of the private sector in providing insurance primarily for price discovery. Since the amount of private capital available to provide such systemic insurance is likely to be limited, most of the insurance would be purchased from the regulator. The idea behind this proposal therefore is that private insurers would help price the insurance, while the government would provide most of the capital underlying the insurance. While some reinsurance schemes along these lines have been looked at by the FDIC, most recently in 1993, and were dismissed based on the conclusion that this market is not viable, there is reason to be more optimistic today. Financial markets, in general, have become much more sophisticated in how they develop niche markets.

A case in point: Coinsurance programs are not without precedent. Motivated by the events of September 11, 2001, the Terrorism Risk Insurance Act (TRIA), first passed in November 2002, offers federal reinsurance for qualifying losses from a terrorist attack. TRIA is a good place to start and includes industry loss triggers and government excess of loss coverage. These features help minimize the insurance industry's losses, yet also provide them with an incentive to monitor and reduce risks. It would work similarly here.

A market solution would require each financial firm to buy insurance against its own losses in a financial crisis. In the event of an insurance payout, payment would not go to the firm itself, but to the government. This contingent capital insurance fee is not equal to the tax, but instead would be used to determine the proportionate share of each financial firm's contribution to the total systemic risk tax. The level of the systemic risk tax would be determined by the expected systemic costs of a financial crisis times the proportionate share of each firm. The important point is that each firm's share would be determined by the private market for insurance.

The reason why a joint public-private insurance plan is needed is that the private insurance sector is not set up to insure against systemic risks. By their very nature, systemic risks cannot be diversified away. The underlying capital required to cover these losses therefore is quite large even though the possibility of such an event is very small.

In the current financial crisis, problems occurred with the monoline insurers, such as Ambac Financial Group and MBIA Inc., and the Financial Products division of AIG. Undercapitalized relative to the systemic event, almost all the monolines and AIG Financial Products were effectively insolvent. Though insolvency of insurers is not necessarily a problem, these insurers may have been systemic due to their counterparty risk. Thus, insurers may have their own too-big-to-fail designation, causing them to take large, directional, systemic bets.

So, in order to avoid this type of problem, a public-private insurance plan is required. Implementation of such a plan would be as follows:

- Each regulated firm would have a target capital of, say, K percent of current assets in the event of a crisis. For every dollar by which the institution's capital falls below the target capital in the crisis, the insurance company would have to pay N cents to the regulator (e.g., a systemic risk fund).[13] This way, the insurance provider would have every incentive to correctly estimate the systemic risk of a firm in a competitive market and charge the firm accordingly.
- The charge would allow the regulator to determine the proportionate share of expected losses contributed by each firm in a crisis—in other words, the relative systemic risk of each firm in the sector. This would be used to determine who pays their share of the overall systemic tax. The regulator would then take this proportionate share of each firm and multiply it by the expected systemic costs of a crisis to determine the level of the tax.
- To avoid double taxation, the fees paid to the insurance company would be subtracted from the firm's total systemic tax bill paid to the regulator.
- The financial firms would need to keep acquiring insurance, and thus pay the tax, on a continuous basis to ensure continuous monitoring and price discovery, and to prevent sudden high insurance premiums from causing funding problems, because the purchases of premiums are spread out over time.
- As described in Section 5.3, the tax proceeds are not meant to bail out failed institutions, but to support the affected real sector and solvent institutions. Future expected bailouts (i.e., government guarantees) need to be priced separately.

The main goal of the tax scheme is to provide incentives to limit systemic risk or to be well capitalized against systemic risk in order to reduce the cost of insurance. Thus, institutions will internalize their externality, and the market price helps measure it.

5.5 SUMMARY

To conclude, even though the Dodd-Frank Act does not directly require a tax on systemic risk contributions of financial firms, there is a chance that implementation by prudential regulators of some of the risk controls, such as capital or liquidity requirements, will eventually be tied to such contributions. Our measures of systemic risk and related ideas to regulate it have been presented and debated actively in the policy circles over the past two years. Our modest hope is that such debates translate eventually into an ex ante Pigouvian tax on systemic risk.

NOTES

1. An analogy can be made to an industrial company that produces emissions that might lower its costs but that pollute the environment.
2. The underlying economics here are presented in Acharya, Pedersen, Philippon, and Richardson (2010a), "Measuring Systemic Risk."
3. A detailed discussion of this methodology, as well as a historical and current analysis of the systemic risk of financial institutions, is provided on the web site http://vlab.stern.nyu.edu/welcome/risk. For additional measures of systemic risk relevant to our analysis, see also Lehar (2005); Gray, Merton, and Bodie (2008); Gray and Jobst (2009); Huang, Zhou, and Zhu (2009); Adrian and Brunnermeier (2008); Tarashev, Borio, and Tsatsaronis (2009); and Segoviano and Goodhart (2009).
4. This section is based on Acharya, Pedersen, Philippon, and Richardson (2010b).
5. As pointed out in Chapter 6, the Dodd-Frank Act calls for countercyclical capital requirements (HR 4173, Title VI, "Improvements to Regulation of Bank and Savings Association Holding Companies and Depository Institutions," Sec. 616, "Regulations Regarding Capital Levels").
6. See, for example, John, John, and Senbet (1991) and Prescott (2002).
7. For resolution authorities, see Scott, Shultz, and Taylor (2009), among others; for contingent capital, see Wall (1989), Doherty and Harrington (1997), and Flannery (2005); and for double liability, see Saunders and Wilson (1992).
8. HR 4173, Title I, "Financial Stability," Subtitle A, "Financial Stability Oversight Council," Sec. 115, "Enhanced supervision and prudential standards for nonbank financial companies supervised by the Board of Governors and certain bank holding companies."
9. Ibid.

10. Putting aside this issue of nonguaranteed liabilities, one could argue that the problem has even worsened for insured deposits, as the guaranteed limits on deposits have been permanently increased from $100,000 to $250,000. If one believes deposit insurance is mispriced, then the mispricing is now 2.5 times worse.
11. HR 4173, Title III, "Transfer of Powers to the Comptroller of the Currency, the Corporation and the Board of Governors," Subtitle C, "Federal Deposit Insurance Corporation," Sec. 331, "Deposit Insurance Reforms."
12. See, for example, the April 2010 IMF Global Financial Stability Report.
13. N cents represents the proportional share of the private market's participation in the insurance component of the public-private plan. If the proposal were simply contingent capital insurance, in which the firm got recapitalized if it were doing poorly in a crisis, then the government's share of the payout to the firm would be $100 - N$ cents on the dollar, and the government would receive $(100 - N)/100$ percent of the insurance premiums.

REFERENCES

Acharya, Viral V., Lasse H. Pedersen, Thomas Philippon, and Matthew Richardson. 2010a. Measuring systemic risk. Working paper, New York University Stern School of Business.

Acharya, Viral V., Lasse H. Pedersen, Thomas Philippon, and Matthew Richardson. 2010b. A tax on systemic risk. Forthcoming NBER publication on Quantifying Systemic Risk, ed. Joseph Haubrich and Andrew Lo.

Adrian, Tobias, and Markus Brunnermeier. 2008. CoVaR. Working paper, Federal Reserve Bank of New York.

Borio, Claudo E.V., and Mathias Drehmann. 2009. Towards an operational framework for financial stability: "Fuzzy" measurement and its consequences. BIS Working Paper No. 284, June.

Brownlees, Christian T., and Robert F. Engle. 2010. Volatility, correlation and tails for systemic risk measurement. Working paper, New York University Stern School of Business.

Caprio, Gerard, and Daniela Klingebiel. 1996. Bank insolvencies: Cross country experience. World Bank, Policy Research Working Paper No. 1620.

Doherty, Neil A., and Scott Harrington. 1997. Managing corporate risk with reverse convertible debt. Working paper, Wharton School.

Flannery, Mark J. 2005. No pain, no gain? Effecting market discipline via "reverse convertible debentures." In *Capital adequacy beyond Basel: Banking, securities, and insurance*, ed. Hal S. Scott. Oxford: Oxford University Press.

Gray, Dale, and Andreas A. Jobst. 2009. Tail dependence measures of systemic risk using equity options data—Implications for financial stability. Working paper, International Monetary Fund, Washington, D.C.

Gray, Dale F., Robert C. Merton, and Zvi Bodie. 2008. New framework for measuring and managing macrofinancial risk and financial stability. Working Paper No. 09-015, Harvard Business School, August.

Hoggarth, Glenn, Ricardo Reis, and Victoria Saporta. 2002. Costs of banking system instability: Some empirical evidence. *Journal of Banking and Finance* 26 (5): 825–855.

Honohan, Patrick, and Daniela Klingebiel. 2000. Controlling fiscal costs of bank crises. World Bank, Working Paper No. 2441.

Huang, Xin, Hao Zhou, and Haibin Zhu. 2009. A framework for assessing the systemic risk of major financial institutions. *Journal of Banking and Finance* 33 (11): 2036–2049.

Jeanne, Oliver, and Anton Korinek. 2010. Managing credit booms and busts: A Pigouvian taxation approach. Working paper, Johns Hopkins University.

John, Kose, Teresa A. John, and Lemma W. Senbet. 1991. Risk-shifting incentives of depository institutions: A new perspective on federal deposit insurance reform. *Journal of Banking and Finance* 15:895–915.

Lehar, A. 2005. Measuring systemic risk: A risk management approach. *Journal of Banking and Finance* 29:2577–2603.

Perotti, Enrico, and Javier Suarez. 2009. Liquidity insurance for systemic crises. *CEPR Policy Insight* 31, February. Also available at www.cepr.org/pubs/PolicyInsights/PolicyInsight31.pdf.

Prescott, Edward S. 2002. Can risk-based deposit insurance premiums control moral hazard? *Federal Reserve Bank of Richmond Economic Quarterly* 88 (Spring): 87–100.

Reinhart, Carmen M., and Kenneth Rogoff. 2008. Is the 2007 U.S. sub-prime financial crisis so different: An international historical comparison. *American Economic Review Papers & Proceedings* 98 (2): 339–344.

Reinhart, Carmen M., and Kenneth Rogoff. 2009. *This time is different: Eight centuries of financial folly*. Princeton, NJ: Princeton University Press.

Saunders, Anthony, and Berry Wilson. 1992. Double liability of bank shareholders: History and implications. *Wake Forest Law Review* 27 (1): 31–62.

Scott, Kenneth E., George P. Shultz, and John B. Taylor, eds. 2009. *Ending government bailouts as we know them*. Stanford, CA: Hoover Press.

Segoviano, Miguel, and Charles Goodhart. 2009. Banking stability measures. IMF Working Paper 09/04, International Monetary Fund.

Tarashev, Nikola, Claudio Borio, and Kostas Tsatsaronis. 2009. Allocating systemic risk to individual institutions: Methodology and policy applications. Working paper, Bank for International Settlements.

Wall, Larry. 1989. A plan for reducing future deposit insurance losses: Puttable subordinated debt. *Federal Reserve Bank of Atlanta Economic Review* 74 (4).

CHAPTER 6

Capital, Contingent Capital, and Liquidity Requirements

Viral V. Acharya, Nirupama Kulkarni, and Matthew Richardson

6.1 OVERVIEW

When a poorly capitalized—or, in other words, highly leveraged—financial firm suffers asset losses and the firm falls into distress, funding gets pulled, forcing the firm to sell its assets, which leads to further funding problems and a downward spiral (see, e.g., Brunnermeier and Pedersen 2009). Due to either direct counterparty relationships or the presence of similar asset holdings at other firms, the failing firm's losses reverberate throughout the financial system, causing an aggregate shortfall of capital. Systemic risk emerges, and the health of the financial system quickly erodes. And because of the debt overhang problem, it is not possible for financial firms to issue new equity capital since the proceeds mostly accrue to the creditors (see Myers 1977). The financial sector then has no choice but to reduce lending, leading to an aggregate credit crunch.

Capital is thus the lifeblood of the financial system when it is under stress. But capital is difficult to raise in such times. How should capital requirements be designed in good times to prevent and manage this risk?

In response to the systemic effect of the failure of the relatively small German bank Herstatt in 1974, the central-bank governors of the G-10 established the Basel Committee on Banking Supervision. While having no statutory authority, the Basel Committee has emerged over the past 35 years as the go-to group to formulate international standards for banking supervision, and especially capital adequacy requirements. The process started with the 1988 Basel Accord (Basel I), which imposed the now-infamous minimum ratio of capital to risk-weighted assets of 8 percent. The committee produced a revised framework in June 1999, which culminated in the implementation of the New Capital Framework in June 2004 (Basel II). Basel II expanded Basel I's capital requirement rules and introduced internal risk assessment processes. As a result of the recent financial crisis, the Basel Committee is at it again with proposals for new capital adequacy and liquidity requirements, denoted Basel III.[1] The long-term implementation of these rules is set to start in November 2010.

While the Dodd-Frank Wall Street Reform and Consumer Protection Act of 2010 provides its own capital guidelines, it is generally assumed that implementation of the Act will, to the extent possible, coincide closely with Basel III. In fact, of the 27 countries party to the Basel agreement in July 2010, the United States signed on (only Germany did not). The impact that Basel I and II had on the financial crisis cannot be understated. While Basel III is clearly an improvement, the Basel approach to prudential regulation remains the same even in light of its utter failure to prevent the financial crisis of 2007 to 2009.

This book takes a very different view of the way to regulate systemic risk. Chapter 5, "Taxing Systemic Risk," argues that the first and best solution to reducing systemic risk is to have financial firms internalize the external costs of this risk. Facing these costs, the firms will organically choose to be less levered (i.e., hold more capital) and to hold less systemically risky assets. Neither Basel III nor the Dodd-Frank Act follows this approach to financial regulation. Nevertheless, we recognize that, even without such pricing and charging for systemic risk, a second-best solution may be to impose binding capital requirements and restrict asset holdings, in other words, to attempt to approximate the optimal policy somewhat directly.[2]

That said, while the Basel process focuses on capital requirements, it ignores the crucial market and regulatory failures of the financial system:

- While recognizing the systemic risk of financial firms, the Basel approach very much remains focused on the risk of the individual institution and not the system as a whole. In other words, the level of a firm's capital requirements in Basel I, II, or III does not depend on its interaction with other financial firms.
- Whatever capital and/or liquidity requirements are placed on one set of financial institutions—say banks and bank holding companies—it is highly likely that the financial activities affected by these requirements will just move elsewhere in the shadow banking system. That is, without the understanding that the whole financial system must be looked at and treated in unison, Basel III will run into the same shadow banking issues that arose with Basel I and II.

- There seems to be no recognition of the role government guarantees play in the allocation of capital. Ceteris paribus, the more guarantees a firm receives, the lower its costs of debt funding. This artificially increases the relative cost of nonguaranteed funding like equity, preferred stock, contingent capital, and possibly subordinated debt (under a credible resolution authority).

Also problematic is that the Basel process sticks with tired old definitions of capital and leverage not entirely suitable for modern-day financial firms and for reducing excessive systemic risk. At the time they were designed, the primary purpose of Basel capital requirements was to guard the retail deposit base of commercial banks from unexpected losses on their loan portfolios. While Basel II has made improvements over Basel I by addressing over-the-counter (OTC) derivative positions, and Basel III has tightened the treatment of off-balance-sheet financing, the focus is still not to measure quantities that actually reflect systemic risk, such as the change in the value of the financial firm's assets given a macroeconomic-wide shock and the impact such a shock has on its liability and funding structure.

More formally, there are two types of risks that cause a financial firm to potentially fail:

1. *Solvency or capital risk*, that is, the market value of the firm's assets falls below its obligations.
2. *Liquidity risk*, that is, the firm cannot convert assets into cash to pay off its obligations because asset markets have become illiquid, or its close cousin, *funding liquidity risk*, that is, the firm is unable to roll over its maturing debt obligations with immediacy at some point in the future.

These risks can spread quickly through fire sales, counterparty risk, or contagious runs, and systemic risk can engulf the financial sector in no time.

As examples of solvency and liquidity risk, note that both these types of risks emerged in the current crisis. With respect to the former, in August 2007, there was a run on asset-backed commercial paper (ABCP) conduits. Because the ABCP conduits had no capital, and the underlying AAA-rated assets fell below par value, investors no longer rolled their funding over, causing these conduits to fail. With respect to the latter, in March 2008 and September 2008, concerns about whether the major broker-dealers would be able to pay their obligations down the road led to an immediate loss of short-term wholesale funding in the form of repo financing and commercial paper. Some of the major investment banks—Bear Stearns, Lehman Brothers, Merrill Lynch, and (almost) Morgan Stanley—thought they had plenty of liquidity, only to see it evaporate literally overnight, and then to run aground the next day.

The goal of this chapter is to evaluate the Dodd-Frank Act (and Basel III) in terms of their approaches to setting capital and liquidity requirements. Section 6.2 outlines the woeful failure of the Basel Accords to lower the systemic risk of the financial system, and, in particular, its causal effect on the financial crisis. Section 6.3 describes and evaluates in some detail the Dodd-Frank Act and Basel III revisions. To the extent that capital requirements are not sufficient (or too costly) to manage systemic risk, Section 6.4 analyzes contingent capital as one possible solution. Contingent capital is cited prominently in both Basel III and the Dodd-Frank Act.

6.2   THE FINANCIAL CRISIS OF 2007 TO 2009

The short account of the final crisis of 2007 to 2009 is that a large number of banks and other major intermediaries managed to shift risks by exploiting loopholes in regulatory capital requirements in order to take an undercapitalized, highly leveraged, one-way bet on the economy—particularly tied to residential real estate, but also to commercial real estate and consumer credit. When the bet went wrong, these large, complex financial institutions (LCFIs) began to suffer considerable losses to the asset side of their balance sheets. Specifically, commercial banks such as Citigroup experienced problems though runs on asset-backed commercial paper issued by their fully leveraged off-balance-sheet investment vehicles. Fannie Mae and Freddie Mac were placed into conservatorship. And on the funding side, all the major investment banks—Bear Stearns, Lehman Brothers, Merrill Lynch, Morgan Stanley, and Goldman Sachs—faced sudden withdrawals of liabilities during this crisis. The $3 trillion plus money market sector also faced a run after Lehman Brothers failed. Many point to these runs as the trigger for the crisis going pandemic. And, shortly after, major bailouts had to be provided to Citigroup, Bank of America, and American International Group (AIG).

As a summary of these losses, Table 6.1 shows the 12 largest writedowns (and credit losses) of U.S. financial institutions from June 2007 (the beginning of the crisis) until March 2010. For example, the top six firms combined for a total of $696 billion in losses. Of some note, five of these six firms received the largest bailouts (Wachovia was acquired by Wells Fargo). Although, prior to their failures, most of these financial institutions were still considered by regulatory agencies to be well-capitalized, the market clearly thought differently. The last column in Table 6.1 shows that, from June 2007 to December 2008, the market values of these six firms dropped precipitously, averaging –88.71 percent. Moreover, during this

TABLE 6.1 Largest Write-Downs for U.S. Financial Institutions (June 2007 to March 2010)

Firm	Write-Downs and Credit Losses ($ Billions)	Equity Return (June 2007– Dec. 2008)	Equity Return (June 2007– Sept. 16, 2008)
Fannie Mae	151.4	−98.14%	−99.23%
Citigroup	130.4	−82.46	−67.20
Freddie Mac	118.1	−97.98	−99.56
Wachovia	101.9	−88.34	−73.18
Bank of America	97.6	−67.79	−34.35
AIG	97.0	−97.57	−94.50
JPMorgan	69.0	−31.51	−12.13
Merrill Lynch	55.9	−85.16	−72.45
Wells Fargo	47.4	−10.77	4.47
Washington Mutual	45.3	−99.95	−90.07
National City	25.2	−94.29	−86.61
Morgan Stanley	23.4	−75.99	−57.65

Source: Bloomberg.

period, major institutions in any part of the financial sector that fell short of capital—special purpose vehicles, such as conduits and structured investment vehicles (SIVs) (in August 2007); independent broker-dealers (in March and September 2008); money market funds (in September 2008); and hedge funds—faced massive runs on their short-term liabilities.[3] By fall 2008 and winter 2009, systemic risk had fully emerged and the real economy was suffering the consequences.

This finding prompts the obvious question, and one that regulators must grapple with: Why, under the Basel core capital requirement of capital to risk-weighted assets ratio of 8 percent, did the top 20 U.S. banks look safe, averaging a ratio of 11.7 percent? And even more striking, and based on their last quarterly disclosure documents, why did the five largest LCFIs that were subject to Basel rules and effectively failed during the crisis—Bear Stearns, Washington Mutual, Lehman Brothers, Wachovia, and Merrill Lynch—all have capital ratios between 12.3 percent and 16.1 percent (e.g., Kuritzkes and Scott 2009)? Something is clearly amiss.

To understand what went wrong from a regulatory capital point of view, note that the LCFIs took their leveraged bet using regulatory arbitrage tricks as a direct result of Basel I and II: First, they funded portfolios of risky loans via off-balance-sheet vehicles (conduits and SIVs). These loans, however, were guaranteed by sponsoring LCFIs through liquidity enhancements that had lower capital requirement by Basel; so the loans were effectively recourse but had a lower capital charge, even though the credit risk never left the sponsoring LCFIs. Second, they made outright purchases of AAA-rated tranches of nonprime securities, which were treated as having low credit risk and zero liquidity and funding risk. Third, they enjoyed full capital relief on AAA tranches if they bought underpriced protection on securitized products from monolines and AIG (both of which were not subject to similar prudential standards). Fourth, in August 2004, investment banks successfully lobbied the Securities and Exchange Commission (SEC) to amend the net capital rule of the Securities Exchange Act of 1934, which effectively allowed for leverage to increase in return for greater supervision. This lobbying was in direct response to the internal risk management rules of Basel II.

Let us consider a few of these observations in greater detail.

One of the two principal means for regulatory arbitrage under the Basel Accords was the creation of off-balance-sheet vehicles, which held on to many of the asset-backed securities they helped issue in the market. With securitized loans placed in these vehicles rather than on a bank's balance sheet, the bank did not need to maintain any significant capital against them. However, the conduits funded the asset-backed securities by asset-backed commercial paper (ABCP)—short-term (typically less than one-week maturity) debt instruments sold in the financial markets, notably to investors in money market instruments. To be able to sell the ABCP, a bank would have to provide the buyers (i.e., the banks' counterparties) with *guarantees* on the underlying credit—essentially bringing the risk back to the banks themselves, even though that risk was not shown on their balance sheets (see Acharya, Schnabl, and Suarez 2009).

These guarantees had two important effects. First, guaranteeing the risk to banks' counterparties was essential in moving these assets off the banks' balance sheets. Designing the guarantees as so-called liquidity enhancements with a maturity less than one year (to be rolled over each year) allowed the banks to exploit a loophole in Basel capital requirements. In fact, almost all of these had a 364-day maturity. The design effectively eliminated the capital charge from retaining the risk of these loans, so that banks achieved a tenfold increase in leverage for a given pool of loans. Second, the guarantees ensured the highest ratings for the off-balance-sheet vehicles from the rating agencies. Indeed, the AAA ratings made it possible for banks to sell ABCP to money market funds, which are required by law to invest mainly in short-term and the highest-rated paper. This allowed banks to fund the ABCP at low interest rates, similar to rates paid on deposit accounts.

Acharya, Schnabl, and Suarez (2009) document an increase in the ABCP market from around $600 billion in 2004 to $1.2 trillion in the second quarter of 2007 (just prior to the start of the financial crisis). When the collapse occurred in the next quarter, the cost of issuing ABCP rose from just 15 basis points over the federal funds rate to over 100 basis points (at its peak being close to 150 basis points). Consequently, the ABCP could no longer be rolled over, and the banks had to return the loans to their balance sheets. Acharya, Schnabl, and Suarez (2009) show that when the crisis hit, of the $1.25 trillion in asset-backed securitized vehicles, only 4.3 percent of the loss was structured to remain with investors. The remaining loss wiped out significant portions of bank capital and threatened banks' solvency.

Off-balance-sheet financing was not the only way banks performed regulatory arbitrage against the Basel rules. In the second approach, a bank would still make loans and move them from its balance sheet by securitizing them. But as Shin (2009) explains, the bank then turned around and reinvested in AAA-rated tranches of the same securitized products it (or other banks) had created.[4] Because of their AAA ratings, these securities had a significantly lower capital requirement under the Basel II arrangement. For commercial banks, the Basel Accord weighted the risk of AAA-rated securities at less than half of the risk of ordinary commercial or mortgage loans, and thus required an even lower capital reserve for them (a 20 percent risk weight compared to 50 percent for mortgages and 100 percent for corporate bonds). In 2004, the Securities and Exchange Commission (SEC) granted stand-alone American investment banks the ability to employ internal models to assess credit risk and the corresponding capital charge. This allowed them to take on even higher leverage than commercial banks, with leverage duly skyrocketing from a 22:1 debt-to-equity ratio to 33:1 within just three years.

In fact, a Lehman Brothers report from April 2008 shows that banks and thrifts, government-sponsored enterprises (GSEs) (Fannie and Freddie), and broker-dealers in 2007 held $789 billion of the AAA-rated collateralized debt obligation (CDO) tranches that were backed by nonprime loans, or approximately 50 percent of the volume outstanding at the time. Moreover, the majority of the subordinated tranches of the CDOs were also held by banks, broker-dealers, and monoline insurers (which insure only one type of bond—e.g., municipal bonds). They collectively held $320 billion of the $476 billion total outstanding.

Last, in terms of regulatory arbitrage to get around the Basel rules, the role played by monoline insurers and AIG cannot be overstated. In particular, credit protection in the form of credit default swaps (CDSs) purchased from AAA-rated insurers on AAA-rated securities led to a 0 percent capital weight on these securities in the portfolios of banks' balance sheets. In other words, even though the spread on the securities over the bank's funding rate adjusted for the CDSs was greater than zero, the capital charge was zero.[5] No wonder LCFIs loaded up on these asset-backed securities. For example, on page 122 of its 2007 annual report, AIG reports that $379 billion of its $527 billion credit default swap exposure on AAA-rated asset-backed securities written by its now-infamous Financial Products group was written not for hedging purposes but to facilitate regulatory capital relief for (mainly European) financial institutions.

The net effect of arbitraging Basel's capital requirements was that global banking balance sheets doubled from 2004 to 2007 with only a minor increase in Basel-implied risk (see the International Monetary Fund's Global Financial Stability Report, April 2008). This fact alone should have signaled a red flag to regulators. When one combines this fact with the growth in short-term shadow banking liabilities from $10 trillion to $20 trillion between 2000 and 2007 (compared to $5.5 trillion to $11 trillion in traditional bank liabilities), it is clear in hindsight that the focus of Basel capital requirements over the prior 30 years has been misplaced. Somewhat surprisingly, rather than the Basel Committee providing a mea culpa, its response has been to offer a new set of rules and guidelines that, in many ways, mirror the previous two attempts.

6.3 BASEL III AND THE DODD-FRANK WALL STREET REFORM AND CONSUMER PROTECTION ACT OF 2010

The financial crisis of 2007 to 2009 was very much a combination of financial firm insolvency (i.e., capital shortfalls) and funding liquidity (or lack thereof), especially in the shadow banking system. Section 6.2 showed that existing regulation, in particular Basel's capital adequacy standards, were more a cause of than a cure for systemic risk problems. The question is whether the Dodd-Frank Act and more generally Basel III are a sufficient step forward to make the financial system more safe and sound without stifling financial innovation.

Consider first the Dodd-Frank Act. As part of the broad mandate given to regulators, the Act calls for stricter prudential standards for systemically important institutions.[6] Moreover, these standards should be increasing in stringency based on factors such as leverage, off-balance-sheet exposures, amount of short-term funding, interconnectedness, and so on.[7] One glaring omission is any direct reference to the comovement of an individual firm's assets with the aggregate financial sector in a crisis. (See Chapter 4, "Measuring Systemic Risk," for an analysis of this issue.)

These additional standards may include:

(A) *risk-based capital requirements;* (B) *leverage limits;* (C) *liquidity requirements;* (D) *resolution plan and credit exposure report requirements;* (E) *concentration limits;* (F) *a contingent capital requirement;* (G) *enhanced public disclosures;* (H) *short-term debt limits; and* (I) *overall risk management requirements.*[8]

Of the nine recommendations for stricter regulation, note that five include additional capital, contingent capital, or liquidity requirements. The basic idea is that, to the extent these stricter standards impose costs on financial firms, these firms will have an incentive to avoid them and therefore be less systemically risky. While the underlying premise is promising from purely a systemic risk viewpoint, our concern is that these standards may not be sufficient to get financial firms to internalize the costs of the systemic risk produced. (See Chapter 5, "Taxing Systemic Risk.")

Also, the details are, perhaps rightly so, left to the regulators. While the Act's recommendations will be implemented later by the Federal Reserve, it is clear that bank holding companies with more than $50 billion in assets, or systemically important nonbank financial companies (as assigned by the Financial Stability Oversight Council), will be subject to these as-yet-unknown additional capital and liquidity adequacy standards.[9]

A reasonable conclusion from Section 6.2's analysis of the financial crisis is that capital and liquidity requirements, especially in their current Basel form, will simply not be sufficient to mitigate systemic risk. The primary reason is that they do not take account of systemic risk. Furthermore, in their current implementations, capital requirements can be readily gamed. So to some extent the financial system must rely on the power and supervisory expertise of the regulator.

That said, it does seem to be the case that some significant improvements are possible by (1) closing major capital loopholes, and (2) relying less on rating agencies. With respect to the loopholes, a good rule of thumb is that if off-balance-sheet financing is effectively a recourse to the banks, then the capital at risk should be treated as such. Moreover, counterparty credit risk exposures to financial firms, including OTC derivatives and securities financing transactions, should also be taken into account. While Basel II did expand the notion of risk for financial institutions, in hindsight the accord chose simplicity over accuracy in the determination of how capital should be treated. As for the reliance on ratings, it seems reasonable to consider not only the credit risk of defaultable assets (as defined by rating agencies), but also liquidity (funding and market) and specification risks.

The Dodd-Frank Act does make considerable progress on these fronts by:

- Addressing the conflict of interest inherent in the rating agency business model and the government's regulatory reliance on ratings (HR 4173, Title IX, "Investor Protection and Improvements to the Regulation of Securities," Subtitle C, "Improvements to the Regulation of Credit Rating Agencies"). (See Chapter 15, "Regulation of Rating Agencies.")
- Including off-balance-sheet activities in computing capital requirements (HR 4173, Title I, Subtitle C, "Additional Board of Governors Authority for Certain Nonbank Financial Companies and Bank Holding Companies," Sec. 165, "Enhanced supervision and prudential standards for nonbank financial companies supervised by the Board of Governors and certain bank holding companies").
- With respect to derivatives: (1) requiring margin requirements that are centrally cleared or over-the-counter, (2) reporting to data repositories and real-time price-volume transparency, and (3) providing authority for prudential regulators to consider setting position limits and penalizing engaging in derivatives whose purpose is "evasive" (see Chapter 13, "Regulating OTC Derivatives").

Missing from the Dodd-Frank Act, however, is any recognition (except in the case of OTC derivatives) that, once these standards are imposed on one set of financial institutions, financial activity most likely will move elsewhere in the financial system to firms not subject to these standards. Of course, this reallocation would not be a problem if the systemic risk is reduced by separating it from core functions of financial intermediaries. The recent financial crisis, however, tells a different tale, as much of the systemic risk emerged from the shadow banking system, which is both less regulated and less subject to capital and liquidity requirements, albeit with weaker government guarantees.

Does Basel III fare any better?

In December 2009, the Basel Committee offered a set of proposals to "strengthen the resilience of the banking sector," which formed the basis for the ongoing Basel III process. Later in July 2010, these proposals were reworked and signed by almost all the countries represented in the Basel process. Before outlining the broad strokes of the Basel III agreement, it is helpful to briefly review the earlier accords, as Basel III works iteratively off these.

The purpose of the Basel Accords is to provide a common risk-based assessment of bank assets and required capital levels. Basel I separated assets into categories and gave risk weights ranging from 0 percent to 100 percent to each category. The risk-weighted assets are calculated by multiplying the sum of the assets in each category by these risk weights. Banks then should hold a minimum ratio of 8 percent of capital to risk-weighted assets (see Elliott 2010). Because the risk analysis of Basel I was quite crude, Basel II refined this by (1) adding further gradation of risk categories,[10] (2) allowing for internal (and more sophisticated) risk models, and (3) incorporating value-at-risk-based capital charges for trading books. Even with the apparent improvements of Basel II, LCFIs, armed with their too-big-to-fail funding advantage, easily exploited the conflict of interests of rating agencies, played off external versus internal risk models, and minimized value at risk, though not systemic risk. Arguably, because the Basel II approach measured individual bank risk but ignored systemic risk (the primary rationale for bank regulation), and in addition did not address the fragility that was developing on the bank liability side in the form of uninsured wholesale deposit funding, the financial sector is in the poor shape it is in today.

Unfortunately, while Basel III tries to correct some of these areas, the basic approach to regulation is essentially a follow-on to Basel II. Specifically, Basel III (1) is stricter on what constitutes capital, (2) introduces a minimum leverage ratio and, to be determined, higher capital requirements (possibly countercyclical in nature), and (3) creates liquidity ratios that banks will eventually have to abide by. With respect to systemic risk—the real issue at hand—the July 2010 Basel Committee report states that the Committee will "undertake further development of the 'guided discretion' approach as one possible mechanism for integrating the capital surcharge into the Financial Stability Board's initiative for addressing systemically important financial institutions. Contingent capital could also play a role in meeting any systemic surcharge requirements." One would think systemic risk *should* be the primary focus of the regulatory guidelines.

However, taken at face value, the Dodd-Frank Act is stronger on this point. And similar to Basel I and II, and for that matter the Dodd-Frank Act, neither shadow banking nor regulatory arbitrage is the spotlight of Basel III. Putting aside these criticisms, which we believe to be of the utmost importance, the next three subsections look at the specifics of capital requirements, liquidity requirements, and capital definitions that can be found in the Dodd-Frank Act and Basel III. The section thereafter explores contingent capital and its potential use as a systemic surcharge to capital requirements.

Capital Requirements

On the one hand, the financial crisis of 2007 to 2009 exposed flaws with using minimum capital ratios based on risk-weighted assets. It is easy for LCFIs to game these weights. On the other hand, it is economically sensible to measure the risk of the assets and use these in determining the capital risk. In an attempt to balance these contrasting views, both the Dodd-Frank Act and Basel III provide explicit minimum leverage ratios (capital over total assets) along with minimum capital ratios (capital over risk-weighted assets). Specifically, the Dodd-Frank Act states:

> *The appropriate Federal banking agencies shall establish minimum leverage (and risk-based) capital requirements on a consolidated basis for insured depository institutions, depository institution holding companies, and nonbank financial companies supervised by the Board of Governors. The minimum leverage (and risk-based) capital requirements established under this paragraph shall not be less than the generally applicable leverage (and risk-based) capital requirements, which shall serve as a floor for any capital requirements that the agency may require, nor quantitatively lower than the generally applicable leverage (and risk-based) capital requirements that were in effect for insured depository institutions as of the date of enactment of this Act.*[11]

In other words, the risk-based capital and leverage capital ratios applicable to Federal Deposit Insurance Corporation (FDIC)–insured depository institutions will be applied to bank holding companies and systemically important institutions. Since these ratios represent a minimum standard, other regulatory guidelines, such as Basel III, could still be viable as long as their rules were stricter. Table 6.2 provides the current ratios for depository institutions. Of some note, these requirements are to be enacted within 18 months, though small institutions are generally exempt. It is also the case that to the extent a financial institution is deemed systemically important, the Federal Reserve may also exempt that institution if the capital and leverage requirements are not appropriate.

While the definitions of capital in the Dodd-Frank Act and Basel III don't perfectly coincide (so the comparison is not perfect), the proposed leverage ratio in Basel III is actually lower (i.e., 3 percent). The Dodd-Frank

TABLE 6.2 Capital Adequacy Standards (Dodd-Frank Act)

	Well Capitalized	Adequately Capitalized
Tier 1 (risk-based capital ratio)	6%	4%
Total (risk-based capital ratio)	10	8
Leverage ratio	5	4

Act goes further still by requiring that bank holding companies with at least $50 billion in assets or systemically important institutions "maintain a debt to equity ratio of no more than 15 to 1 (or a leverage ratio of at least 6.5 percent), upon a determination by the Council that such company poses a grave threat to the financial stability of the United States and that the imposition of such requirement is necessary to mitigate the risk that such company poses to the financial stability of the United States."[12]

In terms of capital requirements, comparing Basel II to Table 6.2, note that the current Basel II total capital ratio of 8 percent is expected to increase under Basel III. Currently, there has been no agreement to what the increase would be, though the final decision is slated for the fall of 2010. Nevertheless, given Basel III's new requirements, it might be reasonable to assume that U.S. bank holding companies will face even higher requirements than Table 6.2 shows.

Along with the possible recommendation for more stringent capital requirements for systemically important financial institutions, the Act explicitly calls for additional capital requirements for depository institutions, bank holding companies, and systemically important nonbank financial companies that address systemic risk arising from "(i) significant volumes of activity in derivatives, securitized products purchased and sold, financial guarantees purchased and sold, securities borrowing and lending, and repurchase agreements and reverse repurchase agreements; (ii) concentrations in assets for which the values presented in financial reports are based on models rather than historical cost or prices deriving from deep and liquid two-way markets; and (iii) concentrations in market share for any activity that would substantially disrupt financial markets if the institution is forced to unexpectedly cease the activity."[13]

One specific, and generally sensible, rule that appears in both the Dodd-Frank Act and Basel III is that "in establishing capital regulations . . . , the Board shall seek to make such requirements countercyclical, so that the amount of capital required to be maintained by a company increases in times of economic expansion and decreases in times of economic contraction, consistent with the safety and soundness of the company."[14] While Basel III is currently short on specifics, it is clear that countercyclical capital adequacy standards will be a key component.

In terms of the underlying economics of capital requirements, as a crisis approaches and financial firms begin to struggle to meet their regulatory minimum, these firms are forced to sell assets and/or raise capital. Of course, the firms are being forced to take these actions, such as fire sales, during the least advantageous times, thus increasing the risk of a liquidity spiral. Countercyclical capital requirements will mitigate this problem; however, there is a drawback of having time-varying capital buffers. The incentive for financial institutions to shift risk is greatest when asset volatility or leverage is at its highest. Asset volatility tends to be very countercyclical—high in a crisis, low in normal times. Thus, if capital requirements are relaxed in a crisis, financial firms will have an even greater incentive to take excessive risk.

To summarize, the Dodd-Frank Act provides substantial leeway for the regulator to impose additional capital requirements on systemically important institutions. Regardless of how this will be implemented, the Act requires LCFIs to have a floor for their leverage ratio and capital ratio at least consistent with insured depository institutions. The capital ratio is expected to be countercyclical, so it will be higher than the floor in good times. While the Act's capital adequacy standards are reasonable and a step forward toward financial reform, the Act still suffers from two problems.

The first is that there is a general belief at the outset that higher capital requirements are quite costly. While this ultimately depends on the definition of capital, define for the moment capital as equity capital. The most basic theorem in finance (Modigliani and Miller 1958, hereafter denoted as M&M) shows that the value of the firm's assets will be independent of how those assets are financed; in other words, choosing investments should be based on whether the return on the project's assets exceeds the cost of capital for those assets. Increasing the return on equity via leverage is just a wash. Given that the systemic costs to leverage are so high, this suggests that higher capital requirements will not be so socially costly. (See Miller 1995.)

While M&M is not reality, it is a useful starting point. The implication is that if M&M doesn't hold, we need to look at its underlying assumptions, such as no taxes; no agency, bankruptcy, or transaction costs; and no limits to arbitrage. Putting aside the tax benefits of debt, the issue of how costly it is to raise equity mostly depends on whether one believes the agency problems of LCFIs are due primarily to conflicts of interest between shareholders and managers, or to conflicts between shareholders and creditors/regulators.[15] With respect to the risk-taking incentives of financial firms, much of the focus by policymakers both here and abroad has been on the type and level of compensation within financial firms. It has been argued that in the period leading up to the crisis bankers were increasingly paid through short-term cash bonuses based on volume and on marked-to-market profits, rather than on the long-term profitability of their bets. Coupled with the fact that shareholders of the failed (or near failed) institutions lost most of their equity value, policymakers see this as prima facie evidence of massive failure of corporate governance at the equity level (i.e., between shareholders and managers). While clearly this view cannot be completely discounted, we believe it is second-order. A review of the theory and evidence suggests that shareholders were for the most part aligned with managers. (See Chapter 17, "Reforming Compensation and Corporate Governance.")

So why do banks fight so hard against capital requirements? That is, why is equity financing so much more costly than debt financing? The most plausible argument is that the main conflict of interest is between shareholders and creditors, and due to the existence of mispriced government guarantees, the true source of conflict is between shareholders and taxpayers. Fixing this problem (i.e., charging for the guarantees and systemic risk) is tantamount to charging for higher leverage, which will in turn put the cost of capital for debt and for equity on equal footing. Without correction of the mispricing of deposit insurance or the too-big-to-fail guarantee, LCFIs will have an incentive to lever up by borrowing at government-subsidized rates and investing in spread (or carry) trades.

The fact that neither the Dodd-Frank Act nor Basel III tries to investigate the question of why equity financing is more costly than debt financing is rather disappointing. This would seem to be the first step in developing a new framework for capital requirements.

The second point is whether leverage can really be measured at the institutional level. As we pointed out earlier in the chapter, the recent crisis has exposed significant problems with capital requirements as Wall Street firms consistently exploited loopholes to get around them. While we described in detail how leverage was artificially reduced through off-balance-sheet financing (see Acharya, Schnabl, and Suarez 2009), there are numerous other examples:

- It is now well documented that a number of firms, Lehman Brothers in particular, used an accounting loophole with certain repo transactions, Repo 105s, to temporarily reduce reported leverage (Lehman Brothers Chapter 11 Proceedings, 2010). In brief, Repo 105s allowed Lehman to treat repo transactions as sales, which in turn allowed the cash from the sales to temporarily pay down liabilities for reporting purposes, only to repurchase back the assets after the reports were released. At some points during the crisis, Lehman's Repo 105 activities reduced reported leverage by as much as $50 billion. (See Chapter 11, "The Repurchase Agreement (Repo) Market," for a detailed analysis.)
- On the flip side, firms can arbitrarily decrease their leverage through overstating of asset values or delaying recognition of losses (Huizinga and Laeven 2009).
- In an April 2010 report, the New York Federal Reserve Bank documented that over the period December 2008 to March 2010 the 18 largest banks reduced their net short-term borrowings in the repo market just before their quarterly reporting, only to ramp up immediately after. The numbers are startling—the debt levels used to fund these securities fall an average of 42 percent at the end of the quarter relative to the peak during the next quarter.

When one takes into account the added complexity of OTC derivatives, the issue of hedging, and challenges with respect to the measurement of risk-weighted assets, the question of how to think about and then measure leverage is nontrivial. Again, like the conclusions with regard to the first point, the existing framework seems flawed and would suggest a new paradigm.

One interesting idea has been put forth by Geanakoplos (2009). He argues that the current crisis is just a manifestation of what he calls the leverage cycle. While part of his framework calls for the government to manage these cycles, one of his main points is that legislation should focus on collateral underlying each transaction. In other words, rather than try to regulate firm leverage—and we have seen that this is difficult to do—he argues that leverage, in other words margins, should be legislated at the transaction or security level. While this brings up the question of how to treat transactions used for hedging risk as opposed to risk taking, it seems a fruitful area to study. In fact, one can view the legislative debate on OTC derivatives as such an exercise. (See Chapter 13, "Regulating OTC Derivatives.")

Liquidity Requirements

As described in Section 6.1 of this chapter, financial distress arises not just from capital risk but also from liquidity risk. The financial crisis of 2007 to 2009 shows that liquidity risk deserves equal footing. The problem arises because regulated institutions as well as their unregulated siblings have fragile capital structures in that they hold assets with long-term duration or low liquidity but their liabilities are highly short-term in nature. Arguably, the current crisis went pandemic when there was a run on the investment banks and money market funds after Lehman Brothers failed.

One solution is to impose liquidity requirements on financial institutions that are similar in spirit to the way capital requirements are imposed, with the intention of reducing runs. The basic idea would be to require that a proportion of the short-term funding must be in liquid assets—assets that can be sold immediately in quantity at current prices. This requirement might be sufficient to prevent runs as it will in effect increase the cost of financial institutions taking on carry trades and holding long-term asset-backed securities.

While the Dodd-Frank Act explicitly calls for the regulator to take into account "the amount and types of the liabilities of the company, including the degree of reliance on short-term funding" in setting prudential standards for systemically important institutions, and for these standards to include among others "liquidity requirements" and "short-term debt limits," there are no other specifics. These are left to the Federal Reserve and other regulators. It is reasonable to infer, however, that the U.S. regulators will look to the new liquidity requirements as part of Basel III.

The original December 2009 proposal in Basel III outlined two new ratios that financial institutions would be subject to:

1. *Liquidity coverage ratio (LCR):* the ratio of a bank's high-quality liquid assets (i.e., cash, government securities, etc.) to its net cash outflows over a 30-day time period (i.e., outflows in retail deposits, wholesale funding, etc.) during a severe systemwide shock.[16] This ratio should exceed 100 percent.
2. *Net stable funding ratio (NSFR):* the ratio of the bank's available amount of stable funding (i.e., its capital, longer-term liabilities, and stable short-term deposits) over its required amount of stable funding (i.e., value of assets held multiplied by a factor representing the asset's liquidity). This ratio should exceed 100 percent.

While there was broad agreement on the need for liquidity requirements, it is not clear when these requirements will be implemented or what the precise rules will be. For example, the push-back by the banking sector led to the NSFR being delayed until January 1, 2018.

Nevertheless, the introduction of the LCR and NSFR as prudential standards has merit. Consider the example of the supersenior AAA-rated tranches of collateralized debt obligations (CDOs) relative to a more standard AAA-rated marketable security (say, a corporate bond). Specifically, assume that the probability and magnitude of losses (i.e., the expected mean and variance) associated with default are similar between the two classes of securities. What are the implications of LCR and NSFR on these holdings?

Liquidity risk refers to the ability of the holder to convert the security or asset into cash. Even before the crisis started, the supersenior tranches were considered to be less liquid than standard marketable securities and more of a hold-to-maturity type of security. The fact that these securities offered a spread should not be surprising, given that there are numerous documentations of a price to illiquidity. For instance, consider the well-documented spread between the off-the-run and on-the-run Treasuries (Krishnamurthy 2002). The LCR would most likely count the AAA-rated CDO less favorably in terms of satisfying liquidity risk.

Funding risk refers to the mismatch in the maturity of the assets and liabilities. There is a tendency for financial institutions to hold long-term assets using cheap short-term funding, a kind of carry trade. But this exposes the institution to greater risk of a run if short-term funding evaporates during a crisis. Indeed, some researchers have argued for capital requirements to take into account this particular funding risk (see Geneva Report 2009).

These two points suggest that it would be useful to know the liquid assets the financial institution holds against short-term funding. One could imagine that the higher the ratio, the less an institution is subject to a liquidity shock, and therefore the less risky it is. The NSFR would help answer this question, and again would be less favorable for the AAA-rated CDO versus the AAA-rated marketable security.

That liquidity risk is now at the forefront of Basel III, and presumably future financial regulation in the United States as a result of the Dodd-Frank Act, is clearly a step forward. The LCR and NSFR liquidity adequacy standards are reasonable approaches toward the regulation of liquidity risk. For example, the focus of the LCR on a systemwide stress scenario is the appropriate way to think about the systemic consequences of holding less liquid assets and/or funding those assets with short-term liabilities.

That said, the approach is eerily similar to that of Basel I, II, and III for setting capital requirements. All the adjustment factors and weights used in calculating the LCR and NSFR have their counterpart in the risk weights of capital ratios. Without a doubt, implementation of the liquidity ratios will push banks toward regulatory arbitrage of the liquidity weights—in particular, to the *best-treated* illiquid securities and systemically risky funding. The unintended consequence will then be a concentration into these activities. Regulators should be acutely aware of this problem and be prepared ex ante to adapt in an expedited way.

The other problem is that the liquidity rules do not seem to take into account the impact a liquidity crisis at one bank has on the financial sector as a whole, especially in a crisis. In other words, banks that contribute more to systemwide liquidity events (in a crisis) should be charged for this negative externality, similar to the arguments we provided in Chapter 5, "Taxing Systemic Risk."

Finally, though now sounding like a broken record, regulators need to be aware that once the LCR and NSFR are imposed on a subset of financial institutions, then these activities will migrate to a part of the financial sector not subject to these requirements. A central theme of this book, and certainly this chapter, is that regulators need to look at the financial system in the aggregate. To the extent systemically risky short-term funding remains in the financial sector, this may have to be ring-fenced away from investing in illiquid assets.

What Is Capital?

New capital requirements (and for that matter liquidity requirements, too) raise the question of how to measure a financial institution's capital. A bird's-eye view of regulatory capital is that it represents the buffer against a decline in the value of a firm's assets against its obligations. Thus, one common definition of capital is that it does not contain a significant debt feature, such as a commitment for future repayment—common equity being the obvious example.

Both the Dodd-Frank Act and Basel III take another look at the question of what constitutes capital for the purpose of setting capital and liquidity standards. In particular, Tier 1 capital would no longer include innovative hybrid securities, such as the popular trust preferred securities (TruPSs). More generally, the Act suggests that "the Comptroller General of the United States, in consultation with the Board of Governors, the Comptroller of the Currency, and the Corporation, shall conduct a study of the use of hybrid capital instruments as a component of Tier 1 capital for banking institutions and bank holding companies."[17]

Basel III provides even greater detail. The rules also exclude hybrid securities as part of Tier 1 capital, but, in general, go further. For example, Basel III will allow only a fraction (e.g., 15 percent) of Tier 1 capital to include such items as equity investments in other financial institutions, mortgage servicing rights, and deferred tax assets.

Rather than describe all the specific details of Basel III, let us consider TruPSs as a case study of the new rules. Trust preferred securities (TruPSs) are hybrid securities that have both debt and equity characteristics. The holding company (usually a bank holding company) issues junior subordinated debt to a trust, which then issues preferred securities. The bank holding company has 100 percent ownership of the trust and usually guarantees the interest and principal payments of the TruPSs. Supervisory concerns regarding prudent risk-management practices have led regulators to reconsider the inclusion of TruPSs as part of Tier 1 capital. (The appendix at the end of this chapter provides a detailed description and economic analysis of TruPSs, especially with respect to the financial crisis of 2007 to 2009.)

The regulatory consensus has been that TruPSs, which have significant debt attributes, do not have the necessary characteristics required for securities included in Tier 1 capital. However, a major concern for regulators has been how to phase out TruPSs from Tier 1 capital while not drastically reducing banks' ability to raise capital as they unwind these positions. The approach has been to grandfather these securities and give banks a transition period to phase out existing TruPSs.

The Dodd-Frank Act requires banks to phase out the use of TruPSs as part of Tier 1 capital. It gives banks with more than $100 billion in capital up to five years to phase out these securities and up to 10 years for institutions with capital between $15 billion and $100 billion. As a compromise, the amendment exempts small banks with capital less than $15 billion and allows them to continue to treat existing TruPSs on the balance sheet as Tier 1 capital. Any new trust preferred securities issued by all banks will be excluded from Tier 1 capital. In terms of magnitude, Moody's Investors Service estimates that in total nearly $118 billion of TruPSs will be disqualified from Tier 1 treatment across all bank holding companies (Reuters 2010).

TruPSs are an interesting example of the kind of capital banks would like to hold from a private standpoint, debtlike in principle but accounted for as capital for regulatory purposes. It begs the question of whether bank capital is socially costly or only privately costly for bank shareholders. A proposal that has recently been floated, called "contingent capital," concerns a hybrid claim that is economically like debt in good times but automatically converts into an equity claim in bad times (for the bank and/or for the system as a whole). We discuss its usefulness as a form of bank capital in the next section.

6.4 CONTINGENT CAPITAL: A SOLUTION?

Contingent capital (often referred to as reverse contingent convertible bonds or CoCo bonds) constitutes a form of uninsured debt that converts automatically into equity when certain prespecified triggers are hit. In terms of requiring banks, and especially systemically important ones, to hold additional capital, this appears to be one of the preferred routes taken by regulators in Canada and the United Kingdom. For example, Lloyds Bank, which is owned by the UK government, issued such capital in November 2009 as part of its capital-raising program, whereby whenever its Tier 1 capital ratio falls sufficiently low, this debt will convert to equity (refer to Box 6.1). Rabobank issued similar contingent capital in March 2010 (refer to Box 6.2). Discussions have been held between the Federal Reserve and the banking industry to introduce slivers of such contingent capital in the U.S. banks.

Contingent capital is designed to facilitate a transfer of losses when a firm's equity is being depleted by converting some debt into equity, thereby ensuring that the bank still maintains a sufficient level of capitalization. When equity prices are falling sharply, management and shareholders try to avoid recapitalization since most of the new capital injected creates value only for the creditors of the firm. Moreover, the new capital is costly and dilutes existing shareholders, who may force a management turnover. In fact, the managers may lose, too, if they are compensated in equity. Thus, left to its own devices, the firm's management would prefer to wait, hoping that the good times will return soon. A possible solution to the agency problems is to convert some of the firm's debt into equity. However, once distress has materialized, no creditor would want to convert without extracting a pound of flesh. And in case the firm is systemically important, the creditors may prefer to simply follow the path of least resistance, that is, allow the firm to get distressed so that regulators have little choice but to backstop the debt of the firm and pass on the costs to taxpayers. In the case of LCFIs, there are additional contingent creditors such as derivatives counterparties. In essence, any expedient resolution is ruled out unless it is prepackaged in the design of the firm's debt and equity.

Contingent capital forces banks facing a deteriorating credit quality to recapitalize in a prearranged manner, thereby lowering the point of default. Imposing losses on creditors would partially restore market lending discipline and lower the point of default, thereby reducing the need for regulatory forbearance, which in turn would reduce the too-big-to-fail or the too-interconnected-to-fail problem.

Contingent capital can thus be understood as a step (i.e., a part of a living will arrangement; see Chapter 8, "Resolution Authority") toward orderly winding down or resolution of a firm that is likely to be distressed in the near future by forcing some of its debt—in a prearranged manner—into equity, and effectively postponing or preempting default.

BOX 6.1   LLOYDS BANK ISSUE OF ENHANCED CAPITAL NOTES

In November 2009, Lloyds Bank issued £5.5 billion of contingent capital. These securities, called enhanced capital notes (ECNs), are debt securities that convert to common equity when the bank's Tier 1 capital ratio falls to 5 percent. The ECN issue was intended to inject much-needed capital and to avoid the government taking larger stakes in the company.

The issue was significantly oversubscribed and the bank decided to increase the issue amount from the initial £5.5 billion to £7.0 billion. Vermaelen and Wolff (2010), however, point out that the Lloyds Bank CoCo bond issue was an exchange offer wherein investors in the ECN received 1.5 percent to 2.5 percent of additional coupon income in exchange for senior capital. Additionally, while European Union rules restricted payments to hybrid capital securities for firms receiving financial aid, the newly issued ECNs were not subject to such restrictions. In effect, hybrid security holders who were eligible for the exchange offer had the choice of either forgoing income or switching to the ECNs. It is unclear how markets would have reacted in the absence of such incentive.

Issuer	Lloyds TSB Bank/Lloyds Banking Group
Status and Ranking	Direct, unsecured, and subordinated obligations of the relevant issuer and rank pari passu
Maturity	10, 12, or 15 years depending on existing security exchanged for
Interest	Premium of between 1.5 percent and 2.5 percent above the interest rate or dividend rate
Trigger Event	Bank's Tier 1 capital ratio falls to 5 percent
Conversion Price	At market price of stock when trigger is hit

Source: Lloyds Banking Group (2009).

BOX 6.2 RABOBANK ISSUE OF SENIOR CONTINGENT NOTES

In March 2010, Rabobank issued €1.25 billion of benchmark 10-year fixed-rate senior contingent notes (SCNs). The securities were priced at an annual coupon of 6.875 percent. The issue was more than twice oversubscribed at €2.6 billion.

The SCNs convert to equity when the equity capital ratio falls below 7 percent. Unlike the Lloyds Bank ECNs, the Rabobank SCNs, when triggered, convert to 75 percent of original principal. Conversion is based on market value but at a discount, making it antidilutive. The Rabobank bond can be thought of as a catastrophe bond (cat bond), which when triggered transfers the risk from the issuer to the investor.

Issuer	Rabobank Nederland
Status and Ranking	Senior unsecured—ranking senior to all subordinated (Tier 2 and Tier 1) capital of the issuer
Maturity	5/10-year bullet—March 2015/2020
Interest	Fixed rate 6.875 percent paid annually
Trigger Event	Equity capital ratio is less than 7 percent
Conversion Price	To 75 percent of the original principal amount plus accrued and unpaid interest

Source: Rabobank Group (2010).

The Dodd-Frank Act

As described in Section 6.3, the Dodd-Frank Act calls for the possible issuance of contingent capital as an additional standard for systemically important institutions. The Act charges that:

> *The Council shall conduct a study of the feasibility, benefits, costs, and structure of a contingent capital requirement for nonbank financial companies supervised by the Board of Governors and bank holding companies . . . , which study shall include—(A) an evaluation of the degree to which such requirement would enhance the safety and soundness of companies subject to the requirement, promote the financial stability of the United States, and reduce risks to United States taxpayers; (B) an evaluation of the characteristics and amounts of contingent capital that should be required; (C) an analysis of potential prudential standards that should be used to determine whether the contingent capital of a company would be converted to equity in times of financial stress; (D) an evaluation of the costs to companies, the effects on the structure and operation of credit and other financial markets, and other economic effects of requiring contingent capital; (E) an evaluation of the effects of such requirement on the international competitiveness of companies subject to the requirement and the prospects for international coordination in establishing such requirement; and (F) recommendations for implementing regulations.*[18]

The Act requires the Council to submit the recommendation report within two years of passing the Act. Depending on the recommendations submitted to Congress, after allowing for an appropriate transition period, the Board of Governors may then require bank holding companies and nonfinancial institutions to "maintain a minimum amount of contingent capital that is convertible to equity in times of financial stress."

By restoring some market discipline and reducing the likelihood of default of financial firms when adverse shocks materialize, contingent capital can be a valuable tool for averting the need to bail out systemically important firms. But in our opinion, there are some important limitations that must be borne in mind. These include: (1) its ability to limit ex ante risk taking and buildup of systemic risk; (2) its usefulness in dealing with distress when complex contingent and off-balance-sheet liabilities characterize a financial firm's balance sheet; (3) its relative attractiveness to standard capital and liquidity requirements; and (4) the limitations to coming up with an international standard of bank regulation tied to contingent capital.

First, the primary purpose of contingent capital seems to be to avoid a regulatory bailout ex post. Its ability to control bank risk taking in good times is, however, limited. In such times, banks can—as they have in the past—take bets on the tail risk of the economy by selling deep out-of-the-money options, such as AIG writing credit default swaps on mortgage and corporate portfolios, Citigroup's selling of undercapitalized liquidity puts to conduits, and large holdings of AAA-rated tranches by investment banks, Fannie and Freddie, and other LCFIs. A property of taking on such tail risk is that the only outcomes possible are boom or bust, and the intermediate region of risky outcomes over which contingent capital might have some bite is essentially rendered rather unlikely or inconsequential. Such tail-risk seeking would likely have to be addressed through means other than pure reliance on a contingent capital requirement.

It is also important to recognize that the real problem is not between unsecured creditors and bank shareholders, but between the government and uninsured capital providers. While resolution plans can be designed to limit the extent of government transfers to uninsured capital providers, some such transfers will necessarily arise in future, especially if firms experience abrupt distress due to the tail nature of their risks (as explained earlier). The moral hazard arising from such transfers is best addressed by imposing a fee—possibly countercyclical—that is based on systemic risk contributions of individual institutions. Unless banks are appropriately charged for losses they impose on the system during aggregate crises, they will not internalize these losses. Thus, we recommend that in addition to contingent capital and resolution plans, an explicit fee be charged to banks in good times based on their expected losses and their systemic risk contributions (measured as described in Chapter 4, "Measuring Systemic Risk"; implementation of the fee is explained in Chapter 5, "Taxing Systemic Risk").

Second, we believe that contingent capital is not adequate even for containment of ex post distress in all contingencies, especially in the form it is proposed whereby there will be a one-time conversion of part of a firm's debt into equity. If instead, and depending on how deteriorated the conditions are, there was a requirement of progressive conversion of debt into equity all the way down the capital structure of financial firms, then indeed all firm losses could eventually be passed on to creditors. Such progressive conversion could be a part of the firm's living will or resolution plan. (See Chapter 8, "Resolution Authority.") Nevertheless, we envision several scenarios in which, before such a plan can be fully executed, some counterparty risk or large-scale liquidation risk may arise, necessitating receivership or bankruptcy of some form. In other words, we should not rule out yet the possibility that there will be systemic crises in the future that, for lack of any other choice, involve bailouts of certain systemically important financial firms. Furthermore, some part of bank debt is explicitly insured, and this debt cannot be converted to equity ex post.

Thus, without progressive debt-for-equity conversion, contingent capital does not fully address the fact that beneath both contingent capital and equity capital of banks lies a significant portion of debt—deposits, secured debt (repos), noncontingent debt of other types, liabilities to derivatives transactions—that will remain explicitly and, in some cases, implicitly guaranteed by governments. The cost of such debt in good times will not reflect the true risks of banks, and as long as this is true, both contingent capital and equity capital will find it desirable to undertake excessive risks at the expense of guaranteed debt (taxpayer money). Moreover, the amounts of contingent capital being considered currently do not appear to be sufficiently large. Consider investment banks that were operating at leverage ratios of 25:1 to 35:1 in terms of debt to equity before many of them collapsed. With such leverage, even a small quantity of abrupt and adverse negative news about assets will be sufficient to wipe out equity capital and the slivers of contingent capital that are currently being talked about. Such leverage ratios need to be prudentially controlled at the outset.

Third, the attractiveness of contingent capital relative to the alternative of a leverage constraint needs to be evaluated. Indeed, another alternative to contingent capital is simply to increase equity or Tier 1 capital requirements, tying them to systemic risk contributions of firms. The usual argument against this is that demandable debt (bank notes or checking accounts) provides far more discipline on bankers—who can alter risks at fast speeds—than equity capital does. It is time to establish the magnitude of this assumed social cost of equity capital. For one, reliance on short-term debt for market discipline comes at a huge social cost of systemic financial fragility. Second, we have offered huge tax advantages to debt. And third, there are better mechanisms available for shareholder governance today than in times when demandable debt grew in fashion.

Put together, these arguments suggest that contingent capital is a part of the big puzzle of rewriting financial sector regulation, and needs to be complemented with other measures. Hence, we endorse the Act's recommendation that all aspects of contingent capital—its merits and limitations, individually and in relation to other possible (systemic) risk controls—be carefully evaluated. Every crisis is different and to the extent that contingent capital would not yet have stood the test of time when the next crisis hits, it seems prudent to combine it with other, more direct, ex ante risk-control measures such as fees based on systemic risk, direct leverage restrictions, or enhanced Tier 1 capital requirements.

Finally, contingent capital is likely to work well in developed countries with well-developed corporate bond markets, but is perhaps not feasible elsewhere. From this standpoint, too, some leverage restrictions or systemic-risk-based capital and liquidity requirements standards are more likely to emerge as international norms evolve.

Globally, countries have been divided on the issue of whether contingent capital is the right tool to deal with systemically important firms. While Europe and the United States have pushed for a bank tax, countries such as Canada have been promoting contingent capital as the right alternative. The Canadian alternative recommends that essentially all subordinated debt and preferred shares sold by banks have a conversion feature that would be triggered when a regulator determines that the firm is no longer viable. However, Canadian officials have conceded that many of the details regarding implementation and execution need to be ironed out before the contingent capital approach is feasible. The global consensus, as of now, seems to be that while contingent capital may help address some of the systemic problems posed by large financial institutions, international coordination will be required to ensure that financial institutions across countries have an equal competitive landscape. At the G-20 summit held in Toronto in June 2010, countries recommended that the Basel Committee consider the contingent capital option, and have left it to the Committee to determine the benefits and costs of including contingent capital as part of regulatory capital. What may in the end take the contingent capital proposal off the table altogether is the fact that bankers like it only if it is capital for regulatory purposes and debt for tax purposes, but with the conversion features being proposed, the tax deductibility of contingent capital is unlikely to be approved by the Internal Revenue Service (IRS) (and other national tax agencies).

Summary and Evaluation of Specific Contingent Capital Proposals

One key issue concerning the design of contingent capital is how the triggers are defined. The Lloyds issue in the United Kingdom includes a trigger based only on its own Tier 1 capitalization levels. In contrast, the current discussions at the Federal Reserve include not only an institution-level capitalization trigger, but also a systemwide trigger. To the extent that the purpose of contingent capital is to address *systemic* risk taking, rather than risk taking per se, it is economically more meaningful to employ a systemwide trigger. However, the systemwide trigger must be rule-based—for example, when the average Tier 1 ratios in the financial system fall below 5 percent, rather than at the discretion of regulators. If discretionary, the systemwide trigger when hit would convey severe adverse news to the market, causing a possible downward spiral. In contrast, a rule-based trigger would be well-anticipated and would avoid such consequences.

Another important issue concerning the design of contingent capital is whether the required capitalization below which conversion is triggered should be based on book measures of equity or market measures of equity. While market measures of equity are somewhat vulnerable to short squeezes and manipulative efforts, book measures of equity are somewhat under managerial discretion and often lag true capitalization of firms. On balance, we prefer the market-based trigger as it is likely to lead to more timely responses to distressed financial firms.

Finally, there is also the issue of whether the triggers should be based on equity market valuations or credit market signals. Again, there is an important trade-off between equity- and credit-based triggers: Equity is more likely to be wiped out even if the firm is bailed out, whereas credit-market signals such as credit default swap (CDS) premiums will be adversely affected if there is anticipated forbearance. However, CDS premiums are, by construction, market prices (and thus assessments) of tail events—in particular, default of the underlying firms. To this extent, they have the potential to better reflect the downside risks than do equity prices.

Broadly, existing proposals can be classified into three categories: contingent capital injection (the main scheme we have discussed so far), contingent capital insurance, and liability-enhanced equity. In contingent capital injections, debt is converted to equity when a trigger is hit, thereby recapitalizing firms when distressed. Contingent capital insurance schemes resemble disaster insurance and pay out when triggered by a systemic event. Liability-enhanced equity increases the liability associated with equity, thereby reducing the need for inefficient bailouts and also addressing the agency problems associated with debt.

We discuss each of these schemes in light of the issues concerning design of triggers. Table 6.3 provides a summary of the various schemes and their key features.

Contingent Capital Injection Most proposals fall under this category. Flannery (2005, 2009a, 2009b), Squam Lake Working Group (2009), and Duffie (2009) propose schemes based on reverse convertible debenture (RCD). RCD is essentially debt that converts into equity when triggered. The schemes differ on the type of trigger used. Some use rule-based triggers based on book or market values, whereas others prefer discretionary triggers based on aggregate market measures. Flannery (2005) suggests using the issuer's equity ratio based on the current market value as opposed to book values, which are biased upward for firms in distress and are thus not appropriate. However, as we mentioned earlier, a market-value-based trigger is subject to opportunistic manipulation by bondholders who can force conversion at low prices by shorting stocks at the expense of existing shareholders. Even in

TABLE 6.3 Summary of Specific Contingent Capital Proposals

Source	Type	Trigger	Equity/ Credit Market Trigger	Book/ Market Value Trigger	Drawback
I. Contingent Capital					
Duffie (2009)	1. Reverse convertible debenture (RCD)	1. Market value of equity	Equity	Market	Equity holders may demand excessive premiums in rights, limiting liquidity raised
	2. Mandated rights offering	2. Liquidity measures			
Flannery (2005)	Reverse convertible debenture	Market capital ratio	Equity	Market	Manipulation by bondholders
Flannery (2009a)	Contingent capital certificates (CCC)	Equity ratio. Fixed share premium conversion	Equity	Market	Dilutes the disciplining effect of debt
Flannery (2009b)	Contingent capital certificates (CCC)	Equity ratio	Equity	Market	Manipulation by bondholders
Hart and Zingales (2009)	Equity injection based on CDS prices	CDS prices and regulator discretion	Credit	Market	Regulator reluctance, death spiral
McDonald (2010)	Debt-to-equity conversion with double trigger	1. Stock price 2. Financial institution index	Equity	Market	Manipulation by bondholders

Squam Lake Working Group (2009)	Debt-to-equity conversion with double trigger	1. Systemic event determined by regulator 2. Bank capital adequacy measures	Equity	Book	Regulator reluctance, death spiral
Vermaelen and Wolff (2010)	Call option enhanced reverse convertible (COERC)	Market value based	Equity	Market	Dilutes disciplining effect of debt
II. Contingent Capital Insurance					
Acharya, Pedersen, Philippon, and Richardson (2010b)	Contingent capital insurance based on firm's losses in a systemic event	Aggregate market or financial institution index		Market	Counterparty risk of insurance sector
Kashyap, Rajan, and Stein (2008)	Contingent capital insurance based on risk-weighted asset value	Aggregate bank losses except covered bank		Book	Regulator reluctance
III. Liability-Enhanced Equity					
Acharya, Mehran, and Thakor (2010)	Liability-enhanced equity	Bankruptcy		Book	Liability increased only if firm has significant earnings
Admati and Pfleiderer (2009)	Liability-enhanced equity	Face value of liabilities		Book	Cumbersome to implement

the absence of such short selling, existing shareholders may sell their shares in the fear that other shareholders may do the same, thereby further pushing down stock prices. Such a self-fulfilling prophecy resulting in a rapid decline in prices is referred to as a death spiral. To address this, Flannery (2009a) suggests using a high conversion price, P, wherein each dollar of principal of debt is converted to $1/P$ shares. Further, the conversion trigger price of equity is set at a level lower than P. Thus, conversion is antidilutive and reduces the likelihood of manipulation.

One criticism of the Flannery proposal is that it reduces the disciplining effect of leverage since conversion is triggered regardless of whether there is a financial crisis. Thus, the threat of bankruptcy is not enough to discipline managers, as the firm is assured of recapitalization even when the firm is performing badly due to poor management. The Squam Lake Working Group (2009) proposal recommends conversion only in the case of a systemic event. The group proposes a double trigger scheme wherein conversion is triggered when there is a systemic event (determined by a regulator) and, in addition, the bank also breaches a covenant. The dual trigger ensures banks are recapitalized only in the event of a systemic crisis. The Group recommends triggers based on banks' capital adequacy measures as opposed to market values. However, since these may be subject to manipulation by management, conversion to a fixed number of shares is suggested. The Group argues that management will not intentionally force conversion unless stock prices are much lower than bond payments since conversion is to a fixed number of shares. Additionally, it also avoids the problem of a death spiral.

The declaration of a systemic crisis by regulators is fraught with political complications. McDonald (2010) suggests using predefined rules based on market values for both systemic and firm-level triggers. Debt to equity conversion takes place when both the bank's stock price and the financial institution index fall below minimum threshold values.

The RCD schemes just described dilute the original shareholders' equity ownership. Vermaelen and Wolff (2010) propose enhancing RCD with a call option to make them more palatable to existing equity holders. Call option enhanced reverse convertibles (COERCs) allow equity holders to pay back debt when conversion is triggered. The call option also makes these securities less susceptible to market manipulation by bondholders.

Duffie (2009) also suggests issuing a mandated rights offering that forces existing shareholders to invest in the firm at lower prices. The risk of a liquidity crisis is thus reduced since new cash is available to the firm when a rights offering is triggered. Bank runs are thus avoided since creditors assume that a liquidity crisis is unlikely. Due to the time lag between the rights offering and cash settlement, Duffie suggests using sufficiently high trigger levels based on cash liquidity measures.

While these schemes rely on the equity markets to signal a systemic event, Hart and Zingales (2009) suggest a credit-market-based trigger that forces firms to issue new equity when CDS prices rise above a threshold level. One advantage of this proposal is that tail contingencies might be better captured through credit market indicators such as credit default swap premiums, rather than equity markets. The rationale is simply that a CDS premium is the fee for insuring against a tail event—the risk of the firm defaulting—in contrast to equity, which is a relatively smooth claim not tied just to the firm's risk of default. Indeed, our research at NYU Stern (see Acharya, Pedersen, Philippon, and Richardson 2010a) suggests that CDS markets were far better than equity markets at capturing systemic risk—that is, predicting which firms will underperform when the market as a whole goes down—especially for insurance firms (e.g., see Chapter 9, "Systemic Risk and the Regulation of Insurance Companies").

Contingent Capital Insurance Contingent capital insurance is designed along the same lines as catastrophe bonds and is triggered when a systemic event occurs. Banks essentially buy insurance policies, which pay off in the event of a systemic crisis. The schemes differ based on the specific methods used to determine the fee charged by the insurers, the systemic event triggers, and who receives the insurance payoffs.

In the Kashyap, Rajan, and Stein (2008) proposal, financial institutions have the option of purchasing contingent capital insurance in exchange for lower regulatory capital requirements. Payout is triggered when a regulator declares a systemic event based on aggregate bank losses. To reduce the risk of default, insurers are required to set aside the payment amount at inception in a lockbox. Since aggregate measures are not based on market values, a death spiral is potentially avoided.

Acharya, Pedersen, Philippon, and Richardson (2010b) propose a tax based on a bank's own contribution to systemic risk. Taxes go to a regulator, and when a systemic event occurs the regulator determines which firms receive support—for instance, only solvent ones and those suffering from a spillover from the weak banks. Instead of an automatic recapitalization upon trigger, the proposal recommends regulators reward firms that take low aggregate risk, thereby getting firms to internalize their systemic risk contributions.

The two proposals are similar except that the Acharya, Pedersen, Philippon, and Richardson (2010b) proposal better addresses moral hazard by charging a firm for its *own* losses in a systemic risk event and by requiring that insurance payoffs do not go to the firm purchasing insurance but to a systemic regulator (or the taxpayers).

Liability-Enhanced Equity   Liability-enhanced equity increases the liability associated with equity. In this scheme, regulators effectively impose higher capital requirements. Additionally, the liability of equity addresses some of the firm-level agency problems associated with debt, such as risk shifting wherein equity holders benefit from excessive risk taking, and the debt-overhang problem wherein equity holders put off recapitalization when the firm is distressed.

The Admati and Pfleiderer (2009) proposal separates equity into unlimited liability equity and limited liability equity. Unlimited liability equity will need to fulfill all the obligations of debt, thus making debt risk-free. The unlimited liability equity is retained at the firm level. To back this unlimited liability equity, an equity liability carrier (ELC) is created. The role of the ELC is to ensure that the obligations of the unlimited liability equity will be fulfilled. The ELC holds limited liability equity as well as safe liquid assets. Only the limited liability equity is tradable in the market. The ELC is strictly regulated and funds can be transferred from the ELC to the financial institution only under limited conditions. Similarly, dividends and debt issuance are subject to constraints based on how well funded the ELC is.

While the Admati and Pfleiderer (2009) proposal reduces the need for inefficient liquidation, it does not specifically address recapitalization issues during a systemic crisis. Acharya, Mehran, and Thakor (2010) suggest building a buffer of safe assets by diverting dividends in good times to a special capital account. The special capital account is invested in safe assets such as Treasuries, which are transferred to a regulator when a bank goes bankrupt. That is, the special capital account cannot be levered up by the firm for risk-taking purposes. By requiring capital be built through dividend restrictions and resulting retained earnings in good times, this proposal addresses the tail-risk-seeking problem well. An institution selling deep out-of-the-money options in good times and collecting premiums faces restrictions on the distribution of these premiums as bonuses to employees and dividends to shareholders, effectively using the premiums as provisions for future losses, including systemically risky scenarios.

Both these proposals increase the liability of equity to downside risks, and can be enhanced to deal explicitly with systemic risk taking by making the extent of such equity liability contingent on some measure of systemic risk contribution of firms.

■ ■ ■

In summary, the three existing proposals for contingent capital style arrangements serve slightly different purposes. The contingent capital injection best deals with reducing ex post distress and bailout likelihood in a systemic crisis. The contingent capital insurance is better suited to getting firms to pay up front for their exposure to a systemic crisis. The equity liability schemes put restrictions on strategies that generate short-term carry for shareholders while dumping long-term risks on creditors and taxpayers. If designed well, they can all contribute to reduction of systemic risk in the financial sector.

However, in a world of imperfect information on the underlying structure of risks and actions of agents undertaking the risks, systemic risk triggers and contributions cannot be precisely measured or judiciously defined. Hence, from a standpoint of prudential regulation of systemic risk, the effectiveness of contingent capital proposals must itself be considered a risk, and therefore other mechanisms such as plain-vanilla leverage restrictions and capital requirements should be employed as safeguards.

APPENDIX: TRUST PREFERRED SECURITIES

The main advantages of using TruPSs are their favorable tax and accounting treatment. The interest paid by the issuing company is tax deductible since it appears as subordinated debt on the issuer's balance sheet. Essentially, in this structure, dividend payments of the preferred securities have been replaced by tax-deductible interest payments for the banks, thereby lowering the cost of capital.

A more important reason for their popularity, especially among bank holding companies, is their classification as Tier 1 capital. To qualify as Tier 1 capital, certain criteria need to be fulfilled, such as the security must allow for deferral for at least five consecutive years, and the loan issued by the trust must be subordinated debt and have the longest feasible maturity (a 30-year maturity usually suffices for this condition). In addition, to be qualified as Tier 1 capital the total amount of trust preferred capital and cumulative preferred shares cannot exceed 25 percent of the sum of all core capital, including restricted core capital elements, net of goodwill, less deferred tax liability (Salutric and Willcox 2009).

A major disadvantage of trust preferred securities is that they are costly to implement. As a result, the structure is usually more popular among bank holding companies, which can treat TruPSs as Tier 1 capital.

The Federal Reserve approved the inclusion of trust preferred stocks as Tier 1 capital in October 1996. Within a year of this announcement, nearly 100 banks had issued trust preferred securities (*ICBA Independent Banker* 2008). Figure 6.1 shows the growth of trust preferred securities since they were first allowed to be classified as Tier 1 capital in 1996 to the third quarter of 2007.

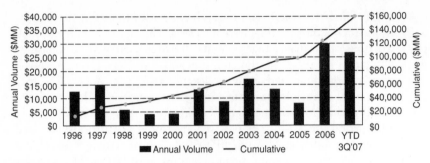

FIGURE 6.1 Trust Preferred Volume from 1996 to 3Q 2007.
Source: ICBA Independent Banker (2008).

TruPSs help banks strengthen their financial positions during good times by providing bank holding companies access to a cheaper source of funding. However, in times of financial distress, limitations on including TruPSs as Tier 1 capital can further exacerbate an already bad situation. This was especially true of the small banks that raised large amounts of capital through TruPSs during the boom period of 2000 to 2006.

In the period from 2000 to 2006, banks issued TruPSs to fund mergers, acquisitions, buybacks, and expansion projects. Figure 6.1 shows steady activity in TruPS issuance for this period. In 2006, the total TruPS volume issued during the year jumped to an astounding $30 billion. This was largely due to an increase in refinancing activity. When initially issued, these securities had a standard 10-year no-call period. As a result, refinancing activity for TruPSs was limited for the 10-year period following 1996. As these securities became callable, refinancing activity picked up in 2006. However, there was an abrupt halt in TruPS issuance when the subprime crisis hit in August 2007. The impact was particularly severe for small banks.

Initially, due to the high costs of issuing TruPSs, small banks were left out of this market. However, the advent of pooling enabled small banks to issue TruPSs in a more cost-efficient way as most of the costs were borne by the bigger banks in the pool. Pooling combined the trust preferred securities from a number of banks and securitized them into collateralized debt obligations (CDOs), which were then divided into tranches and sold to the market. This process helped small banks access the TruPS market as a source of funding, as investors were willing to buy into a diversified pool of securities. From 2000 to 2008, it is estimated that nearly 1,500 small and regional banks issued nearly $50 billion in TruPSs (*Wall Street Journal* 2010).

However, the subprime crisis in July 2007 resulted in a sudden decline in CDO market activity as investors started pulling out due to market uncertainty. The pools could not be securitized and thus markets were unable to absorb newly issued TruPSs. While the market for TruPSs slowed down for larger banks, the condition was far worse for small banks, which were considered too small by private equity firms and other sophisticated investors. Unable to raise capital and facing deteriorating bottom lines, many deferred their interest payments. As of February 2010, nearly 270 U.S. small banks had deferred interest payments on their trust preferred securities. Most of these TruPSs remain on the banks' balance sheets, as these firms find it difficult to track down the original investors. In most cases when the banks manage to locate the investors, the investors are unwilling to sell at a significant discount. As a result, most small banks have retained the TruPSs on their balance sheets, and few have made public announcements to buy them back (*Wall Street Journal* 2010).

NOTES

1. For a comparison of Basel I, II, and III, see Elliott (2010).
2. For restrictions on financial activity, see Chapter 7, "Large Banks and the Volcker Rule."
3. See Acharya, Philippon, Richardson, and Roubini (2009) for a detailed account of the financial crisis of 2007 to 2009.
4. Chapter 15, "Regulation of Rating Agencies," describes this regulatory arbitrage in more detail. In brief, because the issuer pays the rating agency that rates the security, there is a huge conflict of interest to shop the security around until the issuer gets the desired rating, leading to inflated ratings. There is a plethora of academic evidence documenting this effect for structured products. Because the government (and Basel) sets its regulatory structure around these ratings, investors like AIG, Citigroup, ABN Amro, UBS, Fannie Mae, Freddie Mac, and, for that matter, Merrill Lynch and Lehman, among others, got to engage in risky activities without having to hold any capital buffer due to the inflated ratings.
5. Note that the spread was greater than zero not only because the rating agencies gave AAA status to risky securities, but also because LCFIs received a funding advantage due to their government guarantees, either implicit such as too-big-to-fail or explicit such as deposit insurance and government-backed GSE debt.
6. HR 4173, Title I, "Financial Stability," Subtitle A, "Financial Stability Oversight Council," Sec. 115, "Enhanced supervision and prudential standards for nonbank financial companies supervised by the Board of Governors and certain bank holding companies."
7. HR 4173, Title I, Subtitle A, Sec. 113, "Authority to require supervision and regulation of certain nonbank financial companies."
8. HR 4173, Title I, Subtitle A, Sec. 115.

9. There is an out clause to the extent that the Federal Reserve must take into account the international competitive landscape. Presumably, if other countries have not adopted such rules and the financial firm competes with firms in those countries, then the stricter rules may no longer go into effect.
10. A consequence of the increase in risk-weight categories led to greater reliance on rating agencies, which, as we point out, played an important part in the regulatory arbitrage engaged in by financial institutions.
11. HR 4173, Title I, Subtitle C, Sec. 171, "Leverage and risk-based capital requirements."
12. HR 4173, Title I, Subtitle C, Sec. 165, "Enhanced supervision and prudential standards for nonbank financial companies supervised by the Board of Governors and certain bank holding companies."
13. HR 4173, Title I, Subtitle C, Sec. 171.
14. HR 4173, Title VI, "Improvements to Regulation of Bank and Savings Association Holding Companies and Depository Institutions," Sec. 616, "Regulations Regarding Capital Levels."
15. There is a considerable literature, including Acharya, Mehran, and Thakor (2010), Calomiris and Kahn (1991), and Diamond and Rajan (2000), among others, that looks at bank capital structure under various conflicts. For instance, the Acharya, Mehran, and Thakor paper combines the discipline of short-term debt financing of banks with possible correlated risk-shifting and loss of market discipline due to systemic risk bailouts.
16. The stress event assumes, among other outcomes, a rating downgrade of the bank, a loss of both unsecured and secured wholesale funding, higher market volatility, and drawdowns of credit commitments. The agreement outlines specific assumptions like a 5 percent run-off on stable (10 percent on less stable) retail deposits, 25 percent for secured wholesale funding of nongovernment securities, and so on. Of some note, by the time Basel III was agreed to in July 2010, a number of these assumptions had been watered down.
17. HR 4173, Title I, Subtitle C, Sec. 174, "Studies and reports on holding company capital requirements."
18. HR 4173, Title I, Subtitle C, Sec. 165.

REFERENCES

Acharya, Viral V., Hamid Mehran, and Anjan Thakor. 2010. Caught between the Scylla and Charybdis?—Regulating bank leverage when there is rent seeking and risk shifting. Working paper, NYU Stern and Federal Reserve Bank of New York.

Acharya, Viral V., Thomas Philippon, Matthew Richardson, and Nouriel Roubini. 2009. A bird's-eye view—The financial crisis of 2007–2009: Causes and remedies. Prologue of *Restoring financial stability: How to repair a failed system*, ed. Viral V. Acharya and Matthew Richardson, 1–56. Hoboken, NJ: John Wiley & Sons.

Acharya, Viral V., Lasse H. Pedersen, Thomas Philippon, and Matthew Richardson. 2010a. Measuring systemic risk. Working paper, New York University Stern School of Business.

Acharya, Viral V., Lasse H. Pedersen, Thomas Philippon, and Matthew Richardson. 2010b. A tax on systemic risk. Forthcoming NBER publication on Quantifying Systemic Risk, ed. Joseph Haubrich and Andrew Lo.

Acharya, Viral V., Philipp Schnabl, and Gustavo Suarez. 2009. Securitization without risk transfer. Working paper, New York University Stern School of Business.

Admati, Anat R., and Paul Pfleiderer. 2009. Increased-liability equity: A proposal to improve capital regulation of large financial institutions. Working paper, Stanford University.

Brunnermeier, Markus, and Lasse Pedersen. 2009. Market liquidity and funding liquidity. *Review of Financial Studies* 22:2201–2238.

Calomiris, Charles W., and Charles M. Kahn. 1991. The role of demandable debt in structuring optimal banking arrangements. *American Economic Review* 81 (3): 497–513.

Diamond, Douglas W., and Raghuram G. Rajan. 2000. A theory of bank capital. *Journal of Finance* 55 (6): 2431–2465.

Duffie, Darrell. 2009. Contractual methods for out-of-court restructuring of systemically important financial institutions. Submission requested by the U.S. Treasury Working Group on Bank Capital.

Elliott, Douglas. 2010. Basel III, the banks, and the economy. Brookings Institution Report.

Flannery, Mark J. 2005. No pain, no gain? Effecting market discipline via "reverse convertible debentures." In *Capital adequacy beyond Basel: Banking, securities, and insurance*, ed. Hal S. Scott. Oxford: Oxford University Press.

Flannery, Mark J. 2009a. Market-valued triggers will work for contingent capital instruments. Working paper, University of Florida.

Flannery, Mark J. 2009b. Stabilizing large financial institutions with contingent capital certificates. Working paper, University of Florida.

Geanakoplos, John. 2009. The leverage cycle. Cowles Foundation Discussion Paper No. 1715.

Hart, Oliver, and Luigi Zingales. 2009. A new capital regulation for large financial institutions. Working paper, University of Chicago.

Huizinga, Harry, and Luc Laeven. 2009. Accounting discretion of banks during a financial crisis. International Monetary Fund Working Paper 09/207.

ICBA Independent Banker. 2008. Raising capital via trust preferred securities.

Kashyap, Anil, Raghuram Rajan, and Jeremy Stein. 2008. Rethinking capital regulation. Prepared for the Federal Reserve Bank of Kansas City symposium on "Maintaining Stability in a Changing Financial System," Jackson Hole, Wyoming, August 21–23.

Krishnamurthy, Arvind. 2002. The bond/old-bond spread. *Journal of Financial Economics* 66 (2–3): 463–506.

Kuritzkes, Andrew, and Hal Scott. 2009. Markets are the best judge of bank capital. *Financial Times*, September 23.

Lehman Brothers Chapter 11 Proceedings. 2010. Report by the examiner.

Lloyds Banking Group. 2009. Publicly available documents, company web site.

McDonald, Robert L. 2010. Contingent capital with a dual price trigger. Working paper, Northwestern University.

Miller, Merton H. 1995. Do the M & M propositions apply to banks? *Journal of Banking and Finance* 19 (3–4): 483–489.

Modigliani, Franco, and Merton Miller. 1958. The cost of capital, corporation finance and the theory of investment. *American Economic Review* 48 (3): 261–297.

Myers, Stewart. 1977. Determinants of corporate borrowing. *Journal of Financial Economics* 5 (2): 147–175.

Rabobank Group. 2010. Senior contingent roadshow, March 8–12.

Reuters. 2010. Banks get more time to meet new capital rules.

Salutric, Jennifer, and Joseph Willcox. 2009. Emerging issues regarding trust preferred securities. *SRC Insights.*

Shin, Hyun. 2009. Securitization and financial stability. *Presented at the Economic Journal Lecture at the Royal Economic Society meeting, Warwick, UK,* March 2008.

Squam Lake Working Group on Financial Regulation. 2009. An expedited resolution mechanism for distressed financial firms: Regulatory hybrid securities.

Vermaelen, Theo, and Christian Wolff. 2010. How next time to save banks without taxpayers' money: The case for COERCs. Working paper, Insead.

Wall Street Journal. 2010. Big problem for small banks: Trust-preferreds. February 12.

CHAPTER 7

Large Banks and the Volcker Rule

Matthew Richardson, Roy C. Smith, and Ingo Walter[*]

7.1 OVERVIEW

In announcing an agreement between the House and Senate on the Dodd-Frank Wall Street Reform and Consumer Protection Act of 2010, Senator Christopher Dodd noted that "the American people have called on us to set clear rules of the road for the financial industry to prevent a repeat of the financial collapse that cost so many so dearly."

Most of the systemic risk in the United States today emanates from the six largest bank holding companies—Bank of America, JPMorgan Chase, Citigroup, Wells Fargo, Goldman Sachs, and Morgan Stanley.[1] Critics have argued that the Act does not adequately address this risk. For example, none of these institutions are to be broken up, and efforts to lower their systemic risk, such as charging them up front for the risk they create, have been heavily diluted. Indeed, as a result of the crisis some of the leading U.S. financial institutions have become even bigger, broader, and more complex.

Moreover, these large, complex financial institutions (LCFIs) will still report to the same regulators as before, whose effectiveness in averting prior crises was sorely lacking. To impose serious sanctions on the banks, the regulators will now have to go through a lengthy process involving a two-thirds vote of the new 10-member Financial Stability Oversight Council, which is subject to appeal in the courts. They will still escape having to pay a market price for the implicit cheap-money subsidy they receive from government

---

[*]The authors benefited from discussions in the "Is Breaking Up the Big Financial Companies a Good Idea?" Working Group for the NYU Stern e-book *Real Time Solutions for Financial Reform*, which also included Viral Acharya, Thomas Cooley, Kose John, Charles Murphy, Anthony Saunders, Anjolein Schmeits, and Eiten Zemel.

guarantees. They will probably have to face tougher capital adequacy standards in the future, but not for a number of years—plenty of time to devise innovative ways to avoid them. They will be subject to more consumer-products regulation in the future, but will probably be able to pass the cost on to their clients. And although subject to an orderly liquidation authority, there is enough uncertainty about putting LCFIs through a receivership process that its credibility to impose market discipline is questioned.

LCFIs can be defined as financial intermediaries engaged in some combination of commercial banking, investment banking, asset management, insurance, and/or the payments system, whose failure poses a systemic risk to the financial system as a whole (see, for example, Saunders, Smith, and Walter 2009; Duffie 2010). Banks and other LCFIs enjoyed many years of deregulation, globalization, consolidation, and the freedom to engage in multiple business lines and to invest their own capital in a variety of nonbanking activities. This activity helped encourage the great disintermediation from bank balance sheets to increasingly efficient capital markets that widened access and lowered capital costs to market users. It also drove LCFIs to engage in mergers and other corporate actions that greatly increased their size, complexity, and influence.

Table 7.1 lists the market value and assets of the largest 24 U.S. financial firms in June 2007, just prior to the start of the financial crisis. The top 13 names cover two-thirds of all the assets of the top 100 firms ($21 trillion), and constitute a who's who of the crisis that subsequently emerged. Specifically, we have, in order of size, Citigroup, Bank of America, JPMorgan Chase, Morgan Stanley, Merrill Lynch, American International Group (AIG), Goldman Sachs, Fannie Mae, Freddie Mac, Wachovia, Lehman Brothers, Wells Fargo, and MetLife. Bear Stearns and Washington Mutual come in at Nos. 15 and 17, respectively. Of these 13 firms, one could convincingly argue that nine of them either failed or were about to fail in the absence of government intervention during the financial crisis.

Table 7.1 also shows that U.S.-based LCFIs include not just commercial banks but other such financial colossi as AIG and MetLife in the insurance sector; the government-sponsored enterprises Fannie Mae (FNMA) and Freddie Mac (FHLMC); finance subsidiaries tied to real-economy firms such as General Motors Acceptance Corporation (GMAC) and General Electric (GE) Capital;[2] and, putting aside their newly minted bank holding company status, the two premier investment banks Goldman Sachs and Morgan Stanley. None of these firms in early September 2008 were subject to banking regulations, but all were considered large and interconnected enough to be too big to fail (TBTF) and thus were covered by an implicit government guarantee that turned out to save the day.

TABLE 7.1 Largest Financial Firms (by Total Assets, $ Billions, June 2007)

Financial Firm	Assets	Market Equity	Assets/ Equity	Contribution	Cumulative Proportion
Citigroup Inc.	$2,347.4	$253.7	9.3	10.9%	10.9%
Bank of America Corp.	1,618.4	217.0	7.5	7.5	18.4
JPMorgan Chase & Co.	1,504.3	165.5	9.1	7.0	25.4
Morgan Stanley Dean Witter & Co.	1,250.0	88.4	14.1	5.8	31.2
Merrill Lynch & Co. Inc.	1,111.3	72.6	15.3	5.2	36.4
American International Group Inc.	1,111.2	181.7	6.1	5.2	41.6
Goldman Sachs Group Inc.	996.4	88.5	11.3	4.6	46.2
Federal National Mortgage Ass'n	889.7	63.6	14.0	4.1	50.3
Federal Home Loan Mortgage Corp.	843.1	40.2	21.0	3.9	54.2
Wachovia Corp.	748.7	98.1	7.6	3.5	57.7
Lehman Brothers Holdings Inc.	625.3	39.5	15.8	2.9	60.6
Wells Fargo & Co.	610.0	117.5	5.2	2.8	63.5
MetLife Inc.	566.8	47.8	11.9	2.6	66.1
Prudential Financial Inc.	483.9	45.0	10.7	2.2	68.3
Bear Stearns Companies Inc.	427.0	16.7	25.6	2.0	70.3
Hartford Fin'l Services Group Inc.	358.2	31.2	11.5	1.7	72.0
Washington Mutual Inc.	326.1	37.6	8.7	1.5	73.5
Berkshire Hathaway Inc.	272.8	119.0	2.3	1.3	74.8
U.S. Bancorp.	260.5	57.3	4.5	1.2	76.0
Countrywide Financial Corp.	224.0	21.6	10.4	1.0	77.0
American Express Co.	196.4	72.7	2.7	.9	77.9
Lincoln National Corp Inc.	195.0	19.2	10.2	.9	78.8
Suntrust Banks Inc.	194.0	30.6	6.3	.9	79.8
Allstate Corp.	176.3	37.4	4.7	.8	80.6

Table 7.1 lists the 24 largest financial firms in terms of assets in June 2007, prior to the emergence of the financial crisis. Assets are quasi-market values, calculated by book value of assets minus book value of equity plus market value of equity. Also provided are market value of equity, leverage (i.e., quasi market value of assets divided by market value of equity), % contribution of assets to the total assets of the largest 100 firms (based on their market value of equity), and the cumulative proportion based on the firm's ranking. *Data source*: Bloomberg.

7.2 LCFIs AND THE FINANCIAL CRISIS OF 2007 TO 2009

The global financial crisis of 2007 to 2009 was, beyond doubt, the worst episode of financial distress since the 1930s. It was also a clear example of systemic failure, despite two decades of effort by central bankers around the world to put into effect risk-adjusted minimum capital adequacy standards for banks. The crisis spread from the banking sector through the whole of the financial world to the real economy, driving it into a steep recession—and U.S. LCFIs, deregulated less than a decade before, as well as Europe-based LCFIs, stood at the epicenter.

Why? The short version is that a large number of banks and other major intermediaries managed to shift risks by exploiting loopholes in regulatory capital requirements to take an undercapitalized, highly leveraged, one-way bet on the economy—particularly tied to residential real estate, but also to commercial real estate and consumer credit. (See, for example, Acharya and Richardson 2009; Acharya, Cooley, Richardson, and Walter 2010.) This massive bet was financed largely by debt holders who correctly antici-pated de facto government guarantees. They included insured and uninsured depositors and creditors of Fannie Mae, Freddie Mac, and too-big-to-fail banks, which figured they would be bailed out no matter what. They were more or less indifferent to the consequences if they were wrong.

Things turned out pretty much as the creditors expected. Except for Lehman Brothers (and long-term debt holders of AIG and WaMu), there was a bailout of creditors of virtually all the heavily exposed financial inter-mediaries, including Bear Stearns, Fannie Mae, Freddie Mac, Merrill Lynch, Citigroup, Bank of America (through its purchase of Merrill Lynch), Wells Fargo (via Wachovia), and, to a lesser extent, GMAC and GE Capital—as well as Goldman Sachs and Morgan Stanley—which were all in danger without government support.

As necessary as it may have seemed after the fact, the moral hazard from government guarantees has only become worse. The emergency mergers and acquisitions during the crisis have created even larger systemic institutions, exacerbating the problem: Bank of America merging with Countrywide and Merrill Lynch; JPMorgan with Bear Stearns and Washington Mutual; and Wells Fargo with Wachovia. MetLife, the largest U.S. life insurer, entered into an agreement to buy AIG's international life insurer, ALICO, for $15.5 billion, which allowed the nation's largest life insurer to expand its business into Japan, Europe, and the Middle East. The deal increased MetLife's assets by almost 15 percent. Even if many of these firms are well run in the future, it would take only a few isolated cases to again put the entire system at risk.

7.3 THE ECONOMICS OF LCFIs

The LCFI Business Model

The industrial economics of financial intermediation suggests that the structural form of competition between firms active in a given financial intermediation function or in multiple functions should follow the dictates of institutional comparative advantage. If there are significant economies of scale or economies of scope with respect to either costs or client segments, we would expect to see the advantages reflected in, respectively, the size, the range of activities, or the geographic scope or client breadth of those firms that are the most successful.

Figure 7.1 depicts the market for financial services as a matrix of clients, products, and geographies (e.g., Walter 1988). Financial firms clearly will want to allocate available financial, human, and technological resources to those cells in the matrix (market segments) that promise to yield the highest risk-adjusted returns. In order to do this, they will have to attribute costs, returns, and risks appropriately to specific cells in the matrix, and the cells themselves must be linked together in a way that recognizes and maximizes what both analysts and practitioners commonly call synergies.

- *Client-driven linkages* (horizontal arrows) exist when a financial institution can, as a result of serving a particular client or client group, supply financial services more efficiently to either the same or another client in the same group in the same or different geographies. Risk mitigation results from spreading exposures across clients, along with greater earnings stability to the extent that income streams from different clients or client segments are not perfectly correlated.

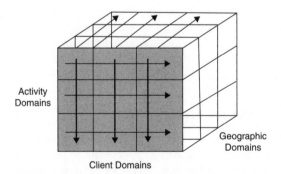

FIGURE 7.1   LCFI Strategic Positioning Matrix: Extracting Size, Scale, and Scope Economies

- *Product-driven linkages* (vertical arrows) exist when a firm can supply a particular financial service in a more competitive manner because it is already providing the same or a similar financial service in other client or geographic dimensions. Here again, there is risk mitigation to the extent that net revenue streams from different products are not perfectly correlated.
- *Geographic linkages* (lateral arrows) are important when an institution can service a particular client or supply a particular service more efficiently in one geography as a result of having an active relationship with that client, or presence in that financial product, in another location. Once more, the risk profile of the firm may be improved where business is spread across different currency, macroeconomic, and interest-rate environments.

To extract maximum returns from this strategic positioning matrix, firms need to understand the size, growth, and competitive dynamics of specific market segments, as well as the costs and the risks embedded in their overall portfolio of activities. Optimizing the linkages between the cells—in order to maximize potential joint cost and revenue economies—can be an especially challenging task, although the market dominance of LCFIs in many areas of financial activity suggests that these operating economies must have some degree of traction in the real world. At the same time, exploiting the potential of the market matrix across revenue, cost, and risk synergies engages the firm in higher levels of managerial complexity, conflicts of interest, and other issues that could well be value destroying.

The existence of large and complex systemic financial intermediaries suggests one of several possibilities: (1) that the benefits of size and complexity do in fact exceed their costs, (2) that there are widespread failures in market discipline and effective corporate governance, or (3) that size and complexity give rise to an unpriced subsidy representing a transfer of wealth from society at large to the shareholders and employees of financial intermediaries. Before discussing these issues, it is worthwhile to take a step back and consider the emergence of LCFIs from a historical perspective.

Glass-Steagall and the History of LCFIs

For almost seven decades, LCFIs were virtually banned from the U.S. financial system, decades that for the most part spanned periods of robust growth and relative financial stability. The Glass-Steagall provisions of the Banking Act of 1933 mandated a virtually complete separation of investment banking from deposit-taking activities. The Act thus eliminated involvement by firms with a commercial banking charter in the securities business—specifically, underwriting and dealing in corporate debt and equity securities, a business that expanded dramatically during the investment bubble of the late 1920s, and was dominated by an amalgam of universal banks such as J.P. Morgan, Chase Manhattan, and National City Corporation and broker-dealers such as Goldman Sachs and Lehman Brothers. The former were listed companies engaged in a full array of universal banking activities, and the latter were private partnerships engaged mainly in securities underwriting and trading and in investing their partners' capital. (See Walter 2010.)

Senator Carter Glass and other contemporary critics of the universal banking model feared that bank involvement in securities underwriting had directly and indirectly led banks to ramp up (warehouse) their holdings of long-term financial instruments, exposing themselves to potentially danger-ous market, credit, and liquidity risk. When this risk materialized with a vengeance, it was thought to have contaminated the entire U.S. financial system by triggering the collapse of banks nationwide, which in turn had disastrous consequences for the real economy. About 40 percent of all U.S. banks failed during this period, undermining their role as financial interme-diaries and cutting off the air supply to the real economy.

The fact is that the big universal banks did increase their holdings of equities and long-term debt securities during the 1920s, but there is little evidence that the quality of bank securities holdings was responsible for the cascading bank failures of 1930 to 1933. Under the circumstances that existed at the time, most of the banks that failed would have collapsed even if they had held no long-term bonds at all (e.g., Walter 1985). Evidence that commercial banks' securities activities somehow directly caused the Great Depression has remained elusive. The indirect causality, however, is an entirely different matter.

The Glass-Steagall Act forced the dissolution of the universal banks—for example, the breakup of J.P. Morgan into the Morgan Bank (which in 1959 merged with the Guaranty Trust Company to form the Morgan Guaranty Trust Company of New York) and Morgan, Stanley & Company. Continen-tal Europe, in contrast, engaged in no such functional separation and largely continued with the universal banking tradition. The United Kingdom went its own way with a commercial banking structure centered on a short list (determined by the Bank of England) of publicly listed clearing banks and a long tradition in the securities sector of single-capacity jobbers (dealers), brokers, and merchant banks. In 1948, Japan was forced under the U.S. occupation to adopt a version of the Glass-Steagall Act, which contained strict separation of commercial and investment banking.

Without access to the markets for deposits and commercial loans, but protected from competition by commercial banks, U.S. investment banks' share of financial intermediation grew rapidly as financial flows progressively shifted to the financial markets. They in turn had a great deal to do with accelerating this process. Commercial paper markets, high-yield securities, asset securitizations, money market mutual funds, and similar innovations were in part the products of investment banks' successful incursions into the market share of credit institutions, aided by the substantially lighter regulatory burdens they bore as (nonbank) securities dealers.

By the 1980s, the U.S. financial system had become heavily market-dominated while other financial systems remained dominated by universal banks. For example, local banks in continental Europe were strongly resistant to cannibalization of profitable business at home. While this structural difference may have had something to do with a persistently higher U.S. rate of economic growth during the 1980s and 1990s, the so-called Anglo-Saxon financial architecture was arguably more efficient, more disciplined, and more innovative than the bank-dominated system of continental Europe. If true, then the Glass-Steagall legislation may have paid handsome growth dividends for over half a century, dividends that might have been forgone if the United States had persisted with a universal banking model after 1933.

Internationally as well, a consequence of Glass-Steagall may have been the progressive dominance of U.S. investment banks in rapidly evolving global capital markets. American broker-dealers, whose competitiveness was enhanced by the disappearance of fixed brokerage commissions in the New York Stock Exchange's "Mayday" financial reforms in 1975, began a sustained offensive in foreign and offshore financial markets. Penetrating the fortresses of universal banking in one country after another, they mounted a sustained 20-year battle to wean European and later Asian corporations from their reliance on *Hausbank* relationships with universal banks, offering lower funding costs and innovative financings. Meanwhile, they cultivated the buy side of the market—insurance companies, pension funds, and other institutional investors—with new investment alternatives and ideas to improve portfolio efficiency. The offensive was so successful that virtually all the major universal banks in Europe mounted vigorous efforts to develop investment banking divisions of their own, but without having been battle-tested or having a viable footprint in the United States, the world's largest securities market.

By the early 1990s, American investment banks basically dominated their industry worldwide, with a market share of about two-thirds. Investment banking developed into one of the top U.S. export industries—arguably another fortuitous consequence of Glass-Steagall. Had universal banking remained in place in the United States after 1933, the lack of competitive pressure across very different strategic cohorts might well have involved significant opportunity costs for the U.S. economy.

Predictably, U.S. wholesale commercial banks—notably Morgan Guaranty, Bankers Trust, Chase Manhattan, and Citicorp—began to agitate for reinstatement of universal banking powers to redress what they had come to regard as a debilitating competitive disadvantage. While they could and did compete vigorously in government bond, foreign exchange, and other permitted markets as well as corporate advisories, they were hamstrung in the corporate securities sectors of the market. So the 1980s saw a spate of political initiatives to get the rules changed. These included high-road arguments that the structure of financial intermediaries should be driven by competitive and strategic consideration, not anachronistic legislation (e.g., Saunders and Walter 1996). They also included low-road initiatives such as Bankers Trust's technically illegal underwriting of commercial paper in 1985, and then letting the courts decide on the merits (Bankers Trust won).

By the late 1980s, commercial banks had gained the limited right to sell investment and insurance products to retail customers, as well as the right to operate separately capitalized, size-constrained wholesale securities subsidiaries under various safeguards—so-called Section 20 subsidiaries—to prevent their commercial banking units from contamination by possible investment banking losses. This came in the form of administrative rulings on the part of the regulators, not legislative change. Perhaps a dozen of the major wholesale commercial banks took early advantage of this progressive liberalization to build significant securities subsidiaries, especially in the bond business, to complement their powerful wholesale commercial banking and government bond activities and their emerging presence in corporate advisory work.

One key area in which the commercial banks made little headway was equities, a highly profitable growth market that was far removed from their traditional expertise in debt finance, and in which they had little sales and trading expertise and few natural relationships with companies undertaking initial public offerings (IPOs). Moreover, lack of a market presence in equities seriously hampered their ability to build a competitive fee-based corporate finance business. This gap in their activity range lent even more urgency to removal of the remaining Glass-Steagall restrictions through legislative action.

With the political landscape lined up for deregulation and many large banks already engaging in broker-dealer-type services through subsidiaries, the merger in April 1998 of Citicorp and Travelers—illegal at the time but permitted under a two-year extendable grace period—simply ignored the remaining functional barriers on the assumption that they would soon be lifted. This bold preemptive strike was soon validated by passage of the Gramm-Leach-Bliley Financial Services Modernization Act of 1999 (GLB), which repealed Glass-Steagall.

Passage of GLB by an overwhelming congressional vote of 343 to 86 put the final nail in the coffin of functional separation in U.S. financial intermediation. At the retail level, it allowed commercial banks to gather assets into both bank deposits and securities accounts such as money market mutual funds, helping to stem the incursion by broker-dealers into their traditional client base and broadening their ability to respond to changes in client preferences. At the wholesale level, GLB allowed commercial banks to underwrite and trade in corporate debt, corporate equities, and municipal revenue bonds and to compete head-on with the broker-dealers. Together with repeal of the McFadden Act (which had limited interstate branching) through passage of the Riegel-Neal Interstate Banking and Branching Efficiency Act of 1994, this set the stage for a return to full-blown universal banking in the United States with few regulatory constraints on scale and scope in financial intermediation.

Among the remaining constraints, the 1999 deregulation did not remove the restrictions on banks under the Bank Holding Company Act of 1956 (BHC), which prevented financial institutions from owning nonfinancial corporations. It conversely prohibits corporations outside of the banking sector from entering deposit taking and commercial lending. This prompted many nonfinancial corporations such as General Electric and BMW to set up industrial loan corporations (ILCs), mainly chartered in Utah, which enabled them to take Federal Deposit Insurance Corporation (FDIC)–insured deposits and make commercial loans despite the BHC prohibition. It also allowed broker-dealers and investment banking units of financial conglomerates to set up FDIC-insured ILCs to offer their clients in the form of brokerage sweep accounts. Remaining in place was a cap of 10 percent on total U.S. deposits booked by any single bank holding company, although the largest financial conglomerates soon lobbied for the cap to be lifted. Bank of America, for example, argued that the cap rendered U.S. banks vulnerable to foreign acquirers by limiting their ability to buy non-U.S. banks that have significant domestic deposits.[3]

As with the imposition of Glass-Steagall 66 years earlier, GLB's reversal of functional separation in financial services had some dramatic, if unintended, consequences. Within two years of deregulation, every major commercial bank that took full advantage of its new access to investment banking was involved in the most serious spate of corporate scandals of modern times—including the collapse of Enron and WorldCom—resulting in large losses for the banks themselves and their investor clients, major fines and legal settlements, and a general erosion of confidence in financial markets. Using their enormous balance sheets, the new financial conglomerates had become fee-chasing Goliaths, with clients playing them off against each other and against the five remaining independent investment banks—Bear Stearns,

Goldman Sachs, Lehman Brothers, Merrill Lynch, and Morgan Stanley. As well, each was embroiled in major regulatory violations and exploitation of conflicts of interest, including corrupted equity research, facilitation of late trading and market timing by hedge funds against the interests of ordinary shareholders of in-house mutual funds, and acting simultaneously as investor and intermediary in corporate transactions.

Moreover, less than a decade after deregulation, these same financial conglomerates were at the epicenter of the global financial crisis that began in 2007 as they chased market share in the securitization business and aggressively followed along as the action increasingly involved riskier credits ranging from subprime mortgages to leveraged loans. Besides encountering securitization pipeline exposure to market, credit, and liquidity risk in pursuit of a booming business, the financial conglomerates also took substantial "warehouse" exposure on their balance sheets or in off-balance-sheet conduits set up to avoid regulatory capital requirements (see Acharya and Richardson 2009). Most would have failed in 2008 had they not by then become systemic institutions and beneficiaries of the largest corporate bailouts in U.S. history, passing on to the public the massive risks that they had assumed in executing their financial conglomerate strategies.

The archetype of U.S. financial firms, Citigroup, soon became the poster child for failed financial conglomerates, virtually wiping out its shareholders, depending entirely on taxpayer life support for its continued existence during the worst of the crisis, and ultimately being partially nationalized with a 34 percent government shareholding.

Systemic Risk of LCFIs

The size and power of LCFIs is worrisome. For example, in 2009, the world's five largest wholesale banks were responsible for the origination of nearly 60 percent of all capital market transactions and, as mentioned earlier, the six largest U.S. banks (in order, Bank of America, JPMorgan Chase, Citigroup, Wells Fargo, Goldman Sachs, and Morgan Stanley) accounted for $8.97 trillion of assets, or approximately 55 percent of all assets held in the entire U.S. banking system.

They operate aggressively because they have to—the global financial marketplace is now extremely competitive, and mandates are won or lost based less on the ideas proposed than on the tightness of the pricing and the willingness to bear risk. Their big balance sheets allow for diversification of risk, but only as long as risks do not become highly correlated (as they now tend to be in moments of panic that engender liquidity crises).

Without government restraint, how can anyone be sure that LCFIs won't repeat the behavior they exhibited in the financial crisis of 2007 to 2009 in the next period of rising asset prices and liquidity? The idea that LCFIs can or will regulate themselves prudently has been shown to be distorted by the industry's competitive dynamics, embedded agency conflicts, and ever-present moral hazard.

Chapter 5 of this book, "Taxing Systemic Risk," argues that the optimal policy for systemic risk regulation of LCFIs is for the regulator to charge a premium that forces the LCFI to internalize the costs of its guaranteed liabilities and the systemic risk they produce. The Dodd-Frank Act, however, does not follow this route. The Act remains largely dependent, as it is now, on effective on-the-spot regulation by systemic regulators and the insulating bulwark of revised capital adequacy standards. These approaches were not particularly effective in averting the most recent crisis. Indeed, they may have sent false signals of comfort based on the banks' having met certain capital metrics that proved to be illusory in the midst of a full-scale liquidity and solvency crisis.

If imposing regulatory incentives on LCFIs—as the most likely form of too-big-to-fail financial organization—is unlikely to succeed in reducing the systemic risk they generate, it may not be premature to ask what options will have to be considered after the next major financial crisis. Specifically, what are the relevant trade-offs of a return to some form of Glass-Steagall, functionally separated world of banking?

It seems clear that the regulator must weigh the systemic risk of a particular functional activity undertaken by a financial institution against the benefit of that activity. Before presenting these trade-offs in more detail, it is useful to provide a framework for thinking about this issue.

First and foremost, most activities of financial institutions have some degree of systemic risk associated with them. We can consider breaking up their functions into several areas in order to better understand the nature of their systemic risk. Specifically, these firms:

- Act as intermediaries, that is, dealers in security markets, repos, and over-the-counter (OTC) derivatives.
- Conduct commercial banking—deposit taking and lending to individuals and institutions.
- Operate investment banking businesses—underwriting security issues and providing advisory services.
- Offer asset management services—managing assets for institutions and individuals.
- Offer brokerage services to individuals, and particularly prime brokerage for hedge funds and other professional investors.
- Conduct proprietary trading—trading on their own accounts, which may include internal hedge funds, private equity partnerships, or asset holdings of unhedged securities.

Some of these activities, like proprietary trading and lending to individuals and institutions, directly risk the firm's capital. To the extent that the portfolio of trading positions and loans generates aggregate market risk—and that leverage is used to accumulate the holdings—systemic risk emerges.

At first glance, it may seem that activities based solely on fee revenue, such as asset management, advisory roles, or brokerage services, are not systemic in nature. This is incorrect. If the stream of revenues from these businesses is capitalized by the equity market and the firm can borrow against this capitalization, then a loss in the present value of revenues can have an effect similar to investing one's own capital.

Consider the asset management business. Since, through its fee structure, asset management revenues are a function of the value of the underlying assets being managed, any market risk of these assets will get passed through to the value of the asset management business. If the market risk of the assets is high, then this can be a particularly systemic activity, not only because of asset risk, but also because of the risk that the underlying business can fall off.

Moreover, some activities are a combination of capital- and fee-based business (e.g., dealer activities, underwriting, and prime brokerage). Consider financial firms acting as dealers. While a majority of their revenue may derive from the spread between buying and selling securities, this activity is rarely without some capital at risk. The firm may have to hold a security for a time while it searches for a counterparty to the trade and thus exposes itself to both idiosyncratic and market risk. Of course, to reduce this risk, firms could hedge the macro or aggregate risk of such a position. The systemic risk would then emerge only from the impact of a systemic crisis on the franchise value of the dealer business. In other words, in a systemic event, OTC derivative trading and other security markets might dry up, causing a loss in revenues.

A secondary issue is that regulators need to identify the relevant cost-benefit analysis of combining different financial activities. It is not clear that one size fits all, so the same rule applied to many institutions may be highly inefficient. As noted earlier, our preferred approach is for financial institutions to be forced to internalize the systemic risk externalities they produce through being charged a fee, or tax, or surcharge, or levy, or whatever one wants to call it. Nevertheless, for the discussion to follow, we are going to put this particular argument aside and focus on the underlying value of promoting functional separation on the part of systemic financial firms.

One of the arguments favoring LCFIs is that the securities markets, especially debt markets, have become highly integrated and fluid as a result of securitization, global linkages, derivatives, and new forms of market innovation. This integration has been beneficial to capital markets, increasing competition, arbitrage trading, and price discovery. Giving up these efficiency gains by going back to a variant of the Glass-Steagall world might seem like a risky strategy. And in any case, it is now almost impossible to draw distinctions between loans and securities, differences that were essential in imposing and enforcing Glass-Steagall in its time.

A second argument is that to return to some sort of Glass-Steagall world in today's globalized marketplace, universal banking would have to be prohibited everywhere, not just in the United States. Otherwise separated American banks and investment banks would be forced to give up their market leadership positions in global finance, something they would surely object to. Even so, the industry would simply reform itself outside of the United States as affected American banks are sold to foreigners and relocated to Europe, or the bankers are recruited away. The LCFIs would still be there. They just wouldn't come under the American regulatory purview. They would still impose systemic risk, but if that risk is concentrated outside the U.S. governmental safety net, they could pose an even more dangerous situation.

On the other hand, countries that would be home to non-U.S. LCFIs (notably Switzerland, the United Kingdom, Germany, Italy, France, Spain, and Japan—and possibly China in the future) are if anything less well positioned than the United States in serving as a credible lender of last resort. Based on the socialization of risk in the 2007 to 2009 crisis, it seems doubtful that taxpayers in these countries would be rushing to provide unpriced or underpriced guarantees for their universal banks to gain global market share.

Restricting activities along the lines of a new Glass-Steagall Act would be particularly detrimental if these activities were ones that created value to the financial system (i.e., diversification or synergies that could not occur outside the LCFI model). What does the existing evidence suggest in this respect?

In terms of systemic risk, the diversification argument seems particularly weak. The fundamentals of modern finance tell us that there are two types of risk: idiosyncratic or firm-specific risk, which is diversifiable, and systematic or marketwide risk, which is not. While it is certainly true that the expansion of financial firms into multiple business lines may reduce the volatility of their overall asset portfolios, this is not necessarily what society most cares about. Because an economic crisis is the realization of marketwide risk, the problem society really cares about is whether banks—large and small—can withstand such risk and continue to perform critical intermediation functions. When the economy craters, banks' loans become impaired, the value of their securities holdings falls, their underlying investment banking business produces far less revenues, and the value of their asset management business plummets. So in a crisis do banks collapse along with everything else?

Wagner (2009) argues that, while diversification makes individual bank default (and distress costs) less likely, it actually increases the likelihood of systemic risk. (See also Freixas, Loranth, and Morrison 2007.) Recent empirical work supports this theory. For example, De Jonghe (2009) documents that the tail betas of diversified financial institutions are higher and therefore these firms create more systemic risk. In a series of papers, DeYoung and Roland (2001), Stiroh (2004, 2006), and Stiroh and Rumble (2006) find that movement away from traditional banking activities toward other financial services increases the volatility and market risk of the firms. This work argues that the costs more than outweigh the benefits. Chapter 4 of this book, "Measuring Systemic Risk," also documents that the systemic risk of LCFIs is higher compared to the risk associated with simpler organizational structures.

The argument for synergies has a better grounding. At face value, if one puts conflicts between shareholders and the firm's managers aside, as noted earlier, the very growth of LCFIs suggests that shareholders believe there is some synergistic value when a firm engages in multiple business lines. It is a reasonable position to take. For example, many analysts would argue that it is important for firms that are active in the primary market for securities (i.e., underwriting) to be important participants in the secondary market (i.e., dealers). Nevertheless, the empirical evidence remains decidedly mixed.

Notably, Laeven and Levine (2007) report evidence that contradicts the existence of wide-scale synergies in LCFIs in the banking sector. They argue that there is a financial conglomerate discount; in other words, the whole is worth *less* than the sum of the parts. See also Delong (2001), who performs an event study on diversifying bank mergers. In a study that goes beyond banks and looks at all financial intermediaries, Schmid and Walter (2009) document similar evidence. Interestingly, they find a premium for the very large firms, indicating that there is most likely a too-big-to-fail guarantee that supports the market value of these firms. Therefore, the reason for the growth in LCFIs may simply be due to the below-market cost of financing through the central bank or public guarantee agency.

From a societal point of view, the benefits to LCFIs of a too-big-to-fail guarantee are clearly not a valid reason to oppose reinstitution of some form of Glass-Steagall, since too-big-to-fail standing encourages moral hazard. In contrast, Baele, De Jonghe, and Vander Vennet (2007) and Elsas, Hackethal, and Holzhauser (2009) provide evidence that the LCFI model does improve bank profitability, and generally argue that these gains are due to economies of scale. The reasons for the different findings can be attributed to both different data sources and different methodologies. In this chapter, we are not going to be able to resolve this current debate. Indeed, the recent studies mirror the findings of the survey article by Berger and Humphrey (1997) some 15 years earlier, which argued there was no predominance of evidence either for or against economies of scale in the financial sector.

What is less controversial in the literature, however, is that the expansion to multiple functions, the LCFI model, produces greater systemic risk. As noted earlier, there is now a plethora of research—including Chapter 4 of this book, DeYoung and Roland (2001), Stiroh (2004, 2006), Stiroh and Rumble (2006), De Jonghe (2009), and even papers loosely in support of the LCFI model such as Baele, De Jonghe, and Vander Vennet (2007)—that finds the LCFI model more risky. Unless the financial legislation along the lines described in Chapter 5 (bank levies) and Chapter 6 (capital and liquidity requirements) are successful in reducing the LCFIs' asset risk and leverage, there is a strong economic case for some form of return to Glass-Steagall and functional separation.

The foregoing analysis aside, the Dodd-Frank Wall Street Reform and Consumer Protection Act of 2010 does not in fact represent a return to a Glass-Steagall world. There is no call for a breakup of today's massive, complex financial conglomerates as a way to reduce the likelihood of future financial crises. The functional separation argument may not have won the day in the ongoing array of financial reforms, but it is likely to be resurrected after the next major financial crisis down the road. That said, written into the 2010 legislation are some Glass-Steagall-like restrictions.

7.4 THE DODD-FRANK WALL STREET REFORM AND CONSUMER PROTECTION ACT OF 2010

Size Constraints

First, there is the prohibition on the size of financial institutions through mergers if the combined firm's total liabilities exceed 10 percent of aggregate consolidated liabilities of all financial companies in the United States. As noted, only Bank of America and JPMorgan Chase would surpass this rule, with Citigroup and Wells Fargo representing additional candidates if a future merger or acquisition were sufficiently large. We have also noted the (perhaps inevitable) irony that government actions in the 2007 to 2009 crisis have encouraged even larger systemic institutions (e.g., Bank of America merging with Countrywide and Merrill Lynch, JPMorgan Chase with Bear Stearns and Washington Mutual, and Wells Fargo with Wachovia). Going forward, expected intense lobbying activity by firms actually or potentially subject to the 10 percent ceiling could well succeed in having the limit raised, triggering even greater industry consolidation and exposure to systemic risk.

If implemented as written, the U.S. size constraint does reduce the growth prospects of such entities into ever larger firms even though it does not call for breaking up large financial institutions into smaller (not-too-big-to-fail) entities. Restricting growth of the liabilities of the very largest institutions is entirely reasonable, in our view. It is almost certainly true that any institution with more than 10 percent of the entire financial sector's liabilities is systemic. The size cap would therefore help limit the too-big-to-fail problem. Of course, the reverse is not true, as a number of institutions with less than 10 percent of liabilities in the system are also systemic. Thus, hard-and-fast rules like the 10 percent ceiling may carry with them potential costs and unintended consequences.[4]

In terms of a more restrictive approach, we do not know enough about the optimum size of a financial institution conducting a multitude of activities in our contemporary global financial system to feel comfortable about advocating an across-the-board breakup of banks and financial conglomerates. Moreover, certain activities like dealer functions and intermediation between large institutions require a high degree of interconnectedness and scale for firms to compete effectively and reduce risks by diversifying them across a number of counterparties. So blanket size constraints are likely to involve substantial efficiency losses. They would also be unilateral in the sense that only a few U.S. and perhaps UK and continental European banks would be subject to such scale reductions.

Breaking Up LCFIs

The Dodd-Frank Act provides that if, after new prudential standards have been implemented, a financial firm is deemed to represent a systemic threat, activities that constitute the source of that threat could be terminated, carved out, or sold to separate unaffiliated financial firms. Possible remedies include terminating one or more activities; imposing conditions on the manner in which a financial holding company subject to stricter standards conducts one or more activities; limiting the ability to merge with, acquire, consolidate with, or otherwise become affiliated with another company; and restricting the ability to offer a financial services or products.

According to the legislation, preemptive breakups and the disposal of specific LCFI holdings are last-resort measures that have to be approved by a two-thirds vote of the Financial Stability Oversight Council (described in Chapter 1) on recommendation of the Federal Reserve, based on their presenting a grave threat to the financial stability of the United States. It also envisages bringing nonfinancial companies posing a systemic threat under the Federal Reserve regulatory umbrella, again by a two-thirds vote of the Financial Stability Oversight Council.

This part of the legislation recommends a breakup based on *activities* of financial firms and possibly nonfinancial firms. It includes two qualifiers. The first allows for judicial review of the regulator's decision. The second requires that any decision made by the regulator must take into account the international competitiveness of the U.S. financial services industry in the context of comparable regulatory developments taking place elsewhere.

This loophole leaves open the possibility that firms will lobby success-fully against any structural interference on the grounds that it affects their global competitiveness. It is of course arguable whether the taxpayers in other countries that are home base for major financial intermediaries would be willing to underwrite the safely and soundness of LCFIs or their affiliated units following the massive losses and risk bearing forced on them during the crisis of 2007 to 2009. So the competitiveness loophole may in the end represent a red herring.

The Modified Volcker Rule

The provision of the Dodd-Frank Act that comes closest to reinstating the 1933 Glass-Steagall provisions is the so-called Volcker Rule. Paul Volcker, the highly respected former Federal Reserve chairman, had long urged that the scope of any implicit federal guarantee be limited to a relatively small number of important banking institutions and to core banking functions, rather than extended across the spectrum of financial intermediaries and risky activities. In exchange for the banking safety net, Volcker recom-mended that banks be allowed to engage in the full range of commercial and investment banking functions as financial intermediaries, but not be permitted to engage in such nonbanking activities as proprietary trading, principal investing, commodity speculation, and hedge fund and private equity fund management. These activities would be spun off to nonbank asset-management firms and would be subject to whatever regulation is nec-essary for those types of institutions. The legacy banks would be allowed to have no economic interest in the spun-off entities.

Paul Volcker's proposals were the subject of hefty debate as the House and Senate bills advanced though the legislative process and ultimately the reconciliation of the two versions for the President's signature. Popular opinion seemed heavily in favor of the rule, and LCFIs were in vociferous opposition, supported by many in the administration. Slowly but surely the pendulum swung in the Volcker direction, propelled by resurgent bank earnings, renewed revelations of LCFI conflicts of interest, and several local elections that made clear the depth of popular antipathy to the dominant banks. This opened the way for Blanche Lincoln of Arkansas to amend the legislation to limit bank derivative transactions to separately capitalized affiliates whose failure would presumably be less likely to cause a systemic crisis. The Lincoln Amendment was likewise heatedly opposed by the banks, convinced that capitalizing a separate derivatives subsidiary would be far more costly that running a derivatives book on the bank's core capital.

As written, the Dodd-Frank Act requires federal agencies to issue rules that prohibit systemic banks and other financial firms from engaging in proprietary trading or investing and sponsoring hedge funds or private equity funds incorporating coinvestments in excess of 3 percent of their capital. Additionally, banks are prohibited from lending and other exposures to sponsored hedge funds and private equity funds. Specifically, the firms covered by these provisions include all depository institutions, their holding companies, any company treated as a bank holding company as defined by the Bank Holding Company Act (such as foreign banks with U.S. operations), and any of their subsidiaries. The rule is also extended to nonbank financial institutions that are systemically important albeit in a different fashion. In particular, while not banning proprietary trading, the Federal Reserve is required to impose greater capital requirements and some limits on these activities. In general, the restrictions would be phased in over a period of seven years.

There are several exemptions to the proprietary trading provisions, most notably:

> *the purchase, sale, acquisition, or disposition of securities and other instruments . . . in connection with underwriting or market-making related activities, to the extent that any such activities permitted by this subparagraph are designed not to exceed the reasonably expected near term demands of clients, customers, or counterparties . . . risk-mitigating hedging activities in connection with and related to individual or aggregated positions, contracts, or other holdings of a banking entity that are designed to reduce the specific risks to the banking entity in connection with and related to such positions, contracts, or other holdings.[5]*

Moreover, any trading in government-issued obligations—U.S. government bonds and obligations of government agencies, government-sponsored enterprises (GSEs), and state and municipal issuers—is also exempt. While the Volcker Rule does in theory cover insurance companies, for the most part their trading is exempt as long as it is consistent with insurance regulations and the Financial Stability Oversight Council. Proprietary trading and investing and sponsoring hedge or private equity funds offshore by a foreign company are likewise not covered by the legislation.

While the Dodd-Frank Act called for the Financial Stability Oversight Council to undertake a six-month study to make recommendations regarding restrictions on proprietary trading, it is clear from the legislation that the Council does not have authority to substantially change the rule. Moreover, *sponsorship* is defined explicitly as serving as a general partner, managing director, or trustee of a private equity fund or hedge fund, and except for the coinvestment provision contains little leeway. These changes would have to be enacted within two years of the legislation's enactment.

Like the hedge funds and private equity funds restrictions proposed by the Volcker Rule, the Lincoln Amendment on derivatives trading through separately capitalized subsidiaries was likewise softened. Banks are only required to spin off swaps desks for equities, commodities, and low-grade credit default swaps into separately capitalized subsidiaries. There is an exemption for foreign exchange derivatives, high-grade credit default swaps, gold, silver, and other asset classes considered relatively low-risk—see Chapter 13 for a detailed discussion.

Given the wide variety of activities performed by financial companies, why choose to restrict only proprietary trading, certain derivatives trading, and limited investments in sponsored hedge funds and private equity funds? And will these functional restrictions actually make a difference when the thunderheads begin to form in advance of the next financial crisis?

We have argued earlier that regulators must weigh the systemic risk of a particular functional activity of a financial institution against the benefit of that activity. Based on this type of cost-benefit analysis, proprietary trading seems like a reasonable choice for a Glass-Steagall-type restriction. Many proprietary trading operations housed within large financial institutions are already subject to so-called Chinese walls and insulated from the information flow within the firm. So a form of separation has already existed. This is not to argue that there are no possible synergies from having proprietary trading in-house. For example, proprietary trading and other functional areas might share common inventories of securities and infrastructure, such as information technology and trade settlement operations, which would lead to economies of scale. Equally, proprietary trading may improve access to financial information like market prices and liquidity, which can help the firm serve investor clients or even as an issuer.

But are such synergies important enough to offset the argument that proprietary trading adds systemic risk to the activities of a financial conglomerate? Academic research has found few credible economies of scope. This argues against investment management (either internal or external funds) being located inside a financial conglomerate. And there are systemic costs when one activity's failure endangers performance of others (see, for example, DeYoung and Roland 2001; Stiroh 2004; De Jonghe 2009).

Moreover, there are well-developed capital market specialists that focus on proprietary trading activities. Numerous hedge funds, private equity funds, and other alternative asset managers can perform these functions outside the corporate boundaries of large financial institutions. This is in addition to the key systemic disadvantage of such activities being housed within LCFIs in light of the low cost of funding attributable to government guarantees, enabling these institutions to take on risky activities that would be unprofitable in the absence of such guarantees.

Proprietary Trading   The first practical issue in implementing this part of the Dodd-Frank Act is what exactly defines proprietary trading.

The intuitive definition is that proprietary trading constitutes any trading conducted by the firm for its own account. The Dodd-Frank Act states that:

> *The term "proprietary trading," when used with respect to a banking entity or nonbank financial company supervised by the Board, means engaging as a principal for the trading account of the banking entity or nonbank financial company supervised by the Board in any transaction to purchase or sell, or otherwise acquire or dispose of, any security, any derivative, any contract of sale of a commodity for future delivery, any option on any such security, derivative, or contract, or any other security or financial instrument that the appropriate Federal banking agencies, the Securities and Exchange Commission, and the Commodity Futures Trading Commission may . . . determine.*[6]

While the aforementioned exemptions for excluding customer-related trading and hedging are logical, they create a gray area for implementing the rule. For example, when an LCFI acts as intermediary between buyers and sellers, especially for less liquid securities, the firm will often be exposed to one side of the transaction. In fact, a number of normal market- and client-oriented transactions, such as trading in foreign exchange, fixed-income securities, and derivatives, as well as services like bridge financing, prime brokerage, and the like, might result in the firm technically trading on its own account but doing so to serve client needs.

This gray area also invites manipulation. What is to prevent a bank from accumulating a large exposure in a given security or derivative in expectation of an eventual customer demand for the asset? How are regulators to distinguish between identical trades where the intent of one is clearly customer-driven and the intent of the other is proprietary? Should there be a time limit set on holdings related to customer-related trading? Should there be the requirement that the aggregate market exposure associated with these holdings be hedged? How can such holdings be differentiated from those related to pure trading bets in the real world?

Skeptics are right to worry about the distinction between permissible and impermissible trading, and most LCFIs have already moved some of their proprietary traders to client desks that nevertheless use the firm's own capital. Equally troubling, traders in that position now have privileged insight into client trades and, by stretching the rules, can front-run them. It seems doubtful that highly compensated practitioners, backed by phalanxes of lawyers and lobbyists well versed in putting pressure on regulators, will take very long to find ways to erode the practical force of the Volcker Rule's proprietary trading restrictions. Time will tell.

LCFIs had already prepared the ground by arguing that proprietary trading operations were not the cause of the 2007 to 2009 financial crisis and that, in addition, proprietary trading is not an important part of the banking business. To the contrary, trading on the firm's account has everything to do with the crisis and the misaligned incentives in the financial system. These activities involve risky position taking (such as the substantial, nearly fatal proprietary investments in asset-backed securities made by Citigroup, UBS, Merrill Lynch, Lehman Brothers, and Bear Stearns), and were arguably not necessary for banking operations.

To better understand this point, it is helpful to focus on the business model of the government-sponsored enterprises (GSEs), Fannie Mae and Freddie Mac. As Chapter 14 shows, the GSEs invested approximately $1.5 trillion in bank-originated pools of mortgages at a leverage ratio of roughly 25 to 1. Because of the implicit government guarantee of their debt (made explicit in September 2008 when they were brought into conservatorship), the GSEs were able to take these bets at a low financing cost. It is now widely recognized that this model was a recipe for disaster, since it combined private profit taking with socialized risk.

The banking sector during the crisis looked almost identical to the GSEs. A Lehman Brothers report from April 2008 shows holdings of residential mortgage-backed securities of U.S. banks and thrifts. These holdings included $901 billion of agency securities and $483 billion of subprime AAA-rated securities, versus $741 billion and $308 billion held by the GSEs. In addition, broker-dealers held a further $230 billion of subordinated subprime securities, exposures even the GSEs refused to touch. And like Fannie Mae and Freddie Mac, these positions held by the banks and thrifts were funded at a lower cost of capital than the underlying risk because of either explicit government guarantees of bank deposits or implicit (and now explicit) too-big-to-fail guarantees.

Beyond this access to cheap financing, the banking sector ended up holding these types of securities because, through regulatory loopholes, the warehousing of ill-fated securities required less regulatory capital and, as a result, the financial intermediaries were free to lever up to the hilt. These securities offered a large spread over the financing rate precisely because they were less liquid and faced systemic risk.

This point is just as relevant after the financial crisis. A quick look at the 2009 balance sheets of the four largest banks—JPMorgan Chase, Bank of America, Citigroup, and Wells Fargo—shows holdings of $1.1 trillion worth of available-for-sale securities. While banks will argue these holdings are necessary for liquidity, if this were in fact the case, then they would be holding Treasuries or cash. Instead, many of these available-for-sale securities are asset-backed securities funded using overnight repos.

However, in the unlikely event that bad times occur and liquidity and market risk surface, these securities would lose value. Since there is little or no capital underlying these positions—and bank-type levered entities would already be facing trouble from loan losses—systemic risk emerges. Commingling systemically risky security holdings with economically important financial intermediation at banks and other large financial institutions was one of the main causes of the recent crisis. This is why finance theory argues persuasively that the business model of securitization never intended asset-backed securities to be held on banks' balance sheets, and especially not to skirt capital requirements. Not all researchers, however, agree with this assertion about the securitization model (see, e.g., Gorton and Metrick 2009).

This aside, an expanded Volcker Rule that extends the definition of proprietary trading to asset-backed security holdings by financial intermediaries represents a logical fix. Other institutions without guarantees such as mutual funds, pension funds, hedge funds, sovereign wealth funds, and nonsystemic insurance companies can step into the breach as banks withdraw from the asset-backed security market.

But there is reason to be less than optimistic. Written into the Dodd-Frank Act is the definition of a firm's proprietary trading account:

> *any account used for acquiring or taking positions in the securities and instruments ... principally for the purpose of selling in the near term (or otherwise with the intent to resell in order to profit from short-term price movements), and any such other accounts as the appropriate Federal banking agencies, the Securities and Exchange Commission, and the Commodity Futures Trading Commission may, by rule ... determine.*[7]

This description reads like a green light for continuing carry trades, in other words longer-term holdings of spread bets between liquid versus illiquid assets, market credit versus idiosyncratic credit, long maturity versus short maturity, and so forth. Of course, as described earlier, carry trades are particularly dangerous for financial institutions with government guarantees.

Hedge Funds and Private Equity Funds   With respect to the second Volcker Rule issue—ownership or sponsorship of hedge funds and private equity funds—these businesses can be highly leveraged and are likely to falter in a crisis, thus adding to the systemic risk of the firm. This is especially the case to the extent that these internal businesses have access to leverage at below-market financing costs. Indeed, the first major institutional collapse of the 2007 to 2009 financial crisis was Bear Stearns, a part of the failure being triggered by problems in two of its hedge funds.

A recent study by Fang, Ivashina, and Lerner (2010) provides some confirmation of this view by looking at private equity funds managed within banks. They find that between 1983 and 2009 these bank-affiliated funds were responsible for almost 25 percent of all private equity investments. As expected, it turns out that private equity investments are financed at better rates when an affiliated bank is involved, consistent with the bank's access to cheap financing. The study also documents that these investments are more likely to go bankrupt and generally do a little worse than private equity funds not affiliated with banks. Given such findings and the well-developed market for private equity outside the LCFI model, the systemic costs of private equity within LCFIs would seem to outweigh any benefits. We conclude that the Volcker Rule applied to private equity is consistent with common sense.

One could make a similar argument for hedge funds, especially those supported by the banking firm's own capital. If the primary advantage for running internal hedge funds arises from their access to cheap financing due to implicit government guarantees of their debt, then both the benefits (i.e., the guarantee) and the costs (i.e., the added systemic risk) are carried by taxpayers. Given the well-developed external market for hedge funds, again the Volcker Rule would seem to be reasonable.

The more controversial case is that of sponsoring hedge funds and private equity funds—that is, funds run by the LCFIs exclusively using outside investors' capital. As described earlier in this chapter, the argument that these activities are not systemic is wrong. In the case of managing alternative investment funds, the LCFI income generated from running these funds represents a proportion of its assets under management (AUM). The value of managing such funds is equivalent to a contingent claim on the underlying assets (see Boudoukh, Richardson, Stanton, and Whitelaw 2005). Such values therefore inherit the respective risk-return characteristics of the AUM. Moreover, because the amount of AUM depends on performance, the valuation has properties that resemble a levered claim on the assets, further increasing systematic risk. If the value of this business is capitalized in its market value of assets, and the LCFI can borrow against this value, then the distinction between running the LCFI's capital and outside investors' capital is not material.

More to the point, what is special about hedge funds versus mutual funds? Many LCFIs have large-scale asset management businesses. The argument for or against them being housed in an LCFI is virtually identical to that of hedge funds and private equity fund sponsorship—arguments that may have contributed to divestitures of asset management businesses by firms like Barclays and Citigroup in the aftermath of the financial crisis.

The New York University Stern School of Business Vlab (at http://vlab .stern.nyu.edu/welcome/risk) provides systemic risk calculations for the 100 largest financial institutions, some of which are publicly traded money management firms. (See Chapter 4, "Measuring Systemic Risk," for a description of Vlab.) Estimates attained from NYU Stern's Vlab show that the per-dollar risk of these firms is quite high. This is because such firms have high tail betas in a crisis. For example, of the 102 largest financial firms in June 2007, four money management firms—T. Rowe Price, Janus Capital Group, Franklin Resources, and Legg Mason—were in the top 20 in terms of their expected relative equity losses in the crisis, the "marginal expected shortfall" (MES). And when tracking these same four firms ex post during the crisis from July 2007 to December 2008, the firms' equity fell 29.8 percent, 71.1 percent, 51.2 percent, and 77.0 percent, respectively. The relevant question therefore is whether the capitalized value of asset management business within LCFIs is leveraged. If so, then these results for the MES and ex post crisis performance of asset management firms argue for the ban to be extended beyond just hedge funds and private equity funds to asset management activities in general.

The Dodd-Frank Act fails to incorporate the original Volcker Rule objective that LCFIs cease their sponsorship of hedge funds and private equity funds, implying that the risks of such affiliations exceed the gains in an environment that includes vibrant hedge fund and private equity fund cohorts to carry out these functions. Instead, LCFIs can continue to sponsor such funds and indeed invest in them up to an amount equal to 3 percent of their capital. We have argued that the actual exposures associated with in-house hedge funds and private equity funds, including exposure to reputational risk, is far in excess of the nominal exposure, and that the original Volcker Rule should have been applied as a matter of public interest.

Derivatives Trading   Chapter 13 of this book considers the impact of the derivatives provisions of the Dodd-Frank Act, concluding that their social benefits significantly exceed their social costs. The surviving Lincoln Amendment in the Act takes a belt-and-suspenders approach on the interface between derivatives markets and involvement in them on the part of LCFIs. As noted, under the Act, banks can conduct business in foreign exchange derivatives, high-grade credit default swaps, gold, silver, and other asset classes considered relatively low-risk within the bank itself. They are only required to spin off swaps desks for equities, commodities, and low-grade credit default swaps into separately capitalized subsidiaries.

In our view, the Lincoln Amendment in its original form was probably unnecessary, since the associated risks are already covered by other safety and soundness provisions of the Act, notably capital adequacy and beefed-up systemic risk regulation. However, nobody knows where the next source of risk to the financial system will come from (e.g., commodities markets), so an extra ounce of prevention probably outweighs the incremental costs with respect to exceptionally risky derivatives. This assumes, of course, that the separately capitalized derivatives unit can be ring-fenced from the capital of the parent institution.

Overall, we view those components of the Volcker Rule incorporated into the Dodd-Frank Act as a moderate success. Success of the proprietary trading ban will depend on the hard slog of successful implementation and enforcement in the real world of political economy against the smartest guys in the room and their lawyers and lobbyists. Continued hedge fund and private equity fund involvement by LCFIs, albeit with limited equity participation, is a clear failure. There is no shortage of independent firms conducting these businesses, and the residual risks facing LCFIs as sponsors are potentially damaging. And we view the limited segregation of certain risky derivatives transactions in separately capitalized subsidiaries as a potentially useful firewall in an uncertain future trading environment.

International Perspective

In terms of international legislation on possible activity limitations and LCFI restructuring, the Group of Twenty (G-20), Bank of England (BoE), Financial Services Authority (FSA), European Central Bank (ECB), Bank for International Settlements (BIS), Financial Stability Board (FSB), International Monetary Fund (IMF), Organization for Economic Cooperation and Development (OECD), and European Commission (EU) have all considered the regulatory options and the need for international coordination. But given the universal banking traditions in most other countries, there is little appetite for reductions in the scope of systemic financial firms.

The one exception is the EU Commissioner for Competition, which has mandated carve-outs by bailed-out financial conglomerates in order to restore a more competitive playing field—in contrast to the Antitrust Division of the U.S. Department of Justice, which has been conspicuously silent on the issue.

Breaking up the largest LCFIs into smaller firms, however, has been proposed by the governor of the Bank of England, by the chairman of the Financial Services Authority of the United Kingdom, and by a number of others in Europe. Further, the European Commissioner of Competition sued ING Group, a Dutch bank holding company now substantially owned by the Dutch government, after bailout funds were received, to break up the group because EU antitrust rules prohibit government assistance to large privately owned businesses. In response to the suit, in October 2009 ING raised additional capital to reduce government ownership, and split itself into two companies. The EU competitive distortion principle, however, would appear to apply to several other LCFIs with substantial government ownership, including the Royal Bank of Scotland (RBS), Lloyds Banking Group, and Citigroup.

Without some type of international cooperation on restrictions such as the modified Volcker Rule, one could argue that such activity limits applied only in the United States would provide a competitive advantage to foreign financial companies. Under the Dodd-Frank Act, foreign financial companies that are active in the United States could continue to own or sponsor hedge funds and private equity funds, and/or engage in proprietary trading as long as it is offshore with respect to the United States. Of course, if there is little evidence in support of these activities being housed within LCFIs in the first place, then it is not clear what is being given up, other than the ability to take excess risk backed by implicit government guarantees and the unpriced negative externality of systemic risk.

7.5 THE DODD-FRANK ACT AND LCFIs: LOOKING FORWARD

As part of any effort to seriously address excessive systemic risk, we find the logic of limiting government guarantees to core banking activities and segregating nonbanking risk-taking businesses to be fundamentally sound and in the public interest. This approach is akin to that of the 1930s, but adapted to the modern financial activities and the ready availability of financial specialists to conduct proprietary activities in a way that can be effectively regulated. It is a development that would be in line with the public interest as well as common sense, and one that is unlikely to trigger significant social costs in terms of financial efficiency and innovation. Indeed, based on a careful reading of the unintended consequences of the Glass-Steagall restrictions of 1933, quite the opposite could be the case. The Dodd-Frank Act represents a small step forward in this direction.

Similar to the Dodd-Frank Act, we do not favor breaking up large, complex financial institutions based on arbitrary size restrictions. But in contrast to the Act, we do favor more stringent market concentration limits as a matter of competitive structure as well as systemic risk exposure. We also support targeted scope restrictions on functional activities conducted by systemic financial firms, certainly in line with the Volcker Rule but with additional reach.

For example, an additional rule would require a complete separation of not only proprietary trading but also asset management businesses—activities that facilitate high-powered and opaque risk taking and are also highly cyclical—from commercial banking operations, which have access to government-guaranteed deposits and lender-of-last-resort support in crises, and which provide financial intermediation services to the real economy. Any commingling of these activities is harmful to the public interest.

It is most important, however, to assess guarantee insurance premiums on LCFIs that are commensurate with the systemic risk contributions of various activities and then let financial firms break up organically if they find it profitable to do so.[8] This approach considers that commingling of different activities may be socially desirable for at least some firms but not for others, and faced with higher premiums for riskier activities, the latter group of firms (or some of them) may carve out these activities as a matter of strategic redirection.

For their part, the wholesale financial industry has argued that the major changes in regulatory structure of the Dodd-Frank Act—likely to suppress earnings in the interest of preserving systemic integrity—already achieve this goal. A recent research report issued by Goldman Sachs before the Dodd-Frank Act was signed estimated that all large banks will incur regulatory cost increases equal to approximately 7 percent of net income, but the cost to the four or five largest U.S. banks would rise to about 15 percent, even before taking into account higher costs of capital after Basel III, which could increase the estimate by several additional percentage points. JPMorgan Chase, in a similar research report, estimated that—after allowing for all of the costs of reforms proposed so far—the return on investment of the largest banks would drop to 5.4 percent from 13.3 percent. The final version of the Dodd-Frank Act was less restrictive and less costly than these early estimates, but there is no doubt that complying with the new law will involve considerable additional expense to LCFIs over the next decade that will reduce their returns on investment.

Perhaps, because of the expectation of such added costs and restrictions, the stock market has turned to a very skeptical view of LCFIs and their ability to recover the economic power, political influence, and stock market valuations they enjoyed before the crisis began. At the time of the announcement of their second quarter results in 2010, the six largest U.S. LCFIs traded at an average price-to-book value ratio of 0.9 times (ranging from a high of 1.28 for Wells Fargo—an LCFI that is not a global wholesale player—to a low of 0.33 for Citigroup), well below the 2 to 3 times price-to-book ratio they enjoyed before the crisis.[9] The more erratic and volatile price-to-earnings ratios of these six LCFIs averaged 14.7 in July 2010. By contrast, these ratios compare poorly with an average price-to-book ratio of 7.8 and a price-to-earnings ratio of 20.5 for nine leading publicly traded asset management firms measured at the same time. Some observers (Baele, De Jonghe, and Vander Vennet, 2007) have suggested that the stock market has never attributed value to large banks for diversification.

In summary, while the commingling of commercial banking with investment banking activities such as underwriting and market making was ruled out in the financial reforms of the 1930s, such commingling did not contribute to the recent financial crisis. Our position falls short of narrow commercial banking (which would be stripped of any investment banking activity altogether), but regulators should prudentially observe, and wherever possible keep in check, likely spillovers from investment banking to the payment system and real-sector lending. The Volcker Rule as originally proposed—banning both proprietary trading and the sponsoring of hedge funds and private equity funds by firms benefiting from access to the government safety net—has been watered down in the Dodd-Frank Act. We support the original Volcker proposals as the best chance for limiting the spillovers. Even so, the modified Volcker Rule that allows proprietary trading in certain public obligations and sponsorship with limited equity interest of hedge funds and private equity funds seems a defensible second-best solution. The same is true of the limited requirement for trading high-risk derivatives through separately capitalized subsidiaries.

Even so, the structural basis for significant systemic risk exposure is likely to remain. Along with their commercial banking activities, restructured and slimmed-down banking institutions (or hedge funds) will continue to perform normal market-oriented and client-oriented transactions, such as trading in foreign exchange, fixed-income securities, and derivatives, as well as intermediation services like bridge financing, prime brokerage, and the like. The key benefit of the U.S. regulatory outcome, despite its limitations and loopholes, is that it may cause key firms to rethink their business models, and the population of less systemic financial specialists in the financial system will increase. Chances are the surviving businesses would be far simpler and their accounts far more transparent (and more easily subject to regulation) than those of today's LCFIs, a business model that appears to have outlived its purpose. This, in turn, would give banking regulators a better shot at understanding and containing the risks that might result in a need for future bailouts.

Perhaps most important, the firms' ability to abuse government guarantees intended for one activity by supporting riskier ones would be limited. Either way, the endemic problem of government guarantees having the effect of compromising market discipline and engendering future crises would have been alleviated.

NOTES

1. Chapter 4, "Measuring Systemic Risk," describes a methodology for estimating the percent contribution of a financial firm to the systemic risk of the financial sector. As of July 2009, putting aside government-backed institutions like AIG, Fannie Mae, and Freddie Mac, these six bank holding companies capture over 50 percent of the systemic risk of the financial sector and are ranked among the nine most systemic firms with insurers Prudential Financial, Hartford Financial Services, and MetLife included in the mix.
2. Table 7.1 does not include GMAC and GE Capital, given that these entities were subsidiaries of larger real-economy firms.
3. Sybil White, "Riegle-Neal's 10% Nationwide Deposit Cap: Arbitrary and Unnecessary," http://studentorgs.law.unc.edu/documents/ncbank/volume9/cybilwhite.pdf.
4. Suppose a large financial firm wished to increase its size. The firm could break into two firms and accomplish this goal. It is not clear that the systemic risk of the former conglomerate, and thus the de facto government guarantee, would not carry over in some way to the collection of surviving firms.
5. HR 4173, Title VI, "Improvements to Regulation of Banks and Savings Association Holding Companies and Depository Institutions," Sec. 619, "Prohibitions on proprietary trading and certain relationships with hedge funds and private equity funds."
6. HR 4173, Title VI, Sec. 619.
7. Ibid.
8. See Chapter 5, "Taxing Systemic Risk."
9. Many bank executives consider price-to-book value ratios to be a better valuation standard than price-to-earnings ratios.

REFERENCES

Acharya, Viral, Thomas Cooley, Matthew Richardson, and Ingo Walter. 2010. Manufacturing tail risk: A perspective on the financial crisis of 2007–09. *Foundations and Trends in Finance* 4 (4): 247–325.

Acharya, Viral, and Matthew Richardson. 2009. Causes of the financial crisis. *Critical Review* 21 (2–3): 195–210.

Acharya, Viral, Gustavo Suarez, and Philipp Schnabl. 2010. Securitization without risk transfer. Working paper, NYU Stern School of Business.

Baele, Lieven, Olivier De Jonghe, and Rudi Vander Vennet. 2007. Does the stock market value bank diversification? *Journal of Banking and Finance* 31 (7): 1999–2023.

Berger, A. N., and D. B. Humphrey. 1991. The dominance of inefficiencies over scale and product mix economies in banking. *Journal of Monetary Economics* 28:117–148.

Boudoukh, Jacob, Matthew Richardson, Richard Stanton, and Robert Whitelaw. 2005. The economics of asset management. Working paper, NYU Stern School of Business.

De Jonghe, Olivier. 2009. Back to the basics in banking? A micro-analysis of banking system stability. Forthcoming in the *Journal of Financial Intermediation*.

Delong, Gayle. 2001. Stockholder gains from focusing versus diversifying bank mergers. *Journal of Financial Economics* 59 (2): 221–252.

DeYoung, Robert, and Karin Roland. 2001. Product mix and earnings volatility at commercial banks: Evidence from a degree of total leverage model. *Journal of Financial Intermediation* 10 (1): 54–84.

Duffie, Darrell. 2010. The failure mechanics of dealer banks. Working paper, Graduate School of Business, Stanford University.

Elsas, Ralf, Andreas Hackethal, and Markus Holzhauser. 2009. The anatomy of bank diversification. *Journal of Banking and Finance* 34 (6): 1274–1287.

Fang, Lily, Victoria Ivashina, and Josh Lerner. 2010. "An unfair advantage"? Combining banking with private equity investing. Working paper, Harvard Business School.

Freixas, Xavier, Gyongyi Loranth, and Alan Morrison. 2007. Regulating financial conglomerates. *Journal of Financial Intermediation* 16 (4): 479–514.

Gorton, Gary B., and Andrew Metrick. 2009. Securitized banking and the run on repo. NBER Working Paper No. w15223.

Laeven, Luc, and Ross Levine. 2007. Is there a diversification discount in financial conglomerates? *Journal of Financial Economics* 85 (2): 331–367.

Saunders, Anthony, Roy Smith, and Ingo Walter. 2009. Enhanced regulation of large, complex financial institutions. In *Restoring financial stability: How to repair a failed system*, ed. Viral Acharya and Matthew Richardson, chap. 5. Hoboken, NJ: John Wiley & Sons.

Saunders, Anthony, and Ingo Walter. 1996. *Universal banking in the United States.* New York: Oxford University Press.

Schmid, Markus, and Ingo Walter. 2009. Do financial conglomerates create or destroy economic value? *Journal of Financial Intermediation* 18 (2): 193–216.

Stiroh, Kevin. 2004. Diversification in banking: Is noninterest income the answer? *Journal of Money, Credit and Banking* 36 (5): 853–882.

Stiroh, Kevin. 2006. A portfolio view of banking with interest and noninterest activities. *Journal of Money, Credit and Banking* 38 (5): 1351–1361.

Stiroh, Kevin, and Adrienne Rumble. 2006. The dark side of diversification: The case of US financial holding companies. *Journal of Banking and Finance* 30 (8): 2131–2161.

Wagner, Wolf. 2009. Diversification at financial institutions and systemic crises. Forthcoming in the *Journal of Financial Intermediation*.

Walter, Ingo, ed. 1985. *Deregulating Wall Street: Commercial bank penetration of the corporate securities market.* New York: John Wiley & Sons, Chapter 1.

Walter, Ingo. 1988. *Global competition in financial services: Market structure, protection and trade liberalization.* New York: Harper & Row.

Walter, Ingo. 2010. The new case for functional separation in wholesale financial services. Department of Finance, Stern School of Business, Working Paper FIN-09-17. Available at http://papers.ssrn.com/sol3/papers.cfm?abstract_id= 1500832.

CHAPTER 8

Resolution Authority

Viral V. Acharya, Barry Adler, Matthew Richardson, and Nouriel Roubini

8.1 OVERVIEW

With losses of 50 percent over the prior six months, by August 31, 1998, the largest hedge fund at the time, Long-Term Capital Management (LTCM), had just $2.3 billion in capital remaining, yet still held over $125 billion in assets on its balance sheet. In addition, it was the sixth largest player in over-the-counter (OTC) derivative positions, including $500 billion of futures positions, $750 billion of swaps, and $150 billion of options. Conditions deteriorated over the month of September, until on Monday, September 21, 1998, LTCM's repo and OTC derivative counterparties demanded increasing collateral by widening the daily margins on these contracts. These extra cash demands put such a strain on LTCM that default was imminent. Over the next few days, through the prodding (and some would argue pressure) of the Federal Reserve Bank of New York, a group of LTCM's 14 major counterparties agreed to inject capital into LCTM—in effect, an out-of-bankruptcy reorganization of the fund.

Just a few weeks later, in testimony to the Committee on Banking and Financial Services of the U.S. House of Representatives, then president of the New York Federal Reserve Bank of New York, William McDonough, explained the reason for the government's participation in the process for winding down LTCM:

> *Two factors influenced our involvement. First, in the rush of Long-Term Capital's counterparties to close-out their positions, other market participants—investors who had no dealings with Long-Term Capital—would have been affected as well. Second, as losses spread to other market participants and Long-Term Capital's counterparties, this would lead to tremendous uncertainty about how far*

*prices would move. Under these circumstances, there was a likeli-
hood that a number of credit and interest rate markets would experience extreme price moves and possibly cease to function for a
period of one or more days and maybe longer. This would have
caused a vicious cycle: a loss of investor confidence, leading to a
rush out of private credits, leading to a further widening of credit
spreads, leading to further liquidations of positions, and so on. Most
importantly, this would have led to further increases in the cost of
capital to American businesses.*[1]

Less than a year later, in an April 1999 report by the President's Working
Group on Financial Markets, ironically made up of regulators who are now
to sit on the Financial Stability Oversight Council as designated by the
Dodd-Frank Act of 2010, the conclusion was that:

*The events in global financial markets in the summer and fall of
1998 demonstrated that excessive leverage can greatly magnify the
negative effects of any event or series of events on the financial
system as a whole. The near collapse of LTCM, a private sector
investment firm, highlighted the possibility that problems at one
financial institution could be transmitted to other institutions, and
potentially pose risks to the financial system.... Although LTCM is
a hedge fund, this issue is not limited to hedge funds. Other financial
institutions, including some banks and securities firms, are larger,
and generally more highly leveraged, than hedge funds.*

Along with recommendations on leverage, the April 1999 report especially highlighted what its drafters believed to be the inadequacy of the U.S.
bankruptcy code to deal with large, complex financial institutions (LCFIs)
that are highly interconnected to the international financial system. As one
of the largest players in OTC derivatives, LTCM was considered a prime
example. The report argued for two major reforms:

1. An expansion and improvement of existing law as to the right of counterparties to close out, net, and liquidate underlying collateral of OTC
   derivatives and repos in the event of a bankruptcy without regard to
   the bankruptcy code's automatic stay (or related provisions).[2] This
   expansion would eventually come into law in the Bankruptcy Abuse
   Prevention and Consumer Protection Act of 2005 (also known as the
   Bankruptcy Act of 2005).
2. Greater legal certainty for dealing with the bankruptcies of LCFIs when
   they are transnational in nature.

With respect to the first point, some have argued that the provisions dealing with financial contracts in the Bankruptcy Act of 2005 actually increased the systemic risk in the system; for example, see Edwards and Morrison (2004) (predicting such increase), Miller (2009), Faubus (2010), Roe (2010), and Tuckman (2010), among others. That is, the legislation designed to address the failure of LTCM may actually have made matters worse. The arguments are complex and discussed in some detail in this chapter. And with respect to the second point, while the Bankruptcy Act of 2005 repealed Section 304 of the bankruptcy code in favor of a new Chapter 15 of the code to deal with international bankruptcy issues in a more consistent and predictable manner, these changes were not sufficient to deal with LCFIs that operated in multiple jurisdictions.

Just 10 years later almost to the date of the LTCM reorganization, the words quoted from McDonough's testimony and the April 1999 report would ring true again with the implosion of a massive real estate bubble and consequent collapse or near collapse of LCFIs with vast interconnections throughout the global economy. The names of these firms are familiar and include Bear Stearns, Lehman Brothers, Merrill Lynch, Fannie Mae, Freddie Mac, American International Group (AIG), and Citigroup, among others. The prospect of failure by these and other institutions led to a wide-scale freezing of capital markets and runs on various types of institutions, causing credit markets to falter. While there was only a single set of losses to be borne when the bubble burst, no one knew where these losses would rest and thus failure appeared to be around every corner. Put another way, the demise or threatened demise of large, interconnected firms imposed significant systemic risk. Over the next six months, regulators worldwide engaged in recapitalizing these and other firms in their respective financial sectors, but the panic and uncertainty caused by the failures of these institutions prevailed as stock markets worldwide and economies in terms of gross domestic products (GDPs) fell off a cliff, with drops not seen for decades.

In the section that follows, we describe the types of systemic risk that arose during the recent financial crisis, and the implications this risk has for designing the resolution of failed financial institutions in the future.

8.2 THE FINANCIAL CRISIS OF 2007 TO 2009

The fear of systemic risk in the LTCM episode and the emergence of this risk in the 2007 to 2009 financial crisis show that the failure of a significant part of the financial sector—one large institution or many smaller ones—can lead to a reduction in credit availability, and this adversely affects the real economy. And like the LTCM failure demonstrated, systemically important companies can generally be defined as financial intermediaries that are not only commercial banks taking deposits and making loans, but also include investment banks, money market funds, mutual funds, insurance firms, and potentially even hedge funds, whose failure poses a systemic risk or externality to the financial system. This externality can come through multiple forms, including counterparty risk on other financial institutions, asset liquidations that can produce a depressing effect on asset prices, liquidity hoarding that raises funding costs in interbank markets even for safe firms (inducing them in turn to hoard liquidity too), and an information contagion effect resulting in a significant reduction in overall market liquidity.

With respect to counterparty risk, the failure of a highly interconnected firm can have a ripple effect throughout the system. For example, consider the over-the-counter derivatives market. The main reason for systemic risk in OTC markets is that if bilaterally set collateral and margin requirements in OTC trading prove insufficient, the loss is not just to the two firms immediately affected by the transaction. That is, bilateral requirements do not take account of the counterparty risk externality that each trade imposes on the other firms in the system, which might fail if their counterparties fail.[3] Put simply, to contain counterparty risk externality, it is necessary to know what else is being done by firms other than the transaction at hand, but such knowledge is simply unavailable in opaque OTC markets. This, in turn, allows systemically important exposures to be built up without sufficient capital to mitigate associated risks.

The prime example in the current crisis is AIG, which built up a $500-plus billion of one-sided credit default swap (CDS) exposure on the AAA-rated tranches of securitized products. These positions were established with little or no capital support. Because all the trades were in the same direction, once the trades lost value, it meant that AIG's failure would be passed on throughout the financial system. Chapter 9 of this book, "Systemic Risk and the Regulation of Insurance Companies," provides a case study of AIG and documents in detail the magnitude of the counterparty exposures.

The second, and related, way systemic risk can enter the market is through spillover risk that arises as one institution's trouble triggers liquidity spirals, leading to depressed asset prices and a hostile funding environment, pulling others down and thus leading to further price drops and funding illiquidity, and so on, causing a death spiral. In essence, fire sales of assets generate a pecuniary externality on other financial firms.

Consider the plight of a weak—potentially insolvent—financial firm. If such a firm is not immediately subjected to prompt corrective action or resolution, the firm can hoard liquidity, anticipating that it would struggle to raise liquidity in markets when it needed it. If such firms are an important part of interbank markets (for example, in payment and settlement systems), then liquidity can get trapped in a few pockets of the financial system rather than finding its way to the most valuable user, as would be the expected normal-time function of interbank markets. What is worse, such hoarding of liquidity—and induced stress in interbank markets—can force safer firms to hoard liquidity, too. The result is a strong reluctance of financial firms to transfer liquidity to each other that can disrupt financing of long-term projects in the real economy. Acharya and Merrouche (2008) document such severe funding stress in the UK interbank markets, showing in particular that settlement banks that had experienced substantial capital write-downs were hoarding more liquidity on days of greater payment activity, and charging higher interbank rates for releasing their liquidity—even when secured by UK gilts—to other (safer) settlement banks.

The flip side of hoarding is banklike runs to which financial institutions operating in the shadow banking system are subject. Such runs have a contagious aspect to them. The new model of banking relied heavily on the short-term, wholesale funding market and was especially vulnerable to such contagion risk. Examples that illustrate this point are (1) the volume of repo transactions going from $2 trillion daily in 1997 to $6 trillion a decade later in 2007, and (2) money market funds accumulating over $4 trillion in assets compared to the $8 trillion of deposits in the banking sector. Since these funds are rolled over on a short-term basis, sudden withdrawal of these funds due to uncertainty about a financial institution's health can cause the institution to fail. When a particular institution fails in this manner, uncertainty about the health of similar institutions can lead to a wide-scale run, and therefore otherwise well-capitalized firms can face runs on their short-term liabilities, causing a systemic crisis.

Two examples of the crisis surrounding Lehman Brothers' bankruptcy filing on September 15, 2008, illustrate this risk:[4]

1. When Lehman Brothers filed for bankruptcy, debt it had issued collapsed in price. One of the largest money market funds, Reserve Primary Fund, was highly exposed to Lehman Brothers short-term paper and the next day "broke the buck"; that is, the fund's net asset value (NAV) fell below par. Since money market funds offer stable NAV and investors can redeem anytime at par value, there was an immediate run on the Reserve Primary Fund, causing it to shut down. Its failure, however, opened up the possibility that other money market funds were similarly exposed, causing a run on money market funds. Since money market funds are a primary source for the commercial paper market, this run opened the possibility of capital shortfalls at many financial institutions that needed to roll over commercial paper. (Chapter 10, "Money Market Funds," discusses this episode in some detail.)

2. With the Lehman bankruptcy on September 15, 2008, the repo market on even U.S. government debt, federal agency debt, corporate debt, and federal agency mortgage-backed securities came to a near halt and settlement fails of primary dealers skyrocketed. The run on the repo market may be interpreted as large withdrawals from the broker-dealer shadow banks in the repo market. In practice, this pushed otherwise solvent firms, like Morgan Stanley, to the verge of bankruptcy, and questionable firms, like Merrill Lynch, to be acquired. Chapter 11, "The Repurchase Agreement (Repo) Market," describes the run on repos.

The preceding discussion highlights the problem of having an LCFI fail and go into bankruptcy. The analysis therefore suggests that any regime set up by the government to deal with the insolvency of LCFIs must follow four basic principles:

1. The counterparty risk of the LCFI must be contained. While the hope is that this risk is mitigated through ex ante prudential regulation (including the imposition of capital requirements, margin rules, and limitations on risky investments, each as provided for by the Dodd-Frank Act), the question arises what happens if this regulation fails.
2. There needs to be a procedure for dealing with a large amount of illiquid assets. As mentioned above, forced asset sales of financial institutions can have a catastrophic effect on the system.
3. The regime should identify insolvent firms promptly as they can become pockets where financial resources of the economy can get trapped, potentially creating funding problems even for otherwise solvent firms.
4. There must be well-defined rules for what happens to the liabilities of the financial firm when it fails, otherwise a run on most of the firm's liabilities will occur. A general reduction in uncertainty about the insolvency process, and greater transparency, will also contain the system-wide run.

The preceding chapters—Chapter 5, "Taxing Systemic Risk"; Chapter 6, "Capital, Contingent Capital, and Liquidity Requirements"; and Chapter 7, "Large Banks and the Volcker Rule"—strongly argued for legislation that charges the LCFIs a premium for the government guarantees they receive and a tax for the negative externality of the systemic risk they produce. In other words, the first line of defense against systemic risk is to have LCFIs internalize these costs and thereby to encourage them to be less systemically risky in order to avoid these costs. As described in Chapters 5 to 7, the Dodd-Frank Act on the whole does not take this approach.

Instead, the Dodd-Frank Act places its emphasis on the ability of a resolution authority to wind down financial institutions in a credible way so as to precommit to no future bailouts of financial firms. Without the too-big-to-fail guarantee, the creditors of these institutions will impose market discipline and financial firms will engage in less risky activities. So the theory goes.

Nevertheless, it is a balancing act for a resolution authority to handle both moral hazard underlying the too-big-to-fail problem and the resulting systemic risk that might emerge when an LCFI fails during a crisis. On the one hand, a credible resolution authority that makes creditors, and not taxpayers, pay for the losses of an LCFI has the potential for removing the too-big-to-fail subsidy and making LCFI debt financing more market-based. On the other hand, if an LCFI does run into trouble in a crisis, such a resolution authority—usually designed in the aftermath of a previous crisis—may not be equipped to handle the exact form of systemic risk that emerges next time.

To understand this trade-off, consider depository institutions. Although subsidized by FDIC deposit insurance priced at below market rates,[5] a number of large deposit institutions, such as Washington Mutual, were not likely viewed as being too big to fail and their long-term debt generally reflected higher spreads than their too-big-to-fail counterparts. As an illustration, Figure 8.1 graphs the CDS premiums of three firms that effectively failed during the financial crisis—Washington Mutual, Wachovia, and Citigroup—during the period January 1, 2007, through the date of Lehman's bankruptcy filing

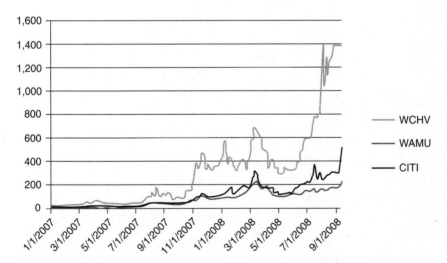

FIGURE 8.1 Credit Default Swap (CDS) Spreads of Failing Financial Firms, January 2007 to September 2008
Source: Bloomberg.

on September 15, 2008. The latter two firms, especially Citigroup, many considered too big to fail, and differences between their CDS spreads and Washington Mutual's seem to reflect this point. Ex post, market participants judged the situation correctly and Citigroup was bailed out during the crisis while Washington Mutual entered receivership. As a thought exercise, imagine a world in which Citigroup's CDS spreads looked like Washington Mutual's and bankruptcy of Citigroup was viewed as highly likely. How much additional systemic risk would have been created? The failures of Lehman Brothers and AIG suggest that the systemic risk level may have been so great that a credible commitment to allow failure would have been impossible. So even if an ex ante commitment not to bailout a failed firm would prevent firms from growing too big to fail, the inability of government to make such a commitment leaves rescue as an option, which is, in turn, anticipated by market participants.

Having highlighted this difficult trade-off, we describe in the next section the specific details of the resolution authority outlined in the Dodd-Frank Act and, in particular, evaluate the legislation with respect to the efficiency of the process and its ability to mitigate moral hazard and systemic risk.

8.3 THE DODD-FRANK WALL STREET REFORM AND CONSUMER PROTECTION ACT OF 2010

The question at hand is whether the Dodd-Frank Act serves the stated purpose, the elimination or containment of systemic financial risk. The discussion here largely focuses on this issue. A central objective of the legislation is to bring large nonbank financial institutions such as bank holding companies and insurance holding companies within the Federal Deposit Insurance Corporation (FDIC) insurance model. The FDIC is a government entity that guarantees deposits at member banks and savings and loan institutions. If an insured deposit-taking institution fails, it is taken over by the FDIC, which pays the guaranteed deposits and oversees disposition of the institution's assets. To expand the FDIC insurance model, the proposed legislation would extend the reach of the FDIC itself. The Dodd-Frank Act would create an orderly liquidation authority (OLA).

In this section, we break our analysis into four components: (1) a general description of the OLA and its implications, (2) the powers and process of the OLA, (3) the funding of the OLA, and (4) the treatment of qualified financial contracts, such as swaps, repos, commodity and forward contracts, and certain other OTC derivatives, given their role in generating systemic risk.

General Implications for Covered Financial Companies within the Orderly Liquidation Authority

Before describing how a financial institution becomes a covered financial company (CFC) within the orderly liquidation regime, it is important to point out that the Dodd-Frank Act institutes major changes for how financial institutions can (or for that matter cannot) access the Federal Reserve Bank's lender-of-last-resort function. Chapter 2 of this book, "The Power of Central Banks and the Future of the Federal Reserve System," provides a detailed analysis, so we just briefly review the argument here.

As described in that chapter, the Fed used its emergency lending powers (i.e., loans to nonbanks) throughout the financial crisis, most notably with respect to Bear Stearns and AIG. The Dodd-Frank Act greatly limits this possibility by prohibiting loans to failing financial firms unless the lending is systemwide. Moreover, innovative programs designed to create liquidity would now need Treasury approval, which could slow the process and create some uncertainty. Our view is that, with respect to the trade-off between creating moral hazard and reducing systemic risk, the legislation gets this wrong.[6]

While access to the lender of last resort allows firms to hold less liquid assets and therefore increases moral hazard on that one dimension, this would appear to be a small cost against the benefit of allowing the Fed to provide liquidity to solvent but illiquid institutions. An appropriate charge for this access could also mitigate the perverse incentives of LCFIs.

With respect to a resolution authority, the Dodd-Frank Act considers financial companies quite broadly, including bank holding companies, systemically important nonbank financial companies, such as large hedge funds, supervised by the Federal Reserve under the Dodd-Frank Act, and generally any similar company engaged primarily in finance activities. In terms of what happens when such a financial institution fails, the presumption is that the institution would go through normal bankruptcy or other applicable insolvency law.

However, upon the recommendation of the Federal Reserve Board (by a two-thirds vote) and a similar vote by the FDIC (or, in some cases, the Securities and Exchange Commission for broker-dealers or the director of the Federal Insurance Office for insurance companies), the secretary of the Treasury could determine that the financial institution should be subject to the OLA. Such financial institutions are designated CFCs. The secretary would have to establish a number of conditions, including that the CFC had defaulted on its obligations or was about to and that failure of the company under procedures outside the OLA (such as under the bankruptcy code) would seriously undermine the stability of the U.S. financial system.

If the board of the CFC does not acquiesce to an orderly liquidation, the Treasury secretary must petition the U.S. District Court for the District of Columbia. If the District Court does not find that the secretary's petition is "arbitrary and capricious," the petition must be granted. All of this must take place within 24 hours of the petition being filed. Further appeals are possible. Once appointed as a receiver, the FDIC would have broad powers to manage the CFC's affairs, including the authority to transfer or sell assets and to satisfy claims. The FDIC would not be able to use any funding, however, unless an orderly liquidation plan has been approved by the Treasury secretary.

The Dodd-Frank Act is clearly a way to formalize the somewhat ad hoc process that took place with respect to Bear Stearns and AIG, and might have taken place with respect to Lehman Brothers, Citigroup's bank holding company, or other such institutions. At first glance, the Act sets up high hurdles for the OLA to take control of a financial firm. For instance, there has to be widespread agreement among the relevant regulatory agencies and the Treasury secretary, and there is judicial review. In the midst of a financial crisis, it is hard to imagine that these will be roadblocks. Looking forward, however, there are several major concerns.

First, to repeat the fears mentioned earlier with respect to the Dodd-Frank Act's restriction of the Fed's emergency powers to provide liquidity support to a nondepository institution during a crisis, regulators may wait too long to intervene—this despite the authority to initiate an OLA prior to a CFC's collapse, if there is a mere danger of default—and have no choice but to put the bank holding company or similar financial firm through the OLA liquidation process. This seems like a very risky proposition in terms of systemic risk.

Second, while there has been a clear attempt to expedite the CFC determination process (e.g., 24-hour judicial review), the procedure—a two-thirds vote by the relevant regulators, the determination by the Treasury secretary, and the approval of the CFC's board, without which there is the judicial review in the U.S. District Court and potential appeals to the U.S. Court of Appeals and the Supreme Court—may not be sufficiently fast to contain the ensuing run on liabilities that can be pulled immediately.

In sum, because of the uncertainty underlying the OLA process, it seems possible that prior to the OLA determination:

- Runs on these and other short-term liabilities will occur in anticipation of such determination, creating a self-fulfilling OLA event.
- Holders of the firm's longer-term debt and equity will try to sell their holdings in secondary markets, putting pressure on the financial firm's position in capital markets.

- Runs on similar financial firms may occur, essentially leading to the regulators having no choice but an OLA determination for a significant part of the financial sector.

While any insolvency procedure is subject to these problems, the Dodd-Frank Act provides little guidance on how the OLA will address them. This is significant because, after all, the main concern is the systemic risk of LCFIs, not their individual risk. Uncertainty inherent in the process, counterparty risk contagion, and resulting fire sales when an LCFI fails should have been addressed systemwide in the legislation. The Act does require that certain systemically important financial institutions prepare customized resolution plans to be implemented should they fail, so-called living wills. As we explain in Section 8.4, we propose that in response to this obligation firms adopt capital structures divided into priority hierarchies of tranches (e.g., debt and equity in the simplest case), along with a mechanism through which junior tranches would be sequentially eliminated to restore the firm to solvency for the benefit of senior tranches when a firm becomes unable to pay all of its obligations. Such living wills, if properly structured, could provide a truly orderly transformation of distressed financial institutions and thus limit the spread of a financial crisis. But, as we also explain, this would be only one part of the solution, since to contain the spread of the crisis when unavoidably even senior tranches of firms must take some losses, temporary liquidity assistance—such as lender-of-last-resort facilities of the central bank or emergency lending from a resolution authority—would also be necessary.

Powers and Process of the Orderly Liquidation Authority

The Dodd-Frank Act is fairly clear on its stated goal for the OLA applied to financial institutions:

> It is the purpose of this title to provide the necessary authority to liquidate failing financial companies that pose a significant risk to the financial stability of the United States in a manner that mitigates such risk and minimizes moral hazard. The authority provided in this title shall be exercised in the manner that best fulfills such purpose, so that—(1) creditors and shareholders will bear the losses of the financial company; (2) management responsible for the condition of the financial company will not be retained; and (3) the Corporation (FDIC) and other appropriate agencies will take all steps necessary and appropriate to assure that all parties, including management, directors, and third parties, having responsibility for

the condition of the financial company bear losses consistent with their responsibility, including actions for damages, restitution, and recoupment of compensation and other gains not compatible with such responsibility.[7]

In trying to achieve these goals, the Dodd-Frank Act shapes the OLA on the receivership model of the FDIC (though specialized alternative provisions apply where the CFC is a broker-dealer or insurance company). Consistent with the FDIC's current and continuing role in resolving depository institutions, the FDIC would have the power to take over the assets and operate the CFC, including the power to transfer those assets or liabilities to a third party or bridge financial company. It is worth noting here that the essence of the Act's receivership model is also consistent with the bankruptcy process. In each case a financially distressed firm becomes subject to the supervision of an administrator—the FDIC or a bankruptcy judge, respectively—and in each case the administrator oversees the operation of the firm and the disposition of its assets. There are differences, however, in the way creditors are paid, for example, and in the procedures applied.

Take, for instance, the order of payments to creditors, which generally follows state law priorities under the bankruptcy code. Under the Act, the FDIC would be able to cherry-pick among obligations (paying some out of priority order or treating obligations with similar priorities differently) under the proviso that no creditor gets less than what it would have received in a liquidation under the bankruptcy code,[8] and subject to certain provisions for qualified contracts. (See the discussion in the following pages.)

Beyond priority, under the provisions of Title II of the Dodd-Frank Act, the OLA's procedures do in some cases follow those prescribed by the bankruptcy code. For example, secured debt, contingent claims, preferential payments, and fraudulent conveyances are treated under the OLA largely as they would be treated under bankruptcy law. But not all provisions are the same under the FDIC receivership model and the bankruptcy code. For example, the settlement of qualified contracts is subject to a stay of up to one business day after the commencement of an FDIC receivership but not subject to the stay at all under the bankruptcy code. And setoffs, which are generally honored under the bankruptcy code, are subject to alteration under FDIC receivership.

There is the potential for a mismatch between the insolvency regimes, and even where the substantive rules are effectively identical, the implementation of them under the new law may be uncertain. In general, at least initially, there could be great uncertainty as to how the new statute would be interpreted, and uncertainty can be costly.

One wonders, moreover, whether the FDIC has the institutional capacity to deal with dissolution of covered firms, which are by definition large and complex. The FDIC has been a receiver for banks and savings and loan associations, which are simpler by comparison, in that as the deposit insurer and holder of the depositors' claims by subrogation, the FDIC is the natural location for the firm's assets. This is not a reason to have the FDIC administer the insolvency of CFCs. By contrast to the OLA, the bankruptcy code, while imperfect and also subject to some uncertainty, has well-established provisions tested by litigation. And the bankruptcy courts are experienced with the management of large cases—Enron, General Motors, and Lehman Brothers recently among them.

That said, it is indisputable that LCFIs are in an important respect special. By definition, the failure of these firms presents significant systemic risk and it is unclear whether the current bankruptcy process can handle such risk, if for no other reason than the fact that the creditors' focus is on the LFCI in question and not the financial system as a whole. In addition to the discussion here, see, for example, Morrison (2009). Furthermore, despite the speed at which recent bankruptcy cases have been resolved, there is a concern that the bankruptcy process might be too slow to deal with LCFIs, whose funding is fragile, whose creditworthiness is essential for dealing with numerous counterparties, and whose complexity might place them at the center of the financial system with, as the current crisis showed, many unintended consequences.

Some experts, notably Jackson (2009), therefore, have argued for a revision to the bankruptcy code for systemically important (and possibly even all) financial institutions, termed Chapter 11F.[9] The basic premise of bankruptcy reorganization, and, to be fair, one that the Dodd-Frank Act recognizes, is that it:

> *follows (for the most part) non-bankruptcy priority rules—"the absolute priority rule"—with useful predictability, sorts out financial failure (too much debt but a viable business) from underlying failure, and shifts ownership of residual claimants, through the certainty that can be provided by decades of rules and case law. (Jackson 2009, 217–218)*

In recognizing the shortfalls of the current bankruptcy code, Jackson (2009) suggests a number of modifications:

- In order to address the issue that creditors' incentives may differ from those of the system, the relevant government agency would be able to file an involuntary petition to place the LCFI into Chapter 11F, subject to judicial review.
- Assuming the petition were granted, the case would be assigned to special masters who have experience with financial institutions and

bankruptcy law. There would be a single bankruptcy proceeding for LCFIs as entire entities as opposed to having some parts (such as the bank holding company) administered in bankruptcy, and other parts (like the depository bank) administered by the FDIC outside of bankruptcy. Expedited procedures would be employed where necessary.

- Qualified financial contracts would be divided into two types: (1) Those for which underlying collateral is cash-equivalent would receive safe harbor treatment and the exemption from bankruptcy's automatic stay (and related provisions), and (2) all others would be subject to the stay (and related provisions). (See later in this chapter for a detailed discussion of this important topic.)
- If there is a need to inject capital into the LCFI, the relevant government agency could provide debtor-in-possession (DIP) financing, which would be subject to the normal rules of priority.

The trade-offs between FDIC receivership and bankruptcy, in addition to forbearance and living wills, are discussed further in Section 8.4. The general point is that the inadequacy of the current bankruptcy code to deal with LCFIs does not imply that the code should be scrapped and be replaced by FDIC-like powers for the OLA. The FDIC generally deals with very specific and narrowly defined institutions. The bankruptcy code, and years of practice under it, is broader in its design and reach.

Funding and Financial Implications of the Orderly Liquidation Authority

As a receiver, the FDIC would be authorized to draw on what the Dodd-Frank Act calls the Orderly Liquidation Fund. This fund would be housed in the U.S. Treasury. Originally, in the proposed bill, this fund was to be financed ex ante by risk-based assessments of covered financial institutions; the more systemically interrelated the institution, the larger the assessment. In the signed law, however, this provision was dropped. Instead, the FDIC will issue debt securities to the Treasury and will repay the borrowings from:

- Creditors who receive funds in the OLA process that are greater than what they would have received in normal liquidation under the bankruptcy code.

And, if this is not sufficient, the FDIC will repay from:

- Ex post assessments on bank holding companies with total assets of $50 billion or more and on any nonbank systemically important financial institution.

As described earlier, in its mere imposition of the FDIC as a receiver, the OLA process is unremarkable. Outside the process, a failed nonbank financial company would land in bankruptcy, and a bankruptcy court, perhaps aided by a trustee rather than the FDIC, would oversee the liquidation of the firm (assuming that reorganization were not possible). And, as noted, the intended process of liquidation under the OLA largely mimics the same process under the bankruptcy code. Specifically, the OLA adopts numerous provisions modeled on the bankruptcy code, including provisions that address secured debt, contingent claims, voidable preferences, and fraudulent conveyances, among other issues. What most importantly distinguishes the OLA from the otherwise applicable bankruptcy regime is the ability to borrow against the Treasury's Orderly Liquidation Fund.

The receiver's use of the fund is discretionary. Perhaps the FDIC will use the fund as intended, just as a source of finance for the failed CFC, supplying the company with liquidity but retaining for the fund assets equal in value to the new loans extended. If so, however, the OLA might not, by itself, offer a significant containment of the risk that the failure of a large, interconnected financial company might undermine the financial system. If such a company has failed because it lacks assets to pay its obligations, and it is not subsidized in receivership, then the company's counterparties will not be paid in full and the risk of contagion remains.

One might expect, therefore, that the FDIC as a CFC receiver will use the Orderly Liquidation Fund not merely, as the fund's name suggests, to achieve an orderly liquidation, but rather will use it as a bailout source for creditors. That is, to prevent contagion effects the FDIC might be expected to satisfy counterparty claims that could not be paid from the assets of the CFC even if liquidated in a leisurely fashion, removed from the crisis.

Bailout (what we call "forbearance" in the following pages) might indeed stem contagion and we argue that the federal government should have greater authority to make loans when the risk of systemic failure is great. But, depending on the size of the risk, bailout has a potentially unacceptable cost. Even if systemically important financial institutions were heavily regulated, as the Dodd-Frank Act provides with its provisions for the imposition of minimum capital requirements, for example, the incentives created by insurance tend to encourage the very sorts of risk the legislation aims to avoid. For evidence of this, one needs to look no further than the collapse of already insured deposit-taking institutions in the recent financial crisis. For more evidence, consider the savings and loan debacle of the late 1980s, where insured and regulated (albeit insufficiently regulated) deposit-taking institutions failed spectacularly and at great cost. Insurance creates moral hazard.

Who would foot the bill for the moral hazard that insurance creates? The answer, at first blush, is the creditors themselves. If credible, the claw-backs in the Dodd-Frank Act would help realign incentives. The question remains whether systemically risky liabilities (i.e., those primarily short-term in nature such as uninsured deposits, foreign deposits, interbank loans, etc.), which are protected during a financial crisis, can be clawed back afterward. If this is the case, then, by rational expectations, a bailout will have no effect. The moment it seems remotely possible that a financial institution will be subject to the OLA, there would be a wide-scale run on the systemically risky liabilities of the company and likewise institutions.

The second source of funding for the bailout is the financial industry itself. But the ex post fund assessments would essentially require that prudent financial companies pay for the sins of the others. This would be bad enough even from merely an ex post perspective once a crisis has begun, as the costs to the financial system could be substantial, and would weigh against the ability of the system to provide credit. Ironically, an illiquid financial system is the very evil the proposed legislation is intended to avoid. But it gets worse. The Act's plan for successful financial institutions to pay the creditors of failed institutions leads to a free rider problem. This will encourage even well-managed banks to take excessive risk. The "heads I win, tails you lose" proposition just gets passed around in the financial sector, creating an even more risky and fragile financial system, making a crisis more likely in the first instance.

Chapter 5, "Taxing Systemic Risk," called for a quite different approach. In that chapter, we argued that the optimal policy was to (1) charge the LCFI for any government guarantees it receives, and (2) tax the systemic risk produced by the LCFI. With respect to (1), if there are liabilities that are deposit-like and subject to runs, and these will be effectively guaranteed in a financial crisis, then this should be made explicit and the LCFI should be charged a premium as such. These premiums would go into a fund similar to the one for FDIC-insured deposits. All other liabilities would be subject to a bankruptcy mechanism. As outlined in the next section, we prefer a living will design, but other approaches like the aforementioned Chapter 11F are also possibilities. For (2), the taxes would go into a systemic risk fund but not be used to bail out failed financial institutions. The purpose of such a fund would be to let these institutions fail and instead pay for the systemic costs of such a failure. In other words, the fund would be used to support solvent financial institutions and, for that matter, non-financial corporations impacted by a systemic crisis. In many ways, this feature should be the differentiating aspect of the resolution authority as it addresses the unique characteristic of LCFIs, namely systemic risk. Of course, such a systemic risk fund could be administered independent of the bankruptcy process.

Treatment of Qualified Financial Contracts

The difficulty in writing insolvency law for systemically important financial institutions is perhaps no better exemplified than by the issue of how to treat qualified financial contracts (QFCs). QFCs cover swaps, forwards, repo transactions, and some other OTC derivative contracts, and are essential for the inner workings of LCFIs. In fact, one could argue that what differentiates LCFIs from other financial institutions is their presence in the market for QFCs.

The current version of the bankruptcy code, enacted in 1978, initially provided a safe harbor from the automatic stay (and related provisions) of bankruptcy for commodity and forward contracts. To reflect the growth in the OTC markets from 1978 through the most recent major bankruptcy reform in 2005, the safe harbor exception has been broadly expanded to cover repurchase agreements, cross-netting provisions, credit swaps, interest rate swaps, and margin loans, among other arrangements (Krimminger 2006). The safe harbor clause allows the counterparty to the failed financial institution to terminate the QFC and take control of what it is owed from the failed institution's assets.

Tuckman (2010) provides an excellent discussion of the advantages and disadvantages of the safe harbor clauses for QFCs, and we briefly review these later in this subsection. See also Edwards and Morrison (2004), Jackson (2009), Miller (2009), Faubus (2010), and Roe (2010), among others. The original motivation for the QFCs' special status in the bankruptcy code was to reduce the systemic risk in the financial system. Because derivatives are hedged (or used as hedges) continually, tying up a counterparty's derivative positions in bankruptcy would make it difficult to manage risk going forward, leading to wide-scale risk exposures for leveraged institutions. Moreover, if the underlying collateral is tied up, the loss in potential liquidity for the counterparty might also have serious consequences. Either of these problems, coupled with uncertainty about when the failed institution's derivatives would be cleared, could cause the derivatives market to freeze. Chapter 11 of this book, "The Repurchase Agreement (Repo) Market," provides a detailed discussion of these issues as they pertain to repos.

As the aforementioned articles have argued, however, the reduction in systemic risk due to QFCs avoiding the automatic stay (and related provisions) in bankruptcy is replaced by another form of systemic risk involving fire sales of QFCs and liquidity funding spirals. Specifically, consider the sale and repurchase or repo agreements. Many repo financiers are money market funds subject to restrictions on average maturity of their investments. When they face default on a repo of a long-term asset such as mortgage-backed security (MBS), their (typically overnight) role as a lender in a repo financing gets translated into being the holder of a long-term asset. As a result, the financier may be forced to liquidate the asset upon a repo counterparty's failure. Similarly, counterparties of a failing firm in a derivative contract might need to reintermediate the contract right away, as it might be serving as a hedge of some underlying commercial risks. Then, due to counterparties all liquidating the repo collateral at once, or terminating and replacing their derivative positions at the same time, money markets and derivatives markets can be destabilized due to the pure number of trades and multiple participants. In the current crisis, there was considerable angst that a bankruptcy of LCFIs like AIG, Merrill Lynch, or Citigroup would have forced large amounts of mortgage-backed derivatives to be sold on the marketplace. Given widespread exposure to these securities by other financial institutions, these losses would have caused a funding liquidity issue, causing even more sales and losses, leading to a death spiral of large parts of the financial system.

An equally strong argument against the safe harbor is that it creates regulatory arbitrage within the system. Specifically, counterparties can build up large concentrated exposures without much consequence, and, because most QFCs can be transformed to mimic the underlying asset, there exist two classes of claims with essentially the same economic purpose, yet subject to different rules and thereby having different implications for ex ante risks. By way of example, consider again a repo against an AAA-rated MBS. If the MBS is held on the *banking* book of an LCFI, it gets treated as a long-term holding subject typically to capital requirement against one year's potential credit risk. If the MBS is instead on the *trading* book as an available-for-sale security that is being rolled overnight in repo markets, then it would be treated as being sold and repurchased each day, so that it would be subject to only one day's market risk as far as its capital requirement goes. The transformation of a long-term asset holding to overnight holding is primarily due to the repo financier having the right to take over the asset in case of the LCFI's failure. However, as explained before, in many cases repo financiers themselves cannot own these assets in the long run and must liquidate them upon the LCFI's failure. Effectively, the migration of the MBS from the banking to trading book lowers the capital requirement against it throughout the system since no institution is holding capital for the scenario in which there is systemic illiquidity and someone must hold the asset for the long run (most likely someone who incurred a huge illiquidity discount in its fire sale). Such distortions push counterparties toward designing complex products that can help shift assets from the banking to the trading book, which are then financed using short-term repos in the shadow banking system, away from the monitoring of regulators and at substantially lower capital requirements. The effective outcome is tremendous liquidity in repo markets for these products in good times, with systemic stress and fragility when the products are anticipated to experience losses. The expansion of safe harbor to repo transactions with underlying mortgage-based assets in the Bankruptcy Act of 2005 has been cited as one of the reasons for the growth in mortgage-based derivatives over the period from 2005 to 2007.

The Dodd-Frank Act essentially treats QFCs the same way the FDIC treats them in receiverships not covered by the Act. That is, at the end of the first business day after a receivership commences, as a general matter counterparties would be able to exercise their rights against the CFC such as to terminate, net out, set off, and apply collateral with respect to all their QFCs. So, although the provision of a safe harbor under the Act is not identical to that of the bankruptcy code, QFCs still generally benefit from special protection. An exception is that until the end of the first business day after commencement, the FDIC would be allowed to transfer all (and only all) of the QFCs between the CFC and a given counterparty.

Exceptions to the safe harbor clause like those in the Dodd-Frank Act make some sense to the extent the systemic risk of financial institutions might vary from one situation to the next. Faubus (2010), Jackson (2009), and Tuckman (2010) all argue for a narrowing of the safe harbor provision, albeit differently than the Dodd-Frank Act. If one takes as given the presence of systemic risk, then the following seems reasonable:

- QFCs that are liquid should keep the exemption. Liquid QFCs will cause less systemic risk in a fire sale situation, yet still allow counterparties to manage their risk without the uncertainty generated by the bankruptcy of a LCFI. Moreover, in order to get the exemption, counterparties will have an incentive to trade in liquid QFCs.
- QFCs that are illiquid—or potentially illiquid (such as repo contracts on MBSs)—would be subject to the ordinary rules of bankruptcy, including the automatic stay. The systemic risk underlying fire sales would be avoided, especially given that complex, illiquid transactions are more difficult to unwind. Of course, this would come at the cost of general liquidity of the counterparties and impact their ability to manage risk. To the extent regulators impose capital and liquidity standards, QFCs subject to the stay should apply higher liquidity standards to the counterparty.

8.4 LOOKING FORWARD: WHAT IF A LCFI FAILS? RECEIVERSHIP, BANKRUPTCY, LIVING WILLS, AND FORBEARANCE

Putting aside the question of whether the existence of a resolution authority is sufficient to induce market discipline and mitigate moral hazard, there is a major problem with the resolution authority proposed by the Dodd-Frank Act. The Act focuses on the individual risk of the institution and not the systemic risk imposed on the sector and the economy. So even if, and it is a big if, market discipline is restored, there will still be too much systemic risk present, and, more important, no way for the OLA to manage this risk. Specifically, the Act provides no real authority to the OLA to provide liquidity support to the financial system in a crisis. Rather, it is clear that the Act does the opposite—no prefunding, the ability to borrow funds from the Treasury for expenses generally associated only with liquidating the CFC, and so on. And the Fed's emergency powers that allow it to be a lender of last resort to nonbanks is greatly narrowed.

The discussion in Section 8.3 provided a detailed comparison of a bankruptcy regime compared to the FDIC-receivership model of the OLA. It seems worthwhile extending this discussion to other approaches for resolving the distress or failure of LCFIs, such as regulatory forbearance and living wills. At one end of the spectrum, while bankruptcy helps resolve the affairs of insolvent institutions and provides discipline, it may not work well in dealing with liquidity problems and systemic risk during a crisis. At the other extreme, blanket regulatory forbearance achieves almost the opposite outcome, simply blunting systemic spillovers during a crisis but at the cost of not addressing insolvency issues and fostering severe moral hazard. On balance, we prefer the idea of a living will, which offers a market-based solution that prevents moral hazard, but avoids the potentially severe costs of bankruptcy.

Table 8.1 summarizes the abilities of different resolution mechanisms to handle some of the main economic issues underlying the failure of an LCFI.[10]

Consider first the strategy of regulatory forbearance, which is largely what the government used to address the financial crisis in the fall of 2008. At its most zealous use, the idea is to provide government aid to an insolvent bank or other financial institution, in effect throw good money after bad, subsidize the bank or institution, and hope that it earns its way out of trouble. This is sanctioning private profit taking with socialized risk. Although unseemly, this solution deserves a fair hearing even if it has potentially exacerbated the moral hazard distortions of government bailouts.

In particular, there may well be a positive externality to spending taxpayer money to save a few systemic institutions so that the entire system can be saved. Many would argue that the approach was successful in preventing a complete financial and economic disaster in September and October 2008. Furthermore, forbearance helped stabilize the system, as the economy seems to be working through its troubles in 2009 and 2010.

That said, at the heart of the debate between forbearance and more drastic action like receivership or bankruptcy liquidation is the question of

TABLE 8.1 Different Resolution Approaches and Their Relative Merits

Resolution Mechanism/ Economic Issue	Bankruptcy	Forbearance	Receivership	Living Wills
Minimizes taxpayer losses	Yes	Yes (if liquidity crisis, though some moral hazard) No (if solvency crisis)	No (if liquidity crisis) Yes (if solvency crisis)	Yes
Deals with insolvent institutions	Yes	No	Yes	Yes
Deals with ex post systemic risk	No (unless the bankruptcy code is reworked, e.g., Chapter 11F)	Yes	Yes (uncertainty about priority of claims might cause systemic risk to emerge)	Could lead to contagious failures unless government funding is introduced
Manages failed institutions during resolution	Yes	Yes	May stretch government skills and resources	Yes
Deals with ex ante moral hazard	Yes	No	Greater flexibility of receivership might suggest implicit bailouts	Yes

whether a financial crisis is a pure panic—one of fear and illiquidity—or one of fundamentals and insolvency. By their nature, fear and illiquidity are temporary states of the world. As risk aversion reverts back to more normal levels and markets open up, a bank's or financial institution's general condition is likely to improve. This would suggest that forbearance is the natural strategy. Forbearance avoids both the sudden impact of a bank failure causing systemic risk and the deadweight losses associated with the bank failure itself.

For economists specializing in the field of banking, however, the forbearance approach has a familiar, less auspicious ring. In Japan's lost decade of the 1990s, Japanese banks kept lending funds to bankrupt corporate firms so as not to write down their own losses, which resulted in the government supporting insolvent banks supporting insolvent firms. This unsustainable progression has often been described as the primary cause for Japan's lost decade of zero growth.

And one cannot ignore the fact that forbearance creates moral hazard. With forbearance and its fond memories, the financial sector is likely to continue in the future to take asymmetric one-way bets. Exploiting rules of regulatory capital requirements, the financial sector will load up on securities that offer small spreads, albeit at the cost of low-probability, but significant, tail risks, the so-called carry trades. Of course, these trades offer spreads because of market credit risk, liquidity risk, and funding risk, all of which showed up during the current crisis. Managed funds buy up the debt of financial institutions under the assumption that these firms are too big to fail, although, in theory, these funds should be the ones imposing market discipline on the behavior of financial firms, not pushing them to become bigger and more unwieldy. The moral hazard from forbearance is thus ultimately one of lack of sufficient market discipline and risk-sensitive pricing from creditors of the financial sector.

In comparison to forbearance, receivership and bankruptcy regimes place their emphasis on mitigating moral hazard.[11] Section 8.3 provided a detailed discussion, and we simply review the arguments here. It is certainly true that a receivership approach allows for greater flexibility than standard bankruptcy to deal with systemic risk. But the orderly liquidation authority of the Dodd-Frank Act is, to say the least, a suboptimal receivership model. The OLA lacks the flexibility to provide funding outside its narrow scope, yet its new, untested procedures provide creditors less certainty as to outcome than would the bankruptcy code. Better legislation would leave the bankruptcy code and the bankruptcy courts to handle the demise of covered firms. Consistent with Jackson's (2009) proposal for a Chapter 11F, a financial institution's bankruptcy could be initiated by a Treasury petition to a qualified panel of judges, a process similar to that under the Dodd-Frank Act. But the result of a successful petition would be the commencement of a bankruptcy case under the bankruptcy code, not an FDIC receivership. The bankruptcy case once commenced need not be ordinary, however. The Orderly Liquidation Fund could exist as a source of capital to financial institutions in bankruptcy, that is, as a debtor-in-possession (DIP) lender much in the same way the Treasury served as a DIP lender in the Chrysler and General Motors cases. That is, one could advantageously strip away the process portions of the orderly liquidation authority and leave its only truly unique element, the Orderly Liquidation Fund.

There would be an additional benefit to segregating the Orderly Liquidation Fund, if it is to exist, from the OLA. As an entity devoted to the prevention of systemic financial crisis, rather than a mere liquidation facilitator, the fund could lend not only to failed firms but struggling ones, perhaps to prevent their failure. Put another way, the fund could focus on liquidity rather than liquidation and a crisis might be prevented earlier rather than later when it is more expensive to address. It is in this sense, moreover, that the Dodd-Frank Act misses the mark by not assessing systemically risky institutions up front. In order to avoid the charge, firms would organically choose to be less systemically interconnected, but, to the extent systemic risk remained, the prefunding could be used to support solvent financial institutions and the real economy at large.

Finally, there is a provision of the Dodd-Frank Act that suggests an alternative to the use of the OLA or the ordinary bankruptcy process when a financial institution fails. The bill requires that certain systemically important financial companies file, in advance of failure, with the Federal Reserve Board and FDIC an acceptable financial distress resolution plan (a plan that has come to be known as a financial institution's living will or funeral plan). While the legislation requires a description of the firm's assets and obligations, and provides that the plan should facilitate bankruptcy resolution, it does not offer great detail on what a financial distress plan must include to receive approval. There is, however, a developed academic literature on just such an arrangement. Significantly, the sort of living will suggested in the literature can accomplish an orderly liquidation in automated fashion, more quickly and more surely than would be possible under either the OLA or the bankruptcy code.

The academic concept of a corporate living will is, in essence, to divide a firm's capital structure into a hierarchy of priority tranches. In the event of an uncured default (after ample opportunity for cure) on a firm's debt obligation, the equity of the firm would be eliminated and the lowest-priority debt tranche would be converted to equity.[12] If elimination of the lowest-priority debt tranche created enough liquidity to pay the firm's remaining debt obligations, then there would be no need for further restructuring. If obligations to the higher debt tranches remained in default (after opportunity for cure), the process would repeat until either all defaults were cured or the highest-priority tranche was converted to equity. Only at the point where a firm defaulted on its most senior obligations, after the elimination of all junior debt, would holders of those senior obligations have reason to foreclose on collateral, as elimination of the junior debt classes would, until that point, provide liquidity that could stabilize the firm and perhaps stem any run on the firm's assets.

Significantly, in no case would there be a need for a judicial valuation or determination of which obligations were or were not entitled to satisfaction. The prospect of default-driven transformations of the tranches from debt to equity would provide firms eternal solvency—or at least solvency until a class of secured claims was impaired—and without the need for bankruptcy restructuring beyond simple adherence to the prescribed capital structure or, to use the terminology of the current debate, without need for bankruptcy beyond simple adherence to the firm's living will. Therefore, although the Dodd-Frank Act envisions living wills as blueprints for the bankruptcy process, a living will with the automatic conversion features we favor would largely eliminate the need for that process. Such an automated mechanism could uniquely provide the speed of resolution that financial markets require, particularly in time of systemic crisis.

There are potential drawbacks to the living will concept, however. For the proposal to be effective, the transformation, or winding down, of the firm must be triggered by an easily verifiable signal such as default on obligations rather than a difficult one such as inherent asset value. The key to the proposal, after all, is to provide swift rescue and payment of those obligations still in-the-money despite the firm's inability to make good on all its obligations. Such a transformation, or winding down, runs the risk that a firm in financial crisis will eliminate an interest that might have later proven to be valuable in a traditional bankruptcy reorganization, where time and the debtor's continued search for liquidity might resolve the crisis. But there are costs, too, to a traditional reorganization, including uncertainty and the potential paralysis of the financial markets that has led to the recent proposal that regulated financial institutions have living wills. Moreover, the market has recently shown an appetite for the idea, or something like it; Lloyds Bank, for example, issued reverse convertible debt, which would be transformed into equity in the event the firm failed to maintain a specified capital requirement. Chapter 6, "Capital, Contingent Capital, and Liquidity Requirements," provides a detailed analysis of various debt-to-equity schemes, which, of course, are related to the living will concept.

Living wills such as the one proposed here could quickly resolve a failed firm's affairs, freeing all but its impaired obligations (which would be transformed or eliminated) to trade at solvency values. This result limits the scope of a firm's failure and reduces the extent to which a firm's insolvency can spread through the financial system. In other words, the instant transformation of the lower-priority tranches will restore the higher-priority tranches to in-the–money status, which would cabin the contagion to the lower tranches. Thus, even though living wills are primarily focused on resolving distress of individual firms, they would not be entirely powerless in dealing with contagion. Nevertheless, some impairment of a firm's obligations would remain unavoidable under living wills, so ultimately living wills are limited in their ability to stem contagion completely. For instance, a living will unaccompanied by a subsidy—such as favorable loans in advance of default offered by the Orderly Liquidation Fund or similar entity—would not entirely eliminate the contagion from a firm's failure if key assets such as unsecured overnight funds were not paid and were transformed or eliminated as a result of default. In such a scenario, central-bank or government-sponsored liquidity will ultimately be needed for a more complete remedy for contagion. But absent such subsidization, which imposes taxpayer and moral hazard costs as outlined earlier, or in conjunction with such subsidization where such costs are acceptable, the living will solution may be the best available option.

8.5 SUMMARY

We have been critical of the orderly liquidation authority (OLA) provided by the Dodd-Frank Act primarily because it lacks the flexibility to have the government provide needed finance in the next financial crisis, because the funding of the OLA will exacerbate moral hazard, and because the resolution of covered financial companies' (CFCs') insolvencies may not be as orderly or certain as is possible. This does not imply that we altogether oppose the new Act. The resolution authority cannot be considered in isolation. There are provisions that we admire, including the Act's proposal for a new Financial Stability Oversight Council that would, through the Federal Reserve Board, have the authority to constrain the activities of systemically important companies. The prescribed forms of potential constraint usefully include the imposition of capital requirements, as observed earlier, and restrictions on risky investments (the so-called Volcker Rule). The provision of oversight is designed to prevent financial distress of large, interconnected firms in the first place rather than to manage their demise, and there is merit in this proposed reform, though we would also include direct ex ante assessments on systemic risk imposed by these firms.

There are, moreover, provisions of the new Act that address the failure contagion problem more effectively than the OLA would in isolation. The Dodd-Frank Act, for example, provides for the regulation of critical payment, clearing, and settlement functions. Effective clearing standards could go a long way toward easing systemic risk when a large, interconnected firm failed. As noted, part of the reason for the cascade of distress in the recent financial crisis was that no financial institution could be sure whether its counterparty was the bearer of a crippling loss, and thus virtually every financial institution was suspect. Such uncertainty would not exist to the same extent if a chain of offsetting obligations could be collapsed instantly, revealing the identity of a single obligor and obligee; if the revealed obligor is insolvent, its counterparties would face a problem, of course, but the location of the risk would be confined to that obligor. Central clearing is particularly appropriate for plain-vanilla derivatives that have hitherto remained over-the-counter and needlessly opaque with respect to exposures across financial institutions.

In sum, the Dodd-Frank Act of 2010 takes some steps in the right direction, but also some in the wrong direction. And a number of opportunities for more complete reform were missed.

NOTES

1. There is not universal agreement either at the time of LTCM's collapse or even after subsequent reflection that LTCM was systemically risky. For example, Furfine (2001) finds that levels of unsecured borrowing by LTCM's counterparties were not greatly affected leading up to LTCM's collapse. Interestingly, he documents a possible increase in the too-big-to-fail effect after the LTCM rescue.
2. Exemption from the automatic stay allows a counterparty on a derivative to close out, net, or liquidate a position even after a bankruptcy petition is filed. The bankruptcy code also extends the exemption to other provisions, such as those for voidable preferences, constructively fraudulent conveyances, and ipso facto clauses, that might otherwise permit a debtor in bankruptcy to claw back assets if acquired by a counterparty prior to or in the event of bankruptcy.
3. See Acharya and Engle (2009), which introduces the notion of counterparty risk externality, and Acharya and Bisin (2010) for its formal modeling.
4. See Summe (2009) for a discussion of the Lehman Brothers bankruptcy and its implications for various insolvency frameworks.
5. As described in Chapter 5, because the FDIC insurance fund was viewed as well capitalized, many FDIC-insured institutions were not charged at all from 1995 to 2005.
6. The Dodd-Frank Act also allows the FDIC, in consultation with the Treasury secretary and by two-thirds vote of the FDIC and Board of Governors, to create a systemwide program to guarantee obligations of solvent depository institutions and holding companies for a fee that offsets projected losses and expenses. However, in addition to these procedural hurdles, the creation of such a program requires a determination that a liquidity crisis is underway, and so any relief may come too late.
7. HR 4173, Title II, "Orderly Liquidation Authority," Sec. 204, "Orderly Liquidation of Covered Financial Companies."
8. Even though the Dodd-Frank Act provides this flexibility, the intent is generally to "ensure that unsecured creditors bear losses in accordance with the priority of claim provisions" (HR 4173, Title II, Sec. 206, "Mandatory Terms and Conditions for Orderly Liquidation Actions"). After postreceivership financing, and subject to exceptions such as priority above ordinary unsecured claims for lost setoff rights and special rules in the case of a broker-dealer CFC, the order

of priority for unsecured claims or junior interests includes (1) expenses of the receiver; (2) amounts owed to the U.S. government; (3) specified wages, salaries, or commissions of ordinary employees; (4) specified obligations to employee benefit plans; (5) other general or senior liabilities of the CFC; (6) obligations subordinated to general creditors; (7) wages, salaries, or commissions of senior executives or directors; and (8) interests of shareholders and the like.

9. It should be pointed out, however, that other experts view receivership as the only viable option to deal with these issues (e.g., Hoenig, Morris, and Spong 2009).

10. Acharya, Richardson, and Roubini (2009) discuss the various approaches in dealing with LCFIs during the financial crisis in early 2009. Parts of this section are based on that discussion.

11. A hybrid model is that of government- (or central-bank) assisted sales, wherein there is some forbearance in the form of creditor or asset guarantees in order to facilitate a purchase. Many transactions by the FDIC, especially in the midst of a crisis, resemble this hybrid model. Bear Stearns's resolution in March 2008 is another leading example. As such, almost all of its properties in terms of efficiency are also hybrid between the extremes of forbearance and receivership.

12. See, for example, Adler (1993) and Merton (1990).

REFERENCES

Acharya, Viral V., and Alberto Bisin. 2010. Counterparty risk externality: Centralized versus over-the-counter markets. Working paper, NYU Stern School of Business.

Acharya, Viral V., and Robert Engle. 2009. Derivatives trades should all be transparent. *Wall Street Journal*, May 15.

Acharya, Viral V., and Ouarda Merrouche. 2008. Precautionary hoarding of liquidity and inter-bank markets: Evidence from the subprime crisis. Working paper, NYU Stern School of Business.

Acharya, Viral V., Matthew Richardson, and Nouriel Roubini. 2009. What if a large, complex financial institution fails? Mimeo, NYU Stern School of Business.

Adler, Barry E. 1993. Financial and political theories of American corporate bankruptcy. *Stanford Law Review* 45:311.

Edwards, Franklin, and Edward Morrison. 2004. Derivatives and the bankruptcy code: Why the special treatment? Columbia Law and Economics Research Paper No. 258.

Faubus, Bryan. 2010. Narrowing the bankruptcy safe harbor for derivatives to combat systemic risk. *Duke Law Journal* 59:802–842.

Furfine, Craig. 2001. The costs and benefits of moral suasion: Evidence from the rescue of Long-Term Capital Management. BIS Working Paper No. 103.

Hoenig, Thomas M., Charles S. Morris, and Kenneth Spong. 2009. The Kansas City plan. In *Ending government bailouts as we know them*, ed. Kenneth E. Scott, George P. Shultz, and John B. Taylor, chap. 10. Stanford, CA: Hoover Press.

Jackson, Thomas H. 2009. Chapter 11F: A proposal for the use of bankruptcy to resolve financial institutions. In *Ending government bailouts as we know them*, ed. Kenneth E. Scott, George P. Shultz, and John B. Taylor, chap. 11. Stanford, CA: Hoover Press.

Krimminger, Michael. 2006. The evolution of U.S. insolvency law for financial market contracts. Federal Deposit Insurance Corporation paper.

Merton, Robert C. 1990. The financial system and economic performance. *Journal of Financial Services Research* 4:263.

Miller, Harvey. 2009. Too big to fail: The role of bankruptcy and antitrust law in financial regulation reform. Testimony before the Subcommittee on Commercial and Administrative Law of the House of Representatives Committee on the Judiciary, October 22.

Morrison, Edward. 2009. Is the bankruptcy code an adequate mechanism for resolving the distress of systemically important institutions? *Temple Law Review* 82:449.

Roe, Mark J. 2010. Bankruptcy's financial crisis accelerator: The derivatives players' priorities in Chapter 11. Harvard Public Law Working Paper No. 10-17.

Summe, Kimberly Anne. 2009. Lessons learned from the Lehman bankruptcy. In *Ending government bailouts as we know them*, ed. Kenneth E. Scott, George P. Shultz, and John B. Taylor, chap. 5. Stanford, CA: Hoover Press.

Tuckman, Bruce. 2010. Amending safe harbors to reduce systemic risk in OTC derivative markets. CFS Policy paper.

CHAPTER 9

Systemic Risk and the Regulation of Insurance Companies

Viral V. Acharya, John Biggs, Hanh Le,
Matthew Richardson, and Stephen Ryan

The social welfare created by insurance is unquestionable. Traditionally, insurers pool and diversify idiosyncratic risks with potentially catastrophic consequences for individuals and businesses. In competitive markets, insurers price diversifiable risks on an actuarial basis, yielding tremendous utility gains to the previously exposed individuals and businesses. The broad role of insurance in the global economy is therefore not surprising. For example, premiums collected by life, health, and property-casualty (PC) insurers totaled $1.28 trillion or 9.0 percent of nominal gross domestic product (GDP) in the United States in 2008, according to the National Association of Insurance Commissioners (NAIC).

More recently, however, some insurers have deviated from this traditional business model by providing insurance or similar financial products protecting against macroeconomic events and other nondiversifiable risks. These nontraditional insurance activities are far more systemically risky than insurers' traditional activities. For example, in the years leading up to the recent financial crisis, the monoline insurers and American International Group (AIG) wrote financial guarantees on structured financial products tied to subprime mortgages.[1] They provided these guarantees in the form of both insurance policies and significantly substitutable credit derivatives. These guarantees played a crucial role in creating and sustaining the subprime mortgage boom that began around 2004. With the decline in house prices that started around mid-2006 and accelerated in late 2007, the guaranteed assets declined significantly in value, yielding huge losses and/or liquidity requirements for the insurers. Downgrades in the monoline insurers' credit ratings led to declines in the value of the guaranteed bonds and contributed to the overall dysfunction in debt markets. Had the government not put AIG into receivership and thereby assumed its obligations, there surely would have been sizable adverse spillover effects on AIG's financial institution counterparties. Mortgage insurers such as MGIC Investment Corporation, PMI Group, and Radian Group experienced similar problems during the financial crisis.

As another example, some large life insurers, notably AIG, Hartford Financial Services Group (HFSG), and Lincoln National, aggressively wrote investment-oriented life insurance policies with minimum guarantees and other contract features that exposed them to equity and other investment markets. These insurers experienced large losses as these markets declined during the financial crisis. In addition to its massive support of AIG, during June 2009 the federal government provided Capital Purchase Program (CPP) funds in the amount of $3.4 billion to HFSG and $950 million to Lincoln National. As a consequence of the strong rebound in financial markets since then, HFSG was able to repay the funds it received on March 31, 2010, while Lincoln National announced on June 14, 2010, its plan to issue $1 billion new shares and debt to retire its CPP funds.

The systemic risks posed by the nontraditional insurance activities just described demand strengthened financial regulation. It is hard to fathom, therefore, why the Dodd-Frank Wall Street Reform and Consumer Protection Act signed by President Obama on July 21, 2010, does not focus to any significant extent on the insurance sector, beyond mandating a few preliminary steps.

In this chapter, we argue that the Dodd-Frank Act is inadequate when it comes to the financial regulation of the insurance industry, and we present our recommendations for reform of this regulation.

9.1 EXISTING STRUCTURE AND REGULATION OF THE U.S. INSURANCE INDUSTRY

There are two broad types of insurance—life and health and property-casualty—that exhibit substantial differences in how insurers operate and are regulated.

Life and health insurers (hereafter, life insurers) sell insurance protection against human life contingencies. For example, life insurance protects financially against unexpected death, annuities protect against living longer than expected, and health insurance covers unexpected medical care, disability, and long-term care costs. Many types of life insurance, such as variable annuities, include substantial investment aspects. As seen in Panel A of

TABLE 9.1 Insurance Direct Premiums in U.S. Dollars, United States, 2008

Panel A: Life and Fraternal Insurance	
Life insurance	$153,849,638,239
Annuity considerations	264,122,255,361
Totals for life insurance, annuity considerations, deposit-type contract funds, other considerations, and accident and health insurance	$787,748,498,852

Panel B: Property-Casualty Insurance	
Homeowners' multiple peril	$ 65,682,086,696
Medical malpractice	11,136,796,122
Workers' compensation	45,571,879,791
Other liability	52,695,252,309
Total private passenger auto	164,254,746,128
Total commercial auto	26,986,027,510
All business lines (including those not shown above)	$495,171,362,005

Source: National Association of Insurance Commissioners.

Table 9.1, in 2008, life insurance accounted for 19.5 percent of total industry premiums, annuity considerations for 33.5 percent, and the remainder, including health, for 47 percent. Table 9.2 shows the top 25 life insurers by premiums. These insurers capture almost three-quarters of industry total premiums. The top three life insurers—Metropolitan Life, AIG, and Prudential—capture almost 23 percent of total industry premiums. It takes only 11 insurers to capture 50 percent of total industry premiums.

Property-casualty insurers sell insurance protection against a wide and mostly familiar set of risks such as auto, fire, and homeowners' insurance. Other major lines of business include tort liability, flood, hurricane and earthquake, medical malpractice, workers' compensation, officers' and directors' liability, marine coverage, and reinsurance. Panel B of Table 9.1 shows the distribution of PC premiums in 2008. Table 9.3 shows that the top 25 PC insurers by premiums capture almost two-thirds of total industry premiums. The top three PC insurers—State Farm, AIG, and Zurich Insurance—capture around 22 percent. Similar to life insurers, only 11 insurers cover 50 percent of all premiums in the PC insurance business.

Unlike other financial regulation, most insurance regulation is carried out by the states, as has been the case since the nineteenth century. Several legal attempts have been made over time to bring insurance regulation under the federal government as part of its power to regulate interstate commerce.

TABLE 9.2   Life and Fraternal Insurance Industry, 2008: Top 25 Companies by Countrywide Premiums

Company	Premiums	Market Share	Cumulative Share
Metropolitan Group	$ 85,412,088,151	10.84%	10.84%
American Int'l Group	54,180,274,203	6.88	17.72
Prudential of America Group	40,073,876,394	5.09	22.81
ING Amer. Ins. Holding Group	35,142,085,489	4.46	27.27
Aegon U.S. Holding Group	32,184,994,461	4.09	31.35
John Hancock Group	31,506,631,544	4.00	35.35
UnitedHealth Group	31,432,339,997	3.99	39.34
New York Life Group	27,941,620,703	3.55	42.89
Principal Fin. Group	25,472,023,815	3.23	46.12
Hartford Fire & Casualty Group	24,669,677,233	3.13	49.26
Lincoln Nat'l Group	21,071,574,017	2.67	51.93
Axa Ins. Group	18,612,297,406	2.36	54.29
Aetna Group	15,820,347,491	2.01	56.30
American Family Corp. Group	15,369,985,151	1.95	58.25
Jackson Nat'l Group	14,368,161,503	1.82	60.08
Mass. Mutual Life Ins. Group	14,220,222,781	1.81	61.88
Humana Group	13,879,154,337	1.76	63.64
TIAA Group	13,798,508,923	1.75	65.40
Pacific Life Group	12,882,759,966	1.64	67.03
Allstate Ins. Group	11,115,233,740	1.41	68.84
Genworth Fin. Group	10,983,637,992	1.39	69.84
Nationwide Corp. Group	10,833,330,409	1.38	71.21
Ameriprise Fin. Grp	10,670,739,020	1.35	72.57
Northwestern Mutual Group	10,414,519,410	1.32	73.89
Aviva Group	9,490,647,446	1.20	75.09
Industry total	**$787,748,498,852**	**100.00%**	**100.00%**

Source: National Association of Insurance Commissioners.

Notably, in *Paul v. Virginia* (75 U.S. 168) in 1869, the Supreme Court ruled that insurance was not commerce and thus not subject to federal regulation. In *United States v. South-Eastern Underwriters Association* (322 U.S. 533) in 1944, the Supreme Court ruled that insurance was commerce, overruling *Paul v. Virginia,* and thus the regulation of insurance was a federal responsibility. In response to this ruling, in 1945, Congress passed the McCarron-Ferguson Act, which deferred insurance regulation to the states. This act reserved the federal government's right to oversee and, if necessary, to take greater responsibility for, insurance regulation.

TABLE 9.3 Property-Casualty Insurance Industry, 2008: Top 25 Companies by Countrywide Premiums

Company	Premiums	Market Share	Cumulative Share
State Farm Group	$ 49,944,110,234	10.09%	10.09%
American Int'l Group	31,947,476,41	6.45	16.54
Zurich Ins. Group	28,157,387,522	5.69	22.22
Allstate Ins. Group	26,880,105,440	5.43	27.65
Liberty Mutual Group	26,331,557,661	5.32	32.97
Travelers Group	21,807,760,469	4.40	37.37
Berkshire Hathaway Group	16,225,291,933	3.28	40.65
Nationwide Corp. Group	15,826,371,498	3.20	43.85
Progressive Group	13,776,834,518	2.78	36.63
Hartford Fire & Cas. Group	11,049,580,528	2.23	48.86
Chubb & Son Inc. Group	9,836,727,259	1.99	50.85
United Serv. Automobile Ass'n Group	9,575,491,347	1.93	52.78
Ace Ltd Group	8,656,266,131	1.75	54.53
I Ins. Group	8,528,226,320	1.72	56.25
Allianz Ins. Group	6,093,099,134	1.23	57.48
American Family Ins. Group	5,835,203,659	1.18	58.66
Auto Owners Group	4,409,410,913	0.89	59.55
American Financial Group	4,091,749,579	0.83	60.38
Assurant Inc. Group	3,853,077,113	0.78	61.16
Erie Ins. Group	3,799,901,584	0.77	61.92
WR Berkley Corp. Group	3,579,386,081	0.72	62.65
Old Republic Group	3,219,625,816	0.65	63.30
Cincinnati Fin. Group	3,180,460,976	0.64	63.94
Metropolitan Group	3,050,105,058	0.62	64.55
XL Amer. Group	3,035,011,919	0.61	65.17
Industry total	**$787,748,498,852**	**100.00%**	**100.00%**

Source: National Association of Insurance Commissioners.

Insurance regulation comprises several major activities. In this chapter, we focus on financial regulation and accounting and disclosure requirements. Insurance regulation also involves the formation and licensing of companies, affiliation and holding company considerations, the licensing of agents and brokers, product approval, marketing methods, on-site examinations, and investment restrictions.

An important function of state insurance regulation is the establishment and management of guarantee funds to pay the claims of policyholders of insolvent insurers. Every state has such funds, usually one for life and another for PC insurers. Not all lines of insurance business are covered. When an insurer fails, the state of domicile takes over and liquidates or rehabilitates the insurer. Policyholders are guaranteed benefits up to a cap. The costs of providing these benefits are covered through assessments against the healthy insurers licensed in that state, with the share of each insurer based on complex formulas. The state guarantee funds do not charge ex ante premiums, so no preexisting fund exists before these assessments. With considerable variation among states, insurers typically pay their assessments over time, and they often earn credits against their state premium taxes. To the extent insurers earn such credits, state taxpayers ultimately bear the costs of insurer insolvency.

While the state insurance guarantee funds have some similarities to the fund of the Federal Deposit Insurance Corporation (FDIC), which insures bank depositors up to a threshold level of $250,000 per depositor per bank, these state insurance funds also exhibit important differences. First, the FDIC charges banks premiums ex ante based on their insured deposits, providing rebates when the fund exceeds a targeted percentage of insured deposits.[2] The fund allows the FDIC to act quickly when bank failures occur, although the FDIC usually has to collect additional premiums in the event of a systemic crisis, such as the thrift crisis in the early 1990s or the financial crisis of 2007 to 2009. Second, state insurance guarantee funds have no responsibility to take "prompt corrective action" regarding failing insurers, comparable to the responsibility of the FDIC regarding failing banks. Prompt corrective action preserves assets and prevents capital depletion prior to failure, thereby reducing the costs of resolving failures through liquidation or other means.

Each state has an insurance department and a commissioner of insurance. The commissioner usually is appointed by the governor of the state, but in 10 states the insurance commissioner is elected. The National Association of Insurance Commissioners (NAIC) promotes the effective performance of state regulation by developing model state laws and regulations, by codifying statutory accounting principles, and in various other ways. The NAIC also rates investments for regulatory purposes. The NAIC's efforts have reduced, though not eliminated, the frictions resulting from state-level regulation of interstate insurers.

The federal government sometimes intervenes in states' insurance regulation. For example, the Employee Retirement Income Security Act (ERISA) preempted state supervision of pensions and health plans administered by insurers. The Securities and Exchange Commission (SEC) regulates insurers' offerings of variable annuities and other performance-based investment products, as well as the financial reporting of publicly traded insurers. When the insurance industry's capacity is challenged by large unexpected shocks or ongoing uncertainty, the federal government may take actions to free up industry capacity or provide insurance itself. For example, the terrorist attacks of September 11, 2001, yielded large property liability claims that reduced insurers' capital and, more importantly, very high uncertainty about potential future terrorist events that effectively froze terrorism reinsurance markets. The Terrorism Risk Insurance Act (TRIA) solved the latter problem by providing government reinsurance of losses from a terrorist attack when the industry's aggregate losses reach a certain level.[3]

Interstate insurers and others have criticized the high cost and inefficiency of state-level regulation, preferring a national insurance charter and federal insurance regulation. However, Congress generally has resisted changing the existing system except when faced with force majeure issues, such as terrorism and Hurricane Katrina. The states vigorously defend their performance in regulating local issues (consumer protection, complaints, etc.), and they point to far fewer failures of insurers versus partly or wholly federally regulated banks.

The financial crisis revealed weaknesses in the financial regulation of insurance companies. Notwithstanding, while the Dodd-Frank Act has stipulated extensive regulatory reform of the financial industry, it has come up with only modest preliminary steps for insurance.

9.2 THE DODD-FRANK WALL STREET REFORM AND CONSUMER PROTECTION ACT IN RELATION TO INSURANCE REGULATION

The Dodd-Frank Act contains several stipulations regarding the regulation of insurance. First, it establishes within the Department of the Treasury the Federal Insurance Office with the following mandates:

> (A) To monitor all aspects of the insurance industry, including identifying issues or gaps in the regulation of insurers that could contribute to a systemic crisis in the insurance industry or the United States financial system; (B) To monitor the extent to which traditionally underserved communities and consumers, minorities . . . , and low- and moderate-income persons have access to affordable insurance products regarding all lines of insurance, except health insurance; (C) To recommend to the Financial Stability Oversight Council that it designate an insurer, including the affiliates of such insurer, as an entity subject to regulation as a nonbank financial company supervised by the Board of Governors pursuant to title I of the Restoring American Financial Stability Act of 2010; (D) To assist the Secretary in administering the Terrorism Insurance

*Program established in the Department of the Treasury under the
Terrorism Risk Insurance Act of 2002 ... ; (E) To coordinate Federal efforts and develop Federal policy on prudential aspects of
international insurance matters, including representing the United
States, as appropriate, in the International Association of Insurance Supervisors (or a successor entity) and assisting the Secretary
in negotiating International Insurance Agreements on Prudential
Measures; (F) To determine whether State insurance measures are
preempted by International Insurance Agreements on Prudential
Measures; (G) To consult with the States (including State insurance
regulators) regarding insurance matters of national importance and
prudential insurance matters of international importance; (H) To
perform such other related duties and authorities as may be assigned to the Office by the Secretary.*[4]

This list indicates that the Federal Insurance Office would investigate
and represent the insurance industry but have no direct regulatory powers.
Instead, it would refer any regulatory problems it identifies to other regulators. For example, it would recommend to the Financial Stability Oversight Council any insurance companies that it believes to be systemically
important.

Second, the Act stipulates the creation of a systemic risk regulator, the
Financial Stability Oversight Council. Nevertheless, the Act gives inadequate
recognition to the potentially systemically risky nature of insurance. For
example, the voting membership of the Council would have a "member
appointed by the President, by and with the advice and consent of the Senate,
having insurance expertise," but not from the Federal Insurance Office.
In this regard, the Act only goes as far as mandating a study considering
systemic regulation with respect to insurance.

Third, the Act provides mechanisms to bring strong federal regulatory
authority over any bank or financial holding company with significant systemic risk. This would presumably include AIG-like diversified financial institutions offering insurance, but not other large insurance companies such
as HFSG, Metropolitan Life, and Lincoln National. Feasibility of federal
regulation of insurance is only mentioned as a subject of a study to be
carried out by the Federal Insurance Office.

Fourth, while the director of the Federal Insurance Office plays an important initial role if, and when, a systemically important insurance company
becomes distressed, there is no follow-on function. Specifically, for a failing
insurance company to go through the Act's orderly liquidation authority,
the director and at least two-thirds of the Federal Reserve Board of Governors must make the recommendation to the Treasury secretary.[5] In contrast

to bank holding companies and broker-dealers, however, the liquidation and/or receivership would be carried out by the state regulator, who most likely does not have either experience or expertise at managing systemic risk.

Finally, the Act contains specific proposals for reform of state-based insurance regulation. It focuses on two wholesale types of insurance: (1) "nonadmitted insurance" accepted by an insurer who "with respect to a state, is not licensed to engage in the business of insurance in such state," and "does not include a risk retention group," and (2) reinsurance, meaning "the assumption by an insurer of all or part of the risk originally undertaken by another insurer." While the proposals regarding nonadmitted insurance generally reinforce state regulatory authority, they simplify the fee structure, eligibility requirements, and application for surplus lines brokers who procure or place nonadmitted insurance for commercial purchasers. The proposals regarding reinsurance preempt certain aspects of the regulation of insurers purchasing reinsurance (ceding insurers) by states other than their states of domicile. With respect to state-based guarantee funds, the Act requires the director of the Federal Insurance Office to conduct a study and make recommendations on the operation of these funds, and the potential costs and benefits of a federal resolution authority.

9.3 EVALUATION OF STIPULATIONS ABOUT INSURANCE REGULATION AND RECOMMENDATIONS FOR REFORM

The Dodd-Frank Act contains little discussion of the financial regulation of insurance companies relating to their systemic risk. We recommend that insurance companies should not be able to offer protection against macroeconomic events and other nondiversifiable risks unless the insurance is backed by adequate capital and liquidity. Such protection would cover credit default swaps on AAA-rated tranches of collateralized debt obligations (CDOs), insurance against a nuclear attack, the systemic portion of insurance on municipal bonds, minimum guarantees on equity indexes, and so forth.

We support the creation of the Federal Insurance Office but recommend that the legislation go further and create a National Insurance Regulator and either an optional or mandatory federal charter for financial institutions with significant insurance operations. The National Insurance Regulator would develop deep expertise in insurance and in the institutions it regulates. It should have equal status in the systemic risk regulator (i.e., the Financial Stability Oversight Council) as the regulators in the commercial banking, securities, and asset management industries. The creation of a

National Insurance Regulator and federal charter would be less costly and yet more efficient than the current state-level regulation for insurers operating nationally.

There is no mention in the Act about the state guarantee funds, which have proven inadequate to deal with multiple insurer insolvencies. Worse still, the Act leaves the tasks of liquidating and rehabilitating insurance firms that are deemed systemic by the secretary (under recommendation from the director of the Federal Insurance Office) to the states' regulators, which have to depend on these guarantee funds. We recommend that these funds be replaced with a National Insurance Guarantee Fund analogous to the FDIC that imposes ex ante premiums on insurers. Such an entity would be in a better position to anticipate and manage insurer insolvencies. Currently, there is an implicit federal guarantee for large insurance companies without any adequate funding to fulfill such guarantees when needed.

We support a dedicated regulator for financial institutions that increase the systemic risk of the financial system. This regulator should have the mandate and expertise to cover all of the functional areas of the financial system, including insurance. We are surprised that the Act does not mention that insurance companies (besides diversified financial holding companies like AIG) are potentially systemically risky. Six of the top 30 systemically important global institutions as identified by the Financial Stability Board of the Bank for International Settlements are insurance companies. A primary focus of this regulator should be understanding the interconnectedness of the activities of these institutions and anticipating how they could lead to systemic risk. This regulator should also charge these institutions a fee for their systemic risk contributions.

On the accounting front, the Act does not consider disclosure and measurement issues regarding systemically risky products. We recommend that financial reporting by insurance companies provide regulators and investors with better information about insurance policies that effectively are written put options on macroeconomic variables and other nondiversifiable risks. These disclosures should clearly indicate concentrations of risk, how historical data are used to value the positions, and other important estimation assumptions.

Some additional accounting changes are necessary for insurance companies: The accounting for insurance policies should be made at least reasonably consistent with the accounting for risk-transferring financial instruments such as derivatives. Fair value accounting, the usual accounting approach for these financial instruments, is the best way to do this, but a discounted expected cash flow measurement approach, such as the Financial Accounting Standards Board (FASB) and the International Accounting Standards Board (IASB) are currently considering, would be adequate. In particular, the income-smoothing mechanisms in statutory accounting principles (SAP) should be eliminated.

9.4 REGULATION OF INSURANCE COMPANIES' SYSTEMIC RISK

In this section, we describe traditional insurers and their relatively low systemic risks. We then describe nontraditional insurance products, which resemble written put options on macroeconomic variables. We argue that insurers offering these nontraditional products are both more exposed to systemic risks and more interconnected with other systemically important financial institutions. Consequently, the existing lax liquidity and capital regulation on nontraditional insurance products increases the systemic risk of the financial system. We argue that insurance firms need to be regulated regarding their systemic risk and provide a schema for insurance regulation.

Traditional Insurers

By traditional insurers, we mean insurers that do not write and retain large and concentrated amounts of nontraditional insurance or similar risk management products with exposure to macroeconomic variables, and that also behave normally in other respects. Traditional insurers' primary liability is the obligation to pay future policy claims. Traditional insurance usually protects policyholders against risks that they deem significant but that are at least reasonably idiosyncratic and thus diversifiable from the insurers' perspective. However, different types of policies differ in the diversifiability of claim payments. For example, automobile claims are more diversifiable than product liability claims. Moreover, some policies with generally diversifiable risks exhibit specific risks that are not diversifiable. For example, life insurers are exposed to pandemics, which occur rarely but can devastate life insurers when they do occur.

Traditional insurers typically hold fairly high-quality securities and other financial assets. Traditional insurers with riskier claim liabilities usually hold less risky assets, so that their overall risk is not too high. For example, PC insurers generally hold less risky assets than do life insurers. During the 2007 to 2009 financial crisis, however, some securities believed to be of high quality, such as AAA-rated structured securities, turned out to be of considerably lower quality than what insurers believed.

Traditional insurers usually closely match the duration of their assets to the duration of their claim liabilities. The duration of claim liabilities varies considerably across types of policies. It can be short, as is the case for automobile and other short-tailed PC insurance policies, as well as nonrenewable term life and health insurance. In contrast, it can be long, as is the case for long-tailed product liability and other long-tailed PC insurance policies as well as investment-oriented life insurance policies.

Because traditional insurers typically hold assets for the duration of their claim liabilities, they generally are a stabilizing influence on the markets for financial assets. However, if necessary for traditional insurers to dump assets in large quantities to pay claims (as would be the case for life insurers exposed to a serious epidemic), they could destabilize those financial markets.

Traditional insurers and banks differ in two important respects. Both pertain to the fact that traditional insurers' risks usually reside more with their claim liabilities than with their typically high-quality and well-matched assets. In contrast, banks' risks usually reside primarily with their assets, which usually are loans with longer duration and less liquidity than deposit and wholesale liabilities.

First, the underwriting risks of traditional insurers' claim liabilities usually are better diversified than are the credit risks of banks' loan assets, which typically are exposed to the macroeconomy, geographical regions, industries, or lines of business. When this is the case, traditional insurers need to hold relatively smaller amounts of capital relative to the face amount of insurance in order to maintain an adequate solvency cushion against adverse claim outcomes. In contrast, when claims are less diversifiable, insurers need to hold more capital. Insurance regulators focus on ensuring that insurers hold adequate capital given the diversifiability of claims. Insurance regulators generally set quite high capital requirements given the diversifiability of claims, in part because they measure capital using very conservative statutory accounting principles (SAP) discussed in Section 9.6.

Second, traditional insurers typically experience illiquidity only when they make poor business decisions rather than as an inevitable result of their business model.[6] Such poor business decisions include investing in inappropriately long-duration, low-quality, or illiquid assets, given the uncertainty about the magnitude and timing of claim payments,[7] or writing inadequately diversified and reinsured policies.[8] In contrast, banks' illiquidity risk arises from their business model of investing in less liquid assets than liabilities.

Traditional insurers' relative lack of exposure to illiquidity results from three specific features of their business model:

1. Insurance policies require premiums to be received before claims are paid, often many years before. Moreover, policy renewal rates usually are very high, even for less solvent and less liquid insurers.
2. Traditional insurers' assets and liabilities are linked in the sense that when policyholders cancel their insurance policies, the insurer both

refunds any unused premiums and eliminates any related claim liabilities. In contrast, when depositors withdraw deposits, banks have to liquidate unrelated loan assets.

3. For investment-oriented life insurance policies with accumulated policy values, policyholders who cash out those policies early are often subject to substantial surrender charges or have the investment values of the policies paid out over prolonged periods (e.g., as annuities). In contrast, when depositors withdraw deposits, cancellation fees and waiting periods are generally nonexistent or minimal.

Because of these distinct features, most traditional insurers weathered the financial crisis considerably better than did most banks and other financial institutions. The main source of traditional insurers' losses during the crisis resulted primarily from the general decline in the markets for securities and other financial assets. In fact, most traditional insurers experienced little or no problem with illiquidity.

Nontraditional Products

While most insurers remained focused on the traditional insurance activities described previously, in the years leading up to the financial crisis, some insurers or their affiliates wrote and retained increasingly large and concentrated amounts of nontraditional insurance policies or similar risk management products with exposure to macroeconomic variables. In this section, we discuss the three examples of this migration from traditional insurance that were most affected by the financial crisis: (1) credit default swaps (CDSs) and other financial guarantees, (2) mortgage insurance, and (3) minimum guarantees and other contract features in investment-oriented life insurance policies.

Credit default swaps and other similar financial guarantees expose insurers or their affiliates to economy-wide risks in part because the default is correlated with the business cycle (see Figure 9.1). As of June 2008, AIG had written a notional value of $307 billion regulatory capital CDSs that exposed itself to significant correlated risks such as a European or worldwide recession.[9] In addition, leading up to the financial crisis, AIG's Financial Products division (AIG FP) and monoline insurers[10] wrote large and concentrated amounts of CDSs and other financial guarantees on structured asset-backed securities, which are typically supersenior CDOs backed primarily by subprime mortgages and mortgage-backed securities.[11] House price depreciation, a macroeconomic variable with significant adverse effects on the overall economy, drove losses on the guaranteed securities and thus on these CDSs and other financial guarantees during the financial crisis.[12]

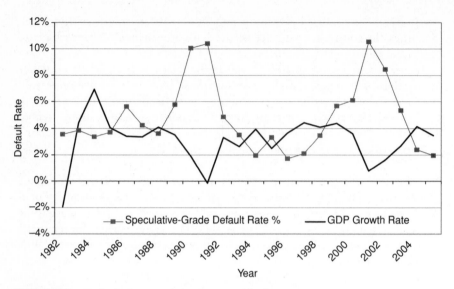

FIGURE 9.1   Default Rate and the Business Cycle

When the writers of these guarantees provided them in the form of CDSs, as AIG FP did, the guarantees resulted in large collateral requirements as they moved into-the-money and/or as the writers' credit ratings were downgraded.

   Mortgage insurers, such as MGIC Investment Corporation, PMI Group, and Radian Group, guarantee high loan-to-value ratios or otherwise risky mortgages, typically as a prerequisite for banks to issue those mortgages. These insurers effectively are a specialized type of financial guarantor. Similar to AIG FP and the monoline insurers, these insurers were adversely affected by house price declines during the financial crisis. For example, from 2007 through the first half of 2009, the largest mortgage insurer—MGIC—lost about $3.5 billion after tax, about 80 percent of its end-of-2006 book value of $4.3 billion. In addition, Figure 9.2 shows that such big mortgage insurers as MGIC and Radian experienced significant widening in CDS spreads during the crisis.

   Minimum guarantees and other contract features in investment-oriented life insurance policies[13] expose insurers to declines in equity markets (and to a lesser extent in debt, real estate, and other investment markets), as well as to decreases in interest rates.[14] Like house price depreciation, equity price declines have significant adverse effects on the overall economy. Over time, aggressive competition led the writers of variable annuities to offer increasingly generous and complex minimum guarantees. As a consequence,

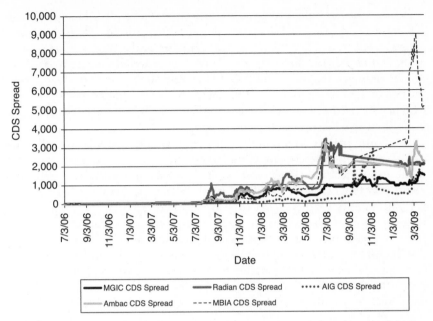

FIGURE 9.2 Five-Year Credit Default Swap Spreads on Monolines and AIG

many of these writers, notably AIG, HFSG, and Lincoln National, all of whom received funds from the federal government during the financial crisis, experienced large losses when equity markets declined sharply during the crisis, particularly in late 2008 and early 2009. While in principle insurers can reinsure or hedge their minimum guarantees, these risk management alternatives involve nontrivial costs and basis risks, and in practice, most insurers offering products with these features have not been fully hedged.

HFSG is a good example. The fair value of HFSG's liability for its U.S. guaranteed minimum withdrawal benefits (its most important but not its only significant guaranteed benefit) increased from $1.4 billion at the beginning of 2008 to $6.5 billion at the end of 2008. Of the $5.0 billion gross loss on HFSG's guaranteed minimum withdrawal benefits during 2008, $962 million was covered by reinsurance and $3.4 billion by hedge derivatives. The $631 million net loss on these guarantees during 2008 equaled 3.3 percent of the book value of HFSG's owners' equity of $19.2 billion at the beginning of 2008.

HFSG was exposed to the decline in investment markets during 2008 in other significant ways as well. During that year, it recorded $5.9 billion of realized losses in net income and $11.5 billion of unrealized losses in other comprehensive income, primarily on debt investments. It also experienced a $301 million falloff in fee income because of its decline in assets under management from $372 billion at the beginning of the year to $298 billion at the end of the year. In total, HFSG's owners' equity declined by over half to $9.3 billion at the end of 2008 and by almost 60 percent to $7.9 billion at the end of the first quarter of 2009. This decrease in HFSG's owners' equity explains its need for the $3.4 billion of federal Capital Purchase Program funds it received in June 2009.

Importantly, variable annuity writers generally have not become illiquid as a direct result of these minimum guarantees and other contract features, because these features usually defer and/or spread out insurers' required payments over time. However, HFSG, Lincoln National, and a number of other variable annuity writers have experienced liquidity problems for indirectly related reasons, such as declining fees from assets under management and impairment losses on assets in their general accounts. In fact, Figure 9.3 shows that both HFSG and Lincoln National were under substantial stress: Their CDS spreads increased remarkably from July 2007 and continued to shoot up during the crisis period. Had some significant unexpected source of additional claim payments, such as an epidemic, occurred during this financial

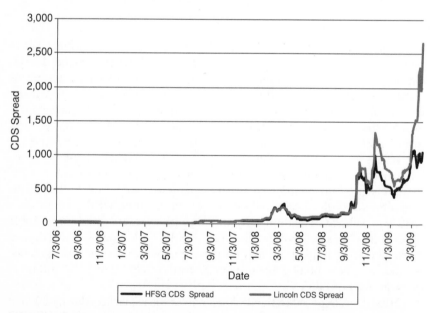

FIGURE 9.3   Five-Year Credit Default Swap Spreads for Two Major Variable Annuity Writers (HFSG and Lincoln)

crisis, it is conceivable that life insurers writing variable annuities would have become unable to honor their minimum guarantees. This could have led to the affected insurers having to sell assets in fire sales and/or to policyholder runs on these insurers.[15] Since a number of very large life insurers write variable annuities, such effects could have exacerbated systemic risk.[16]

In summary, these nontraditional products are similar in that they all involve insurers or their affiliates writing put options explicitly or implicitly tied to macroeconomic variables. Such put options on macroeconomic variables are nondiversifiable and pay off in times of macroeconomic downturns. Financial guarantees also provide direct interconnections between insurers and other systemically important financial institutions, as well as the functioning of systemically important capital markets. For these reasons, these products are far more systemically risky than is traditional insurance.

Interconnections between Insurers and Systemically Important Financial Institutions and Markets

As a result of their increasing nontraditional activities, certain insurers have become deeply interconnected with other systemically important financial institutions and capital markets (e.g., securitization markets). The most direct interconnection results from insurers writing financial guarantees that protect other financial institutions against default or nonperformance on their assets. While these interconnections have long existed to some extent—for example, PC insurers provided surety insurance[17] and monoline insurers provided financial guarantees long before the financial crisis of 2007 to 2009—they strengthened considerably during the years immediately prior to the financial crisis. These strengthened interconnections provided channels for systemic risk to flow between insurers and other financial institutions and markets. Figure 9.4 depicts one such channel between insurers and banks, showing that monoline reinsurers and insurance firms are net sellers of credit derivatives, while banks are net buyers of these derivatives. When an insurer that provides financial guarantees to other financial institutions fails, then those institutions find themselves exposed to risks they believed they had hedged. This creates or exacerbates any existing systemic risk in those other institutions. Conversely, the failure of the insurer could arise in part or whole from its need to pay under these financial guarantees.

These interconnections are most likely to yield systemic risk when both of two conditions hold: (1) the financial guarantees are concentrated in specific insurers and (2) payments on the guarantees are highly correlated. The second condition is likely to hold when the guarantees are explicitly or implicitly tied to macroeconomic variables. Both of these conditions held for

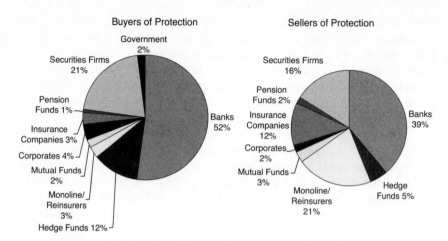

Buyers of Protection

Sellers of Protection

FIGURE 9.4 Who Uses Credit Derivatives?
Source: Credit Derivatives Report 2006 © British Bankers' Association,
www.bba.org.uk.

AIG FP's $450 billion written CDS exposure and monoline insurers' large written CDS and financial guarantee exposures.

Once significant interconnections exist between an insurer and other systemically important financial institutions and markets, then anything that reduces the insurer's ability to pay claims on its credit-risk-related guarantees can create or exacerbate its systemic risk and the systemic risk of the other financial institutions and markets for which it provides guarantees. AIG experienced very large losses in its insurance operations due to repurchase agreements involving structured securities and aggressive writing of variable annuities and other insurance products. These losses contributed to AIG's systemic risk.

Summary and a Schema for Insurance Regulation

Traditional insurance has low systemic risk. Insurance claims typically are idiosyncratic and diversifiable. To the extent that insurance claims are not diversifiable, insurance regulators set capital requirements to ensure that traditional insurers hold more than adequate capital. Traditional insurance claims generally involve relatively low liquidity requirements except in rare and extremely adverse claim outcomes. Traditional insurers typically are not significantly interconnected with systemically important financial institutions or capital markets.

The nontraditional products written and held by some insurers or their affiliates, as discussed earlier, involve considerably higher systemic risks. Even so, these products were often less burdened by regulatory capital and liquidity requirements than traditional insurance products. This is most apparent for AIG FP's written CDSs, which imposed no regulatory capital and liquidity requirements on this noninsurance subsidiary of AIG but ultimately required massive amounts of capital and liquidity provided by the federal government. This also is true to a lesser extent for the monoline insurers' financial guarantees, for mortgage insurance, and for the minimum guarantees and other contract features in investment-oriented life insurance policies, because of the underappreciated high positive correlation of claims under these policies.

Figures 9.5 and 9.6 provide a useful schema for insurance regulation. Figure 9.5 depicts the regulatory capital and liquidity requirements of traditional insurance policies compared with the various types of nontraditional products. Figure 9.6 shows the economic capital and liquidity that these products require to pay claims that arise as a result of adverse movements in the macroeconomic variables involved. Comparison of the two figures

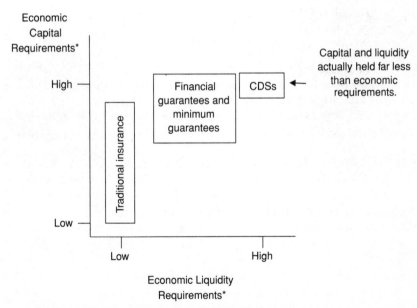

*Amounts needed to cope with adverse circumstances when they occur.

FIGURE 9.5 Economic Capital and Liquidity Requirements of Traditional Insurance Policies Compared with Nontraditional Insurance Products

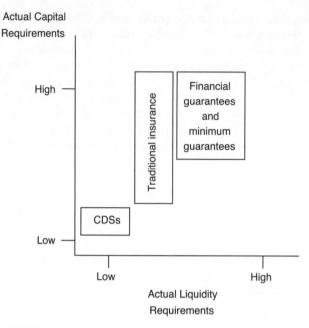

FIGURE 9.6 Actual Capital and Liquidity Requirements of Traditional Insurance Policies Compared with Nontraditional Insurance Products

indicates that nontraditional products require capital and liquidity far beyond what are currently mandated by insurance or other regulators.

Insurance industry regulators could address this problem using the following approaches:

- Raise regulatory capital and liquidity requirements for these products to levels commensurate with the amount of capital and liquidity that will be required to make the required payments on these products when the macroeconomic variables involved move unfavorably.
- Restrict insurers from writing and holding too much of these products; within financial holding companies, fully seal off insurance subsidiaries from affiliates offering these products.
- Require daily settlement or another mechanism that requires writers of these products to adjust their capital and available liquidity frequently.
- Require insurers to disclose concentrations of these products and the extent of their capitalization and collateralization or the dedicated liquidity available to make payments. This disclosure could be made in financial reports, through market clearinghouses/registries, or other means.

9.5 THE IMPORTANCE OF FEDERAL REGULATION FOR INSURANCE COMPANIES

Our insurance regulatory proposals in Section 9.4 ("Summary and a Schema for Insurance Regulation") do not fully address the systemic risks of insurers offering nontraditional insurance products. We argue in this section that the existence of too-interconnected-to-fail insurers that must be bailed out by taxpayers' money in a financial crisis and that exert externalities on the entire financial system requires a federal regulator with the authority and resources to regulate these companies. State insurance regulators are inherently limited in their ability to do so, for various reasons. These regulators generally will not have access to all of the relevant information about the insurers operating in multiple states and the overall financial system in which they operate, and so will not be able to see the potential magnitude of and avenues for insurers' systemic risk. With considerable variation across states, state regulators lack the financial resources and technical skills to measure the systemic risk contributions of individual insurers, as well as the ability to levy premiums for these contributions. Were a state to levy higher premiums or otherwise treat insurers' systemic risk contributions more onerously, insurers would have the incentive to redomicile in more lenient states (i.e., engage in regulatory arbitrage).

In the first two parts of Section 9.5, we argue that some insurance companies are too-interconnected-to-fail, imposing significant systemic risk on the economy and overwhelming state guarantee funds' ability to resolve the potential failures of these companies. In the third part of Section 9.5, we explain the reasons why additional federal regulation is necessary beyond the creation of the Federal Insurance Office, stipulated by the Dodd-Frank Act. We argue for the creation of a National Insurance Regulator and an associated federal charter, the establishment of a National Insurance Guarantee Fund, and the regulation of some insurance companies by a dedicated systemic risk regulator.

Are Some Insurance Companies Too Interconnected to Fail?

Systemic risk can be conceived as the potential failure of a significant part of the financial sector—one large institution or many smaller ones—leading to reductions in the availability of credit and/or critical risk management products such as insurance, thereby adversely affecting the real economy. Because of the interconnectedness of the modern financial sector, for the purposes of systemic risk regulation one must view the financial sector broadly as composed of not just commercial banks taking deposits and making loans, but also investment banks, money market funds, mutual funds, insurers, and potentially even hedge funds and private equity funds.

The potential failure of too-interconnected-to-fail companies poses a systemic risk or externality to the financial system as a whole.[18] This externality can be manifest through an informationally contagious effect on other financial institutions, a decline in asset prices, a reduction in overall market liquidity, and other ways. The insurance sector can generate several specific types of systemic risk.

The first type is counterparty risk. If a financial institution is highly interconnected with other financial institutions, then its failure can ripple throughout the system. For example, consider over-the-counter (OTC) derivatives markets. The main reason for systemic risk in these markets is that bilaterally set collateral and margin requirements in OTC trading do not incorporate the counterparty risk externality that concentration of trades with specific counterparties with insufficient liquidity and capital to absorb the potential losses imposes on the rest of the financial system.[19] The prime example in the 2007 to 2009 financial crisis is AIG, which wrote $450 billion of CDSs on the so-called supersenior (i.e., senior to AAA-rated) tranches of securitized products with little or no capital support. Because all AIG's trades were in the same direction and highly correlated, once the trades lost value, AIG did not have sufficient liquidity to post collateral and capital to absorb the losses on the trades. AIG's failure would have passed through the financial system had the federal government not put AIG into receivership and assumed its obligations (see Appendix A).

Another example is the ratings downgrades of major insurers that took place in the first six months of 2008. Figure 9.2 showed a deterioration of credit quality of some of the major insurers: CDS spreads jumped at the start of the crisis in July 2007, increased gradually through the first half of 2008, and spiked in June 2008. As the major rating agencies downgraded these insurers during 2008, thousands of municipal bonds and structured products that had been guaranteed by the insurers were downgraded. The downgraded bonds, in turn, required financial institutions owning the bonds either to hold more capital or to sell them, putting additional downward pressure on the pricing of the bonds.

Reinsurance exhibits many of the same characteristics as the OTC derivatives markets just described. Reinsurance contracts are opaque, bilaterally negotiated contracts. The contracts provide a means for insurers to become interconnected, and thus to pass on systemic risk. Most reinsurers are large and global entities that primarily are regulated indirectly through their interactions with the primary insurers that cede insurance to them. It is critical that reinsurers hold adequate capital and liquidity to pay claims on their contracts, and that concentrations of exposures in reinsurers be observable to market participants and regulators. A partial solution to the opacity problem is a centralized clearinghouse for standardized reinsurance contracts along the lines under consideration for OTC derivatives. Since it is likely that many reinsurance contracts will be nonstandardized, however, a federal regulator should have access to *all* of the contracts (through a national registry).

The second type of systemic risk is spillover risk. This is the risk that one institution's losses or illiquidity cause it to sell assets, thereby depressing asset prices and causing losses and funding illiquidity for other financial institutions, leading to further price drops and illiquidity.[20] Indeed, the high probability of fire sales of assets was one of the reasons the government put both Fannie Mae and Freddie Mac into conservatorship. The two institutions together held over $1.4 trillion of mortgage-backed securities, $250 billion of which were less liquid, nonprime securities.

Insurance companies, as one of the major holders of illiquid long-term securities, pose a similar threat to the system. For example, according to the NAIC and the American Council of Life Insurers, life insurers held assets of $5.1 trillion at the end of 2007. These assets were distributed across all areas of financial markets: 38 percent in corporate bonds, 33 percent in stocks, 11 percent in government bonds, 6 percent in commercial mortgages, and 12 percent across a variety of assets. Life insurers are the largest source of corporate bond financing, providing further evidence of their overall importance to the financial system. Table 9.4 provides a list of the top 25 life insurance companies by total assets at the end of 2007. Almost 24 percent of the assets are concentrated in just three firms—Metropolitan Life, Prudential, and AIG—and the largest 25 life insurance companies hold almost 79 percent of industry assets. Containment of this second type of systemic risk requires ex ante measurement of systemic risk and a type of tax for systemic risk contributions. (We discuss two useful ex ante measures of systemic risk in detail in Appendix B.)

The third type of systemic risk is the possibility of runs resulting from many financial institutions' fragile capital structures, which finance long-duration or low-liquidity assets with shorter-term or more liquid liabilities. For example, the collapse of Lehman Brothers and the value of its short-term debt caused the largest money market fund, the Prime Reserve Fund, to "break the buck," leading to a run on the entire money market system. Only the government's 100 percent backstop of money market funds reversed the slide.

While insurers' liabilities are not as subject to large-scale runs due to the stickiness of the majority of their funding (i.e., their premiums), it is not beyond the realm of possibility that there could be a run on insurance companies. Insurance contracts (even long-term ones based on life insurance

TABLE 9.4 Largest Life Insurance Entities by Total Assets, December 31, 2007

Company	Assets ($ Billions)	Market Share	Cumulative Share
Metropolitan Life	$ 457	8.9%	8.9%
Prudential Financial	387	7.6	16.5
American Int'l Group	364	7.1	23.6
Hartford Life	264	5.2	28.8
Manulife Financial	218	4.3	33.0
TIAA	199	3.9	36.9
Aegon USA	198	3.9	40.8
New York Life	193	3.8	44.6
ING North America	191	3.7	48.3
AXA Financial	159	3.1	51.4
Northwestern Mutual	157	3.1	54.5
Lincoln Financial	155	3.0	57.5
Principal Financial	136	2.7	60.2
Massachusetts Mutual	132	2.6	62.8
Nationwide	111	2.2	64.9
Pacific Life	99	1.9	66.9
Allstate	89	1.7	68.6
River Source Insurance	85	1.7	70.3
Jackson National	77	1.5	71.8
Allianz	70	1.4	73.2
Genworth Fin. Group	68	1.3	74.5
Sun Life Assurance	62	1.2	75.7
Thrivent Financial for Lutherans	57	1.1	76.8
Aflac	56	11	77.9
State Farm	45	09	78.8
Industry total	**$5,114**	**100.00%**	**100.00%**

Source: National Association of Insurance Commissioners, American Council of Life Insurers.

with withdrawal penalties) generally can be cashed in or simply closed out and reopened elsewhere. Many types of insurance are commodities sold by numerous insurers in a highly competitive industry. If policyholders do not have adequate faith in state guarantee funds because they do not collect up-front premiums or for other reasons, then policyholders likely would move their policies elsewhere when insurers' solvency becomes suspect. A run on a major insurance company could lead to the types of systemic problems mentioned earlier and, with enough opacity in the system, could lead to runs on other similar insurers. The potential for such contagion was one of the primary reasons cited by AIG for not letting AIG fail during the fall of 2008 (see Appendix A).

In summary, insurers' systemic risks require regulation. Systemic risk is a negative externality imposed by each financial firm on the system. While each insurer is motivated to prevent its own collapse, it is unlikely to act to prevent a collapse of the system as a whole. So when an insurer attempts to increase its expected return by holding large amounts of illiquid assets (e.g., structured subprime mortgage-backed securities), or concentrating its risk into particular exposures (e.g., guarantees of those securities), or holding less collateral or capital, its incentive is to manage its own risk-return trade-off and to ignore the spillover risk it imposes on other financial institutions.

Too-Interconnected-to-Fail, Systemic Risk, and Issues with the State Guarantee Funds

State guarantee funds are the current way to deal with the failure of an insurer. These funds have been strengthened and extended in response to federal threats to create federal charters, regulation, or federal guarantee funds for insurance companies (as in the bills proposed by Representative John Dingell in 1992 and 1993). They have coped with numerous insurance failures, mostly small PC insurers, but also a few large life insurers—Mutual Benefit in 1992 and the largest, Executive Life, in the late 1980s. The life guarantee funds disbursed over $6 billion between 1988 and 2007 to policy holders of failed insurers.

Questions about the guarantee funds have existed since well before the recent financial crisis. Clearly, the state funds misprice risk by not assessing ex ante risk-based premiums. How serious is this economic distortion? A similar mispricing exists for the Federal Deposit Insurance Corporation (FDIC) and the Pension Benefit Guaranty Corporation (PBGC), although Congress has partially addressed the issue.

The practice of assessing the healthy insurers operating in each state for the costs of paying the claims of policyholders of the state's failed insurers and granting the healthy insurers premium tax credits for those assessments moves much of the cost onto the states' taxpayers. Is this the right way to finance such guarantees? Shouldn't the insurance industry price its products to cover guarantee costs? The answer is yes, because otherwise insurance companies will not internalize the systemic costs they impose on markets. The fact that these systemic costs cut across state and even international lines renders state regulation problematic.

The financial crisis of 2007 to 2009 raises other questions about the adequacy of the state guarantee funds. The total one-year capacity nationwide of the life and health insurance associations is $10 billion. The maximum paid is limited to $600,000 per policyholder in most states.[21] The money has to be gathered state by state for policyholders in those states—a process that would take years to accomplish. This capacity is clearly much lower than insurers' potential losses from systemically risky events. For example, as described in Appendix A, AIG's insurance companies (i.e., not AIG FP) incurred losses of $40 billion during the crisis. In addition, Metropolitan Life (with $400 billion in assets) was considered too big to fail and probably too interconnected to fail, and the state guarantee funds would have been inadequate to prevent such a failure and to cover policyholder claims in an insolvency.[22] Furthermore, HFSG and Lincoln National's receipt of federal CPP funds—something state guarantee funds could not do—reduced the threat of failure of those companies.

In summary, many large (particularly PC) insurers are deemed to be too interconnected to fail or constitute systemic risks because of their interconnectedness with other financial firms. State-level regulation through guarantee funds is inadequate to deal with these risks. Who, then, should regulate the systemic risk in the insurance sector?

Federal Regulation of the Insurance Sector

The issues raised in the first two parts of this section suggest the need for federal regulation of the insurance sector. In fact, proposals for *optional* (not mandatory) federal chartering for insurance companies have frequently been made in the post-McCarran-Ferguson Act period. The proposals have come in response to perceived failures of state regulation and have usually been followed by efforts by the states to mitigate those concerns.

In the 1960s, Senator Edward Brooke of Massachusetts, with a number of cosponsors in the Senate, sponsored an alternative Federal Charter Bill, motivated primarily by the states' assessing 2 percent premium taxes on annuity premiums. This tax made it virtually impossible for insurers to compete against new noninsurance companies entering the pension business. TIAA-CREF was the principal company supporting the bill since the company did primarily a pension annuity business. The rest of the insurance industry vigorously opposed the bill. Subsequently, the states imposing the taxes relented, removing the bill's motivation.

In 1992 and 1993, Representative John Dingell introduced a bill entitled the Federal Insurance Solvency Act (HR 1290 in 1993) in response to a spate of insurer insolvencies in the 1970s and 1980s, under the assumption that the federal government was ultimately liable for the industry losses. Since a federal insurance guarantee ultimately requires full regulation of insurers, the insurance industry opposed the legislation and successfully blocked it.

Once the threat of federal regulation was removed, the states responded with a strengthening and broadening of state guarantee funds.

During the several years of negotiation for the Gramm-Leach-Bliley bill in the mid-1990s, the insurance industry changed its position on having an optional federal charter. It advocated a bill akin to the banking regulation framework of coexisting federal and state bank regulation, which arguably offers the benefits of healthy regulator competition. This bill, introduced in 2001, was rejected by Congress, which at the time was dominated by an antiregulation view that opposed creating another federal regulatory agency.

The pros and cons of federal regulation were discussed thoroughly at an American Enterprise Institute (AEI) conference in June 1999, with papers published the following year.[23] The interests of the insurance industry and of supporters of the bill were briefly as follows:

- The balkanization of 50 state regulators was extremely inefficient. An evaluation of the extra costs of the regulators themselves, the costly compliance with the many variations in the 50 states, and the market-related inefficiencies suggested that the first two costs were large but did not seem sufficient to dictate a major regulatory change. The market-related inefficiencies were impossible to measure but would loom large as new noninsurance competitors entered the insurance business with the simplicity of a single regulator.
- Optional chartering for companies would not eliminate the states' roles since only the large multistate insurers would be likely to opt for a federal charter. Advocates noted the benefits and successes of the dual-regulation format in the banking system, and the regulatory progress embodied in healthy regulatory competition.
- Proponents expected that the federal regulator would abandon many state features such as policy form approvals (substantial delays in coming to market occur when 50 states must approve a new product), rate setting (primarily in the property-casualty business), and possibly the requirement to produce two complex and very different sets of financial statements—under generally accepted accounting principles (GAAP) for investors and under state-defined statutory accounting principles for state safety and soundness regulation.
- Another common concern was that no agency in the federal government had an in-depth knowledge of the insurance business. "In a time of economic difficulty or crisis, a federal insurance agency may be a critical player" (C. F. Muckenfuss [Wallison 2000]).

In rebuttal, state insurance regulators cited the historical success of their safety and soundness regulation, with their "50 eyes" on insurers, the progress made by the states and the NAIC in meeting industry concerns, and the local nature of consumer protection. One of the success stories state regulation advocates often quote is the state-run bailout of General American Life, a very large but probably not too-big-to-fail or very systemic company. The company had entered into an imprudent set of transactions, with the approval of the Missouri Insurance Department, that produced a high-yielding money market return but were dependent on the company keeping its AA rating. The rating went down, and the rush to the exit was a classic run, rendering the company unable to meet its obligations. The state engineered a bailout by Metropolitan Life that saved the state guarantee fund from doing anything. In a recent meeting, the former CEO of New York Life cited the General American Life experience to prove that the states' resolution authority worked just fine. Some academics also noted the fundamental theoretical proposition in public finance that regulatory functions are best implemented at the lowest level of government possible in order to be closer to the people and firms affected.

These were the fundamental arguments regarding insurance regulation made in 1999. The concerns have not gone away—and in fact, some predictions of danger have come true with alarming force. Moreover, 10 years later, we have significant new issues. In particular, systemic risks were not a concern of the insurance industry or its regulators in 1999. Too-interconnected-to-fail status was considered an issue for the major banks at that time, but not for insurance entities. In fact, insurance regulators generally supported the rapid consolidation of the industry proceeding at the time.

The AIG case study in Appendix A illustrates a number of serious regulatory lapses regarding that firm. While some of these problems have now been addressed (e.g., bringing derivatives under the jurisdiction of the Commodity Futures Trading Commission [CFTC] in mid-2009 by reversing the 2000 statute exempting them from any form of regulation), most remain. For instance, the state guarantee funds still are inadequate to deal with losses of the magnitude incurred by AIG's insurance businesses, which were as large as those in AIG FP. None of the state regulatory agencies, even New York's, have the technical staff—actuarial or legal—to comprehend AIG's conglomeration of insurance businesses, complex financial entities like AIG FP, and the largest airplane leasing business in the world. State regulators could not have responded as dramatically and as quickly to the problems of AIG or other large insurers as the federal government did during the financial crisis.

The need for the federal government to step in during the financial crisis for AIG and other large insurers suggests that it is ultimately responsible for significant insurance company failures. However, because the federal government has no ongoing FDIC-like insurance guarantee program and no regulatory authority, it has no understanding of the insurance business.

While we support the Dodd-Frank Act for the creation of the Federal Insurance Office to gather information about the industry and identify its problem areas, this Office will have no regulatory power. Therefore, we believe that a federal regulator for the insurance sector, with strong expertise in insurance and in the institutions that have a focus on insurance, is imperative.[24] The creation of a national insurance regulator will automatically raise a host of other issues that policymakers would have to address:

- Should the federal regulator identify important insurance firms and require or allow them to be federally chartered and regulated? Given the jurisdictional shopping risk, we prefer making this a requirement, not an option.
- Would the federal charter lead to a federal FDIC-like guarantee—with ex ante premiums that are sensitive to systemic risk—for federally chartered insurers or perhaps for all insurers, replacing the state guarantee funds? We believe this is important, as state guarantee funds are inadequate to deal with the multiple insurer insolvencies that could result in a financial crisis. A national guarantee fund would be in a better position to anticipate and manage insurer insolvencies.
- How would consumer protection issues be dealt with?
- And finally, what model of regulation would be adopted? Should it be *prescriptive*, like the present state system where every new policy form must be approved, or *prudential*, like the British Financial Services Authority (FSA)'s safety and soundness-oriented system?

The Act also stipulates the establishment of a systemic risk regulator for those financial institutions viewed as imposing systemic risk exposure to the financial system. Our view is that some insurance companies should be included in the list of institutions to be regulated by such a systemic risk regulator. In Chapter 5, "Taxing Systemic Risk," we argued that because systemically risky firms create externalities on the entire financial system, this regulator should charge these institutions a fee for their systemic risk contribution. In Appendix B, we show how to measure insurers' systemic risk contributions.

9.6 INSURANCE ACCOUNTING

The purpose of financial accounting is to provide information about a firm's performance and prospects not just to investors but also to regulators. Given the lessons learned from the 2007 to 2009 crisis, is the current accounting system adequate for this purpose? This section discusses the crucial issues related to insurance accounting. Our main suggestions related to the insurance regulatory issues arising in the financial crisis are as follows:

- Despite the nontransferability of insurance policies, to mitigate incentives for contract structuring and to promote the usefulness and comparability of insurers' financial statements, the accounting for these policies should be made more consistent or reasonably consistent with the accounting for substitutable risk-transferring financial instruments, such as derivatives. Fair value accounting, the usual accounting approach for these other financial instruments, is the best way to do this, but a discounted expected cash flow measurement approach such as the FASB and IASB are currently considering would be adequate. This proposal is particularly important for financial guarantees, given their substitutability with credit derivatives and other credit-risk-transfer products, but it is also important for minimum guarantees and other contract features in investment-oriented insurance policies.
- Relatedly, to promote timely regulatory response to emerging solvency problems, statutory accounting principles (SAP) preferably should reflect fair value accounting or a similarly timely alternative. At a minimum, the income-smoothing mechanisms in SAP should be eliminated.
- Better financial report disclosures are needed for insurance policies and other financial instruments that are written put options on macroeconomic variables, including financial guarantees tied to asset-backed securities and minimum guarantees in investment-oriented life insurance policies. These disclosures should clearly indicate concentrations of risk, how historical data are used to value the positions, and other important estimation assumptions.

While less directly related to the financial crisis, we also make these additional suggestions:

- Accounting for different types of insurance policies should be made more consistent. Again, fair value accounting is the best way to do this, but a discounted expected cash flows measurement approach would be adequate.
- Accounting for insurance policies currently governed by Financial Accounting Standard (FAS) 60 (property-casualty and traditional life insurance) should not reflect the illusion that insurance policies are not financial instruments for which the time value of money and other critical economic factors are irrelevant.

Accounting Implications of Differences between Insurance Policies and Other Financial Instruments

Insurance policies exhibit three characteristics that may imply that these policies should be accounted for differently from other financial instruments. First, insurance policies generally are nontransferable by the insurer. For example, even when an insurer reinsures an insurance policy, the insurer remains on the hook to the policyholder if the reinsurer defaults. This lack of transferability creates a sort of market illiquidity that makes exit value, the measure of fair value applied in the accounting for other financial instruments, a largely hypothetical notion even under normal market conditions. As discussed later, in ongoing projects the FASB and IASB are considering requiring insurance policies to be measured at a firm-specific expected discounted cash flow measure that does not allow for profit to be recognized at the inception rather than at exit value.

Second, the initial sale of insurance policies often involves large commissions and other acquisition costs. Insurers are willing to bear large acquisition costs because many insurance policies renew with high probability, thereby yielding an internally developed intangible (i.e., noncontractual) asset. While GAAP for insurance in the United States requires this intangible asset to be recognized as "deferred acquisition costs," the recognition of this asset is hard to reconcile with accounting concepts and practices outside of insurance, and both the FASB and IASB propose to eliminate this asset. Relatedly, a high policy renewal probability implies that the boundaries of insurance policies differ economically and contractually.

Third, investment-oriented life insurance policies often contain minimum guarantees and various other contract features that typically are inseparable from the host policy, cannot be obtained separately in insurance or other markets, exhibit significant joint value, and are marketed by insurers and purchased by policyholders as a package. Some of these contract features meet the accounting definition of a derivative, and so are required under FAS 133 to be bifurcated from the host policy and accounted for at fair value. However, for the reasons just listed, such bifurcation is even more problematic for insurance policies than for other financial instruments. A simpler and perhaps more attractive alternative to bifurcating the embedded derivatives in an insurance policy is to account for the entire policy at fair value or a similar alternative.

Accounting and Its Role in Insurance Regulation Currently

In the United States, capital requirements and other aspects of insurance regulation are based on SAP, not GAAP. The two accounting systems have jointly evolved over time and, as a result, overlap in many respects. For example, GAAP for property-casualty insurance and term and whole-life insurance was based substantially on SAP, whereas SAP for investment-oriented life insurance and reinsurance was based substantially on GAAP. Compared with banks' regulatory accounting principles, which are primarily based on GAAP with a limited number of deviations, SAP contains more numerous and significant deviations from GAAP.

Where they differ, SAP generally is more conservative than GAAP, yielding lower capital for all insurers and lower net income for growing insurers. The most important ways in which SAP is more conservative than GAAP are:

- Policy acquisition costs are expensed immediately under SAP but capitalized and amortized under GAAP.
- Insurance liabilities are calculated under SAP using statutory assumptions that generally are conservative.
- An asset valuation reserve is recorded under SAP based on statutory assumptions that generally are conservative.
- Various illiquid assets are not admitted as assets under SAP.

This conservatism reflects insurance regulators' focus on insurers' solvency and the fact that excessive growth by insurers can threaten their solvency.

The following aspects of SAP yield lower capital and income volatility than GAAP:

- Unrealized gains and losses on available-for-sale securities are excluded from SAP capital (as is the case for banks' regulatory accounting principles).
- Realized gains and losses arising from changes in the level of interest rates are recorded in an interest maintenance reserve and amortized into interest income over time.

Why insurance regulators prefer less volatile net income than GAAP provides is unclear; perhaps it is to allow insurers some time to replenish their capital when investment losses occur.

SAP generally is consistent across states, because the National Association of Insurance Commissioners (NAIC) worked to codify SAP in its *Accounting Practices and Procedures Manual.*[25] This manual first became effective in January 1, 2001, and is reissued annually. Although all states have accepted it for implementation, the manual does not override state laws and regulations, so differences in the implementation of SAP remain across states. The biggest change in SAP brought about by the NAIC's codification project was to recognize deferred taxes. Because most insurers have deferred tax assets, this change worked to increase their capital.

Problems with Current Insurance Accounting

Insurance GAAP is almost nonexistent internationally. The IASB issued the minimalistic IFRS 4 in 2004 simply to satisfy the European Union Accounting Regulation requirement that European companies listed in a European securities market use IFRS to prepare their consolidated financial statements starting in 2005. This standard provides few restrictions on insurers' financial reporting. This state of affairs will change when the IASB completes its ongoing insurance accounting project and issues a final standard, currently scheduled for 2011.

In contrast, U.S. insurance GAAP is extensively specified but exhibits significant problems, four of which we briefly describe next.

Different Types of Insurance Policies Are Accounted for Inconsistently

U.S. GAAP requires very different accounting measurements, financial statement classifications, and footnote disclosures by insurers for each of the following broad types of policies or policy features: (1) short-duration property-casualty, accident and health, nonrenewal term life, and group life policies governed by FAS 60; (2) long-duration renewable term life and whole-life policies governed by FAS 60; (3) investment-oriented life insurance policies (universal life and annuities) governed by FAS 97; (4) financial guarantees governed by FAS 163; (5) embedded derivatives and other contract features in investment-oriented life insurance policies governed by FAS 133 and Statement of Position (SOP) 03-1, respectively; (6) ceded reinsurance policies governed by FAS 113; and (7) assumed reinsurance policies governed by SOP 93-6 and SOP 98-7.

These different approaches make it difficult for regulators to understand the aggregate positions, performance, and risks of insurers offering diversified sets of policies. One of the attractive features of an insurance accounting model based on fair value or a similar alternative is that it would require insurers to account consistently for different types of insurance policies.

Financial Guarantees Accounted for as Insurance versus Other Financial Instruments Are Substitutable but Accounted for Inconsistently

FAS 163 defines financial guarantees that should be accounted for as insurance policies under its guidance as "contracts issued by insurance enterprises that provide protection to the holder of a financial obligation from a financial loss in the event of a default." The standard defines an event of default as "nonpayment (when due) of insured contractual payments (generally principal and interest) by the issuer of the insured financial obligation." The financial guarantees issued by insurers may not meet FAS 163's definition either because the counterparty does not currently hold the guaranteed financial obligation or because the guarantees provide protection against something other than an event of default. Under FAS 163, financial guarantees yield gross recognized assets equal to the expected future premiums discounted at the risk-free rate and gross recognized liabilities equal to the expected future claim payments discounted at the risk-free rate.

Insurers account for financial guarantees that do not meet FAS 163's definition of a financial guarantee as derivatives if the guarantees meet FAS 133's definition of a derivative. Under FAS 133, financial guarantees that are deemed derivatives are measured and presented on the balance sheet at a net fair value amount, in contrast to FAS 163's gross presentation. Gross presentation bulks up insurers' balance sheets compared with net presentation, thereby reducing insurers' capital ratios. While gross presentation highlights the expected payments that insurers have to make, it ignores the fact that in many cases insurers will not have to make any payments if policyholders cease paying premiums.

If a financial guarantee issued by an insurer does not meet either FAS 163's definition of financial guarantees or FAS 133's definition of derivatives, then the insurer generally accounts for the guarantee as a loss contingency under FAS 5. This standard's "probable" and "reasonably estimable" thresholds for recognition often yield understated liabilities for financial guarantees.

Time Value of Money Is Accounted for Problematically and Inconsistently

FAS 60 accounting for short-duration insurance policies ignores the time value of money altogether. FAS 60 accounting for long-duration traditional insurance policies incorporates the time value of money in measuring claim liabilities but classifies the economic interest on those liabilities as insurance expense, not interest. FAS 97 for investment-oriented life insurance policies properly accounts for and classifies the time value of money.

This problematic and inconsistent treatment of the time value of money is difficult to fathom given that the up-front receipt of premiums is a fundamental aspect of insurance.

FAS 60's Lock-In Assumption Ignores Changes in Expected Cash Flows

FAS 60 requires insurance liabilities for long-duration contracts to be based on original assumptions unless the actual experience is sufficiently unfavorable that the contract becomes unprofitable to the insurer (i.e., a premium deficiency exists). In this case, the original assumptions are unlocked and the liability is reestimated using new assumptions.

This requirement artificially smooths an insurer's book value and net income in the absence of an unlock, and yields artificially volatile book value and net income in the period of an unlock.

Proposed Changes in Insurance Accounting

The FASB and the IASB have joint but separate projects under way to develop new approaches for insurance accounting. All of their decisions through the date of this writing in July 2010 are tentative and can be reversed or otherwise altered.[26] Both standard setters have considered but jettisoned the idea that insurance policies should be measured at fair value defined as exit value, because insurance policies generally cannot be transferred by the insurer.

Instead, both standard setters are considering measuring insurance policies at an insurer-specific expected discounted cash flow value that allows for no initial profit on policies. Initial profit is eliminated by discounting expected cash flows at the internal rate of return, which equals the appropriate economic discount rate plus the abnormal profit margin expected at inception. Both standard setters have decided that insurers should update the economic discount rate each period but should not update the abnormal profit margin. This measurement basis exhibits some of the attractive features of fair value—most notably, the use of current expected cash flows rather than probable and reasonably estimable or locked-in cash flows.

Both standard setters have decided to expense acquisition costs as incurred. Hence, they do not propose to use deferred acquisition costs to capture the aforementioned intangible asset created by the sale of insurance policies. Acquisition costs may affect the calculation of the abnormal profit margin and thus the measurement of insurance policies in some yet-to-be-determined fashion.

Two Insurance Accounting Issues Raised by the Financial Crisis

The financial crisis has raised two issues regarding insurance accounting. The first issue is whether it is possible to define insurance policies in a way that clearly distinguishes them from substitutable financial products and, relatedly, whether it is desirable to account for insurance policies differently from other financial instruments.

Oddly, given its extensive nature, U.S. GAAP does not include an explicit definition of an insurance policy. However, IFRS 4 contains a definition of an insurance policy along with guidance distinguishing insurance risk from other types of financial risk. Under IFRS 4's definition of an insurance policy, the insured party must be exposed to and not speculating on the insured risk, and the insured event specified in the contract must pertain directly to, not simply be correlated with, that exposure. IFRS 4's definition encompasses various credit-risk-transfer products that are structured as derivatives or other financial instruments, up to the limit of the insured party's exposure.

For example, a written credit default swap that pays off in the event of default on a financial asset held by the purchaser of the CDS is an insurance policy under this definition. The same swap would not be an insurance policy if the purchaser did not hold the financial asset. A swap that pays off based on an index correlated with the default on the financial asset would also not be an insurance policy under this definition, regardless of the correlation of default on the financial asset and the index.

It is inherently difficult to distinguish insurance policies from substitutable financial products. Accordingly, similar accounting for insurance policies and substitutable financial products is necessary to avoid providing insurers and other firms with incentives to structure contracts to achieve desired accounting outcomes.

The second issue is: Can the accounting for insurance policies that pay off in highly correlated fashion in rare circumstances be made more robust?

The financial crisis led to large write-downs being recorded by AIG Capital Markets on its credit default swaps (which it accounted for as derivatives, not insurance policies), by the financial guarantors on their financial guarantees, and by a number of large life insurers (including AIG) on their minimum guarantees and other contract features on investment-oriented life insurance policies. Each of these positions can be viewed as an initially out-of-the-money written put option tied directly or indirectly to a macroeconomic variable, specifically, house price or equity price indexes. In the cases just listed, insurers accumulated sizable concentrations of these positions.

The insurers' initial valuations of these put options and the large losses they subsequently recorded on these positions during the crisis all reflect the following statistical issue. These put options pay off rarely, but when they pay off, they pay off in a highly correlated fashion, since they are tied to the same or similar indexes. In the absence of good market information about the value of these positions, accounting for them is prone to large ex post errors, especially when the historical data inevitably used to value them have been accumulated during a prolonged period in which the indexes have risen, suggesting that these put options are less valuable than in fact they are. When insurers rely too heavily on such historical data in accounting for these positions, they will record large losses when such a period ends. Insurance regulators need to be aware of this fact. Disclosures of insurers' concentrations of such put options and the assumptions they use to value those put options are of critical importance.

9.7 SUMMARY

The traditional economics literature on insurance focuses on potential insureds' moral hazard and adverse selection incentive problems. In equilibrium, these problems cause insurers to underprovide insurance and to hoard liquidity and capital, behaviors with adverse implications for economic growth.

In contrast, the financial crisis of 2007 to 2009 revealed that during the period of 2004 to 2007, if not before, insurers provided excessive insurance on structured financial products and other exposures tied to macroeconomic variables, and were undercapitalized and insufficiently liquid given the correlated risks of that insurance. In this chapter, we argued that these problems resulted from insurers' (not insureds') ignoring their systemic risk externalities, which are particularly severe for too-interconnected-to-fail insurers. We evaluated the Dodd-Frank Wall Street Reform and Consumer Protection Act of 2010 in relation to insurance industry regulation and made several recommendations regarding regulation of insurance accounting. Most importantly, because the current state regulation and guarantee funds are inadequate to assess and manage the systemic risk of large insurers, we advocate a federal regulator that will manage, both ex ante and ex post, the large insurers' systemic risks. In Appendix B, we propose two possible measures of systemic risk based on market data and suggest one way to tax insurers for their contributions to systemic risk. These proposals, if implemented, would ensure that going forward the provision of insurance is not effectively backstopped by taxpayer funds. They would enable markets appropriately to price the systemic risk externalities as well as the insurance risk, and in turn, ensure efficient allocation of resources to profitable investments.

APPENDIX A: THE CASE OF AIG

Was AIG too big to fail, and what does its de facto failure tell us about insurance regulation going forward?

AIG is often called the largest insurance entity in the world. Depending on how *large* is defined, it was the largest under most definitions, but was only number two or three in some specific categories of insurance (say, in terms of assets as a life insurance company). But no other company had the combination of life, property-casualty, global reach, and noninsurance product lines as did AIG.

AIG's assets totaled $860 billion on December 31, 2008, dwarfing any other insurance entity, with 116,000 employees, operating in 130 countries, with 71 U.S.-based insurance companies, and 176 other companies representing non-U.S. insurers and other financial services.[27] Many regulatory issues are raised by AIG's structure: regulatory arbitrage in its multitude of companies and countries and its selection of a Gramm-Leach-Bliley regulator, its extreme unregulated systemic risk, and its complete lack of regulation of certain insurance-like components.

In this Appendix, we first look at AIG's lines of businesses, and then evaluate their systemic risk using the three criteria: interconnectedness, spillover risk, and causing systemwide runs.

Summary of Lines of Business

It is useful to break down the analysis of AIG into the four major components, as AIG describes itself in its 10-K presentation (see the 349-page 10-K for the year ended December 31, 2008).

General Insurance   AIG's General Insurance segment encompasses a large number of property-casualty businesses—both commercial and personal lines, international reinsurance, a mortgage guarantee business, and operations in virtually all global markets. The company was founded in 1916 in Shanghai as an Asian insurance agency and grew significantly after World War II to cover the rest of the world. Acquisitions in the past decade led it to further dominance. The 10-K lists 10 principal companies through which AIG conducts its general business segment.

The state of Pennsylvania takes the lead in regulating AIG's U.S. general insurance companies, of which 11 are based in Pennsylvania (no AIG life insurance companies are regulated in Pennsylvania). Many other companies are domiciled in other states, and many in foreign countries.

As AIG or other insurers write certain special types of insurance policies, they can pick a state or country that permits or is favorable to writing that type of contract. For example, the controversial finite insurance contract, written by General Reinsurance Company to accommodate AIG, was written through General Re's Irish subsidiary. This was the contract that led to prison terms for several General Re officers and the forced resignation of Chairman Hank Greenberg of AIG in 2005.

No major issues of solvency have been raised by the groups of General Insurance companies in AIG, but overall coordination and regulatory arbitrage remain concerns. Joel Ario, the insurance commissioner of Pennsylvania, in his testimony on March 13, 2009, before the House Subcommittee on Capital Markets, defended the multiple-state regulation of AIG's general insurance segment, stating:

> *Our critics may question the efficiency of having multiple eyes on a complex enterprise such as AIG, but the reality is that these multiple eyes have served policyholders well by probating the solvency of the AIG insurance companies' deposits turmoil at the AIG holding company level.*

Other critics of the multistate and multicountry regulation have attributed the regulation success to the strong personal control that Chairman Greenberg had over all activities of the company, and particularly the AIG Capital Markets (CM) entities, for "protecting their solvency."

The operating loss in 2008 for AIG's General Insurance segment was $5.7 billion.

Life Insurance and Retirement Services   AIG's Life Insurance and Retirement Services segment had serious losses in 2008, of $37.5 billion, almost as much as AIG Financial Products' loss of $40.8 billion. These losses came from its failed securities-lending businesses, aggressive variable annuity death benefit provisions, and investment losses on its over $500 billion asset portfolio ($489.6 billion as at December 31, 2008).

Securities lending is typically not considered a very risky business, as the collateral is invested in safe short-term assets. Other life insurance companies, such as Metropolitan Life, also run similar businesses. In AIG's case, however, state filings show that roughly two-thirds of its cash collateral was invested in mortgage-backed securities very similar to the AAA-rated tranches it was insuring in its Financial Products group. Moreover, over one-half of the collateral was invested in assets that had maturities ranging from 3 to 10 years, a much different duration than the short-term loans provided by AIG via its debt securities. This opened up AIG to a maturity mismatch if the borrowers of AIG's securities did not roll over their loans.

The AIG 10-K lists eight "financial" life companies for its foreign businesses, and 10 "principal" life companies for its U.S. business.

Eric Dinallo, in his testimony on March 5, 2009, before the Senate Banking Committee, describes the New York Insurance Department as primary regulator of 10 of AIG's 71 U.S. insurance companies. Other states are primary for all others.

Asset Management   AIG's Asset Management business is not regulated by states but is overseen by the federal agencies: primarily the SEC and the Office of Thrift Supervision. It has four principal companies related to its major life insurance acquisitions and the varied products (including mutual funds) offered to individuals and institutions. No regulatory problems have developed under those businesses, but its operating loss in 2008 was $9.2 billion.

Financial Products What AIG calls its Financial Products business includes three primary entities: the International Lease Finance Corporation (ILFC) (the world's largest airplane leasing business), a consumer finance business, and a capital markets operations business called AIG Capital Markets (AIG CM).

The ILFC was profitable in 2008 with operating income of $1.2 billion. The consumer finance business lost $1.3 billion.

A major factor in AIG's collapse was the $40.5 billion loss on AIG CM, out of the total loss of over $100 billion (see page 116 of the 10-K).

Federal Reserve Chairman Ben Bernanke said in congressional testimony: "AIG had a financial products division which was very lightly regulated and was a source of a great deal of systemic trouble." He further called the Financial Products unit "a hedge fund basically that was attached to a large and stable insurance company that made large numbers of irresponsible bets, and took huge losses."

It is true that AIG CM had an operating loss of $40.8 billion in 2008, but the other businesses of AIG had losses of $67.9 billion, for a total of $108.8 billion. The "large and stable insurance company" had losses of $43.2 billion (page 71 of the 10-K). Clearly AIG would have needed to join the other insurance companies (Prudential, Hartford, Principal, Lincoln National, etc.) for federal Troubled Asset Relief Program (TARP) support, even without the "hedge fund" losses.

AIG, in its 10-K, reports that the loss related "primarily" to its "super senior multi-sector CDO credit default swap portfolio." Downgrades of AIG's credit ratings and "extreme market conditions" drove the losses (page 117 of the 10-K). The "very lightly regulated" part of Chairman Bernanke's quote arose mainly from two causes:

1. Credit default swaps were exempted from regulation under the Commodity Futures Modernization Act of 2000, which prevented the SEC or the New York Insurance Department from regulating the instruments.
2. Both regulators had tried to assert authority. Brooksby Born, the head of the Commodity Futures Trading Commission, testified before Congress 17 times, arguing that such derivatives posed an unknown and growing risk to the world's financial system. She was vigorously opposed by Federal Reserve Chairman Alan Greenspan, ex-Treasury Secretary Robert Rubin, and ex-SEC Chairman Arthur Levitt.

AIG purchased a savings and loan company in 1999, enabling it to select the Office of Thrift Supervision (OTS) as the "consolidated supervisor" under Gramm-Leach-Bliley. AIG Financial Products is not a licensed insurance company; it is based primarily in London and escaped regulation by the British Financial Services Authority since AIG had an "equivalent regulator," the OTS.

Accordingly, a "large and stable insurance entity," combined with a sophisticated hedge fund, making "large numbers of irresponsible bets," was ultimately regulated by the regulatory agency for U.S. home loan companies.

Briefly, AIG Financial Products started business with AIG in 1987 and offered complex hedge products successfully for 10 years.[28] The founders left in 1993 and the first credit default swap was written in 1998. The product relied heavily on the support of AIG's AAA credit rating. The credit default swap business accelerated after 1998 when JPMorgan introduced, jointly with AIG CM, a CDO product that relied on the insurance provided by an AIG credit default swap.

Systemic Risk of AIG

Section 9.5 outlined three ways systemic risk can materialize in the financial sector. It seems worthwhile to explore each of these possibilities as it pertains to AIG.

Interconnectedness By far, the degree of AIG's interconnectedness to the financial system was its greatest contributor to systemic risk. Through its Financial Products unit, AIG had $1.6 trillion in notional derivatives exposures, linking itself to over 1,500 corporations, governments, and institutional investors. And, as widely reported, AIG had $450 billion of one-sided credit default swap exposures on the so-called AAA tranches of securitized products. The problem with OTC derivatives markets, like the ones AIG participated in, is that bilateral collateral and margin requirements in OTC trading do not take into account the counterparty risk externality that each trade imposes on the rest of the system, allowing systemically important exposures to be built up without sufficient capital to mitigate the risks.

The AAA tranches of the securitized products would only be affected by a very rare market event, but, if the event occurred, most of the AAA tranches would be hit. In other words, the risk underlying these tranches was almost all systematic, and therefore none of it was idiosyncratic and diversifiable.[29] It is therefore not surprising that such an event—the massive drop in housing prices and collapse of the credit market—caused (1) widespread losses at AIG, (2) the failure of AIG due to its undercapitalization at the parent level from its exposure to its Financial Products unit, and (3) these losses to be passed back to the counterparties of AIG (without government support).

Systemic risk arises because the losses passed back to the counterparties may cause those counterparties to sell assets, leading to a rapid downward spiral in the value of these assets, which leads to further losses and funding difficulties, causing more asset sales, and so forth. In the most extreme case, if AIG's failure leads to the failure of another financial institution and that institution has counterparties, then those counterparties are put at risk. In effect, AIG's counterparty risk extends way beyond the 1,500 institutions it had arrangements with.

To give an idea of the magnitude of the losses and the depth of the counterparties, Table 9.5 provides the 10 largest payments of AIG to its various counterparties from September 16, 2008, to December 31, 2008, as a result of government aid. The payments are broken down into (1) collateral postings under credit default swap contracts,[30] (2) the outright purchase

TABLE 9.5 AIG Financial Products Counterparty Payments, September 16 to December 31, 2008 ($ Billions)

Collateral Postings under AIG FP CDSs		Maiden Lane III Payments to AIG FP CDS Counterparties		Payments under Guaranteed Investment Agreements	
Société Générale	$ 4.1	Société Générale	$ 6.9	California	$ 1.02
Deutsche Bank	$ 2.6	Goldman Sachs	$ 5.6	Virginia	$ 1.01
Goldman Sachs	$ 2.5	Merrill Lynch	$ 3.1	Hawaii	$ 0.77
Merrill Lynch	$ 1.8	Deutsche Bank	$ 2.8	Ohio	$ 0.49
Calyon	$ 1.1	UBS	$ 2.5	Georgia	$ 0.41
Barclays	$ 0.9	Calyon	$ 1.2	Colorado	$ 0.36
UBS	$ 0.8	Deutsche Zentral-Genossenschaftsbank	$ 1.0	Illinois	$ 0.35
DZ Bank	$ 0.7	Bank of Montreal	$ 0.9	Massachusetts	$ 0.34
Wachovia	$ 0.7	Wachovia	$ 0.8	Kentucky	$ 0.29
Rabobank	$ 0.5	Barclays	$ 0.6	Oregon	$ 0.27
Top 20	$18.3			Top 20	$ 7.00
Total	$22.4	Total	$27.1	Total	$12.10

Source: AIG.

of collateralized debt obligations that AIG had written CDS contracts on via Maiden Lane III,[31] and (3) guaranteed investment agreements held by municipalities.[32] As can be seen from the table, without government support, the losses across the financial community from these three sources alone would have been staggering, reaching a total of $61.6 billion.

Spillover Risk　Whether the realization of these losses by all of AIG's counterparties would have caused the unraveling of the global financial system remains an open question. However, even without these losses, AIG's failure or, in fact, rating downgrade, had the potential to cause a systemwide collapse. Similar to the Long-Term Capital Management (LTCM) crisis a decade earlier, AIG's holdings of $1.6 trillion in derivatives would have led to an unwinding of positions that could have created a deathlike spiral where asset values decline in response to liquidity pressure, which in turn leads to funding liquidity issues, which in turn lead to further declines in asset prices, and so forth.

An additional question is whether AIG's failure at the parent level could lead to fire sales on its vast holdings of assets beyond the derivative products mentioned. Going into the crisis, AIG was the fifth-largest institutional asset manager worldwide. If one were to include all of AIG's investments just described, AIG was the largest investor in corporate bonds in the United States, and the second-largest holder of U.S. municipal bonds through its commercial insurance business, worth $50 billion. Any significant forced sale of these bond portfolios would have put substantive stress on the respective financial markets.

Since the assets of AIG's insurance companies were legally separated from AIG CM, however, it is not clear that a failure at the parent level would indeed have caused a fire sale of its asset holdings elsewhere in the organization. In case of default, the AIG parent company had guaranteed the contracts at AIG CM; this effectively meant the counterparties had a claim on the underlying businesses owned by AIG though not ahead of the policyholders. It is quite possible that the businesses would have continued as normal.

However, as mentioned earlier, there were significant losses from AIG's investments in the cash collateral derived from its securities-lending business in which it lent out securities held in its life insurance and retirement service businesses. These losses were mostly attributable to AA-rated and AAA-rated tranches of nonprime mortgage-backed securities. The losses from September 16 to December 31, 2008, totaled $43.7 billion, and included a number of systemically important counterparties. The top 10 in order of their losses were: Barclays ($7 billion), Deutsche Bank ($6.4 billion), BNP Paribas ($4.9 billion), Goldman Sachs ($4.8 billion), Bank of America

($4.5 billion), HSBC ($3.3 billion), Citigroup ($2.3 billion), Dresdner Klein-wort ($2.2 billion), Merrill Lynch ($1.9 billion), and UBS ($1.7 billion). In addition, AIG offered investment-oriented life insurance policies with min-imum guarantees and other contract features that yielded losses for AIG when equity and bond markets fell as a result of the financial crisis.

It is quite likely that, like other life insurance companies, AIG would have required capital infusions from the government even without AIG CM as a result of these investment losses. A failure of AIG at the core business level would have resulted in a massive fire sale of its assets and a possible run by policyholders on some of its operations. Either of these could have systemic consequences.

"Bank" Run　Even if AIG were not failing at the individual insurance com-pany level, it is possible that its failure at the parent level, and weaknesses described earlier at the insurance company level, could cause a classic run on the "bank." Since AIG has more than 81 million life insurance policies worldwide, with a face value of $1.9 trillion, a large-scale run could have wide-scale effects.

For example, in one scenario, policyholders would cash in their policies, forcing AIG to raise cash, primarily through asset sales, leading to the type of spillover risk described earlier. The only protection AIG would have in this case is the surrender charges or cancellation penalties, or untapped value of the policies. In another scenario, the sudden jump in the number of uninsureds would put temporary pressure at least on the ability of other life insurance companies to meet the insurance demands of these potential new customers.

Of course, the largest concern of a bank run is that it leads to a sys-temwide run on the sector. Such runs are catastrophic, as they lead to a freezing of the market these institutions operate in, and cause severe exter-nalities toward related individuals and businesses. Given the importance of the life insurance sector to the overall economy, a systemwide run would be very damaging.

In the current financial crisis, systemwide runs have occurred in many parts of the shadow banking sector, starting with subprime lenders, moving on to asset-backed paper conduits, then investment banks and money market funds, and ending with hedge funds. The two criteria for a run are that (1) similar institutions operate in the same space, and (2) there is opacity (or information asymmetry) about each institution's operations. This can lead to healthy institutions' also facing runs on their liabilities. A run on a failing institution, assuming it is not systemic in its own right, is bad only to the extent that it leads to runs on healthy institutions.

It remains an open question whether a run on some of AIG's insurance businesses would lead to a run on other insurance companies. To many analysts, AIG was a unique company, so its troubles may be seen as specific to its circumstances—the failure of AIG CM and the collateral investments of its securities-lending business—and not a more endemic characteristic of life insurance companies such as investment-oriented life insurance policies with minimum guarantees.

Analysis of AIG

The AIG case study raises at least the following six regulatory questions and issues:

1. How can the systemic risks imposed by a company like AIG be regulated?
2. Was Gramm-Leach-Bliley poorly conceived or administered, so as to permit the regulatory arbitrage of AIG selecting the OTS as its consolidated supervisor?
3. Can a very large, too-big-to-fail insurance entity be adequately regulated by any existing federal regulator?
4. Should the scale and reach of an AIG-type entity be limited by regulation?
5. Could the state guarantee associations have coped with the insurance losses incurred by AIG in 2008?
6. Credit default swaps are essentially insurance. Is some form of insurance regulation needed for such products?

In answer to question 6, what is clear is that AIG's capital markets group did not offer typical insurance. As described in the opening paragraph of this chapter, insurance works because insurers pool and diversify large idiosyncratic risks faced by individuals and businesses. But there is no diversifiable risk on the AAA tranche of credit portfolios; it is all systematic. In practice, this means that if a systemic event occurs, then all policies written on this event require a payout; or, in AIG's case, $450 billion worth of payouts are required in the highly unlikely case that the underlying bonds are worth nothing.[33] This reasoning suggests that insurance companies should not be able to offer insurance protection against systemic events unless the insurance is fully capitalized. This would cover CDSs on AAA-tranche CDOs, insurance against a nuclear attack, the systematic portion of insurance on municipal bonds, and so forth.

APPENDIX B: SYSTEMIC RISK MEASUREMENT: AN EXAMPLE

Can we quantify and measure the systemic risk of financial institutions?[34] In this section, we argue that significant progress can be made even by relying exclusively on market information. The first part of this section shows how one can measure systemic risk of a financial institution over time using stock market information. The second part shows the success of a systemic risk measure computed from credit default swaps data in predicting the performance of insurance firms during the 2007 to 2009 financial crisis.

Measuring Systemic Risk of Insurance Firms Using the Stock Market

To measure the systemic risk of insurance firms using the stock market, we propose a measure called the Marginal Expected Shortfall (MES). Suppose that the economy incurs a systemic cost (a negative externality of the financial sector) whenever there is a crisis, measured as the return to the financial sector or overall economy being sufficiently bad, say in the 5 percent left tail of the market return distribution. Furthermore, suppose that the cost is proportional to the extent of loss incurred below the 5 percent cutoff. Then the contribution of each individual financial institution to this cost is proportional to its size, and to its MES, defined as the percentage loss or negative return it suffers when the market is in its 5 percent left tail. The tax to be imposed on each institution could thus be the average of this contribution, or in other words, its MES multiplied by its (dollar) weight in the economy and multiplied by the likelihood of the crisis (in our example, 5 percent). To summarize, MES of a financial institution can be interpreted as the per-dollar systemic risk contribution of that institution when a systemic crisis materializes.

The idea behind MES is that one calculates the losses experienced by each firm when aggregate losses are large. The MES is the contribution of each firm to the aggregate losses. For the example to follow, we calculate the losses of the market value of equity of financial firms in the prior year's 5 percent worst-case periods of aggregate stock market losses (measured on a daily basis). We focus on financial firms with at least $5 billion in market capitalization (as of June 2007), leaving us with 102 financial firms. Of these 102 financial firms, 36 are considered insurance companies based on their two-digit Standard Industrial Classification (SIC) in the Center for Research in Security Prices (CRSP)–Compustat database.

Table 9.6 presents the dollar MES of these insurance companies, as well as their MES as a percentage of the market value of their equity. In addition,

TABLE 9.6 Systemic Risk and Balance-Sheet Characteristics of Insurance Firms in Year Prior to July 2007

Ranking in Insurance Sector	Company	Ticker	$MES5	MES5	Assets ($ Billions)	Market Cap ($ Billions)	BEA	LDA	STA	Ranking in Top 102 Financials
1	AIG	AIG	1.044	0.57%	$1,033.87	$181.67	0.101	0.138	0.761	10
2	MetLife	MET	0.741	1.55	552.56	47.82	0.061	0.030	0.909	13
3	Prudential Financial	PRU	0.575	1.28	461.81	45.02	0.050	0.024	0.926	17
4	Berkshire Hathaway Inc. Del.	BRK-A	0.546	0.46	269.05	119.00	0.428	0.118	0.454	19
5	UnitedHealth Group	UNH	0.485	0.71	53.15	68.53	0.396	0.131	0.473	22
6	Countrywide Financial Corp.	CFC	0.453	2.10	216.82	21.57	0.066	0.358	0.575	26
7	Loews Corp.	L	0.386	1.41	79.54	27.38	0.215	0.062	0.722	28
8	Wellpoint Inc.	WLP	0.383	0.78	54.19	48.99	0.461	0.141	0.398	29
9	Travelers Companies	TRV	0.372	1.05	115.36	35.52	0.218	0.050	0.732	31
10	HFSG Inc.	HIG	0.350	1.12	345.65	31.19	0.054	0.014	0.932	33
11	Aetna Inc. New	AET	0.339	1.34	49.57	25.31	0.195	0.049	0.755	34
12	Allstate Corp.	ALL	0.284	0.76	160.54	37.36	0.134	0.035	0.831	43
13	Lincoln National Corp.	LNC	0.252	1.31	187.65	19.21	0.063	0.022	0.915	51
14	Principal Financial Group	PFG	0.252	1.61	150.76	15.61	0.053	0.010	0.937	52
15	Chubb Corp.	CB	0.233	1.07	51.73	21.74	0.267	0.080	0.653	55
16	Berkshire Hathaway Inc. Del.	BRK-B	0.220	0.45	269.05	49.29	0.428	0.118	0.454	57
17	Genworth Financial	GNW	0.216	1.44	111.94	14.96	0.116	0.066	0.818	59
18	Aflac Inc.	AFL	0.213	0.85	60.11	25.14	0.136	0.023	0.841	60
19	Progressive Corp. OH	PG	0.207	1.19	21.07	17.42	0.261	0.103	0.636	61
20	Marsh & McLennan Cos.	MMC	0.195	1.14	17.19	17.15	0.329	0.210	0.461	63
21	Cigna Corp.	CI	0.171	1.14	41.53	15.03	0.097	0.043	0.860	66
22	Aon Corp.	AOC	0.149	1.19	24.79	12.51	0.216	0.088	0.696	71

(Continued)

TABLE 9.6 Systemic Risk and Balance-Sheet Characteristics of Insurance Firms in Year Prior to July 2007 (*Continued*)

Ranking in Insurance Sector	Company	Ticker	$MES5	MES5	Assets ($ Billions)	Market Cap ($ Billions)	BEA	LDA	STA	Ranking in Top 102 Financials
23	Humana Inc.	HUM	0.142	1.39	13.33	10.24	0.253	0.089	0.658	72
24	MBIA Inc.	MBI	0.136	1.67	43.15	8.14	0.157	0.690	0.153	73
25	Unum Group	UNM	0.134	1.50	52.07	8.95	0.142	0.044	0.814	75
26	CNA Financial Corp.	CNA	0.127	0.98	60.74	12.95	0.165	0.033	0.802	77
27	Ambac Financial Group	ABK	0.115	1.29	21.06	8.89	0.287	0.484	0.229	79
28	W.R. Berkley Corp.	BER	0.112	1.78	16.63	6.32	0.215	0.082	0.703	81
29	Loews Corp.	CG	0.096	1.15	2.84	8.38	0.138	0.344	0.518	85
30	Cincinnati Financial Corp.	CINF	0.091	1.22	18.26	7.46	0.374	0.043	0.583	89
31	Safeco Corp.	SAF	0.078	1.18	13.97	6.61	0.287	0.061	0.652	92
32	Health Net Inc.	HNT	0.071	1.19	4.73	5.93	0.412	0.084	0.504	94
33	Assurant Inc.	AIZ	0.065	0.92	25.77	7.13	0.148	0.039	0.813	96
34	Coventry Health Care	CVH	0.059	0.66	6.41	9.01	0.457	0.151	0.392	98
35	Torchmark Corp.	TMK	0.058	0.91	15.10	6.40	0.215	0.048	0.737	99
36	Fidelity National Fin'l Inc. New	FNF	0.050	0.95	7.37	5.25	0.483	0.069	0.449	101

The 36 insurance firms considered are from a list of 102 U.S. financial firms based on a market capitalization in excess of $5 billion as of June 2007. MES5 is the Marginal Expected Shortfall of a stock given that the market return is below its fifth percentile. It was measured for each individual company's stock using the period July 2006 through June 2007. $MES5 is MES5 multiplied by the market capitalization, the product of outstanding shares and stock price as of the end of June 2007. The accounting data are: book value of assets, book equity divided by total assets (BEA), total long-term debt divided by total assets (LDA), short-term liabilities relative to total assets (STA) as given by (1 − BEA − LDA). All balance sheet data are based on latest available quarterly CRSP-Compustat merged data as of end of June 2007. The left column gives the within-insurance-sector systemic risk ranking by $MES5 whereas the right column gives the ranking within the 102 U.S. financial firms.

various accounting data are also provided. The far-left column gives the within-insurance-sector systemic risk ranking by $MES5, whereas the far-right column gives the ranking within the 102 U.S. financial firms, also by $MES5. The top five most systemic firms in order were AIG, Metropolitan Life, Prudential, Berkshire Hathaway, and UnitedHealth, achieving ranks of 10, 13, 17, 19, and 22, respectively, among the 102 largest financial firms.

Table 9.7 presents the insurance companies that fall into the top 20 of the list in Table 9.6 based on their dollar MES each year from June 2004 through June 2007—just prior to the crisis. Although more than one-third of the top 100 financial firms are insurance companies, a smaller percentage shows up in the top 20 most systemic list. For example, there are only three firms in 2004, seven in 2005, five in 2006, and four in 2007. Of these firms, AIG is always most systemic with rankings of 2, 2, 3, and 10 among all financial institutions over the years 2004 to 2007, respectively. Prudential Financial is in the top 20 in three of the four years, while Berkshire Hathaway, Metropolitan Life, and UnitedHealth are present half the time. In total, nine insurance companies show up as being among the top 20 systemic financial firms at some point over this four-year period.

To compare across different types of institutions, Figures 9.7 and 9.8 graph the MES across depository institutions, broker-dealers, nondepository institutions, and insurance companies over the period 1963 to 2008. To adjust for different sizes across these financial entities, we divide each

TABLE 9.7 Insurance Companies' Systemic Risk Rank (2004 to 2007)

2004	2005	2006	2007
AIG (2)	AIG (2)	AIG (3)	AIG (10)
Berkshire Hathaway (13)	UnitedHealth (10)	Allstate (13)	Metropolitan Life (13)
HFSG (18)	Well Point (13)	UnitedHealth (16)	Prudential Financial (17)
	St. Paul Travelers (16)	Prudential Financial (17)	Berkshire Hathaway (19)
	Prudential Financial (17)	Metropolitan Life (18)	
	Aetna (18)		
	Berkshire Hathaway (20)		

This table reports the insurance companies that feature in the top 20 systemic financial institutions from the largest 102 firms based on market capitalization (as of June 2007). The systemic risk measure is based on each firm's Marginal Expected Shortfall in dollars from the previous year's 5 percent worst days.
Source: Acharya, Pedersen, Philippon, and Richardson (2009).

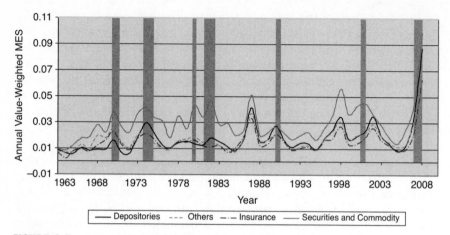

FIGURE 9.7   Annual Value-Weighted Marginal Expected Shortfall (5 percent) by Groups of Financial Institutions

The chart depicts for each year from 1963 until 2008 the market-cap-weighted MES (5 percent) for each of the four categories of financial institutions conditioned on at least 22 days of trading within a year.

Source: Acharya, Pedersen, Philippon, and Richardson (2009).

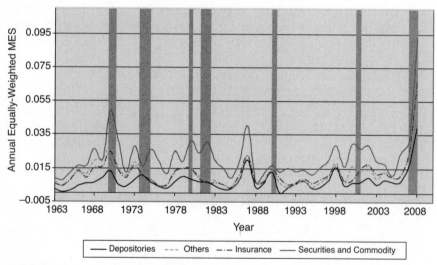

FIGURE 9.8   Annual Equally-Weighted Marginal Expected Shortfall (5 percent) by Groups of Financial Institutions

The chart depicts for each year from 1963 until 2008 the equally weighted MES (5 percent) for each of the four categories of financial institutions conditioned on at least 22 days of trading within a year.

Source: Acharya, Pedersen, Philippon, and Richardson (2009).

dollar MES by the firm's market capitalization, and present findings for both value-weighted and equal-weighted averages of the MES return. Three observations are noteworthy: First, while securities firms clearly have the highest MES among the different type of financial institutions, insurance companies do not stand out as being the least systemic. In fact, insurance companies are generally at least as systemic as the depository institutions (commercial banks). Second, there are clear fluctuations in the degree of systemic risk through time, reaching its highest point during the recent crisis but also spiking during periods in the 1970s, the market crash of 1987, and the LTCM crisis in 1998. Third, while recessions are clearly an important factor, they are neither a necessary nor a sufficient condition for systemic risk to be present.

As an additional comparison of insurance companies alone, we graph the relationship between the systemic risk measure, the MES as a percentage of market value of equity, and various accounting characteristics of the insurance company, including book equity to assets, long-term debt to assets, short-term liabilities to assets, log assets, and market equity capitalization. To save space, we only present the plots for the first two accounting characteristics in Figure 9.9.[35] One implication of these (and unreported) figures is that leverage, irrespective of the way it is measured, has a negative impact on systemic risk.

Systemic Risk Measure Computed Using the Credit Default Swaps Market Data and the Financial Crisis of 2007 to 2009

Insurance firms experienced significant stress during the financial crisis of 2007 to 2009. Figure 9.10 shows the time series of daily levels of the CRSP value-weighted index and the daily average levels of CDS spreads for 20 insurance firms whose spread data are available from Bloomberg.[36] Noticeably, the stock market declined gradually from the onset of the crisis in the middle of 2007, only to take a big plunge in the summer of 2008. Meanwhile, insurance firms showed serious signs of stress from as early as the fourth quarter of 2007, when their CDS spreads remarkably widened from around 20 basis points to over 600 basis points. These spreads remained considerably high throughout the crisis, peaking at around 1,300 basis points right before the trough of the stock market.

The magnitude of stress, nevertheless, was not homogenous across firms. This point is clearly illustrated in Figure 9.11, which plots the levels of CDS spreads for five big insurance firms, namely Ambac Financial Group, MBIA Inc., Hartford Financial Services Group (HFSG), Metropolitan Life, and AIG. Of these five firms, the two monoline insurers, Ambac and MBIA,

a

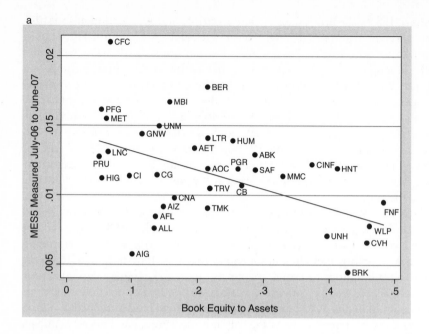

b

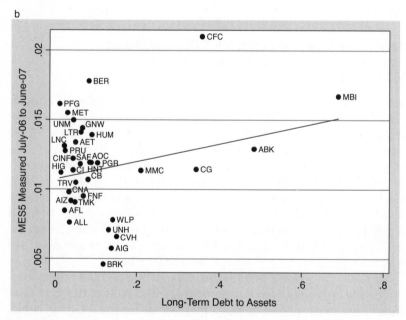

FIGURE 9.9 Systemic Risk per Dollar (Marginal Expected Shortfall) and Balance Sheet Characteristics of Insurance Firms in the Year Prior to July 2007

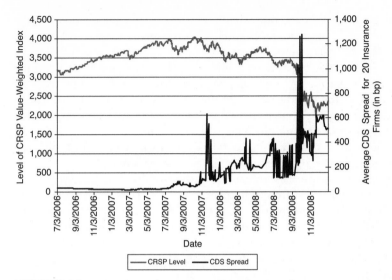

FIGURE 9.10 CDS Spread versus CRSP Index Level
The chart depicts a plot of the daily average CDS spread for 20 insurance firms included in the sample, and CRSP index level over the July 2006 to December 2008 period.

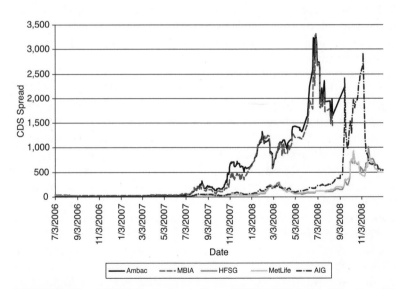

FIGURE 9.11 CDS Spreads for Ambac, MBIA, HFSG, Metropolitan Life, and AIG
The chart depicts a plot of the daily levels of CDS spreads for five big insurance firms over the July 2006 to December 2008 period.

experienced the earliest and most significant increase in CDS spreads. From a level of around 12 basis points in 2006, CDS spreads of these two firms rose to above 1,000 basis points in early 2008 and peaked at over 3,000 basis points in June 2008. Spreads on AIG CDSs also increased over the same time period, but to a much smaller degree. However, the firm's troubles became clear in the summer of 2008 when its CDS spreads shot up from well under 500 basis points to over 2,000 basis points. In contrast, HFSG and Metropolitan Life were the least stressed of the five firms, seeing their CDS spreads widen to only about 200 basis points in the midst of the crisis and peak at just over 800 basis points in November 2008.

How can we measure ex ante which insurance firms are relatively more systemic than others and thus will undergo greater stress during a systemic crisis? We show that information from the credit default swaps market can offer a good answer to this question. In particular, we find that a measure of systemic risk computed from CDS spreads, namely CDS Marginal Expected Shortfall (CDS MES), can successfully predict the performance of insurance firms during the 2007 to 2009 financial crisis.

The idea of using MES based on stock market data as a measure of firm-specific systemic risk is discussed in the preceding section. Given that information from CDS data is informative about the level of stress experienced by insurance firms over the crisis, we employ a similarly defined measure of MES computed from CDS spread data. Acharya, Pedersen, Philippon, and Richardson (2010) argue that this measure can approximate expected systemic risk contribution given that the change in CDS spreads attaches smaller weight to safer firms.

As a proxy for the market of insurance firms, we initially consider the 102 U.S. financial firms with at least $5 billion in market capitalization (as of June 2007). Data on CDS spreads are available from Bloomberg for 40 of these firms, 20 of which are insurance firms. To compute CDS MES for each insurance firm, we take the 5 percent worst days over the one-year precrisis period (from June 30, 2006, to July 1, 2007) for an equally weighted portfolio of CDS returns on the 40 financial firms, then calculate CDS MES for each individual firm as the average daily logarithmic returns on CDS spreads over these days.[37] The CDS MES obtained is our measure of systemic risk for each of the 20 insurance firms examined. Table 9.8 provides the ranking for these 20 firms based on their CDS MESs. At the top of the list is Genworth Financial Inc., whose systemic risk measure is as high as 16.40 percent. Ambac Financial Group Inc., MBIA Inc., and AIG are next. By contrast, Aetna Inc., Cigna Corp., and Marsh & McLennan Cos. Inc. are the least systematically risky firms, with negative CDS MESs.

Results from Table 9.8 coupled with Figure 9.11 reveal at a preliminary level the success of CDS MES as a predictor of how stressful each firm was

TABLE 9.8 CDS MES Ranking of 20 Insurance Firms

Company	Ticker	CDS MES Ranking	Realized CDS SES (July 2007– June 2008)	Realized CDS SES (July 2007– Dec. 2008)	CDS MES
Genworth Financial	GNW	1	145.38%	403.03%	16.40%
Ambac Financial Group	ABK	2	424.10	389.12	8.05
MBIA Inc.	MBI	3	383.11	303.44	6.71
American International Group	AIG	4	277.42	369.20	3.40
Allstate Corp.	ALL	5	183.66	271.38	2.97
Loews Corp.	L	6	136.79	175.47	2.67
Prudential Financial	PRU	7	240.25	394.44	2.33
Lincoln National Corp.	LNC	8	234.94	403.58	2.27
Aon Corp.	AOC	9	32.41	55.10	2.26
HFSG Inc.	HIG	10	212.09	368.41	2.03
Travelers Companies	STA	11	124.68	171.62	1.95
Chubb Corp.	CB	12	164.91	192.52	1.73
Unum Group	UNM	13	118.33	165.43	0.98
Safeco Corp.	SAF	14	123.95	155.92	0.85
CNA Financial Corp.	CNA	15	105.34	218.89	0.84
MetLife Inc.	MET	16	220.59	362.62	0.75
Torchmark Corp.	TMK	17	24.69	182.45	0.34
Aetna Inc. New	AET	18	127.42	192.96	−0.12
Cigna Corp.	CI	19	124.73	267.69	−0.56
Marsh & McLennan Cos.	MMC	20	31.82	33.43	−0.63

This table contains the list of 20 U.S. insurance firms with a market capitalization in excess of $5 billion as of June 2007. The firms are listed in descending order according to their CDS Marginal Expected Shortfall at the 5 percent level (MES), calculated over the July 2006 through June 2007 period. Realized CDS SES is the return on CDS spread during the crisis.

during the crisis. Specifically, Ambac Financial Group and MBIA, which rank the highest among the five big insurance firms, are those that were the most seriously hurt during the crisis. As described earlier, their CDS spreads skyrocketed from the beginning of the crisis and continued to increase over time. In contrast, HFSG and Metropolitan Life, which have the lowest CDS MESs, also experienced widening CDS spreads but to a much smaller magnitude and at a much slower pace.

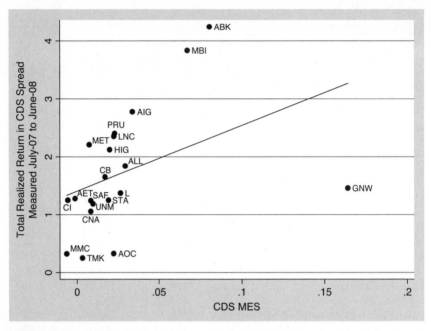

FIGURE 9.12   CDS Marginal Expected Shortfall (MES) versus Total Realized
Return in CDS Spreads Measured July 1, 2007, to June 30, 2008
The chart depicts a scatter plot for 20 insurance firms of the CDS MES computed
during the July 1, 2006, to June 30, 2007, period versus the total realized return on
CDS spreads during the period from July 1, 2007, to June 30, 2008. CDS MES is
the average CDS returns on the 5 percent worst days from July 1, 2006, to June 30,
2007, when the average CDS returns of the 20 companies are the highest.

Figures 9.12 and 9.13 show at a more detailed level how well CDS MES
can predict the realized systemic risk contribution of the 20 insurance firms
during the July 2007 to June 2008 crisis period. This realized contribution
is measured using both the percentage change in CDS spreads (Figure 9.12),
and the total percentage change in stock returns (Figure 9.13). As can be
seen from the figures, CDS MES as an ex ante measure of systemic risk contribution does very well ex post. There is indeed a clear positive association
between CDS MES as a measure of systemic risk and realized systemic costs
over the crisis. Firms that had higher systemic risk ex ante were under greater
stress ex post; that is, they experienced larger increases in CDS spreads and
lower stock returns over the crisis.

In unreported results, we also measured realized performance over the
July 2007 to December 2008 period. We argue that CDS MES should explain
ex post performance better when the realized systemic risk contribution

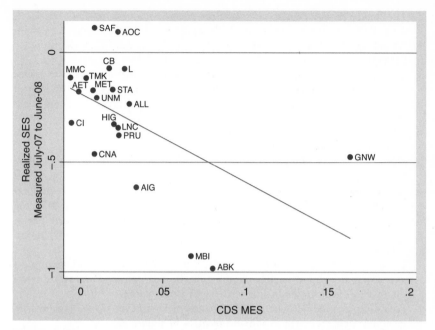

FIGURE 9.13 CDS Marginal Expected Shortfall (MES) versus Total Realized Stock Returns Measured July 1, 2007, to June 30, 2008
The chart depicts a scatter plot for 20 insurance firms of the CDS MES computed during the July 1, 2006, to June 30, 2007, period versus the total realized stock return during the period from July 1, 2007, to June 30, 2008. CDS MES is the average CDS returns on the 5 percent worst days over the July 1, 2006, to June 30, 2007, period, when the average CDS returns of the 20 companies are the highest.

is measured for the July 2007 to June 2008 period, as the government bailout programs introduced during the latter part of 2008 could have had a stabilizing effect on CDS spreads and stock returns. In fact, we document the same patterns as in Figures 9.12 and 9.13. To confirm our conjecture, these effects are, nevertheless, weaker when realized CDS spreads or stock returns are measured up until December 2008.

NOTES

1. AIG also incurred larger losses on its insurance subsidiaries in 2008 than on the Financial Products group, and these losses were due largely to its securities lending, certain repurchase agreement transactions, and its direct purchase of the supersenior tranches of subprime mortgage-based CDOs, which were the same type as those insured by the CDSs sold by the FP group.

2. The Dodd-Frank Act eliminates this rebate provision; for example, see HR 4173, Title III, "Transfer of Powers to the Comptroller of the Currency, the Corporation, and the Board of Governors," Subtitle C, "Federal Deposit Insurance Corporation," Sec. 332, "Elimination of Procyclical Assessments."

3. To be precise, the insurer pays all losses up to a deductible and pays coinsurance of 15 percent for losses above the deductible up to an aggregate event limit of $100 billion. Above the event limit, the government covers all losses at no charge.

4. HR 4173, Title V, "Insurance," Subtitle A, "Office of Insurance," Sec. 502, "Federal Insurance Office."

5. HR 4173, Title II, "Orderly Liquidation Authority," Sec. 203, "Systemic Risk Determination."

6. An exception to this statement occurs when insurers experience rare and extremely adverse underwriting outcomes. For example, epidemics that kill large numbers of people in short periods of time are rare—the last significant one in the United States was the Spanish flu in 1918 and 1919—but when they occur, they can devastate life insurers.

7. For example, Mutual Benefit Life was seized by regulators in 1991 because its assets were disproportionately illiquid policyholder loans and real estate assets that were difficult to sell in a depressed real estate market.

8. For example, some PC insurers failed because they wrote too many homeowners' insurance policies in catastrophe-prone areas like Florida.

9. Source: 2008 OTS targeted review of AIG, available online at www.fcic.gov/hearings/pdfs/2010-0701-2008-OTS-Targeted-Review.pdf.

10. Monoline insurers guarantee the payment of bond principal and interest when an issuer defaults. Since insurance regulations generally prevent PC and life insurers from offering financial guaranty insurance (but not somewhat substitutable surety insurance), monolines get their names from this being the sole form of insurance they write. Historically, these companies insured municipal bonds, which have faced mostly idiosyncratic and therefore diversifiable default risk. Whether this diversifiability would persist in times of widespread revenue shortfalls for municipalities is a question worthy of serious regulatory consideration. Warren Buffett muses about the moral hazard risk that municipalities might try to solve such shortfalls by defaulting on their bonds in his 2008 Letter to Shareholders as Berkshire Hathaway's chairman (pp. 12–15). However, over time, the monolines expanded their business to insure structured products.

11. A supersenior CDO is an unrated CDO senior to at least one AAA-rated CDO created in the same securitization.

12. According to the 2008 OTS report, the housing market deterioration and global credits market disruption contributed to AIG's losses of $49 billion as of March 31, 2008.

13. There are four general types of minimum guarantees in variable annuities and other investment-oriented life insurance policies: (1) guaranteed minimum death benefits, which guarantee the policyholder's heirs a minimum payment upon the policyholder's death; (2) guaranteed minimum income benefits, which guarantee

the policyholder a minimum income stream when the policyholder annuitizes the policy in the future; (3) guaranteed minimum withdrawal benefits, which guarantee that the policyholder can withdraw specified percentages of a guaranteed value of the policy each year (without the requirement to annuitize); and (4) guaranteed minimum accumulation benefits, which guarantee that the policyholder's account value will be a certain amount at a specified future date. Other contract features in these policies include no-lapse guarantees and minimum or ratchet interest crediting. We do not attempt to distinguish the effects of these different types of minimum guarantees and other contract features.

14. Equity securities are the primary assets in the separate accounts that insurers create for variable annuities. In contrast, the primary assets in life insurers' general accounts are corporate bonds, other debt instruments, and real estate.

15. While slower than bank deposit runs due to certain contractual features of investment-oriented life insurance policies (significant surrender charges and restrictions on the speed of withdrawals), significant policyholder runs did occur at various life insurers, such as Executive Life, in the early 1990s. HFSG discloses in its financial reports that it experienced unusual withdrawal behavior in 2008 and 2009. It is likely that the federal government's injection of $3.4 billion of Capital Purchase Program funds into HFSG, made in June 2009 but under discussion beginning in November 2008, mitigated such behavior.

16. The possibility of systemic risk goes beyond variable annuity writers. U.S. life insurers hold over $5 trillion of various types of long-term debt and equity securities that they typically try to duration match to their usually long-term claim liabilities. Some of these securities—such as the structured asset-backed securities in which AIG, HFSG, and some other insurers seeking additional yield invested significant amounts—are illiquid or can become so during a financial crisis. Should life insurers collectively have to dump enough illiquid assets during a crisis, the values of those assets would fall further than they would have otherwise.

17. Surety insurance protects policyholders against contractual nonperformance by a counterparty to a contract.

18. For a general analysis of the regulation of these companies, see Walter, Smith, and Saunders (2009).

19. For the introduction and formal discussion of the concept of counterparty risk externality, see, respectively, Acharya and Engle (2009) and Acharya and Bisin (2009).

20. See, for example, Brunnermeier and Pedersen (2008).

21. The total amount called from 1988 through 2008 was $6 billion compared to the capacity over that same period of $115 billion. The largest draw in the associations' history was $875 million in 1995.

22. It is, therefore, for a good reason that the states, by law, prohibit the advertising by the life and health companies of the existence of the guaranty funds.

23. See Wallison (2000).

24. For a discussion of what the regulatory structure would look like, see Walter, Smith, and Saunders (2009).

25. National Association of Insurance Commissioners, Kansas City, Missouri.

26. This discussion is based on the insurance contract project update on the FASB web site dated April 15, 2010.
27. Note 3 of the 10-K outlines the operating segments of AIG in considerable detail.
28. The history of AIG Financial Products is outlined in a three-part series written by Robert O'Harrow and Brady Dennis for the *Washington Post* in December 2008 and January 2009.
29. See Jurek, Coval, and Stafford (forthcoming).
30. Collateral postings were required by a number of credit default swap contracts as the underlying collateralized debt obligations lost value and/or AIG itself suffered a ratings downgrade.
31. Maiden Lane III was an investment company designed to purchase the underlying collateralized debt obligations that AIG had written credit default swap contracts on, effectively closing out the credit default swaps. It was created in September 2008 when AIG was effectively taken over by the U.S. government.
32. Guaranteed investment agreements are investments with a guaranteed rate of return that municipalities use to invest the proceeds from their bond issues, and are effectively used to cement high ratings at the issuance level.
33. One could argue that the possibility that all bonds have a recovery rate of zero is in fact zero, so the amount at risk is less than $450 billion. It is clear, however, that because the probability of a AAA-rated tranche being affected is very low, the actual dollars at risk may have been quite high given the level of CDS premiums. For the product to be considered insurance, this amount would need to be covered.
34. The methodology proposed in this subsection and the resulting calculations are based on Acharya, Pedersen, Philippon, and Richardson (2009).
35. Plots for the remaining variables are available from the authors upon request.
36. CDS data for this study is the spread on the five-year senior unsecured credit default swaps.
37. CDSs are not as frequently traded as stocks. Hence, to eliminate the effect of CDS return on a given day being the aggregated return over many nontrading days, we use only returns on days when CDS spread information is available for that day and the previous trading day. No return is used for a day when no spread information can be obtained for the trading day immediately preceding it. The worst days of the CDS index are defined as days when returns on the CDS index are the highest.

REFERENCES

Acharya, V. V., and A. Bisin. 2009. Centralized versus over-the-counter markets. Working paper, NYU Stern School of Business.

Acharya, V. V., and R. Engle. 2009. Derivative traders should all be transparent. *Wall Street Journal*, May 15.

Acharya, V. V., L. Pedersen, T. Philippon, and M. Richardson. 2009. Regulating systemic risk. In *Restoring financial stability: How to repair a failed system*, ed. Viral V. Acharya and Matthew Richardson. Hoboken, NJ: John Wiley & Sons.

Acharya, V. V., L. Pedersen, T. Philippon, and M. Richardson. 2010. Measuring systemic risk. Working paper, NYU Stern School of Business.

Brunnermeier, M., and L. Pedersen. 2008. Market liquidity and funding liquidity. *Review of Financial Studies* 22 (6): 2201–2238.

Jurek, J., C. Coval, and E. Stafford. Forthcoming. The economics of structured finance. *Journal of Economic Perspectives*.

Wallison, P. J., ed. 2000. *Optional federal chartering and regulation of insurance companies*. Washington, DC: AEI Press.

Walter, I., J. Smith, and A. Saunders. 2009. Enhanced regulation of large, complex, financial institutions. In *Restoring financial stability: How to repair a failed system*, ed. V. V. Acharya and M. Richardson. Hoboken, NJ: John Wiley & Sons.

Three

Shadow Banking

CHAPTER 10

Money Market Funds

How to Avoid Breaking the Buck

Marcin Kacperczyk and Philipp Schnabl*

10.1 OVERVIEW

A money market fund is a financial intermediary that manages funds on behalf of investors who wish to invest in low-risk securities while being able to withdraw funds at short notice. The primary objective of a money market fund is to maintain the value of the principal of its assets. Thus, money market funds invest only in low-risk, short-term securities, such as commercial paper, certificates of deposit, and Treasuries. From the investors' perspective, holding shares of money market funds is similar to depositing cash in a bank, because investors can withdraw money from a fund anytime without a penalty. The benefit relative to bank deposits is that money market funds earn a slightly higher yield relative to what cash yields in bank deposit accounts. The cost relative to bank deposits is that money market funds are not insured by the government. The money market funds sector is large, with more than $3 trillion of assets under management in 2007.

---

*This chapter is partly based on the authors' article "When Safe Proved Risky: Commercial Paper during the Financial Crisis of 2007–2009," published in the *Journal of Economic Perspectives* in winter 2010. We thank the editors, Matt Richardson and Viral Acharya, for their help in preparing this chapter. We also benefited from discussions in the "Money Market Funds" Working Group, which also included Stanley Kon, Anthony Lynch, Antti Petajisto, Kermit L. Schoenholtz, and Robert Whitelaw.

10.2 PRIMER ON MONEY MARKET FUNDS

Money market funds emerged in the 1970s as an alternative to bank deposits. The driving force behind their emergence was restrictive regulation of bank deposits. Until the early 1980s, the government set a maximum interest rate on bank deposits, which limited the returns to investors. Money market funds allowed investors to circumvent this regulation by directly investing in money market instruments, such as commercial paper, which yielded higher returns than bank deposits.

Even after the government lifted the interest rate ceiling, rates on bank deposits typically remained below rates on money market deposits. As shown in Figure 10.1, interest rates on money market deposits closely followed the federal funds rate, but bank deposits' rates usually remained below the Fed funds rate. As a result, money market funds offer a yield advantage over bank deposits, and total money market deposits increased steadily over the past three decades from $500 billion in 1987 to $3 trillion in 2007, as shown in Figure 10.2.

A possible explanation for the difference between the two interest rates is that money market deposits are riskier, because, unlike bank deposits, they do not have government insurance. Hence, even though money market funds seek to preserve the value of an investment at $1.00 per share, it is possible that investors in money market funds can suffer a loss on their investments.

To limit the risks of money market fund investments, the government regulates holdings of money market funds under Rule 2a-7 of the Investment Company Act of 1940. The regulation specifies the type of instruments money market funds can invest in. For example, Rule 2a-7 limits commercial

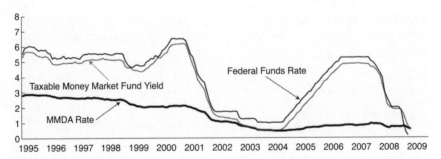

FIGURE 10.1 Comparison of Annual Bank Rates and Money Market Fund Yields (Percent, Monthly)
Source: Bank Rate Monitor, Federal Reserve Board, and iMoneyNet.

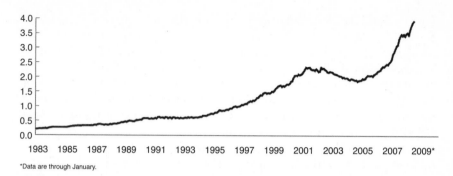

*Data are through January.

FIGURE 10.2   Total Net Assets of Money Market Funds (Trillions of Dollars, Monthly)
Source: Report of the Money Market Working Group (Figure 2.2), Investment Company Institute, March 17, 2009.

paper holdings of money market funds to commercial paper that carries either the highest or second-highest rating for short-term debt from at least two of the nationally recognized credit rating agencies. Further, money market funds must hold not more than 5 percent of their assets in securities of any individual issuer with the highest rating and not more than 1 percent of their assets in securities of any individual issuer. Also, holdings of securities with the second-highest rating must not exceed 5 percent of the funds' assets. Rule 2a-7 also contains regulation of other asset classes to limit risks of money market funds (Stigum and Crescenzi 2007).

We use a novel data set provided by iMoneyNet to analyze the holdings of money market funds. This data set provides the most comprehensive source of information on money market funds' asset holdings. Our subsequent analysis focuses on taxable money market funds, which represent 84.5 percent of money market fund holdings in 2007.

As of January 2007, there were 473 taxable money market funds holding assets worth $1.95 trillion. About one-third of the funds were Treasury funds, which almost exclusively invest in government debt and government-backed agency debt. The remaining two-thirds were prime funds that invest primarily in nongovernment assets, such as commercial paper. The largest asset class held by taxable money market funds was commercial paper, accounting for $634 billion or 32.5 percent of total asset holdings. The remaining asset classes included government debt and government-backed agency debt ($585 billion), repurchase agreements ($390 billion), bank obligations ($297 billion), and other assets ($45 billion).

Most large money market funds are geared toward institutional investors. A study by Moody's Investors Service (2007) shows that in

January 2007 the 15 largest institutional prime funds accounted for a total of $459 billion of assets. Institutional prime funds hold a large number of different money market instruments, and these money market funds are therefore considered well diversified. Nevertheless, money market funds are highly exposed to risks in the financial industry as a whole. Assets originated by the financial industry—measured as the total of financial commercial paper, structured securities, bank obligations, and repurchase agreements—accounted for 91.4 percent of money market fund assets.

Outside the United States, most countries have no regulation similar to Rule 2a-7. As a result, money market funds developed only recently, when changes in the regulatory environment in Europe led to a more favorable treatment of money market fund deposits. Over the past several years, money market funds in Europe have grown significantly. As of January 2008, European money market funds had about €350 billion of assets under management. In terms of currency, the market was about evenly split between euros and British pounds (see International Capital Market Association 2008).

Given that most money market funds are based in the United States, we focus our discussion on money market funds in the United States. However, we note that most of our analysis also applies to European money market funds.

10.3 MONEY MARKET FUNDS DURING THE FINANCIAL CRISIS

Prior to Lehman's bankruptcy, most investors regarded money market funds as a safe asset class. The only time a money market fund ever defaulted prior to the financial crisis was in the early 1990s during the Orange County bankruptcy. However, it was a small fund and other funds weathered the bankruptcy without breaking the buck. This is probably why, during the early phase of the financial crisis, most investors perceived money market funds as a safe haven. Even though a large number of prime money market funds had invested in asset-backed commercial paper, these funds barely suffered any losses from those investments, as most issuers of asset-backed commercial paper had credit guarantees from large commercial banks (Acharya, Schnabl, and Suarez 2009). In case a fund did face some losses, the management company often voluntarily purchased impaired assets at face value.

It was not until September 2008 that money market funds faced significant pressure. After the bankruptcy of Lehman Brothers on September 15, 2008, many investors were surprised to learn that the Reserve Primary

Fund—one of the largest money market funds, with more than $65 billion in assets under management—owned more than $785 million of Lehman's commercial paper. In fact, the founder of the Reserve Primary Fund, who had been one of the pioneers of the money market industry, had publicly expressed the view that money market funds should not invest in commercial paper because it was too risky. In line with this view, until September 2005 the Reserve Primary Fund holdings' reports with the Securities and Exchange Commission (SEC) did not include any investment in commercial paper. This commitment was subsequently abandoned and, from 2006 onward, the reports filed by the Reserve Primary Fund indicated that the fund began acquiring significant amounts of commercial paper, probably to boost its performance (Stecklow and Gullapalli 2008).

The revelation of the Reserve Primary Fund's exposure to Lehman during its bankruptcy triggered an immediate run on the fund. On September 16, 2008, the Reserve Primary Fund was forced to pay out $10.8 billion in redemptions, and it faced about $28 billion of further withdrawal requests. The run quickly spread to other money market funds with commercial paper holdings. Our analysis based on iMoneyNet data shows that within a week institutional investors reduced their investments in money market funds by more than $172 billion. To stop the run on money market funds, on September 19, 2008, the U.S. Department of the Treasury instituted a temporary deposit insurance covering all money market investments. This announcement stopped the run on money market funds, and redemption requests promptly receded.

Nonetheless, investors interpreted Lehman's bankruptcy as a signal that commercial paper issued and sponsored by financial institutions was far riskier than investors had previously thought. As shown in Figure 10.3, financial commercial paper outstanding dropped by 29.5 percent, from $806 billion on September 10, 2008, to $568 billion on October 22, 2008. Over the same time period, asset-backed commercial paper outstanding dropped by a smaller 9.8 percent, from $741 billion to $668 billion. Also, the spreads on both asset-backed and financial paper significantly increased, though the change for financial commercial paper was more temporary.

Money market funds were a leading force in the decline of the commercial paper market. Alhough money market fund investments were considered safe because of the newly introduced deposit insurance, money market funds themselves decided to reduce their holdings of commercial paper. As Figure 10.4 shows, within one month after Lehman's bankruptcy, as a percentage of money market funds, commercial paper holdings fell from 24.2 percent to 16.9 percent. The decrease in commercial paper holdings was accompanied by money market funds' expansion of their holdings of government debt from 36.7 percent to 44.5 percent of asset holdings.

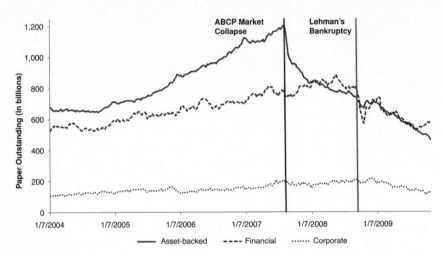

FIGURE 10.3   Commercial Paper Outstanding, January 2004 to October 2009
Note: Weekly commercial paper outstanding based on Federal Reserve Board data.

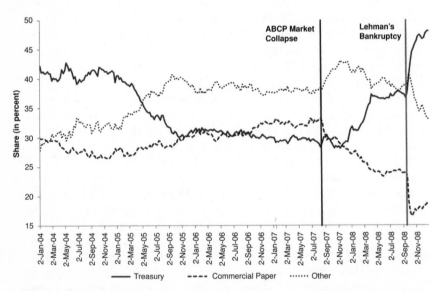

FIGURE 10.4   Money Market Funds' Asset Shares in Total Holdings, January 2004 to December 2008
Note: Authors' own analysis using iMoneyNet data on money market funds' holdings.

10.4 GOVERNMENT RESPONSE TO LEHMAN'S BANKRUPTCY

In response to the run on money market funds, the government decided to roll out a number of new policy initiatives to contain the situation. On September 19, 2008, the U.S. Treasury announced that the U.S. government would temporarily guarantee assets of money market funds (U.S. Department of the Treasury 2008). Around the same time, it announced a new lending program—the Asset-Backed Commercial Paper Money Market Mutual Fund Liquidity Facility (AMLF). The AMLF—administered by the Federal Reserve Bank of Boston—was supposed to provide loans to commercial banks so that they could purchase high-quality asset-backed commercial paper from money market funds. These are nonrecourse loans, which implies that if the asset-backed commercial paper defaults, the Federal Reserve takes over the commercial paper instead of requiring repayment of the loan. As Figure 10.5 illustrates, the AMLF started buying commercial paper on September 24, and its first two weeks of activity amounted to approximately $150 billion worth of purchases. Over time, the AMLF reduced its purchases, and by October 2009, its holdings had gone down to almost zero.

On October 7, 2008, the Federal Reserve announced that, in addition to buying through the AMLF, it would purchase three-month commercial

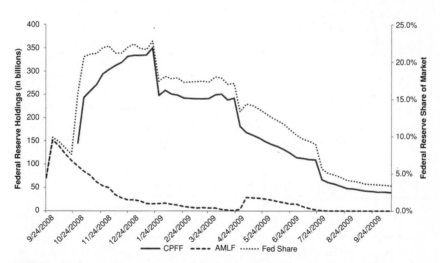

FIGURE 10.5 Holdings of Fed Funding Facilities, September 2008 to October 2009

Note: Based on Federal Reserve Board and New York Federal Reserve data.

paper directly from eligible issuers through the Commercial Paper Funding Facility (CPFF). Only U.S. issuers of commercial paper, including U.S. issuers with a foreign parent, were eligible to sell commercial paper to this facility. This was important because many issuers of commercial paper are located outside of the United States, but they maintain funding facilities in the United States (Acharya and Schnabl 2009). The interest rate on corporate and financial commercial paper was the three-month overnight indexed swap rate—a standard measure of borrowing costs in money markets—plus 200 basis points. Likewise, the interest rate on asset-backed commercial paper was the overnight indexed swap rate plus 300 basis points.

As shown in Figure 10.5, the CPFF started purchasing commercial paper on October 26, 2008. The value of financial commercial paper outstanding came back to its precrisis level. Also, the spreads on all types of commercial paper significantly decreased. By the end of 2008, the total value of commercial paper purchased under the CPFF program equaled $335 billion, of which one-third was asset-backed commercial paper. As a result, the Federal Reserve was the single largest buyer of commercial paper (Federal Reserve Bank of New York 2008). Initially, the program purchased only assets with maturities over 15 days, and only from January 2009 on did it expand to shorter-maturity assets. Also, like the AMLF, the value of assets purchased under the CPFF has been gradually declining; it reached about $40 billion in October 2009.

Finally, on October 21, 2008, the Federal Reserve announced another lending program—the Money Market Investor Funding Facility (MMIFF)—intended to complement the AMLF. Similar to the AMLF, the new program was supposed to provide nonrecourse loans to money market funds. The main difference was that it was restricted to money market instruments other than asset-backed commercial paper, such as certificates of deposit, bank notes, and financial and corporate commercial paper. The New York Fed began funding eligible money market instruments under this program on November 24, 2008. However, the facility never took off, and as of August 2010 it had not provided a single loan to money market funds.

10.5   NEW REGULATION AND ASSESSMENT

The SEC adopted new regulation for money market funds in March 2010. The new regulation aims to reduce the risk-taking behavior of money market funds by restricting their investments to the highest-quality securities, reducing the average maturity of their holdings, requiring funds to maintain a portion of their portfolios in instruments that can easily be converted into cash, and requiring them to provide monthly holdings reports. Regarding the funds' liquidations, the new regulation allows money market funds that have broken the buck to suspend redemptions to allow for an orderly unwinding of the fund (see Securities and Exchange Commission 2010; Maxey 2010).

In an earlier proposal, the SEC was also seeking comments on whether money market funds, like other mutual funds, should be priced at a floating net asset value rather than at a fixed net asset value of one dollar. The reasoning for this proposed change was that investors would put less focus on whether a fund breaks the buck if net asset values also fluctuated under normal circumstances (see Securities and Exchange Commission 2009).

In evaluating the new SEC regulation, it is important to recognize that money market funds perform two important functions in the economy. First, they effectively form a part of the payment system, because money market fund investors can redeem their shares on demand. Second, money market funds primarily invest in short-term securities issued by the financial sector. Hence, they are an important source of short-term financing for other financial intermediaries.

Why should the government regulate money market funds? During a financial crisis, concerns are usually voiced about the viability of the payment system and access to short-term financing for financial intermediaries. If either the payment system fails or financial intermediaries cannot refinance themselves, there can be large negative effects on the rest of the economy. Given that money market funds provide both payment services to investors and refinancing to financial intermediaries, there is a strong case for the government to support money market funds during a financial crisis by guaranteeing the value of money market fund investments. As a result of such support, money market funds have an ex ante incentive to take on excessive risk, similarly to other financial institutions with explicit or implicit government guarantees.

Prior to Lehman's bankruptcy, guarantees to money market funds may have been perceived as unlikely. However, after the guarantees were provided in September 2008, most investors will expect similar guarantees during future financial crises, independent of whether the guarantees are made explicit. Hence, we evaluate the new regulation in terms of its suitability to address the prospect of government support during financial crises.

The key provisions of the new money market fund regulations are as follows:

- Improved portfolio liquidity (e.g., 30 percent of money market funds' holdings must be liquid within one week).
- Higher credit quality (e.g., maximum of 3 percent invested in second-tier securities).

- Shorter portfolio maturity (e.g., maximum weighted average maturity of a fund's portfolio restricted to 60 days).
- Introduction of periodic stress tests to evaluate funds' ability to withstand shocks.
- Enhanced disclosure (monthly reporting of money market fund holdings).
- Authorization of a fund's board of directors to suspend redemptions if the fund breaks the buck.

Importantly, the SEC decided against the introduction of a floating net asset value and instead maintained the stable net asset value for pricing.

We believe that the new regulation is sensible and should increase the safety of the money market fund sector. However, we point out that the new regulation cannot entirely eliminate runs on money market funds. Like other financial intermediaries, money market funds transform illiquid securities (e.g., commercial paper) into liquid demand deposits. As long as the regulator does not impose liquidity requirements of 100 percent—and thereby effectively outlaw money market funds—there will always be a possibility of a run. In fact, several money market funds satisfied the regulation even during the financial crisis and were still subject to runs after Lehman's bankruptcy. Hence, even though the new regulation makes the money market fund sector more secure (and also less profitable), it will not eliminate the issue of government support during systemic crises.

Our key observation is that the new regulation does not address the critical issue of likely government guarantees during future financial crises. We therefore recommend considering the following alternative proposals.

Glass-Steagall for Money Market Funds

Our first solution is based on the principle that money market funds inherently look just like banks and are engaged in maturity mismatch. Under this alternative, we envision that the government explicitly recognizes its commitment to support money market funds during a systemic crisis. The provision of guarantees should be restricted to large systemic crises and can be at the discretion of a financial regulator. In exchange for the expected cost of the guarantee, the government should charge a fee to money market funds. The fee should be charged in normal times and not after the crisis has arisen. To preclude risk taking at the expense of the guarantee, the SEC should require investment restrictions on portfolio maturity and eligibility. In addition, we recommend restrictions on exposure to a single issuer, by aggregating exposure across securities. (See Kacperczyk, Sialm, and Zheng 2005 for implications of such rules for equity funds.) The fee charged against the guarantee would thus typically be lower than the cost of the guarantee provided on bank deposits, because investments by money market funds would be more restrictive than those of banks benefiting from deposit insurance.

Discount Window for Money Market Funds

Our second alternative is based on the idea that even though money market funds in principle can be treated differently from banks—that is, without explicit guarantees to deposits—in a systemic crisis, when several financial institutions are in trouble, there will invariably be a collective run on money market funds since they primarily invest in short-term commercial paper and a large part of the market for this paper consists of issuance by banks and financial institutions. Recognizing this possibility, some resolution of such collective runs must be planned for in advance. Individual runs on funds may be easy to resolve through requiring that funds in trouble simply liquidate their assets and pass on their losses to investors. However, such a resolution may be difficult when several funds are in trouble simultaneously, as it would require large-scale liquidations of commercial paper all at once.

Hence, under the second alternative, we propose that the government would announce that it will *not* provide guarantees to money market funds during a systemic crisis. To make such an announcement credible, the government needs to outline a clear procedure for stopping runs on money market funds. First, the government should allow money market funds to place a stay on redemptions in the case of a run—that is, a temporary suspension of the rights of investors to redeem their invested funds. The primary purpose of the stay is to allow for an orderly liquidation of the fund. This measure recognizes that putting a stay on a single fund's redemptions can trigger a run on the rest of the money market fund sector, leading to a stay on the entire industry.

Second, the government should establish a liquidity window (similar to the discount window for banks), which lends to money market funds freely against liquid collateral (such as bonds of governments of the highest credit quality). On illiquid assets, either the central bank could lend through the liquidity window against a fee and a sizable haircut (depending on current market conditions) or, preferably, the illiquid assets should be liquidated in an orderly manner during the period of the stay. These three features—a stay, the liquidity facility, and the orderly liquidation of illiquid assets—should allow investors to withdraw money during the liquidation process, but only after first paying for losses on liquidations and fees to the central bank.

In addition, the regulator can require money market funds to purchase guarantees from affiliated financial intermediaries. Before Lehman's bankruptcy, several fund families supported their funds to avoid breaking the buck. The regulator could require fund families explicitly to recognize—and suitably capitalize—such guarantees. Funds lacking support from their fund families would be required to purchase guarantees from financial institutions of comparable financial strength as fund families providing support.

Require Floating Net Asset Value

Our third alternative is to require money market funds to use a floating net asset value instead of a stable net asset value. However, we recognize that under such regulation, money market funds would lose their special status of being almost equivalent to cash or bank deposits and instead would become more like short-term bond funds. Hence, this proposal would effectively outlaw money market funds.

Moreover, to the extent that investors value the stable net asset value, we would expect the emergence of money market funds that have (nominally) floating net asset values but effectively provide a stable net asset value. Such

TABLE 10.1 Money Market Proposals

New SEC Regulation	Option 1: Glass-Steagall	Option 2: Discount Window	Option 3: Floating Net Asset Value
Minimum liquidity, maximum maturity	Recognize government support during systemic crisis	No guarantee during systemic crisis	No guarantee during systemic crisis
Restrict to first-tier securities	Charge insurance fee	Allow funds to suspend redemptions (SEC)	Require floating net asset value
Periodic stress tests	Restrict liquidity and maturity (SEC)	Lend against illiquid securities	
Monthly disclosure	Limit exposure to single issuer		
Authorize fund to suspend redemptions			

funds would break the buck only during a systemic crisis, which would effectively make them equivalent to money market funds with stable net asset values. Hence, this proposal would require the regulator to ensure that net asset values are indeed floating during normal times.

10.6 RECOMMENDATIONS

We believe that one of these three approaches is needed to address the issue of government guarantees to the money market fund sector during a systemic crisis (see Table 10.1). In order to choose among the three approaches, we recommend undertaking more research on the costs and benefits of each approach, allowing policymakers to make an informed choice. The key message of our chapter is that money market funds benefit from an implicit government guarantee and that no regulatory reform will succeed without explicitly addressing this issue.

REFERENCES

Acharya, Viral, and Philipp Schnabl. 2009. Do global banks spread global imbalances? The case of asset-backed commercial paper during the financial crisis of 2007–2009. *IMF Economic Review* (forthcoming).

Acharya, Viral, Philipp Schnabl, and Gustavo Suarez. 2009. Securitization without risk transfer. Working paper, NYU Stern School of Business.

Federal Reserve Bank of New York. 2008. Commercial Paper Funding Facility LLC.

International Capital Market Association. 2008. Money market funds—Draft report. December 12.

Investment Company Institute. 2009. Report of the Money Market Group. March 17.

Kacperczyk, Marcin, and Philipp Schnabl. 2010. When safe proved risky: Commercial paper during the financial crisis of 2007–2009. *Journal of Economic Perspectives* 24 (1): 29–50.

Kacperczyk, Marcin, Clemens Sialm, and Lu Zheng. 2005. On the industry concentration of actively managed equity mutual funds. *Journal of Finance* 60 (4): 1983–2011.

Maxey, Daisy. 2010. Money funds exhale after SEC rules; should they?" *Wall Street Journal*, February 2.

Moody's Investors Service. 2007. Portfolio management activities of large prime institutional money market funds. Special report.

Securities and Exchange Commission. 2009. 17 CFR Parts 270 and 274, money market fund reform: Proposed rule. July 8.

Securities and Exchange Commission. 2010. 17 CFR Parts 270 and 274, money market fund reform: Final rule. *Federal Register* 75, no. 42 (March 4): 10060–10119.

Stecklow, Steve, and Diya Gullapalli. 2008. A money-fund manager's fateful shift. *Wall Street Journal*, December 8.

Stigum, Marcia, and Anthony Crescenzi. 2007. *Stigum's money market*. 4th ed. New York: McGraw-Hill.

U.S. Department of the Treasury. 2008. Treasury announces temporary guarantee program for money market funds. Press release, September 29.

CHAPTER 11

The Repurchase Agreement (Repo) Market

Viral V. Acharya and T. Sabri Öncü*

11.1 OVERVIEW

The U.S. shadow banking system played a significant role in the financial crisis that started in August 2007. The shadow banking system is a system of "financial institutions that mostly look like a bank, borrow short term in rollover debt markets, leverage themselves significantly, and lend and invest in longer-term and illiquid assets" (see Acharya, Gale, and Yorulmazer 2009). Unlike banks, however, the shadow banking system is much less regulated.

Shadow banking is a recently minted term. However, the emergence of a shadow banking system in the United States may be traced as far back as the early 1970s.[1] Its most important component is securitized debt, or simply debt secured by underlying assets (many of which are debt securities themselves), such as U.S. Treasuries, agencies, corporate bonds, commercial paper, mortgage-backed securities (MBSs), equities, and so on. By the fourth quarter of 2009, the amount of outstanding securitized debt in the United States totaled $11.6 trillion, about one-third of the entire U.S. debt market.[2]

*We would like to thank Antoine Martin and Joseph Sommer of the Federal Reserve Bank of New York for helping us improve our understanding of the legal aspects of the repos. None of their comments are necessarily the opinion of the Federal Reserve Bank of New York or any other component of the Federal Reserve System. We are grateful to Anjolein Schmeits and Darrell Duffie for helpful comments and suggestions.

Much of this securitized debt is in the form of what are called repurchase agreements. A *repurchase agreement* (also known as a *sale and repurchase agreement*, or more popularly as a *repo*) is a short-term transaction between two parties in which one party borrows cash from the other by pledging a financial security as collateral. A series of regulatory changes in the 1980s made the repo market an attractive source of short-term—typically overnight—financing for primary dealers to finance their positions in the debt of the U.S. government, federal agencies, corporations, and federal agency mortgage-backed securities. Later, it also became a funding source for others to lend and invest in relatively illiquid mortgage-backed securities.

The lack of official statistics precludes an accurate estimation of the size of the repo market. However, Gorton and Metrick (2009a) and also Gorton (2009) estimate that the repo market totaled about $12 trillion as of 2009 (although this estimate likely includes some double counting). Based on the average daily amount outstanding, the Federal Reserve Bank of New York put the primary dealer repo financing of U.S. government, federal agency, corporate, and federal agency mortgage-backed securities at $6.5 trillion in 2008. This amount fell to $4.4 trillion in 2009. This substantial collapse has rendered the shadow banking system of the United States crippled. And notably, the collapse was also central to the financial crisis of 2007 to 2009, featuring, among others, a significant repo run on Bear Stearns in the first two weeks of March 2008. In the repo run on Bear Stearns, the money market funds that financed Bear Stearns's holdings of AAA-rated mortgage-backed securities in the overnight repo market refused to roll over the financing, forcing Bear Stearns to draw down on its liquidity pool, and ultimately ending in its Federal Reserve–assisted sale to JPMorgan Chase.

Despite its central role in the shadow banking system—and in the recent financial crisis—there was almost no mention of the repo market in the recently passed U.S. House of Representatives bill (HR 4173). Neither does there appear to be any significant mention of this market in the Senate bill or the final Dodd-Frank Wall Street Reform and Consumer Protection Act of 2010. In this chapter, we explain why the silence about dealing with the possibility of future runs in the repo market is a significant mistake. In particular, we explain that, unlike the liquidity risk that unsecured financing may become unavailable to a firm, the liquidity risk that secured repo financing may become unavailable to a firm is inherently a systemic risk: The repo markets are likely to become illiquid precisely when a large part of the financial sector is experiencing stress. Unless this systemic liquidity risk of the repo market is resolved, the risk of a run on the repo market will remain.

In this chapter, we provide a primer on the U.S. repo market (Section 11.2), describe how it came to play such a significant role in securitized banking (Section 11.3), discuss its critical role in the form of repo runs in the crisis (Section 11.4), argue a case for reforming the repo market infrastructure based on an understanding of the fundamental source of repo runs (Section 11.5), outline our proposal for such reform (Section 11.6), and articulate implications for the future (Section 11.7).

11.2 A PRIMER ON THE U.S. REPO MARKET

Consider the following transaction between a primary securities dealer and one of its clients, say a municipality. The primary securities dealer in need of money calls the municipality and, in exchange for an MBS worth, say, $100, borrows $100 for a week. The understanding is that a week later, the primary securities dealer will return with $105 to get the MBS back. The extra $5 is the interest on the $100 principal, whereas the MBS is the collateral securing the loan. From the municipality's perspective, the municipality lends $100 to the primary securities dealer at $5 interest by borrowing the MBS for a week. If the primary securities dealer fails to come back with $105 at the end of the week, the MBS becomes the property of the municipality. If the municipality sells the borrowed MBS before the end of the week, then the municipality will need to buy the MBS back to return it to the primary securities dealer. If it is acceptable to the dealer, the municipality may instead buy a substitute (and most likely a cheaper) MBS.[3] If the municipality fails to return the MBS or an acceptable substitute to the primary securities dealer, then the dealer keeps the $100 without paying any interest.

In this transaction, the primary securities dealer enters into a sale and repurchase agreement or, in short, a repo. The municipality enters into a *purchase and resale agreement*, or a *reverse repo*. Thus, every repo is also a reverse repo and vice versa; the perspective depends on who is the seller and who is the purchaser. The day the repo is initiated is called the sale date, and the day the repo is terminated is called the purchase date. Since repos are essentially secured loans and the interest on the loan is also usually very small compared with the principal, the counterparty risk on the loan is usually not an issue. The counterparty risk can, however, be an issue on the collateral, because the value of the collateral may deviate from the principal of the loan. When there is such counterparty risk on the collateral, one of the parties is usually subject to a haircut.[4] That is, if the MBS is worth $100, the loan might be worth only $90, giving rise to a 10 percent haircut to the primary securities dealer. This $10 haircut is the margin required by the municipality as protection against the potential value loss of the MBS in case the primary securities dealer fails to come back and the municipality has to take ownership of the MBS, sell it, and recover the loss. If the primary securities dealer does not own the MBS, then the dealer needs to find $10 elsewhere or earn the $10 by the sale date in order to buy the MBS. The $10 is the dealer's equity and $90 is the debt on the total loan of $100. The asset of the primary securities dealer is the MBS, and therefore, the dealer's leverage is 10 times, where leverage is defined as the value of the asset divided by the value of the equity.

If, however, the MBS is worth $90 and the loan is worth $100, then there is a 10 percent haircut to the municipality. This $10 haircut is the margin required by the primary securities dealer as protection against the potential value gain of the MBS in case the municipality fails to deliver the MBS on the purchase date so that the dealer has to buy a substitute MBS to replace the old one. Therefore, there can be a haircut either to the debtor (primary securities dealer) or to the creditor (municipality), although most of the time it is the debtor who is subject to the haircut, if any. If the municipality has only $10, then the municipality needs to sell the MBS for $90 to someone else in order to lend $100 to the primary securities dealer; in this case, $10 is the equity, the MBS is the debt, and the $100 loan is the municipality's asset, making the leverage of the municipality 10 times. If the primary securities dealer does not have the MBS, the municipality does not have the money, and there is no haircut, then both the primary securities dealer and the municipality are infinitely leveraged.[5]

In the U.S. repo market, loans are mostly extended overnight; that is, they are one-day transactions. *Overnight repos* constitute about half of all repo transactions, and most of them are open; they roll over automatically until either party chooses to exit. Other repo transactions, called *term repos*, have terms longer than one day but shorter than one year, although the vast majority have maturities of three months or less. Participants in the repo market include commercial banks, investment banks, hedge funds, mutual funds, pension funds, money market funds, municipalities, corporations, and other owners of large amounts of idle cash, as well as the Federal Reserve and primary securities dealers.

The Fed participates in the repo market mainly to implement its monetary policy; primary securities dealers participate mostly to finance their market making and risk management activities. Owners of large amounts of idle cash engage in the repo market mainly for two reasons: (1) to get better interest rates in the repo market compared with deposits at commercial banks, and (2) for insurance purposes; while large deposits at commercial banks are not insured,[6] deposits at so-called repo banks are secured by debt used as collateral.

11.3 EVOLUTION OF THE U.S. REPO MARKET

Although loans secured by some type of collateral have been traced back at least 3,000 years to ancient China, repos as we know them were introduced to the U.S. financial market by the Federal Reserve in 1917.[7] Repos allowed the Fed to extend credit to its member banks, after a wartime tax on interest payments on commercial paper had made it difficult for banks to raise funds in the commercial paper market. Later in the 1920s, the New York Fed used repos secured with bankers' acceptances to extend credit to dealers to encourage the development of a liquid secondary market for acceptances. Repos fell from grace during the Great Depression after massive bank failures and low interest rates, only to make a comeback after the Treasury–Federal Reserve Accord of 1951 "that renewed emphasis on controlling inflation rather than keeping interest rates low" (Garbade 2006).

Early repos in the United States had two distinguishing features. First, accrued interest was excluded from the price of the repo securities. Second, even though the creditor could sell or deliver the repo securities to settle a prior sale at prices that included the accrued interest during the term of the repo, ownership of the repo securities rested with the debtor. These features had the following implications: (1) the repo securities were underpriced; (2) the creditor had to remit to the debtor any coupon payments on the repo securities during the term of the repo; and (3) in the event of a bankruptcy of the debtor, the repo securities were subject to automatic stay; that is, the creditor could not take ownership of the repo securities and sell them immediately.[8] These features remained intact until the early 1980s.

During the period of high inflation in the 1970s and early 1980s, rising short-term interest rates made repos a highly attractive short-term investment to holders of large amounts of idle cash. Increasing numbers of corporations, local and state governments, and, at the encouragement of securities dealers, even school districts and other small creditors started depositing their idle cash in repo banks to earn interest rather than depositing money in commercial banks that did not pay interest on demand deposits. Furthermore, the U.S. Treasury started borrowing heavily after 1974, eventually changing the status of the United States from a creditor to a debtor nation and increasing the volume of marketable Treasury debt significantly. This led to a parallel growth in government securities dealers' positions and financing, and the repo market grew by leaps and bounds. Figure 11.1 depicts the size of the market from January 1970 to January 1986, as reported by the Federal Reserve Board.

The first important change to repo contracts was brought about after the spectacular collapse of Drysdale Government Securities Inc. in 1982. Despite

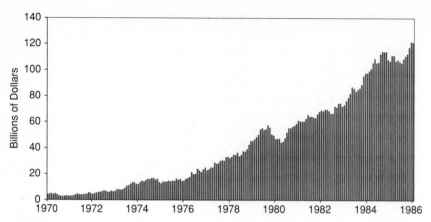

FIGURE 11.1   Monthly Averages of Daily Outstanding Overnight and Term Repos, 1970 to 1986
Source: Federal Reserve Board.

its limited equity, Drysdale had been acquiring substantial amounts of debt securities through reverse repos and at prices that excluded the accrued interest. Drysdale then sold short these debt securities to third parties at prices that included the accrued interest. Drysdale used the surplus thus generated to raise more capital and to make interest payments to its reverse repo counterparties. However, when interest rates moved against Drysdale in May 1982, the cumulative losses on its interest rate bets depleted its capital. On May 17, 1982, Drysdale failed to pay the interest on the securities it had borrowed. When that news hit the repo market, it came to a near halt, forcing the Fed to intervene as a lender of last resort to calm fears and prevent a collapse. This near collapse exposed the systemic risk associated with the exclusion of accrued interest, and therefore, largely at the encouragement of the Federal Reserve Bank of New York, inclusion of accrued interest in the invoice price of repo securities became standard market practice; for details, see Garbade (2006).

    The foundation for the second important change in repo contracts was laid when another government securities dealer, Lombard-Wall, with $2 billion in assets and comparable liabilities, collapsed three months later in August 1982. Prior to Lombard-Wall's August 12, 1982, filing with the Federal Bankruptcy Court of New York, there had been no precedent court case in which the question of whether repos were secured loans or independent sale and repurchase agreements was directly addressed. If repos were classified as independent sale and repurchase agreements, then creditors could take immediate possession of the repo securities; if, by contrast, they were classified as secured loans, then repo securities would have been subject to automatic stay. On August 17, 1982, the Federal Bankruptcy Court of New York announced that Lombard-Wall's repos were secured loans and issued a restraining order prohibiting the sale of these repo securities. Although submissions by the Federal Reserve Bank of New York and several others argued that this decision would undermine the liquidity of the repo market, the court reaffirmed its decision a month later (Garbade 2006). This removed the vagueness associated with whether repos were secured loans or independent sale and repurchase agreements. Despite this ruling, investment banks, mutual funds, and other large financial institutions favored the exception of repo securities from the application of automatic stay, although they seemed unwilling to write contracts that clearly stated that a repo was a pair of outright sale and repurchase transactions.[9]

Debates continued until another securities dealer, Lion Capital Group, collapsed in May 1984 and a bankruptcy court placed an automatic stay on Lion's repo securities.[10] Shortly thereafter, Congress ended the debates about the classification of repos by enacting the Bankruptcy Amendments and Federal Judgeship Act of 1984, exempting repos on Treasury and federal agency securities, as well as those on bank certificates of deposit and bankers' acceptances, from the application of automatic stay. Since then, repos on these securities have been exempt from automatic stay. Curiously, prior to its collapse on September 15, 2008, Lehman Brothers appears to have treated the so-called Repo 105 contracts differently. Repo 105 contracts, and the role they played in Lehman's demise, are discussed in Box 11.1.

Dealer delivery failures in the 1980s also gave rise to the emergence of *tri-party repos*, in which the counterparties used a third agent, called the tri-party agent, to manage the collateral.[11] The tri-party agent ensured that the collateral pledged was sufficient and met eligibility requirements, and all parties agreed to use the collateral prices supplied by the tri-party agent. Today, there are only two tri-party agents in the United States, called the *tri-party clearing banks*: Bank of New York Mellon and JPMorgan Chase. Because these two clearing banks have a huge amount of exposure on an intraday basis, regulators expressed concerns that fears regarding the financial health of a major dealer or clearing bank could quickly spread contagion throughout the market. Indeed, the Fed's decision to extend its lender-of-last-resort support to the systemically important primary dealers during the recent financial crisis through the Primary Dealer Credit Facility (PDCF) was partly a result of these concerns. (We discuss the runs on the repo market that occurred during the crisis in detail in the next section.)

On May 17, 2010, the Federal Reserve Bank of New York Task Force on Tri-Party Infrastructure published a white paper (Federal Reserve Bank of New York 2010) addressing these concerns and proposed potential solutions that may prevent a bank run on tri-party repos.[12] In Box 11.2, we present excerpts from Moody's Investors Service's May 25, 2010, assessment of the FRBNY white paper.

BOX 11.1   REPO 105 AND THE LEHMAN BANKRUPTCY

On March 13, 2010, the *Wall Street Journal* reported:

> *Six weeks before it went bankrupt, Lehman Brothers Holdings Inc. was effectively out of securities that could be used as collateral to back the short-term loans it needed to survive. The bank's subsequent scramble to stay alive exposed the murky but crucial role that short-term lending, done in a corner of Wall Street known as the repo market, plays in the financial world.*
>
> *The report by Lehman's court-appointed bankruptcy examiner, which runs thousands of pages, recounts efforts by the bank to use sleight-of-hand accounting transactions to spiff up its financial picture and sometimes use low-quality collateral to get loans.*[13]

As discussed in the main text, in the United States, repo transactions are secured loans, at least for *accounting* purposes, so that ownership of the repo securities belongs to the debtor. Despite this, prior to its bankruptcy Lehman was treating some of its repo transactions, Repo 105 transactions, as outright sales. Put differently, since it is *legally* determined that repo transactions resemble outright sales, followed by outright repurchases, Lehman was trying to make the accounting treatment follow the legal treatment.

At the root of Repo 105 is a Financial Accounting Standards Board (FASB) rule, called FAS 140, which was approved in 2000. FAS 140 allowed securitized debt to be removed from the issuer's balance sheet so that the loans backing the securities were no longer assets of the issuer and therefore the purchasers of the securities were protected in case the issuer fell into financial distress and filed for bankruptcy.

FAS 140 was passed to improve the securitization market; it was not intended for the repo market. It contained a provision that stated that the issuer could report the securities as assets on its balance sheet as long as the issuer agreed to buy the securities back for a price between 98 percent and 102 percent of the sale price. If the repurchase price was outside this band, then the securities could not be reported as assets until the repurchase date.[14]

It was this provision that Lehman used as a loophole. Lehman was doing precisely what the primary securities dealer in the main text was doing: borrowing $100 at $5 interest by lending securities worth $100 irrespective of the term of the repo—except that Lehman was removing the securities from the asset side of its balance sheet and using the borrowed cash to pay some of its debt temporarily. By engaging in this kind of activity toward the end of every fiscal quarter since 2001, Lehman was able to decrease its assets while keeping its equity unchanged. As a result, Lehman's reported leverage appeared much lower than it actually was. In some quarters, Lehman's Repo 105 transactions were as much as $50 billion. This was the use "to spiff up its financial picture" mentioned in the quoted *Wall Street Journal* article.

BOX 11.2   MOODY'S COMMENTS ON THE FRBNY TASK FORCE ON TRI-PARTY INFRASTRUCTURE WHITE PAPER

Tri-party repo is similar to bilateral repo except for the involvement of a third party—a tri-party agent (Bank of New York Mellon or JPMorgan Chase, the two major clearing banks) provides custody, valuation, and settlement services for the exchange of cash and collateral between the borrower and the cash investor. Although nearly 40% lower than its peak size in 2008, at $1.7 trillion the tri-party repo market remains a key source of funding for primary dealers (see figure following). The collateral funded in this market (see figure following) mostly consists of Treasuries and agencies. At $320 billion, less liquid collateral is still a large portion, although this has decreased 65% since the start of the financial crisis.

An "unwind" occurs every morning, when the tri-party agent returns the collateral to the dealer-borrower and the cash to the cash

Part A
Triparty Repo Market's Size Is $1.7 Trillion
The Collateral Is Mostly Liquid and
High-Quality

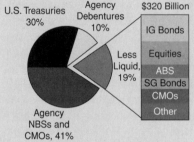

Part B
A Major Funding Source for Primary Dealers
PDs get –50 Percent of Secured Funding *
through Triparty Repo

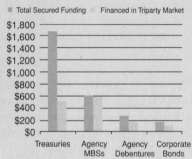

For both exhibits, triparty data is shown
as of April 7, 2010. For Part B, total secured funding
is as of April 9, 2010.

* Applies only to collateral types shown, which represent
the majority of collateral used in secured borrowing.

Source: New York Federal Reserve Bank.

investor. Until the transaction (whether a term repo or a rolling overnight repo) is "rewound" in the afternoon, it is the tri-party agent that is lending to the dealer on a secured basis. The purpose of the unwind is to allow the dealer access to the securities in its collateral pool to settle sales, which occur throughout the day. Such intraday credit extension, while normal, is not guaranteed in the clearing agreement and can be withdrawn at any point, particularly if the dealer's creditworthiness deteriorates.

In order to reduce the gigantic amount of intraday credit extended by the clearing banks, the Task Force proposed developing an "auto-substitution" functionality. This would allow dealers to access and substitute their encumbered collateral, thus facilitating settlement without the need for the daily unwind. Any remaining intraday credit would be extended under well-defined bilateral agreements between dealers and the clearing banks.

While this is a sensible solution for both the dealers and the clearing banks, its implementation is only targeted for June of 2011. Prior to the full implementation of auto-substitution, the Task Force has recommended several tactical improvements. The first is a more robust and disciplined process for confirming repo trades between dealers and cash investors than exists today. The idea is to establish a "three-way" point-of-trade confirmation process that would ensure that clearing banks always have an accurate, up-to-date picture of all outstanding repo trades. By knowing exactly what the dealer's position is (e.g., what collateral is already encumbered, at what haircut, and for how long), the clearing banks would have a greater degree of confidence in extending secured credit to dealers. With less uncertainty as to the level of collateralization they can count on, the odds of a rapid withdrawal of credit by the clearing banks would also be reduced.

The final implementation of a marketwide trade confirmation solution is targeted for April 2011, although incremental improvements will likely occur along the way.

The second tactical recommendation is to eliminate the unwind process from as much of the term tri-party market as possible. The logic is that collateral being funded on a term basis is not as actively traded. Therefore, not having access to it during the day poses less of a challenge for the dealers. With lower aggregate exposure, the clearing banks might be less driven to severely reduce the amount of remaining daylight credit to dealers. Still, pending the full implementation of auto-substitution and the elimination of uncertainty associated with daylight credit extension, the market is structurally vulnerable to a repo run for two reasons. First, many cash lenders (primarily money market funds) continue to make lending decisions based on the counterparty's credit risk rather than on the quality of the collateral. And second, the market as a whole has a tendency for pro-cyclical haircuts—that is, lower haircuts when liquidity is abundant, and higher haircuts when liquidity is scarce. If cash investors pulled away in a stress environment, the clearing banks would be faced with a choice—as they were in several cases in 2008—of taking on large secured credit exposure to dealers or severely constraining intraday credit to them.

Source: Moody's Investors Service.

The tri-party settlement is one of two settlement methods used in the United States. The other is the delivery versus payment (DVP) method. For example, the Federal Reserve's reverse repos are settled via the DVP method, wherein securities are moved against simultaneous payment. The Federal Reserve sends collateral to the clearing bank of its reverse repo counterparty, triggering a simultaneous movement of money against the collateral on the sale date. On the purchase date, the counterparty sends the collateral back to the Fed, which triggers the simultaneous return of the counterparty's funds. Such repo transactions are called bilateral repo transactions.

Although the repo market grew rapidly after the Bankruptcy Amendments and Federal Judgeship Act of 1984, until the mid-1990s it remained confined mostly to U.S. government debt, federal agency debt, corporate debt, and federal agency mortgage-backed securities. However, since the mid-1990s, it has grown to include a broad range of debt instruments as collateral: all types of private-label MBSs, such as residential mortgage-backed securities (RMBSs) and commercial mortgage-backed securities (CMBSs); all types of asset-backed securities (ABSs), such as automobile loans, credit cards, and student loans; and tranches[15] of structured products such as collateralized mortgage obligations (CMOs), collateralized loan obligations (CLOs), collateralized debt obligations (CDOs), and the like (see Gorton 2009b).

The last significant change to the repo contracting conventions came in 2005. In April 2005, Congress enacted the Bankruptcy Abuse Prevention and Consumer Protection Act of 2005 (BAPCPA), which took effect in October 2005. BAPCPA expanded the definition of repurchase agreements to include mortgage loans, mortgage-related securities, and interest from mortgage loans or mortgage-related securities. This meant that as of October 2005, repo contracts on even MBSs, CMOs, CMBSs, and CDOs backed by mortgages and the like as collateral became exempt from automatic stay. We summarize the milestones in the evolution of the U.S. repo market in Box 11.3.

BOX 11.3   TIME LINE OF IMPORTANT U.S. REPO MARKET DEVELOPMENTS

1917	Federal Reserve introduces repos; accrued interest is excluded from the invoice price of repo securities, and repo securities are subject to automatic stay.
1929	Use of repos declines with the onset of the Great Depression.
1951	Congress enacts the Treasury–Federal Reserve Accord of 1951, bringing repos back into favor.
1982	Accrued interest is included in the invoice prices of repo securities.
1984	Congress enacts the Bankruptcy Amendments and Federal Judgeship Act of 1984 to exempt repos on Treasury and federal agency securities, as well as on bank certificates of deposit and bankers' acceptances from the application of automatic stay.
2005	Congress enacts the Bankruptcy Abuse Prevention and Consumer Protection Act of 2005 to expand the definition of repos to include mortgage loans, mortgage-related securities, and interest from mortgage loans and mortgage securities; all mortgage-related repo securities become exempt from the application of automatic stay.[16]

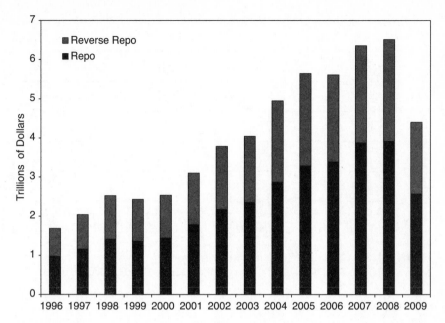

FIGURE 11.2 Annual Averages of Daily Financing by U.S. Government Securities Primary Dealers
Source: Securities Industry and Financial Markets Association.

No official statistics of the actual size of the repo market have been collected since inclusion of almost all types of securitized debt as collateral was allowed in repo agreements. Therefore, there is no official information on the evolution of the size of the repo market over the past quarter century. Figure 11.2 depicts the evolution of financing by primary dealers in the U.S. government securities market from 1996 through 2009 and offers a feel for the exponential growth of the repo market since the mid-1990s. Meanwhile, Figure 11.3 and Table 11.1, reproduced from the FRBNY Task Force on Tri-Party Infrastructure White Paper (2010), show the growth of the tri-party repo market from May 2002 through May 2010 (Figure 11.3), as well as the composition and concentration of tri-party repo collaterals (Table 11.1).

Last, Figures 11.4 and 11.5 depict the exponential growth of the U.S. debt market over the same period. It should be noted that ABS issuance surpassed corporate debt issuance in 2005 and remained higher in 2006, only to decline in 2007 after the onset of the financial crisis. In 2008 and 2009, ABS issuance returned to levels last seen in the early 1990s.

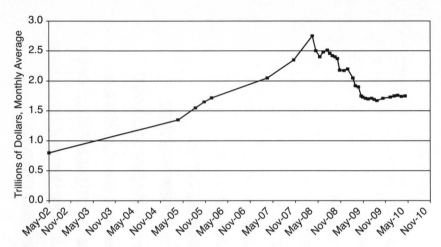

FIGURE 11.3   Growth of Tri-Party Repo Market
Source: FRBNY Task Force on Tri-Party Infrastructure White Paper (2010).

11.4   THE CRISIS

The financial crisis of 2007 to 2009 was a crisis not only of the traditional banks, but also of the shadow banks. Unlike traditional banks, shadow banks did not have access to the safety nets designed to prevent wholesale runs on banks—deposit insurance and the central bank as the lender of last resort—until 2008. Although there was no wholesale run on the traditional banking system in this period, we effectively observed a run on *shadow* banks that led to the demise of a significant part of the shadow banking system.[17] Since repo financing was the basis of most of the leveraged positions of the shadow banks, a large part of the run occurred in the repo market. Other important runs that occurred in this period were on mortgage lenders, asset-backed commercial paper (ABCP) programs, structured investment vehicles (SIVs), and money market funds, to name a few (see Acharya, Gale, and Yorulmazer 2009).

When the housing market changed course in the first quarter of 2006, the subprime mortgage market began to deteriorate. While there is no secondary market for subprime mortgages and, therefore, there are no publicly observable subprime mortgage prices, the ABX index provides a publicly observable market that prices subprime risk.[18] The ABX index, introduced by dealer banks in January 2006, is traded via credit default swap (CDS)

TABLE 11.1   Tri-Party Repo Statistics as of April 9, 2010

Composition and Concentration of Tri-Party Repo Collateral

Asset Group	Collateral Value ($ Billions)	Share of Total	Concentration by Top Three Dealers
ABS (Investment and Non–Investment Grade)	$ 41.7	2.4%	45%
Agency CMOs	112.7	6.6	46
Agency Debentures (Including STRIPS)	179.5	10.5	33
Agency MBSs	584.9	9.3	45
CMOs Private-Label (Investment Grade)	25.2	1.5	48
CMOs Private-Label (Non–Investment Grade)	18.9	1.1	47
Corporates (Investment Grade)	79.6	4.7	39
Corporates (Non–Investment Grade)	34.7	2.0	54
Equities	73.3	4.3	59
Money Markets	27.4	1.6	74
U.S. Treasuries (Excluding STRIPS)	474.4	27.7	39
U.S. Treasury STRIPS	38.7	2.3	46
Other	19.5	1.1	—
Total	**$1,710.5**	**100.0%**	**38%**

Distribution of Investor Haircuts in Tri-Party Repo

Asset Group	Collateral Value ($ Billions)	Haircuts		
		10th Percentile	Median	90th Percentile
ABSs (Investment and Non–Investment Grade)	$ 41.7	0%	5%	8%
Agency CMOs	112.7	2	3	5
Agency Debentures (Including STRIPS)	179.5	2	2	5
Agency MBSs	584.9	2	2	4
CMOs Private-Label (Investment Grade)	25.2	2	5	7
CMOs Private-Label (Non–Investment Grade)	18.9	0	8	8
Corporates (Investment Grade)	79.6	2	5	8
Corporates (Non–Investment Grade)	34.7	5	8	15
Equities	73.3	5	8	20
Money Markets	27.4	2	3	5
U.S. Treasuries (Excluding STRIPS)	474.4	2	2	2
U.S. Treasury STRIPS	38.7	2	2	2
Other	19.5	—	—	—
Total	**$1,710.5**			

Source: Reproduced from the FRBNY Task Force on Tri-Party Infrastructure White Paper (2010).

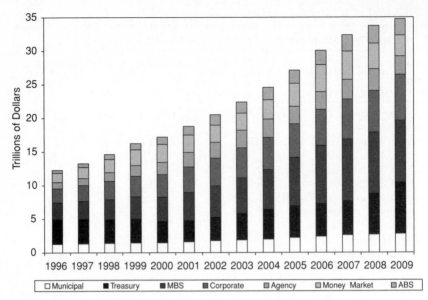

FIGURE 11.4 Size of the U.S. Debt Market, 1996 to 2009
Source: Securities Industry and Financial Markets Association.

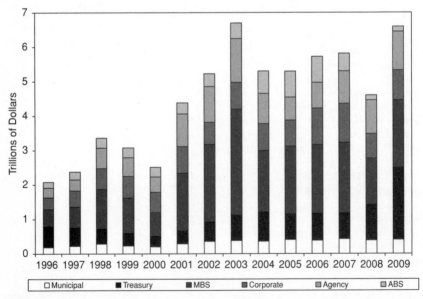

FIGURE 11.5 Issuances in the U.S. Debt Market, 1996 to 2009
Source: Securities Industry and Financial Markets Association.

contracts and allows investors to take positions in subprime mortgage-backed securities. Figure 11.6 displays the ABX spread—that is, the CDS spread (labeled ABX) on the BBB-rated ABX tranche of the first vintage of the ABX in 2006. This vintage is representative of riskier levels of subprime securitization. Figure 11.6 also shows the London Interbank Offered Rate (LIBOR)–overnight index swap (OIS) spread (labeled LIB-OIS). The LIB-OIS is the spread between the three-month LIBOR and the three-month overnight index swap rates, and provides a proxy for the state of the repo market. Larger values of the LIB-OIS spread indicate higher perceived counterparty risk in the banking system; see Gorton and Metrick (2009a) for a detailed discussion.

Figure 11.6 depicts the steady deterioration of the subprime mortgage market from January 2007 to January 2009 and compares this with the deterioration in the interbank markets. There were two easily identifiable large jumps in the LIB-OIS: on August 9, 2007—from 13 basis points to 40 basis points, when BNP Paribas suspended redemptions on three of its SIVs—and on September 15, 2008—from 87 basis points to 105 basis points, when Lehman declared bankruptcy. The most significant move in the ABX, in contrast, appears to have occurred from 669 basis points at the end of June 2007 to 1,738 basis points at the end of July 2007, following the collapse on June 20, 2007, of two highly levered Bear Stearns hedge funds

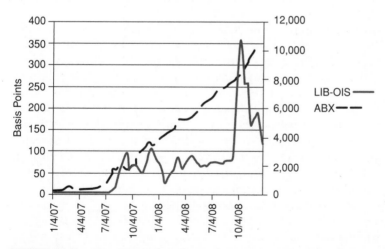

FIGURE 11.6 LIB-OIS (Left Scale) versus ABX (Right Scale; Measured in Basis Points)
Source: Reproduced from Gorton and Metrick (2009b).

that invested in subprime mortgages. The collapse of these two hedge funds was indeed a run on a shadow bank in the repo market. The two funds (one of which at its peak was levered 10 times its equity) were speculating mostly in CDOs on subprime mortgages; they borrowed funds in the repo market and pledged their CDOs as collateral.

With the deterioration of the subprime market in the first half of 2007, creditors began asking the two Bear Stearns funds to post more collateral to back the repos by mid-June 2007. When the funds failed to meet these margin calls, creditors, led by Merrill Lynch, threatened to declare the funds in default of repo agreements and to seize the investments. In fact, on June 19, 2007, Merrill seized $850 million of the CDOs and tried to auction them. When Merrill was able to sell only about $100 million worth of CDOs, the illiquid nature and the declining value of subprime assets became evident (see Acharya et al. 2009). Bloomberg reported that at least seven other lenders, including Lehman Brothers and Deutsche Bank, also circulated lists of CDOs and other bonds that they were planning to sell.[19] The rapid increase of the ABX spread during July 2007 appears to be a response of the subprime market to this run on the shadow banks in the repo market. This shadow bank run and the systemic crisis that followed illustrate the significance of the exemption of repo securities from the application of automatic stay; had the repo securities been subject to automatic stay (or alternatives proposed later in this chapter), the Bear Stearns funds could have filed for bankruptcy and the forced fire sale of their assets could have been avoided.

Eventually, the subprime mortgage decline became systemic. In early August 2007, a run ensued on the assets of three SIVs of BNP Paribas. On August 9, BNP Paribas suspended redemptions from these SIVs. BNP Paribas's SIVs were bankruptcy-remote entities financing their subprime holdings through the issuance of ABCPs that had essentially lost their liquidity and become nontradable. The announcement of the suspension of redemptions by BNP Paribas gave rise to counterparty risk concerns and caused the ABCP market to freeze. This freeze coincided with the first major jump in the LIB-OIS spread. When fears of counterparty risk spread through markets, all short-term debt markets—including the repo market—froze, only to open after central banks injected massive amounts of liquidity into the system (see Acharya and Richardson 2009).

Based on a data set obtained from dealer banks, Gorton and Metrick (2009b) studied the repo spreads and haircuts for various types of repo securities, and their results are reproduced in Table 11.2. Of note, the spreads and the haircuts reported in this table are only for dealers; non-dealer counterparties may have been subject to other spreads and haircuts.

The repo spreads are the spreads between the three-month repo and the three-month OIS rates. Table 11.2 demonstrates clearly how a crisis that started in the subprime market spread like a wildfire to other types of comparable nontransparent securitized debt, such as automobile, credit card, and student loan asset-backed securities, as well as the high-credit-rated structured products, such as AAA- and AA-rated CLOs and CDOs.

As Gorton and Metrick claim, the increasing haircuts in the repo market may be interpreted as a run on shadow banks. Figure 11.7, reproduced from Gorton and Metrick (2009a), shows how that run evolved. The data they examine are the interbank repo haircuts for the following asset classes: (1) AA–AAA auto/credit card/student loan ABS; (2) AA–AAA RMBS/CMBS; (3) <AA RMBS/CMBS; (4) AA–AAA CLOs; (5) unpriced ABS/MBS/all subprime; (6) AA–AAA CDOs; (7) unpriced CLOs/CDOs (where *unpriced* means that the collateral does not have public pricing on either Reuters or Bloomberg). Of these, the categories (1)–(4) do not contain subprime mortgages and are labeled "Non-Subprime-Related" by Gorton and Metrick. In particular, the RMBS referred to in categories (2) and (3) are prime mortgages. The categories (5)–(7) are either directly subprime or contain subprime mortgages. CDOs, in particular, contain some subprime mortgages. Finally, using all seven categories, they also construct an equal-weighted average repo haircut index for structured bonds.

As can be seen from Figure 11.7, the run on the shadow banking system in the repo market occurred in two phases. Although Bear Stearns's hedge funds were the first victims, it was BNP Paribas's suspension of redemptions on its three SIVs that triggered the first phase. After Bear Stearns collapsed in March 2008, the Federal Reserve introduced its most radical change in monetary policy since the Great Depression by extending its lender-of-last-resort support to the systemically important primary dealers through the new Primary Dealer Credit Facility (PDCF). However, even this extension of the lender-of-last-resort facility did not prevent the run on Lehman Brothers, as investors realized that this support was not unconditional and unlimited (see Acharya et al. 2009). While the largest haircut jump in Figure 11.7 corresponds to the collapse of Lehman on September 15, 2008, the second-largest jump, which came in the summer of 2008, corresponds to traditional bank runs on likely insolvent banking institutions, such as IndyMac, Washington Mutual, and Wachovia.

With the Lehman bankruptcy on September 15, 2008, the repo market on even U.S. government debt, federal agency debt, corporate debt, and federal agency mortgage-backed securities came to a near halt, and settlement fails of primary dealers skyrocketed. Table 11.3 shows a quarterly summary of the primary dealer settlement fails from the first quarter of

TABLE 11.2 Three-Month Repo Rate—OIS Spreads (Basis Points) and Haircuts (Percentage) from January 1, 2007, to December 31, 2008

Series	Period	Mean	Median	Standard Error	Maximum	Minimum	Mean Haircut
BBB+ to A Corporates	Whole period	86.50	82.14	83.15	429.43	0.50	0.50%
	First half of 2007	2.01	1.95	0.61	5.30	0.50	0.00
	Second half of 2007	61.85	65.49	36.29	126.35	1.70	0.00
	All of 2007	32.28	2.70	39.53	126.35	0.50	0.00
	All of 2008	136.19	103.63	81.61	429.43	44.33	0.90
AA to AAA Corporates	Whole period	77.59	74.78	78.42	409.43	-3.50	0.50%
	First half of 2007	-1.69	-2.05	1.90	10.44	-3.50	0.00
	Second half of 2007	55.27	58.95	34.53	116.35	-2.30	0.00
	All of 2007	27.13	-1.35	37.64	116.35	-3.50	0.00
	All of 2008	123.86	92.11	77.57	409.43	39.33	0.90
AA to AAA ABS— Auto/CC/SL	Whole period	105.22	94.76	101.00	479.43	1.70	5.20%
	First half of 2007	4.44	4.00	1.77	11.00	1.70	0.00
	Second half of 2007	68.44	71.78	40.93	141.35	3.70	0.90
	All of 2007	36.82	5.25	43.29	141.35	1.70	0.50
	All of 2008	167.92	119.81	98.07	479.43	54.33	9.50
AA to AAA ABS— RMBS/CMBS	Whole period	124.04	107.78	120.11	520.30	3.70	9.40%
	First half of 2007	6.41	6.00	1.76	13.00	3.70	0.00
	Second half of 2007	76.35	81.78	43.92	151.35	5.70	1.80
	All of 2007	41.80	7.00	46.92	151.35	3.70	0.90
	All of 2008	199.44	145.08	117.27	520.30	64.33	17.10

<AA ABS—RMBS/CMBS	Whole period	135.90	117.78	129.02	550.30	6.70	10.60%
	First half of 2007	9.41	9.00	1.76	16.00	6.70	0.00
	Second half of 2007	84.55	88.20	48.62	166.35	8.70	3.70
	All of 2007	47.43	10.00	51.08	166.35	6.70	1.90
	All of 2008	217.01	153.95	125.56	550.30	69.33	18.60
Unpriced ABS/MBS/All Subprime	Whole period	108.94	109.69	84.64	295.38	7.70	37.30%
	First half of 2007	10.41	10.00	1.76	17.00	7.70	0.00
	Second half of 2007	95.62	97.83	58.54	196.35	9.70	7.70
	All of 2007	53.52	11.00	59.59	196.35	7.70	3.90
	All of 2008	187.28	197.88	42.23	295.38	99.33	68.00
AA to AAA CLO	Whole period	134.46	117.14	127.18	545.3	3.70	10.20%
	First half of 2007	6.41	6.00	1.76	13.00	3.70	0.00
	Second half of 2007	85.93	92.65	51.27	171.35	5.70	1.80
	All of 2007	46.64	7.00	53.98	171.35	3.70	0.90
	All of 2008	214.96	148.76	121.61	545.30	79.33	18.70
AA to AAA CDO	Whole period	130.09	124.69	107.46	380.38	4.70	30.00%
	First half of 2007	7.41	7.00	1.76	14.00	4.70	0.00
	Second half of 2007	107.77	109.35	69.56	226.35	6.70	8.30
	All of 2007	58.19	8.00	70.48	226.35	4.70	4.30
	All of 2008	231.72	241.39	56.52	380.38	129.33	53.50
Unpriced CLO/CDO	Whole period	148.32	142.60	123.54	413.75	6.70	32.40%
	First half of 2007	9.41	9.00	1.76	16.00	6.70	0.00
	Second half of 2007	122.63	124.42	80.14	256.35	8.70	10.50
	All of 2007	66.69	10.00	80.34	256.35	6.70	5.40
	All of 2008	268.39	256.58	63.03	413.75	154.33	57.30

Source: Reproduced from Gorton and Metrick (2009b).

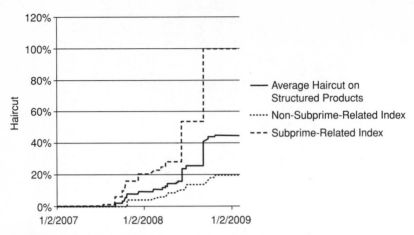

FIGURE 11.7   Repo Haircuts on Different Categories of
Structured Products
Source: Reproduced from Gorton and Metrick (2009a).

2007 to the last quarter of 2009. Figure 11.8 provides a quarterly summary
of the effects of the run on the repo market on the financing of primary
dealers after Lehman's collapse. As shown, it was the *borrowing* ability of
the primary dealers that went down significantly, not their *lending* ability.
Since this may be interpreted as large withdrawals from the broker-dealer
shadow banks in the repo market, Figure 11.8 also illustrates the disappear-
ing confidence in the shadow banking system and the severity of the run on
shadow banks. When the Fed and the U.S. government let Lehman collapse,
the next in line for a run, Merrill Lynch, had to merge with Bank of America.
Shortly thereafter, the two remaining independent broker-dealers, Morgan
Stanley and Goldman Sachs, were forced to convert to bank holding companies and were formally put under supervision and regulation of the Federal
Reserve. In fact, the entire Wall Street system of independent broker-dealers
collapsed in a matter of seven months (see Acharya et al. 2009).

11.5   A CASE FOR REFORMING THE REPO MARKET

As Acharya and Krishnamurthy (2010) clarify, the primary issue with financing risky securities (such as mortgage-backed securities) through repo
markets is that such financing is likely to freeze or experience stress in times
of aggregate (economy-wide or financial-sector-wide) stress, and on their
own, financial firms do not have the incentive to internalize the costs of such

TABLE 11.3 Settlement Fails of U.S. Government Securities Primary Dealers during the Financial Crisis, 2007 to 2009 ($ Billions)

	Treasury		Agency		MBS		Corporate	
	Receive	Deliver	Receive	Deliver	Receive	Deliver	Receive	Deliver
2007								
Q1	$ 738.1	$ 586.8	$ 91.2	$ 76.6	$ 474.6	$ 473.8	$356.1	$404.2
Q2	726.8	528.3	117.7	118.2	595.8	617.7	498.0	572.9
Q3	834.4	549.7	239.5	231.7	805.6	819.7	822.9	884.3
Q4	1,373.0	1,085.4	202.8	192.5	757.8	686.8	488.4	547.5
2008								
Q1	$ 3,946.2	$ 3,835.7	$234.7	$221.8	$1,023.3	$ 952.1	$364.8	$413.4
Q2	3,762.9	3,726.3	202.4	192.6	596.1	566.5	361.3	407.2
Q3	3,077.4	2,784.0	238.1	228.4	463.1	425.5	199.4	214.9
Q4	16,824.6	16,266.6	586.6	600.7	971.9	863.5	271.7	337.8
2009								
Q1	$ 1,442.9	$ 1,286.0	$143.1	$167.1	$ 867.8	$ 950.3	$168.0	$225.8
Q2	806.6	764.8	95.4	100.9	1,078.9	1,319.4	151.6	215.6
Q3	617.7	536.8	62.1	76.7	1,283.9	1,553.2	145.2	192.4
Q4	245.0	184.4	141.9	163.9	3,128.6	3,945.1	156.7	192.2

Source: Federal Reserve Bank of New York.

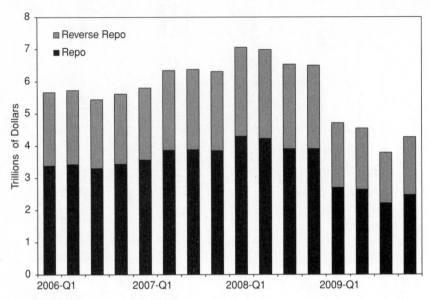

FIGURE 11.8 Quarterly Averages of Daily Financing by U.S. Government Securities Primary Dealers, 2006 to 2009
Source: Securities Industry and Financial Markets Association.

a freeze or stress. By virtue of being secured and being typically short-term financing arrangements, repo markets, by and large, function smoothly; in other words, repos usually get rolled over. When the underlying assets, such as Treasury or agency debt, are essentially safe, the repo lender is undeterred from rolling over the financing even in stressful times. Indeed, Treasury and agency debt might even experience a flight to safety in such times.

In contrast, if the underlying collateral is a mortgage-backed security and an economic downturn ensues, the risk of an already illiquid market for MBSs gets compounded; this is because many financial institutions' portfolios are crowded with MBSs or have lost capital. In this scenario, repo lenders run the real risk of being forced to sell their collateral in illiquid markets. The repo lender may respond by raising the required haircut or simply refusing to roll over. The resulting fall in repo financing ability against the collateral is perverse, as it sets up an adverse dynamic: The future buyers of assets anticipate that they are likely to face steep haircuts, too, and thus will not offer attractive prices for assets; in turn, the collateral's ability to be financed with repo today falls even further. A complete market freeze can arise, as it did during the crisis of 2007 to 2009 and as theoretically modeled by Acharya, Gale, and Yorulmazer (2009).

To summarize, unlike the liquidity risk that *unsecured* financing may become unavailable to a firm (a risk largely specific to the credit risk of the firm), the liquidity risk that *secured* repo financing may become unavailable to a firm is inherently a systemic risk, materializing in circumstances where other financial firms are also experiencing stress and the markets for assets held predominantly by the financial sector are rendered illiquid. Federal Reserve Chairman Ben Bernanke has noted this important difference, along with the fact that current practices for bank liquidity risk management do not take into sufficient account the likely freezes in secured repo financing.[20]

This leads to the problem that while in good times financial firms may not fully internalize the costs imposed on the system by being excessively financed through short-term repo markets, in bad times they charge excessively high haircuts on repo financing and do not internalize the pecuniary externalities imposed on other firms through the resulting fire sales of assets. Indeed, to support financial firms facing a repo freeze or to support the assets directly, the likely lender of last resort would only accentuate a problem that firms ignore in good times—namely, the systemic risk associated with repo financing. Viewed this way, in good times there is a case for subjecting repo-financed risky securities to a capital charge—effectively a *regulatory haircut*—which takes into account the security's systemic risk and maturity mismatch relative to the repo tenor. Equally important, there is a case for a better design of the bankruptcy of a repo-financed debtor than simply granting its repo lender the full right to seize the collateral and liquidate it at will in an illiquid market.

11.6 PROPOSED REFORMS

Somewhat surprisingly, the House and the Senate bills are both quiet on how to reform the repo markets. The only concrete proposal has come from the FDIC chair, Sheila Bair, who has proposed that repo counterparties of Federal Deposit Insurance Corporation (FDIC)–regulated banks be subject to a 10 cents per dollar (originally proposed as 20 cents per dollar) haircut in case of a bank being taken over by the FDIC. The Federal Reserve Bank of New York (2010) and the Basel Committee on Banking Supervision (2010) have both taken on the issue and are in touch with industry and academia to devise a better architecture for the functioning of these markets. Later, we discuss the proposed reforms and also propose an alternative, from both an ex ante as well as an ex post perspective, that addresses these issues.

Possible reforms of the repo market can be put into three categories: a full government-guarantee scheme, a full market-discipline scheme, and a combination of the two. Our preferred alternative is the combination.

At one extreme, some (most notably, Gorton 2009) have suggested that repo financing is akin to demandable deposits in many ways and thus is similarly vulnerable to the information-sensitive panics when adverse information about underlying collateral (or counterparties) hits markets. His proposal is thus to treat repo financing in a similar way—that is, offer federal deposit insurance to the repo contracts, at least against securities that are relatively safe, such as the supersenior tranches of securitization pools. Under this proposal, it is recognized that repo financing has the inherent systemic fragility akin to demandable deposits, and in all likelihood the government would end up backing up repo counterparties were the fragility to materialize. Hence, by explicitly recognizing the guarantee up front, it becomes possible to charge repo financiers for the guarantee. As with any insurance premium, the objective is not just to collect fees for an ex post guarantee, but also to get repo financiers to internalize the systemic fragility inherent in repo contracts.

At another extreme, others (most notably, Roe 2009) have proposed that repo financiers should not be allowed unrestricted access to collateral even in case of default of the counterparty. That is, there should be some sort of automatic stay on repo financiers' claims, and they should join the bankruptcy of the defaulting counterparty as a secured creditor, as in the case of corporate bankruptcies. The rationale for this is twofold: First, it prevents the fire sales of the repo collateral by the financiers and avoids the adverse dynamic we highlighted before; and second, by exposing the repo financiers to credit risk of the counterparty (and not just that of the collateral), the financiers would subject the borrowers to much greater market discipline. In particular, financiers would opt for safer counterparties, all else being equal, or charge higher haircuts to riskier ones—either way, discriminating ex ante between safer and riskier borrowers.

The advantage of the government guarantee scheme is that it resolves virtually all ex post uncertainty by transferring the risk of repo contracts away from financiers to the government agency for an up-front fee. However, its disadvantages are more subtle and somewhat pernicious. The charging of FDIC premiums has been heavily influenced by the banking industry, and no premiums are charged to most banks when the FDIC's reserve fund is capitalized above 1.25 percent to 1.35 percent of the insured deposits. This kind of a fee structure gives rise to a highly procyclical risk-taking incentive, because, as far as the risk-return trade-off is concerned, the risks are backloaded. There is no guarantee that repo insurance premiums would work any differently. Perhaps, and somewhat more disturbingly, such a guarantee scheme effectively amounts to transferring the credit risk of virtually most parts of the securitization market to the government's balance sheet. While conforming mortgages in the United States are already being backstopped by Fannie Mae and Freddie Mac, the proposed guarantee scheme would extend such a backstop to subprime securitized pools, corporate loans, automobile receivables, credit card receivables, and so on. Given the inability of the government to control the urge to get Fannie and Freddie to engage in other kinds of activities, and the inclination of Fannie and Freddie, in turn, to undertake greater risks at the expense of taxpayers, the idea of extending guarantees to practically all risks of the economy should be viewed with caution. Such caution would be even more necessary for governments other than the United States, whose balance sheet is already heavily stretched.

The advantage of market discipline through the automatic stay approach is that it transfers the entire risk of the repo transaction to the repo financier—to some extent the risk of the collateral but also that of the borrower's ability to pay. This way, other than through ex post forbearance, private markets are allowed to function—bear and price risks—and thereby provide incentives to take account of relevant risk-return trade-offs. There are, however, several countervailing issues that arise. First, since the primary issue with repo contracts is their systemic externality, it is unclear that private market outcomes would be necessarily efficient from a risk-return standpoint of the economy as a whole. Second, automatic stay introduces *basis risk* in the repo contract, since its eventual payoff is linked not just to the underlying asset but to the whole pool of assets of the borrower and the rest of its capital structure. In general, this may create sufficient ex ante, as well as ex post, uncertainty to reduce the financier's willingness to lend against certain assets to all types of borrowers. The result might be a significant reduction in ex ante liquidity in some parts of repo-financed securitized markets. Third, a rationale for the bankruptcy exemption of the repos has been that when the borrower defaults, counterparty risk transmission is reduced as far as the repo contract goes, because it is protected from any spillover of the borrower's remaining risks and liabilities.

Given this relative assessment, our preferred approach is one that facilitates a ready winding down of the repo contracts and eliminates disorderly fire sales of underlying assets. In particular, the approach consists of the following four pieces:

1. In case of default of a borrower, its repo counterparties on Treasuries, and perhaps agency-backed securities (assuming the agency-backed securities are effectively government-backed), are allowed to take their collateral as under the current arrangements. However, repo counterparties on other kinds of risky collateral, such as ABSs and MBSs, are subjected to a stay.
2. Immediately upon default, repo counterparties of risky collateral are paid by a *repo resolution fund*, which could simply be within the FDIC

or the Federal Reserve, a recovery amount that is based on a conservative value assessment of the collateral.[21] Such a value assessment could be based on market intelligence, historical estimates, projected valuations obtained from a poll of dealers, and so on. The important issue is that the assessment should be conservative.

3. The underlying repo collateral is taken over by the repo resolution fund and liquidated in an orderly manner over a prespecified period, say, not more than six months (but with some flexibility to deal with unexpected circumstances). If the eventual recovery on the collateral is above the conservative estimate paid to the repo lenders (see step 2), then the time-value-adjusted difference is paid to the repo lenders. Conversely, if the eventual recovery is lower than the conservative estimate paid to the repo lenders, the time-value-adjusted difference is clawed back from the repo lenders. The claw-back feature is explicitly legislated (as with the current mechanism used by the FDIC to deal with uninsured depositors of failed FDIC-regulated banks).

4. In effect, steps 2 and 3 resemble a lender-of-last-resort operation, whereby risky collateral in times of a systemic crisis would be provided liquidity, albeit conservatively at a haircut or penalty rate. However, the claw-back feature implies that the repo resolution authority—the lender of last resort—takes on the credit risk of repo lenders, as well as of the underlying collateral (but limited to the difference between realized recovery and the conservative estimate at the time of the borrower's bankruptcy). To manage this credit risk, the repo resolution authority should do the following:

   - Include as eligible only relatively high-quality collateral.
   - Charge repo lenders an ex ante fee for the lender-of-last-resort facility, commensurate with the residual credit risk borne by the facility.
   - Require that eligible repo lenders for the lender-of-last-resort facility meet prespecified solvency criteria.
   - Impose a concentration limit at the level of individual repo lenders, as well as on the lender's overall portfolio size.

Thus, our preferred approach provides ex post liquidity to the repo market rather than a complete guarantee of underlying risks. This approach also charges ex ante for this liquidity facility and ensures that the risks undertaken by the market participants do not expose the taxpayers to losses beyond a certain size. It combines the attractive features of full insurance and full market-discipline schemes, avoiding their weaknesses. Furthermore, in contrast to Ms. Bair's proposal of a fixed haircut for resolving all repo collateral, it allows the haircut to be determined ex post based on conservative value assessments at the time of the borrower's bankruptcy.

11.7 GOING FORWARD

The current financial legislation proposals are completely silent on how to reform the repo market. We believe this is a mistake in light of the systemic nature of the repo market and its structural weaknesses. As we mentioned, unlike the liquidity risk that *unsecured* financing may become unavailable to a firm, the liquidity risk that *secured* repo financing may become unavailable to a firm is inherently a systemic risk: The markets for the repo securities may become illiquid precisely when a large part of the financial sector is experiencing undercapitalization or funding stress.

Unless this systemic liquidity risk of repo market is resolved, the risk of a run on the repo market will remain. Our proposed solution—similar to our proposed reform for money market funds (Chapter 10, "Money Market Funds") and orderly winding down of dealers and other financial firms (Chapter 8, "Resolution Authority")—addresses the externality of systemic risk of repo contracts on risky and potentially illiquid collaterals. Such a solution can be exercised without overly compromising market discipline, market liquidity, or taxpayer funds. Admittedly, our proposed solution is one among many possibilities; other alternatives may be possible.

Finally, although we have focused on the U.S. repo markets, our discussion and proposed reforms apply to other countries as well. Repo markets exist around the globe, from China to Japan to Hungary to Turkey, to name but a few countries, although their histories are much shorter and their sizes much smaller than that of the U.S. repo market. Many emerging countries' repo markets date back to the early 1990s. The largest repo market outside the United States is the European repo market, which was established with the introduction of the euro in 1999 and stood at €5.6 trillion based on the amount outstanding on December 9, 2009.[22] The European market is the only repo market outside the United States where potentially illiquid financial assets are used as repo collateral, and therefore our proposed reforms are also relevant to the European repo market. In other repo markets, the repo collateral generally represents government bonds issued by the sovereign states, so that in these markets, the repo lenders do not appear to run a substantial risk of being forced to sell their collateral in illiquid markets in the event of financial crises. This may change, however, if potentially illiquid collateral were to become acceptable in repo transactions in these countries. Indeed, when sovereign credit risk is an issue, even the repo markets for government bonds may be vulnerable.

At any rate, leaving the repo markets out of the discussion of financial reform is not an alternative; if these markets are not reformed and their participants not made to internalize the liquidity risk, runs on the repo market will occur in the future, potentially leading to new systemic crises.

NOTES

1. The term *shadow banking system* was coined in September 2007 by Paul McCulley, a managing director at PIMCO. It was later popularized by Bill Gross, the chief investment officer of PIMCO, and Professor Nouriel Roubini of the NYU Stern School of Business.
2. www.sifma.org/uploadedFiles/Research/Statistics/SIFMA_USBondMarketOutst anding.pdf.
3. Most often, a cheaper but equivalent substitute is acceptable to the primary securities dealer (the borrower) in the U.S. repo market. If it is not, then the interest goes up.
4. A haircut is not the only tool that is used to manage the counterparty risk in the U.S. repo market. Another tool is marking the repo securities to market. The collateral is valued at current market levels, and the trade is adjusted through a margin call (debtor sends more collateral) or repriced (funds are delivered to creditor). See www.sifma.org/services/stdforms/pdf/master_repo_agreement.pdf.
5. In other words, both the MBS and money are borrowed.
6. Since the start of the crisis, large deposits held at commercial banks are insured up to a limit of $250,000.
7. www.roaths.com/pawnbroking.htm.
8. However, there appears to have been some deliberate vagueness about this until a government securities dealer, Lombard-Wall, collapsed in 1982, and the Federal Bankruptcy Court of New York imposed an automatic stay on the repo securities that Lombard-Wall had used as collateral. See www.nytimes.com/ 1982/12/17/business/lombard-wall.html. This point had always been uncertain until the 1982 and 1984 amendments to United States Code, Title 11. In a true sale, the buyer is not subject to the automatic stay. For instance, if an automobile dealer bought a car from General Motors the day before it filed for bankruptcy, it could resell the car without asking for permission of the court. However, if the deal were financed by GM, the dealer would need a court order to sell the car. The repo transactions are structured formally as a true sale, free of the automatic stay. The question was, and still is, whether courts would reclassify a repo transaction as a secured transaction. Before 1982/1984, this would inflict the stay on the collateral taker. After 1982/1984, it would only affect the rights of a secured party, which are more limited than the rights of a buyer.
9. Even if they did, a court would be free to reclassify them.
10. "Lion Capital's Collapse Raises Issue of Unresolved Legal Status of 'Repos,'" *Wall Street Journal*, May 8, 1984.
11. See Copeland, Martin, and Walker (2010) for a fuller discussion of the tri-party repo market and its various sources of vulnerability and fragility before the 2010 reforms.
12. As of April 2010, the size of the tri-party repo market was $1.7 trillion.
13. http://online.wsj.com/article/SB10001424052748703447104575118150651790066.html.
14. http://knowledge.wharton.upenn.edu/article.cfm?articleid=2464.

15. *Tranche* means slice in French.
16. It should be mentioned that the repo banks have gone beyond BAPCPA. Parties that engage in such repos are relying on the general Section 555 of United States Code, Title 11, rather than the repo-specific Section 559 of United States Code, Title 11.
17. Isolated runs, such as the September 2008 run on the Seattle-based savings and loan Washington Mutual, did occur.
18. The index is overseen by Markit Partners. See www.markit.com/information/products/abx.html.
19. www.bloomberg.com/apps/news?pid=20601087&refer=home&sid=aYDTeH YnV3ms.
20. From Ben Bernanke's remarks to the Risk Transfer Mechanisms and Financial Stability Workshop at the Bank for International Settlements, May 29, 2008: "[U]ntil recently, short-term repos had always been regarded as virtually risk-free instruments and thus largely immune to the type of rollover or withdrawal risks associated with short-term unsecured obligations. In March, rapidly unfolding events demonstrated that even repo markets could be severely disrupted when investors believe they might need to sell the underlying collateral in illiquid markets. Such forced asset sales can set up a particularly adverse dynamic, in which further substantial price declines fan investor concerns about counterparty credit risk, which then feed back in the form of intensifying funding pressures.... In light of the recent experience, and following the recommendations of the President's Working Group on Financial Markets (2008), the Federal Reserve and other supervisors are reviewing their policies and guidance regarding liquidity risk management to determine what improvements can be made. In particular, future liquidity planning will have to take into account the possibility of a sudden loss of substantial amounts of secured financing."
21. The repo resolution fund should clearly be eligible for participating in the lender-of-last-resort facilities of the central bank. If such participation is not clear a priori, uncertainty concerning it could lead to a breakdown of our proposed resolution plan.
22. According to the survey conducted by the International Capital Market Association with 53 financial institutions located in 14 European countries, as well as the United States and Japan.

REFERENCES

Acharya, Viral V., Douglas Gale, and Tanju Yorulmazer. 2009. Rollover risk and market freezes. Working paper, NYU Stern School of Business.
Acharya, Viral V., and Arvind Krishnamurthy. 2010. Why bankers must bear the risk of "too safe to fail" assets. *Financial Times*, March 17.
Acharya, Viral V., and Matthew Richardson, eds. 2009. *Restoring financial stability: How to repair a failed system.* Hoboken, NJ: John Wiley & Sons.

Basel Committee on Banking Supervision. 2010. BCBS-CGFS working group on systemic liquidity risk.

Copeland, Adam, Antoine Martin, and Michael W. Walker. 2010. The tri-party repo market before the 2010 reforms. Working paper, Federal Reserve Bank of New York.

Federal Reserve Bank of New York. 2010. Tri-party repo infrastructure reform. FRBNY Task Force on Tri-Party Infrastructure White Paper, May 17.

Garbade, K. D. 2006. The evolution of repo contracting conventions in the 1980s. *FRBNY Economic Policy Review* (May): 27–42.

Gorton, G. 2009. Slapped in the face by the invisible hand: Banking and the panic of 2007. Federal Reserve Bank of Atlanta's 2009 Financial Markets Conference: Financial Innovation and Crisis, May 11–13.

Gorton, G., and A. Metrick. 2009a. Haircuts. Yale ICF Working Paper No. 09-15.

Gorton, G., and A. Metrick. 2009b. Securitized banking and run on the repo. Yale ICF Working Paper No. 09-14.

Roe, Mark. 2009. End bankruptcy priority for derivatives, repos and swaps. *Financial Times*, December 16.

CHAPTER 12

Hedge Funds, Mutual Funds, and ETFs

Stephen Brown, Anthony Lynch, and Antti Petajisto*

Hedge funds and mutual funds are major participants in the so-called shadow banking system, which runs parallel to the more standard banking system. Mutual funds, intended for a retail clientele, are heavily restricted—both in terms of their regulatory regime and in terms of the strategies they may employ. Hedge funds, by contrast, are directed to high net worth individuals and institutions and have both a more relaxed regulatory regime and a wider range of investment strategies available to them. These funds add value to the financial system in several ways: First, they act as primary providers of liquidity and a source for sophisticated capital. Second, they allow the investor to achieve well-diversified portfolios. Hedge funds adopt a variety of investment strategies that generate returns with low correlation to the overall market, thus allowing even better diversification. Third, these funds, along with other institutional investors, play an important corporate governance role in firms in which they hold significant equity stakes. Finally, by trading on margin and taking extensive short positions, certain hedge fund strategies provide their investors with access to significant leverage they would not otherwise have access to.

But at what cost? Regulators, particularly in Europe, are concerned that hedge funds generate significant systemic risk through their extensive use of leverage and short positions. Hedge funds are a remarkably diverse category, and some use little or no leverage. However, certain hedge fund strategies

---

*We benefited from discussions in the "Hedge Funds and Mutual Funds" Working Group for the NYU Stern e-book *Real Time Solutions for Financial Reform*, which also included Marcin Kacperczyk, Matthew Richardson, Philipp Schnabl, and Robert Whitelaw.

are highly levered, which means that they can generate the counterparty risk associated with net asset value (NAV) going negative. This counterparty risk can be systemic if the hedge funds are highly interconnected to other financial firms. Fire sales of illiquid assets may become necessary as NAV declines, which can also generate systemic risk. Do these concerns justify the regulatory proposals concerning hedge funds that have recently been discussed in Washington, D.C., and in the European Union (EU)? Mutual funds are typically not levered but are usually subject to daily redemptions, so they too can be susceptible to runs that generate systemic risk.

In contrast to hedge funds and mutual funds, exchange-traded funds (ETFs) do not sell or redeem individual shares for cash, but instead allow authorized participants—typically large financial institutions—to purchase or redeem large blocks of shares in kind by contributing or receiving, respectively, the same basket of securities as held by the ETF. For this reason, ETFs are likely less susceptible to conventional runs than are hedge funds or mutual funds, though authorized participants that redeem large blocks of ETFs may be doing so to sell the underlying security basket. Most ETFs are structured like mutual funds and are regulated in a similar way. ETFs add value by providing investors with easy access to various market segments and asset classes, including alternatives such as commodities and currencies. They generally offer very low fees and provide a vehicle for selling short the underlying security basket, which is useful for both active trading and hedging purposes. Thus, an ETF provides liquidity to the markets for the securities in its basket by allowing market participants to trade, and even short sell, the basket at very low trading costs. The unique trading mechanism of ETFs also avoids the problem of stale NAVs that caused significant market timing and value destruction in mutual funds until a scandal broke out in 2003.

There is no evidence that unregulated hedge funds caused or contributed in any way to the severity of the recent financial crisis. Rather, it was highly regulated money-center banks that were the source of the problem. A case could be made that hedge funds, by investing in other financial products, actually reduced systemic risk in the crisis, both by providing necessary liquidity and by taking otherwise troubled assets off the balance sheets of the banking system. Aragon and Strahan (2010) examine the impact of the Lehman Brothers bankruptcy of September 15, 2008, and find that stocks held by Lehman-connected hedge funds suffered relatively larger drops in liquidity than stocks not held by these funds during the last quarter of 2008. Lehman was providing custodial services, securities lending services, and financing to their hedge fund customers, and thus its bankruptcy severely hampered the ability of these funds to provide liquidity to markets. These results suggest that hedge funds are an important source of liquidity during times of low liquidity like the recent crisis.

However, the collapse of Long-Term Capital Management in 1998 shows that there are circumstances under which hedge funds and mutual funds may impose externalities on the financial system. It is important to note that there are no hedge funds today that are as large and economically significant as Long-Term Capital Management, perhaps because the market has learned from that episode: Prime brokers and counterparties are paying closer attention to the potential insolvency of hedge funds and not allowing nearly as high levels of leverage. Consequently, we did not observe similar systemically important hedge fund blowups in 2008, despite market conditions that were even more extreme than in 1998. While it is true that a group of smaller hedge funds could present the same risk if their strategies were sufficiently correlated, there are substantial differences across strategies. According to Brown and Goetzmann (2003), accounting for style differences alone explains about 20 percent of the cross-sectional dispersion of hedge fund returns. Finally, long-only hedge funds would be expected to have similar systemic risk characteristics as mutual funds.

Tables 12.1 and 12.2 and Figures 12.1 and 12.2 are taken from the Investment Company Institute's 2010 *Fact Book* and provide information about the net flows, total net asset value, and total number of mutual funds and ETFs. Figure 12.3 is based on data taken from the Lipper TASS Asset Flows Report for the Fourth Quarter 2009 and provides information about net flows for the hedge fund industry. First, Table 12.1 shows that total net asset value of mutual funds declined sharply in 2008 from $12,001 billion at the end of 2007 to $9,603 billion at the end of 2008, after growth in net asset value every year from 2003 through 2007. However, the total net flow to mutual funds in 2008 was actually positive at $412 billion (see Figure 12.1), and the number of mutual funds increased too (see Table 12.2). So the decline in total net asset value of mutual funds during 2008 was driven by negative returns in 2008. It was not until 2009 that the total net flow went negative, with an outflow of $150 billion, and the number of mutual funds declined. However, in that year, the total net asset value of mutual funds increased to $11,121 billion, despite the outflow. Figure 12.3 shows a redirection from mutual funds into hedge funds starting in 2003 but ending abruptly in 2008, as hedge fund investors fled to safety with the onset of the financial crisis. According to Lipper TASS, these outflows, together with negative returns, caused total net assets to decline from $1.80 trillion at the end of the second quarter of 2008 to $1.18 trillion at the end of the first quarter of 2009. This represents a loss of one-third of total net asset value in only three quarters—which is certainly a significant decline.

TABLE 12.1 Investment Company Total Net Assets by Type (Billions of Dollars, Year-End, 1995–2009)

	Mutual Funds[1]	Closed-End Funds	ETFs[2]	Unit Investment Trusts	Total[3]
1995	$ 2,811	$143	$ 1	$73	$ 3,028
1996	3,526	147	2	72	3,747
1997	4,468	152	7	85	4,712
1998	5,525	156	16	94	5,791
1999	6,846	147	34	92	7,119
2000	6,965	143	66	74	7,248
2001	6,975	141	83	49	7,248
2002	6,383	159	102	36	6,680
2003	7,402	214	151	36	7,803
2004	8,095	254	228	37	8,614
2005	8,891	277	301	41	9,510
2006	10,397	298	423	50	11,167
2007	12,001	313	608	53	12,975
2008	9,603	188	531	29	10,350
2009	11,121	228	777	38	12,164

[1]Mutual fund data include only mutual funds that report statistical information to the Investment Company Institute. The data do not include mutual funds that invest primarily in other mutual funds.
[2]ETF data prior to 2001 were provided by Strategic Insight Simfund; ETF data include investment companies not registered under the Investment Company Act of 1940 and exclude ETFs that primarily invest in other ETFs.
[3]Total investment company assets include mutual fund holdings of closed-end funds and ETFs.
Sources: Investment Company Institute and Strategic Insight Simfund.
Note: Components may not add to the total because of rounding.

Table 12.1 shows that total net assets for ETFs also dipped in 2008, before rebounding in 2009, while Table 12.2 shows that the number of ETFs has increased every year since 1995. Although the total net asset value of ETFs has been growing faster than that of mutual funds, the total net asset value of ETFs at the end of 2009 was still less than 10 percent of that of mutual funds at the same time. The total net asset value of ETFs as a fraction of the NAV of mutual funds has increased from zero in 1993 (the inception of the first ETF) to 7 percent at the end of 2009. The reason for the growth in ETFs is an influx of capital: Figure 12.2 shows that net issuance of ETF shares has been positive every year since 1999. While size is only one of many determinants of an entity's ability to generate systemic risk, the

TABLE 12.2 Number of Investment Companies by Type (Year-End, 1995–2009)

	Mutual Funds[1]	Closed-End Funds	ETFs[2]	Unit Investment Trusts	Total[3]
1995	5,761	500	2	12,979	19,242
1996	6,293	497	19	11,764	18,573
1997	6,778	487	19	11,593	18,877
1998	7,489	492	29	10,966	18,976
1999	8,004	512	30	10,414	18,960
2000	8,371	482	80	10,072	19,005
2001	8,519	492	102	9,295	18,408
2002	8,512	545	113	8,303	17,473
2003	8,427	584	119	7,233	16,363
2004	8,419	619	152	6,499	15,689
2005	8,451	635	204	6,019	15,309
2006	8,721	647	359	5,907	15,636
2007	8,749	664	629	6,030	16,072
2008	8,888	642	743	5,984	16,257
2009	8,624	627	820	6,049	16,120

[1]Mutual fund data include only mutual funds that report statistical information to the Investment Company Institute. The data do not include mutual funds that invest primarily in other mutual funds.

[2]ETF data prior to 2001 were provided by Strategic Insight Simfund; ETF data include investment companies not registered under the Investment Company Act of 1940 and exclude ETFs that primarily invest in other ETFs.

[3]Total investment company assets include mutual fund holdings of closed-end funds and ETFs.

Sources: Investment Company Institute and Strategic Insight Simfund.

Note: Components may not add to the total because of rounding.

fact that the ETF industry is so much smaller than the mutual fund industry means that the ETF industry is likely to be much less capable of generating systemic risk than the mutual fund industry.

Going forward, there are three channels through which hedge funds may potentially generate systemic risk when they suffer losses: (1) by causing prices to move away from fundamentals with their trades (e.g., forced liquidations due to redemptions or tightening credit constraints); (2) by no longer being able to provide liquidity to the market because of their capital erosion (when other market participants have come to rely on this liquidity provision in normal times); and (3) by generating counterparty risk when their NAVs go negative. Sections 12(c)1 and 12(c)3 of the Investment Company Act of 1940 explicitly limit mutual funds' access to leverage and their

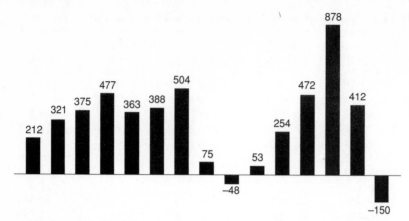

FIGURE 12.1 Net Flows to Mutual Funds ($ Billions, 1995–2009)
Source: Investment Company Institute's 2010 *Fact Book*.

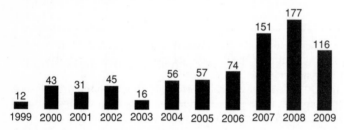

FIGURE 12.2 Net Issuance of ETF Shares ($ Billions, 1999–2009)
Source: Investment Company Institute's 2010 *Fact Book*.

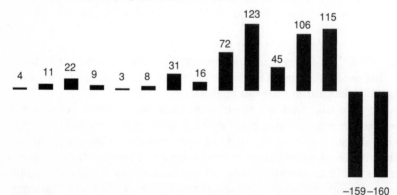

FIGURE 12.3 Net Flows to Hedge Funds ($ Billions, 1995–2009)
Source: Lipper, a Thomson Reuters Company. *Asset Flows Report*, Fourth Quarter 2009.

ability to establish short positions. This suggests that they can generate systemic risk only through the first two channels. However, competition from hedge funds has led to the emergence of long/short mutual fund strategies, which at first sight appear difficult to reconcile with these sections of the Act. Some mutual funds short against established asset positions ("shorting against the box") and are therefore not net short in violation of Section 12(c)3 and do not create counterparty risk. Others achieve similar ends using derivative positions, which if unhedged may represent more of a problem. Leverage and short positions are more common for ETFs than for mutual funds. Since their portfolios are rebalanced daily, the risk of a negative NAV is negligible. The only source of systemic risk for ETFs is in-kind redemptions followed by large-scale selling of the underlying portfolio, which is akin to, but not the same as, the first channel. ETFs provide liquidity to markets through a different channel than mutual funds and hedge funds, by allowing units of the underlying baskets of securities to be traded at low cost, which explains why the second channel does not apply either.

For hedge funds and mutual funds, the following factors are likely the most important for determining whether a fund or group of funds is capable of generating systemic risk: (1) the NAV of the fund or group, (2) the leverage of the fund or group, (3) the illiquidity of the assets of the fund or group, and (4) the extent to which the value of the fund or group moves with the positions of other financial institutions.

Mutual funds, ETFs, and hedge funds are major participants in the shadow banking system, along with insurance companies, broker-dealers, money market funds, pension funds, structured investment vehicles (SIVs), conduits, and so forth. Within this system, it is quite possible for participants such as hedge funds and mutual funds to provide functions more typically associated with banking. While some criticize this system because of the ability of its participants to conduct regulatory arbitrage, it should be noted that many of these participants, including hedge funds, mutual funds, and ETFs, are provided no explicit government guarantees, but compete with regulated banks that have advantages like the explicit guarantee of deposit insurance and the implicit too-big-to-fail guarantee.

The case for hedge fund, mutual fund, and ETF regulation can be built on two separate justifications: the potential for systemic risk and investor protection in general. Regulation that limits the ability of hedge funds and mutual funds to impose externalities by generating systemic risk often constrains their ability to add value to the financial system and their investors. Balancing these considerations is important. Since mutual fund NAVs essentially never go negative because of their long-only mandates, mutual funds have far less potential to generate systemic risk than do hedge funds. Since ETFs typically require redemptions in kind, and the total net asset value of

ETFs is still much smaller than those of hedge funds and mutual funds, ETFs appear to have much less potential to generate systemic risk than do hedge funds or mutual funds. Therefore, the case for regulating them further to limit systemic risk is much weaker than even the weak case for regulating mutual funds for this reason. Regulation designed to protect investors is also costly, and these costs need to be taken into account when deciding how much regulation is optimal. Last, many hedge funds can easily leave the United States if regulation becomes too burdensome, a factor that limits the amount of regulation that can be imposed on the U.S. hedge fund industry.

12.1 U.S. LEGISLATION AND THE EU PROPOSAL

The Dodd-Frank Wall Street Reform and Consumer Protection Act of 2010, passed by the U.S. House and Senate, requires hedge funds to register with the Securities and Exchange Commission (SEC) as investment advisers. Section 410 raises the assets threshold for federal regulation of investment advisers from $25 million to $100 million, a move expected to significantly increase the number of advisers under state supervision. According to Section 404 of the Dodd-Frank bill, the SEC may require any investment adviser registered with the SEC to maintain such records and file such reports "as necessary and appropriate in the public interest and for the protection of investors, or for the assessment of systemic risk by the Financial Stability Oversight Council" (FSOC). This data is to be shared with the FSOC. The records and reports required to be filed with the SEC will include a description of: (1) the amount of assets under management and the use of leverage; (2) counterparty credit risk exposure; (3) trading and investment positions; (4) valuation methodologies of the fund; (5) types of assets held; (6) side arrangements, whereby certain investors in a fund obtain more favorable rights or entitlements than other investors; (7) trading practices; and (8) such other information as the SEC, in consultation with the FSOC, deems necessary and appropriate in the public interest and for the protection of investors or for the assessment of systemic risk. Further, the SEC will conduct periodic inspections and other inspections prescribed as necessary by the SEC of all records maintained by an investment adviser registered with the SEC.

Section 408 specifies the threshold for registration of hedge funds (advisers of "private funds" in the language of the Act) to be $150 million. This section also requires hedge funds to maintain such records and provide to the SEC such annual or other reports as the SEC determines necessary or appropriate in the public interest or for the protection of investors. Finally, Section 408 says that the SEC, in prescribing regulations to carry out the requirements of Section 203 of the Investment Advisers Act of 1940 with respect to investment advisers to midsize private funds, will take into account the size, governance, and investment strategy of such funds to determine whether they pose systemic risk, and will provide for registration and examination procedures with respect to the level of systemic risk posed by such funds. Based on the language of the section, it is not clear exactly what constitutes a midsize private fund.

The requirement that hedge funds with assets under management of more than $150 million register with the SEC as investment advisers will affect only a small minority of hedge funds currently operating. According to data provided by Lipper TASS, as of the end of December 2009, a majority of U.S. hedge funds (56 percent) had less than $25 million of assets under management. The new registration threshold of $150 million excludes 82 percent of all funds. The original Senate bill also required investment advisers to use independent custodians for client assets to prevent Madoff-type frauds, but the latest version no longer includes this requirement.

In addition, family offices are exempt from reporting requirements under Section 409 of the Dodd-Frank Act. This exemption appears to be written very broadly, since the definition of family office is left to the rule, regulation, or order of the SEC. Consequently, there is a real danger that this exception could become a loophole that swallows the entire hedge fund reform effort. This particular exemption is interesting. Miller (2010) shows that the original Section 3(c)1 exemption in the 1940 Investment Company Act that allowed for the growth and development of hedge funds was originally designed to protect the interests of family offices.

The final version of the bill does not include a tax for systemic risk. However, such a provision did exist in the bill until a last-minute compromise to cut it out. If the provision had remained in the bill, hedge funds above $10 billion in assets would have been subject to a tax on systemic risk.

Turning to mutual funds, the Dodd-Frank bill only asks for studies into the financial literacy of retail investors and into mutual fund advertising, both with a view to generating recommendations to improve investor protections. Yet the issues associated with regulating mutual funds overlap substantially with those associated with regulating hedge funds. The major differences are that hedge funds can use leverage, whereas mutual funds cannot, and hedge funds can slow or even halt redemptions, whereas mutual funds cannot. It is important to realize that long-only hedge funds have the same systemic risk characteristics as mutual funds.

The EU's proposed hedge fund directive goes considerably further than the U.S. bill, suggesting significant regulatory oversight and control for all hedge funds with assets in excess of €100 million. It also restricts the ability of "third country" (non-EU) funds to market themselves within the EU. The so-called third country elements of the draft EU directive would force non-EU hedge funds to comply with the new rules if they wish to market themselves at all within the EU.

12.2 U.S. LEGISLATION CONCERNING THE SYSTEMIC RISK IMPOSED BY HEDGE FUNDS

Transparency to regulators can help them measure and manage possible systemic risk and is relatively costless. Consequently, we support the Dodd-Frank bill's requirement that hedge funds provide information to the SEC about their trades and portfolios necessary to assess systemic risk. The information needs to be provided in a regular and timely fashion about both their asset positions and their leverage levels. However, a hedge fund will be required to provide information to the SEC if it falls within one of three different categories:

1. Section 404 of the bill requires any investment adviser registered with the SEC to provide information that the SEC determines to be necessary and appropriate in the public interest and for the protection of investors, or for the assessment of systemic risk by the FSOC; the asset threshold for registration of private fund advisers with the SEC is $150 million.
2. Section 408 of the bill says that hedge funds with assets under management between $100 million and $150 million are exempt from registration, but can be required by the SEC to provide such information that it determines to be necessary or appropriate in the public interest or for the protection of investors.
3. Section 408 of the bill also states that the SEC shall provide for registration and examination procedures with respect to the investment advisers of midsize private funds that reflect the level of systemic risk posed by such funds.

It is important that there is consistency and coherence in the information provision requirements across these three categories. Ensuring this will be an important implementation challenge. Moreover, it is not clear what constitutes a midsize private fund, so it not clear exactly which funds not registered with the SEC will be required to provide information to the SEC to assess systemic risk. U.S. legislators—or the SEC—need to clarify what constitutes a midsize private fund.

For all three categories, the Dodd-Frank Act gives the SEC the authority to require any information it deems necessary to achieve its objectives. Given that the SEC likely has its own conflicts of interest and has been prone to ineffectiveness in the past, it would have been better if the SEC's mandate had been instead limited to prespecified items that had been clearly described in the bill.

If a hedge fund or group of hedge funds generates systemic risk for the financial system, then that hedge fund or group of hedge funds needs to be treated as a systemic institution and regulated (and taxed) as such. However, NAV alone is not sufficient to determine if a hedge fund (or mutual fund) is generating systemic risk. The Dodd-Frank bill recognizes this by explicitly listing a number of factors to be taken into account by the regulator when determining the ability of a hedge fund to generate systemic risk. While it is critical that the regulator take all these factors into account when regulating hedge funds, we think it is important to remember that determining appropriate measures of hedge fund systemic risk is a real challenge.

Hedge funds, or groups of hedge funds, that generate systemic risk may need regulation that discourages investors from withdrawing funds after bad performance, since bad performance by a fund may lead to a run on the fund's assets under management. However, many hedge funds decided to put up gates during the crisis, so the question is whether the externality created by withdrawals after poor performance distorts when and how fund managers put up gates relative to the social optimum. While the current Dodd-Frank bill does not address this issue, the need for any such regulation is unclear, given the incentives of hedge funds to put up gates during times of crisis.

12.3 U.S. LEGISLATION CONCERNING PROTECTION OF HEDGE FUND INVESTORS

It is not at all clear that additional regulation is needed to improve protections for hedge fund investors. There are several important considerations: (1) such regulation is costly to funds; (2) the effectiveness of regulators like the SEC is questionable; (3) private information providers play an important role in the dissemination of information to investors; and (4) fiduciaries who are investing money in hedge funds on behalf of pension funds and other investors have the primary responsibility to do due diligence. However, we support the requirement in the original Senate bill, which is not in the final Dodd-Frank Act, that investment advisers use independent custodians for client assets, since it is a simple way to prevent misappropriation of the hedge fund assets.

While the new threshold under the Dodd-Frank bill for required registration as an investment adviser with the SEC is $100 million, the threshold for registration of private fund advisers is $150 million. If the argument for registration is to provide investors with necessary information about the operational characteristics of hedge funds, it is not clear why this requirement should be limited to hedge funds over $150 million, since doing so excludes from consideration all but the largest hedge funds. Section 408 of the bill is a step in the right direction, saying that the SEC can require private fund advisers with assets under management of between $100 million and $150 million to provide necessary information in the public interest or for the protection of investors.

According to the latest data from Lipper TASS, 25 percent of all hedge funds have less than $10 million assets under management. It is these funds, excluded under the Dodd-Frank bill, that we would anticipate seeing the most serious operational problems. According to Brown and Goetzmann (2009), operational risk is a more significant explanation of fund failure than is financial risk. They find that financial risk events typically occur within the context of poor operational controls. It would be better to have all hedge funds register with the SEC and file the mandated Form ADV disclosure, as all mutual funds are required to do, without artificial limitations on asset size or lockup period exception. Form ADV does not reveal competitive concerns, such as positions taken and strategies used, but it does reveal conflicts of interest, both internal and external to the fund, and the existence of past legal or regulatory issues.

In addition, registration opens the fund up to possible audit by the SEC. The mandated disclosures do not convey much information, but Brown, Goetzmann, Liang, and Schwarz (2008) have shown that this information is material to investors and an indicator of fund quality. The mandated disclosures would have the additional benefit of shifting the burden of proof to fiduciaries who would otherwise claim, "Nobody told us; we did not know." For a token $12,500 per fund, investors can obtain far more detailed information (including positions taken and strategies used) from private information providers. It may make sense to increase sanctions on fiduciaries who violate their duty of due diligence by not bothering to obtain one of these due diligence reports.

If the SEC uses its newly established authority to write new rules with the purpose of protecting investors, we support greater disclosure of all expenses charged to fund investors, as well as greater transparency about any fund-level tax discrimination between investors. This is because both fees and taxes have a first-order impact on the investors' net return, and neither is well disclosed in today's hedge fund business. For example, in a practice known as "stuffing," some hedge funds allocate short-term capital gains to some investors (such as liquidating partners), while allocating long-term capital gains to others (such as the general partner). If such arbitrary tax treatment is indeed allowed, it should be clearly disclosed to investors, just like any other aspects that will significantly impact an investor's net return.

One argument justifying limited disclosure is that small investors do not have access to hedge funds, as they do not meet the $1 million net worth test to be an accredited investor. Indeed, this test has become more stringent as the investor's primary residence is now excluded from the net worth test. While it does make sense to adjust the accredited investor thresholds for inflation going forward, it is less clear why the threshold should suddenly be increased today, say from $1 million to $2.5 million, by excluding the investor's primary residence from the net worth test. On average, investors who had access to hedge funds fared better in the 2008 crisis than investors who invested in the public equity markets, so it is hard to justify this by arguing investor protection. However, while a pension fund may easily satisfy the accredited investor threshold, it does not guarantee that the pension fund's manager is capable or qualified to evaluate a given hedge fund product.

12.4 EU DIRECTIVE CONCERNING U.S.-BASED FUNDS

Concern that U.S.-based financial institutions were conduits for systemic risk from the United States to Europe has prompted the EU proposal calling for strict regulation of hedge funds there and a requirement that would force non-EU funds to comply with these regulations. Yet the evidence attests to the much more significant role of money-center banks in this transfer of risk.

In a letter sent to Europe's internal market commissioner, Michel Barnier, U.S. Treasury Secretary Timothy Geithner argues that compelling non-EU funds to comply with the new rules in the directive is likely to be a protectionist law that will create barriers to the entry and continued presence of non-EU funds in the EU marketplace. We strongly oppose any legislation that inhibits the ability of investors to obtain access to the full menu of available investment vehicles, and so we share Geithner's concerns about the protectionist flavor of the "third country" elements of the draft EU directive. The highly publicized failures of Luxalpha and other European Madoff feeder funds point less to the malfunction of existing regulation than the failure of European fiduciaries to do the normal and customary due diligence on fund custodians and subcustodians.

It is important that the regulatory responses to the crisis are coordinated across nations to preserve, as much as possible, equal access to all markets. Moreover, the potential for regulatory arbitrage across markets needs to be limited.

12.5 VOLCKER RULE

The so-called Volcker Rule is a provision in the U.S. legislation proposed by Paul Volcker, the highly respected former Fed chairman, which limits the scope of any implicit federal guarantee to a relatively small number of important banking institutions and to core banking functions, rather than extending it across the spectrum of financial intermediaries and risky activities. In exchange for the banking safety net, Volcker recommends that banks be allowed to engage in the full range of commercial and investment banking functions as financial intermediaries, but not be permitted to engage in such nonbanking activities as proprietary trading, principal investing, commodity speculation, and hedge fund and private equity fund management. These other activities would be spun off to nonbank asset-management firms and would be subject to whatever regulation is necessary for those types of institutions. The legacy banks would have no economic interest in the spun-off entities.

As written, the legislation requires federal agencies to issue rules that prohibit certain financial companies from engaging in proprietary trading or investing in or sponsoring hedge funds or private equity funds. The companies covered include all depository institutions, their holding companies, any company treated as a bank holding company as defined by the Bank Holding Company Act (such as foreign banks with U.S. operations), and any of their subsidiaries.

It is essential to remember that the spun-off entities may still generate systemic risk for the financial system even after being spun off. In fact, the spun-off entities likely will impose more counterparty risk after being spun off than before when they were owned by the large financial institutions, since any diversification benefits associated with being part of a large financial institution will be lost. Implementation of the Volcker Rule will likely cause the pool of hedge funds and mutual funds to increase in size and in the range of strategies offered. Consequently, the Volcker Rule further increases the importance of having a mechanism to assess levies on hedge funds if they impose systemic risk on the financial system going forward.

That said, while the Volcker Rule does not extend to nonbank financial institutions that are systemically important, these firms will be subject to additional capital and quantitative limits on such activities as set forth in future rules by the Federal Reserve. Therefore, any hedge fund considered to be systemically important will be subject to these new rules.

The Volcker Rule also means that hedge funds and mutual funds will no longer be competing directly with banks and other members of the banking system. However, the hedge fund industry is likely to become more competitive with the public availability of funds whose operations were previously owned by banks.

12.6 CONCLUSIONS

The U.S. legislation only allows for the possibility that a hedge fund or group of hedge funds may need to be treated as a systemic institution and regulated (and taxed) as such. Mutual funds and ETFs are not explicitly mentioned in the Dodd-Frank bill as possible systemic institutions. Distinguishing hedge funds from mutual funds and ETFs in this way seems reasonable to us in light of their greater potential to generate systemic risk going forward.

In our view, the U.S. legislation would benefit from a lighter regulatory approach that is more focused on those hedge funds most likely to create systemic risk. At the same time, we would favor a broader regulatory approach that extends operational disclosure to a larger fraction of hedge funds. Certainly, the additional reporting requirements imposed on hedge funds with more than $150 million in assets under management (requiring them to register with the SEC as investment advisers) are not onerous. Moreover, the reporting requirements are unlikely to materially affect the cost of these hedge funds doing business going forward. However, investor confidence could be bolstered significantly, since operational risk appears to be a major issue with hedge funds, and the mandated forms have been found to provide information that investors find useful. The SEC's ability to require private fund advisers with assets under management of between $100 million and $150 million to provide necessary information for the protection of investors may also play a role in improving investor confidence. The family office exemption (Section 409 of the Dodd-Frank Act) appears to be written so broadly that it could end up swallowing the entire hedge fund reform effort.

Turning to mutual funds, the increase in the NAV threshold for registration as an investment adviser with the SEC to $100 million could have the opposite consequence—namely, a reduction in investor confidence—since many small mutual funds that previously were required to file Form ADV and other mandated forms would no longer be required to do so. However, the existence of private information providers, which supply much more information than that required by the SEC and for a very modest fee, dampens considerably the effect that the changes in the criteria for registration as an investment adviser might have on investor confidence in the hedge fund and mutual fund industries.

The proposed EU hedge fund directive will make it more difficult for sophisticated capital to provide liquidity to the market. This is a goal that is difficult to understand. The recent crisis highlights just how important liquidity provision is for a well-functioning financial market.

REFERENCES

Aragon, G., and P. Strahan. 2010. Hedge funds as liquidity providers. Working paper, Arizona State University.

Brown, Stephen, and William Goetzmann. 2003. Hedge funds with style. *Journal of Portfolio Management* 29: 101–112.

Brown, S., W. Goetzmann, B. Liang, and C. Schwarz. 2008. Mandatory disclosure and operational risk: Evidence from hedge fund registration. *Journal of Finance* 63 (6): 2785–2815.

Brown, S., W. Goetzmann, B. Liang, and C. Schwarz. 2009. Estimating operational risk for hedge funds: The ω-score. *Financial Analysts Journal* 65 (1): 43–53.

Miller, J. 2010. Inventing hedge funds: A cross-cultural comparative study of institutional and individual entrepreneurship in ambiguously regulated environments. Unpublished doctoral dissertation, NYU Stern School of Business.

CHAPTER 13

Regulating OTC Derivatives

Viral V. Acharya, Or Shachar, and Marti Subrahmanyam*

13.1 OVERVIEW

Over-the-counter (OTC) derivatives account for a significant proportion of overall banking and intermediation activity. On the one hand, they enable end users like corporations, including industrial and financial firms, to hedge their underlying risk exposures in a customized manner. For example, an airline may hedge the price of its future commitments to buy jet fuel or a mutual fund may reduce its portfolio's exposure to exchange rate movements using such products. On the other hand, they enable banks and other financial intermediaries—the providers of hedging services to end users—to earn profits, as they in turn hedge the customized OTC products they sell, either by diversifying the risk across different end users or by shedding the risk to other intermediaries via liquid markets for standardized derivatives. The profit earned by the intermediaries is, in part, a compensation for the mismatch between the risks of the standardized and the customized products. It is clear that there is value to the economy from trading in derivatives, which enables users to hedge and transfer risk by altering the patterns of their cash flows. Interest rate swaps, for example, are the largest segment of OTC derivative markets and have contributed remarkably to the management of interest rate risk on corporate and commercial bank balance sheets. It is not surprising, therefore, that the use of derivatives has grown

*We received useful inputs and comments on earlier drafts from Menachem Brenner, Rob Engle, Steve Figlewski, Matt Richardson, and Raghu Sundaram. We are also grateful to Darrell Duffie, Pablo Salame of Goldman Sachs, and Til Schuermann of the Federal Reserve Bank of New York for useful discussions. Opinions expressed herein are entirely our own.

drastically in many countries, covering equity, interest rate, foreign exchange, commodity, and credit markets.

The financial crisis of 2007 to 2009 has, however, highlighted two aspects of the OTC derivatives market that deserve attention and potential reform. The first aspect is that, while financial innovation—the design of new, customized products—typically occurs in the OTC space, this is also the arena in which banks can tailor their own risk taking and leverage buildup, since some of these positions are not reflected on their balance sheets either from a regulatory or statutory disclosure perspective. This is especially true since, thus far, regulatory capital requirements have not been suitably adjusted to reflect all aspects of OTC exposures, such as their illiquidity and their counterparty and systemic risks. The lack of such adjustment implies that risk taking is often more attractive for banks through off-balance-sheet OTC derivatives than via on-balance-sheet or exchange-traded products. For instance, the so-called toxic derivative assets (such as synthetic credit default swaps bought and sold on mortgage pools of dubious quality) that brought down many banks and insurance firms required, in retrospect, far too little regulatory capital relative to the risks incurred.

The second aspect that deserves attention concerns the opacity of exposures in OTC derivatives. By definition, an OTC derivative market does not have a central marketplace where all trades occur. This contrasts with exchange-traded derivatives, which are both traded on an exchange and cleared through a clearinghouse. Unlike cleared derivatives, where the clearinghouse monitors the risk of the positions of the various participants and imposes margins and other risk-mitigating devices, the risk-monitoring function in OTC markets is left to the individual counterparties. Since, for the most part thus far, OTC derivatives have not been centrally cleared, neither market participants nor regulators have accurate knowledge of the full range of the exposures and interconnections of the various market participants. This leads to a *counterparty risk externality* (see Acharya and Engle 2009; Acharya and Bisin 2010) that while each trade's counterparty risk is affected by other trades that are being done by the counterparties, this information is not visible. This prevents adequate risk controls against counterparty risk and a suitable conditioning of contract terms on precise measures of counterparty risk, and thereby results in a greater risk of leverage buildup ex ante and uncertainty about fallout of a counterparty's default ex post.

Primary concerns surrounding the failures or near failures of Bear Stearns, Lehman Brothers, and American International Group (AIG) all had to do with uncertainty about how counterparty risk would spread through the web of OTC connections, particularly in the market for credit default swaps (CDSs), and in the case of AIG, how so much counterparty risk got built up in the first place. In the end, all this presented a fait accompli to regulators to engage in massive government bailouts of two of these three corporations. Indeed, much of the dislocation of the global economy after the financial crisis in 2008 can be traced to these spectacular failures.

The task of the Dodd-Frank Wall Street Reform and Consumer Protection Act of 2010 as far as derivatives reform is concerned can thus be considered to address these issues of leverage and opacity in those derivatives that are traded over the counter. In this chapter, we provide a condensed version of the reforms legislated by the Act relating to derivatives (the original text of this section of the Act is more than 450 pages) and our overall assessment of the reforms, followed by a more detailed discussion and implications for the future.

13.2 THE WALL STREET TRANSPARENCY AND ACCOUNTABILITY PART OF THE DODD-FRANK ACT OF 2010

In the fall of 2009, the U.S. House of Representatives Financial Services Committee chaired by Congressman Barney Frank approved a bill, the Wall Street Reform and Consumer Protection Act of 2009, to regulate the massive OTC derivatives business. The proposed legislation called for sweeping changes in the structure (centralized trading versus over-the-counter trading) and regulation (margin requirements and transparency) of derivatives, but with exemptions for commercial end users. Then, in the spring of 2010, the Restoring American Financial Stability Act, proposed by the U.S. Senate Banking Committee under Senator Christopher Dodd, required similar reforms of the derivatives markets targeted at improving their transparency and accountability.

In a controversial move, however, the revised Senate bill, the Wall Street Transparency and Accountability Act of 2010 (approved April 21, 2010), proposed prohibiting U.S. federal assistance, including Federal Reserve advances and access to the discount window, as well as emergency liquidity or debt guarantee program assistance, to any dealer, major market participant, exchange, or clearing organization in connection with derivatives or other activities (with limited exceptions for hedging activities by banks and derivatives involving certain financial asset classes). This provision would potentially have spurred financial institutions to separate their derivatives businesses from their U.S. bank or U.S. branch office in order for the bank or branch to be eligible for these forms of federal assistance. Such separation was, in fact, explicitly proposed in Senator Blanche Lincoln's amendment, which would remove government-backed financial firms (notably, the commercial banks) from any derivatives markets. As per the Lincoln Amendment, the affected institutions could still hold swaps and other derivatives, but they would have to be contained in separate legal entities that could not be used to fund or manage their banking businesses. Equally important, the affected lenders could not use their bank capital reserves to provide a backstop for their derivatives businesses.

While the clearing and transparency proposals of the House and the Senate bills were considered relatively uncontroversial, the restricted federal assistance and the Lincoln Amendment were both unexpected twists, and the conference version of the Dodd-Frank Act was keenly awaited to clarify the final legislation on these two issues. Unfortunately, the Act leaves key aspects of implementation to be determined by the Securities and Exchange Commission (SEC), the Commodity Futures Trading Commission (CFTC), and other financial regulators, with substantial scope for interpretation in the coming years.

What follows is a summary of the Wall Street Transparency and Accountability Act of 2010—the part of the Dodd-Frank Wall Street Reform and Consumer Protection Act that deals with the derivatives markets. In this description, we follow closely the original language of the Act to minimize subjective translation of any of the provisions. The Act covers several key aspects: which derivatives will be affected; clearing, transparency, and reporting requirements; bankruptcy-related issues; trading and risk mitigation; and extraterritorial enforcement and international coordination.

Which Derivatives Will Be Affected?

1. **Coverage of derivatives:** The Act repeals the provision under the Gramm-Leach-Bliley Act (GLBA), also known as the Financial Services Modernization Act of 1999, that prohibited the regulation of OTC derivatives. In this sense, it expands the scope of regulation for the first time to the completely unregulated OTC market. There is, however, an important exception being considered: The foreign exchange (FX) derivatives (forwards and swaps, among others) could be excluded based on the decision of the Treasury secretary. Specifically, "He/she may exempt FX swaps based on a) systemic risk, opacity, leverage, evasion and their consequences, b) whether existing regulations are sufficient, c) bank regulators can do the job, d) other effects." The Treasury secretary will be required to report to Congress within a year if and why FX derivatives are different from others, and if and why they should be exempted from the Act.[1] The Act also contains a specific clause that states that derivative contracts ("swaps") are not "insurance" contracts and precludes them being regulated as such.

Clearing

2. Clearing requirements: The default treatment of derivatives under the Act will be that they remain uncleared. Nevertheless, the exemption process to this default treatment has been clearly laid out with the intention that several plain-vanilla products will, over time, in fact be centrally cleared. In particular, the Act requires that within a year from its enactment, the "Commission" (the SEC and the CFTC[2]) shall adopt rules for reviewing a derivatives clearing organization's bid for the kind of derivatives it seeks to accept for clearing. If a set of derivatives is to be allowed for central clearing (based on outstanding interest, liquidity, pricing, trading infrastructure, mitigation of systemic risk taking account of the size of the market and clearing resources, the effect on competition, and clarity on resolution of insolvency of the clearing agency), then the Commission will allow a 30-day comment period before the clearing commences. Further, there will be periodic reviews of derivatives that are cleared and of those that remain uncleared to assess whether clearing of some products needs to be stayed and whether other derivatives should be brought into the space of cleared derivatives.

An important issue concerns how the clearing requirements will be imposed on existing positions in a product viewed as "to be cleared." The Act clarifies that all positions, existing and new, need to be reported to a "swap data repository." Subject to this requirement, however, existing contracts need not be cleared if they are reported within specified time frames. Also, the clearing requirement will not be imposed on positions for which "one of the counterparties to the swap: (i) is not a financial entity;[3] (ii) is using swaps to hedge or mitigate commercial risk; and (iii) notifies the Commission, in a manner set forth by the Commission, how it generally meets its financial obligations associated with entering into uncleared swaps." The Act, however, permits regulators to consider further extending the exemption to small banks, savings associations, farm credit system institutions, and credit unions, including those with less than $10 billion of total assets.

3. Clearinghouse management: The Act recognizes that clearinghouses must be approved and reviewed based on their ability to provide needed financial resources for clearing as well as operational expertise. It requires the clearinghouses to provide public disclosure of contract terms, fees, margin methods, daily prices, volumes, open interest, governance structure, conflicts of interest, and so on, for the products they clear. The Act also stipulates that a "clearinghouse will have adequate collateral to cover the default by a member/participant creating the largest financial exposure for that organization in extreme but plausible conditions (plus operational costs on a rolling basis for each year)." To this end, clearinghouses will have to ensure required record keeping of positions, conduct monitoring and daily credit risk assessment of all counterparties, and impose risk-based margins that provide coverage of their exposures in normal times.

The Act charges the clearinghouses with keeping collateral funds with minimum market, credit, and liquidity risks. This recognizes the excessive counterparty credit risk created by some large swap counterparties that deployed the collateral backing their bilateral contracts for investments in risky securities. While the exact collateral-sharing rules across clearinghouses in case of a counterparty's insolvency are not clearly laid out (and presumably left to evolution of such practices in due course), the Act contains specific language to rule out counterparty risk across clearinghouses from each other's insolvency: "In order to minimize systemic risk, under no circumstances shall a derivatives clearing organization be compelled to accept the counterparty credit risk of another clearing organization."

Finally, the Act provides for the usual governance requirements of centrally cleared products pertaining to the regulation of insider trading, incentives for whistle-blowers, and containment of conflicts of interest at the clearinghouse management level. On the latter, the Act requires the Commission to adopt numerical limits on the control or the voting rights of clearinghouses by any one institution, singling out systemically important financial firms.

4. Uncleared swaps: This is the default option for a derivative under the Act. Uncleared swaps will, however, be regulated for the first time. In particular, they may be subject to *margin and collateral requirements* in order to offset the risks they pose, and will also be subject to *transparency requirements* (outlined below in point 5). Furthermore, the Act explicitly recognizes that regulatory arbitrage—trading in uncleared clones to avoid clearing or trading in derivatives outside of the United States—may undermine the intended purpose of the Act. Hence, it allows regulators to take corrective actions to prevent such behavior. In fact, the Act gives unrestricted rights to the Commission and prudential regulators to require adequate margin on clones and abusive swaps that are used to evade clearing requirements; the required margins may be in line with, if not identical to, their cleared counterparts. The exact actions available to the Commission and the prudential regulators are not detailed in the Act.

Transparency and Reporting Requirements

5. Transparency: First and foremost, the Act requires that all existing derivative positions (both cleared and uncleared swaps) be reported to a swap data repository[4] within 180 days of its enactment, and all new positions (both cleared and uncleared) starting 90 days after the enactment (or an alternative legislated period). The repository, as the recipient of the trade information, will be tasked with providing data to the regulatory agencies (including foreign and international agencies, if applicable), to minimize systemic risk, and to publish certain aggregate market information (trading and clearing in major swap categories and participants and developments in new products) to the public twice a year. In addition to this transparency at the position level, the Act requires *real-time public reporting*, meaning "to report data relating to a swap transaction, including price and volume, as soon as technologically practicable after the time at which the transaction has been executed." Such public reporting will, however, not include counterparty or customer information, and will also have a delay exemption for "block trades" (to be defined by the Commission for particular markets and contracts), taking account of the likely impact of disclosure of such trades on market liquidity.

Bankruptcy-Related Issues

6. Bankruptcy exemption: Under the Act, a security-based swap is treated as a sale and repurchase transaction in case of bankruptcy of one of the counterparties. Thus, derivatives contracts will continue to enjoy the exemption from bankruptcy of counterparties—as in the case of sale and repurchase transactions (repos)—as far as netting arrangements and segregation of collateral are concerned.

7. Collateral segregation: For cleared derivatives transactions, the Act requires both segregation of a counterparty's collateral and prohibition of commingling of such collateral with own funds, effectively requiring that a customer's collateral be treated, dealt with, and accounted for strictly as belonging only to the customer. For uncleared derivative transactions, the Act requires the segregation of initial margin, but not of variation margin payments (i.e., daily margin requirements based on mark-to-market changes), upon request of a counterparty. If a counterparty does not ask for its collateral to be segregated in an uncleared derivative transaction, the Act requires a swap dealer[5] or a major swap participant[6] to report on a quarterly basis regarding the back-office procedures of the swap dealer or major swap participant in compliance with the agreement between the parties with respect to the handling of collateral. Also, there is no requirement that a counterparty request to segregate margin be made at the time the swap is executed.

Trading and Risk Mitigation

8. Systemically important institutions in derivatives markets: Major swap participants and swap dealers will be required to register with the Commission, which, in turn, will define what constitutes a "substantial position," that is, the threshold that the Commission determines to be prudent for the effective monitoring, management, and oversight of entities that are systemically important or that can significantly impact the U.S. financial system. In addition, major swap participants and swap dealers must meet periodic reporting requirements, minimum capital requirements, minimum initial and variation margin requirements (which, in certain instances, may include noncash collateral), and business conduct standards. In particular, major swap participants and swap dealers will be subject to capital requirements based on their total risk—including their uncleared transactions—by a prudential regulator (or by the Commission in the absence of a prudential regulator).

Unlike some of the prior versions of the legislation, the Act does not provide an explicit exemption from the margin requirement for end users. Nonetheless, in a letter from Chairs Christopher Dodd and Blanche Lincoln to Chairs Barney Frank and Colin Peterson (June 30, 2010), Senators Dodd and Lincoln expressed their view that the legislation was not intended to impose margin requirements on end users.

9. Position limits, position accountability, and large trade reporting: The Act requires the Commission to establish limits, taking account of the hedge-exemption provisions, on the size of a position in any swap that may be held by any person or institution. In establishing such limits, the Commission is authorized to aggregate positions in (1) any security or loan or group of securities or loans on which the swap is based, or (2) any security or group or index of securities, the price, yield, value, or volatility of which, or of which any interest therein, is the basis for a material term of such swap and related group or index of securities. The Commission may exempt, conditionally or unconditionally, any person or class of persons, any swap or class of swaps, or any transaction or class of transactions from the prescribed position limits. In addition to limits that may be established by the Commission, the Act also requires self-regulatory organizations to establish and enforce position limits or position accountability requirements in any security-based swap that may be held by their members.

10. De minimis investment requirement: It should be noted that derivatives trading activity does not necessarily qualify as "proprietary trading" as far as the Volcker Rule is concerned. Under this rule, banks retain the right to engage in hedge fund and private equity fund investments subject to a cap limiting those investments to 3 percent of the funds' capital and no more than 3 percent of the banks' Tier 1 capital. Importantly, the banking entity is prohibited from bailing out these investment funds in case of their insolvency.[7] Since derivatives are not necessarily included in the activities restricted by this de minimis investment requirement, they are also not subject to the additional capital requirements, nor to the quantitative limits applicable to proprietary trading under the Act (unless the appropriate federal bank agency, the SEC or the CFTC, determines that such additional requirements or limitations are appropriate to protect the safety and soundness of the banking entities engaged in such activities). Of course, derivative positions are subject to the requirements stipulated under the derivatives reforms, as described earlier.

11. Leverage limitation requirement: The Act requires the Federal Reserve to impose a maximum debt-to-equity leverage ratio of 15:1 on any financial company that the Council determines poses a "grave threat" to the U.S. financial stability. The leverage and risk-based capital requirements applicable to insured depository institutions, depository institution holding companies, and systemically important nonbank financial companies must be not "less than" the "generally applicable risk-based capital requirements" and the "generally applicable leverage capital requirements," and not "quantitatively lower than" the requirements that were in effect for insured depository institutions as of the date the Act was enacted. However, it is unclear how leverage undertaken through derivatives contracts will affect the adoption of the maximum debt-to-equity ratio of 15:1 for systemically important firms.[8] The Act does not specify how the implicit leverage in derivatives contracts would be taken into account in the calculation of the overall leverage ratio.

12. The Lincoln Amendment (Section 716): The originally proposed Lincoln Amendment would have prevented insured depository institutions from engaging in derivatives activity by requiring them to spin off this activity. The Dodd-Frank Act enacts a diluted version that allows insured depository institutions to engage in "bona fide hedging and traditional bank activities" on their books—that is, hedging transactions and positions in plain-vanilla interest rate, FX, and centrally cleared CDSs. All other derivatives activity can be managed by the depository institutions only in independent and well-capitalized "swap entities" as affiliates (swap dealers, major swap participants, exchanges, and clearinghouses).

13. Prohibition on lender of last resort support:[9] This aspect of the Act constitutes the most far-reaching implication in terms of the resolution of derivatives exposures in case of insolvency. The Act imposes that from two years after the Act becomes effective (with some flexibility for extension up to one additional year) "no Federal assistance (e.g., advances from any Federal Reserve credit facility or discount window, FDIC insurance, or guarantees) may be provided to any swaps entity with respect to any of its activities." However, the Financial Stability Oversight Council can override the prohibition on Federal Reserve assistance with a two-thirds majority vote. Another important exception is made for affiliates of insured depository institutions: "The prohibition on Federal assistance contained does not apply to and shall not prevent an insured depository institution from having or establishing an affiliate which is a swaps entity, as long as such insured depository institution is part of a bank holding company, or savings and loan holding company, that is supervised by the Federal Reserve and such swaps entity affiliate complies with sections 23A and 23B of the Federal Reserve Act and such other requirements as the CFTC or the SEC, as appropriate, and the Board of Governors of the Federal Reserve System, may determine to be necessary and appropriate." To be eligible for such assistance, however, the insured depository institution must be engaged in only "bona fide hedging and traditional bank activities" (see point 12). The Lincoln Amendment (Section 716), besides allowing insured depository institutions to engage in bona fide hedging and traditional bank activities, also permits them to engage in separately well-capitalized swap entities as affiliates. The federal assistance to insured institutions, however, requires such affiliates, if any, to be spun off, but allows the insured depository institution up to 24 months to divest the swaps entity or cease the activities that require registration as a swaps entity.[10]

Extraterritorial Enforcement and International Coordination

14. Foreign platforms (boards of trade): The Act provides the Commission authority to require registration of foreign boards of trade that provide direct access to U.S. market participants to their electronic trading and order matching system. In adopting specific rules and regulations, the Commission is directed to consider whether comparable regulation exists in the foreign board of trade's home country. If offering linked contracts, which are contracts that are priced against a contract that is traded on a U.S. exchange, for which the Commission has not granted direct access permission, a foreign board of trade must adopt daily trading information requirements, record keeping, position limits, and oversight requirements that are comparable to those on U.S. exchanges. In addition, foreign boards of trade would be required to have the authority to liquidate or reduce market positions to protect against market manipulation and must notify the Commission should it adjust its reporting requirements or position limits or any other area of interest to the Commission.

15. International harmonization: The Act provides for the right levels of international harmonization in terms of setting standards for the regulation of derivatives and information sharing about derivatives positions: "In order to promote effective and consistent global regulation of swaps and security-based swaps, the Commodity Futures Trading Commission, the Securities and Exchange Commission, and the prudential regulators, as appropriate, shall consult and coordinate with foreign regulatory authorities on the establishment of consistent international standards with respect to the regulation (including fees) of swaps, security-based swaps, swap entities, and security-based swap entities and may agree to such information-sharing arrangements as may be deemed to be necessary or appropriate in the public interest or for the protection of investors, swap counterparties, and security-based swap counterparties."

In addition to these main issues, the Act requires studies to be conducted on the effectiveness of position limits as a regulatory tool, international harmonization of margining standards for swaps, and the possibility of developing algorithmic language to standardize electronic reporting of derivatives, among others. These are listed in detail in Appendix A, along with a table providing a time line of these future studies.

13.3 EVALUATION OF PROPOSED REFORMS

The main market failures in the OTC derivatives market are the buildup of excess leverage, opacity, and difficulties of resolution when a large counterparty gets into trouble. Does the Wall Street Transparency and Accountability part of the Dodd-Frank Act on financial reforms address these issues? Our overall assessment is that while there are a lot of positives, a measured evaluation can be made only after specific details of implementation of the reforms are laid out by regulators over the next few years.

It should be noted at the outset that there are several aspects of the Dodd-Frank Act that seek to contain risk taking by systemically important institutions, not all of which are directly aimed at derivatives activity (for example, the Volcker Rule and leverage limitation described in Section 13.2, points 10 and 11). Clearly, hedge funds, as a group, have a significant presence in the derivatives markets. Hence, for some banking firms, such as Goldman Sachs, which has significant investments in hedge funds, the de minimis investment restrictions under the Volcker Rule could have a major impact on their aggregate level of derivatives exposure. If estimated correctly, the leverage limitation requirement of 15:1 would also restrict overall derivatives exposure of banks.

We focus our discussion, however, on those aspects of the Act that *directly* address derivatives activity that would remain on banks' books even after passage of the Act. These are: (1) derivatives that are standardized and have reasonable trading volumes would be considered for central clearing, and those that continue to trade OTC would be regulated in a "comparable" manner (points 1 through 4, 8, and 9); (2) transparency of all derivatives trades (point 5); and (3) bankruptcy issues relating to derivatives, the modified Lincoln Amendment, and the restriction of federal assistance for swap entities (points 6, 7, 12, and 13). The Act's proposals concerning international harmonization (points 14 and 15) are, by and large, reasonable, and we discuss them only briefly in concluding remarks.

First and foremost, many important details concerning clearing requirements for derivatives remain unspecified and subject to further examination by various regulators, including the SEC, the CFTC, and the secretary of the Treasury. Over the next year or so, regulators will decide the particular types of derivatives that would be required to be centrally cleared. At one level, these tasks require detailed market knowledge and are not suitable for congressional debate and legislation. At another level, however, they will require significant human resources to be allocated to the relevant regulators (especially the CFTC) and will enlarge the gray area of regulatory discretion, which will inevitably lead to significant lobbying efforts from the industry. Hence, the new legislation places a great deal of faith in—and burden on—the prudential regulators to get it right. Given the existing pressures facing regulators and the substantial new burden imposed on them under the Act, it is not obvious how they will carry out their responsibilities. Furthermore, the challenges of recruiting appropriate talent to discharge these duties remain daunting.

The exact implementation of clearing provisions should be such that it contains the moral hazard of the clearinghouses, given their systemic importance. This moral hazard may arise when clearinghouses would take risks for their own private profit; as they become more systemically important, we run the risk of a replay of the recent crisis should the clearinghouses become the future government-sponsored enterprises (GSEs). Therefore, although their limited risk choices relative to private institutions make the moral hazard issue easier to deal with, given their systemic importance it is critical that their risk standards be constantly maintained. A consistent margin requirement across clearinghouses is also critical for avoiding a competitive race to the bottom. Otherwise, risky counterparties could migrate to clearinghouses that have the least stringent requirements; this would have the undesirable effect of concentrating systemic risk, rather than distributing it across multiple clearinghouses.

At the very outset, however, exception is potentially provided for not expanding the scope of the derivatives reform to FX derivatives. The exact guiding principle behind this exception is not spelled out, but the proposal presumably reflects the fact that banks deal in FX derivatives primarily to help their customers manage their business risks. Whether to regulate these derivatives is to be decided by the secretary of the Treasury after a detailed evaluation of the risks involved. Still, it is unclear why FX derivatives have been singled out, since a similar argument—that they aid hedging risks for ultimate users who have an offsetting business risk—could be made for a large fraction of overall positions in interest rate and commodity derivatives.

Concerning the Act's exemption for hedging transactions, we will provide direct evidence in this chapter that the primary systemic risk in the OTC derivatives market lies with dealers and not with end users. Hence, we endorse the Act's separate treatment of end-user positions. The Act, however, leaves out one rather important detail. The exempted positions must demonstrably be so for hedging purposes, and this should be verified on a regular basis through an audit procedure by the regulators, combined with the ability to penalize in case of unsatisfactory audit results (what we call the "audit and penalize" principle). Recognizing the limits to efficacy of such auditing in the case of large and complex organizations, we recommend that large swap participants, even in the end-user space, be subject to similar transparency requirements as dealers to avoid regulatory arbitrage of large scale and dimensions.

The Act relies heavily on margin requirements as the first line of defense against the buildup of leverage through derivatives. In particular, clearinghouses are required to charge margins such that they can withstand the failure of their largest exposure among the various members. Potentially, this is a sound way of determining margin requirements—rather than requiring that margins be raised uniformly across all positions on the clearinghouse. The simple rationale is that the Act will effectively require clearinghouses to ask members to fully collateralize their largest exposure in a given risk class (e.g., the largest exposure in single-name CDSs). Assuming that it is highly unlikely that two single names will default on the same day, this would mean the clearinghouse is reasonably well protected most of the time, and yet offers substantial collateral efficiency to its members. Indeed, requiring fully collateralized largest exposures might be a better way of imposing position limits (which the Act recommends for consideration following an evaluation study of their potential efficacy). The implicit position limit in this case is based on members' ability to generate collateral rather than an exogenous quantity restriction.

Recognizing the scope for creation of OTC clones simply to get around clearing requirements, the Act requires the regulators to charge margins for OTC positions also, in a manner that would be similar—even if not identical—for cleared varieties of these positions, and also empowers them to take adequate actions against evasive positions. However, there are likely to be several OTC products that are customized and without any similar cleared products. On this front, expecting regulators to get the margins right for each product's risk is likely to meet disappointment. It will also give rise to a "catch me if you can" game between industry and the regulators, not to mention the substantial workload on the regulators to react to changes in derivative positions of individual dealers in a timely manner.

Here, transparency in the OTC derivatives space could play a vital role. Fortunately, the Act does well on this front. *The Act's biggest strength lies in legislating counterparty-level transparency for the regulators, price-volume-level transparency for all market participants, and aggregated transparency of positions and players in different derivatives markets (twice a year).* By requiring that this transparency standard be applied right away to all OTC derivatives and not just to centrally cleared ones, the Act helps ensure that regulators will have the required information on interconnectedness of financial institutions in future systemic crises. Also, the time delay between execution and reporting of "block trades" that the Act permits is reasonable, as it will allow market makers sufficient time to unwind a position before the information about that position becomes public and will not deter them from supplying liquidity to the market.[11] Nevertheless, the transparency standard could be improved (as we will explain in detail) by gathering information on: (1) collateral backing different contracts (so as to ascertain the counterparty risk "exposure"), (2) potential exposures in stress scenarios rather than just current exposures that tend to be small in good times, and (3) the largest such potential exposures of a derivatives player to different counterparties. Some aggregated versions but at the level of each institution (that is, the largest potential uncollateralized exposures of each institution without revealing names of its counterparties or customers) should be made available to all market participants. In principle, with such a transparency standard, the counterparty risk externality could be mitigated and each derivative contract would better reflect—through price and collateral requirements—the counterparty risk arising from other trades and exposures of the involved parties.[12]

Consider next the modified Lincoln Amendment. The underlying rationale for requiring derivatives to be separately capitalized is to ease the resolution of the bank holding company that gets into trouble: The derivatives affiliate could simply be spun off, given its adequate capitalization. The rationale for exempting plain-vanilla interest rate, FX, and credit derivatives from being separately capitalized is that these products are currently employed in significant quantities by banks for the purpose of hedging risks on their books—of loans, global transactions, and counterparty risk in bilateral contracts. However, there is no explicit recognition of this hedging motive, and thus no recognition of its natural corollary that regulators "audit" over time, "penalizing" abuses and requiring that nonhedging transactions be better capitalized or moved to the well-capitalized subsidiary. *Not requiring—or even recommending—"audit and penalize" treatment of exemptions that are based on hedging motives is an important weakness of the Act.* It also raises the possibility of potential arbitrage by banks of the Act's intentions to contain leverage, for instance, by establishing large derivatives positions in the plain-vanilla segment on the bank's own balance sheet. And in case of a large bank's failure, if large uncollateralized exposures are discovered to be in this plain-vanilla space, the system may face a rerun of the Bear Stearns, Lehman, and AIG episodes: Yes, there would be the well-capitalized derivatives subsidiary, but all the risk might in fact be on the bank's main book!

In our assessment, however, the Act's proposals for derivatives are the weakest in the area of bankruptcy resolution relating to derivatives and swap entities. There are three issues that raise concerns.

First, the restriction on federal assistance to swap entities, including clearinghouses, seems to rule out an important mechanism to deal ex post with systemic risk. The Act should recognize that once most derivative contracts move to centralized clearing platforms, clearinghouses will become important concentrations of systemic risk. While their capitalization levels can be monitored, there is always the small chance that those levels will prove inadequate when there is an unexpected shock to a large member or to several markets at once. In this case, there should be little hesitation to provide temporary liquidity assistance to the clearinghouse and resolve its situation in due course. But without such assistance, capital markets may freeze in the same way they froze when Bear Stearns, Lehman, and AIG experienced problems. While the Act potentially allows for federal assistance to swap entities if the Council managing systemic risk approves so by a two-thirds vote, this is unnecessary discretionary uncertainty in the midst of a crisis and may cause costly delays in an emergency similar to September 2008.

Second, in the event that a clearinghouse gets to the point of insolvency, the Act explicitly prohibits its positions from being transferred to another clearinghouse. While every effort should be made to produce an orderly resolution, if there is a sufficiently healthy clearinghouse that manages similar products to those of the failing one, it might be far more orderly to have this clearinghouse deal with some—if not all—of the outstanding positions, especially the ones that may be difficult to liquidate or close out sufficiently quickly. Again, the Act seems to overly restrict ex post resolution options for stress scenarios at a clearinghouse. Even under more normal circumstances, transfer of positions across clearinghouses may in fact reduce systemic risk. Hence, a prohibition on such transfers may not be prudent.

Third, as we argue elsewhere in the book in the case of sale and repurchase agreements (repo markets), there is a case for softening the bankruptcy exemption for derivative transactions in scenarios where there is a systemically important counterparty that is going bankrupt. By granting exemption from bankruptcy—primarily from automatic stay on a secured or collat-eralized part of the transaction—derivative counterparties effectively ob-tain a short-term, immediately demandable claim on the distressed firm. The derivatives positions then become equivalent to those of short-term creditors who join the run. In all systemic crises—the panics before the formation of the FDIC in 1934, the Continental Illinois failure of 1984, the collapse of Long-Term Capital Management in 1998, and the crisis of 2007 to 2009—ultimately short-term creditors of distressed firms had to be stayed (respectively) through suspension of demandable deposits in commercial bank clearinghouse certificates, a government bailout, a Federal Reserve–orchestrated conversion of debt into equity, or a federal backstop. All this was to avoid fire-sale liquidations and liquidity dry-ups in markets. While the benefit of bankruptcy exemption is clear—it reduces counterparty risk and contagion risk, in turn generating greater liquidity for trades in good times—it comes at the expense of inducing more precipitous runs, and when these occur for systemically important firms, this invariably compro-mises taxpayer funds and entrenches the too-big-to-fail problem. A systemic exception to the bankruptcy exemption for derivatives for a prespecified period would buy the regulators some time to plan for orderly resolutions.

Leaving aside the uncertainty of exact implementation and the few crit-ical weaknesses we have flagged, we believe that, in principle, many of the proposed changes have the potential to stabilize the derivatives markets and improve their functioning and their regulation over time. By requir-ing standardized products (which trade in large volumes and are sufficiently commoditized) to trade on exchanges or centralized clearinghouses (existing or newly formed), the Act makes progress on the front of containing lever-age buildup through OTC derivatives positions. By requiring that not just cleared but even OTC derivatives be subject to high levels of transparency, the Act goes quite some distance in reducing the systemic risk of the OTC derivatives business and the systemic costs of bankruptcy of a major market participant. However, implementing these changes all at once may prove to be a major task. Hence, as a cautious step-by-step approach to getting the details right, *our overall recommendation is to start with applying changes to the credit derivatives market that was the primary source of OTC market stress in this crisis.* Following this, the costs and benefits of the migration from OTC to centralized clearing can be considered and evaluated for other markets, such as interest rate, FX, and commodity derivatives. The main reason for this view is that the credit derivatives market is where most of the systemic consequences manifested themselves in the current crisis and where the underlying risk transfers are largely between financial firms, while other markets such as interest rate and FX derivatives were largely unaffected in the crisis and represent a larger amount of risk transfer between financial firms and end users.

Having provided our overall assessment of the derivatives reforms under the Dodd-Frank Act, we proceed as follows. In Section 13.4, we discuss the specifics of moving OTC markets to centralized exchanges or clearinghouses, the trade-off between relying on margin requirements versus transparency, why it is important to deal with the risk of dealers first, and why the proposed reforms would help end users. In addition, we discuss the systemic risk that arises due to setting up centralized clearing platforms and whether the reforms adequately provide for dealing with this risk. We conclude in Section 13.5 with a look ahead at how the reforms may shape global derivatives arena in the future. In Appendix C, we also discuss the issue of sovereign credit derivatives and whether there is any need to ban them as has been called for in some parts of Europe.

13.4 CLEARING, MARGINS, TRANSPARENCY, AND SYSTEMIC RISK OF CLEARINGHOUSES

Migration to Centralized Clearing Should Start with Credit Derivatives

The growth of OTC derivatives in recent years, particularly in the CDS market, makes them top candidates for proposed regulations.[13] A key issue with any derivative contract is that of collateral (or margin) requirements. If collateral requirements are too low, then counterparty risk issues manifest themselves; in contrast, if they are too high, they may remove any advantage of the derivative relative to managing risks simply by holding cash reserves. As such, setting the precise level of collateral requirements will ultimately be a practice that evolves over time in each exchange or clearinghouse (possibly also coordinated across exchanges and clearinghouses). However, some guidelines are necessary, especially as to how to margin the many customized CDSs that will continue to remain OTC.

We would like to stress that the risk exposure for credit derivatives is fundamentally of a different nature from that associated with traditional derivative products, such as interest rate swaps. Like other swaps, the mark-to-market value of a single-name CDS, a type of a credit derivative, fluctuates from day to day as the market's assessment of the underlying entity's credit risk varies. Although these daily fluctuations are similar to daily price movements for other derivatives and can be handled adequately within a standard margining system, the potential liability of the protection seller to its counterparty upon the occurrence of a credit event suddenly jumps to as much as 100 percent of the contract's notional principal. In nearly every case, this liability will greatly exceed the value of the collateral posted to cover daily margin flow variations and will leave the protection buyer exposed to significant counterparty risk.

Under central clearing, this *jump to default* liability would ultimately lie with the clearinghouse. One possible way to eliminate the counterparty risk, then, would be to require collateral equal to the full notional principal amount on all of a protection seller's swaps, but that would be prohibitively expensive. A more feasible and cheaper alternative that would also eliminate most of counterparty risk in the case of a credit event would be to require the protection seller to post margin equal to 100 percent of its single *largest* exposure to an individual reference entity. This additional margin would guarantee that the protection seller could always cover the potential liability from any *single* credit event that it has sold protection against. Only in the case of simultaneous defaults by multiple entities covered by the same protection seller would there be any residual counterparty risk. This margin requirement can be considered a *concentration charge* and would be in addition to posting the margin required to cover daily fluctuations in the values of all of the protection seller's open positions in the absence of a credit event.[14]

Another feature of CDS contracts that distinguishes them from other derivatives is that there are no obvious sellers of protection who are naturally hedged by other positions as end users. This is in contrast to FX and interest rate derivatives, where there could be end users whose positions are opposite to each other, so that the hedging activity actually reduces systemic risk. Furthermore, CDS trades inherently feature wrong-way exposures for protection buyers, as credit risk is tied to the macroeconomic cycle so that it materializes precisely when the counterparty (the protection seller) has also most likely become riskier. Hence, CDS regulation *must* move first, since the materialization of counterparty risk in CDSs, and potentially systemic risk in the financial sector, is likely to coincide with an economic downturn. A pragmatic approach for rolling out proposed regulation would be gradually to move single-name and index CDSs first to central clearing while adopting margin requirements, as discussed earlier for those CDSs that remain OTC. To minimize regulatory overload, other derivative markets could be added over time. Moreover, while CDS reforms are being put in place, regulators should require disclosures by the concerned parties to understand the quality of bilateral margining and risk management in interest rate, currency, and commodities derivatives. Based on such information, policymakers would be able to better assess whether and what kind of additional regulation is needed in these markets.

Margin Requirements versus Transparency

Does the Act fully deal with the difficulty of opacity in OTC derivatives markets? The answer to this question is somewhat mixed. On the one hand, it is clear that single-name CDSs on corporations and sovereigns will likely move to central clearing platforms (as has already happened to some extent through industry-initiated efforts) and possibly over time move to exchanges. This would significantly reduce the opacity of these products. Nevertheless, since the bill requires transparency primarily for cleared derivatives, the status of uncleared derivatives markets remains open. Instead of requiring mandatory disclosures of these remaining OTC positions, the Act puts the burden on regulators to impose margins or capital requirements, hoping that they would be large enough to contain risks, and, wherever possible, to get trading to move to centrally cleared products.

Before discussing the Dodd-Frank Act's proposal to require margins for uncleared derivatives, let us review the current use of collateral by dealers to mitigate counterparty credit risks. The overall picture that emerges is that while there is clearly a substantial amount of collateral being posted on OTC derivative contracts between counterparties, the uncollateralized portions remain large enough to cause concern about counterparty risk and the attendant systemic risk issues.

More specific details on the state of collateral use in the OTC derivatives market emerge from the examination by the International Swaps and Derivatives Association (ISDA) of the state of the global marketplace for collateral in recent years. The ISDA conducted its first survey of collateral use in the OTC derivatives industry among its 67 member firms, including the top five banks—Goldman Sachs, Citigroup, JPMorgan Chase, Bank of America, and Morgan Stanley—in 2000. Since that time, the reported number of collateral agreements in place has grown from about 12,000 to almost 151,000, while the estimated amount of collateral in circulation has grown from about $200 billion to an estimated $2.1 trillion at the end of 2008 and an estimated amount of almost $4 trillion at the end of 2009.

Not only has there been a continuing trend toward increased collateral coverage, in terms of both amount of credit exposure and the number of trades (Figures 13.1 and 13.2), but the use of cash collateral has also continued to grow in importance among most financial firms, and now stands at almost 84 percent of collateral received and 83 percent of collateral delivered, up from 78 percent and 83 percent, respectively, at the end of 2008. The use of government securities as collateral also grew. The increase in cash and government securities was balanced by a decline in the use of other forms of collateral, such as corporate bonds and equities. These trends are a reflection of the heightened demand for high-quality collateral post–Bear

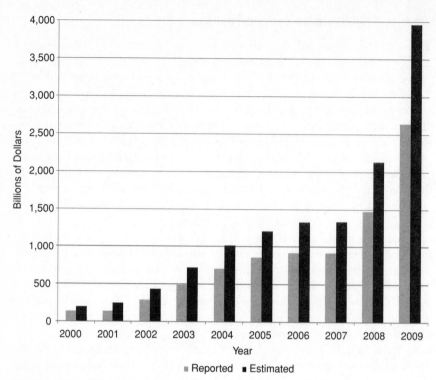

FIGURE 13.1 Growth of Value of Total Reported and Estimated Collateral, 2000 to 2009 ($ Billions)

Source: International Swaps and Derivatives Association, Margin Surveys 2000 to 2009.

Stearns and especially after Lehman's collapse, while the supply of collateral has been reduced due to the hoarding of collateral as reserves by dealers (e.g., Goldman Sachs).[15] By some counts, according to an article in *Barron's*, fees earned on lending collateral contribute about a third of dealers' overall profits on derivatives trades.[16]

When collateralized transactions are categorized by size, there is a significant variation in the counterparty mix relating to collateral arrangements (see Figure 13.3). Most collateral agreements among large firms are with hedge funds and institutional investors (50 percent), followed by corporations (15 percent), banks (13 percent), and other (21 percent). At the other extreme, small financial firms—the survey respondents with the least number of collateral agreements outstanding—deal mostly with other banks.[17] Approximately one-half of the collateral agreements at medium-sized financial firms are with other banks and corporations. Medium firms also deal with

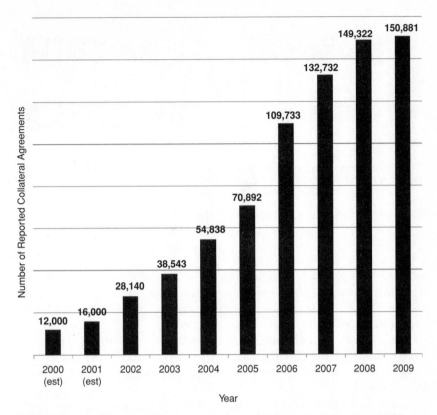

FIGURE 13.2 Growth of Reported Collateral Agreements, 2000 to 2009
Source: International Swaps and Derivatives Association, Margin Surveys
2000 to 2009.

hedge funds and institutional investors, but to a relatively smaller extent
than large firms. Other counterparties, which include commodity trading
firms, special purpose vehicles, sovereigns, supranationals, private banking
clients, and municipalities, represent 21 percent of counterparties at large
firms, 10 percent at medium firms, and only 1 percent at small firms.

In addition to this substantial variation in the nature of counterparties
involved in collateral arrangements, the percentage of trades subject to collateral arrangements varies across different types of underlying contracts (see
Table 13.1). These differences are, in part, reflective of the variation in the
risk of the underlying trades and counterparties, as well as the specific size
of the market segment and its development. As illustrated, credit and fixed
income are the most collateralized types of OTC derivative contracts (fea-
turing 60 to 70 percent of trade volume and exposure that is collateralized),

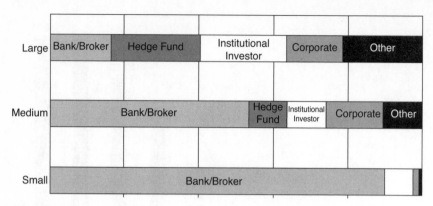

FIGURE 13.3 Counterparties of Collateralized Transactions
Source: International Swaps and Derivatives Association, Margin Surveys
2000 to 2009.

whereas FX, equity, and commodities show less collateralization (between
45 and 50 percent of trade volume and exposure). This likely reflects the
fact that FX and commodities derivatives are used more often for hedging
purposes and have end users as one counterparty, whereas fixed income
and credit have a higher component of dealer-to-dealer trades. However,
closer scrutiny of the detailed data, which unfortunately are not readily
available today, would permit a more granular characterization of these
major markets.

Given this evidence on collateralization of OTC derivatives, recent International Monetary Fund (IMF) research on the counterparty risk stemming
from OTC derivatives finds that a large part of the counterparty risk in
this market remains undercollateralized (i.e., up to $2 trillion) relative to
the risk in the system.[18] This estimate is close to the $2 trillion net credit
exposure figure presented by the Bank for International Settlements (BIS)
in its semiannual derivatives survey,[19] but is higher than a recent ISDA
survey cited by the BIS in its September 2009 quarterly review that puts the
volume of undercollateralized derivatives at $1 trillion. Using information
from the 10-Q quarterly statements, the IMF report estimates that the five
key U.S. banks mentioned before are jointly carrying almost $500 billion
in OTC derivative payables exposure as of the third quarter of 2009. The
five largest European banks—Deutsche Bank, Barclays, UBS, Royal Bank of
Scotland (RBS), and Credit Suisse—had about $600 billion to $700 billion
in undercollateralized risk (measured by residual derivative payables) as of
December 2008.

This residual exposure arises for two reasons, according to the IMF
report. First, sovereigns, as well as AAA-rated insurers, corporations, large
banks, and multilateral institutions "do not post adequate collateral since

TABLE 13.1 Trade Volume and Exposure Collateralized, 2003–2009 Survey

	Trade Volume Requiring Collateral							Exposure Collateralized						
	2009	2008	2007	2006	2005	2004	2003	2009	2008	2007	2006	2005	2004	2003
OTC Derivatives	65	63	59	59	56	51	30	66	65	59	63	55	52	29
Fixed Income	63	68	62	57	58	58	53	71	66	65	57	58	55	48
FX	36	44	36	37	32	24	21	48	55	44	44	43	37	28
Equity	52	52	51	46	51	45	27	52	56	56	56	61	52	24
Metals	39	38	37	37	31	24	18	47	41	34	34	44	40	18
Energy	39	40	42	48	36	26	16	47	39	41	44	37	30	15
Credit	71	74	66	70	59	45	30	66	66	66	62	58	39	25

Source: International Swaps and Derivatives Association, Margin Surveys 2000 to 2009.

they are viewed by large complex financial institutions as privileged and (apparently) safe clients." Second, based on the bilateral nature of the contracts, dealers have agreed not to mandate adequate collateral for dealer-to-dealer positions. In fact, creditworthy dealers typically post no collateral to each other for these contracts.

It is estimated in the report that if the two-thirds of OTC contracts that are "standardized" were shifted into clearinghouses, as policymakers propose, banks would need to find over $200 billion in initial margins and guarantee funds: An extra $80 billion would be needed to cover clearing of CDSs; $40 billion to $50 billion for interest rate swaps; and $90 billion for equities, foreign exchanges, and commodities. In addition, if regulators charged an ad hoc capital levy of 10 percent to 20 percent on the remaining third of (nonstandard) OTC contracts retained by dealers on their own books, this would require the banks to hold an additional $70 billion to $140 billion of capital to reflect these risks adequately. Moreover, in such a scenario, nonstandardized derivatives could no longer be netted against standardized ones, which implies that banks would need to hold even more capital against nonstandardized contracts to immunize them against default. An estimate of the additional capital to be raised by banks would be in the range of $150 billion to $250 billion.

While some increase in initial collateral requirements seems unavoidable given the manifestations of counterparty risk witnessed in the recent crisis, the lack of adequate netting of collateral across different platforms and products raises the questions of whether margins or capital requirements are the best mechanism to deal with remaining OTC contracts and whether they can even be designed effectively. At one extreme, it is clear that the current undercollateralization of uncleared derivatives poses substantial systemic risk. At the other, where uncleared OTC positions are required to be fully collateralized, counterparties would most likely find it cheaper to take on basis risk by trading in standardized products that are cleared rather than the customized ones they desire.[20] Hence, if the goal is to shrink the size of opaque OTC markets, regulators can simply raise their margin requirements to prohibitive levels, effectively making these products unattractive to hedgers. In reality, in many cases, customized OTC products used for hedging by end users are unlikely to have any centrally cleared counterparts. How should the regulators deal with such products? We know that elsewhere in bank regulation, capital requirements designed by regulators have fallen woefully short of containing systemic risk and leverage, as they are too coarse and easily arbitraged. There is no reason to believe that the outcome here would be any different. A solution that does not pose large systemic risk, while at the same time making the use of customized OTC derivatives cost effective, is therefore required.

Toward a Transparency Standard

A better solution than increased margin requirements would therefore be to require transparency of the exposures of dealers and large swap players to all OTC products, not just centrally cleared ones, and at regular intervals. The information overhead can be minimized by requiring all dealers as well as large swap players to produce frequent risk reports on their OTC derivatives positions as follows:

- *Classification of exposures* into:
  - Product types (such as single-name or index CDSs, interest rate swaps, currency swaps, etc.).
  - Type of counterparty (bank, broker-dealer, corporation, monoline, etc.).
  - Maturity of contracts.
  - Credit rating of counterparties.
- *Size of exposures* should be reported:
  - As gross (maximum notional exposure).
  - As net (taking account of bilateral netting arrangements).
  - As uncollateralized net (recognizing collateral posted by counter-parties).
  - In fair-value terms (to account for mark-to-market changes).
  - By major currency categories.
- Uncollateralized net exposures should be further modified and stated also as *potential exposures* based on stress tests that take account of replacement risk for the exposures, assuming severe market conditions such as replacement time of two to four weeks.
- *Concentration reports* should be provided, and detail the aforementioned information for the entity's largest counterparty exposures (say, the largest 5 or 10) that account for a substantial proportion of the total exposure, say 75 percent.
- *Margin call report* that lists the additional collateral liabilities of the firm as:
  - Total additional liability in case the firm experiences one, two, or more notch downgrades.
  - The largest such liabilities aggregated by different counterparties (e.g., the five largest).

Although this list appears to involve a large amount of information, the costs of such disclosure are not likely to be that onerous. Investment banks already maintain this information for internal risk management purposes; indeed, they publish some of it in their quarterly reports (see Appendix B for an overview of Goldman Sachs's and Citigroup's disclosure levels as of August 2010). Therefore, it would not be a huge additional burden for them to disclose this information to regulators in a standardized format at frequent intervals, say monthly. Some aggregated versions that respect customer confidentiality can then be made transparent to markets at large, for example on a quarterly basis, to help enhance market discipline against uncollateralized exposure buildup.[21] In particular, market transparency of counterparty exposures will create a tiering of financial firms in each OTC market, making it possible for new trades to be directed toward the least risky counterparty.

Overall, we recommend that the effective functioning of the OTC markets should rely more on transparency and less on rules designed by regulators, such as those based on capital, collateral, or position limits, which could prove to be too rigid in some circumstances and could invite regulatory arbitrage.[22] This would be more in line with the spirit of market-based risk mitigation mechanisms that may be more flexible than regulation by fiat. However, even if regulators were to design margin requirements themselves, which may be less desirable, the proposed OTC transparency would still help. For instance, if regulators required that exposures to the (e.g., five) largest counterparties of each financial firm be sufficiently well collateralized, then they would have effectively mitigated a significant part of the systemic risk in OTC markets at a reasonable cost. And in case of failures, regulators would know the exposures with precision and could take anticipatory action to contain systemic contagion, since they would possess the necessary information ahead of time.

Deal with the Dealers First

The main participants in the overall derivatives landscape are large financial firms: commercial and investment banks, mutual funds, pension funds, hedge funds, and insurance companies. For instance, in the United States, the derivatives market is dominated by the financial industry and five banks in particular. JPMorgan Chase, Bank of America, Goldman Sachs, Citigroup, and Morgan Stanley account for more than 96 percent of the total industry notional amount and about 80 percent of industry net current credit exposure, as per Fitch Ratings' July 2009 report. Figure 13.4 depicts the shares of these top five banks in different markets and Figure 13.5 shows the outstanding notional amounts of derivative contracts by each bank, with JPMorgan Chase alone accounting for more than 30 percent of market trading volume.

It is clear from these numbers that reform of OTC derivatives should first and foremost be applied, and with some urgency, to these major dealer banks. Importantly, these banks not only serve as intermediaries and dealers

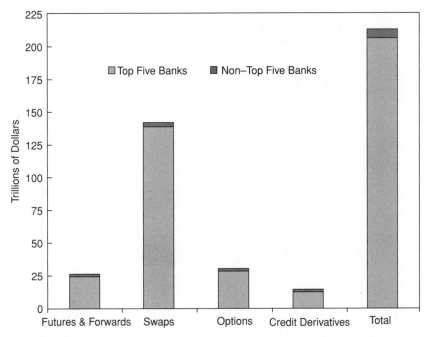

FIGURE 13.4 Concentration of Derivative Contracts—All Commercial Banks, 4Q09 (\$ Trillions)
Source: Call Reports, Office of the Comptroller of the Currency, 4Q09.

in the derivatives market, but they also buy and sell derivatives to manage risks on their own balance sheets, and to undertake speculative positions in their proprietary trading desks. Furthermore, they directly or indirectly control several other investment vehicles, such as asset management/private banking entities, including hedge funds, which are likely to be significant users of OTC derivative products. Current reporting standards are insufficient to separate both the *proprietary and asset management*–based derivative trading from *hedging*-related trading, and, in turn, to separate all these activities from derivatives trades initiated in the banks' capacity as dealers and intermediaries. Once the Lincoln Amendment under the Dodd-Frank Act (see points 12 and 13 in Section 13.2 for details) will be enacted in practice, it will effectively create segregation between the banking subsidiary that can apply for "hedger exception" and be subject to hedge documentation of its positions, with supervision and audit by bank regulators at daily frequency (as with its other risk reports), and the market making or pure dealer subsidiary, which will be subject to higher collateral or capital requirements.

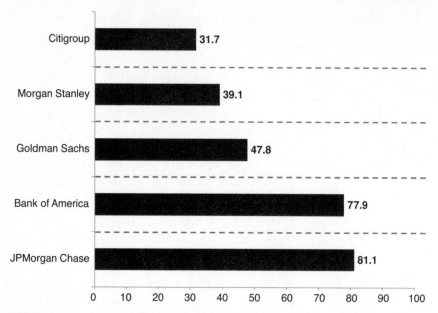

FIGURE 13.5 Notional Value of Derivatives Contracts Outstanding Held by U.S. Banks as of 1Q09 ($ Trillions)
Source: Deutsche Bank, *Wall Street Journal*, Office of the Comptroller of the Currency.

Proposed Reforms Will Help End Users

The end users of OTC derivatives, including some of the largest corporations on both sides of the Atlantic (such as Caterpillar and Lufthansa), have expressed concerns about the proposed reforms. Some of them have sent memoranda to their respective regulators suggesting that the proposed reforms to the OTC derivatives markets would ultimately increase their business risks, reduce investment capital, and slow economic growth. To better evaluate the validity of their concerns, one should first recognize the relative importance of end users in the OTC derivatives markets and their motivation for accessing such products.

According to a 2009 ISDA survey, 94 percent of the world's 500 largest companies, located in 32 different countries, made use of derivatives. That included 92 percent of U.S. companies, 100 percent of UK companies, 97 percent of German companies, 100 percent of French companies, and 100 percent of Japanese companies. The broad use of derivatives by companies of various sizes is documented in a more detailed analysis conducted by Fitch Ratings in July 2009 based on the quarterly reports of a sample of 100 companies from a range of industries in the Standard & Poor's (S&P) 1,500 universe. The report sheds light on the trends in derivatives use within various industries. Table 13.2 details the assets and liabilities for the selected companies in each industry.

In the financial services industry, the most important user segment (the top five banks put aside), 36 companies were reviewed in the Fitch report. Of these 36, only four institutions had no exposure to derivatives.[23] In addition, Fitch reviewed 13 regional banks, and it seems that trading activity in derivatives by these banks is not as extensive as by the larger national banks. Furthermore, the study shows that interest rate derivatives make up an average 85 percent of total net exposure, while currency derivatives make up an average 7 percent of total exposure. In the insurance industry, interest rate derivatives dominate on the balance sheets of the four reviewed companies. However, and not surprisingly, AIG and MBIA Inc. show sizable total notional amounts for net credit derivatives written (AIG $256 billion; MBIA $165 billion).

Fitch also reviewed the derivatives disclosure of 14 utilities and power companies. Utilities traditionally have used derivatives to hedge pricing exposures within regulated business lines. In response to deregulation and the development of active energy trading markets, many power and gas companies also developed proprietary trading operations that allowed them to speculate on derivatives, above and beyond what was necessary to hedge their own production and purchasing. However, since the Enron bankruptcy (which was, at least in part, attributed to derivatives trading using complex special purpose vehicles), the resulting changes to accounting rules governing energy contracts require more detailed disclosure; consequently, many of these companies have either disbanded or sold their trading functions. Of the 14 utilities reviewed, only three companies (Dominion Resources Inc., Exelon Corporation, and FPL Group Inc.) disclosed the use of derivatives for proprietary trading. Proprietary trading may be used for the purpose of price discovery or to benefit from superior market knowledge. However, for the companies reviewed it appears that the scale of trading activities is limited in relation to their overall activities.

Similar to power companies, the oil industry also has had extensive experience in the use of derivatives over the past several decades. Of the seven energy companies reviewed, six had exposures to derivatives, with a 97 percent concentration in commodity derivatives. Surprisingly, according to Fitch's review of energy companies, Exxon Mobil Corporation—the largest energy company in the United States—had no derivatives exposure at the end of the first quarter of 2009. Furthermore, two companies (ConocoPhillips and El Paso Corporation) had trading operations in addition to using derivatives for risk management of their operations. Non-trading activities typically include hedging of crude oil and natural gas production. Although oil companies actively market natural gas, crude oil, and other products to customers, their knowledge of the market gained through this marketing effort is useful for trading on the prices of these basic commodities. As a result, oil companies may engage in trading activities for the purpose of generating profit from exposure to changes in the market prices of these products, rather than merely hedging.[24]

Thus, while end users of OTC derivatives do represent a significant proportion of the market in terms of the number of participants, their usage is dominated by the activities of a few large firms, in particular the large insurers. Nevertheless, these end users have expressed several concerns regarding the reform of OTC derivatives. The first concern is that an increase in the overall cost of dealer activities—due to transparency and greater margin requirements—may raise end users' own hedging costs, as dealers will, in one form or another, pass on the costs to these end users. The second concern is that reforms that force a dealer preference for standardized products cleared centrally would reduce the ability of end users to find customized hedges, thus increasing their basis risk. For example, an airline may not be able to hedge jet fuel prices, but only the price of crude oil, which may not move perfectly in line with the airline's fuel costs.

Will end users' hedging costs necessarily increase? We are unable to quantify this, as we explain in detail later. However, even if end users' costs were to go up, it may be argued that this is a fair price that society requires to balance economic growth and financial stability. The experience with the CDS market during the financial crisis highlights the systemic risks imposed by OTC contracts that did not adequately price risk to balance economic growth and financial stability. In some cases, such as FX, it may be argued that the opposite is the case and the basis risk borne by market participants swamps the systemic consequences of using customized, noncleared derivatives.

In our view, enhanced transparency and reduced counterparty risk of derivatives dealers ought to benefit end users directly in terms of the risks and costs they ultimately bear. Currently, end users manage the counterparty risk of dealers either by distributing their hedges across different dealers or by buying protection on counterparties through CDSs. Both these methods are not only inefficient but also deceptive. As the current crisis has made clear, dealers themselves are often taking similar positions. In this case, buying protection against default of the first dealer from a second dealer is not that different from bearing the default risk of the first dealer.

In contrast to current practices, up-front capital injections into central clearinghouses along with greater margin requirements on OTC positions

TABLE 13.2 Derivative Assets and Liabilities as of June 6, 2009 ($ Millions)

	Company	Total Assets	Total Derivative Assets[a]	Total Derivative Liabilities[a]
Selected Insurance Companies	American International Group	819,758	10,192	5,197
	MetLife, Inc.	491,408	9,351	4,009
	Prudential Financial	427,529	7,430[b]	4,621[b]
	MBIA Inc.	27,907	1,126	5,332
Selected Utilities and Power Companies	Duke Energy Corporation	53,584	491	649
	Southern Company	49,557	20	461
	Exelon Corporation	48,863	1,437	506
	American Electric Power	45,865	710	353
	FPL Group, Inc.	45,304	1,016	1,762
	Edison Int'l	44,429	950	948
	Dominion Resources, Inc.	41,687	2,219	2,219
	PG&E Corporation	41,335	298	542
	Entergy Corporation	36,613	351	91
	AES Corporation	34,838	202	467
	Consolidated Edison, Inc.	34,224	279	464
	FirstEnergy Corporation	33,557	383	869
	Progress Energy, Inc.	30,903	5	935
	Centerpoint Energy, Inc.	19,676	142	221
Selected Energy and Oil Companies	Exxon Mobil Corporation	222,491	NA	NA
	ConocoPhillips	143,251	7,442	7,211
	Anadarko Petroleum Corporation	48,154	533	84
	XTO Energy, Inc.	37,056	2,397	66
	Chesapeake Energy Corporation	29,661	1,978	635
	El Paso Corporation	22,424	873	896
	Spectra Energy Corporation	21,417	26	22

[a]Includes the impact of netting adjustments.
[b]Presented gross without netting benefits.
Source: Fitch Ratings, quarterly filings.

held directly by dealers would reduce the default risk that end users face. One still cannot rule out the possibility, however remote, that a clearinghouse may itself collapse (see the next subsection). But there are mechanisms in place—such as the lender of last resort—to deal with such an extreme scenario. It would be better from a systemic perspective for the Federal Reserve to lend to a clearinghouse, effectively lending to its strongest member firms, than to the weakest ones that brought it down. Furthermore, since the risks are clearly visible from the marketwide information available within the clearinghouse, it may be possible to take preventive action earlier than under the previous regime, where the risks were largely under the regulators' radar.

Under the proposed reforms, dealer activities are intended to be efficiently margined by regulators to contain the systemic risk they pose on others. Thus, it is only fair that end users also pay at least a part of this price. The alternative scenario where these risks are not borne and paid for by the beneficiaries—dealers and end users—but are underwritten by taxpayers at large if dealers default is suboptimal. Indeed, such perverse incentives were the root cause of the credit bubble just witnessed and must be curbed before they lead to another crisis.

Another point of contention is about whether the derivatives reform should extend directly to the end users or they should be exempt. It may be reasonable to argue that end users should receive exemption from the detailed transparency reports and margin requirements that dealers will be subject to. It may also be appropriate that the margin requirements should take into account the hedged positions that the end users aim to maintain. Such exemptions, however, cannot be left entirely open-ended by regulators. It is important to recognize that once dealers are subject to higher capital requirements and transparency, and end users enjoy a hedger exception, the most likely place for buildup of excessive risks in the OTC markets would be in the space of end users. Of course, the regulations should take cognizance of the hedges that the end users maintain with their operational positions.

It is important, as proposed in the Act, that end users that choose not to be classified as dealers be brought under the same set of regulations as dealers if these end users violate certain criteria regarding their hedging status. In particular, end users should be required to provide hedge documentation of their derivatives trades detailing their underlying exposures. This hedge documentation must be subject to regular audits. End users whose audits reveal shortcomings in hedge documentation, or who are found to be maintaining substantial one-way derivatives position bets more appropriate for a dealer's warehouse or a speculative desk, should be subject to penalties and potentially have their hedger exception revoked for a sufficiently long period, effectively subjecting them to additional transparency requirements and margins.

Nevertheless, the "audit and penalize" system is not perfect and will not prevent all abuse of the hedger exception. The risk from any such abuse will be greater in case of "major swap participants," who therefore deserve greater scrutiny. Large corporations may have greater hedging needs and require larger OTC positions for hedging. However, their ability to use derivatives under the hedger exception carries the risk of ending up in a levered, too-big-to-fail position. Like dealers, they too must pay for this systemic risk.

Centralized Clearinghouses: Too Systemic to Fail?

Momentum is gathering—partly through industry consensus on some products such as standard credit derivatives and partly through legislation in the Dodd-Frank Act—for the establishment of a central counterparty (CCP) clearinghouse for OTC derivatives as a way to reduce counterparty credit risk. The CCP would stand between the two original counterparties, acting as the seller to the original buyer, and as the buyer to the original seller. Because its long and short positions are automatically offsetting, a CCP has no losses or gains on a derivatives contract so long as the original counterparties to the trade continue to perform. The CCP is, however, exposed to a counterparty credit risk from each of its participants. To minimize this risk, a CCP relies on a range of controls and methods, including stringent membership access, a robust margining regime, clear default management procedures, and significant financial resources that back its performance.

A clearinghouse, through its opportunity to net across different asset classes and across dealers, can lead to a substantial reduction in risk and a substantial improvement in allocational efficiency. It potentially also allows market participants to reduce the amount of margin to post against their exposures if many contracts clear through the same clearinghouse. Therefore, a joint clearing of different derivative products in the same CCP would not only improve the opportunity to net counterparty exposures, but also increase the incentives for market participants to clear their derivatives trades without increasing systemic risk. At the same time, if there are too many clearinghouses, regulators run the risk of increasing the systemic risk posed by OTC derivatives due to fragmented trading (for example, if default management procedures are not coordinated in advance or if there is lack of sufficient information sharing on exposure data) and excessive use of collateral (unless there is a collateral-sharing arrangement across different clearinghouses). Nevertheless, forcing the establishment of a single clearinghouse may concentrate the risks due to the monopolistic position that it would create for clearing.

Finding the optimal number of CCPs is not the only hurdle for establishing a central clearing of OTC derivatives. One also needs to take into account the difficulties of clearing OTC trades. First, while multilateral netting can be the main advantage of a CCP in reducing counterparty risk, multilateral netting can be limited or even impossible, when the contracts traded are nonuniform and when the terms of the contract remain largely undisclosed to other participants. Moreover, if an OTC trader defaults on its promise to pay the CCP, the CCP faces a large replacement cost risk. The less standardized the contract, the larger this cost.

Even after a successful migration of derivatives trading from the OTC market to central exchanges, CCPs are not immune to the risk of failing on their obligations; if many of its trading counterparties default together or are vulnerable at once, a CCP may not have enough resources to cover all its outstanding positions. While clearinghouses have functioned well in general, a few clearinghouse failures have occurred around the world from time to time. For example, in 1974, a sharp price increase in the Paris White Sugar Market with a subsequent correction prompted the default of participants on margin calls; as a result, the Caisse de Liquidation market was closed by the French commerce ministry. Similar incidents occurred in Kuala Lumpur (Commodity Clearing House, 1983) due to defaults in palm oil contracts and in Hong Kong (Futures Guarantee Corporation, 1987) due to failures in futures trades.[25]

There are also a few instances in recent U.S. history when exchanges were on the brink of collapse. In the 1970s, two short episodes in the commodity futures market caused serious liquidity problems with settlement delays. In 1976, as a result of a manipulation in the Maine potato futures contract on the New York Mercantile Exchange (NYMEX), the largest default in the history of commodity futures trading occurred on some 1,000 contracts that covered 50 million pounds of potatoes. A similar market disruption occurred at the end of 1979, when the price of silver jumped to an all-time record. At that time, the Hunt brothers were estimated to hold one-third of the entire world supply of silver (other than that held by governments). A change of the Commodity Exchange (COMEX) rules regarding leverage spurred a series of margin calls, causing COMEX to increase margin levels to 100 percent, which further dried up market liquidity. An SEC report on the silver crisis later stated that "for six days late in March 1980, it appeared to government officials, Wall Street, and the public at large that a default by a single family on its obligations in the fomenting silver market might seriously disrupt the U.S. financial system."

Central counterparties in the equity arena also have experienced similar problems. In the aftermath of the 1987 stock market crash, a big counterparty of the Chicago Mercantile Exchange (CME) failed to make a large payment by the settlement date, leaving the exchange $400 million short. Its president, Leo Melamed, called its bank, Continental Illinois, to plead for the bank to guarantee the balance, which was well in excess of its credit lines. Only three minutes before the exchange was due to open, the bank authorized the backstop. Melamed has said repeatedly that if the Merc had not opened that morning, it would not have opened again. To make matters worse, the head of the New York Stock Exchange (NYSE) also noted that if the Merc had not opened that morning, the NYSE would not have, either, and the NYSE might have never reopened again.[26] Even the remote possibility of such an incident being repeated is too high a risk for the system to bear.

The collapse of Lehman Brothers in September 2008 resurfaced concerns of the likelihood, however small, of clearinghouse failures. Lehman had $4 billion in margin accounts to backstop commitments for customers and also had large proprietary bets on energy, interest rate, and stock index futures on the CME. A court-appointed examiner, Anton Valukas, presented a report that reveals details about the scramble at the CME, the world's biggest futures exchange, as Lehman filed for bankruptcy. The CME ordered Lehman to liquidate bets made with Lehman's own money, but rather than selling off these positions, Lehman continued to add to them for another two days. Thereafter, the CME convened an emergency committee that conducted a forced transfer of the bank's positions, the first and only time this has been done by the exchange operator.

While the CME has dealt with a failure of clearing members before, including the 2005 unraveling of the broker Refco, the risk that the Lehman crisis posed to the CME does raise the issue that the growing pressure from regulators to shift more derivatives contracts to centralized clearing concentrates the risk of several counterparties defaulting in one place—namely, the clearinghouse. This recent episode gives some support to the concerns that the failure of a CCP could suddenly expose many major market participants to substantial losses.

As the previous examples show, oversight and intervention are often necessary to avoid the failure of a clearinghouse. Given that central clearing in some form is likely to be an important aspect of OTC derivatives, if a single party were to default, the clearinghouse would settle the outstanding trades and prevent a cascade of failures. In many cases, the centralized counterparty would be a privately owned corporation belonging to a consortium of dealers and other market participants. While this may ensure that the clearinghouse has relatively deep pockets, the risks must still be monitored the same way as any other entity with systemic risk. The risks that the centralized counterparty will naturally have to bear could be mitigated by setting margins, as discussed before, but adequacy of the initial and variation margining procedures of the CCPs must be a part of the task entrusted to the systemic risk regulator.

In this context, it is important to note that looking back at history, we find that the failure of clearinghouses due to poor risk management or excess risk taking has been relatively rare. This is in striking contrast to the case of banks and large financial institutions, where it is relatively an exception to find an example where failure is not linked to poor risk management or excessive risk taking. So, while clearinghouses are clearly systemic and perhaps too-big-to-fail members of the financial sector, their risk-taking activities have a limited scope, and on balance the moral hazard in their case is also somewhat limited. Hence, in the central clearing arena, competition among exchanges does not appear to have caused a race to the bottom in terms of risk management and control, in which clearinghouses settle for excessively low levels of contractual guarantees in an attempt to increase volume; if anything, there is a race to the top (see Santos and Scheinkman 2001).

In the unfortunate case when a centralized counterparty itself faces default, there should be little hesitation to rescue it with taxpayer resources, rather than being subject to the mercy of an individual financial institution. Such systemic risks are indeed exactly what the lender of last resort should focus on, since from a moral hazard standpoint it is far more prudent to rescue a clearinghouse than a private risk-taking institution that blows up due to its risky trades and endangers its in-house public utility function as a market maker (a case in point being Bear Stearns, which was de facto a clearer of a large number of CDS contracts). Thus, while some of the moral hazard remains, it would be much more muted than in the case of individual financial institutions, both because the clearing corporation is more transparent and because of active supervision by the systemic risk regulator. The regulatory apparatus appears well designed to reduce this risk, so that wherever there is sufficient standardization of contracts, we welcome the migration from OTC to CCPs.

13.5 CONCLUSION: HOW WILL THE DERIVATIVES REFORMS AFFECT GLOBAL FINANCE IN FUTURE?

We conjecture that there are four key areas where the proposed OTC reforms of the Dodd-Frank Act will have the greatest global impact. These concern: (1) consolidation within the United States and across countries of clearinghouses and exchanges, and potentially also of large dealer banks;

(2) emergence of global transparency platforms and services related to processing of newly made available data on derivatives transactions and positions; (3) gradual transition of (some) end-user hedging demand to centralized platforms and exchanges; and (4) separation of market making and proprietary trading/asset management positions in large financial institutions.

There are two sound economic reasons why consolidation across clearinghouses and exchanges is likely to take off following the proposed OTC reforms. First, in the early years, centralized clearing will likely occur separately within the individual product spaces (e.g., credit derivatives, interest rate derivatives, etc.). We believe that centralized clearing will first occur with credit derivatives, and then with relatively standardized interest rate and FX products. Customized products will probably remain in the uncleared space, at least for some time until market innovations permit them to be moved to clearinghouses at a reasonable cost. However, absent rules across clearing platforms to share collateral in case of a dealer's default, there will most likely be a reduced portfolio margining benefit, and in the short run, an increase in collateral requirements from dealers. Yet, market infrastructure and organization will likely respond to the enhanced collateral requirement and costs. Clearinghouses and exchanges may be spurred to merge and thereby work out collateral-sharing arrangements in case of default, and in turn, offer more cost-effective collateral arrangements to dealers. Dealers may themselves find it advantageous to merge in order to ensure that they can provide as much portfolio margining to clients as possible, rather than see clients getting fragmented across dealers in different markets. Moreover, while greater transparency and trade registry at the level of individual platforms would aid regulators in the event of a large financial firm's default, such information would have to be shared across different platforms. This should also spur consolidation across platforms, especially globally, and should be partly encouraged by national regulators. Of course, such consolidation implies that systemic risk will likely get concentrated on a few platforms and in the hands of a few dealers, unless their leverage and risks are managed well. This will be a key challenge for central banks and systemic risk oversight councils in the future, particularly in order to forestall the potential failure of a large clearinghouse or exchange.

Second, related to the point on the need to coordinate transparency, a market response to such need is likely to emerge in the form of global clearing services being provided by players such as the Depository Trust & Clearing Corporation (DTCC), as well as in the form of global information gathering and dissemination provided by players such as Markit.

Greater standardization of products would facilitate such global aggregation, and the consolidation proposed earlier would also necessitate such global data repositories. Furthermore, to the extent that new information would become available—even if with some delay and coarseness—third-party vendors, which mine these data and refine them into more directly useful measures of counterparty exposures and risks, may emerge. Indeed, central banks and systemic risk oversight councils may find it efficient to outsource some processing of data in this form rather than managing such risk data entirely themselves. The Office of Financial Research (OFR), proposed in the Dodd-Frank Act in the United States, will also be charged with the task of collecting transaction-level data and organizing it in forms that aid understanding of systemic risk. It would be desirable for a climate to be created for a healthy exchange—and even some competition—among the OFR, third-party vendors, policy institutions, and academic research in figuring out how best to analyze the new data that are commonly available to all.

Third, it is plausible that, over time, the migration of standardized products to centralized clearinghouses and exchanges will allow entry of new dealers such as large hedge funds and specialized derivatives trading firms (the initial push for consolidation notwithstanding). This will simply be the outcome of greater pretrade and posttrade transparency offered by such platforms relative to the current veil that precludes such transparency of OTC markets. Such entry should reduce the costs of trading in these products, and end users (the hedgers) would be induced to move some of their hedging away from customized products with dealer banks to the centralized platforms, perhaps with some market innovations in combining customization with centralized clearing. There is a chance that such a movement may significantly enhance liquidity on these platforms, and in some cases, make it possible—even if not in the near future—to allow retail access to certain derivative products that are close to cash markets. For example, a CDS is best visualized as a standardized corporate bond, and ability to trade credit risk this way—with appropriate risk controls—might be valuable to retail traders and provide depth to credit markets (as we currently have with equities). Nevertheless, given the basis risk involved in hedging production schedules with standardized products, some market for customized hedging will remain in the OTC space. Overall, we believe that end users will likely face lower counterparty risk and pay for it more efficiently given the proposed reforms.

Last, but not least, there is bound to be a greater separation on the books of banks between the pure market-making function that is properly combined with traditional banking products, especially in the interest rate and

FX area, and positions taken through proprietary trading and investment in asset management entities, such as hedge funds. The former cluster of businesses will be offered the traditional support under the Dodd-Frank Act through privileged access to funding and deposit insurance. The risk-taking activities, however, would be separated so that the moral hazard issues are mitigated to a large extent. It is not necessary for this separation to take place in the context of separate companies, as long as there is a separate accounting for risk, capital adequacy, and regulatory oversight. One approach that we have stressed in this chapter is to organize the hedging and the dealer functions of derivatives into separate subsidiaries and adopt the "audit and penalize" strategy (explained in this chapter) to ensure that the hedging subsidiary is not a speculative arm.

While all these are interesting trends to look out for over the next decade or two, it is unlikely that the debate on derivatives will be closed anytime soon. There will always be the occasional backlash against derivatives when large defaults are imminent and some powerful firms, policy institutions, or countries are at the suffering end. Perhaps such debate is useful in the sense that each time it is raised, the marketplace is reminded that while derivatives have their natural use in hedging when markets are incomplete, they also facilitate leverage, which has been found to be a key contributor to systemic risk in past financial crises. Regulating leverage thus will require certain improvements in the trading infrastructure of derivatives and possibly some restrictions on derivatives positions of large players (whose leverage contributes more to systemic risk). In the end, will we get the balance in regulating derivatives right? We will know only when the next crisis hits us, but most likely it will be where we do not anticipate it—perhaps in a new "green energy" asset class, or in the currently nascent derivatives markets in Asia, or in some other pocket that we cannot even imagine today!

APPENDIX A: ITEMS CONCERNING OTC DERIVATIVES LEFT BY THE DODD-FRANK ACT FOR FUTURE STUDY

1. Study on the Effects of Position Limits on Trading on Exchanges in the United States.
   a. The CFTC shall conduct a study of the effects (if any) of the **position limits** imposed pursuant to the other provisions of this title on excessive speculation and on the movement of transactions from exchanges in the United States to trading venues outside the country.

    b. Report to the Congress:
- Within 12 months after the imposition of position limits pursuant to the other provisions of this title.
- The Chairman of the CFTC shall prepare and submit to the Congress biennial reports on the growth or decline of the derivatives markets in the United States and abroad, which shall include assessments of the causes of any such growth or decline, the effectiveness of regulatory regimes in managing systemic risk, a comparison of the costs of compliance at the time of the report for market participants subject to regulation by the United States with the costs of compliance in December 2008 for the market participants, and the quality of the available data.
- Required hearing within 30 legislative days after the submission to the Congress of the report.

2. Study on Feasibility of Requiring the Use of Standardized Algorithmic Descriptions for Financial Derivatives
    a. The SEC and the CFTC shall conduct a joint study of the feasibility of requiring the derivatives industry to adopt standardized computer-readable algorithmic descriptions which may be used to describe complex and standardized financial derivatives.
    b. Goals: The algorithmic descriptions defined in the study shall be designed to facilitate computerized analysis of individual derivative contracts and to calculate net exposures to complex derivatives.
    c. The study will also examine the extent to which the algorithmic description, together with standardized and extensible legal definitions, may serve as the binding legal definition of derivative contracts. The study will examine the logistics of possible implementations of standardized algorithmic descriptions for derivative contracts. The study shall be limited to electronic formats for exchange of derivative contract descriptions and will not contemplate disclosure of proprietary valuation models.
    d. Report to the Committees on Agriculture and on Financial Services of the House of Representatives and the Committees on Agriculture, Nutrition, and Forestry and on Banking, Housing, and Urban Affairs of the Senate within eight months after the date of the enactment of this Act.

3. International Swap Regulation and Harmonization of Margining Methods
    a. The CFTC and the SEC shall jointly conduct a study relating to:
        i. Swap regulation in the United States, Asia, and Europe.
       ii. Clearinghouse and clearing agency regulation in the United States, Asia, and Europe.

    iii. Identifying areas of regulation that are similar in the United States, Asia, and Europe and other areas of regulation that could be harmonized.

  b. The CFTC and the SEC shall submit to the Committee on Agriculture, Nutrition, and Forestry and the Committee on Banking, Housing, and Urban Affairs of the Senate and the Committee on Agriculture and the Committee on Financial Services of the House of Representatives a report not later than 18 months after the date of enactment of this Act, including:

    i. Identification of the major exchanges and their regulator in each geographic area for the trading of swaps and security-based swaps including a listing of the major contracts and their trading volumes and notional values as well as identification of the major swap dealers participating in such markets.

    ii. Identification of the major clearinghouses and clearing agencies and their regulator in each geographic area for the clearing of swaps and security-based swaps, including a listing of the major contracts and the clearing volumes and notional values as well as identification of the major clearing members of such clearinghouses and clearing agencies in such markets.

    iii. Description of the comparative methods of clearing swaps in the United States, Asia, and Europe.

    iv. Description of the various systems used for establishing margin on individual swaps, security-based swaps, and swap portfolios.

4. Stable Value Contracts[27]

  a. Not later than 15 months after the date of the enactment of this Act, the SEC and the CFTC shall, jointly, conduct a study to determine whether stable value contracts fall within the definition of a swap. In making the determination required under this subparagraph, the Commissions jointly shall consult with the Department of Labor, the Department of the Treasury, and the State entities that regulate the issuers of stable value contracts.

  b. If the Commissions determine that stable value contracts fall within the definition of a swap, the Commissions jointly shall determine if an exemption for stable value contracts from the definition of swap is appropriate and in the public interest. The Commissions shall issue regulations implementing the determinations required under this paragraph. Until the effective date of such regulations, and notwithstanding any other provision of this title, the requirements of this title shall not apply to stable value contracts.

TABLE 13.3 Time Line of the Future Studies

Study	Deadline	Section
Study on the Effects of Position Limits on Trading on Exchanges in the U.S.	12 months after imposition of position limits	719(a)
Study on Feasibility of Requiring the Use of Standardized Algorithmic Descriptions for Financial Derivatives	8 months after enactment of the Dodd-Frank Act	719(b)
International Swap Regulation and Harmonization of Margining Methods	18 months after enactment of the Dodd-Frank Act	719(c)
Stable Value Contracts	15 months after enactment of the Dodd-Frank Act	719(d)
Study on Impact of FOIA Exemption on Commodity Futures Trading Commission	30 months after enactment of Section 748	748
Study on Oversight of Carbon Markets	6 months after enactment of the Dodd-Frank Act	750

There are two studies that are within the bill, but are unrelated directly to our discussion:

5. Study on Impact of FOIA Exemption on Commodity Futures Trading Commission
   a. The Inspector General of the Commission shall conduct a study:
      i. Whether the exemption under section 552(b)(3) of title 5, U.S. Code (known as the Freedom of Information Act) established in paragraph (2)(A) aids whistleblowers in disclosing information to the Commission.
      ii. On what impact the exemption has had on the public's ability to access information about the Commission's regulation of commodity futures and option markets.
      iii. To make any recommendations on whether the Commission should continue to use the exemption.
   b. Not later than 30 months after the date of enactment of this clause, the Inspector General shall submit a report on the findings to the Committee on Banking, Housing, and Urban Affairs of the Senate and the Committee on Financial Services of the House of Representatives.

6. Study on Oversight of Carbon Markets
   a. The interagency group shall conduct a study on the oversight of existing and prospective carbon markets to ensure an efficient, secure, and transparent carbon market, including oversight of spot markets and derivative markets.

APPENDIX B: CURRENT OTC DISCLOSURE PROVIDED BY DEALER BANKS

To help investors gauge the financial implications for companies that have sold CDSs, the Financial Accounting Standards Board (FASB) in the United States introduced a new standard that eliminates the inconsistency between two existing accounting standards, effective for fiscal years that end after November 2008. One of these rules covers financial guarantees, which are similar in terms of their economic risks and rewards to credit derivatives. It requires an extensive disclosure of contracts in which the buyer of the insurance owns the underlying instrument that the contract is protecting. However, if the guaranteed party does not own the asset or the instrument that is insured, then the protection is classified as a derivative and falls under another accounting standard that does not require disclosure. This is in spite of the fact that the risks of a financial guarantee and a credit derivative being undertaken by a firm under either of these kinds of instruments are the same in economic terms.

The FASB's new standard covers sellers of CDS instruments, namely the entities that act as insurers by selling protection. They have to disclose such details as the nature and term of the credit derivative, the reason it was entered into, and the current status of its payment and performance risk. In addition, the seller needs to provide the amount of future payments it might be required to make, the fair value of the derivative, and whether there are provisions that would allow the seller to recover money or assets from third parties to pay for the insurance coverage it has written.

We detail the collateral data, fair value, and notional value of credit exposures in OTC derivatives for Goldman Sachs (Figure 13.6) and Citigroup (Figure 13.7), two of the major players in these markets. As is clear from the disclosures, there is a fair deal of difference in reporting standards:

- Goldman Sachs reports CDS exposures by:
  - Maturity.
  - Credit rating (AAA/Aaa, AA/Aa2, etc.) of counterparty.
  - Gross, net, as well as net of collateral.

OTC Derivative Credit Exposure
($ Millions)

As of September 2009

Credit Rating Equivalent	0–12 Months	1–5 Years	5–10 Years	10 Years or Greater	Total	Netting	Exposure	Exposure Net of Collateral
AAA/Aaa	$ 1,482	$ 3,249	$ 3,809	$ 2,777	$ 11,317	$ (5,481)	$ 5,836	$ 5,349
AA/Aa2	6,647	12,741	7,695	9,332	36,415	(20,804)	15,611	11,815
A/Aa2	31,999	46,761	29,324	31,747	130,831	(111,238)	28,503	24,795
BBB/Baa2	4,825	7,780	5,609	8,190	26,404	(12,069)	14,335	8,041
BB/Ba2 or lower	3,049	13,931	2,903	1,483	21,366	(5,357)	16,009	9,472
Unrated	666	1,570	387	148	2,771	(224)	2,547	1,845
Total	$48,668	$86,032	$49,727	$53,677	$238,104	$(155,173)	$82,931	$61,317

As of June 2009

Credit Rating Equivalent	0–12 Months	1–5 Years	5–10 Years	10 Years or Greater	Total	Netting	Exposure	Exposure Net of Collateral
AAA/Aaa	$ 2,743	$ 4,524	$ 4,623	$ 3,209	$ 15,099	$ (6,221)	$ 8,878	$ 8,520
AA/Aa2	6,989	20,669	9,252	9,252	46,162	(32,641)	13,521	9,759
A/Aa2	36,715	39,178	28,307	28,760	132,960	(103,597)	29,363	25,539
BBB/Baa2	5,091	10,211	3,435	7,238	25,975	(11,908)	14,067	8,492
BB/Ba2 or lower	5,849	11,576	2,814	1,983	22,222	(5,965)	16,257	10,160
Unrated	859	1,386	623	446	3,314	(83)	3,231	2,808
Total	$58,246	$87,544	$49,054	$50,888	$245,732	$(160,415)	$85,317	$65,278

FIGURE 13.6 Goldman Sachs's Accounting Disclosures of Credit Default Swap Exposures

Source: Goldman Sachs's annual balance sheets.

OTC Derivative Credit Exposure
($ Millions)

As of March 2009

Credit Rating Equivalent	0–12 Months	1–5 Years	5–10 Years	10 Years or Greater	Total	Netting	Exposure	Exposure Net of Collateral
AAA/Aaa	$ 4,699	$ 6,734	$ 5,994	$ 2,964	$ 20,391	$ (8,178)	$12,213	$11,509
AA/Aa2	18,619	40,015	22,228	10,095	90,957	(71,881)	19,076	16,025
A/Aa2	21,148	33,369	16,955	19,767	97,239	(66,342)	30,897	25,220
BBB/Baa2	8,185	19,413	6,833	12,571	47,002	(31,280)	15,722	10,358
BB/Ba2 or lower	8,734	9,922	3,568	1,652	23,976	(8,116)	15,760	10,339
Unrated	2,670	1,007	312	360	4,349	(371)	3,978	3,314
Total	$64,055	$116,460	$55,890	$47,409	$283,814	$(186,168)	$97,646	$76,765

As of November 2008

Credit Rating Equivalent	0–12 Months	1–5 Years	5–10 Years	10 Years or Greater	Total	Netting	Exposure	Exposure Net of Collateral
AAA/Aaa	$ 5,519	$ 3,871	$ 5,853	$ 4,250	$ 19,493	$ (6,093)	$ 13,400	$12,312
AA/Aa2	26,835	30,532	33,479	18,980	109,826	(76,119)	33,707	29,435
A/Aa2	25,416	27,263	17,009	24,427	94,115	(59,903)	34,212	28,614
BBB/Baa2	11,324	17,156	8,684	14,311	51,475	(29,229)	22,246	16,211
BB/Ba2 or lower	11,835	10,228	4,586	3,738	30,387	(12,600)	17,787	11,204
Unrated	808	803	916	215	2,832	(11)	2,821	1,550
Total	$81,737	$89,943	$70,527	$65,921	$308,128	$(183,955)	$124,173	$99,326

FIGURE 13.6 (Continued)

The following tables summarize the key characteristics of the Company's credit derivative portfolio as protection seller (guarantor) as of September 30, 2009, and December 31, 2008:

In millions of dollars as of September 30, 2009	Maximum Potential Amount of Future Payments	Fair Value Payable[1]
By industry/counterparty:		
Bank	$ 860,437	$ 46,071
Broker-dealer	301,216	17,661
Monoline	—	—
Nonfinancial	2,127	96
Insurance and other financial institutions	151,326	12,753
Total by industry/counterparty	$1,315,106	$ 76,581
By instrument:		
Credit default swaps and options	$1,314,282	$ 76,383
Total return swaps	824	198
Total by instrument	$1,315,106	$ 76,581
By rating:		
Investment grade	$ 759,845	23,362
Non–investment grade	422,865	33,231
Not rated	132,396	19,988
Total by rating	$1,315,106	$ 76,581

[1]In addition, fair value amounts receivable under credit derivatives sold were $23,324 million.

The following tables summarize the key characteristics of the Company's credit derivative portfolio as protection seller (guarantor) as of June 30, 2009, and December 31, 2008:

In millions of dollars as of June 30, 2009	Maximum Potential Amount of Future Payments	Fair Value Payable
By industry/counterparty:		
Bank	$ 899,598	$ 71,523
Broker-dealer	322,349	30,798
Monoline	123	89
Nonfinancial	4,805	231
Insurance and other financial institutions	138,813	14,756
Total by industry/counterparty	$1,365,688	$117,127
By instrument:		
Credit default swaps and options	$1,363,738	$116,600
Total return swaps and other	1,950	527
Total by instrument	$1,365,688	$117,127
By rating:		
Investment grade	$ 813,892	49,503
Non–investment grade	342,888	46,242
Not rated	208,908	21,382
Total by rating	$1,365,688	$117,127

FIGURE 13.7 Citigroup's Accounting Disclosures of Credit Default Swap Exposures
Source: Citigroup's annual balance sheets.

In millions of dollars as of March 31, 2009	Maximum Potential Amount of Future Payments	Fair Value Payable
By industry/counterparty:		
Bank	$ 919,354	$123,437
Broker-dealer	345,582	56,181
Monoline	139	91
Nonfinancial	5,327	5,121
Insurance and other financial institutions	135,729	21,581
Total by industry/counterparty	$1,406,131	$206,411
By instrument:		
Credit default swaps and options	$1,404,928	$206,057
Total return swaps and other	1,203	354
Total by instrument	$1,406,131	$206,411
By rating:		
Investment grade	$ 808,602	88,952
Non–investment grade	362,851	79,409
Not rated	234,678	38,050
Total by rating	$1,406,131	$206,411

In millions of dollars as of December 31, 2009	Maximum Potential Amount of Future Payments	Fair Value Payable[1]
By industry/counterparty:		
Bank	$ 943,949	$118,428
Broker-dealer	365,664	55,458
Monoline	139	91
Nonfinancial	7,540	2,556
Insurance and other financial institutions	125,988	21,700
Total by industry/counterparty	$1,443,280	$198,233
By instrument:		
Credit default swaps and options	$1,441,375	$197,981
Total return swaps	1,905	252
Total by instrument	$1,443,280	$198,233
By rating:		
Investment grade	$ 851,426	$ 83,672
Non–investment grade	410,483	87,508
Not rated	181,371	27,053
Total by rating	$1,443,280	$198,233

[1] In addition, fair value amounts receivable under credit derivatives sold were $5,890 million.

FIGURE 13.7 (*Continued*)

- Citigroup reports the exposures by:
  - Nature of counterparty (bank, broker-dealer, monoline, etc.).
  - Type of instrument (CDSs, total return swaps, etc.).
  - Fair value as well as maximum notional payable.

The new regulatory regime should require that these reports be more standardized.

APPENDIX C: SOVEREIGN CREDIT DEFAULT SWAPS MARKETS

Since the mid-1990s, Fitch Ratings has recorded a total of eight sovereign defaults. The list of sovereign defaults includes Indonesia and the Russian Federation (both in 1998), Argentina (2001), Moldova (2002), Uruguay (2003), the Dominican Republic (2005), Ecuador (2008), and Jamaica (2010). In the wake of Greece's recent debt crisis and with the eroding credit quality of other sovereign issuers, particularly in Europe, the need for targeted regulations of the sovereign CDS market has been called into question. In May 2010, the German securities regulator, BaFin, took unilateral action by banning naked short sales of certain sovereign bonds and related CDS contracts, as well as equity securities.

From virtual nonexistence only a few years back when sovereign CDSs were mostly traded on emerging market economies, the sovereign CDS market has grown rapidly to $1.76 trillion, according to data from the end of June 2009 published by the BIS (compared with $22.4 trillion for nonsovereign contracts). Given the large quantity of sovereign bonds outstanding, there is a substantial body of natural buyers of protection. Yet the lack of natural sellers of protection in the sovereign CDS market has capped its growth. The launch of SovX, the European index of 15 equally weighted sovereign entities, in July 2009 has provided an additional avenue for investors to express views on the sovereign market and has significantly improved liquidity. SovX has been seeing a steady pickup in activity relative to corporate CDS index contracts such as those of CDX and iTraxx, and is now ahead of the financial sector CDS index (see Figure 13.8). Still, the sovereign CDS market accounts for a relatively small share of the overall CDS market, and exposures to sovereign CDSs are modest relative to the size of government bond markets. That remains the case despite a notable growth in turnover in sovereign CDSs, especially in terms of net dealer exposures (Figure 13.9) over the past year in which there has been increasing attention on public finances of a number of countries. Figure 13.10 shows, however, that wherever sovereign credit risk is more in question (e.g., recently

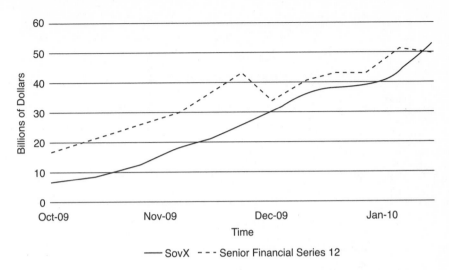

FIGURE 13.8 Gross Notional Outstanding of SovX versus Financials
($ Billions)
Source: Morgan Stanley Research, "Credit Derivatives Insights: Sovereign CDS
Markets—A Corporate Perspective," January 29, 2010; DTCC.

in the cases of Greece, Portugal, Spain, Italy, and Ireland), the ratio of CDSs
to government bond markets is greater, relative to safer countries (e.g., the
United States and the UK). Indeed, some of the safest countries such as the
UK and France have also shown signs of stress in this context.

Concerns about the market implications of large fiscal deficits came to
the fore in late 2009 and early 2010. Investors' attention was first drawn
to the issue of sovereign risk in the aftermath of the financial difficulties en-
countered by the government-owned Dubai World in late November 2009.
More recently, though, the focus has shifted to the euro-zone periphery,
where large budget deficits have led to the prospect of rapidly increasing
government debt/gross domestic product (GDP) levels in several countries
(see Figure 13.11). In October 2009, as it became evident that Greece might
lose European Central Bank (ECB) funding for Greek banks and the use of its
sovereign bonds as collateral at the ECB, CDS premiums and yield spreads
on Greek government debt shot up, both in absolute terms and relative to the
benchmark German bunds. Simultaneously, while sovereign CDS premiums
shot up across the board since that period, it was primarily the European
banks who suffered in terms of market valuation of their equity as well as
their own corporate CDSs (more so than Asian or U.S. counterparts), both
due to reduced value of government guarantees and exposures to sovereign
credit risk through their government bond holdings (Figure 13.12).

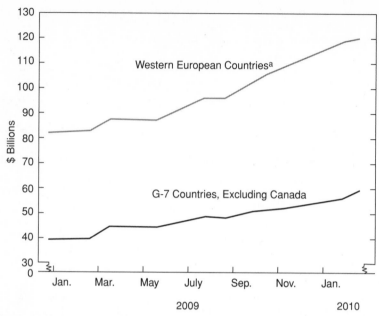

ᵃThe Western Europe series includes the 15 members of the Markit iTraxx SovX Western Europe
Index, excluding Portugal and Norway.

FIGURE 13.9   Net Notional Dealer Exposures to Sovereign CDS Contracts
Source: Depository Trust & Clearing Corporation; Bank of England
1Q10 Bulletin.

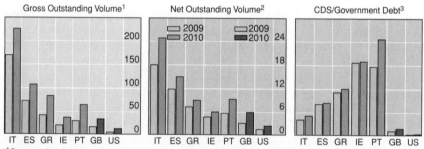

¹Gross notional values are the sum of CDS contracts bought or sold for all warehouse contracts in aggregate;
in billions of U.S. dollars.

²Net notional values are the sum of net protection bought by net buyers; in billions of U.S. dollars.

³Net notional CDS volume as a percentage of government debt.

FIGURE 13.10   Gross Sovereign CDSs
Source: Organization for Economic Cooperation and Development; Depository
Trust & Clearing Corporation; BIS Quarterly Review, March 2010.

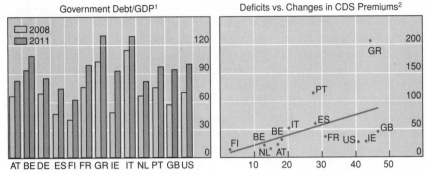

AT = Austria; BE = Belgium; DE = Germany; ES = Spain; FI = Finland; FR = France;
GR = Greece; IE = Ireland; IT = Italy; NL = Netherlands; PT = Portugal;
GB = United Kingdom; US = United States.

[1]Actual data for 2008 and projections for 2011.

[2]Horizontal axis shows the sum of government deficit as percentage of GDP for 2007–2011; vertical axis represents change in CDS premiums between October 26, 2009, and February 17, 2010. Actual data for 2007–2009 and projections for 2010–2011 for government deficit as percentage of GDP.

FIGURE 13.11 Government Debt, Deficits, and Sovereign Credit Premiums
Source: Organization for Economic Cooperation and Development; Depository Trust & Clearing Corporation; BIS Quarterly Review, March 2010.

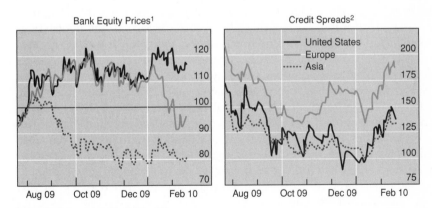

[1]In local currency; July 31, 2009 = 100.

[2]Equally weighted average senior five-year CDS spreads for the banking sector.

FIGURE 13.12 Bank Equity Prices and CDS Premiums
Source: Datastream, Markit, Bank for International Settlements calculations; BIS Quarterly Review, March 2010.

In general, sovereign CDSs are traded by a wide variety of market participants, including banks, asset management firms, and hedge funds. These market participants have a multitude of reasons to trade in sovereign CDSs: trading of the basis and hedging of a specific government bond exposure, hedging of a direct exposure to sovereign credit, or simply isolating single-name corporate risk from the risk of the sovereign where the corporate is located. However, recent events in the sovereign credit markets have brought sovereign CDSs under intense market scrutiny, and have led EU politicians to call for a ban on naked sovereign CDS trades.

As a knee-jerk reaction to the Greek woes, policymakers and commentators in Europe have quickly questioned the sovereign CDS market's effect on the levels at which heavily indebted countries, such as Greece, were able to refinance in the capital market. They have, in fact, given notice that they would consider banning CDS use for speculative bets in the markets. Nevertheless, as of today, there is no compelling evidence that activity in the sovereign CDS market has led to wider spreads and has limited governments' ability to borrow money, as even the German regulator, BaFin, acknowledged as it moved to restrict naked short selling. First, examination of the DTCC's reports since the beginning of 2010 shows that the net outstanding CDS position on Greece has changed little over the course of the year. The net position for Greece was $8.7 billion in the week of January 1, 2010, and has ranged between $8.5 billion and $9.2 billion since then (compared to $7.4 billion a year ago). None of the data suggests that there has been a surge of open interest in either 2009 or 2010. Second, the no-arbitrage relationship between CDSs and bonds implies that while it is relatively easy for CDSs to drive bond prices higher and yields lower, it is much harder for CDSs to force bond prices lower and yields higher, since bonds become hard to borrow and then it becomes increasingly difficult to short the bond against selling protection. The fact that basis has remained stable—that is, the government bond and CDS spreads have remained essentially in line (for most countries, including Greece) and outstanding positions have remained constant—strengthens the assertion that naked short selling activity in the CDS market has had little or no impact on the government bond market.

Another piece of evidence supporting our view that the CDS market was an effect of the euro-zone crisis, rather than its cause, is Altman's bottom-up analysis to assess sovereign risk (see Box 13.1). Using corporate financial health data of a nation's private sector to find its aggregate default risk, Altman's metric has signaled early warnings of a domestic economic slowdown in Greece and Portugal well before May 2010 (see Table 13.4).

While there is no global consensus for a ban or even restrictions on short selling of sovereign bonds or the purchase of related CDSs, it is clear that the side effects of such a ban might be significant. Banks would need

TABLE 13.4 Financial Health of the Private Sector of Selected Countries—The Z-Metrics Assessment

Country	Number of Listed Companies	Five-Year Public Model[a]			Median PD from CDS Spreads[b]	One-Year Public Model[c]		
		Median PD	Standard Deviation PDs	Median Rating	Five-Year[b]	Median PD	Standard Deviation PDs	Median Rating
Netherlands	61	3.33%	7.52%	ZB	2.83%	0.153%	1.020%	ZB–
United Kingdom	442	3.62	11.60	ZB–	6.52	0.218	2.580	ZC+
Canada	368	3.70	12.20	ZB–	4.15	0.164	3.350	ZB–
United States	2,236	3.93	9.51	ZB–	3.28	0.139	2.320	ZB
France	297	5.51	9.72	ZC+	3.75	0.290	2.060	ZC+
Germany	289	5.54	13.10	ZC+	2.67	0.268	3.960	ZC+
Spain	82	6.44	9.63	ZC	9.39	0.363	1.360	ZC
Italy	155	7.99	10.20	ZC	8.69	0.493	1.650	ZC
Portugal	30	9.36	7.25	ZC–	10.90	0.482	0.827	ZC
Greece	79	10.56	14.40	ZC–	24.10	0.935	3.660	ZC–

[a]Based on Z-Metrics PDs from January 1, 2010, to April 1, 2010.
[b]Assuming a 40 percent recovery rate, based on CDS spreads observed from January 1, 2010, to April 2010.
[c]Probability of default (PD) is computed as $1 - e^{(-5*s/(1-R))}$.
Sources: RiskMetrics Group, 2010; Markit; Compustat.

to use other ways to hedge country-specific risks, such as creating a short position in that country's debt or shorting a relevant stock index. Short-selling activity directly in government bonds will certainly have a greater effect on government bond prices, as it involves selling the actual instruments in the market. A ban might also remove potential demand for government debt from so-called negative basis traders (investors who buy bonds and short the associated CDSs, pocketing the difference), hindering the liquidity of the government debt market. Furthermore, the blanket restriction on naked positions would have unanticipated effects on basis hedges such as the purchase of a sovereign CDS to hedge a position in corporate bonds of the country.

BOX 13.1: SOVEREIGN DEFAULT RISK ASSESSMENT FROM THE BOTTOM UP

*Edward I. Altman**

Periodically, sovereign economic conditions spiral out of control and require a massive debt restructuring and/or bailout accompanied by painful austerity programs in order for the country to function again in world commercial and financial markets. Recent instances involving several Latin American countries in the 1980s, Southeast Asian nations in the late 1990s, Russia in 1998, and Argentina in 2000 are examples of situations in which a nation's severe problems not only impacted its own people and markets but created seismic financial tremors the likes of which we are now experiencing from the situation involving Greece and several of its southern European neighbors.

The dire condition of these nations usually first manifests as a surprise to most, including the agencies that rate the default risk of sovereigns and the companies that reside in these suddenly threatened nations. Similar to Greece, which was investment grade not long ago, South Korea, considered in 1996 to be one of the "Asian Tigers" with an AA– rating, one of the best credit ratings possible, was downgraded within one year to BB–, one of the so-called junk rating categories, and would have defaulted if not for a $50 billion bailout from the International Monetary Fund (IMF).

Academics and market practitioners simply have not had an impressive record of providing adequate early warnings of impending sovereign economic and financial problems using the usual macroeconomic indicators, such as GDP growth, debt levels relative to GDP, trade and financial deficits, unemployment, and productivity. While there is no absolute guarantee of providing the magic formula for early warning transparency of impending doom, we believe that one can learn a great deal about sovereign risk by analyzing the health and aggregate default risk of a nation's private corporate sector—a type of bottom-up analysis. Models such as Altman's established Z-Score technique (1968), and more recently (2010) RiskMetrics' Z-Metrics system, can provide an important additional measure of sovereign vulnerability.

The Z-Metrics system combines several fundamental measures of corporate default risk—such as profitability, leverage, and liquidity—with equity market value measures and a few macroeconomic stress variables. Each factor is assigned a weighting, which when tallied up gives a measure of default probability for one- and five-year horizons. By aggregating these measures for listed companies in each country and calculating median credit scores and default probabilities, one can assess the overall health of the nation's private sector. Our Z-Score tests showed that South Korea was the riskiest country in all of Asia at the end of 1996, which was before the Asian crisis started in Thailand and spread east and north to cover most countries. Thailand and Indonesia followed South Korea closely as the next most vulnerable countries. And yet, South Korea was, as noted, considered to be an excellent credit by traditional methods.

The current situation in Europe is also instructive. In a recent test of default probabilities (see Table 13.4), using our new Z-Metrics measure, Greece clearly has the most risky and the least healthy private sector profile, with a five-year median cumulative default probability of over 1,000 basis points (10.56 percent), followed by Portugal (9.36 percent), Italy (7.99 percent), and Spain (6.44 percent). Germany and France display a moderate overall credit risk cohort (5.5 percent), with the United Kingdom (perhaps a surprise) and the Netherlands rounding out our survey as the least risky corporate sectors. The United States and Canada also display healthy metrics. With the most notable exception of Greece, our five-year median default probabilities for corporates are quite close to the median for sovereigns. Default probabilities are derived from the credit default swap (CDS) market's five-year contract over the past few months in 2010. The CDS market's default probability assessment for Greece is more than twice our median default probability for its corporate sector. Similar differences can be observed for the United Kingdom and Spain, although at lower

---

default probability levels. Of course, 50 percent of the corporations in these countries have default probabilities greater than the median.

So, in prescribing difficult sanctions to governments in order for them to qualify for bailouts and subsidies, we should be careful to promote, not destroy, private enterprise valuations. Improving corporate health can be an early indicator of a return to health of the sovereign.

*Dr. Altman is the Max L. Heine Professor of Finance at the NYU Stern School of Business and an adviser to several financial institutions, including the RiskMetrics Group.

Regardless, the proposed reforms to the OTC derivatives markets should reassure the governments that they would have unfettered access to trading information should it be desired to rule out market manipulation motives. This is but just one of the useful roles that the much-needed transparency of OTC derivatives can serve. The transparency of the OTC derivatives market would shine a much-needed light on the market and obviate the need for desperate measures such as banning naked short selling.

NOTES

1. Even if the Treasury ultimately determines to exclude FX swaps and forwards, the bill provides that parties to such transactions are subject to certain business conduct standards and requires these transactions to be reported to a swap data repository or to the CFTC.
2. The Act divides jurisdiction over the derivatives markets between the CFTC and the SEC. The CFTC will have jurisdiction over "swaps" and certain participants in the swap market, while the SEC will have similar jurisdiction over "security-based swaps." The definition of *swap* under the Act includes interest rate, currency, equity, credit, fixed-income, and commodity derivatives, with certain exceptions for physically settled commodity forwards and certain securities transactions (such as security options). Note that over-the-counter FX swaps and forwards are included in the definition of swap, but the secretary of the Treasury has the authority to exempt them from the definition of the term swap. The term *security-based swap* is defined as a swap on a single security (or loan) or index composed of a narrow group of securities.
3. *Financial entities* includes swap dealers, major swap participants, commodity pool operators, a private fund under the Investment Advisers Act of 1940, an employee benefit plan, or an entity predominantly engaged in activities related to banking or that is financial in nature.

4. Under the Act, a *swap data repository* is "any person that collects and maintains information or records with respect to transactions or positions in, or the terms and conditions of, swaps entered into by third parties for the purpose of providing a centralized recordkeeping facility for swaps."

5. A *swap dealer* is "any person who (i) holds itself out as a dealer in swaps; (ii) makes a market in swaps; (iii) regularly enters into swaps with counterparties as an ordinary course of business for its own account; or (iv) engages in any activity causing the person to be commonly known in the trade as a dealer or market maker in swaps, provided, however, in no event shall an insured depository institution be considered to be a swap dealer to the extent it offers to enter into a swap with a customer in connection with originating a loan with that customer."

6. A *major swap participant* is "any person who is not a swap dealer, and (i) maintains a substantial position in swaps for any of the major swap categories (as determined by the Commission), excluding (I) positions held for hedging or mitigating commercial risk; and (II) positions maintained by any employee benefit plan (or any contract held by such a plan) as defined in the Employee Retirement Income Security Act of 1974 for the primary purpose of hedging or mitigating any risk directly associated with the operation of the plan; (ii) whose outstanding swaps create substantial counterparty exposure that could have serious adverse effects on the financial stability of the U.S. banking system or financial markets; or (iii) (I) is a financial entity that is highly leveraged relative to the amount of capital it holds and that is not subject to capital requirements established by an appropriate Federal banking agency; and (II) maintains a substantial position in outstanding swaps in any major swap category as determined by the Commission."

7. The provisions of the Volcker Rule are to take effect on the earlier of 12 months after the issuance of the final rules or two years after the enactment of the Act, at which point a two year transition period begins, with the possibility of additional extensions thereafter.

8. A *systemically significant institution* is a bank holding company with total consolidated assets equal to or greater than $50 billion or a nonbank financial company supervised by the Board of Governors.

9. This prohibition on lender-of-last-resort support is commonly referred to as the "swaps push-out provision," as it effectively forces many derivatives activities to be pushed out of insured banks into separately capitalized entities.

10. The prohibition on federal assistance does not prevent an insured depository institution from acting as a swaps entity for swaps or security-based swaps involving CDSs, if those are cleared. Therefore, a beneficial consequence of this provision, which essentially allows banks to retain *cleared* CDSs in their books without losing the benefits of federal assistance, is the push toward central clearing of CDSs.

11. The Commission will have to decide on the provisions: "(i) to ensure such information does not identify the participants; (ii) to specify the criteria for determining what constitutes a large notional swap transaction (block trade) for particular markets and contracts; (iii) to specify the appropriate time delay

for reporting large notional swap transactions (block trades) to the public; and (iv) that take into account whether the public disclosure will materially reduce market liquidity."

12. It is equally important for regulators to have information on derivatives' risk exposures not just in clearinghouses and exchanges in their own jurisdiction, but also in other global financial centers. The Act recognizes this and provides sufficient latitude in international information sharing across clearinghouses and data repositories. However, the implementation issues will be fairly complex and remain largely unknown.

13. Industry and regulatory sources offer varying estimates of the size of the OTC market, but they all underscore similar past and current trends. Over the past decade, the OTC derivatives market, both in the United States and internationally, registered exponential growth (over 20 percent compound annual growth rate since 1998), with credit derivatives as a significant force behind it. Today, based on recent statistics from the Bank for International Settlements, the OTC segment accounts for 90 percent of the overall derivatives market size in terms of notional amount outstanding, and the total notional amount of all types of OTC contracts outstanding globally almost doubled to $605 trillion in the four years to June 2009.

14. In effect, our recommendation amounts to imposing a position limit, but one whose size—as it applies to each market participant—is determined by the participant, subject to the requirement that its largest position in the clearinghouse be fully collateralized. In case the clearinghouse has concerns about a particular group of firms, for example those in one industry, the definition of the single largest exposure could be broadened to include this group.

15. "Goldman Sachs Demands Collateral It Won't Dish Out," Bloomberg, March 15, 2010.

16. "The Case for Regulating Financial Derivatives," *Barron's*, March 22, 2010.

17. A total of 67 ISDA member firms responded to the 2009 Margin Survey. The Survey classifies respondents into three size groups based on the number of collateral agreements executed. The threshold for classification as a large program is 1,000 agreements; under this criterion, 20 firms are classified as large. Financial firms with 51 to 1,000 agreements are considered to be medium (25 firms fall into this classification); and the rest, financial firms that have fewer than 50 agreements, are classified as small (22 firms fall into this classification).

18. www.imf.org/external/pubs/ft/wp/ 2010/wp1099.pdf.

19. BIS Derivatives Statistics, June 2009, Table 19, memo item (www.bis.org/ statistics/derstats.htm).

20. Another, somewhat more subtle device would be to legislate that, in the event of a default, OTC counterparties are junior to any centrally cleared or exchange-traded claim. This would ensure that uncleared OTC products still exist but are subject to substantial counterparty risk or high margins; in turn, these products would be worthwhile only if customization gains are sufficiently large.

21. Aggregated reports for credit derivatives are currently being published by the Depository Trust & Clearing Corporation (DTCC), but it is clear that they fall

short of the transparency standard we deem necessary to assess counterparty and systemic risks with sufficient granularity (without compromising anonymity).

22. Some economists argue that it is possible that increased transparency might destroy incentives to gather information and actually deter market makers from operating in these markets, which, in turn, might decrease liquidity. We note, however, that the illiquidity costs need to be weighed against the financial fragility costs arising when large players fail. We hold the view that suitably *aggregated* information on exposures should be disseminated to the market at large.

23. The four financial institutions without exposure to derivatives are: New York Community Bancorp Inc., Hudson City Bancorp, Vornado Realty Trust, and ProLogis.

24. Typically, an oil company's trading risk position will be net short the commodity, offset by the company's natural long position as a producer.

25. See Hills, Rule, Parkinson, and Young (1999) for further details.

26. Panel on the Stock Market Crash of 1987 with Nicholas Brady and Gerald Corrigan (Brookings-Wharton Papers on Financial Services, First Annual Conference, Washington, DC, October 29, 1997).

27. The term *stable value contract* means any contract, agreement, or transaction that provides a crediting interest rate and guaranty or financial assurance of liquidity at contract or book value prior to maturity offered by a bank, insurance company, or other state or federally regulated financial institution for the benefit of any individual or commingled fund available as an investment in an employee benefit plan subject to participant direction, an eligible deferred compensation plan that is maintained by an eligible employer, an arrangement described in section 403(b) of the Internal Revenue Code of 1986 (tax-sheltered annuity), or a qualified tuition program.

REFERENCES

Acharya, Viral V., and Alberto Bisin. 2010. Counterparty risk externality: Centralized versus over-the-counter markets. Working paper, NYU Stern School of Business.

Acharya, Viral V., and Robert Engle. 2009. Derivatives trades should all be transparent. *Wall Street Journal*, May 15.

Hills, Bob, David Rule, Sarah Parkinson, and Chris Young. 1999. Central counterparty clearing houses and financial stability. *Bank of England Financial Stability Review*.

Santos, T., and José A. Scheinkman. 2001. Competition among exchanges. *Quarterly Journal of Economics* 116 (3): 1027–1062.

PART Four

Credit Markets

CHAPTER 14

The Government-Sponsored Enterprises

Viral V. Acharya, T. Sabri Öncü, Matthew Richardson,
Stijn Van Nieuwerburgh, and Lawrence J. White*

14.1 OVERVIEW

Despite the ongoing congressional efforts to rewrite the U.S. financial regulations after the onset of the ongoing global financial crisis, there is no attempt to reform the two mortgage giants—Fannie Mae (or, more formally, the Federal National Mortgage Association [FNMA]) and Freddie Mac (or, more formally, the Federal Home Loan Mortgage Corporation [FHLMC]), both of which are government-sponsored enterprises (GSEs)—in the bill that was passed by the U.S. Congress and signed into law by President Obama in July 2010.

In fact, the only mention of Fannie Mae and Freddie Mac is hidden in a subsection of a miscellaneous subtitle of the mortgage reform section of the Dodd-Frank Act.[1] Rather than enacting legislation, this subsection presents a series of findings about the GSEs in terms of their foray into the subprime mortgage market, ending with the following conclusion:

> *The hybrid public-private status of Fannie Mae and Freddie Mac is untenable and must be resolved to assure that consumers are offered and receive residential mortgage loans on terms that reasonably*

---

*We benefited from discussions in the "Towards a New Architecture for U.S. Mortgage Markets: The Future of the Government Sponsored Enterprises" Working Group for the NYU Stern e-book *Real Time Solutions for Financial Reform*, which also included Stanley Kon.

reflect their ability to repay the loans and that are understandable and not unfair, deceptive, or abusive. . . . It is the sense of the Congress that efforts to enhance by the protection, limitation, and regulation of the terms of residential mortgage credit and the practices related to such credit would be incomplete without enactment of meaningful structural reforms of Fannie Mae and Freddie Mac.

According to a recent *Financial Times* article,[2] Federal Reserve Chairman Ben Bernanke believes that a blueprint for Fannie Mae and Freddie Mac should have been outlined in the spring of 2010, but Treasury Secretary Timothy Geithner put the final resolution of Fannie and Freddie a year off. We believe that this delay is a major policy mistake, as we argue in this chapter.

Although Fannie Mae and Freddie Mac are not the only GSEs,[3] our references to GSEs in this chapter will refer to only these two companies. The key policy question is: Given the central role that they played in this crisis, what is to be done to fix them? We provide a few suggestions that may help answer this important question. Our earlier suggestions, together with an analysis of the GSE crisis as it unfolded in mid to late 2008, can be found in Jaffee, Richardson, Van Nieuwerburgh, White, and Wright (2009).

14.2 THE BEGINNINGS

Fannie Mae was created as part of the New Deal in response to the Great Depression of the 1930s. It was chartered by the Federal Housing Administration (FHA) in 1938 as a government agency to help stabilize the mortgage market for the FHA. While the purpose of the FHA, created as part of the National Housing Act in 1934, was to insure mortgage loans to low-income and middle-income borrowers by private lenders, the primary purpose of Fannie Mae was to purchase, hold, or sell FHA-insured mortgage loans. In 1948, Fannie Mae's authority was expanded to include the Veterans Administration (VA)-guaranteed home mortgages.

The Federal National Mortgage Association Charter Act of 1954 removed government backing for borrowings that were used to fund Fannie Mae's secondary market operations. It also stipulated that Fannie Mae be exempt from all local taxes except property taxes, and provided for the Federal Reserve banks to perform various services for Fannie Mae. This act also opened the path through which Fannie Mae's secondary market operations could be transferred to the private sector.

In 1968, Fannie Mae was quasi-privatized, so as to remove its activity from the annual budget and balance sheet of the U.S. government. All direct government subsidy activities of the old Fannie Mae were transferred to the FHA and to a contemporaneously established government agency, the Government National Mortgage Association (GNMA or Ginnie Mae), and the bulk of secondary market operations of the old Fannie Mae were spun off to the new Fannie Mae, which was owned by private shareholders. Yet the new Fannie Mae has never become a fully private corporation, because it maintained the privileges given to the old Fannie Mae by the Federal National Mortgage Association Charter Act of 1954.

In 1970, the U.S. Congress chartered the Federal Home Loan Mortgage Corporation (Freddie Mac), another privately owned corporation, to provide competition to Fannie Mae. As described by the Federal National Mortgage Association Charter Act of 1954, both of the GSEs have the following purposes:

(1) to provide stability in the secondary market for residential mortgages;

(2) to respond appropriately to the private capital market;

(3) to provide ongoing assistance to the secondary market for residential mortgages (including activities relating to mortgages on housing for low- and moderate-income families involving a reasonable economic return that may be less than the return earned on other activities) by increasing the liquidity of mortgage investments and improving the distribution of investment capital available for residential mortgage financing; and

(4) to promote access to mortgage credit throughout the Nation (including central cities, rural areas, and underserved areas) by increasing the liquidity of mortgage investments and improving the distribution of investment capital available for residential mortgage financing.

Like Fannie Mae, Freddie Mac had been exempt from state and local income taxes and certain Securities and Exchange Commission (SEC) requirements, had access to U.S. Treasury funding up to $2.25 billion, and was given the right to use the Federal Reserve as its fiscal agent, as well as several other special privileges (see, for example, Frame and White 2005 and Jaffee and Quigley 2007 for details).

14.3 THE CRISIS

The GSEs perform two separate roles. Their first function—the guarantee function—is arguably the most important: guaranteeing the credit risk of *conforming mortgages* that the GSEs bundle into securities. Conforming mortgages are those mortgages that meet the criteria that are set by the regulator of the GSEs.[4] Among other criteria defining a conforming mortgage is the maximum loan size; loans that exceed the established size limit are called jumbo loans. The GSEs buy conforming mortgages from mortgage originators, bundle them into pass-through[5] mortgage-backed securities (MBSs), and sell the MBSs to private investors.[6] However, the GSEs bear all of the default risk of these mortgages. They charge a small fee for this guarantee (e.g., averaging 22 basis points in 2007), and they hold \$0.45 of capital for every \$100 of mortgage face value that they guarantee.

Ex post, it appears that the GSEs received inadequate compensation and held inadequate capital for the default risk they were bearing. The small fee and 45 basis points of capital were for the most part designed for prime mortgages.[7] But, based on reports by the GSEs in the fall of 2009, Jaffee (2010) documents that Fannie Mae had guaranteed \$8 billion of subprime mortgages, \$259 billion of Alt-A (alternative-to-agency) mortgages, and \$591 billion worth of other high-risk mortgages. Freddie Mac had not guaranteed any subprime mortgages, but had guaranteed \$156 billion of Alt-A mortgages and \$407 billion worth of other high-risk mortgages. (See also Moore 2010.) This is one reason why their overall capitalization was inadequate relative to the risks they undertook.

Their second role is essentially that of a hedge fund: purchasing both prime and nonprime (Alt-A as well as subprime) mortgage securities. They financed these asset purchases by issuing so-called agency debt.[8] Because of an implicit government guarantee, which has now become an explicit guarantee, the GSEs are able to borrow at interest rates that are below the levels that the market would demand in the absence of the guarantee. The leverage ratio of the GSEs on these purchased assets was a stunning 30:1 at the height of the housing boom, again illustrating that GSEs—through their own choice of leverage—have been inadequately capitalized. Further, while their mortgage portfolios were of long maturity, the agency debt that they issued was of shorter maturity, so their assets were more sensitive to the shifts in interest rates than were their liabilities. While the GSEs hedged these risks, the maturity mismatch exposed them to model misspecification error of their mortgage pricing models.

Despite critics' fears that these interest rate risks were not fully hedged and would eventually cause financial difficulties for the GSEs, it was the credit risks of their guarantees and of the mortgages that they held in their portfolios that led to their downfall. Jaffee (2010) reports that, in addition to the riskier mortgages that they had guaranteed (mentioned earlier), Fannie Mae held in its portfolio $22 billion of subprime mortgage portfolios and $25 billion of Alt-A mortgages, whereas Freddie Mac held $64 billion of subprime mortgage portfolios, $22 billion of Alt-A mortgages, and $18 billion worth of other high-risk portfolio holdings, for a combined total of $151 billion.

After the housing bust that began in late 2006, Fannie Mae and Freddie Mac experienced unprecedented losses on their mortgage portfolios and their guarantees, and this wiped out their thin capital. In 2001, Fannie and Freddie had started buying risky private-label securities, and their holdings started to swell significantly after 2003 (e.g., Jaffee 2010; Moore 2010). For example, Jaffee (2010) documents that as a percentage of their new business, their high-risk lending increased from 21 percent in 2003 to 44 percent in 2004, 45 percent in 2005, and 51 percent in 2006. Some of the mortgage loans that underlay the securities in their mortgage portfolios were made to low-income households and thus helped the GSEs meet their affordable housing goals, as determined by their then "mission" regulator, the U.S. Department of Housing and Urban Development (HUD).

Let us look at the hedge fund function of the GSEs closely. For every $1 of mortgage-backed securities purchased with equity, they borrowed heavily to purchase additional mortgage-backed securities. Figure 14.1 shows

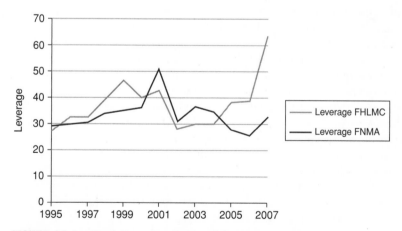

FIGURE 14.1 Book Leverage Ratio of the GSEs, 1995 to 2007
Source: Office of Federal Housing Enterprise Oversight (OFHEO) Annual Report, Bloomberg.

the book leverage ratios of the GSEs, measured as total assets divided by common equity, over the period 1995 to 2007. What needs to be noted is the GSEs' ability to maintain such a high leverage (book leverage exceeding 20:1 throughout this period) given that they were investing in risky, relatively illiquid mortgage-backed securities. This provides an idea of the importance of the implicit government guarantee.

In fact, studies have estimated the transfer from taxpayers to the GSEs to be in the billions of dollars even before the crisis ignited. For example, in a May 2001 study, the Congressional Budget Office (CBO) calculated an annual implicit subsidy that increased from $6.8 billion in 1995 to $13.6 billion in 2000. While the GSEs questioned the methodology of that analysis, later academic studies confirmed the findings. Using a standard discounted earnings model based on the implicit government subsidy, Passmore (2005) estimates that the gross value lies somewhere between $119 billion and $164 billion, of which shareholders receive respectively between $50 billion and $97 billion. Using an alternative approach based on options pricing, Lucas and McDonald (2006) report a somewhat smaller value of $28 billion, though a recent update by the authors in Lucas and McDonald (2010) shows that this value can increase with more realistic modeling. Of some interest, they show a value at risk at the 5 percent level for Fannie Mae of $165 billion and for Freddie Mac of $112 billion, eerily close to their losses in the current crisis if one is to believe the CBO estimates.

The liabilities of Fannie Mae and Freddie Mac also give some idea of the importance of this implicit government guarantee. The GSE debt is typically issued at interest rates that are somewhere between AAA-rated corporate and U.S. Treasury debt obligations, and is bought by domestic institutional investors, as well as foreign central banks and sovereign wealth funds that treat GSE debt as U.S. Treasury equivalents. An estimate of the cost of this implicit federal subsidy for the debt issued by the GSEs can be derived from the spread between the interest rates that are paid by the GSEs on the agency debt that they sell and the rates that are paid by comparable (roughly, AA–) private institutions. Quigley (2006) gives a detailed review of estimates of this spread that are reported in different studies using different methodologies. On the basis of this evidence, the Congressional Budget Office has concluded that the GSEs enjoy an overall funding advantage of about 41 basis points. Passmore (2005) documents a similar subsidy of 40 basis points from 1998 to 2003, while Lucas and McDonald (2010) again come in a little lower at 20 to 30 basis points.

The implicit government guarantee backing the agency debt as well as MBSs issued by the GSEs played a significant role in the increased foreign demand for these securities. Flow of funds data show that the amount of U.S. agency securities, including those of Fannie Mae and Freddie Mac, held by foreign countries tripled to $1.46 trillion in 2008 (21.1 percent of the total), from $492 billion in 2002 (10.8 percent of the total). This is particularly troubling because, irrespective of claims to the contrary by Treasury officials through the years, the GSE debt de facto became government debt. Default on this debt may well therefore have had consequences for official sovereign U.S. debt. Figure 14.2 gives a breakdown of the foreign holders of the agency and GSE-backed securities.

As mentioned before, on the assets side, the investment portfolio of the GSEs became markedly riskier through time as they loaded up on nonprime mortgages under pressure from Congress and various administrations. Successive secretaries of the Department of Housing and Urban Development (HUD) mandated that the GSEs increase the share of mortgage loans to low-income households from 40 percent in 1996 to 50 percent in 2001 to 56 percent in 2008. It has been argued by some analysts (see, for example, Pinto 2008) that the GSEs' nonprime bets were even larger.

In response to turmoil in the housing and mortgage markets, the Housing and Economic Recovery Act of 2008 (HERA) gave the U.S. Treasury the power to buy an unlimited amount of securities from Fannie Mae and Freddie Mac if the Treasury secretary determined that such actions are necessary to:

- Provide stability to the financial markets.
- Prevent disruptions in the availability of mortgage finance.
- Protect the taxpayer.

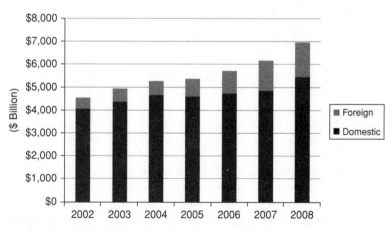

FIGURE 14.2 Foreign Holders of Agency Securities ($ Billions)
Source: Federal Reserve Statistical Release Z.1, Flow of Funds Accounts of the United States.

The unlimited authority was to assure investors that the two GSEs would be kept solvent by the federal government. When the substantial losses that Fannie Mae and Freddie Mac faced threatened their solvency, the newly established Federal Housing Finance Agency (FHFA) under HERA placed them into conservatorships on September 7, 2008, eight days before the Lehman Brothers collapse of September 15, 2008.

As documented by the CBO, as of May 2010 the Treasury had injected a total of $144.9 billion into the two entities, and the CBO projects that an additional $65 billion may be required to keep Fannie Mae and Freddie Mac solvent until 2019. The CBO has further estimated that the total tax-payer losses might ultimately reach somewhere between $300 billion and $400 billion.

14.4 RECOMMENDATIONS

Since their collapse in September 2008, the issue of whether the GSEs were too big to fail has been debated by various analysts and politicians. Shareholders and preferred stockholders lost almost all of their value while creditors were bailed out. As unseemly as this latter action was, there can be little doubt that the GSEs were systemically risky and too big to fail. The argument for why this is can be broken down to four reasons:

1. As Figure 14.2 shows, the debt was widely held by foreigners who, rightly or wrongly, treated the debt as U.S. government-backed. Default on this debt might have been taken as a signal that U.S. government backing was no longer assured, having severe consequences for U.S. sovereign debt issuance.
2. The GSEs guarantee approximately $5.4 trillion worth of mortgages (27 percent of which is retained in their portfolios). The loss of these guarantees might have had significant counterparty repercussions throughout the financial sector. Moreover, as this crisis showed, the GSEs are effectively the prime mortgage market. The disappearance of the GSEs during the crisis would have seriously curtailed the housing market without any backup.
3. The GSEs held over $1.5 trillion worth of mortgage-backed securities. Liquidation of these securities (or the mere threat of liquidation) would have led to fire sales of these securities and caused a collapse in their values. The collapse would have meant substantial further losses on the balance sheets of other financial institutions, leading to further fire sales and loss in value, and so forth, with the potential for a death spiral in the financial sector.

4. Because of their size and presence in the mortgage market, the GSEs were also one of the largest participants in derivatives markets, primarily in the interest rate swap market for hedging interest rate risk. The failure of the GSEs would have exposed their counterparties in the derivatives markets to possible losses on their derivatives books. The magnitude of this counterparty risk and uncertainty about who had exposure to the GSEs could have caused a run on many financial institutions and a freezing of the derivatives market.

Combined, these reasons imply that the GSEs in their current form will always be considered too big to fail. No risk management practice, regulatory oversight, or resolution authority will ever be able to handle them. Unlike the absence of structural reform for large financial institutions in the rest of the financial reform bill, the GSEs need to be put through a radical metamorphosis of their business model and practices.

We believe that there are three key issues that need to be dealt with by the Obama administration and Congress:

(1) **First and foremost, the hedge fund function of the GSEs needs to be discontinued entirely.** There is no role for a gigantic government-sponsored hedge fund, trading in mortgage-related contracts. The original rationale for this activity was to promote liquidity in the secondary mortgage market. This reasoning is obsolete, because markets have now had more than 30 years of experience in investing in and trading conforming MBSs. We envision that the government could slowly wind down the assets on the GSEs' balance sheets—for example, by corralling them into a kind of Resolution Trust Corporation like the one that was created during the savings and loan crisis in the late 1980s and early 1990s. This entity could hold MBSs until maturity or slowly sell them into the private market. Private investors could raise private capital and purchase the assets from the GSEs. Under the conservatorship agreement, the current plan is to reduce the portfolio by 10 percent each year from its 2009 limit of $900 billion until it reaches $250 billion. This is a step in the right direction, but does not go far enough.

(2) **Second, the guarantee function of the GSEs should be revisited and possibly discontinued.** This could be accomplished in several ways:

- One option is to fully nationalize the guarantee business for conforming loans. The rationale for such nationalization is that in the next large mortgage crisis, the government would inevitably bail out any private securitization firm—say, the privatized Freddie Mac or Fannie Mae. A downside of this approach is that no market information is available to ensure that the government receives the correct insurance fee and that the guarantee function remains economically viable. The current guarantee fee is too low and needs to be recalibrated in case this option is employed.

- A second option is to fully privatize the guarantee business. In this scenario, the GSEs would be completely dismantled. This would eliminate the distortions that arise because of the implicit government guarantees, such as artificially low financing costs and artificially low mortgage rates. Note that conforming mortgages are loans that are conservatively underwritten: For example, all of the pooled conforming loans in a mortgage-backed security have loan-to-value ratios of 80 percent or less (or are covered by private mortgage insurance) and have documented debt-payment-to-income ratios of 35 percent or less. Therefore, these loans will normally have low credit risk to begin with.

  The idea is to structure the cash flows from these pooled loans into tranches. The most senior tranche would effectively have no credit risk, and therefore would not need any credit guarantees. This tranche could be as large as 80 percent of all conforming loans; the default rate would need to exceed 40 percent with only a 50 percent recovery rate before the senior tranche would take its first dollar loss. Such losses for conforming mortgages are unprecedented, even in the worst housing market since the Great Depression. Under this scenario, the remaining 20 percent of loans would be securitized as subordinated tranche(s) that would contain (some) credit risk, and trade as such in private markets. Subordinated tranches may or may not contain insurance from private companies, such as the monolines.

- A third option, which is a public-private hybrid, would see the GSEs disappear, but it would keep all conforming mortgage-backed securities guaranteed. From the investors' side, one potential advantage of keeping all conforming mortgage-backed securities guaranteed (credit risk-free) is that an investment community with substantial human capital was built up around default-free mortgage-backed securities. Under this scenario, private mortgage securitizers would purchase mortgage loans from originators and issue default-free mortgage-backed securities. Instead of bearing the credit risk, private securitizers would purchase mortgage default insurance for the mortgage-backed securities. In practice, this would be necessary for only the 20 percent subordinated debt mentioned before. However, it still may require too much private capital to insure the credit risk of all conforming mortgages in mortgage-backed securities.

  We believe that there may be an important role for the government here. In particular, mortgage default insurance would be offered through a new public-private partnership structure, modeled after the Terrorism Risk Insurance Act of November 2002. Specifically, the securitizer would purchase, say, 25 percent of its insurance from a large monoline insurance company and 75 percent from a newly formed government entity. As with terrorism risk insurance, the private insurance market would help to establish a market price for mortgage default risk. The newly formed government entity would charge a fee based on this market price. This would ensure that the government also receives adequate compensation for the credit risk, a key difference from the pre-crisis approach.

In the private scenarios, regulation would need to be imposed to prevent securitizers from bulking into large systemic hedge funds that would pose the same risks as do Fannie Mae and Freddie Mac and to ensure that monoline insurance companies that provide private insurance are well capitalized.

In principle, the public-private insurance could not only be provided for conforming loan pools, but also be extended to nonconforming loans (prime jumbo, Alt-A, and subprime). Indeed, such a structure may help to revitalize the nonprime mortgage market. Consequently, we recommend that such an approach be explored for the nonconforming mortgage market, as well. It would ensure that the government receives compensation for the systemic credit risk, which it ultimately bears on all mortgages. As in the 2008 crisis, most of that default risk in the event of a major housing crisis is, in fact, concentrated in the nonprime mortgage segment.

(3) **Third, the GSEs should get out of the business of promoting home ownership for low-income households and underserved regions.** We believe that whatever decision is made about the future of the GSEs, the two current mandates of making mortgage markets liquid and well-functioning and of promoting access to mortgage credit by underserved groups or regions are incompatible.

The current approach of government intervention through the GSEs—to keep mortgage interest rates artificially low for all households—is both too expensive and ineffective. If the policy objective is to promote and subsidize low-income home ownership, then the Federal Housing Administration and its securitizer, Ginnie Mae, as well as the Department of Housing and Urban Development (HUD) are much better suited to perform the role for the underserved groups or regions, rather than for all households at large. Such a focused approach would be both more transparent and more effective.

In general, we recommend that the government reassess the efficacy of housing subsidies as a tool to curb inequality. Housing subsidies, whether they are home-mortgage interest tax deductibility or the tax-free status of the income (rent) derived from owning a home, distort the price of housing relative to other consumption and investment goods. As such, they may lead the U.S. economy to overinvest in relatively unproductive housing assets instead of in more productive business capital.

14.5 WAY FORWARD: PROJECTIONS TO THE FUTURE IF THE GSEs ARE NOT FIXED

The current financial legislation proposals are completely silent on the future of Fannie Mae and Freddie Mac. We believe that this is a mistake given the central role they played in the crisis, their systemic nature, and their structural weaknesses, all of which will persist unless addressed with urgency.

Although the GSEs are currently under government control through the conservatorships, and the losses that accrue are mostly due to the souring of the mortgages that were acquired and/or guaranteed prior to September 7, 2008, nevertheless the longer that the GSEs remain under government control, the harder it will be to establish any new structure. We especially fear an inertial reversion to their former quasi-government/quasi-private structure. This would simply be a recipe for a repeat of their inadequately capitalized status, their excessive risk taking, and then their financial collapse. This surely cannot be a sensible route for the Obama administration—or any other administration—to pursue.

Viewed slightly differently, the implicit guarantee of the GSE debt represents a major off-balance-sheet debt of the U.S. government. The ratio of government debt to gross domestic product (GDP) in the United States is now approaching 100 percent (and by some other measures, close to 120 percent, its level in 1945 following World War II). The steady rise in government debt-to-GDP ratio since 2001 (when it was under 40 percent) is a cause for concern as the economy's recovery remains practically jobless, households remain indebted, house prices are stagnant, and the global economy stays fragile. Any further rise in federal indebtedness is unlikely to be sustainable in the wake of a significant global shock (such as further weakening of sovereigns in the euro zone or a slowdown of economic growth in Asia).

The U.S. government should at the outset consolidate on its balance sheet the nontrivial quantity of guarantees that it has provided to the financial sector, notably to the GSEs. This would discipline fiscal planning to take account of these guarantees and recognize that the government's contingent leverage is significantly higher than its current leverage. In our view, sensible fiscal planning would require the government to plan for a graceful exit from the guarantees. Whether the government sees beyond the next election or passes the buck on to future governments and taxpayers will be the litmus test of the political will in the United States for making short-run sacrifices in the interest of long-run sustainable growth.

A final note of caution: On the assumption that the GSEs are reformed, and their backing from the U.S. government is removed, it is important that their explicit guarantees are not passed on as implicit guarantees elsewhere in the financial system. One can imagine that large, complex financial institutions with too-big-to-fail guarantees, or as-yet-unformed entities in the shadow banking world, may step into the void. Given the size of the mortgage market, regulators should make sure that neither mortgage guarantees nor mortgage-backed securities are held in high concentration by lightly capitalized institutions. Given the addiction of the U.S. financial system to mortgage subsidies, and the historical reluctance to regulate the housing sector (even in the presence of systemic risk in these markets), we have reason not to be optimistic.

NOTES

1. See the Dodd-Frank Wall Street Reform and Consumer Protection Act of 2010, Title XV, "Mortgage Reform and Anti-Predatory Lending Act," Subtitle H, "Miscellaneous Provisions," Sec. 1491, "Sense of Congress regarding the importance of government-sponsored enterprises reform to enhance the protection, limitation, and regulation of the terms of residential mortgage credit."
2. "Freddie Mac Likely to Need More Cash Support," *Financial Times*, February 24, 2010.
3. The Federal Home Loan Bank System is also a GSE.
4. Prior to August 2008 their prudential regulator was the Office of Federal Housing Enterprise Oversight (OFHEO). Their current regulator, the Federal Housing Finance Agency (FHFA), was established by the Federal Housing Finance Regulatory Reform Act of 2008, which is Division A of the larger Housing and Economic Recovery Act of 2008, signed into law on July 30, 2008, by President George W. Bush.
5. That is, the interest and principal payments by the underlying mortgage borrowers are passed through (except for fees) to the MBS investors.
6. Often the GSEs simply arrange a swap with the originator, swapping the securities for the mortgages and then letting the originator decide whether to hold the securities or sell them in the secondary market.
7. Prime mortgages are mortgage loans that are extended to borrowers with high credit scores, whereas nonprime mortgages are mortgage loans that are offered to borrowers who do not qualify for prime mortgage loans. Alt-A (alternative-to-agency) mortgages generally refer to loans that are offered to borrowers with

high credit scores but reduced proof of income. Subprime mortgages are mortgage loans that are extended to borrowers with low credit scores whether they have proof of income or not. The category of "other high-risk mortgages" includes loans that have similar characteristics to subprime and Alt-A, such as high loan-to-value ratios, lower FICO scores, and/or interest-only/option adjustable-rate mortgage (ARM) features, but are not strictly designated as such.

8. Their debt is known as agency debt possibly because when Fannie Mae was first chartered in 1938 it was a government agency, although Freddie Mac has never been one.

REFERENCES

Frame, W. S., and L. J. White. 2005. Fussing and fuming over Fannie and Freddie: How much smoke, how much fire? *Journal of Economic Perspectives* 19:159–184.

Jaffee, D. 2010. The role of the GSEs and housing policy in the financial crisis. U.C. Berkeley working paper prepared for presentation to the Financial Crisis Inquiry Commission.

Jaffee, D., and J. M. Quigley. 2007. Housing subsidies and homeowners: What role for government-sponsored enterprises? *Brookings-Wharton Papers on Urban Affairs*, 103–130.

Jaffee, D., M. Richardson, S. Van Nieuwerburgh, L. J. White, and R. Wright. 2009. What to do about the government sponsored enterprises? In *Restoring financial stability: How to repair a failed system*, ed. V. V. Acharya and M. Richardson. Hoboken, NJ: John Wiley & Sons.

Lucas, D., and R. McDonald. 2006. An options-based approach to evaluating the risk of Fannie Mae and Freddie Mac. *Journal of Monetary Economics* 53 (1): 155–176.

Lucas, D., and R. McDonald. 2010. Valuing government guarantees: Fannie and Freddie revisited. In *Measuring and managing federal financial risk*, ed. D. Lucas. Chicago: University of Chicago Press.

Moore, D. 2010. CBO's budgetary treatment of Fannie Mae and Freddie Mac. *Congressional Budget Office Background Paper*, January.

Passmore, W. 2005. The GSE implicit subsidy and the value of government ambiguity. *Real Estate Economics* 33 (3): 465–486.

Pinto, E. 2008. Statement before the Committee on Oversight and Government Reform. U.S. House of Representatives, December 9.

Quigley, J. M. 2006. Federal credit and insurance programs: Housing. *Federal Reserve Bank of St. Louis Review* 88 (4): 281–310.

CHAPTER 15

Regulation of Rating Agencies

Edward I. Altman, T. Sabri Öncü, Matthew Richardson, Anjolein Schmeits, and Lawrence J. White*

15.1 OVERVIEW

Credit rating agencies (CRAs) are firms that offer judgments about the creditworthiness—specifically, the likelihood of default—of debt instruments that are issued by various kinds of entities, such as corporations, governments, and, most recently, securitizers of mortgages and other debt obligations. It has been widely argued that the rating agencies played a central role as enablers in the financial crisis of 2007 to 2009, due to the following two key features of the ratings process.

First, beginning in the 1930s, financial regulation has mandated that rating agencies be the central source of information about the creditworthiness of bonds in U.S. financial markets. More recently, other countries have adopted similar regulations; for example, Japan's Ministry of Finance imposed a requirement in the mid-1980s that only investment-grade companies (i.e., firms rated BBB or higher) could issue corporate bonds. Reinforcing this centrality was the U.S. Securities and Exchange Commission (SEC)'s creation of the Nationally Recognized Statistical Rating Organization (NRSRO) designation in 1975 and its subsequent protective entry barrier around the incumbent NRSROs. The fact that regulators used ratings as their primary source for measuring risk gave a powerful status to NRSROs; see, for example, White (2010).

*We are grateful to Thomas Cooley for helpful comments and suggestions. We would like to especially thank Laura Veldkamp and Ingo Walter, members of the Stern Working Group on rating agencies, for their input and suggestions.

Second, the prevalent business model of the major rating agencies is the "issuer pays" model. That is, the issuer of a security both chooses and pays the rating agency for rating the security. This leads to a potential conflict of interest because the rating agency has a financial incentive to pander to issuers in order to be chosen as the rater. Of course, this creates tension with the rating agencies' mission of providing an objective analysis of credit risk of the security. This tug-of-war between the rating agencies' reputations for objectivity and their incentives to get business, coupled with their special NRSRO status in regulation, was at the heart of the financial crisis.

In addition, and partly related to the conflict of interest, issues with respect to ratings quality and flaws in the methodology used by rating agencies to rate mortgage-backed securities (MBSs) and structured products were important factors in the crisis.

The Dodd-Frank Act attempts to address these issues comprehensively and contains some significant conceptual improvements to the ratings process by putting in place various measures to improve internal controls and rating accuracy, and by removing regulatory reliance on ratings. The latter is a small step toward shifting the burden of information collection to the users and may improve competitiveness, ratings quality, and innovation in the industry. However, the Act is less forceful in dealing with the problem of incentive misalignment in the "issuer pays" model and in assessing the optimal business model for rating agencies. Furthermore, the legislation appears to substitute heavy oversight and rule making by the SEC for market solutions, which may have some adverse effects. In this chapter, we examine the problematic role of CRAs in the crisis, evaluate the proposals in the Act, and provide suggestions for additional improvements in the ratings process.

15.2 THE CRISIS

The three largest U.S.-based credit rating agencies—Moody's Investors Service, Standard & Poor's (S&P), and Fitch Ratings—were clearly central players in the subprime residential mortgage debacle of 2007 to 2008. Their initially favorable ratings were crucial for the successful sale of bonds that were securitized from subprime residential mortgages and similar debt obligations. The sale of these bonds, in turn, was an important underpinning for the U.S. housing boom and bubble of 1998 to 2006. When house prices plateaued in mid-2006 and then began to fall, default rates on the underlying mortgages rose sharply, and the initial ratings proved to be wildly overoptimistic. The prices of mortgage bonds cratered, and massive downgrades of the initially inflated ratings wreaked havoc throughout the U.S. financial system and damaged the financial systems of many other countries as well.

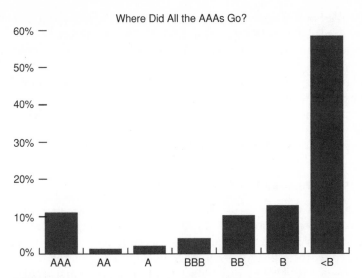

FIGURE 15.1 Ratings Distribution as of June 30, 2009, of Newly Issued AAA-Rated Asset-Backed Securities from 2005 to 2007
Note: S&P rating distribution of 2005 to 2007 issued U.S. AAA-rated ABS CDOs.
Source: International Monetary Fund, *Global Financial Stability Report,* chap. 2, "Restarting Securitization Markets: Policy Proposals and Pitfalls" (October 2009), 93. Web link: www.imf.org/external/pubs/ft/gfsr/2009/02/pdf/text.pdf. (*Data source:* Standard & Poor's.)

Figure 15.1 illustrates the extent of the downgrades that were suffered by securities that were tied to the residential mortgage-backed security (RMBS) market. The chart shows that, of all the senior-most asset-backed security (ABS) and collateralized debt obligation (CDO) tranches that were issued between 2005 and 2007 and were originally rated AAA, only about 10 percent were still rated AAA by S&P by the end of June 2009. Meanwhile, almost 60 percent were rated below B, among the lowest rating levels and well below investment grade. Straight private-label residential MBSs (not shown) experienced a similar ratings decline, with 63 percent of AAA-rated securities issued between 2005 and 2007 being downgraded by August 2009 (and 52 percent downgraded to BB or lower).

A key question, therefore, for regulators of rating agencies and also for prudential regulators of financial institutions is whether evidence like that presented in Figure 15.1 shows an inherent flaw in the ratings process or simply reflects an unexpected macroeconomic shock (i.e., bad luck on the part of the credit rating agencies).

There is a plethora of recent academic research, both theoretical and empirical, that sheds light on this question. In the next few subsections, we discuss the literature and focus on three problem areas:

1. The regulatory dependence on ratings and the role of rating requirements in existing regulation.
2. The conflicts of interest that are associated with the business model of the rating agencies.
3. The quality of ratings independent of this conflict of interest.

Regulatory Dependence on Ratings

The consequences of the errors of the major rating agencies in rating mortgage-backed securities have been so severe because the rating agencies play a central role in the bond markets—a centrality that has been greatly reinforced by the regulatory requirements imposed upon the major institutional investors in these markets. Since the 1930s, prudential regulation has required that banks, insurance companies, pension funds, money market mutual funds, and securities firms must follow the ratings of the major rating agencies in making decisions as to what bonds should be held in their portfolios.

This special role of the rating agencies was crystallized in 1975 when the SEC created a special designation (NRSRO) and immediately ushered the three large rating agencies (Moody's, S&P, and Fitch) into this category. The SEC subsequently became an opaque barrier to entry into the ratings industry, allowing only four more firms to attain the NRSRO designation during the following 25 years. Mergers among the four late entrants and subsequently with Fitch, however, caused the number of NRSROs to shrink back to the original three by year-end 2000. Thus, as the subprime residential mortgage securitization process was gathering steam in the early part of the decade of 2000 to 2009, only three rating firms could provide the ratings—especially the highly valued AAA and AA ratings—that could allow mortgage securitizers' bonds to be held in the portfolios of the prudentially regulated financial institutions.

Sy (2009) provides a good discussion of the Basel Committee on Banking Supervision's analysis of the regulatory uses of credit ratings. This analysis aggregated 17 surveys from a total of 26 separate agencies across 12 different countries, and concludes that credit ratings are an essential part of the regulatory process for identifying assets that are eligible for investment purposes, for determining capital requirements, and for providing an evaluation of credit risk. Key examples include the use of NRSRO ratings in the United States to decide capital charges for broker-dealers and to set credit risk weights for banks under the Basel II Accord.

With respect to the current crisis, this dependence on ratings encouraged prudentially regulated financial institutions to engage in regulatory arbitrage. Specifically, these institutions were encouraged to reach for yield by investing in bonds that were rated as appropriate for the institution but that carried yields that were higher than usual for the bonds in that rating class; the higher yields indicated that the bond markets understood that these bonds were riskier than the rating suggested. Financial institutions could thus take on excessive risk while appearing to abide by the prudential regulatory restrictions. See, for example, the detailed discussion in Calomiris (2009).

Furthermore, since AAA-rated securities were given special status with respect to capital requirements, financial institutions with artificially low costs of funding due to mispriced government guarantees—such as the government-sponsored enterprises (GSEs) Fannie Mae and Freddie Mac, too-big-to-fail institutions, and Federal Deposit Insurance Corporation (FDIC)-insured depository institutions—had a particular incentive to take carry trades and lever up on these AAA-rated securities. Acharya, Cooley, Richardson, and Walter (2010) argue that this manufacturing of tail risk on certain mortgage-backed securities was central to the financial crisis. While there are numerous examples of regulatory arbitrage by financial institutions during the financial crisis, the following four examples are particularly illuminating:

1. On page 122 of American International Group (AIG)'s 2007 annual report, it was reported that $379 billion of its $527 billion credit default swap (CDS) exposure on AAA-rated asset-backed securities sold by AIG's now-infamous Financial Products group was written not for hedging purposes, but to facilitate regulatory capital relief for financial institutions. Regulatory rules had zero capital requirement if an AAA-rated insurance company provided credit enhancement for AAA-rated securities.

2. While the focus of the collapse of AIG has been on its Financial Products division, which lost $40.8 billion in 2008, it has been much less reported that AIG's Life Insurance and Retirement Services division had similar losses of $37.5 billion in the same year. These losses stemmed from the Life Insurance and Retirement Services division's failed securities-lending businesses, aggressive variable annuity death benefit provisions, and investment losses on its over $500 billion asset portfolio. Securities lending is normally considered a low-risk activity because the collateral is invested in safe short-term assets. In this crisis, however, AIG exploited the AAA rating of certain mortgage-backed securities and invested almost two-thirds of its cash collateral in longer maturities ranging from three years to 10 years. This exposed AIG to a maturity mismatch and

consequently large losses if the borrowers of AIG's securities did not roll over their loans (as turned out to be the case in some critical instances, such as Lehman Brothers).

3. Another example of regulatory arbitrage witnessed in the run-up to the crisis was based on exploiting ratings for the purpose of satisfying capital adequacy requirements. Acharya, Schnabl, and Suarez (2010) show that commercial banks established conduits to securitize assets while simultaneously insuring these newly securitized assets using credit guarantees. These credit guarantees were structured to reduce bank capital requirements via the conduits' AAA rating. As we now know, many of the commercial banks involved in this activity became seriously impaired in the crisis. For example, the two largest players, Citigroup and ABN Amro, financed $93 billion and $69 billion, respectively, of AAA-rated securities off balance sheet through so-called special purpose vehicles, and both effectively failed.

4. Similarly, in the 18-month period prior to July 2007 (the beginning of the crisis), UBS increased its holdings of AAA-rated nonprime mortgage-backed securities from $5 billion to more than $50 billion. Merrill Lynch did likewise. But these numbers were actually small compared with the accumulations of Fannie Mae, Freddie Mac, and the Federal Home Loan Bank System (the other housing GSE). The GSEs held almost $300 billion of these securities, according to an April 2008 Lehman Brothers report. In fact, as per this report, of the $1.64 trillion of these securities outstanding, an astonishing 48 percent was held by banks, broker-dealers, and the GSEs.

Conflicts of Interest in the "Issuer Pays" Model

The conflict of interest that is associated with the "issuer pays" model adopted by the major rating agencies in the early 1970s had largely been kept in check by the rating agencies' reputational concerns (see, e.g., Covitz and Harrison 2003). Rating agencies were helped by the fact that there were thousands of issuers of corporate and government debt that they rated, so the threat by any one issuer to take its business elsewhere was not potent. Moreover, the plain-vanilla debt that was being rated was quite transparent, so that errors (accidental or otherwise) would be quickly spotted.

For the mortgage-related structured bonds, however, the conflict of interest was exacerbated, since the volumes of rated bonds were large, the profit margins wide, and issuers far fewer; thus, an issuer's threat to take its business to a different rating agency was far more compelling. For example, Figure 15.2 shows the growing importance of structured products to Moody's during the period from 2002 to 2007. Specifically, the figure

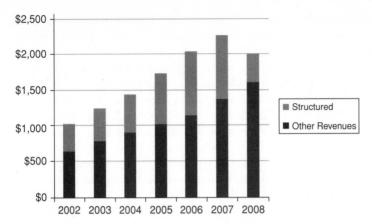

FIGURE 15.2   Moody's Revenues in $ Millions
Source: Moody's Annual Reports 2002 to 2008.

graphs the breakdown of revenues between structured finance products and the rest of Moody's business.

In addition, the rated securities were far more complex and opaque than plain-vanilla bonds, so that errors were less likely to be spotted quickly. The issuers also figured out how to game the ratings criteria and were perceived to receive debt structuring advice from the rating agencies themselves (see International Monetary Fund 2009).

Most financial market analysts would agree that the current business model of the major CRAs can lead to severe conflicts of interest, which tend to reduce the quality of ratings and the accountability of the rating agencies. The conflicts of interest stem not only from who pays for the rating, but also from the fact that the rating agencies provide other revenue-generating services to the rated companies.

Recent papers—such as Bolton, Freixas, and Shapiro (2008); Mathis, McAndrews, and Rochet (2009); Sangiorgi, Sokobin, and Spatt (2009); and Skreta and Veldkamp (2009), among others—provide a theoretical justification for regulation based on the conflict-of-interest argument. The conflicts of interest that are addressed in these papers include ratings inflation due to the fact that the rating agencies are paid by the issuers, as well as the practice of so-called ratings shopping, whereby the issuer can troll the NRSROs for the best rating. Regulatory suggestions that are provided in these papers with respect to the future of the business model of CRAs are discussed at the end of this chapter.

Given the compelling nature of the conflict-of-interest argument, researchers have developed tests of implications of these theories. In particular,

Ashcraft, Goldsmith-Pinkham, and Vickery (2009) provide a detailed analysis of subprime and Alt-A MBS issuance between 2001 and 2007. While they find that credit ratings on MBSs contain useful information, their overall evidence is fairly damning. Specifically, consistent with Bolton, Freixas, and Shapiro (2008) and Mathis, McAndrews, and Rochet (2009), who argue that ratings inflation is more likely to occur during high-volume periods, Ashcraft et al. (2009) show that during the 2005 to mid-2007 period ratings became increasingly inflated even after adjusting for credit risk and deal characteristics.

The authors also report that for a given credit rating, more opaque MBSs, such as those based on loans with less documentation, perform much worse than other MBSs. This result is consistent with the conclusions of Sangiorgi, Sokobin, and Spatt (2009) and Skreta and Veldkamp (2009), who highlight the importance of transparency. Equally telling evidence on the conflict of interest related to ratings shopping is provided by Benmelech and Dlugosz (2009). They find that tranches that are rated by just one agency, a characteristic that is consistent with ratings shopping, are more likely to be downgraded, and more severely at that.

While the aforementioned papers document issues with the ratings of structured products of residential mortgage-backed securities, these issues also appear relevant for other securities, such as commercial mortgage-backed securities (CMBSs). For example, Stanton and Wallace (2010) analyze the performance of CMBSs before and during the financial crisis. They show that loan underwriting standards did not significantly deteriorate in the period leading up to the crisis, but instead that most of the failure in the CMBS market can be attributed to growing ratings inflation of the higher tranches of CMBSs.

To this point, according to an August 2009 Goldman Sachs report, the evolution of the capital structure of CMBSs had changed dramatically during the decade leading up to the crisis. In particular, the report gives the breakdown of the percentages of commercial mortgage pools that are tranched as AAA, AA, A, BBB, BB, and equity. The report provides evidence that the mezzanine subordination level, and therefore credit enhancement, consistently decreased in the decade prior to the crisis. For example, between 1995 and 2007, the range of the pool that was AA-rated went from (26.8%, 21.2%) to (9.5%, 7.2%).

The empirical evidence suggests that conflicts of interest played an important role in the financial crisis. This evidence is supplemented by testimony of employees of the rating agencies to congressional and other regulatory committees. While some of the testimony may be taken with a grain of salt due to different interpretations of events and the fact that some employees may have been disgruntled, the overwhelming part of the testimony strongly supports the conflict-of-interest story with respect to structured products. According to the testimony, the profit margins that were associated with rating these products took center stage over the firms' providing adequate resources given the growth in this market, and rating quality was generally less emphasized. In fact, some testimony went as far as to claim that ratings methodologies were changed in response to losses in market share.[1]

Ratings Quality

Apart from the conflict-of-interest problem, there is another strong argument that can be made against both the quality and the accuracy of the ratings. This was especially the case for structured products, where the CRAs did not seem to fully understand the products that they rated and did not take default correlations into account. Flawed methodologies and data inputs were often used to assign ratings, and investors who relied on these ratings did not always have sufficient information to assess their quality. The methodologies and inputs that were used to rate nonprime residential MBSs (and CDOs backed by RMBSs) were particularly flawed, overestimating the quality of the underlying loans and underestimating the correlation of their performance.

As an example, Hull and White (2009) analyze ex post the risk of MBSs and MBS CDOs that were issued between 2000 and 2007. Using criteria similar to those used by the rating agencies, they look at the variation in AAA tranches under different modeling assumptions, such as loan correlations and recovery rates. They find that, while the AAA ratings assigned to the senior tranches of MBSs were in line with the theoretical models, the AAA ratings assigned to tranches of the mezzanine portion of the MBS CDOs could not be justified. Similar findings are documented by Coval, Jurek, and Stafford (2009) and Griffin and Tang (2009).

Another aspect of ratings quality is the timeliness and accuracy of rating changes. A considerable focus of the regulatory investigation of rating agencies' role in the crisis has been the widespread view that rating agencies were slow to react to the housing collapse in their analysis of structured products. While some see the rigidity of ratings by CRAs in the crisis as evidence of malfeasance, there is a history of CRAs' preference for stable ratings (see, e.g., Altman and Rijken 2004, 2010). CRAs argue that short-term credit quality shifts may lead to rating reversals in the future, and have even cited surveys that show that issuers strongly prefer stability over frequent changes, especially with respect to downgrades. In addition, since there are transaction costs that are associated with changes in portfolio holdings, an institutional investor that is subject to regulatory mandates that are linked to ratings would prefer to avoid the alterations in portfolios that could be driven by a cyclical down-and-up pattern of ratings fluctuation.[2]

15.3 PUBLIC INTEREST OBJECTIVES OF RATING REGULATION

If a credit rating is inflated or of low quality, there is little accountability and, in general, almost no incentive for the rating agencies to compete on quality. In fact, competition may actually lower quality as rating agencies compete under the specter of the conflict of interest; see, for example, Bolton, Freixas, and Shapiro (2008) for a theoretical analysis that makes this point.[3] As an illustration of the effect of competition on rating agencies, Becker and Milbourn (2008) examine the impact of the increase in Fitch's market share on corporate bond ratings that were provided by Moody's and S&P. They document a decrease in ratings quality with competition. Many researchers have argued that the ratings process for structured products is even more vulnerable to this problem.

Even if the business model of rating agencies were switched to an "investor pays" model and the free-rider problem of investors could be solved, there is still potential for a race to the bottom; that is, prudentially regulated institutions will shop around for the lowest rating that will still satisfy regulatory standards and seek the highest yield subject to that constraint (reaching for yield). This will often entail investing in securities that the market (and perhaps the investor) believes are more risky than the (mistaken) rating indicates. As described earlier, during the crisis many institutional investors, especially large, complex financial institutions (LCFIs), used ratings not only to measure risk internally but also to engage in regulatory arbitrage.

The conflict-of-interest argument and the poor quality of initial ratings of RMBSs have encouraged the development of alternative models and products from firms that estimate ratings and default probabilities that are less subject to these issues.[4] However, given the fact that ratings by NRSROs are an important part of the regulatory process and a crucial determinant of investment strategies, there is still need for reform.

Any regulation of the rating industry should have a number of important public interest objectives:

- To completely remove or significantly reduce the power and influence that the incumbent CRAs have on the functioning of global capital markets.
- To provide meaningful and accurate information to investors, issuers, regulators, and other major market participants on the probability of

default and loss given default of debt securities issued by firms, financial institutions, and sovereigns and on the derivative instruments that are related to these primary securities, and, by doing so, restore confidence in CRAs and financial markets.

■ To remove or reduce the potential conflicts of interest that are inherent in the current business model of CRAs, in particular with respect to the "issuer pays" model.

15.4 THE DODD-FRANK WALL STREET REFORM AND CONSUMER PROTECTION ACT (2010)

The severe recent criticism of the rating agencies comes after prior rating debacles involving the Asian crisis of the late 1990s and many fraud-related, but fairly transparent, cases like Enron and WorldCom of the early 2000s. The criticisms in those instances involved the rating agencies' tardiness in downward rating adjustments. In the case of the mortgage securities ratings, however, the major criticism is aimed at the rating agencies' *initial*, overly optimistic ratings. It is therefore no surprise that financial regulatory reform has included specific provisions for regulating the credit rating agencies.

Title IX, Subtitle C, "Improvements to the Regulation of Credit Rating Agencies," proposes legislation to strengthen the regulation of rating agencies and to restore investor confidence in the rating process.

Role of Government

The Dodd-Frank Act (2010) stresses the systemic importance of credit ratings and the public interest nature of the activities and performance of rating agencies as rationales for regulation. A key premise of the Dodd-Frank Act is that conflicts of interest, particularly in the advising of arrangers of structured financial products, as well as the inaccuracy in the rating of such structured financial products, should be addressed.[5]

The Act presents new rules for internal control and governance, independence, transparency, and liability standards. It establishes an Office of Credit Ratings at the SEC to "administer the rules of the Commission (i) with respect to the practices of NRSROs in determining ratings, for the protection of users of credit ratings, and in the public interest; (ii) to promote accuracy in credit ratings issued by NRSROs; and (iii) to ensure that such ratings are not unduly influenced by conflicts of interest."[6]

The Act requires an internal control structure and annual ratings review process, which gives the SEC the right to suspend or revoke the registration of an NRSRO with respect to a particular class or subclass of securities if the NRSRO "has failed over a sustained period of time, as determined by the Commission, to produce ratings that are accurate for that class or subclass of securities . . . or does not have adequate financial and managerial resources to consistently produce credit ratings with integrity," or if rules regarding the separation of ratings and sales and marketing were violated.[7]

The Act further requires that each NRSRO should "publicly disclose information on the initial credit ratings determined by the NRSRO for each type of obligor, security, and money market instrument, and any subsequent changes to such credit ratings, for the purpose of allowing users of credit ratings to evaluate the accuracy of ratings and compare the performance of ratings by different NRSROs."[8] In addition, to enhance transparency in rating performance and methodologies, the Act requires that each NRSRO provide comprehensive disclosures on the information, procedures, and methodologies that are used in estimating and changing credit ratings, and stress the potential limitations of the ratings and the types of risks that are not included in the rating (such as liquidity, market, correlation, and other risks). Moreover, the Act requires the rating agencies to provide an explanation or measure of potential volatility for the credit rating, any factors that may lead to a change in the rating, and the sensitivity of the rating to those factors.

Finally, the Act contains various other provisions, the most notable of which removes credit rating agencies and the firms that issue securities from exemption from the SEC's fair disclosure (FD) rule.[9]

With respect to the role of NRSROs, the legislation is a clear attempt to hold the rating agencies accountable and to open up the system to higher-quality information with respect to the risks of securities. Specifically, we favor the following aspects of the proposals:

- Some regulatory oversight, since regulators are among the largest consumers of ratings through determining capital requirements of financial institutions and prudent rules for investors.
- The periodic audit of ratings that are provided by NRSROs and the ability of the SEC to rescind the NRSRO status based on its findings (at least with respect to a particular class or subclass of securities).

We have concerns, however, about the legislation with respect to the granting and maintenance of NRSRO status. While oversight of NRSROs is needed, some of the provisions are quite onerous in terms of compliance, yet would appear to yield only small benefits. In practice, given their fixed-cost nature, this will impose a relatively heavier burden on innovative start-up NRSROs, thereby strengthening the dominance of the larger rating agencies. Over time, one would hope that the amount of oversight would be streamlined. In addition, the success of the legislation depends on the ability of the SEC to implement effective oversight—an area in which it has not been particularly successful in the past. One suggestion in this respect would be to explore the creation of the equivalent of the Public Company Accounting Oversight Board (PCAOB) for rating agencies. It is unclear how this would substitute for or complement the Office of Credit Ratings at the SEC, but it seems worthy of consideration.

As a final note, the Act's removal of the FD exemption for rating agencies will clearly reduce the market power of the NRSROs, but may also lead to unintended consequences. Empirical evidence suggests that the removal of the exemption from Regulation FD will reduce the information content of rating changes, and thus may negatively impact the efficiency of financial markets (see Jorion, Liu, and Shi 2005).

Reliance on NRSRO Ratings

With respect to the reliance on NRSRO ratings, the Dodd-Frank Act explicitly calls for the removal of statutory references to credit ratings in federal and state law on financial regulation. In particular, the Act mandates replacement of the language "investment grade" and "non–investment grade"; it especially mandates replacement of the latter by "that does not meet standards of credit-worthiness." In addition, the Act proposes that federal agencies undertake a review of their reliance on credit ratings, develop different standards of creditworthiness, and amend their regulations to reflect these different standards.[10]

We strongly support the removal of specific language that requires regulatory agencies to rely on credit ratings. This is quite important, as ratings are not sufficient to measure the risk of fixed-income securities, as we describe in the next section. Furthermore, we endorse the idea that rating agencies should provide more than a single-point estimate of risk by adding potential stressed outcomes. For example, in addition to a single estimate of default risk, there should be a specification of a reasonable distribution of different outcome scenarios.

But the regulator should also look to other sources for risk measurement. Beyond the default risk estimated by rating agencies, both the regulator and investor need to consider model/misspecification error, liquidity/funding risk, and market risk. The specification of a reasonable distribution of outcome scenarios would have been extremely useful in the subprime mortgage structured finance debacle that led to the crisis. For example, estimates of rating migration under different scenarios of real estate price declines might have highlighted the default risk more clearly and alerted investors more effectively than did a single rating designation.

15.5 DODD-FRANK AND CONFLICTS OF INTEREST

In order to incentivize the rating agencies to do their job effectively, the Dodd-Frank Act defines liability standards for failing to investigate or obtain analysis from independent sources. For example, investors can now bring suit against rating agencies for a knowing or reckless failure to conduct a reasonable investigation of the rated security. Rating agencies are now subject to so-called expert liability; in other words, they are no longer exempt on First Amendment grounds from private rights of action.[11] In this respect, the Act proposes that since credit rating agencies effectively play a gatekeeper role in the debt markets and perform commercial evaluative and analytical services on behalf of their clients, they should be subject to the same standards of accountability and liability as are security analysts, investment bankers, and auditors.[12]

As for the independence of rating agencies, the potential conflicts of interest associated with the "issuer pays" model, and the provision of non-rating-related services by rating agencies, the Act prohibits "the sales and marketing considerations of an NRSRO from influencing the production of ratings by the NRSRO." The Act does not allow compliance officers to work on ratings or sales, and installs a one-year look-back review when an employee of an NRSRO goes to work for an underwriter of a security that is subject to an NRSRO rating.[13]

Most important, however, is the Act's provision that calls for a two-year study of the credit-rating process for structured finance products and the conflicts of interest that are associated with the "issuer pays" and the "investor pays" models. In particular, the study is to determine the "feasibility of establishing a system in which a public or private utility or a self-regulatory organization assigns Nationally Recognized Statistical Rating Organizations to determine the credit ratings of structured finance products."[14] The review should include an analysis of mechanisms for determining fees for the NRSROs, metrics for determining the accuracy of credit ratings, and alternative methodologies of creating incentives for the NRSROs to report accurate credit ratings.

While studies are always met with some skepticism, the Act goes further by calling for "a system for the assignment of NRSROs to determine the initial credit ratings of structured finance products, in a manner that prevents the issuer, sponsor, or underwriter of the structured finance product from selecting the NRSRO that will determine the initial credit ratings and monitor such credit ratings. In issuing any rule . . . the Commission shall give thorough consideration to the provisions of . . . section 939D of H.R. 4173 (111th Congress), as passed by the Senate on May 20, 2010, and shall implement the system described in such section 939D unless the Commission determines that an alternative system would better serve the public interest and the protection of investors."[15]

Section 939D calls for a Ratings Board to be housed in the Office of Credit Ratings at the SEC. The majority of the Ratings Board would be composed of investors in structured finance products, and its purpose would be to assign a rating agency to the issuer for the initial rating of a structured security. That is, the Office of Credit Ratings would install a centralized clearing platform for rating agencies. It would work in three steps:

1. A company that wants its structured debt to be rated would go to the Ratings Board. Depending on the attributes of the security, a flat fee would be assessed.
2. From a sample of approved rating agencies, the Ratings Board would choose, most likely via lottery, the rating agency that rates the security. While this choice could be random, a more palatable lottery design could be based on some degree of excellence, such as the quality of the ratings methodology, the rating agency's experience at rating this type of debt, some historical perspective on how well the rating agency has rated this type of debt relative to other rating agencies, past audits of the rating agency's quality, and so forth.
3. For a fee, the rating agency would then proceed to rate the debt. The issuer would be allowed to gather additional ratings, but the initial rating would have to go through this process, which no longer allows the issuer to choose the rater.

Section 939D of HR 4173 was proposed by Senator Al Franken, became known as the Franken Amendment, and was passed by a supermajority of the Senate but watered down in conference in trying to reconcile the House and Senate versions of the financial reform bill. The Congress could not agree on how to allocate rating mandates across the various NRSROs; consequently, in a typical congressional compromise, they simply mandated that the SEC conduct a study to determine how to do that.

The legislation addresses the conflict of interest that is associated with the "issuer pays" model to some extent via Section 939D. This reform reduces the scope for ratings shopping and more generally the incentive to inflate ratings without compromising credit rating agencies' willingness to voice a diversity of opinions. This is because, by construction, removing issuers' choice of rating agency diminishes the scope for ratings shopping and removes the incentive for rating agencies to attract business by offering favorable ratings. If the Ratings Board uses expertise as a criterion, this reform will also more likely spur competition among rating agencies to produce a higher-quality product. That is, to maintain a strong weight in the lottery, the rating agency will have incentives to invest resources, innovate, and perform high-quality work. Right now, there is no incentive for the rating agencies to produce quality ratings, because they are not rewarded for doing so. In fact, since issuers pay the raters, one could argue the reverse, leading to a race to the bottom.

Of course, the issue in the end will come down to the outcome of the study and whether regulators will decide to honor the spirit of the Dodd-Frank Act and implement Section 939D of HR 4173 if no better alternative is found. On the one hand, the Act written this way makes sense. There are a number of implementation issues, not the least of which is the payment scheme and the SEC's ability to execute and administer a system of this type. Moreover, one concern about Section 939D of HR 4173 is that it might lead to unintended consequences, such as enshrining the ratings and the raters that are chosen by the lottery as officially sanctioned ratings and again be the only component of risk assessment. On the other hand, the Act might give the SEC too much leeway to implement a meaningless reform that does not adequately address a major cause of the financial crisis: the breakdown in the ratings process due to the combination of the conflict of interest and regulatory reliance on ratings.

This is especially true because the other reforms that are written in the Dodd-Frank Act do not seem sufficient. For example, while the proposal to force more disclosure of preliminary ratings sounds like a step in the right direction, it is easily circumvented. Investment banks are well aware of the methodologies that raters use and can figure out which agency is likely to offer the highest rating. Imposing more uniformity on ratings—by penalizing rating agencies that perform worse than their peers or by dictating ratings methodologies—may reduce the variance of ratings. However, by making ratings more similar, these measures also diminish the additional information content of multiple ratings, which may leave investors—and, more importantly, regulators—less well-informed.

As a final comment, holding the NRSROs accountable for their errors introduces the notion of legal liability. While expanded legal liability will clearly increase their accountability and thus improve their behavior, it may impose considerable costs on the system. By construction, almost any ex ante credit rating is wrong ex post upon default of the issuer. This could lead to frivolous and unfair lawsuits and may result in a bias toward overestimating the probability of default in published ratings. We therefore prefer to let the market penalize credit rating agencies for inaccurate ratings, which is more along the lines of implementing a business judgment rule and is more consistent with enhanced competition.

In regard to other jurisdictions, given that rating agencies command a special status in terms of regulatory reliance on their product outside the United States, it should not be surprising that rating agencies are also a prominent part of the regulatory agenda worldwide. Specifically, international proposals by the Group of Twenty (G-20), Britain's Financial Services Authority (FSA), the Financial Stability Board (FSB), the International Monetary Fund (IMF), the Organization for Economic Cooperation and Development (OECD), and the European Commission of the European Union (EU) all call for stronger (and internationally coordinated) regulatory oversight of registered rating agencies in order to ensure good governance and manage conflicts of interest, and also require an increase in transparency and quality of the rating process. The G-20, the FSA, and the EU proposals recommend the introduction of differentiated ratings for structured products. The OECD proposal focuses on increasing the competitiveness of the rating industry by lowering barriers to entry through simpler registration requirements and by encouraging unsolicited ratings to stimulate the expansion of small credit rating agencies with new business models. The EU and OECD proposals appear to be more explicit in recommending changes in the business model of rating agencies (e.g., the EU proposal suggests an internationally coordinated switch from the "issuer pays" to the "investor pays" model) and a reduction in the use of NRSRO ratings in financial regulation. As described in our analysis of the Dodd-Frank Act, however, increased competition will not necessarily lead to higher-quality ratings; and a switch to the "investor pays" model does not solve the conflict-of-interest problem as long as investors have an incentive to use ratings to exploit capital regulatory requirements.

More recently (on June 2, 2010), the European Commission proposed amendments to the supervisory framework for CRAs, adopted in April 2009, to improve the international coordination of regulatory oversight at the EU level. Under the Commission's current proposal, a new European supervisory authority, the European Security Markets Authority (ESMA), with direct supervisory powers over CRAs, will be established. The ESMA will be responsible for the registration, supervision, and day-to-day monitoring of CRAs, as well as for taking appropriate supervisory measures that range from the issuance of a public notice to the withdrawal of the registration in the event that a CRA is determined to be in breach of the regulation. Although this proposal transfers all supervisory powers to the ESMA, it allows for the possibility that the ESMA may delegate powers back to national authorities, where appropriate, such as on-site inspections for day-to-day monitoring. Furthermore, the proposal allows for the possibility that national authorities may request the ESMA to examine whether the conditions for the withdrawal of a CRA's registration are met or whether the use of credit ratings issued by a CRA should be suspended based on its assessment of a serious and persistent breach of the regulation. However, the responsibility will remain with the ESMA.[16] While we agree with the European Commission's claim that a single central regulator at the EU level may allow the CRAs to operate in a simpler regulatory environment, we remain concerned about the tremendous faith put in the ability of a central regulator to monitor and evaluate the performance of the rating agencies.

Another aspect of the amendments is that the European Commission requires the issuers of structured finance instruments to provide information not only to the CRA that they choose, but also to all other interested CRAs. This aspect of the amendments appears to be intended to reinforce competition among CRAs, avoiding possible conflicts of interest under the "issuer pays" model, and enhancing transparency and the quality of ratings. We believe that this requirement is a step in the right direction for avoiding possible conflicts of interest and reinforcing competition, and may even form a basis for a hybrid business model in which some of the CRAs disclose their ratings publicly, while others may choose to keep the ratings private and try to sell them to interested investors.

Last, in its June 3, 2010, press release regarding the amendments, the European Commission reiterated its concerns about the lack of competition in the global rating industry and acknowledged its intent to examine further structural solutions, including the establishment of a European CRA or other independent public entities with a stronger role in the issuing of ratings. This acknowledgment confirms our belief that rating agencies will remain present at the top of the regulatory agenda worldwide for quite a while.

15.6 LOOKING FORWARD

In the typical view of the role of ratings in the financial crisis, investors were asleep at the wheel because of the government's seal of approval of rating agencies. But our analysis shows that ultimately it was not investors who were deceived here but instead it was taxpayers who were deceived. This is how it worked: Because the issuer pays the agency that rates the security, there is a huge conflict of interest to shop the security around until the issuer gets the desired rating, leading to inflated ratings. Thanks to several academic studies and recent testimony by rating agency officials, we now know that this took place. And because the government sets its regulatory structure around these ratings, investors like AIG, Citigroup, ABN Amro, UBS, Fannie Mae, Freddie Mac, and, for that matter, Merrill Lynch and Lehman Brothers, among others, were able to engage in risky activities without having to hold a sufficient capital buffer due to the inflated ratings. Rating agencies acquiesced in this unholy alliance between investors and issuers. The crisis, and the taxpayer-funded bailouts that followed, could not have transpired the way it did without rating agencies planted in the center of the financial system.

The Dodd-Frank Act represents a major change in the way that credit rating agencies would be regulated. The legislation addresses the two core problems: first, the central role of NRSRO ratings in financial regulation and the dominance of a few rating agencies in the industry; and second, the conflict of interest in the "issuer pays" model and how some investors use these ratings.

Among the largest consumers of rating agencies are the prudential regulators. But their very reliance, coupled with the existing conflicts of interest and possibility for regulatory arbitrage, has made the system less stable. It seems clear that, going forward, the rating agency model needs to be quite different. While the legislation is a major step in the right direction, one would hope that the Dodd-Frank Act would lead to major changes through its commissioned studies. Next, we address the regulatory reliance and conflict of interest issues.

Regulatory Reliance on Ratings

Ratings are not sufficient to measure the risks of fixed-income securities and therefore the risk profiles of financial institutions. There are generally three risk components that need to be evaluated: default risk and model risk, liquidity/funding risk, and market risk. Although the following comments hold generally for all securities, we illustrate the ideas using structured securities as an example.

Default Risk and Model Risk   We do not know enough yet about the process by which the rating agencies evaluated the default probability and expected losses of structured securities. Was their analysis ex ante poor quality or are we simply judging them in hindsight? Clearly, the conditions were ripe for abuse—the economics involved with rating structured products, the involvement of the rating agencies in also structuring the products, the aforementioned conflicts of interest, and so on. But we will leave this issue of process aside.

Instead, we want to focus on whether structured products can really be rated in a comparable manner to, for example, corporate bonds. We believe that the answer is no, and regulators need to build this into the way that they treat structured products as possible investments for the finance industry. Structured securities are securities that are backed by a portfolio of loans/bonds/mortgages that are issued on a prioritized basis, known as tranches. Mathematically, the payoffs on these structured securities resemble those of option combinations on the underlying portfolio. If one were to further structure the tranches, such as the so-called CDO-squared formulations, then the payoffs resemble options on options, defined as compound options in the academic and practitioner literature.

Understanding this connection to options is very useful. There is an extensive literature that shows that valuation is highly sensitive to the volatility of the underlying asset for option combinations, and to the volatility of volatility for compound options. So, for structured products, unless the analysts have near certainty about the volatility and correlations of the underlying loans in the portfolio that they will have to input into their ratings model, the output from their model will be highly unreliable. In fact, both Hull and White (2009) and Coval, Jurek, and Stafford (2009) simulate the sensitivity of the ratings of structured products to assumptions about default correlations and default probabilities and make this very point of unreliability of the model.[17]

A rating is an estimate of the likelihood of default and the losses that are associated with default. Estimates can be precise or imprecise, and this degree of precision needs to be incorporated into the regulator's perspective on risk. The point here is that there is no way around this issue. Even in a world where the analyst has modeled the structured product perfectly, small changes in the underlying assumptions can have dramatic effects. As such, these securities have fundamentally different properties than do the plain-vanilla corporate and municipal bonds, which are the traditional securities rated by the NRSROs.

Liquidity/Funding Risk   Securities with fundamentally the same risk can offer different rates of return due to different levels of liquidity. A well-known example is provided by off-the-run versus on-the-run Treasury securities.[18] Liquidity is priced because there are times, such as during a crisis, when investors need to convert the securities into cash, and some securities trade in markets where this is difficult to do. Structured products definitely fit into this class, and help explain why some of the so-called supersenior and AAA tranches offered higher yields than were available on plain-vanilla AAA-rated individual securities. Historically, some finance companies may have been holders of illiquid securities because their funding sources (i.e., policyholder premiums, deposits, etc.) were relatively sticky and their overall investment portfolio risk was low. This is not necessarily true anymore. For example, as life insurers have become subject to runs due to the possibility of policyholders' cashing in and increased risk of their investment portfolios due to holdings of variable annuities, a concentration of fixed-income portfolios in illiquid securities may be problematic. Therefore, the regulator should put a higher degree of emphasis on corporate liquidity into portfolio requirements.

Market Risk   Even if securities have the same probability of default and expected loss, and have the same liquidity, these securities can offer different rates of return due to their level of market risk. Market risk is especially damaging to insurance companies because the companies get hit both by their fixed-income securities' falling in value along with their other investments, and because their funding sources begin to dry up as consumers and businesses try to conserve cash. Structured products, especially the safer AA and AAA tranches, are particularly vulnerable in this respect. Almost all of the risk of these securities is market risk, as individual risks of the individual loans/bonds/mortgages have been diversified away (see, for example, Coval, Jurek, and Stafford 2009; Longstaff and Myers 2009). Only in a rare event in which there are widespread defaults will the securities bear losses, but this is when the company can least afford it. Therefore, a corporate bond with the same default probability and expected loss as a structured security should be considered less risky, as much of the former's risk is diversifiable.

■ ■ ■

Understanding risk is not just about an estimate of expected losses, but also about when those losses occur (i.e., involving both credit and market risk); when the portfolio may become impaired (i.e., liquidity); and how accurately we measure those losses ex ante. The regulator needs multidimensional inputs to judge the prudence of the finance company's investment portfolio. This leads to the following implications for the provision of additional information, as pertaining to structured products:

- Along with the rating, a measure of the ex ante accuracy (or confidence) of the rating. It may well be the case that certain structured products should not be rated.
- Along with the rating, and its precision, a measure of the securities' liquidity in the secondary market.
- Along with the rating, its precision, and its liquidity, a measure of its market risk.

As an illustration, the AAA tranche of a CDO-squared on a mortgage pool would get, in addition to its AAA rating, a mark of high imprecision, high illiquidity, and high market risk. Additional useful information would be the current market prices of various related securities. There is extensive evidence that market prices tend to have more and earlier information, albeit with much more volatility, about default probabilities and losses than do ratings.

Alternative Business Models

Clearly, the rating agencies' business model needs to be fixed. This has been talked about for years, and the current crisis shows that these concerns are valid. The focus should be on revamping the system, which will increase competition (and therefore improve quality), and on fixing the conflicts of interest.

However, there is little discussion in the Act of the problem that ratings are currently used by some institutional investors to conduct regulatory arbitrage—that is, simultaneously taking excessive risk while adhering to the regulator's safety standards because of the NRSROs' overly optimistic rating. This suggests that alternative models, such as "investor pays," may suffer from similar abuses and not provide a solution to the rating agencies' problem, and EU proposals of a possible switch to this model may be premature.

While investors may, indeed, try to game the ratings systems through the arbitrage process, it is clear that the recent criticism of agencies has already motivated a number of new entrants to the credit risk rating industry. These new firms and models may not be NRSRO designates, but will provide investors and regulators with additional estimates of, for example, the probability of default of issuers and also possibly the distribution of possible outcomes. Many of these newcomers are likely to advocate point-in-time statistical models for default assessment that will likely provide more timely, albeit also more volatile, estimates of default than will the traditional through-the-cycle rating process of all the major existing rating agencies. The challenge for institutional investors and their boards is to analyze these new methods in order to determine the value added and to compare their benefits with the additional costs involved.

In terms of sticking with the "issuer pays" model, Bolton, Freixas, and Shapiro (2008) argue that up-front payments to credit rating agencies would eliminate the conflict of interest, and enforced disclosure of all ratings would mitigate the shopping-for-ratings problem. An alternative approach, and one that Section 939D of HR 4173 is directly based on and is highlighted for potential implementation by the Dodd-Frank Act, is provided for in Mathis, McAndrews, and Rochet (2009). (See also Raboy 2009 and Richardson and White 2009.) The main idea is that issuers no longer choose the rating agency, but instead must go through a centralized clearing process. The idea is motivated through both theoretical and empirical work that shows the conflict of interest of issuers choosing rating agencies is a first-order problem for structured finance products. The optimal resolution in Mathis, McAndrews, and Rochet (2009) is such a scheme. The proposals in this chapter as well as in Raboy (2009) and Richardson and White (2009) have the advantage of simultaneously solving the following: (1) the free-rider problem, because the issuer still pays; (2) the conflict of interest problem, because the agency is chosen by the regulating body; and (3) the competition problem, because the regulator's choice can be based on some degree of excellence, thereby providing the rating agency with incentives to invest resources, to innovate, and to perform high-quality work. As we mentioned before, however, it does put tremendous faith in the ability of the regulator to monitor and evaluate the rating agencies' performance.

So, we now move forward with new regulation on rating agencies. Many issues are addressed fairly well; others are deferred. We hope that our comments will help in the new studies that are mandated by the new Act.

NOTES

1. See, for example, Financial Crisis Inquiry Commission June 2, 2010, hearings on "Credibility of Credit Ratings, the Investment Decisions Made Based on Those Ratings, and the Financial Crisis," testimony by Mark Froeba and Eric Kolchinsky.
2. In fact, so-called point-in-time models developed by scholars and practitioners, such as structural and Z-Score type procedures, will usually provide more advanced early warning signals of downgrades and defaults than do CRAs that use more conservative through-the-cycle, longer-term criteria. Indeed, Altman and Rijken (2004, 2006) found that rating agencies, on average, wait 1.6 times longer than do multivariate predictive models to signal the rating change; and, when CRAs do change their ratings, the amount of the change (particularly downgrades) is only 0.6 times as much as the change should have been compared with the point-in-time model.
3. In the Skreta and Veldkamp (2009) model, competition also leads to ratings inflation; but this outcome occurs because more (competing) raters—even when they are trying for accurate ratings—provide more opportunities for inadvertent optimistic errors, which the rated firms can then select opportunistically.
4. Indeed, we are aware of at least four new recent efforts in this direction proposed by firms like Morningstar, Inc., Audit Integrity Score, Bloomberg's CRAT score, and the RiskMetrics Group's Z-Metrics approach. One of this chapter's authors (Altman) is involved in the last effort.
5. See Title IX, Subtitle C, Sec. 931, "Findings."
6. See Title IX, Subtitle C, Sec. 932, "Enhanced Regulation, Accountability and Transparency of Nationally Recognized Statistical Rating Organizations."
7. See Title IX, Subtitle C, Sec. 932, "Enhanced Regulation, Accountability and Transparency of Nationally Recognized Statistical Rating Organizations."
8. See Title IX, Subtitle C, Sec. 932, "Enhanced Regulation, Accountability and Transparency of Nationally Recognized Statistical Rating Organizations."
9. See Title IX, Subtitle C, Sec. 939B, "Elimination of Exemption from Fair Disclosure Rule."
10. See Title IX, Subtitle C, Sec. 939, "Removal of Statutory References to Credit Ratings."
11. See Title IX, Subtitle C, Sec. 933, "State of Mind in Private Actions."
12. Note that in this respect the removal of the exemption from Regulation FD for credit rating agencies proposed in the bill and described earlier seems to make

sense, since it will be hard to justify a differentiation in reporting standards between these different gatekeepers in the financial market.

13. See Title IX, Subtitle C, Sec. 932, "Enhanced Regulation, Accountability and Transparency of Nationally Recognized Statistical Rating Organizations."

14. See Title IX, Subtitle C, Sec. 939F, "Study and Rulemaking on Assigned Credit Ratings."

15. See Title IX, Subtitle C, Sec. 939F, "Study and Rulemaking on Assigned Credit Ratings."

16. http://europa.eu/rapid/pressReleasesAction.do?reference=MEMO/10/230.

17. One particularly egregious example was the structuring of synthetic collateralized debt obligations (CDOs) built from BBB-rated mezzanine tranches of multiple residential mortgage-backed securities (RMBSs) in the nonprime area. The BBB-rated tranches already represented options on diversified pools of mortgages, so pooling these BBB tranches from a number of RMBSs would not add much additional diversification, which in turn should have greatly affected the assumptions underlying the synthetic CDOs, especially for the higher-rated tranches.

18. On-the-run Treasury securities are the most recently issued Treasury securities and are more liquid than the other Treasury securities, which are called off-the-run.

REFERENCES

Acharya, Viral, Thomas Cooley, Matthew Richardson, and Ingo Walter. 2010. Manufacturing tail risk: A perspective on the financial crisis of 2007–09. *Foundations and Trends in Finance* 4 (4): 247–325.

Acharya, Viral V., Philipp Schnabl, and Gustavo Suarez. 2010. Securitization without risk transfer. SSRN; available at: http://papers.ssrn.com/sol3/papers.cfm? abstract_id=1364525.

Altman, Edward, and Herbert Rijken. 2004. How rating agencies achieve stability. *Journal of Banking and Finance* 28 (11): 2679–2714.

Altman, Edward I., and Herbert A. Rijken. 2006. A point-in-time perspective on through-the-cycle ratings. *Financial Analysts Journal* 62 (1): 54–70.

Altman, Edward, and Herbert Rijken. 2010. Improving rating agency default predictions by adding outlook and watch list categories: Comparison with point in time models. Vrije University, Amsterdam, Working Paper and NYU Department of Finance Working Paper (Summer).

Ashcraft, Adam, Paul Goldsmith-Pinkham, and James Vickery. 2009. MBS ratings and the mortgage credit boom. Working paper.

Becker, Bo, and Todd Milbourn. 2008. Reputation and competition: Evidence from the credit rating industry. Working paper, Harvard Business School.

Benmelech, Efraim, and Jennifer Dlugosz. 2009. The credit rating crisis. NBER Working Paper No. 15045.

Bolton, Patrick, Xavier Freixas, and Joel Shapiro. 2008. The credit ratings game. NBER Working Paper No. 14712.

Calomiris, Charles. 2009. A recipe for ratings reform. *Economist's Voice*.

Coval, Joshua, Jakub Jurek, and Erik Stafford. 2009. The economics of structured finance. *Journal of Economic Perspectives* 23 (1): 3–25.

Covitz, Daniel, and Paul Harrison. 2003. Testing conflicts of interest at bond rating agencies with market anticipation: Evidence that reputation incentives dominate. FEDS Working Paper No. 2003-68.

Griffin, John, and Dragon Tang. 2009. Did subjectivity play a role in CDO credit ratings? Working paper, University of Texas, Austin.

Hull, John, and Alan White. 2009. The risk of tranches created from residential mortgages. Working paper, University of Toronto.

International Monetary Fund. 2009. *Global financial stability report: Navigating the financial challenges ahead*. Washington, DC: IMF, October. www.imf.org/external/pubs/ft/gfsr/2009/02/pdf/text.pdf.

Jorion, Philippe, Zhu Liu, and Charles Shi. 2005. Informational effects of Regulation FD: Evidence from rating agencies. *Journal of Financial Economics* 76: 309–330.

Longstaff, Francis, and Brett Myers. 2009. How does the market value toxic assets? Working paper, UCLA.

Mathis, Jerome, Jamie McAndrews, and Jean Charles Rochet. 2009. Rating the raters. *Journal of Monetary Economics* 56:657–674.

Raboy, David. 2009. Concept paper on credit rating agency incentives. Congressional Oversight Panel, January 9.

Richardson, Matthew, and Lawrence J. White. 2009. The rating agencies: Is regulation the answer? In *Restoring financial stability: How to repair a failed system*, ed. Viral V. Acharya and Matthew Richardson. Hoboken, NJ: John Wiley & Sons.

Sangiorgi, F., J. Sokobin, and C. Spatt. 2009. Credit-rating shopping, selection and the equilibrium structure of ratings. Working paper, Carnegie Mellon.

Skreta, Vasiliki, and Laura Veldkamp. 2009. Ratings shopping and asset complexity: A theory of ratings inflation. *Journal of Monetary Economics* 56:678–695.

Stanton, Richard, and Nancy Wallace. 2010. CMBS and the role of subordination levels in the crisis of 2007–2009. Working paper, University of California, Berkeley.

Sy, Amadou. 2009. The systemic regulation of credit rating agencies and rated markets. IMF Working Paper.

White, Lawrence J. 2010. Markets: The credit rating agencies. *Journal of Economic Perspectives* 24:211–226.

CHAPTER 16

Securitization Reform

Matthew Richardson, Joshua Ronen, and Marti Subrahmanyam*

16.1 OVERVIEW

Securitization generally refers to the process by which consumer and business loans are pooled and securities backed by these pools are issued in the capital markets. The payments made on these securities thus depend primarily on the performance of the underlying loans in the pool. Securitization has played an expanding role in the U.S. financial system and the broader economy, growing over the past 25 years to be an important source of credit and financing for individuals and businesses.

There is widespread agreement that asset-backed security losses were at the center of the financial crisis of 2007 to 2009. In particular, many policymakers blame the originate-to-distribute model of securitization and the lack of skin in the game for lenders and securitizers. As such, the main recommendation of the Dodd-Frank Wall Street Reform and Consumer Protection Act is that securitizers retain 5 percent of the securitized loans (subject to some discretionary adjustments by the regulators).

While such a requirement normally would be helpful in aligning incentives, and, in fact, might emerge naturally in capital markets, we argue that the absence of skin in the game may not have been the major culprit in the financial crisis: Financial institutions actually held on to large chunks of (mostly senior) tranches of their securitized assets. Rather than potentially preventing the crisis, however, this most likely turned out to be a major

*We are grateful to Thomas Cooley and Anjolein Schmeits for helpful comments and suggestions. We benefited from discussions in the "Securitization Reforms" Working Group for the NYU Stern e-book *Real Time Solutions for Financial Reform*, which also included T. Sabri Öncü, Stephen Ryan, Stijn Van Nieuwerburgh, and Lawrence J. White.

cause. We suspect that two major factors contributed to this behavior: first, the existence of cheap government guarantees (such as via Fannie Mae and Freddie Mac) or implicit guarantees (e.g., too big to fail) that reduced market discipline, and second, regulatory arbitrage—decreasing required capital through off-balance-sheet entities or retaining the less-capital-requiring senior tranches that were overrated by conflicted rating agencies.

Securitization is a relatively new form of banking. The first collateralized mortgage obligations (CMOs) were issued in June 1983 by Freddie Mac and were rapidly replicated by many players in the financial services industry. Between 1990 and 2006, issuance of mortgage-backed securities (MBSs) grew at an annually compounded rate of 13 percent, from $259 billion to $2 trillion a year; and asset-backed securities (ABSs), secured by auto loans, credit cards, home equity loans, equipment loans, student loans, and other assets, grew from $43 billion to $753 billion.

In 2006, nearly $2.9 trillion in mortgage- and asset-backed securities were issued. (Figures 16.1 and 16.2, respectively, show the amount of asset-backed issuance and securitization rates.) It is estimated that securitization is responsible for between 30 percent and 75 percent of lending in various markets, including an estimated 59 percent of outstanding home mortgages. Historically, most banks have securitized their credit card assets and a substantial portion of automobile sales as ABSs (Citigroup 2008, 10–11). Overall, recent data collected by the Board of Governors of the Federal Reserve System (September 2009) show that securitization has provided over 25 percent of outstanding U.S. consumer credit.

The benefits attributed to securitization include enhanced efficiency and a reduced cost of financing. They also include incremental credit creation and, more generally, the development of financing and investment products that match the industry-specific needs of issuers and (mostly institutional)

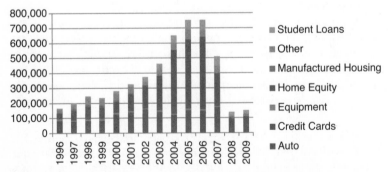

FIGURE 16.1 Asset-Backed Security Issuance ($ Millions)
Source: Securities Industry and Financial Markets Association.

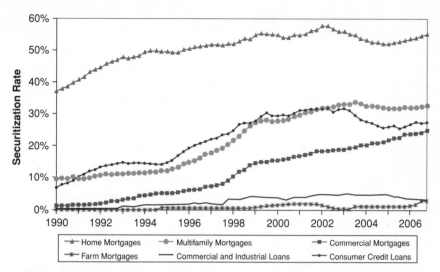

FIGURE 16.2 Securitization Rates in Different Loan Categories Based on U.S. Flow of Funds Data (1990 to 2006)
Source: Data from the Federal Reserve's U.S. Flows of Funds Accounts (Tables L2, L125, L126) for the period Q1 1990 to Q4 2006. Share securitized is calculated as the percentage of loans securitized outstanding over total loans outstanding.

investors. For example, local lenders that are unable to diversify away idiosyncratic risks or aim to attract deposits from other parts of the country could, by securitizing their assets, make it possible for the borrowers to avoid paying premiums for diversifiable risk, thus reducing financing costs and expanding the size of the mortgage market. At the same time, securitization frees up capital on the balance sheets of the originators of the loans, allowing them to make new loans. In underscoring the crucial role of securitization, the G-7 finance ministers declared that "the current situation calls for urgent and exceptional action...to restart the secondary markets for mortgages and other securitized assets" (G-7 Finance Ministers 2008). Also, in its *Global Financial Stability Report* (October 2009), the International Monetary Fund noted that "restarting private-label securitization markets, especially in the United States, is critical to limiting the fallout from the credit crisis and to withdrawal of central bank and government interventions."

At the same time, securitization is viewed as a culprit in creating serious systemic problems that led to large losses in the value of securitized products during the financial crisis of 2007 to 2009. We further explore the role of securitization in the financial crisis in the next section.

16.2 THE FINANCIAL CRISIS AND SECURITIZATION

There is considerable empirical evidence that lending standards in the mortgage market slipped noticeably in the years leading up to the financial crisis. For example, from 2002 to 2006, mortgage loan-to-value (LTV) ratios increased dramatically in all three major loan categories (prime, Alt-A, and subprime), while the prevalence of loans with full documentation decreased dramatically (e.g., Jaffee, Lynch, Richardson, and Van Nieuwerburgh 2009). Figure 16.3 illustrates the declining quality of subprime loans during this period. With the backdrop of this evidence, one explanation for the financial crisis that has received popular attention is the flawed originate-to-distribute model of securitization. This model allowed mortgage lenders (mortgage banks, or brokers working on their behalf) to pass through the loans, lowering their incentive to screen the borrowers and monitor the loans. To use the colloquial expression, it reduced their skin in the game.

While this evidence cannot be ignored, the case for this explanation is not so straightforward. Even with securitization, mortgage lenders do have skin in the game to the extent that a considerable portion of their income derives from mortgage servicing. For example, the largest originator, Countrywide, suffered huge write-downs from the loss of mortgage-servicing rights as the

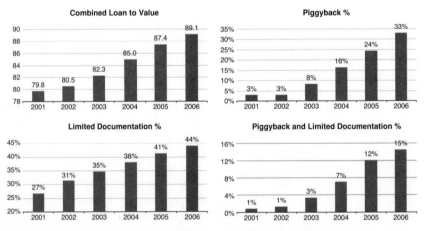

FIGURE 16.3 Declining Subprime Loan Quality, 2001 to 2006
Note: The figure provides three measures of loan quality: loan to value (mortgage as a percent of the appraised value of the house); limited documentation (mortgages in which the borrower states only a limited amount of information, e.g., income, on the mortgage application); and piggyback (a second mortgage on top of a first mortgage, usually in lieu of mortgage insurance).
Source: Loan Performance, Paulson & Co.

crisis unfolded (Gorton 2008). Furthermore, while the banks received large securitization fees, they also faced risk holding on to all the loans during the securitization process, which typically lasts from two to four months.

In addition, while securitizers had no *apparent* skin in the game, many of them were effectively exposed to the inherent risk of the securitized loans due to the fact that they provided equity or credit enhancements that resulted in explicit or implicit recourse to the loan originators. Banks arbitraged regulations by setting up off-balance-sheet entities—such as asset-backed commercial paper (ABCP) conduits, structured investment vehicles (SIVs), and other types of special purpose entities (SPEs)—to hold the securitized assets and provide liquidity or credit guarantees to investors in securities backed by these assets. Such guarantees and other credit enhancements, whether explicit or implicit, shifted some or all of the risk back to the securitizing institutions by providing a backup credit line or commitment to repurchase nondefaulted assets in case of a failure to roll over maturing obligations. However, capital requirements for such off-balance-sheet enhancements were roughly only one-tenth of the requirement if the assets had been held on the balance sheet, and thus would not have been securitized. This regulatory arbitrage allowed financial institutions to increase their effective leverage while appearing to be safe under the Basel I capital regulations (Acharya, Schnabl, and Suarez 2010).

Nevertheless, there are a number of careful academic empirical papers that argue that due to the adverse selection problem of lenders having no skin in the game, they did tend to hold on to the good loans and sell off the poor-quality ones. See, among others, Berndt and Gupta (2009); Dell'Ariccia, Igan, and Laeven (2009); Elul (2009); Jiang, Nelson, and Vytlacil (2010); Keys, Mukherjee, Seru, and Vig (2009, 2010); Mian and Sufi (2009); and Purnanandam (2010).

Consider the Keys, Mukherjee, Seru, and Vig (2010) paper as a representative example. Focusing on the subprime mortgage market, they provide empirical evidence on the slippage of lending standards when banks securitize. Using a large data set of securitized subprime loans in the United States, they empirically confirm that the number of securitized loans varies systematically around a credit cutoff reflected in a FICO score of 620.[1] That is, securitization of loans is more likely if the 620 threshold—established by the government-sponsored enterprises (GSEs), Fannie Mae and Freddie Mac, in their guidelines on loan eligibility—is attained. The authors argue that the adherence to the threshold by investors following the advice of GSEs generates an increasing demand for securitization of loans that are just above the credit cutoff relative to loans below this cutoff. Figure 16.4 shows the delinquencies for low-documentation loans (i.e., loans with no documentation or loans that provide no information about income but some information about assets) around the 620 cutoff point. As can be seen from Figure 16.4,

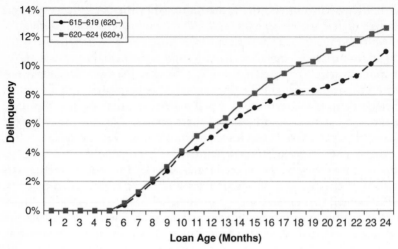

(a)

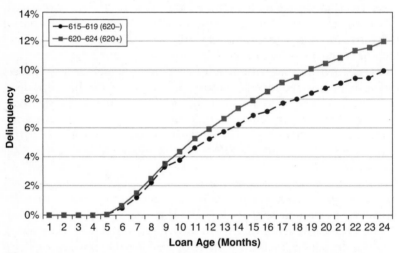

(b)

Delinquencies for low-documentation loans around 620 FICO. These figures present the data for average percent of low-documentation loans (dollar weighted) originated by banks (a) and independents (b) that become delinquent for 2001–2006. We track loans in two FICO buckets—615–619 (620⁻) and 620–624 (620⁺) from their origination dates and plot the average loans that become delinquent each month after the origination date. As can be seen, the higher-credit-score bucket defaults more than the lower-credit-score bucket.

FIGURE 16.4 Delinquencies for Securitized Loans
Source: Reprinted with permission from Elsevier. Benjamin Keys, Tanmoy Mukherjee, Amit Seru, and Vikrant Vig, "Financial Regulation and Securitization: Evidence from Subprime Loans," *Journal of Monetary Economics* 56, no. 5 (2009): 721–724.

higher-credit-score buckets (that are more likely to be securitized) default more than the lower-credit-score buckets.

The higher delinquencies for securitized loans may be explained by the fact that securitization increases the separation between the originator of the loan and the party that bears the default risk inherent in the loan. In contrast to hard information (such as FICO scores), soft information (such as the likelihood that a borrower's job may be terminated, the borrower has upcoming expenses not revealed by current credit reports, or the borrower has income or assets that are costly for investors to process) is unverifiable to a third party (see Stein 2002). The increase in this distance between the lenders and the ultimate investors may induce lenders not to collect soft information about borrowers when they do not have to ultimately bear the risk of loans they originate (i.e., when they securitize). The initial choice of incurring the cost of acquiring soft information is predicated on there being a sufficient chance that the lender would retain the loan on its balance sheet (see Rajan 2008).

Rational investors should, of course, anticipate higher defaults and price the loans accordingly. There is evidence suggesting that this indeed is the case. For example, Jiang, Nelson, and Vytlacil (2010) maintain that low-documentation loans are priced at a 29-basis-point premium. (See also Krainer and Laderman 2009.) Nevertheless, the authors show that loan delinquency rates are higher, even after controlling for the higher interest rate, indicating that investors were not adequately compensated for the additional risk.

The question then arises as to why the private sector—securitization firms and ABS investors—could not enter into contracts with lenders to ensure they had the right incentives to screen borrowers and monitor loans. Such a market failure might occur if the costs of default of poor-quality loans are not fully borne by the holders of the ABSs backed by these loans. The most likely explanation is that many of the parties in the market for securitized products (at least for mortgage-related securities) have some type of implicit or explicit guarantee from the U.S. government.[2] As long as one of these guaranteed entities is active in the securitization process—as a lender, securitizer, or investor—incentives will be distorted somewhere, and potentially everywhere, down the chain. For example, the investor in prime MBSs which are guaranteed by a GSE does not necessarily care about the quality of the loan, because she may be confident that the principal will be guaranteed by the government. Similarly, if the investor is a depository institution with deposit guarantees from the Federal Deposit Insurance Corporation (FDIC), the external discipline to reject risky loans is diminished.

Indeed, Acharya, Cooley, Richardson, and Walter (2010) argue that the manufacturing of tail risk by large, complex financial institutions (LCFIs), much in the way of AAA-rated securitized products, was the major cause of the crisis.[3] LCFIs took this risk because little or no regulatory capital was required, given the high-investment-grade status of these products. Almost all the firms that ran aground were engaged in some form of regulatory arbitrage using AAA-rated securities. These securities offered attractive yields but, because of their AAA status, required little or no regulatory capital. (See Chapter 15, "Regulation of Rating Agencies," for a complete discussion of how the interaction among securitizers, rating agencies, and institutional investors (like LCFIs) put the system at risk.)

Can the regulatory arbitrage argument explain the two seemingly contradictory facts that (1) some securitizers did have skin in the game, and (2) adjusting for loan characteristics, securitized loans performed worse than their nonsecuritized counterparts? With respect to (1), many of the LCFIs were major players in the securitization business. According to the regulatory arbitrage argument, their skin in the game had very little to do with incentive compatibility and almost everything to do with capital relief. This would explain their involvement with predominantly AAA-rated securities as opposed to the lower tranches. While holding AAA-rated assets nonetheless would still have aligned incentives with other investors who bought the same securitized assets, the point is that adverse selection considerations were not the underlying motivation for the securitized holdings of LCFIs.

With respect to (2), because LCFIs had access to a lower cost of capital due to government guarantees, their excess demand pushed the prices of securitized products away from their fundamental value. Thus, ceteris paribus, loans that were securitized were priced favorably because these loans were associated with cheap government guarantees and because they would eventually require less regulatory capital.[4] An interesting question, given their investment in the supersenior and senior tranches of the structures, is whether LCFIs invested in the equity tranches as well. Without such an investment, their incentives would have been somewhat dented relative to what they might have been.

If skin in the game is not the primary issue, and instead it is the regulatory arbitrage that was facilitated by the securitization process, then financial regulation should be redesigned to address this aspect of securitization. Of course, the two issues should be linked: the larger the skin in the game, the more limited should be the regulatory arbitrage. That is, assets on the balance sheet resulting from skin in the game constrain capital, whereas those sold do not. The incentives then would be toward retaining skin in the game in the form of the senior tranches that require relatively less regulatory capital. At the same time, however, without the originators retaining the risky tranches, the senior tranches would not be so senior if credit rating agencies had done their job properly.

Nevertheless, if the private sector cannot contractually solve the adverse selection problem of lenders, regulation should be aimed at requiring securitizers to hold a proportion that is commensurate with the amount of risk inherent in the underlying (securitized) assets. That is, originators may need to be induced to apply sound underwriting standards that minimize expected delinquency rates due to such ownership. But it is also important that capital requirements are tuned to properly cover the *effective* risk (explicit or implicit) assumed by the securitizers. A good rule of thumb is that capital requirements should be neutral between the financial institutions holding the credit risk of the loans themselves and the *effective* credit risk that they are exposed to in connection with the securitized loans. This would ensure that credit creation is not impeded by excessive capital requirements imposed by blunt and/or arbitrary constraints proposed by regulators in an attempt to maintain the safety of the financial institutions, while neglecting the need to provide credit to business and consumers.

16.3 THE DODD-FRANK WALL STREET REFORM AND CONSUMER PROTECTION ACT

With respect to securitization, Title IX, Subtitle D of the Dodd-Frank Act, "Improvements to the Asset-Backed Securitization Process," largely misses the big picture. While it is well intended, the legislation instead focuses on secondary issues: the skin-in-the-game issue, better disclosure rules to increase transparency of securitized products, accounting/regulatory standards for such disclosure, and capital requirements corresponding to the newly issued accounting standards.

The key language in the Act requires that "the Federal banking agencies and the Commission (SEC) shall jointly prescribe regulations to require any securitizer to retain an economic interest in a portion of the credit risk for any asset that the securitizer, through the issuance of an asset-backed security, transfers, sells, or conveys to a third party."[5] Moreover, the regulations require a securitizer to retain "not less than 5 percent of the credit risk for any asset" that is "not a qualified residential mortgage."[6] The exemption for qualified residential mortgages derives from the premise that skin in the game is required only when there is a possibility of bad loans being made. In general, the regulatory agencies are accorded some discretion to apply the requirements to securitizers. To preclude the undoing of the incentives under the risk retention requirement, the stipulated regulations shall "prohibit a securitizer from directly or indirectly hedging or otherwise transferring the credit risk that the securitizer is required to retain with respect to an asset." Also, the Act orders the conduct of a study of the combined impact by classes of asset-backed securities of these requirements and those of the Financial Accounting Standards 166 and 167 issued by the Financial Accounting Standards Board (FASB).

In terms of disclosure requirements, the Act requires "each issuer of an asset-backed security to disclose, for each tranche or class of security, information regarding the assets backing that security."[7] The Act goes on to describe:

- The "standards for the format of the data provided by issuers of an asset-backed security, which shall, to the extent feasible, facilitate comparison of such data across securities in similar types of asset classes."
- Requirements for "issuers of asset-backed securities at a minimum to disclose asset-level or loan-level data if such data are necessary for investors to independently perform due diligence, including data having unique identifiers relating to loan brokers or originators, the nature and extent of the compensation of the broker or originator of the assets backing the security, and the amount of risk retention of the originator or the securitizer of such assets."

As a final part of the Act related to securitization, the chairman of the Financial Services Oversight Council is tasked with carrying out a study on the macroeconomic effects of the risk retention requirements that will include, among other things: (1) analysis of the effects of risk retention on real estate asset price bubbles; (2) analysis of the feasibility of minimizing real estate price bubbles by proactively adjusting the percentage of risk retention that must be borne by creditors and securitizers of real estate debt; and (3) assessment of whether such adjustments should take place independently or in concert with monetary policy, among other suggestions.[8]

To the extent that securitization has been addressed internationally as well, the focus has also been on securitizers' or originators' retaining some portion of the risk of the underlying assets (see, e.g., statements by the Group of Twenty and the European Commission). The Financial Stability Board (FSB)'s proposals instead get to the root cause of the crisis by recognizing that financial institutions used securitization as a way to circumvent capital requirements via off-balance-sheet financing. The FSB calls for the removal of the rules that allowed such activity to take place and the prescription of a clearer definition of capital adequacy to include such off-balance-sheet vehicles.

16.4 EVALUATION OF THE PROPOSALS

Skin in the Game

The guiding principle behind Congress's major proposals for securitization—namely, that securitizers should have skin in the game—is reasonable and is a natural outcome of almost all models of securitization: to align incentives between investors and the securitizers. To the extent that this did not take place—that is, the market failed—there is a need for setting and enforcing standards, provided that capital charges would be assessed only on the amount of risk retained and not on the amount of risk transferred.

To our knowledge, however, there has been no empirical study of the extent to which securitizers had skin in the game. The legislation therefore may be based on a false premise that may be debatable, even if it is true in some cases. And even if lack of skin in the game was a source for the failure of securitization markets, there needs to be a well-constructed argument for why the private sector cannot solve the issue. We believe the best line of reasoning in this respect is the existence of mispriced government guarantees in the financial system, such as deposit insurance, too-big-to-fail guarantees, and GSE debt subsidies.

Of course, a more direct attack of the problem then would call for either the dismantling or the appropriate pricing of government guarantees. These issues are discussed in detail in Chapter 5, "Taxing Systemic Risk"; Chapter 8, "Resolution Authority"; and Chapter 14, "The Government-Sponsored Enterprises." Since the legislation fails to correct mispriced government guarantees, which are the root cause of the incentive problem, a second-best solution for other parts of the financial system may be warranted. To this extent, Title IX, Subtitle D of the Dodd-Frank Act that deals with securitization has some merit. However, there are still some major concerns.

One issue is that the 5 percent skin-in-the-game proposal is "one size fits all."[9] The fixed level of 5 percent of economic interest retained does not vary with the underlying risk or the opacity of the loans, the specific nature of the tranches of the pool, or other risk characteristics of the structure. Clearly, the level of retention should vary with these characteristics. Admittedly, the Act properly accords regulators the discretion to require less than 5 percent to the extent that the institutions complied with regulatory underwriting standards intended to limit the risk of the securitized class of assets. It is not clear, however, whether the regulators will use this discretion to allow a decrease in retention, even when it is merited by the circumstances. Even in cases where institutions originate or securitize loans with relatively safe assets, for which the 5 percent might end up being too high (as a more extreme case, for some securitized products, the underlying assets are bonds and leveraged loans that are traded securities and thus monitored by the market), it is unclear why and how regulators would make an exception, since there is no incentive to do so. They may simply choose to act cautiously to avoid blame if unexpected losses materialize, rather than take the risk. Furthermore, it is not clear that regulators possess the necessary skills or access to the information necessary to determine the optimal amount of skin in the game.

The most notable exception to this is the exemption for qualified residential mortgages. While we applaud the recognition that qualified residential mortgages have different risk characteristics, the aforementioned work by Keys, Mukherjee, Seru, and Vig (2009, 2010) illustrates how easy it is to game the system. If one generally views GSE requirements as qualifying, they show that loans are much lower quality when they *just meet* those requirements as opposed to when they *just miss* them. Regulators will need to be especially vigilant in designing definitions of loan quality, which will be a major challenge.

The economic reasoning behind securitization is that to expand the credit markets one needs to transfer the credit risk from banks to the broader capital market. While banks have expertise in making loans, they either do not have adequate capital or would have too much risk concentration to hold all the loans on their balance sheets. The typical model of securitization, therefore, leads to contracts in which the banks hold a fraction of the risk (i.e., skin in the game) to align incentives but transfer most of it to mutual funds, pension funds, hedge funds, and other capital market investors. Not all researchers agree with this view of securitization, however; Gorton and Metrick's (2009) explanation is that securitization represents a new form of depository banking for institutional investors and corporations.

To the extent that there is generally more demand for safer securities, and therefore, demand for securitized products to be tranched into prioritized risks, the standard model would suggest that banks hold the riskier portion of these securities. Of course, the lesson from the crisis is that LCFIs did the opposite, and held predominantly the AAA-rated tranches in order to exploit regulatory capital requirements. Alternatively, in the Gorton and Metrick (2009) view of banking, LCFIs may have held AAA tranches because they act as collateral for securitized banking.

Thus, one important missing element of Title IX, Subtitle D of the Dodd-Frank Act is a precise discussion of how the 5 percent allocation is spread across the tranches and how this will affect capital requirements. Specifically, would there be any requirement that the allocation be spread across tranches or could it be concentrated in some of them? (See the discussion later in this section on capital requirements.)

Are there substitutes to a skin-in-the-game remedy? The Dodd-Frank Act could, for example, directly specify underwriting standards to be followed by banking institutions, possibly varying across different asset classes with different risk profiles. In this case, the riskiness of the securitized assets could be controlled without need for skin in the game. For instance, the standards could specify a maximum loan-to-value (LTV) ratio, a maximum loan to income that varies with credit history and so on. This approach, in theory, is presumably the idea behind the exemption for qualifying residential mortgages and government-backed security issuance.

Or, more generally, should a combination of underwriting standards and skin in the game be required?

In fact, Title XIV, "Mortgage Reform and Anti-Predatory Lending Act," attempts to do this for the residential mortgage market by applying minimum underwriting standards for mortgages. One of the more important clauses is that "in accordance with regulations prescribed jointly by the federal banking agencies, in consultation with the Commission, no creditor may make a residential mortgage loan unless the creditor makes a reasonable and good faith determination based on verified and documented information that, at the time the loan is consummated, the consumer has a reasonable ability to repay the loan, according to its terms, and all applicable taxes, insurance, and assessments."[10] Moreover, the subtitle of the Act goes on to describe the basis for determining whether the borrower can pay, including typical features such as credit history, income, and their current obligations, as well as income verification and the type of loan if nonstandard (such as variable-rate, interest-only, negative amortization, etc.). While most would agree that a reduction in predatory lending would improve the securitization process, and some of the prescriptions in Title XIV are a step in the right direction, it is not clear that a presumption of loan repayment is realistic.

Surely, some loans, even mortgages, may be economically viable even if there is a chance of default. Of course, the interest rate underlying the loan should reflect the probability of default. Indeed, this is the basis for the market's pricing of credit risk. Direct stipulation of underwriting standards might straitjacket originators, thus preventing the origination of loans that could be made inherently less risky through innovative contractual and monitoring mechanisms or simply different credit terms, such as requiring a higher down payment. In other words, it would prevent originators from using their superior local knowledge of the market environment to make informed judgments about which loans to extend and how to price them.

Disclosure

The portion of the Dodd-Frank Act that deals with better disclosure is reasonable in principle, although the information to be disclosed should be defined more clearly. One of the major problems in the crisis was that, when some financial firms ran aground because of their holdings of securitized products, other firms, which did not have such holdings, suffered from contagion. There was general uncertainty about which firms were holding securitized products and what these securities were worth. This uncertainty was resolved, to a large extent, only after the government performed extensive stress tests on the large financial firms, in order to separate them by asset quality.

It is reasonable to force issuers of asset-backed securities to disclose asset-level or loan-level data, but it is not clear how investors or regulators can use this voluminous information. A more practical solution would be to call for a template to facilitate a comparison of risk metrics across securities of similar types of asset classes. Currently, the ratings provided by the rating agencies are not sufficiently granular. There should be a broader classification that takes into account the following factors: illiquidity (for example, Level 1, 2 or 3, as classified for financial reporting, and the likely status when the overall market does poorly); the concentration/diversification of the underlying loans; the credit risk of the security (related to the rating); the market risk of the security (performance when the overall market does poorly); and the degree of model error possible in these risk estimates. All these quantities are measurable and can be specified by the regulators, who should be charged with the responsibility for designing and implementing such a template. (These and other issues are discussed in detail in Chapter 4, "Measuring Systemic Risk"; Chapter 13, "Regulating OTC Derivatives"; and Chapter 15, "Regulation of Rating Agencies.")

Capital Requirements and the Securitization Model

It could well be that higher skin-in-the-game requirements will cause consolidation, for accounting purposes, of all the transferred assets and the corresponding liabilities, including the parts not retained by the sponsor. In conjunction with this requirement, regulators have decided to base capital requirements on all assets and liabilities thus consolidated. In addition, they reserve the right to treat nonconsolidated transferred assets and liabilities under the securitization as if they were consolidated, hence including them in the computation of required capital. This would impose significant unjustified costs on the securitizers, which may deter future securitizations and reduce the flow of credit. Finally and importantly, this requirement will put U.S. financial institutions at a relative disadvantage to foreign institutions that are not yet subject to these rules.

The Dodd-Frank Act calls for a study of the impact of the skin-in-the-game clause on capital requirements as outlined by Financial Accounting Standard (FAS) 166 and FAS 167. We consider this a relevant issue. The importance of a risk-based approach to capital requirements has been most recently emphasized by the banking regulatory agencies in their issuance on January 28, 2010, of a final rule on "Risk-Based Capital Guidelines; Capital

Adequacy Guidelines; Capital Maintenance; Regulatory Capital; Impact of Modifications to Generally Accepted Accounting Principles; Consolidation of Asset-Backed Commercial Paper Programs; and Other Related Issues."[11] The rule, effective March 29, 2010, "eliminates the exclusion of certain consolidated asset-backed commercial paper programs from risk-weighted assets . . . and provides a reservation of authority to permit the agencies to require a banking organization to treat entities that are not consolidated under accounting standards as if they were consolidated for risk-based capital purposes, commensurate with the risk relationship of the banking organization to the structure."[12]

In particular, the rule reaffirms that a banking organization should hold capital commensurate with the level and nature of the risks to which it is exposed, and that the agencies believe that the effects of FAS 166 and FAS 167[13] and banking organizations' risk-based capital ratios will result in regulatory capital requirements that better reflect exposure to credit risk. Also, asserting that "experiences from the recent financial crisis demonstrate that credit risk exposure of sponsoring banking organizations to such structures (and to the assets of the structures) has in fact been greater than the agencies previously estimated, and more associated with non-contractual risks, including reputational risk, than the agencies have previously anticipated" (page 4640), the agencies concluded that risk-based capital requirements based solely on contractual exposure may underestimate the true exposure of sponsoring banking organizations to the credit risk. This seems to be the rationale for the agencies to include all assets and liabilities consolidated under FAS 167 in the computation of capital requirements, even when some or all of these assets involved no contractual risks on the part of the sponsoring organization. This may also explain the reservation of authority to include assets and liabilities in the computation of required capital even when they are not consolidated under FAS 167.

This rule is consistent with our conclusions regarding the skin-in-the-game remedy. Notwithstanding the agencies' intent to align the new accounting standards with risk-based capital principles, however, the proposed standards omit reference to the provisions of FAS 167 (particularly paragraphs 22A, 23A, A80, and A81), which provide for separate classification of assets and liabilities reflecting the inherent risklessness to the consolidating institution posed by those separately classified assets and liabilities. By not acknowledging that separately classified assets and liabilities should either be excluded from capital ratios or be given a zero risk weight, the proposed standards do not provide for alignment taking into account the inherent risklessness to the consolidating institution of separately classified assets and liabilities.[14] (The appendix at the end of this chapter discusses this issue in greater detail.)

16.5 CONCLUSION

Future reform should focus on the internalization by securitizers of the fair cost of guarantees and the prevention of regulatory arbitrage. To the extent that such reforms are not undertaken, the arguments in favor of the skin-in-the-game retention have validity. That said, the composition of the retained assets in the securitization should subject the securitizers to sufficient risk to ensure incentive compatibility. That is, the composition of the assets retained does in fact matter. Regulators should ascertain that the mix of assets retained includes first loss positions; this would mitigate the regulatory arbitrage effected by holding a larger than merited quantity of the least risky and least-capital-requiring tranches.

An attempt to prevent regulatory arbitrage through off-balance-sheet financing is at the core of the very recent rules enacted by the banking regulatory agencies. Essentially, the rules require that capital requirements be based on all assets and liabilities that are consolidated in accordance with FAS 167, in effect implying that most securitized assets and associated liabilities be brought onto the balance sheets of the securitizers. In addition, the regulators reserve the authority to require consolidation even when not required by FAS 167. This would increase capital requirements and deter regulatory arbitrage.

Unfortunately, the rules may have unintended consequences. By insisting on consolidating all assets and liabilities of the (otherwise) off-balance-sheet entities, the rules lead to overcapitalization imposing unjustified costs that could deter securitization and hence credit creation. We recommend that capital requirements be based only on assets for which the cash rights are owned by the securitizers, and on liabilities for which the securitizers are effectively responsible. This can be accomplished by excluding from the computation of required capital the separately presented assets (the cash rights of assets that are not owned by the securitizers) and the separately presented liabilities (that do not obligate the securitizers). The basic rule of thumb should be that, for every dollar of economic interest in the securitization, that dollar should face the full capital requirements by law. But if the credit risk has truly been transferred, then no capital is required.

APPENDIX: ACCOUNTING STANDARDS FOR SECURITIZATION (FAS 166/167, DODD-FRANK ACT, AND THE BANKING AGENCIES' RULES)

The separate classification of (1) assets that can be used only to settle obligations of the consolidated variable interest entity (VIE) and (2) liabilities of a consolidated VIE for which creditors do not have recourse to the credit of the primary beneficiary necessarily recognizes that the primary beneficiary has neither the right to cash generated by these (separately classified) assets nor the responsibility to settle the (separately classified) liabilities.

The theory embraced by FAS 167 under which the assets and liabilities of the variable interest entity are consolidated into the financial statements of the primary beneficiary is premised on control over the variable interest entity being consolidated, rather than control over the individual assets or the obligation to settle individual liabilities. Indeed, the criterion for consolidation—anchored in Accounting Research Bulletin (ARB) 51—is whether the primary beneficiary has a "controlling financial interest" in the variable interest entity. Accordingly, under paragraph 14A of FAS 167, the essential characteristics for consolidation involve "the power to direct the activities of a variable interest *entity* that most significantly impact the *entity's* economic performance," and "the obligation to absorb the losses of the *entity*... or the right to receive benefits from the *entity* that could potentially be significant to the variable interest *entity*" (emphasis added). The unmistakable emphasis of the FASB on an entity-conceptual approach as a basis for consolidation inevitably results in the commingling of "non-assets" and "non-liabilities" with the otherwise proper assets and liabilities of the primary beneficiary. Hence, the separate classification provisions of paragraphs 22A and 23A of FAS 167 rectify the obfuscation of assets and liabilities caused by commingling, so as to make the financial statements more transparent and permit the accurate measurement of the capital of financial institutions.

A concern that reputational risk may, in some circumstances, result in assuming off-balance-sheet exposures does not detract from the inherent risklessness to the consolidating institution of separately classified assets and liabilities. An assumption of noncontractual (and legally unenforceable) exposure as a result of solely reputational risk can and should be assessed on a case-by-case basis, taking into account the specific nature of the securitized assets and the likelihood of risk assumption. Specifically, reputational risk may materialize over only a narrow range of outcomes: In good times (when underlying assets perform well), there would be no need to make investors whole—they suffered no losses; in bad times, it would not be feasible for a sponsor to make investors whole when the sponsor is not legally obligated to do so, nor would it be rational to do so in order to maintain a reputation that has little or no value when future profitability of securitizations is seen to be low. Presumably, the examinations conducted by the agencies would reveal when an assumption of off-balance-sheet exposures is probable. In that event, the capital ratios may be adjusted accordingly.[15] Indeed, this would be in tune with the recent (September 2009) Joint Forum Report on

Special-Purpose Entities issued by the Basel Committee on Banking Supervision. It recommended that "if at inception or at any point during the life of an SPE there is a likelihood or evidence of support by the financial firm, including non-contractual support, then the activities and risks of that SPE should be aggregated with those of the institution for both supervisory assessment and internal risk management purposes."

Yet another way of approaching this issue is by allowing originators/securitizers to bond themselves by formally committing not to absorb non-contractual risks or losses such that any violation of the commitment would trigger an appropriate penalty.

Recognition that separately presented assets and liabilities under FAS 167 are inherently riskless to the consolidating institution will enable continued use of securitizations as an important part of the financial system. While risk-based asset weights do not affect the calculation of leverage ratios, separately classified assets and liabilities should likewise be excluded from leverage ratios to rectify the consolidation of what essentially are "non-assets" and "non-liabilities" of the consolidating institution. Applying the simple rule of including all consolidated assets and liabilities in the computation of required capital is a blunt instrument that does not consider cross-sectional differences in effective risk exposures of different securitizers.

While the requirements of FAS 167 are subject to interpretation, the standard may require that most securitization vehicles be consolidated. The nonexclusion of the separately classified (riskless) assets and nonrecourse liabilities from this computation has far-reaching implications: increasing required capital to an extent that is bound to impose significant costs on securitizers, leading to a smaller volume of securitizations. Probably, these are the concerns that prompted the requirements in the Act to conduct a study to understand the combined impact of the credit risk retention requirements and the new securitization accounting rules. Given the importance of this issue, it should have been directly acknowledged in the legislation.

NOTES

1. The Fair Isaac Corporation—FICO—provides an analysis of the creditworthiness of an individual by looking at a variety of factors, including payment history, debt ratio, types of credit, and number of credit inquiries. FICO scores range from 300 to 850 with higher scores signifying stronger credits.
2. Examples include the implicit guarantee on the GSEs, the explicit guarantee on deposits by the FDIC for deposit institutions, or the very implicit too-big-to-fail guarantee on large, complex financial institutions (LCFIs).
3. Gennaioli, Shleifer, and Vishny (2010) provide an alternative explanation of the crisis that also centers around securitization. In contrast to regulatory

arbitrage, they argue for a model in which investors simultaneously demand riskless securities and neglect unlikely risks, leading to excess securitization and greater financial instability. Alternatively, Gorton and Metrick (2009) argue that the growth in securitization arose naturally from the need for collateral for a new form of depository banking for institutional investors and corporations. But without any form of insurance analogous to that provided by the FDIC, when the housing collapse led to uncertainty about LCFI exposures and therefore solvency, there was a run on the repo market and the banking sector failed.

4. Note that an important element of this story is the role of the rating agencies. There is considerable evidence that the ratings were inflated due to the conflict of interest of having the issuer of the security both choose and pay the rating firm. (For a detailed analysis, see Chapter 15, "Regulation of Rating Agencies.") This ratings inflation allowed more and more questionable loans to fit into the regulatory arbitrage framework.

5. Title IX, Subtitle D, Sec. 941, "Credit Risk Retention."

6. Qualified residential mortgages are not defined per se in the Dodd-Frank Act. Instead, this section of the Act calls for the federal banking agencies, the Commission, the secretary of Housing and Urban Development, and the director of the Federal Housing Finance Agency to determine the definition jointly. Guidelines provided in the legislation, however, are sensible in that they require such evidence as documentation and verification of the financial resources of the borrower, borrower income, and payment-to-income ratio. Other potential restrictions mentioned are the type of mortgage product such as those that include adjustable rates, balloon payments, negative amortization, or interest-only payments.

7. Title IX, Subtitle D, Sec. 942, "Disclosures and Reporting for Asset-Backed Securities."

8. Title IX, Subtitle D, Sec. 946, "Study on the Macroeconomic Effects of Risk Retention Requirements."

9. Note that many mortgage lenders are not banking institutions, and may not have a source of sustained liabilities, such as deposits. Another possibility would be to require the origination fee of the lenders to be earned over some period of the loan. Thus, if default occurs within a certain period of time (i.e., before the end of the amortization period), the originator would get only a portion of the fee. The mortgage lender would not be able to sell the mortgage servicing rights. Servicing of mortgages typically commands a 0.50 percent fee, and thus the fee incentivizes the lender to choose good loans and monitor them accordingly.

10. Title XIV, Subtitle B, "Minimum Standards for Mortgages."

11. *Federal Register* 75, no. 18, Thursday, January 28, 2010, Rules and Regulations, 12 CFR Part 325, RIN 3064–AD48.

12. The rule "provides for an optional two-quarter implementation delay followed by an optional two-quarter partial implementation of the effect on risk-weighted assets that will result from changes to U.S. generally accepted accounting principles. It further provides for an optional two-quarter delay, followed by an optional two-quarter phase-in, of the application of the agencies' regulatory

limit on the inclusion of the allowance for loan and lease losses (ALLL) in Tier 2 capital for the portion of the ALLL associated with the assets a banking organization consolidates as a result of changes to U.S. generally accepted accounting principles." The delay and subsequent phase-in periods of the implementation will apply only to the agencies' risk-based capital requirements, not the leverage ratio requirement (p. 4636).

13. FAS 166 and FAS 167, among other things, establish new standards for reporting companies' transfers of assets to special purpose entities, known as variable interest entities (VIEs) under GAAP, and for consolidating VIEs. Under FAS 167, banking organizations may be required to consolidate assets, liabilities, and equity in certain VIEs that were not consolidated under the standards that FAS 166 and FAS 167 replaced. Most banking organizations are required to implement the new consolidation standards as of January 1, 2010. The agencies' risk-based capital and leverage rules (collectively, the capital rules) generally would require a banking organization to include assets held by newly consolidated VIEs in its leverage and risk-based capital ratios determined under those rules.

14. Paragraph 22A of FAS 167 addressing separate classification under the title of "Presentation" states the following: "A reporting enterprise shall present separately on the face of the statement of financial position (a) assets of a consolidated variable interest entity that can be used only to settle obligations of the consolidated variable interest entity and (b) liabilities of a consolidated variable interest entity for which creditors (or beneficial interest holders) do not have recourse to the general credit of the primary beneficiary."

15. There is precedent for excluding certain assets that are consolidated from a bank's risk-weighted assets. Section 1(c)(1) of 12 CFR Part 3 states that "even though the assets of the nonfinancial company are consolidated for accounting purposes, these assets (as well as the credit equivalent amounts of the company's off-balance-sheet items) are excluded from the bank's risk-weighted assets."

REFERENCES

Acharya, Viral, Tom Cooley, Matthew Richardson, and Ingo Walter. 2010. Manufacturing tail risk: A perspective on the financial crisis of 2007–09. *Foundations and Trends in Finance* 4 (4): 247–325.

Acharya, Viral, and Philipp Schnabl. 2009. How banks played the leverage game. In *Restoring financial stability*, ed. V. V. Acharya and M. Richardson, 83–100. Hoboken, NJ: John Wiley & Sons.

Acharya, Viral, Philipp Schnabl, and Gustavo Suarez. 2010. Securitization without risk transfer. Working paper.

Berndt, Antje, and Anurag Gupta. 2009. Moral hazard and adverse selection in the originate-to-distribute model of bank credit. *Journal of Monetary Economics* 56:725–743.

Board of Governors of the Federal Reserve System. 2009. G19: Consumer credit. (September). www.federalreserve.gov/releases/g19/current/g19.htm.

Citigroup. 2008. Does the world need securitization? (December), 10–11. www .americansecuritization.com/uploadedFiles/Citi121208_restart_securitization .pdf.

Dell'Ariccia, Giovanni, Deniz Igan, and Luc Laeven. 2009. Credit booms and lending standards: Evidence from the subprime mortgage market. European Banking Center Discussion Paper No. 2009-14s.

Elul, Ronel. 2009. Securitization and mortgage default: Reputation versus adverse selection. FRB of Philadelphia Working Paper No. 09-21.

G-7 finance ministers and central bank governors plan of action. 2008. (October 10). www.treas.gov/press/releases/hp1195.htm.

Gennaioli, Nicola, Andrei Shleifer, and Robert Vishny. 2010. Financial innovation and financial fragility. Working paper.

Gorton, Gary B. 2008. The panic of 2007. Yale ICF Working Paper No. 08-24.

Gorton, Gary B., and Andrew Metrick. 2009. Securitized banking and the run on repo. NBER Working Paper No. w15223.

Jaffee, Dwight, Anthony Lynch, Matthew Richardson, and Stijn Van Nieuwerburgh. 2009. Mortgage origination and securitization in the financial crisis. In *Restoring financial stability*, ed. Viral V. Acharya and Matthew Richardson, chap. 1, 61–82. Hoboken, NJ: John Wiley & Sons.

Jiang, Wei, Ashlyn Nelson, and Edward Vytlacil. 2010. Liar's loan? Effect of origination channel and information falsification on delinquency. Working paper.

Keys, Benjamin, Tanmoy Mukherjee, Amit Seru, and Vikrant Vig. 2009. Financial regulation and securitization: Evidence from subprime loans. *Journal of Monetary Economics* 56:721–724.

Keys, Benjamin, Tanmoy Mukherjee, Amit Seru, and Vikrant Vig. 2010. Did securitization lead to lax screening: Evidence from subprime loans. *Quarterly Journal of Economics* 125:307–362.

Krainer, John, and Elizabeth Laderman. 2009. Mortgage loan securitization and relative loan performance. Working paper, Federal Reserve Bank of San Francisco.

Mian, Atif, and Amir Sufi. 2009. The consequences of mortgage credit expansion: Evidence from the U.S. mortgage default crisis. *Quarterly Journal of Economics* 124:1449–1496.

Purnanandam, Aniyatosh. 2010. Originate-to-distribute model and the subprime mortgage crisis. Working paper, University of Michigan.

Rajan, Raghu. 2008. A view of the liquidity crisis. Mimeo, University of Chicago.

Stein, Jeremy. 2002. Information production and capital allocation: Decentralized vs. hierarchical firms. *Journal of Finance* 57 (5): 1891–1921.

PART Five

Corporate Control

CHAPTER 17

Reforming Compensation and Corporate Governance

Jennifer Carpenter, Thomas Cooley, and Ingo Walter

Other chapters in this volume address the critical issues of macro-prudential and micro-prudential regulation, which in combination are intended to improve the strength of the financial system with minimum damage to the system's efficiency, innovative properties, and competitiveness. It has frequently been argued that such measures are necessary but not sufficient—that underlying patterns of behavior, incentive structures, and governance practices at financial firms are at the root of the problem. With roughly half of the earnings of wholesale banks allocated to their bonus pools in recent years, and with bonuses often paid in shares that are sensitive to short-term fluctuations in value, it is worth rethinking compensation and its role in avoiding future crises that wreak havoc in the financial system and the real economy. This applies equally to senior management and to highly compensated risk-taking employees. To the extent that compensation practices play a role in distorting decision making at the firm level and endanger the financial commons, it is important to address them. Here we examine two key dimensions of the problem—compensation practices and corporate governance—and consider what role, if any, there may be for external regulation.

17.1 KEY ISSUES

Politicians and the general public in the United States and Europe have persistently expressed outrage at massive bonuses paid to employees of banks and other financial institutions, including institutions that clearly would

493

have collapsed had it not been for taxpayer bailouts. Along with financial regulators, they appear to believe that the risk-taking incentives in compensation structures at financial firms are in part to blame for causing the recent financial crisis, and will turn out to be a root cause of the next one. More generally, recent evidence on relative compensation shows a persistent rise in the share of national personal incomes going to employees in banking and financial services—a trend that cannot be explained by a commensurate rise in that sector's share of economic value added.[1] This has been taken to suggest that a significant proportion of financial activity is value-redistributing rather than value-creating, shifting financial wealth from the end users of the financial system to financial intermediaries through excessive trading spreads and commissions, fund management fees, exploitation of asymmetric information, various types of front-running, and persistent speculative gains that cannot be explained by normal returns distributions.[2] It is this suspected primacy of wealth redistribution, rather than wealth creation, in financial markets that has given rise to allegations of "useless finance."[3]

Controversies characterizing the public profile of the wholesale financial services industry are amplified by the share of financial firms' revenues going to employees, with plenty of anecdotal evidence of jaw-dropping compensation packages for rather ordinary individuals even in times of widespread economic malaise. Regardless of merit, this characterization is widely accepted and sets an undercurrent of public anger against which finely balanced discussions of compensation practices in finance must take place. This anger has reached a crescendo in cases where the overpaid individuals have been employees of banks or other financial firms that effectively failed during the crisis and owe their continued existence to taxpayers called upon to bail them out. So the public feels betrayed by the system not once, but twice. An inexplicable tin ear on the part of the leaders of the financial industry—or very bad advice—seems to reject the notion that the legitimacy of the system itself is being called into question, threatening to erode its future role as a generator of income and wealth.

Besides the debates about the value creation at the source of compensation in the financial sector and the sense of privatization of gain and socialization of risk, the third strain of the debate related to compensation deals with incentives and risk. This centers on a widespread view that compensation structures in the financial sector, through the design of bonus pools, have encouraged risk taking, erosion of transparency, and risk-prone business strategies that, when aggregated, ultimately contribute to the systemic risk in the system.

These three elements—set against a broader public outcry about rising levels of executive compensation throughout the corporate world, especially in the United States—have led to widespread populist calls for regulation, punitive taxation, and even caps on compensation at financial institutions. The institutions, in turn, have countered that such constraints would hamper their ability to attract and retain the executive talent needed to steer them back to health, to stabilize the financial system, and, in many cases, to repay taxpayers for the bailouts that rescued them.

17.2 THE CRISIS

To what extent were compensation structures at financial firms to blame for the 2007 to 2009 financial crisis? Although pay practices based on performance measures that failed to account adequately for downside risk clearly created incentives for excessive risk taking, we do not believe that compensation itself was the source of the problem.

Compensation at financial firms is substantially share-based, so the interests of managers and shareholders tend to be closely aligned—although this begs the question whether both public shareholders and share-incentivized managers are equally prone to behave in ways that create systemic risk.[4] As it happened, top employees at these firms incurred enormous losses of personal wealth in the crisis.[5] But the bigger problem for regulators and society is that, because of implicit and explicit taxpayer guarantees of financial firms considered too big or too interconnected to fail, the incentive to take large, potentially systemic risks is built directly into the equity itself. We know that boards of a number of financial firms (presumably under pressure from equity analysts and shareholders) explicitly encouraged the lending and trading practices that ultimately helped lead to the crisis. Consequently, new financial regulation should focus as much on reshaping shareholder risk incentives as on reshaping manager risk incentives.

17.3 SHORT-TERM MEASURES AND EARLY-STAGE PROPOSALS

Several countries have imposed or at least called for compensation limits or punitive taxes on financial sector compensation. In March 2009, the U.S. House of Representatives approved a 90 percent tax on bonuses at firms receiving federal bailout money, although the bill did not pass. In June, the U.S. appointed Kenneth Feinberg as Special Master of Executive Compensation to review and approve pay at bailed-out financial firms. In the lead-up to the Group of 20 (G-20) summit in September 2009, France and Germany called for international limits on bankers' compensation. In December, the United Kingdom announced that it would levy a one-time tax of 50 percent on bonuses of British bankers in excess of £25,000. While France voiced support for this kind of excess compensation tax, the United States and Germany did not follow suit. The international diversity in responses to an issue where there is broad agreement in terms of its contribution to the financial crisis may portend similar dissonance and inconsistency in the compensation environment going forward—especially after things are stabilized and competition for human capital in this industry regains its usual intensity.

Consequently, some believe that international cooperation in regulation is needed to prevent financial firms from arbitraging the market for human capital through choice of jurisdiction. In September 2009, the G-20 collectively endorsed the notion that excessive compensation in the financial sector encouraged excessive risk taking and contributed to the financial crisis. The G-20 put in place a set of agreed principles on compensation that address three layers of governance at significant financial institutions: managerial performance and risk incentives, corporate governance, and regulatory oversight. Perhaps the strongest emphasis of the G-20 principles is on the need to expose executives to downside risk through compensation deferral and claw-backs—"maluses" to operate in tandem with "bonuses." The Financial Stability Board (FSB)'s implementation standards list specific proportions and time periods for deferral, such as a 40 percent to 60 percent lockup of compensation for at least three years. The Board recommended that firms prohibit employees from using personal hedging strategies to undermine the intended risk incentive alignment. The FSB also suggested that at least 50 percent of pay be share-based, along with a share retention policy, as opposed to the use of guaranteed bonuses.

To govern compensation design, the FSB proposed a board remuneration committee that functions independently of management and works with the firm's risk committee to evaluate the risk incentives created by the compensation system. The FSB endorsed a limit on total variable compensation as a fraction of firm revenues, in order to maintain an adequate capital base. It also augmented national reporting standards with required disclosure of specific compensation characteristics, performance measurement, risk adjustment, and quantitative information about the amount and composition of executive compensation. Finally, the FSB called for regulatory supervisors to review firm compensation policies to guard against institutional and systemic risk, and to maintain effective, consistent standards across national jurisdictions. Financial sector supervisors could take corrective action, for example, by imposing higher capital requirements or modifying compensation structure at noncompliant firms. They could also block major strategic initiatives such as mergers and acquisitions on the part of firms with suspect compensation systems.

17.4 U.S. GUIDELINES FOR COMPENSATION AND CORPORATE GOVERNANCE

In June 2010, the U.S. Federal Reserve, in conjunction with the Treasury and the Federal Deposit Insurance Corporation (FDIC), finalized its Guidance on Sound Incentive Compensation Policies for the financial firms that come within its regulatory purview. These are designed to be consistent with the G-20 initiatives.

The Federal Reserve recommends specific compensation and governance structures and reserves the right to enforce them. Specifically, the Fed advocates balanced risk-taking incentives with (1) ex ante risk adjustment in the measures of employee performance that are used to determine compensation, (2) the use of deferred compensation and longer performance periods, with realized compensation depending on risk outcomes, and (3) consideration of the effects of so-called golden parachutes and golden handshakes on employee risk incentives. These guidelines apply not only to senior executives, but also to nonexecutives with the capacity to take large risks, such as traders with large position limits.

The Fed also calls for integration of compensation oversight in banks' risk-management processes and internal controls and active supervision of incentive compensation by boards of directors who would be held responsible for ensuring the organizations' safety. It has also signaled consideration of compensation practices in approving merger and acquisition transactions in the financial sector. In addition, the Fed has initiated a broad review of incentive compensation arrangements at banking organizations to help identify and coordinate the adoption of best practices.

17.5 THE DODD-FRANK ACT

The Dodd-Frank Wall Street Reform and Consumer Protection Act includes the most significant legislation on executive compensation to come out of the U.S. financial crisis. It represents the most important reforms in corporate governance since the 2002 Sarbanes-Oxley Act, with most of its provisions applying to all firms, not just financials. Some of its reforms may be viewed as incremental rather than foundational, for reasons that we will discuss. That said, the Act makes some important recommendations about compensation:

- *Say on pay.* The Dodd-Frank Act requires that shareholders be offered the opportunity to make their views known on the compensation of executives. These ideas have been around for a while and are not particularly radical. They require that proxy statements include a resolution subject to shareholder vote to approve the compensation of executives. Shareholders would also be empowered to make their own compensation proposals. Shareholder votes would not be binding and could not overrule decisions by the board of directors.

- *Structure of compensation committees.* The Act requires compensation committees to be composed of only independent directors with very strict requirements for independence. It would also empower them to hire independent compensation consultants and legal counsel. There is significant language in the legislation in the form of the "rules of construction." Specifically, the Act says the following: "Rule of Construction—This paragraph may not be construed (i) to require the compensation committee to implement or act consistently with the advice or recommendations of the compensation consultant (or legal counsel); or (ii) to affect the ability or obligation of a compensation committee to exercise its own judgment in fulfillment of the duties of the compensation committee."

- *Disclosure of pay versus performance.* The Act also requires firms to describe compensation policies and provide data on the relationship between realized executive compensation, including returns on share-based compensation, and realized financial performance of the firm. In addition, firms would have to disclose total annual CEO compensation, median annual employee compensation, and their ratio.

- *Claw-backs.* The legislation requires firms to attempt recovery of erroneously awarded incentive-based compensation. No listing would be allowed for companies unless they have a clearly articulated policy on claw-backs and recovery for any compensation awarded within the past three years based on an accounting restatement, whether or not there was fraudulent intent in the accounting misstatements.

- *Hedging strategies.* Importantly, the Act mandates that the Securities and Exchange Commission (SEC) require by rule that each public company disclose in the annual proxy statement whether the employees of the issuer are permitted to purchase financial instruments (including prepaid variable forward contracts, equity swaps, collars, and exchange funds) that are designed to hedge or offset any decrease in the market value of equity securities granted to employees by the issuer as part of an employee compensation package. This requirement provides an additional degree of transparency about the relationship between pay and performance. During the period covered by Troubled Asset Relief Program (TARP) support of banks, the U.S. Treasury's compensation monitor, Kenneth Feinberg, banned all hedging of stock-based compensation by executives at banks under his purview.

■ *Regulatory oversight of compensation in financial firms.* In addition to these reforms, which apply to all institutions, the Act also includes some special requirements aimed at financial firms. Specifically, it empowers the Federal Reserve to establish rules that mandate sufficient disclosure of incentive compensation arrangements and that prohibit arrangements that encourage inappropriate risk taking or could lead to material financial losses at these companies.

17.6 ANALYSIS

In general, these reforms do not represent a major change in executive compensation in the United States, for the simple reason that they are not binding. In effect, they encourage a greater degree of transparency and more market discipline without tying the hands of corporate directors. This is sensible.

There is a powerful principle that has shaped corporate governance in the United States for a long time. It is known as the "business judgment rule." Delaware courts, the favorite venue for the incorporation of businesses in the United States, are known for respecting and upholding the business judgment rule. The business judgment rule holds that directors of public companies cannot be held liable for or overruled on decisions, good or bad, that are based on their best business judgment. The rules of construction in the Dodd-Frank compensation reforms basically reaffirm this rule. Why is this a good thing? Consider the alternative. If shareholders or other interested parties could sue or otherwise punish directors for decisions that turn out to be bad, then it would be very difficult to attract people to be directors, and the directors would be reluctant to take significant actions. There is a time consistency problem in corporate governance. To deal with this, shareholders are willing to tie their own hands from the start. This is effectively what they do when they buy shares in Delaware corporations where they know the business judgment rule will be upheld.

This does not mean shareholders' say on pay is an empty reform. To the extent that shareholders are dissatisfied enough to raise a ruckus, it increases the transparency of corporate governance.

The special nature of financial firms raises some additional issues that need clarification. One focuses on the inherent conflicts of interest between shareholders of financial firms and society as a whole. Society needs the banking system to provide smooth functioning of the payments system and the credit markets just as much as it needs utilities to provide an uninterrupted supply of power and water. Financial intermediaries therefore have strong and inescapable public utility characteristics—they are special. The financial disaster of 1929 to 1933 and the crisis of 2007 to 2009 show that a seizing-up of financial markets can be devastating to economic prosperity and difficult and time-consuming to reverse. Evidence from past crises suggests recovery times as long as a decade in the real sector of the economy.

Thus, society's interests may be quite different from those of individual profit-maximizing financial institutions that would not naturally count the cost of the systemic risk their collective actions might create. Moreover, these institutions are extremely highly leveraged and benefit from explicit or implicit guarantees due to their specialness, so equity value maximization calls for even greater risk taking than individual firm value maximization would normally dictate. The incentive to overinvest in subprime mortgage products may have been as much a matter of pressure from shareholders as from managers and traders. To the extent that shareholders' incentives are the problem, some of the regulatory proposals miss the point. For example, tilting away from cash-based compensation toward more share-based compensation and strengthening shareholder governance, without reshaping shareholder risk incentives, may only serve to increase risk-seeking behavior.

Public and political outrage has focused mainly on the level of bankers' pay. But the mere level of pay reflects primarily a wealth transfer from shareholders to managers. Except for any impact on total production and welfare, society has no obvious stake in how profit is divided between shareholders and employees. What is relevant for society is not so much the level of compensation, but rather the risk incentives created by the pay structure. It wasn't the $170 million paid to American International Group (AIG) executives that cost taxpayers so much. It was the $170 billion they had to inject into AIG as a result of its unbridled underwriting of risk. Regulators should be much less concerned with how much these executives are paid, and much more concerned with what kinds of actions their pay induces.

If any group has cause to complain about the level of pay at financial institutions, it is the shareholders of these institutions, since they end up paying most of the bill. The tepid valuations of wholesale financial firms reflected in metrics such as price-to-earnings or market-to-book ratios provide ample testimony even among the most successful firms. Relative to other sectors of the economy, the quality of earnings is poor. Yet instead of embracing calls for pay limits, which could strengthen their hand at the bargaining table, these institutions rushed to pay back bailout money in order to throw off the regulatory constraints on compensation. It would appear that boards that are supposed to represent shareholders feel that the value that star bankers and traders can add to equity is worth the price, and the loss of talent resulting from pay constraints is one of the most serious threats to profitability and long-term survival. Or perhaps shareholders would rather overpay managers to take risks than let compensation regulation channel the firm into safer, less profitable activities.

Reinforcing the view that the financial crisis was not attributable to conflicts between shareholders and managers at financial firms, Fahlenbrach and Stulz (2009) find no evidence that banks where CEO and top executive incentives were better aligned with shareholder interests performed better during the crisis. If anything, their evidence is to the contrary. This further suggests that the problem is not so much the conflict between shareholders and managers; rather, it is the conflict between shareholders and society.

This conflict leaves open the possibility of a role for regulation of compensation. But direct regulation of the pay structure of hundreds of thousands of financial employees with heterogeneous risk preferences, skill sets, and job functions seems wildly ambitious. It seems easier and more efficient to try to align financial shareholders' interests with those of society from the start, and then leave shareholders to design individual contracts to create the right incentives.

For example, the use of claw-backs in compensation contracts has been rare. One might argue that this is because shareholders have simply lacked the bargaining power to impose them. An alternative explanation is that they are very costly and not especially beneficial from the shareholders' perspective. Managers could charge shareholders for exposing them to this downside risk in the form of offsetting features, such as higher salaries, that could make the overall cost of compensation much higher. And the threat of claw-backs might even lead managers to avoid actions shareholders consider beneficial. If regulators can succeed in giving shareholders an interest in limiting systemic risk through correct pricing of guarantees and capital charges, then shareholders or their boards may willingly impose claw-backs or other deterrents to inappropriate risk taking.

Similarly, shareholders may have cause to dislike using deferred cash compensation, or so-called inside debt. A new study[6] shows that at firms where CEOs are heavily compensated with deferred compensation, recently mandated disclosure of the practice precipitated significant declines in equity value, total firm value, and volatility—although bond values rose. This suggests that while greater use of deferred compensation at financial institutions might have socially beneficial effects on firm risk, it would be unwelcome to shareholders, and possibly even value reducing for individual firms. The most effective regulatory approach would be to make it worth shareholders' while to implement such pay schemes and otherwise discourage excessive managerial risk taking.

To the extent that shareholder interests cannot be aligned with those of society, or if shareholders cannot be sufficiently empowered, there may be a role for some degree of flexible, but consistent, regulatory oversight of compensation practices. But it must be weighed against the costs of limiting shareholders' ability to create incentives for performance and innovation, and the risk of unintended consequences.

Elements of a sensible contract include the following:

- Stock-based or other performance-based pay to create an incentive to add value through efficiency and innovation.
- Ex ante risk adjustment of performance measures to discourage the pursuit of illusory profit, or so-called fake alpha.
- Deferred cash compensation, or inside debt, to give managers an interest in the long-term solvency of the firm.
- Claw-backs to give managers an acute interest in controlling downside risk.
- Guaranteed cash compensation to attract and retain talented personnel and compensate them for the downside risks they may be forced to bear.

Sensible regulation does not include caps on pay or limits on cash compensation or prohibition of guaranteed bonuses. Although uniform caps on the level of pay may be popular with voters, they can hamper shareholders' ability to attract and retain the best talent—with *best* being defined only after firm-specific and systemic risk have been properly accounted for and priced. Crude compensation limits thus fail to serve the regulator/taxpayers' interest, because it is not the level of pay per se, but rather the risk-taking incentives in compensation that potentially threaten the safety and soundness of the financial system. Guaranteed bonuses by themselves do not create an incentive for risk taking. If they represent an overpayment to managers, that is not a big problem for society. If they represent the price of attracting the best talent, that may be in society's interest. If they represent compensation to managers who must be forced to bear downside risk, they are essential.

If regulators or boards are to succeed in imposing the threat of claw-backs on talented managers with rich opportunity sets, they might have to pay these managers more, on average, not less. Alternatively, average pay levels at these institutions could decline endogenously if the Volcker Rule and other new restrictions on banking activity ultimately mean that these firms find less use for high-priced talent, and the high-priced talent leaves for better opportunities elsewhere.

Sensible regulation should also avoid mandating specific proportions of any particular form of compensation, since the range of what is optimal in different settings is likely to be very wide. Mandating deferred compensation in the form of restricted stock also misses the point. It is deferred cash compensation that is most likely to make managers value the firm's safety and soundness, since it is very similar to ordinary debt, and carries only downside risk.

However, regulation that requires increased disclosure and transparency of compensation arrangements is more than welcome. Current accounting standards in the United States, for example, require only disclosure of the details of compensation to the top five executives. At financial institutions, however, there may be many more employees with the power to take destabilizing actions—referred to earlier as highly compensated risk-taking employees—who sometimes earn more than top management. A broader and deeper disclosure requirement, at least for the eyes of regulators, is clearly necessary. In fact, regulation that generates a database of common compensation practices and performance outcomes would be of great social value and would provide a basis for judging compensation going forward.

17.7 EVALUATION OF THE DODD-FRANK, FEDERAL RESERVE, AND G-20 COMPENSATION REFORMS

The Dodd-Frank requirements to increase shareholder say on compensation should bring about salutary compensation reform to the extent that shareholder interests are aligned with those of society. So if the conflict of interest between shareholders of financial firms and taxpayers can be resolved—for example, with correct pricing of federal guarantees—it may be enough to strengthen shareholder rights and then leave shareholders to influence managerial compensation accordingly.

The Federal Reserve argues that, because of the federal safety net and unpriced or underpriced systemic risk, shareholder and taxpayer conflicts of interest may not be adequately resolved at banking organizations. It therefore seeks to regulate their compensation policies directly. Its ideas of ex ante risk adjustment, deferred compensation, longer performance periods, and ex post settling up are sound principles for managing risk incentives and reducing moral hazard, as are its proposals to strengthen the role of risk management in firm governance.

But while these objectives should serve as important advisory guidelines, the Fed should be cautious about enforcement. Given the heterogeneity of banking organizations and their employees, and therefore the diversity of contracts that are likely to be appropriate, the Fed should not (and likely could not), in our view, control compensation and governance. Perhaps a reasonable middle ground would be to place the chief risk officer, and perhaps a Fed representative, on the financial firms' boards. The idea of ex ante risk adjustment of performance measures—so that an employee is essentially charged immediately for the risk consequences of his or her actions—is a sound accounting principle. However, where compensation is concerned, it may be difficult to implement effectively because of the complexities of assessing the risks of new activities and the sensitivity of incentives to these measurement errors. For this reason, we believe it is best, whenever possible, to use it in conjunction with the principles of deferred compensation and longer performance periods, with ex post adjustments as needed.

The Fed's plan to continue to review compensation policies and outcomes at banking organizations on a regular basis is excellent. This could generate valuable new information about which schemes work well and which do not. Not only should the review process itself spur voluntary improvements, but it should also provide more concrete information than is currently available about those aspects of the process that need regulation.

Like the Fed guidelines, the FSB's implementation standards contain a number of sound principles, such as the need to impose downside risk on executives, the need to ensure the independence of the compensation committees, and the need for better disclosure. But its opposition to guaranteed bonuses is not constructive, in our view. These bonuses are not likely to lead to destabilizing behavior and may actually be a necessary carrot to give to talented employees who must be forced to bear downside risk. In addition, its proposal of a minimum proportion of stock-based compensation is not likely to be useful. Shareholders will want to use stock-based compensation anyway, to keep managers on their side, and will be better positioned to judge the right proportion case by case. In fact, to the extent that shareholders' risk incentives diverge from those of society, stock and option compensation may only aggravate the problem.

The FSB's call for better disclosure is also well-conceived and long overdue. When managers use products such as equity swaps and collars to hedge their restricted stock and option positions, they undermine the incentive alignment these compensation instruments are supposed to achieve. They also effectively monetize at least part of the value of that compensation, so hedging not only reduces incentive benefits, but also increases the value of the compensation to managers. High-cost option and stock packages are justified if the cost premium induces performance benefits and compensates managers for the additional firm risk they must bear relative to cash compensation. But if managers are permitted to undo the incentive effects and effectively pocket more of the value of these compensation instruments up front, shareholders should at least be made aware.

The Dodd-Frank Act requires all firms to disclose the permissibility of managerial hedging. The G-20 proposal would go further and prohibit managerial hedging at financial firms altogether. Outright prohibition of managerial hedging is probably too restrictive. While in most cases, allowing managerial hedging seems like a bad idea, firms in some sectors, such as the technology industry, appear to use stock and option compensation as a form of funding, not just incentive alignment. This might be justified if market imperfections make outside capital too expensive, and in these cases, permitting managerial hedging might make sense. The Dodd-Frank Act gives firms flexibility on this point.

17.8 INTERNATIONAL COMPENSATION DEVELOPMENTS

Given the global nature of financial markets and competition among major banks, asset managers, and other financial intermediaries, debates on executive compensation comparable to those in the United States have raged elsewhere as well. The United Kingdom went some way toward imposing revised compensation schemes among banks, first and foremost among those bailed out during the financial crisis. Discussions were even more heated in continental Europe, where there was even less understanding about levels and formulas for compensating senior management and risk-taking professionals in wholesale financial intermediaries and asset managers. In some cases, like the United Kingdom, popular sentiment led to major surtaxes on compensation that all market players had to digest.

Discussion of the compensation issue at the European Union level has focused on proposed legislation to recalibrate bank capital requirements. In June 2010, the EU Commission agreed to place limits on bankers' bonuses. The rules were approved by the EU Council of Ministers and voted by the European Parliament. These rules also apply to hedge funds and other asset managers.

Under the EU law, immediate cash bonuses are limited to 30 percent for lower-paid staff and 20 percent for large bonus awards. Between 40 percent and 50 percent of bonuses will be deferred from three to five years, and half of all bonus payments must be paid out in stock or other securities linked to the firm's performance. In addition, bonuses must be more closely linked to base salaries in order to reduce the risk-taking incentive effects of the bonus component. There are also provisions for bonus claw-backs, where individuals or business units are shown to have contributed to major subsequent losses.

In the case of financial firms bailed out by taxpayers, bonus payments cannot be made until the government support has been repaid. While there is some flexibility for national regulators within the EU framework, there is also provision for significant financial and nonfinancial penalties for firms that are deemed to maintain risky compensation policies.

In fact, the EU rules are unlikely to present significant compliance problems for major banks, many of which had already introduced similar features into their bonus practices. Asset managers, in contrast, face much more significant adjustments in the EU effort to place banks and other intermediaries on the same bonus footing—pointing out that financial crisis losses were about evenly split between banks and asset managers, and that unequal treatment represents an invitation to regulatory arbitrage.

Banks and institutional investors nevertheless argue that the EU compensation law would lead to significant migration of financial services activities to the United States, just as these same firms have argued that other features of the Dodd-Frank Act would lead to business migration in the opposite direction. As long as the EU and U.S. regulatory overlay remains in broad balance, it seems doubtful that significant bilateral activity migration will take place. Equally doubtful is the willingness and ability of Switzerland, Singapore, or other financial centers to take on regulatory responsibility for and risk exposure to financial transactions that could lead to large systemic losses.

17.9 IS CORPORATE GOVERNANCE OF FINANCIAL FIRMS SPECIAL?

A basic tenet of modern economic theory is that in perfect capital markets, firms' maximization of profit leads to socially optimal outcomes, and in most industries, government intervention does more harm than good. However, it has long been understood that, like public utilities, the banking industry and financial intermediaries in general are an exception to this rule. It is not an exaggeration to suggest that economic prosperity depends on the availability of credit for risky borrowers on one hand, and default-free lending for certain types of investors on the other. In addition, the financial institutions that provide this socially beneficial intermediation also serve as the transmission belt for monetary policy. Yet ensuring the smooth functioning of financial markets is not a necessary consequence of profit maximization at these institutions and, as we noted earlier, their special privileges as primary dealers can further widen the gap between social interests and individual firm interests.

To bridge this gap, the banking system was heavily regulated in the wake of the Crash of 1929 and the Great Depression of the 1930s. But the past few decades have brought not only outright deregulation but also a new class of institutions that have functioned as banks; they have enjoyed their guarantees implicitly, yet have fallen outside the banking system or have found ways around explicit bank regulation. In addition, the proliferation of new financial products has enabled not only beneficial financial innovation, but also the means for escaping regulatory constraints. The crisis of 2007 to 2009 has brought to light the need to overhaul the regulation of the financial industry. So one element of modern financial regulation must be a specialized structure of corporate governance at financial firms. While the governance of ordinary firms is typically best left to shareholders, society's interest in the solvency of these institutions creates a role for much greater involvement of regulators, risk managers, and unsecured creditors in corporate decision making.

17.10 CONCLUSION

From the perspective of financial regulation, the issue of compensation in financial firms is best seen as problematic—not because there is a conflict between shareholders and managers, but because there is a conflict between shareholders and society. In the current environment, financial firms benefit from a rich patrimony of special privileges and subsidies because of their special role in the economy. This distorts incentives in ways that are best addressed directly. It also distorts compensation levels and structures in the financial services sector. If the primary distortions—specifically those related to systemic risk—can be dealt with, compensation and governance issues will tend to fall into line.

While increased transparency, good guidelines, and frequent oversight are to be applauded, there are two important reasons why more direct intervention in compensation is both unlikely and unwise:

The first is contract law. The ability to write and enforce contracts without being subjected to arbitrary notions about fairness is one of the bulwarks of the U.S. system. It is a critical element of markets for human capital. Any attempts to interfere with employment contracts are not likely to survive legal challenges.

The second is the extraordinary deference the courts have paid to the prerogatives of corporate governance. Although the U.S. Supreme Court established in *Rodger v. Hill* (1933) the right to intervene in matters of compensation deemed excessive, courts since then have been reluctant to overrule decisions made by corporate boards. The overriding consideration is the business judgment rule, holding that directors of public companies cannot be held liable for or overruled on decisions, good or bad, that are based on their best business judgment.

Here is an optimistic scenario: Efforts to reform the financial system successfully come to grips with pricing systemic risks and force these risks back inside the financial firms that engage in them. Through a governance process acutely aware of the duty of care and duty of loyalty, financial firms internally price these risks and incorporate them into the profit-and-loss positions of their various activities. Compensation for both senior management and risk-taking employees is then based on these risk-adjusted profit-and-loss results, with payment in shares with appropriate lockups to ensure that these results reflect reality. Financial conglomerates operating under these rules may decide to break themselves up into stand-alone commercial banks, with commensurate returns to shareholders and compensation to employees, and independent units engaged in other activities. These might include investment banking, private equity, and hedge fund activities, which, to the extent they continue to create systemic risk, would likewise be forced to internalize it—but would exhibit their own unique patterns of returns to shareholders and to employees.

NOTES

1. Viral V. Acharya and Matthew Richardson, eds., *Restoring Financial Stability* (Hoboken, NJ: John Wiley & Sons, 2009), chap. 8. See also Thomas Phillipon and Ariell Reshef, "Wages and Human Capital in the U.S. Financial Industry 1909–2006," NBER Working Paper No. 14644, 2009.
2. In March 2010, Goldman Sachs reported in an SEC filing that the firm earned at least $100 million per day on 131 days in 2009, an extremely unlikely result in the trading world, and one that is far removed from the primacy of an institutional role as a financial intermediary.
3. Willem Buiter, "Useless Finance, Harmful Finance and Useful Finance," *Financial Times*, April 12, 2009.
4. See, for example, Clementi and Cooley (2009).
5. See Rudiger Fahlenbrach and René Stultz, "Bank CEO Incentives and the Credit Crisis," working paper, 2009, www.ssrn.com/abstract=1439859.
6. Chenyang Wei and David Yermack, "Deferred Compensation, Risk, and Company Value: Investor Reactions to CEO Incentives," New York University Working Paper, 2010.
7. J. Carr Bettis, John M. Bizjak, and Swaminathan L. Kalpathy, "Why Do Insiders Hedge Their Ownership and Options?" Working paper available at http://papers.ssrn.com/sol3/papers.cfm?abstract_id=1364810.

REFERENCES

Boni, Leslie, and Kent Womack. 2002. Wall Street's credibility problem: Misaligned incentives and dubious fixes? *Brookings-Wharton Papers in Financial Services* (May).

Byrd, J., and K. Hickman. 2002. Do outside directors monitor managers? Evidence from tender offer bids. *Journal of Financial Economics* 32 (Fall): 195–221.

Clementi, Gian Luca, and Thomas F. Cooley. 2009. Executive compensation: The facts. NBER Working Paper No. 15426 (October). Available at http://papers.ssrn.com/sol3/papers.cfm?abstract_id=1493019.

Erhardt, N., J. Werbel, and C. Shrader. 2003. Board of directors diversity and firm financial performance. *Corporate Governance* 11, no. 2 (Spring): 102–110.

Fahlenbrach, Rüdiger, and Rene M. Stulz. 2010. Bank CEO incentives and the credit crisis. *Journal of Financial Economics*.

Galbraith, John Kenneth. 1973. *Economics and the public purpose.* New York: Macmillan.

Kane, Edward J. 1987. Competitive financial reregulation: An international perspective. In *Threats to international financial stability*, ed. R. Portes and A. Swoboda. Cambridge: Cambridge University Press.

Krozner, Randall S., and Philip E. Strahan. 1999. Bankers on boards, conflicts of interest, and lender liability. NBER Working Paper No. W7319, August.

Saunders, Anthony, Anand Srinivasan, and Ingo Walter. 2001. Price formation in the OTC corporate bond markets: A field study of the inter-dealer market. *Journal of Economics and Business* (Fall).

Shivdasani, A., and D. Yermack. 2003. CEO involvement in the selection of new board members: An empirical analysis. *Journal of Finance* 54, no. 5 (Fall).

Smith, Clifford W. 1992. Economics and ethics: The case of Salomon Brothers. *Journal of Applied Corporate Finance* 5, no. 2 (Summer).

Smith, Roy C., and Ingo Walter. 1997. *Street smarts: Linking professional conduct and shareholder value in the securities industry.* Boston: Harvard Business School Press.

Walter, Ingo, and Roy C. Smith. 2000. *High finance in the euro-zone.* London: Financial Times–Prentice Hall.

White, Lawrence J. 1991. *The S&L debacle: Public policy lessons for bank and thrift regulation.* New York: Oxford University Press.

CHAPTER 18

Accounting and Financial Reform

Joshua Ronen and Stephen Ryan

Comprehensive and informative financial reporting by financial institutions for their financial instruments and transactions is essential to promote long-term stability of the U.S. financial system. Because managers of financial institutions inevitably will be evaluated in part based on reported accounting numbers, they will have the incentive to make these numbers appear favorable (i.e., either value- or income-increasing or risk-decreasing). The goal of financial reporting should not be to skew these incentives in any particular direction, but rather to describe financial instruments and transactions as faithfully and reliably as possible through both conceptually sound accounting methods and illuminating disclosures. Armed with such financial reporting, it is then the task of investors and bank regulators to understand and use these descriptions to promote proper decision making by bank managers and, overall, a well-functioning financial system.

In this chapter, we consider three longstanding financial reporting issues that arose with particular salience during the financial crisis: (1) banks' loan loss reserving under the current incurred loss model, (2) fair value measurement in illiquid markets, and (3) the leverage embedded in derivatives and similarly small-value but high-risk instruments, including residual or otherwise subordinated retained interests from securitizations.

We also discuss the troublesome issue of political interference in setting accounting standards and the current status of convergence of U.S. generally accepted accounting principles (GAAP) with international accounting standards.

Our recommendations are:

- The current incurred loss model for a bank's loan loss reserving should be replaced with an expected loss approach, because the latter is more consistent with economic valuation and with fair value accounting used for some other financial instruments. The proposal for dynamic loss reserving is unsuitable for financial reporting purposes, as it is completely at odds with established accounting concepts. While the goal of dynamic loss reserving—encouraging banks to build up capital during periods of economic strength—is laudable, this goal must not be accomplished by compromising the consistency of GAAP.

- Even in illiquid markets or when systemic risk is a concern, we recommend fair value measurement of financial instruments as superior overall to amortized cost measurement, because the latter suppresses the timely reporting of some or all unrealized gains and losses. Reasonable arguments can be made to measure fair value either as the current construct of exit value or as discounted cash flows. In choosing between these two alternative fair value measurements, accounting standard setters will need to make trade-offs, because the two bases exhibit different strengths and weaknesses when the relevant markets are illiquid. We recommend that accounting standard setters consider requiring firms to present and reconcile the two measurement bases in a columnar format for their illiquid financial instruments, as this information is relevant to bank regulators and investors.

- While limited, the amortized cost of financial instruments is reliable information that is useful for various financial analysis purposes, and for this reason, we support the recent proposal by the Financial Accounting Standards Board (FASB) to require firms to present on the face of the balance sheet (another columnar format would serve the same purpose) both the amortized costs and fair values of financial instruments "that are being held for collection or payment(s) of contractual cash flows" and for which unrealized gains and losses are reported in other comprehensive income.

- The embedded leverage in derivatives and similarly small-value but high-risk instruments should be comprehensively portrayed in financial reports. The most natural and flexible approach is through disclosure, rather than balance sheet grossing up of these positions. We recommend required disclosure of standardized alternative leverage measures including but not limited to: (1) full grossing up of all derivatives and similar positions to the extent they are not subject to contractual netting agreements; and (2) netting of grossed-up positions when they are economically well-hedged by other positions in the firm's portfolio.

- Bank regulators and politicians must not be allowed to meddle in GAAP and financial reporting in their pursuit of more effective bank regulation or other policy goals.

- Accounting convergence, while desirable, should not come at the expense of either high-quality financial reporting now or an accounting-standard-setting process that has the capacity to improve accounting standards over time.

18.1 BANKS' LOAN LOSS RESERVING

Background

Banks currently reserve for loan losses, under both U.S. GAAP and international accounting standards, using the incurred loss model. Under this model, banks accrue allowances (reductions of net loans outstanding) and provisions (expenses) for loan losses only when those losses: (1) are "incurred" (U.S. bank regulators refer to incurred as "inherent" in banks' existing loan portfolios); (2) are "probable"; and (3) "can be reasonably estimated" based on available information. As a proxy for the unobservable losses inherent in banks' loan portfolios, certain accounting guidance provided by U.S. bank regulators allows banks, for their currently performing loans, to accrue only for losses expected to be realized in loan charge-offs over a relatively short horizon (such as a year), even when the remaining life of the loans is considerably longer than that.

Various parties—notably the Financial Stability Forum in an April 2009 report, and the U.S. Treasury in its June 2009 proposals to reform the financial system—have argued that in good economic times, the incurred loss model yields loan loss allowances that are too low to absorb loan losses when the economic cycle turns, thereby exacerbating the cyclicality of the financial system. These parties suggest replacing the incurred loss model with "dynamic" loan loss reserving—in which banks accrue for loan losses based on long-run or through-the-cycle default probabilities and expected losses given default—even when the expected time until the cycle turns is beyond the remaining life of the loans. Dynamic loan loss reserving is intended to induce banks to build up more capital in good economic times so that they are better able to weather periods of economic weakness.

Expected loss reserving is currently under consideration by the International Accounting Standards Board (IASB). A somewhat less complete, but more objective, form of expected loss reserving is proposed in the FASB's May 2010 Exposure Draft, *Accounting for Financial Instruments and Revisions to the Accounting for Derivative Instruments and Hedging Activities.* Expected loss reserving constitutes a middle ground between the incurred loss model and dynamic loss reserving. Under this approach, banks reserve for loan losses expected to occur over the remaining life of their existing loans based on some specified information. The main difference between the IASB's considerations and the FASB proposal is what that specified information is.

The FASB's proposed approach in the Exposure Draft includes the following features, with their likely effects on loan loss reserving indicated.

- The probable threshold to accrual of credit losses on loans would be eliminated. This feature would have a particularly large effect for heterogeneous loan types for which losses are accrued at the individual loan level, making the probable threshold hard to meet.
- Firms would incorporate the implications of all available information relating to past events and existing conditions for the collectibility of all remaining cash flows over the remaining life of the loans. This proposal would prohibit the bank-regulator-sanctioned use of a charge-off horizon shorter than the remaining life of loans in assessing incurred or inherent losses.
- For pools of homogeneous loans, for which losses are accrued at the pool level, firms should determine appropriate historical loss rates for the pools and adjust those loss rates for existing economic factors and conditions. In making these adjustments, firms would assume that the economic conditions existing at the end of the reporting period would remain unchanged for the remaining life of the pools; that is, they would not forecast future events or economic conditions that did not exist at the reporting date. Through these features, the FASB effectively would retain the incurred loss model's requirement that credit losses be incurred or inherent in existing loan portfolios. In contrast, the IASB is considering requiring firms to predict future events and economic conditions over the remaining life of existing loans, which would yield a more complete, but also more subjective, form of expected loss reserving.

To be accrued now, loan losses must be realized over a period no longer than the life of existing loans. The expected time to the turn of the business cycle (by which we mean the time when probabilities of loan default and expected losses given default change significantly) may be shorter or longer than the average life of existing loans. This time difference largely determines the relative magnitude of loan loss accruals under the incurred loss model and the distinct FASB and IASB approaches to expected loss reserving.

Specifically, for banks with loans with an average loan life shorter than the time to the expected turn of the business cycle, both approaches to expected loan loss reserving—FASB and IASB—are similar to the incurred loss model for banks, because the turn in the business cycle is not captured in expected losses. For banks with loans whose remaining life is longer than the time to the expected business cycle turn, the IASB approach to expected loss reserving is similar to dynamic loss reserving, because the turn of the business cycle is captured in those expectations. In contrast, the FASB approach would not capture the turn of the business cycle for these loans, because predictions of future events and economic conditions are not part of this approach.

The Issues

There are two primary issues with the current proposals. The first is whether the incurred loss model in GAAP should be replaced by either a dynamic or expected loss reserving approach. The second consideration is whether GAAP loan loss reserving should be adjusted to induce banks to build up sufficient capital in good economic times to better prepare for the inevitable economic downturn.

We believe that the incurred loss model yields artificially low loan loss accruals, particularly in two cases: (1) when banks accrue for losses on their currently performing loans over a horizon shorter than the remaining expected life of their loans, as allowed by the U.S. bank regulation, and (2) for heterogeneous loans for which it is difficult to meet the model's probable loss condition. Moreover, the expected loss approach is consistent with economic valuation and with fair value accounting used for some other financial instruments. For these reasons, we recommend replacing the incurred loss model with an expected loss approach.

The proposal for dynamic loss reserving should be rejected, because it is completely at odds with accounting concepts—concepts that prohibit accrual for firms' general business risks unrelated to existing exposures—as well as with the accounting methods that banks use for other financial instruments. The contractual or effective maturity of most loans is shorter than the highly uncertain period of the business cycle; as a result, dynamic loss reserving obscures actual credit loss experience and yields artificially smooth earnings. Dynamic loss reserving is an indirect means toward the goal of bolstering bank capital reserves in good economic times. While it appears to be a worthy goal, boosting reserves should be addressed head-on by requiring higher capital ratios when the economy is robust or through regulatory accounting principles, not by compromising the consistency of GAAP and the transparency of financial reports based on GAAP.

Recommendation

The current incurred loss model for banks' loan loss reserving should be replaced with an expected loss approach, because the latter is more consistent with economic valuation and with fair value accounting used for other financial instruments. The proposal for dynamic loss reserving is unsuitable for financial reporting purposes, as it is completely at odds with established accounting principles. While the goal of dynamic loss reserving—encouraging banks to build up capital during periods of economic strength—is laudable, this must not be accomplished by compromising the consistency of GAAP.

Trade-offs exist between FASB's less complete, but more objective, proposed expected loss reserving approach and IASB's more complete and subjective approach. Regardless of which approach is chosen, we recommend requiring firms to disclose the incremental losses associated with forecasted future events and economic conditions over the remaining lives of existing loans.

18.2 MARKET ILLIQUIDITY AND FAIR VALUE MEASUREMENT

Background

In terms of the measurement basis for banks' financial instruments, we believe that fair value is preferable to amortized cost, even when the relevant markets are illiquid and fair value measurement reliability and systemic risk are concerns.[1] Amortized cost accounting suppresses the timely reporting of some or all unrealized gains and losses. It thereby reduces firms' need and/or incentives for voluntary disclosure, for the simple reason that there is little or nothing for firms to explain about amortized costs. This suppression of information prolongs price and resource allocation adjustment processes; while the efficiency of these processes is always important, it is absolutely critical in working through economic crises.

Market illiquidity raises practical problems for estimating fair values that should be addressed by accounting standard setters. This could be via expanded disclosures about firms' use of internal models and unobservable inputs in estimating fair value, and portions of unrealized fair value gains and losses that result from such illiquidity. In April 2009, the FASB required additional disclosures along these lines.

Statement of Financial Accounting Standards (FAS) 157 (Financial Accounting Standards Board 2006) defines fair value as exit value—that is, the value a firm would receive from selling an asset or the value that the firm would pay to retire a liability in an orderly transaction at the measurement date. FASB Staff Position (FSP) FAS 157-3 requires the measurement of exit value for an illiquid financial instrument to incorporate a discount rate premium for illiquidity to the limited extent that the terms of trade of a *hypothetical* orderly transaction in the instrument would incorporate such a premium. Intuitively, exit value incorporates discount rate premiums for illiquidity only to the extent that market illiquidity enables willing buyers to demand and receive better terms from willing sellers in such hypothetical transactions.

Given this limited incorporation of discount rate premiums, the exit value of an illiquid financial asset occupies a hypothetical middle ground between what a firm will receive if it must sell or chooses to sell the asset (i.e., a fire-sale value) and the value a firm will receive if it holds the asset through the recovery of market illiquidity or maturity, whichever comes first. We refer to the latter value as "fulfillment value" and to this holding period as the "liquidity horizon." This hypothetical middle ground does not correspond to the transactions that actually occur in currently illiquid financial instruments, whether through immediate fire sales or through orderly transactions at the liquidity horizon. It also does not capture the fact that transactions will not occur when the relevant markets are so illiquid that buyers and sellers cannot agree on terms of trade.

Many parties have criticized exit value accounting as requiring firms to mark illiquid assets down to fire-sale prices. This view reflects an incorrect interpretation of FAS 157 and FSP FAS 157-3, as already noted. This criticism may accurately reflect auditors' incentives to pressure reporting firms to rely on observable transaction prices, even when those transactions are partly or wholly forced.

However, some have correctly criticized exit value accounting as requiring firms to mark illiquid financial instruments to a value below fulfillment value, even when they have the ability and intent to hold the instruments through the liquidity horizon. These parties typically suggest that firms with this ability and intent should record the financial instruments at fulfillment value or, more reasonably, at a weighted average of fulfillment value and fire-sale value, with the weights reflecting the probability that the firm holds the instruments through the liquidity horizon versus selling them before then. We refer to this weighted average valuation as discounted cash flows.

The Issues

There are two key issues: (1) determining the preferable measurement for illiquid financial instruments for the purpose of accounting recognition—exit value or discounted cash flows, and (2) whether firms should be required to disclose the differences between exit value and discounted cash flows for their illiquid financial instruments.

Resolving the first issue requires accounting standard setters to make trade-offs, because the two alternative bases for financial instrument measurement exhibit different strengths and weaknesses when the relevant markets are illiquid. These trade-offs exist because illiquidity risk pertains to breakdowns in market functioning. Unlike the realization of other (e.g., interest rate, prepayment, and credit) risks in liquid markets, the realization of market illiquidity makes a firm's intent and ability to hold a financial instrument through the liquidity horizon economically significant; the firm cannot sell a financial instrument or acquire an identical instrument without sizable cost. A firm with the ability and intent to hold the instrument through the liquidity horizon will, on average, realize the discounted cash flows, not the exit value.

The strengths of exit value vis-à-vis discounted cash flow measurement are threefold. First, in principle at least, the use of exit value yields identical valuations for identical financial instruments held by different firms; that is, exit value is a more market-specific and less firm-specific measure compared with discounted cash flows. Second, exit value does not incorporate a firm's unobservable and changeable abilities and intents, thus making it a more verifiable measure. Third, by incorporating a discount rate premium for (reducing the accounting valuation of) illiquid financial instruments, exit value diminishes banks' incentive to acquire illiquid instruments instead of otherwise similar but liquid instruments. By comparison, a discounted cash flow measure that incorporates a sufficiently high probability of holding an illiquid instrument through the liquidity horizon would yield reported accounting gains upon inception. While it may be a rational decision for individual banks to load up on illiquid assets, this practice would raise systemic risks, as discussed throughout the book. The main weakness of exit value measurement is that it does not reflect the economic significance of the firm's intent and ability to hold a financial instrument through the liquidity horizon. The discounted cash flows approach has the opposite strengths and weaknesses of exit value.

Valid arguments can be made on both sides as to whether exit value is preferable to discounted cash flows for the accounting recognition of illiquid financial instruments. Some favor exit value because of its superior comparability across firms, verifiability, and incentive properties regarding the acquisition of illiquid financial instruments. However, we emphasize that the discounted cash flows approach has greater relevance for firms with the ability and intent to hold financial instruments through the liquidity horizon, and that it provides management the flexibility to signal that intent and possibly other private information. We recommend that accounting standard setters resolve this trade-off by presenting and reconciling discounted cash flows and exit values—and also amortized costs, which are reliable measurements that are useful for certain financial analysis purposes—in a columnar format, as proposed by Ronen and Sorter (1972) and Ronen (2008).

In fact, the FASB has recently moved in this direction. In the Exposure Draft, the FASB proposes that firms present both fair values and amortized costs on their balance sheets "for instruments that are being held for collection or payment(s) of contractual cash flows." It also proposes that firms provide information reconciling the two measurements. Our recommendation simply expands these presentation and reconciliation requirements to include discounted cash flows. This information would be highly relevant to bank regulators in evaluating the solvency of a bank that holds illiquid financial instruments and has the ability and intent to hold them through the liquidity horizon.

Recommendation

Although reasonable arguments can be made to support the use of either exit value or discounted cash flows, both measurements—along with amortized cost—should be presented and reconciled in financial reports. This will offer a significant improvement over current financial reporting requirements. The differences between exit value and discounted cash flows for banks' illiquid financial instruments are particularly relevant to bank regulators.

18.3 DERIVATIVES AND OTHER INSTRUMENTS WITH EMBEDDED LEVERAGE

Background

Derivatives, residual interests in securitizations, and various other financial instruments (derivative-like instruments) have small value but carry high risk compared with traditional cash instruments. These derivative-like instruments usually settle as a net asset or liability and so are presented net in financial reports. However, these instruments could instead be presented as a gross asset less a gross liability. For example, a retained residual interest in a securitization could be presented as "securitized assets" less the "sold more senior interests in those assets." This gross presentation illustrates that these instruments embed financial leverage.

In the same fashion as discussed in Chapter 13 about securitizations, financial institutions often use the net presentation of these instruments to exploit loopholes in regulatory capital requirements in order to take large undercapitalized bets on credit and other risky instruments.

The Issues

Financial reporting needs to present more transparently the embedded leverage in derivative-like instruments—both by type of instrument and in aggregate. This could be done through balance sheet presentation, footnotes, or management's discussion and analysis (MD&A) disclosure.

Depending on the financial instrument involved, various accounting approaches may achieve gross balance sheet presentation. For example, a retained residual interest from a securitization could be grossed up through required consolidation of the securitization entity. This would record all the assets of the entity as assets of the consolidating firm and all the sold interests of the entity as liabilities of the consolidating firm. (This is the approach taken in FAS 167, as discussed in Chapter 13.) Alternatively, the residual interest could be grossed up to the most comparable offsetting cash instruments without requiring consolidation. The latter approach is more flexible in that it could allow for partial grossing up (for example, when the residual interest does not bear all of the risk of the securitized assets). This approach is more general in that it works for all small-value and high-risk instruments, not just the ones created using special purpose entities.

Recommendation

In our view, the most natural and flexible way to provide information about the embedded leverage in derivative-like instruments is through disclosure rather than balance sheet presentation. We recommend requiring disclosure of standardized alternative leverage measures, including but not limited to: (1) full grossing up of all derivatives and similar positions; and (2) netting of grossed-up positions when they are economically well hedged by other positions in the firm's portfolio.

18.4 BANK REGULATORS SHOULD NOT MEDDLE IN GAAP

Background

During the financial crisis, political pressure on accounting standard setting was intense. This pressure generally was focused on making GAAP more amenable to the goals of bank regulation. These goals were twofold: (1) to require banks to hold more capital in good times, so as to cushion the blow when the economic cycle turns, and (2) to allow banks to record smaller write-downs in bad times to preserve their diminished regulatory capital. An example of the first goal is the proposal to require through-the-cycle loss reserving to induce banks to build up capital during strong economic times in an effort to help them better survive weak economic times when they occur. An example of the second goal is the proposal to suspend fair value accounting during economic crises. Earlier in this discussion, we evaluated these troublesome accounting proposals in detail. Here, we discuss the equally problematic underlying political pressure on accounting standard setting.

Perhaps the most extreme example of this pressure was Representative Edward Perlmutter's (D-CO) proposed amendment to the original Financial Stability Improvement Act that was under consideration by the U.S. House of Representatives' Committee on Financial Services. That amendment would have effectively given a council of bank regulators veto power over GAAP. Fortunately, the proposed amendment was rejected.

Despite this positive development, it would be too optimistic to hope that the political pressure on accounting standard setting is going to disappear. This pressure must be quashed whenever it arises, and in our view, bank regulators should not have any significant power over GAAP.

The most direct way that GAAP requirements might create systemic risk is by reducing banks' regulatory capital ratios below the required levels during difficult economic times, leading to aggregate deleveraging of the banking system and driving down financial asset prices. If banks' regulatory capital were the only concern, however, then the natural approach to deal with it would be to modify either required regulatory capital ratios (e.g., make them higher in good economic times and lower in bad economic times) or the regulatory accounting principles (RAP) on which those ratios are calculated. (Note: We doubt the wisdom of regulatory forbearance in bad economic times, as discussed later.) Intervening in the GAAP that governs financial reporting is not the solution.

The main impediment to these natural approaches is the Federal Deposit Insurance Corporation Improvement Act of 1991 (FDICIA), which includes various provisions that restrict bank regulators' ability to exercise regulatory forbearance. These provisions were included in the FDICIA for the very good reason that forbearance exercised by bank regulators during the 1970s and 1980s delayed, and thereby significantly exacerbated, the costs of resolving the thrift crisis.

In particular, Section 121 of the FDICIA requires that RAP be "consistent with generally accepted accounting principles . . . unless bank regulators determine that the application of any generally accepted accounting principle to any insured depository institution is inconsistent with the objectives described in paragraph (1), [in which case they] may . . . prescribe an accounting principle . . . which is *no less stringent* than generally accepted accounting principles" (emphasis added). Representative Perlmutter's proposed amendment would have de facto repealed Section 121 of the FDICIA and allowed bank regulators to exercise regulatory forbearance opaquely by making GAAP less stringent.

The Issues

Representative Perlmutter's proposed amendment and other political pressures on GAAP would invariably create considerably larger problems than the one they purport to address. The comparative advantages of GAAP and financial reporting are to promote transparency and a well-informed investing public through financial reports that are informative and no more complex than necessary. Transparency plays an essential role in the functioning of financial and other markets, but one that is distinct from the safety-and-soundness role of bank regulation. If potential investors in risky firms and assets do not feel they have transparent information, they will view those firms and assets with fear and loathing, creating illiquid financial markets and exacerbating systemic risk. These problems will exist and weigh on the economy in many ways every day, not just with respect to systemic risk during financial crises.

These political pressures would instead use GAAP for purposes to which it is not suited: to require banks to build up capital during robust economic times and to allow bank regulators to exercise regulatory forbearance during poor economic times. GAAP's potential use to allow the exercise of regulatory forbearance is particularly worrisome. Regulatory forbearance has pernicious effects on banks' incentives. If banks anticipate regulatory forbearance, they will take on more systemic risk ex ante. Therefore, it should be exercised rarely, if at all, and only with extreme caution. When exercised, regulatory forbearance should be implemented in ways that are best understood and most controllable by bank regulators (i.e., through modification of regulatory capital requirements and/or RAP). Regulatory forbearance should also be implemented transparently because bank regulators are not immune to incentive problems. Giving bank regulators the power to cloak their failures through nontransparent financial reporting is a recipe for faulty bank regulation.

In addition, bank regulators exhibit very little understanding of accounting. Accounting standard setting is a difficult process that requires broad and deep understanding of the field. These standards are individually complex and collectively intertwined, and they involve subtle interpretation in practice. This is particularly true for the highly technical standards that govern the accounting for financial instruments and transactions that most significantly affect banks. Given these difficulties, the FASB occasionally makes poor decisions in retrospect. In its defense, however, it has also exhibited a remarkable willingness and ability to accept criticism, to address its mistakes quickly, and to write standards that increase transparency over time.

It is impossible to believe that bank regulators would perform nearly as well as caretakers of GAAP. Even in their own areas of expertise, bank regulators have often acted sluggishly. For example, officials let the thrift crisis fester from the mid-1970s, when interest rates rose, until the early 1990s. Later, bank regulators' failure to appreciate the risks of increasingly undisciplined credit extension and highly leveraged investment and consumption throughout the global financial system over a long period played a crucial role in the recent financial crisis.

Recommendation

Bank regulators and politicians must not be allowed to meddle in GAAP and financial reporting in their pursuit of more effective bank regulations. If politicians want to allow bank regulators to exercise regulatory forbearance, they should sponsor a bill amending Section 121 and other provisions of the FDICIA so that bank regulators can modify RAP, not mess with GAAP.

18.5 CONVERGENCE WITH INTERNATIONAL ACCOUNTING STANDARDS

Convergence of U.S. and international accounting standards has been an expressed goal of the Securities and Exchange Commission (SEC), FASB, and IASB for many years. The FASB and IASB signed a Memorandum of Understanding (MOU) regarding work on joint projects in 2006. The MOU was updated in November 2009 and again in June 2010. The November 2009 MOU targeted June 2011 as the date for the boards to complete a large number of significant and complex joint projects, although the June 2010 MOU retains this target date only for the projects for which "the need for improvement of IFRSs and US GAAP is the most urgent." A number of the projects in the boards' joint work plan involve financial instruments, including fair value measurement, accounting for financial instruments, leases, and insurance contracts; the June 2011 target date applies only to the first three of these projects. Whether or not the boards meet this target, this work plan constitutes an unprecedented and staggering workload for both boards for the coming year.

In principle, accounting convergence is desirable, because it enhances comparability of the financial reports of firms that would otherwise use different accounting standards, and it thereby levels the accounting playing field. In practice, however, convergence should not come at the expense of either high-quality financial reporting now or a process that has the capacity to improve accounting standards over time. While political pressure on accounting standard setting occasionally is significant in the United States, political interference on international accounting standards is more varied and complex, as it is subject to the differing political environments and accounting traditions in many countries. Moreover, the European Union engages in a lengthy and political process of endorsing each IASB standard, as do various other regions and countries. The process constitutes an ex post veto on and thus yields ex ante leverage over IASB standards. Reflecting the heightened politics, IASB standards, in our view, more frequently contain political compromises and exhibit vagueness and implementation flexibility than do FASB standards.

We have also observed that in recent joint projects, the two boards are attempting to converge accounting standards where possible. When they disagree on substantive issues, they are agreeing to disagree and proposing different accounting approaches. One example would be the boards' differing expected loan loss reserving models; the Exposure Draft incorporates many other examples. While these differences undermine the goal of accounting convergence, we believe this agreement to disagree where necessary is sensible given the boards' differing political circumstances. In particular, it is decidedly preferable to the political endorsement of accounting standards in the United States—an outcome that conceivably might result from adoption of (i.e., full convergence with) international accounting standards.[2]

NOTES

1. See Ryan (2009). The executive summary of this Stern White Paper is available online at http://whitepapers.stern.nyu.edu/summaries/ch09.html.
2. For extensive discussion of convergence of U.S. and international accounting standards, see Hail, Leuz, and Wysocki (2009).

REFERENCES

Financial Accounting Standards Board. 2006. *Fair value measurements*. Statement of Financial Accounting Standards No. 157. Norwalk, CT: FASB.

Hail, Luzi, Christian Leuz, and Peter Wysocki. 2009. Global accounting convergence and the potential adoption of IFRS by the United States: An analysis of economic and policy factors. FASB independent research report (February).

Johnson, S. 2008a. The fair-value blame game. www.cfo.com, March 19.

Johnson, S. 2008b. How far can fair value go? www.cfo.com, May 6.

Ronen, J. 2008. To fair value or not to fair value: A broader perspective. *Abacus* 44 (2): 181.

Ronen, Joshua, and George H. Sorter. 1972. Relevant accounting. *Journal of Business* 45 (2): 258.

Ryan, Stephen. 2009. Fair value accounting: Policy issues raised by the credit crunch. In *Restoring financial stability: How to repair a failed system*, ed. Viral V. Acharya and Matthew Richardson, chap. 9. Hoboken, NJ: John Wiley & Sons.

Epilogue

One of the great challenges of writing a book like this is that the whole set of issues it addresses is so dynamic—constantly evolving, constantly updated with new information. The financial system we are talking about regulating is not a fixed environment but one that keeps adapting to attempts to regulate it and to new information about the economies it serves. It is precisely these challenges that have made this book special in the minds of its various contributors and editors.

As we put the finishing touches on the manuscript, the economic world has been rocked by the European sovereign debt problems. We are trying to decipher the results and implications of the publication of the stress test outcomes for 91 European financial institutions. They are an important leading indicator of the willingness of large, complex financial institutions to embrace the market demand for greater transparency. They are an equally important indicator of the willingness of sovereign governments and regulators to engage in the kind of rule making and oversight that will make the financial system safer.

The markets have been somewhat disappointed—not by the fact that all but seven banks cleared the tests, but because the tests were designed in a way that one cannot read much into that success rate. Even though Greek debt restructuring is a foregone conclusion in the minds of most players in the financial marketplace, the stress tests involved much rosier scenarios. French and German banks are known with almost certainty to be owning sovereign bonds of several countries that are experiencing refinancing problems, but the stress tests effectively ignored the risks of such holdings by valuing them at above market-implied rates. Expectations about some large European banks are being revised downward by markets in light of the stress tests' opacity. In the end, the fact that only one Greek bank, five Spanish banks, and one German bank failed the stress tests has hardly been reassuring. These are in fact not the systemically important financial institutions of Europe whose insolvency would threaten the global financial markets were Greece to default.

It is useful to contrast the European exercise to the stress tests conducted by the Federal Reserve in the United States during February to May 2009. While many complained that we had already hit the unemployment rates assumed in the stress scenarios, the housing price decline assumed was in fact worse than what we had seen till then and comparable only to the outcomes in the Great Depression. More importantly, the end goal of the stress tests was clear: to detect the potentially insolvent—or at least undercapitalized—financial firms, and charge them with raising additional capital to meet prudential standards, failing which the government would do so for them along with dilution of existing shareholders and adverse consequences for management in place. A close to fully transparent release of the stress test results had a highly salubrious effect on markets. About half of the 19 banks were found to be wanting, with clear revelation of how much capital shortfall they would face under moderate and extreme stress scenarios. The threat of government ownership stakes, dilution, and job loss induced managements of undercapitalized banks to issue the required capital in no time. Measures of credit risk of all financials—not just the ones that raised capital—seemed to improve. A positive amplifier seemed to take hold of the U.S. financial system, so much so that annual stress tests are currently being considered as part of a future regulatory tool kit.

As far as prudential regulation of systemic risk goes, there is an important lesson to be learned from the disappointment concerning the nature of European stress tests and the success of the American tests that preceded them. The lesson is that systemic risk contributions of financial firms can be assessed in advance using a combination of market data and scenario analysis. These ex ante assessments can be used to predict with reasonable confidence which financial firms are most likely to be undercapitalized in a crisis. In turn, such assessments can be employed to effectively charge a levy (for example, through capital requirements as in the case of the American stress tests, and more generally through taxes) on those that are systemically riskier. If such levies cannot be met by some firms or if they eventually end up being undercapitalized, then a clear resolution plan to wind them down in an orderly fashion or recapitalize them in good time is necessary.

When these two tools are in place, (1) ex ante systemic risk assessments, and (2) credible and orderly ex post resolution, markets remain confident that the system can indeed weather extreme stress. Absent such a tool kit, financial firms remain excessively fragile, financial intermediation is impaired, and there is little that can be done to avoid a buildup of the expectation that in stress scenarios, wholesale failures and ensuing panic will be managed primarily through taxpayer-funded bailouts (as is increasingly the expectation in Europe).

The global financial sector is the plumbing through which capital gets allocated across countries, firms, and households. Several trillions of dollars exchange hands every day. If there is a leak in the pipes, ultimately the plumbing will fail to function efficiently and some taps may run out of capital altogether. We hope we have convinced the readers of this book that the primary leak in the global financial plumbing is that of persistently *mispriced government guarantees*. Until we fix this primary cause of weakness in the global financial sector, we are unlikely to make much progress in restoring financial stability. All else being attempted is likely to end up being much ado about nothing.

The Dodd-Frank Wall Street Reform and Consumer Protection Act of 2010, which we described, analyzed, and critiqued in great detail in this book, identifies—let us say acknowledges—the critical weakness that led to the worst financial crisis of our times: in particular, that too-big-to-fail and too-systemic-to-fail financial firms are currently not paying for the costs they impose on others when they experience trouble. Recognizing this weakness as the basis of future financial reform is in itself a good start. But the Act falls short of addressing the weakness fully. A lot has been left by the Act to be accomplished by the prudential regulators—the Federal Reserve System, the Federal Deposit Insurance Corporation, the Securities and Exchange Commission, and the Commodity Futures Trading Commission. We believe that in one way or another, these regulators will need to shape the Act's implementation using the two key tools we proposed earlier. The results of the European bank stress tests tell us that markets remain skeptical that regulatory attempts to gauge and address systemic risk are still somewhat feeble. They crave good information and sound regulation.

We hope that the time, thought, and spirit of citizenship that we have gathered as a group of New York University Stern School of Business faculty in putting together this book will be useful in some measure as these prudential regulators start their important journey to design a new and robust architecture of global finance. We will follow and, wherever possible, participate in their steps with keen interest.

About the Authors

Viral V. Acharya, Professor of Finance, has research expertise in the regulation of banks and financial institutions, corporate finance, credit risk, liquidity risk, sovereign debt, crises, and growth.

Barry E. Adler, Bernard Petrie Professor of Law and Business and Associate Dean for Information Systems and Technology at NYU Law School, conducts research in bankruptcy, contracts, corporations, and corporate finance.

Edward I. Altman, Max L. Heine Professor of Finance, has research expertise in corporate bankruptcy, high-yield bonds, distressed debt, and credit risk analysis.

John H. Biggs, Executive-in-Residence and Former Chairman, President, and CEO of TIAA-CREF, has research expertise in the financing of retirement, corporate governance, accounting, finance, and investments.

Stephen J. Brown, David S. Loeb Professor of Finance, has research expertise in hedge funds, mutual funds, Japanese equity markets, empirical finance and asset allocation, and investment management.

Christian Brownlees, Postdoctoral Candidate in Financial Econometrics, has research expertise in financial volatility and correlations, financial high-frequency data, nonlinear time series modeling, and statistical computing.

Thomas Cooley, Dean Emeritus and Paganelli-Bull Professor of Economics, has research expertise in macroeconomic theory, monetary theory and policy, and the financial behavior of firms.

Robert F. Engle, Michael Armellino Professor of Finance, has research expertise in financial econometrics and market volatility, and is the recipient of the 2003 Nobel Prize in Economic Sciences for his work in methods of analyzing economic time series with time-varying volatility (autoregressive conditional heteroskedasticity, ARCH).

Farhang Farazmand, PhD Candidate in Finance, has a research interest in empirical asset pricing.

Xavier Gabaix, Professor of Finance and Martin Gruber Chair in Asset Management, has research expertise in asset pricing, executive pay, the origins scaling laws in economics and macroeconomics, and the causes and consequences of seemingly irrational behavior.

Marcin Kacperczyk, Assistant Professor of Finance and NBER Research Fellow, has research expertise in institutional investors, empirical asset pricing, mutual funds, socially responsible investing, and behavioral finance.

Nirupama Kulkarni, PhD Candidate in Real Estate and Finance at the Haas School of Business, has research interests in credit risk, regulation of banks and financial institutions, sovereign debt, crises, and real estate finance.

Hanh Le, PhD Candidate in Finance, has research expertise in corporate finance, corporate governance, and the governance and regulation of financial institutions.

Samuel Lee, Assistant Professor of Finance, has research expertise in financial market liquidity, corporate finance, and corporate governance.

Anthony W. Lynch, Associate Professor of Finance, has research expertise in asset pricing, mutual funds, and portfolio choice.

Thomas M. Mertens, Assistant Professor of Finance, has research expertise in asset pricing, macroeconomics, and computational finance.

Vicki G. Morwitz, Research Professor of Marketing, has research expertise in consumer behavior, marketing research, psychological aspects of pricing, the effectiveness of public health communication, and political marketing.

T. Sabri Öncü, Visiting Assistant Professor of Finance and Assistant Professor in the International Finance Department of Kadir Has University, Istanbul, Turkey, has research expertise in asset pricing, financial econometrics, and empirical industrial organization.

Lasse H. Pedersen, John A. Paulson Professor of Finance and Alternative Investments, has research expertise in liquidity risk, margin requirements, short selling, spiral effects, liquidity crisis, dynamic trading, and the valuation of stocks, bonds, derivatives, commodities, currencies, and over-the-counter (OTC) securities.

Antti Petajisto, Visiting Assistant Professor of Finance, has research expertise in asset pricing, mutual funds, exchange-traded funds, hedge funds, index funds, index design, and performance evaluation.

Thomas Philippon, Associate Professor of Finance, has research expertise in macroeconomics, risk management, corporate finance, business cycles, corporate governance, earnings management, and unemployment.

Matthew Richardson, Charles Simon Professor of Applied Financial Economics and Director of the Salomon Center for the Study of Financial Institutions, has research expertise in capital market efficiency, investments, and empirical finance.

Joshua Ronen, Professor of Accounting, has research expertise in disclosure equilibria, agency theory, and capital markets.

Nouriel Roubini, Professor of Economics and International Business, has research expertise in international macroeconomics and finance, fiscal policy, political economy, growth theory, and European monetary issues.

Stephen G. Ryan, Professor of Accounting, has research expertise in accounting measurement, accounting-based valuation and risk assessment, and financial reporting by financial institutions and for financial instruments.

Shelle Santana, PhD Candidate in Marketing, has research interests in the areas of pricing and emotion, subjective value of money, and numerical cognition. In addition, she has extensive corporate experience in the credit card industry.

Anjolein Schmeits, Clinical Associate Professor of Finance, has research expertise in corporate finance, financial intermediation and banking, corporate governance, information economics, and financial contracting.

Philipp Schnabl, Assistant Professor of Finance, has research expertise in corporate finance, financial intermediation, and banking.

Kermit Schoenholtz, Adjunct Professor, has research expertise in financial markets, monetary policy, and macroeconomics.

Or Shachar, PhD Candidate in Finance, has research interests in credit risk, regulation of financial institutions, and financial econometrics.

George David Smith, Clinical Professor of Economics and International Business and Academic Director of the Langone Program, has research expertise in corporate strategy and structure, regulation, and financial market history.

Roy C. Smith, Kenneth Langone Professor of Entrepreneurship and Finance, has research expertise in international banking and finance, entrepreneurial finance and institutional investment practice, and professional conduct and business ethics.

Marti G. Subrahmanyam, Charles E. Merrill Professor of Finance and Economics, has research expertise in valuation of corporate securities; options and futures markets; asset pricing (especially in relation to liquidity, market microstructure, the term structure of interest rates, and fixed-income markets); family businesses; and real option pricing.

Richard Sylla, Henry Kaufman Professor of the History of Financial Institutions and Markets and Professor of Economics, has research expertise in the history of money, banking, and finance.

Stijn Van Nieuwerburgh, Associate Professor of Finance, has research expertise in finance, macroeconomics, general equilibrium asset pricing, and the role of housing in the macroeconomy.

Paul A. Wachtel, Professor of Economics, has research expertise in monetary policy, central banking, and financial sector reform in economies in transition.

Ingo Walter, Seymour Milstein Professor of Finance, Corporate Governance and Ethics, has most recently focused his research on industrial organization and competitive performance in the global financial services sector.

Lawrence J. White, Arthur E. Imperatore Professor of Economics, has research expertise in the regulation of financial intermediaries.

Robert F. Whitelaw, Edward C. Johnson 3d Professor of Entrepreneurial Finance, has research expertise in market efficiency, stock return predictability, risk and return in the stock and bond markets, and hedging and risk management.

About the Blog

The Dodd-Frank Wall Street Reform and Consumer Protection Act of 2010 mandates the most important changes to financial regulation in nearly a century. While the bill has been passed by both houses of Congress, its implementation is still taking shape. As the implementation and debate continue, we encourage readers to participate in the discussion on the accompanying blog at http://w4.stern.nyu.edu/blogs/regulatingwallstreet/.

There you will find other media coverage about these issues and can engage in the debate with the authors and faculty contributors.

Index